Exam 70-221

MCSE

Windows® 2000
Network Infrastructure
Design

TRAINING GUIDE

que®
CERTIFICATION

MCSE TRAINING GUIDE (70-221): DESIGNING A WINDOWS® 2000 NETWORK INFRASTRUCTURE

International Standard Book Number: 0-7897-2794-3

Library of Congress Catalog Card Number: 2002104976

Printed in the United States of America

First Printing: May, 2002

05 04 03 02   7 6 5 4 3 2 1

Interpretation of the printing code: The rightmost double-digit number is the year of the book's printing; the rightmost single-digit number is the number of the book's printing. For example, the printing code 02-1 shows that the first printing of the book occurred in 2002.

Trademarks

Warning and Disclaimer

PUBLISHER
David Culverwell

EXECUTIVE EDITOR
Chuck Stewart

MANAGING EDITOR
Thomas F. Hayes

ACQUISITIONS EDITORS
Nancy Maragioglio
Ann Quinn
Jeff Riley

DEVELOPMENT EDITORS
Susan Brown Zahn
Laura Loveall
Steve Rowe

SOFTWARE DEVELOPMENT SPECIALIST
Michael Hunter

PROJECT EDITOR
Tonya Simpson

COPY EDITORS
Nancy Albright
Gayle Johnson
Maribeth Echard

INDEXER
John Sleeva

TECHNICAL EDITORS
Mindaugas Balcius
Scott Berkel
Jeff Dunkelburger
Ike Ellis
James Michael Stewart

COVER DESIGNER
Charis Ann Santillie

PROOFREADER
Maribeth Echard

PAGE LAYOUT
Cheryl Lynch

Contents at a Glance

Table of Contents

Part I: Exam Preparation

6 Designing a Management and Implementation Strategy for Windows 2000 Networking   361

Part II: Final Review

Fast Facts   415

Part III: Appendixes

About the Authors

John Alumbaugh, MCSE, CNE, MCT, A+, Network+, is the principal consultant for the operating systems and collaborative solutions team for FrontWay Indianapolis, a network and eBusiness consulting company. John has 13 years of experience in the IT industry and is responsible for Windows 2000 readiness at FrontWay Indianapolis.

Glen Bergen has an extensive background in technical and IT skills, database design, and network infrastructure design. His experience includes knowledge in Unix, Novell, and Microsoft operating systems, and he has authored several books on Windows 2000. His Microsoft certifications include MSCE + Internet, MCDBA, and MCT. For the past four years, he has been employed as a Technical Instructor for PBSC Computer Training. Glen enjoys spending time walking the trails around Edmonton, Alberta, with his wife, Jen.

Damir Bersinic, an MCT, MCSE+Internet, MCDBA, and Oracle Certified DBA and Trainer, has over 17 years of industry experience working with SQL Server, Oracle, Microsoft Windows NT and BackOffice, and other advanced products. He has provided consulting and training on Active Directory and migrating to Windows 2000 to a number of companies. He is President and Founder of Bradley Systems Incorporated, a Microsoft Certified Solution Provider focusing on database, Internet, and system integration consulting and training. His extensive work with Windows NT and BackOffice has allowed him to provide high-level consulting and assistance to clients all over the world. In his spare time, he likes to listen to music and enjoy time with his wife and newborn son. He can be reached via email at damir@bradsys.com.

Dave Bixler is the Technical Services Manager for a Fortune 500 systems integrator. He has been working in the computer industry since the mid-1980s, working on anything from paper tape readers to Windows 2000 servers. Dave has also worked on a number of New Riders books as an author, technical editor, or book reviewer. Dave's industry certifications include Microsoft's MCP and MCSE, as well as Novell's MCNE, and a number of others. When he's not taking tests, he is with his very patient wife, Sarah, and their boys, Marty and Nick.

Michael D. Gambill is an MCSE+I, MCT, and MCNE and works as a Senior Systems Consultant and Trainer at a Microsoft Solution Provider Partner/Certified Technical Education Center. His areas of expertise include Microsoft Exchange, Windows 2000, and Windows NT. He has over ten years of experience in the industry. He lives in Cincinnati, Ohio, with his wife, Dawn, and their three children, Zachary, Brandon, and Paige.

Doug Harrison is an MCSE, MCDBA, and MCNE. Doug has been working with Windows 2000 since Beta 2, and he currently works as the technical education manager at PBSC Computer Training in Toronto, Canada. Doug has been teaching Novell and Microsoft certified training for the past four years. Prior to his career in the training world, he worked as a network administrator and software developer for a consulting engineering firm. Doug currently lives in Toronto with his wife, Tracey, and their daughter, Mikayla.

continues

About the Authors *continued*

Dale Holmes holds MCSE, CNE, CCNA, and Unix/C certification. He is a partner and senior technical consultant for AllNet, LLC, in Baltimore. He is an author of many certification titles, he designs and implements large-scale deployments of Microsoft and Cisco products on a daily basis, and he performs onsite technical training for IT professionals. He can often be seen walking through town with his wife, Emma, his twin girls, Autumn and Winter, and the family dog, Roxanne. He can be reached via email at techtalk@allnetllc.net.

Bill Matsoukas is President of Speed Productions, Inc., a consulting and technical service firm that specializes in the design and implementation of Microsoft networks. He holds MCSE and CNE certification. Bill has been an IT professional for the past 18 years. He lives in Colorado with his wife, Teri, and his son, Bryan. When not making the world a better place for computers, Bill restores old Mustangs and coaches Peewee hockey.

Rob Scrimger is a trainer and consultant who lives and works in Canada. He started with computers in 1979 and, through a lot of luck and on-the-job training, has managed to do everything but design the boards (he is taking an electronics course, though). When he's not working on computers, Rob enjoys good food and good friends, preferably on a boat. Currently Rob is certified in every product in the MCSE stream, holding every Microsoft certification except the MCSD that he plans to add by the time this book goes to press. He is also A+ and Network+ certified.

Mark Verhagen is a Senior Systems Consultant, actively employed by Compugen Systems Limited in Compugen Technical Services (CTS). For the past four years Mark has designed, planned, implemented, and supported Microsoft Server solutions for the corporate, government, and educational sectors on small- to large-scale projects. Keeping one step ahead, Mark has completed all of the Microsoft provided Windows 2000–accelerated training, participated in Windows 2000 Beta testing, and was planning and implementing Windows 2000 for early adopters before its release. Mark is an experienced MCSE, Citrix Certified Administrator (CCA), and Internet Security Specialist (ISS), and also a Technical Forum Host on the leading Virtual Community for IT Professionals, BRAINBUZZ.COM. When he's not going 100mph, Mark makes the most of time at home in Sherwood Park, Alberta, with his wife and two children.

About the Technical Editors

These editors contributed their considerable hands-on expertise to the entire development process for *MCSE Training Guide: Windows 2000 Network Infrastructure Design*. As the book was being written, these dedicated professionals reviewed all the material for technical content, organization, and flow. Their feedback was critical to ensuring that *MCSE Training Guide: Windows 2000 Network Infrastructure Design* fits your need for the highest quality of technical information.

Mindaugas Balcius is an MCSE, MCT, Master CNE, and CNI. He works as a Technical Training Supervisor at the New Horizons Computer Learning Center. His areas of expertise include TCP/IP, Internet technologies, and Web site development. Minda currently lives in Indianapolis, Indiana, with his wife Amy, but they both want to move back to Lithuania.

Scott Berkel is an enterprise consultant, designer, and instructor for customized Microsoft training courses. With more than 14 years of experience in the PC industry, Scott holds over 30 other certifications, including Microsoft's MCSE, MCT, MSS, and MCP; CompTIA's A+ and Network+; IBM's PSE; Novell's CNA; and a multitude of manufacturer-specific hardware certifications. He has authored and edited material on multiple projects for New Riders, including both *A+ Certification Fast Track* and *Top Score* software. Scott works as an independent consultant and trainer in Indianapolis and is available to assist you, your employer, or your clients in all aspects of information technology. For more information, send email to berkelconsulting@home.com or visit the Web site at http://www.berkelconsulting.com.

Ike Ellis, MCNE, MCSE+I, CNI, MCT, is a senior systems engineer for QuickStart Technologies. Ike currently teaches Microsoft courses on topics ranging from Visual Basic to Systems Management Server. Ike has been working on Windows 2000 since Beta 1. He and his wife, Jessica, raise two active boys in San Diego.

Tell Us What You Think!

As the reader of this book, you are the most important critic and commentator. We value your opinion and want to know what we're doing right, what we can do better, what areas you'd like to see us publish in, and any other words of wisdom you're willing to pass our way.

As the Executive Editor for Que Certification I welcome your comments. You can fax, email, or write me directly to let me know what you did or didn't like about this book—as well as what we can do to make our books stronger.

Please note that I cannot help you with technical problems related to the topic of this book, and that due to the high volume of mail I receive, I might not be able to reply to every message.

When you write, please be sure to include this book's title and author as well as your name and phone or fax number. I will carefully review your comments and share them with the author and editors who worked on the book.

Fax: 317-581-4666

Email: certification@quepublishing.com

Mail: Chuck Stewart
          Executive Editor
          Que Certification
          201 West 103rd Street
          Indianapolis, IN 46290 USA

How to Use This Book

Que Certification has made an effort in its *Training Guide Series* to make the information as accessible as possible for the purpose of learning the certification material. Here, you have an opportunity to view the many instructional features that have been incorporated into the books to achieve that goal.

CHAPTER OPENER

Each chapter begins with a set of features designed to allow you to maximize study time for that material.

List of Objectives: Each chapter begins with a list of the objectives as stated by Microsoft.

Objective Explanations: Immediately following each objective is an explanation of it, providing context that defines it more meaningfully in relation to the exam. Because Microsoft can sometimes be vague in its objectives list, the objective explanations are designed to clarify any vagueness by relying on the authors' test-taking experience.

OBJECTIVES

This chapter covers the following Microsoft-specified objectives for the Analyzing Business Requirements section of the Designing a Microsoft Windows 2000 Network Infrastructure exam:

Analyze the existing and planned business models.

- **Analyze the company model and the geographical scope. Models include regional, national, international, subsidiary, and branch offices.**

- **Analyze company processes. Processes include information flow, communication flow, service and product life cycles, and decision-making.**

▶ Often network designers focus on only the technical issues that surround a design project, and they neglect the business-side issues. The first step when considering business impact and issues for a network design project is to examine the basic business model being applied. This objective teaches you how to do this.

Analyze the existing and planned organizational structures. Considerations include management model; company organization; vendor, partner, and customer relationships; and acquisitions plans.

▶ This objective helps you determine issues that will impact your design, stemming from the various business structures in place within your client's organization and from outside customers and partners.

CHAPTER **1**

Analyzing Business Requirements

Chapter Outline: Learning always gets a boost when you can see both the forest and the trees. To give you a visual image of how the topics in a chapter fit together, you will find a chapter outline at the beginning of each chapter. You will also be able to use this for easy reference when looking for a particular topic.

Study Strategies: Each topic presents its own learning challenge. To support you through this, Que Certification has included strategies for how to best approach studying in order to retain the material in the chapter, particularly as it is addressed on the exam.

STUDY STRATEGIES

▶ The material in this chapter is not necessarily Microsoft-specific. The approach to network analysis that you take in this chapter will serve you well on any network project. Remember as you learn these techniques that many of them can be transferred to other non-Microsoft projects.

▶ Much of the material in this chapter dealing with basic networking was previously covered on the MCSE 4.0 exam Networking Essentials. Because Microsoft has eliminated this exam requirement in the MCSE 2000 track, I recommend reviewing *Network+ Certification Guide* (New Riders Publishing, ISBN 073570077X) and *Network+ Fast Track* (New Riders Publishing, ISBN 0735709041).

▶ Pay particular attention to the Case Study that we develop in this chapter. Case studies are an excellent way to learn and begin to understand network design concepts.

▶ As you read the material presented in this chapter, try to associate it with events in your own experience. Think about network projects that you have been involved with, and try to determine if any of the steps described in this chapter were performed for those projects. What was the outcome as a result of design planning strategies?

Exam Tip: Exam Tips appear in the margins to provide specific exam-related advice. Such tips may address what material is covered (or not covered) on the exam, how it is covered, mnemonic devices, or particular quirks of that exam.

EXAM TIP

The Web Proxy Is the Only Service That Caches Remember that the Web Proxy is the only service (except the Reverse Web Proxy) that uses caching technology. Often, users think that the Winsock Proxy and Socks Proxy also use the caching features of Microsoft Proxy Server and are disappointed when the blazing speed typically associated with a proxy server is not there.

INSTRUCTIONAL FEATURES WITHIN THE CHAPTER

These books include a large amount and different kinds of information. The many different elements are designed to help you identify information by its purpose and importance to the exam, and also to provide you with varied ways to learn the material. You will be able to determine how much attention to devote to certain elements, depending on what your goals are. By becoming familiar with the different presentations of information, you will know what information will be important to you as a test-taker and which information will be important to you as a practitioner.

Warning: In using sophisticated information technology, there is always potential for mistakes or even catastrophes that can occur through improper application of the technology. Warnings appear in the margins to alert you to such potential problems.

Chapter 3 · DESIGNING A WINDOWS 2000 NETWORK INFRASTRUCTURE · 149

tools that you can use. One very useful part of the TCP/IP tools is the Dynamic Host Configuration Protocol (DHCP). In the next section, you learn how DHCP is used to facilitate a manageable IP addressing strategy.

WARNING

DHCP Server The DHCP server should *not* be installed on domain controllers.

DEVELOPING DHCP STRATEGIES

Design a DHCP strategy.

The Dynamic Host Configuration Protocol (DHCP) was originally designed to dynamically assign IP addresses to IP network hosts. Currently, DHCP is also capable of assigning other configuration parameters to an IP host, such as default gateways, name server addresses, multicast addresses, and node type. In this section, the tools and technologies required to successfully implement DHCP are covered. The following areas are reviewed:

NOTE

Secure DNS Updates This example assumes that the DNS server is configured to allow only secure updates.

- ◆ IETF standard DHCP
- ◆ Windows 2000 Server implementation of DHCP
- ◆ DHCP integration into routed networks
- ◆ Integration of Windows 2000 DHCP into a legacy DHCP network
- ◆ Designing DHCP services for remote locations
- ◆ Optimizing and measuring DHCP performance

Windows 2000 Server DHCP is standards-based and is compliant with Internet Engineering Task Force (IETF) Request for Comments (RFC). Windows 2000 DHCP has several enhancements (compared to Windows NT DHCP), as defined in several IETF draft standards and RFCs. The Windows 2000 Server DHCP implementation has the following enhancements:

- ◆ DNS/DHCP integration
- ◆ Vendor-specific configuration pushdowns
- ◆ Class ID support
- ◆ Multicast address assignment
- ◆ Unauthorized DHCP server detection

Note: Notes appear in the margins and contain various kinds of useful information, such as tips on the technology or administrative practices, historical background on terms and technologies, or side commentary on industry issues.

Objective Coverage Text: In the text before an exam objective is specifically addressed, you will notice the objective is listed to help call your attention to that particular material.

Figure: To improve readability, the figures have been placed in the margins wherever possible so they do not interrupt the main flow of text.

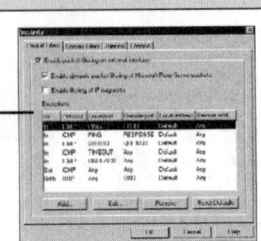

FIGURE 4.10
The Security configuration option, Packet Filters tab of Microsoft Proxy Server 2.0.

STEP BY STEP

4.3 Defining Packet Filters

1. From the Start, Programs, Microsoft Proxy Server menu, select Microsoft Management Console.

2. Packet filters are considered a shared service under Microsoft Proxy Server. You can access the packet filter configuration by right-clicking the Web Proxy, Winsock Proxy, or Socks Proxy service nodes in the MMC and selecting Properties. From the Service tab, click the Security button (as shown in Figure 4.9).

3. By clicking the Security button, you open the Security configuration page for Microsoft Proxy Server (shown in Figure 4.10). Configuration changes made on this tab affect the entire Microsoft Proxy Server.

4. To enable packet filtering, check the Enable Packet Filtering on External Interface option. This configures Microsoft Proxy Server so that no traffic will flow between the public and private interfaces on the Microsoft Proxy Server (except the packet types listed in the exceptions list).

Step by Step: Step by Steps are hands-on tutorial instructions that walk you through a particular task or function relevant to the exam objectives.

Chapter 1   ANALYZING BUSINESS REQUIREMENTS   25

Review Break: Crucial information is summarized at various points in the book in lists or tables. At the end of a particularly long section, you might come across a Review Break that is there just to wrap up one long objective and reinforce the key points before you shift your focus to the next section.

REVIEW BREAK

This part of the chapter discussed many areas of a solid technical assessment. This is the first step in understanding the company's technical environment and providing a foundation for technical design. A technical assessment analyzes several factors in both the premigration environment and post-migration goals. These factors include company size and the geographical distribution of its users; distribution and administration (centralized versus decentralized) of network resources; and analyzing the available connectivity via LAN, WAN, and remote access. Also included are concerns about the network bandwidth of that LAN/WAN/RAS connectivity, its scalability and availability, and how data and network systems are accessed. Finally, we discussed network roles and how security affects these systems. This brings us to the next part of the chapter, where we will review the physical structure of a network in more detail and analyze the impact that various devices and services have on the network.

In the Field Sidebar: These more extensive discussions cover material that perhaps is not directly relevant to the exam, but which is useful as reference material or in everyday practice. In the Field may also provide useful background or contextual information necessary for understanding the larger topic under consideration.

IN THE FIELD

GETTING WORK DONE IN SPITE OF AN AUTOCRATIC MANAGEMENT STYLE

I once worked in a medium-sized company where the owners had sold the company and then agreed to stay on to run it. The former owners maintained close control while pretending to encourage initiative and discussion. Weekly management meetings were held in which each manager was required to discuss his or her progress in meeting rigid goals and to offer suggestions for improving the business.

continues

CASE STUDY: WHIRLED FOODS, INC.

ESSENCE OF THE CASE

Here are the essential elements of this case:

► The company has divisions in Paris, Hong Kong, and New York. They are on the verge of acquiring two large organizations and are planning for further growth.

► To support the merger, a new WAN must be developed.

► To facilitate some of this growth, the company wants to integrate its network with its suppliers and distributors via the Internet for the purposes of e-commerce.

SCENARIO

Whirled Foods, Inc. is a large parent company with five operating companies under its umbrella. Each of the five operating companies has its own network infrastructure and Information Technology standards. Each operating company is currently responsible for its own Information Technology administration. Three of the companies have hired Information Technology administration staff, and two of the companies have outsourced all of their Information Technology administration to the same Information Technology management company. The operating companies comprise a worldwide operation with multiple international sites. Whirled Foods, Inc. would like to connect each of the sites together in

Essence of the Case: A bulleted list of the key problems or issues that need to be addressed in the Scenario.

Scenario: A few paragraphs describing a situation that professional practitioners in the field might face. A Scenario deals with an issue relating to the objectives covered in the chapter, and it includes the kinds of details that make a difference.

CASE STUDIES

Case Studies are presented throughout the book to provide you with another, more conceptual opportunity to apply the knowledge you are developing. They also reflect the "real-world" experiences of the authors in ways that prepare you not only for the exam but for actual network administration as well. In each Case Study, you will find similar elements: a description of a Scenario, the Essence of the Case, and an extended Analysis section.

CASE STUDY: THE NETWORK AT SUNSHINE BREWING

continued

ANALYSIS

Believe it or not, there are companies with networks like this and there are some with larger networks that have even more types of users. The trick to looking at a network is really simple. Break it down. In the end, most users want to get at their files, work with an office suite, and surf the Internet.

From that standpoint, most of the information you need should be in the descriptions of what the users need. The following are key services that will make this network run:

► **Global Catalog servers.** Locate the users' home domain. You need to have one per site, which is the Microsoft recommendation. This is fine; the users should have to query it once if they are traveling and that's it.

► **Lightweight Directory Access Protocol (LDAP).** For those who think this list is familiar, it is. It is copied from the section on monitoring, because in most networks, regardless of size or shape, the process is essentially the same. Let's call these

► **Domain Name System (DNS) name server.** You need the DNS name server because this will be the main name resolution method. For load balancing, you want to have multiple copies of this, and probably one per site would not be out of line—notably if the domain is Active Directory–integrated.

► **Dynamic Host Configuration Protocol (DHCP).** DHCP is also a requirement (even the refrigerator will need this one day). This is a small service and is locked into subnets, so it makes sense to put it at the subnet level. Then you can split the range to provide redundancy.

► **Windows Internet Name Service (WINS).** You probably won't need this service. At the very least, you won't need it forever, so this is not a big issue. To make it easier to remove, you might place it centrally.

► **Routing and Remote Access (RRAS).** RRAS is required and should be monitored. In offices where the Internet connection can stand it—that is, physically accept two

Analysis: This is a lengthy description of the best way to handle the problems listed in the Essence of the Case. In this section, you might find a table summarizing the solutions, a worded example, or both.

EXTENSIVE REVIEW AND SELF-TEST OPTIONS

At the end of each chapter, along with some summary elements, you will find a section called "Apply Your Knowledge" that gives you several different methods with which to test your understanding of the material and review what you have learned.

CHAPTER SUMMARY

KEY TERMS

- Local Area Network (LAN)
- Wide Area Network (WAN)
- virtual private network (VPN)
- Enterprise network
- network infrastructure
- business model
- information flow

Although the business prospectus might seem foreign to many technical engineers, it is essential to a successful deployment of any corporate network and to Windows 2000/Active Directory in particular.

Without an in-depth analysis of the business, you cannot design a flexible, comprehensive, and scaleable network. Geographic boundaries alone do not provide adequate information for determining domain or site boundaries and domain controller placement. You must also understand the business requirements and work flow within and between geographic locations.

Understanding work flow and areas of responsibility helps you deter-

Key Terms: A list of key terms appears at the end of each chapter. These are terms that you should be sure you know and are comfortable defining and understanding when you go in to take the exam.

Chapter Summary: Before the Apply Your Knowledge section, you will find a chapter summary that wraps up the chapter and reviews what you should have learned.

---

46   Part I   EXAM PREPARATION

APPLY YOUR KNOWLEDGE

Exercises

1.1   Documenting Information Flow

This exercise demonstrates the process of documenting information flow for a sample business process. We will use a fictitious company called Speedy Message Service, Inc. for this exercise.

Estimated Time: 15 minutes

Speedy Message Service, Inc. is a company that offers after-hours telephone answering and message delivery services to small businesses. It employs several switchboard operators who answer calls, collect messages, and deliver messages to fax machines and pagers owned by representatives of Speedy Message Service clients.

When a person calls a client of the Speedy Message Service after that client's normal business hours, the phone call is routed to the Speedy Message Service switchboard. One of the Speedy operators answers the call, collects the caller's name and phone number, and determines for which client the call was intended. The operator then reads a prewritten script describing the Speedy Message Service to the caller and asks the caller if he wants to leave a message. If the caller wants to leave a message, the operator requests and records the identity of the intended recipient of the message, as well as the message itself, from the caller. After the caller leaves his message, the call is ended. The operator then looks up the pager or fax number of the recipient of the message and either faxes a typed copy of the message to the appropriate fax number or forwards the text message to the recipient's pager. The transaction is logged in the Speedy Message Service database for billing purposes. The transaction is logged whether or not the caller chooses to leave a message.

From this scenario, document the information flows that take place during the call-answering/message-delivery process. Follow these steps:

1. Determine each individual step of the process.

2. Determine the source and destination of each piece of information that is involved in each step of the process.

3. Document the flow of information from each source to each destination. Indicate the direction of the information flow.

When you have completed step 1, you will have a list that looks like the following:

1. Answer the call and collect the caller's name and phone number.

2. Determine which client the caller wants to reach.

3. Read the script to the caller.

4. Determine if the caller wants to leave a message.

Review Questions

1. What is the major benefit of a formal change-management process?

2. What are some of the benefits of conducting a risk analysis?

3. What characteristics distinguish a WAN from a LAN?

4. What are some of the factors contributing to the TCO of a computer beyond the purchase price?

5. What span of time makes up a product's life cycle?

Exercises: These activities provide an opportunity for you to master specific hands-on tasks. Our goal is to increase your proficiency with the product or technology. You must be able to conduct these tasks in order to pass the exam.

Review Questions: These open-ended, short-answer questions allow you to quickly assess your comprehension of what you just read in the chapter. Instead of asking you to choose from a list of options, these questions require you to state the correct answers in your own words. Although you will not experience these kinds of questions on the exam, these questions will indeed test your level of comprehension of key concepts.

APPLY YOUR KNOWLEDGE

Exam Questions

The first five exam questions refer to the Case Study presented earlier in this chapter.

1. Which business model applies to Whirled Foods, Inc.'s corporate Enterprise network?

   A. Regional

   B. National

   C. Subsidiary

   D. International

2. When you've finished your new network infra-structure design, the Enterprise corporate net-work that connects each of the operating companies in the parent headquarters will be what type of network?

   A. Wide Area Network (WAN)

   B. Metropolitan Area Network (MAN)

   C. Local Area Network (LAN)

   D. Storage Area Network (SAN)

3. What is the structure of Whirled Foods, Inc.'s IT management group?

   A. Centralized

   B. Decentralized

   C. Distributed

   D. Hierarchical

4. What is Whirled Foods, Inc.'s projected growth?

   A. The company plans to reduce its size in the next two years.

   B. The company plans to increase its size in the

   C. The company plans to remain consistent over the next two years.

   D. The company has no plans or strategies with respect to growth.

Answers to Review Questions

1. A formal change-management process allows an organization to carefully analyze proposed changes and let all affected parties give input before a change is implemented in the production environ-ment. This helps avoid implementing changes that have surprising and sometimes disastrous results. See "The Change-Management Process."

2. The major benefits of conducting a risk analysis are the ability to develop plans to prevent risk fac-tors from happening and the ability to develop plans to help mitigate the impact of risk factors that cannot be prevented. See "Acquisitions Plans."

3. Several characteristics distinguish a WAN from a LAN. First is the geographic scope. A WAN occupies a much larger geographic region than a LAN. Another characteristic is bandwidth. WANs typically (but not always) offer much less bandwidth then LANs. Finally, LANs are usually under the complete control of the company that owns them, whereas WANs use leased lines from public carriers and are subject to control by the carrier administrators. MAN stands for Metropolitan Area Network. A MAN is a subset of a WAN, with a shorter area span, usually within the boundaries of a single city. SAN stands for Storage Area Network, which describes the newer technologies available for mass data storage where large arrays of storage are distrib-uted across a building or campus and connected

Exam Questions: These questions reflect the kinds of multiple-choice questions that appear on the Microsoft exams. Use them to become famil-iar with the exam question formats and to help you determine what you know and what you need to review or study more.

Answers and Explanations: For each of the Review and Exam questions, you will find thorough explanations located at the end of the section.

Suggested Readings and Resources

1. Berg, Glenn. *MCSE Training Guide: Networking Essentials, Second Edition.* New Riders Publishing, 1999.

2. Cone, Boggs, Perez. *Planning for Windows 2000.* New Riders Publishing, 2000.

3. Microsoft. *Architecture and Capacity Planning, White Paper.* Microsoft, 1999.

4. Microsoft. *Distributed file system: A Logical View of Physical Storage, White Paper.* Microsoft, 1999.

5. Microsoft. *Dynamic Host Configuration Protocol for Windows 2000, White Paper.* Microsoft, 1999.

6. Microsoft. *Introduction to TCP/IP.* Microsoft Press, 1998.

7. Microsoft. *Microsoft Windows 2000 Windows Internet Name Service (WINS) Overview, White Paper.* Microsoft, 2000.

8. Microsoft. *Windows 2000 DNS, White Paper.* Microsoft, 1999.

9. Microsoft. *Windows 2000 Server Deployment Planning Guide.* Microsoft Press, 2000.

10. Miller, Mark. *Troubleshooting TCP/IP.* M&T Publishing, 1992.

    • Chapter 1: Using TCP/IP and the Internet Protocols

    • Chapter 2: Supporting TCP/IP and the Internet Protocols

11. Scrimger, Rob, and Kelli Adam. *MCSE Training Guide: TCP/IP, Second Edition.* New Riders Publishing, 1998.

Suggested Readings and Resources: The very last element in every chapter is a list of additional resources you can use if you want to go above and beyond certification-level material or if you need to spend more time on a particular subject that you are having trouble understanding.

Introduction

MCSE Training Guide: Windows 2000 Network Infrastructure Design is designed for advanced users, technicians, or system administrators with the goal of certification as a Microsoft Certified Systems Engineer (MCSE). It covers the Designing a Microsoft Windows 2000 Network Infrastructure exam (70-221). This exam measures your ability to analyze the business requirements for a network infrastructure and design a network infrastructure that meets business requirements.

This book is your one-stop shop. Everything you need to know to pass the exam is in here, and Microsoft has approved it as study material. You do not have to take a class in addition to buying this book to pass the exam. However, depending on your personal study habits or learning style, you may benefit from buying this book *and* taking a class.

Microsoft assumes that the typical candidate for this exam has a minimum of one year's experience implementing and administering network operating systems in medium–to–very-large network environments.

HOW THIS BOOK HELPS YOU

MCSE Training Guide: Windows 2000 Network Infrastructure Design takes you on a self-guided tour of all the areas covered by the Designing a Microsoft Windows 2000 Network Infrastructure exam, and teaches you the specific skills you need to achieve your MCSE certification. You'll also find helpful hints, tips, real-world examples, exercises, and references to additional study materials. Specifically, this book is set up to help you in the following ways:

◆ **Organization.** The book is organized by individual exam objectives. Every objective you need to know for the Designing a Microsoft Windows 2000 Network Infrastructure exam is covered in this book, in an order that is as close as possible to that listed by Microsoft. However, we have not hesitated to reorganize the objectives where needed to make the material as easy as possible for you to learn. We have also attempted to make the information accessible in the following ways:

  - The full list of exam topics and objectives is included in this introduction.

  - Each chapter begins with a list of the objectives to be covered.

  - Each chapter also begins with an outline that provides you with an overview of the material and the page numbers where particular topics can be found.

  - The objectives are repeated where the material most directly relevant to it is covered (unless the whole chapter addresses a single objective).

  - The CD-ROM included with this book contains, in PDF format, a complete listing of the test objectives and where they are covered within the book.

◆ **Instructional Features**. This book has been designed to provide you with multiple ways to learn and reinforce the exam material. Following are some of the helpful methods:

  - *Case Studies.* Given the case studies basis of the exam, we designed this Training Guide around them. Case studies appear in each chapter and also serve as the basis for exam questions.

- *Objective Explanations.* As mentioned previously, each chapter begins with a list of the objectives covered in the chapter. In addition, immediately following each objective is an explanation in a context that defines it more meaningfully.

- *Study Strategies.* The beginning of the chapter also includes strategies for approaching the studying and retaining of the material in the chapter, particularly as it is addressed on the exam.

- *Exam Tips.* Exam tips appear in the margin to provide specific exam-related advice. Such tips may address what material is covered (or not covered) on the exam, how it is covered, mnemonic devices, or particular quirks of that exam.

- *Review Breaks and Summaries.* Crucial information is summarized at various points in the book in lists or tables. Each chapter ends with a summary.

- *Key Terms.* A list of key terms appears at the end of each chapter.

- *Notes.* These appear in the margin and contain various kinds of useful information, such as tips on technology or administrative practices, historical background on terms and technologies, or side commentary on industry issues.

- *Warnings.* Using sophisticated information technology increases the potential for mistakes or even catastrophes because of improper application of the technology. Warnings appear in the margin to alert you to such potential problems.

- *In the Field.* These extensive discussions cover material that may not be directly relevant to the exam but that is useful as reference material or in everyday practice. In the Field features may also provide useful background or contextual information necessary for understanding the larger topic under consideration.

- *Exercises.* Found at the end of the chapters in the "Apply Your Knowledge" section, exercises are performance-based opportunities for you to learn and assess your knowledge.

◆ **Extensive Practice Test Options.** This book provides numerous opportunities for you to assess your knowledge and practice for the exam. The practice options include the following:

- *Review Questions.* These open-ended questions appear in the "Apply Your Knowledge" section at the end of each chapter. They enable you to quickly assess your comprehension of what you just read in the chapter. Answers to the questions are provided later in a separate section entitled "Answers to Review Questions."

- *Exam Questions.* These questions also appear in the "Apply Your Knowledge" section. Use them to help you determine what you know and what you need to review or study further. Answers and explanations for them are provided in a separate section entitled "Answers to Exam Questions."

- *Practice Exam.* A Practice Exam is included in the "Final Review" section. The Final Review section and the Practice Exam are discussed later in this list.

- *ExamGear.* The special Training Guide version of the *ExamGear* software included on the CD-ROM provides further opportunities for you to assess how well you understood the material in this book.

◆ **Final Review.** This part of the book provides you with three valuable tools for preparing for the exam:

  - *Fast Facts.* This condensed version of the information contained in the book will prove extremely useful for last-minute review.

  - *Study and Exam Prep Tips.* Read this section early to help you develop study strategies. It also provides you with valuable exam-day tips and information on exam and question formats, such as adaptive tests and case study–based questions.

  - *Practice Exam.* A practice test presents questions written in styles similar to those used on the actual exam. Use it to assess your understanding of the material in the book.

The book includes several other features, such as a section titled "Suggested Readings and Resources" at the end of each chapter that directs you toward further information that could aid you in your exam preparation or your actual work. There are valuable appendixes as well, including a glossary (Appendix A), an overview of the Microsoft certification program (Appendix B), a description of what is on the CD-ROM (Appendix C), and a description of the Que Certification *ExamGear* software (Appendix D).

> **NOTE** For a description of the Que Certification ExamGear, Training Guide software, please see Appendix D, "Using *ExamGear, Training Guide Edition* Software."

For more information about the exam or the certification process, contact Microsoft:

Microsoft Education: 800-636-7544

Internet: `ftp://ftp.microsoft.com/Services/MSEdCert`

World Wide Web: `http://www.microsoft.com/train_cert`

CompuServe Forum: `GO MSEDCERT`

WHAT THE DESIGNING A MICROSOFT WINDOWS 2000 NETWORK INFRASTRUCTURE EXAM (70-221) COVERS

The Designing a Microsoft Windows 2000 Network Infrastructure exam (70-221) covers the Windows 2000 networking topics represented by the conceptual groupings or units of the test objectives. The objectives reflect job skills in the following areas:

- Analyzing Business Requirements (Chapter 1)

- Analyzing Technical Requirements (Chapter 2)

- Designing a Windows 2000 Network Infrastructure (Chapter 3)

- Designing for Internet Connectivity (Chapter 4)

- Designing a Wide Area Network Infrastructure (Chapter 5)

- Designing a Management and Implementation Strategy for Windows 2000 Networking (Chapter 6)

Before taking the exam, you should be proficient in the job skills represented by the following units, objectives, and subobjectives.

Analyzing Business Requirements

Analyze the existing and planned business models:

- Analyze the company model and the geographical scope. Models include regional, national, international, subsidiary, and branch offices.

- Analyze company processes, including information flow, communication flow, service and product life cycles, and decision-making.

Analyze the existing and planned organizational structures. Considerations include management model; company organization; vendor, partner, and customer relationships; and acquisition plans.

Analyze factors that influence company strategies:

- Identify company priorities.
- Identify the projected growth and growth strategy.
- Identify relevant laws and regulations.
- Identify the company's tolerance for risk.
- Identify the total cost of operations.

Analyze the structure of IT management. Considerations include type of administration, such as centralized or decentralized; funding model; outsourcing; the decision-making process; and the change-management process.

Analyzing Technical Requirements

Evaluate the company's existing and planned technical environment and goals:

- Analyze company size and user and resource distribution.

- Assess the available connectivity between the geographic location of worksites and remote sites.

- Assess net available bandwidth and latency issues.

- Analyze performance, availability, and scalability requirements of services.

- Analyze data and system access patterns.

- Analyze network roles and responsibilities.

- Analyze security considerations.

Analyze the impact of infrastructure design on the existing and planned technical environment:

- Assess current applications.

- Analyze network infrastructure, protocols, and hosts.

- Evaluate network services.

- Analyze TCP/IP infrastructure.

- Assess current hardware.

- Identify existing and planned upgrades and rollouts.

- Analyze technical support structure.

- Analyze existing and planned network and systems management.

Analyze the network requirements for client computer access:

- Analyze end-user work needs.

- Analyze end-user usage patterns.

Analyze the existing disaster recovery strategy for client computers, servers, and the network.

Designing a Windows 2000 Network Infrastructure

Modify and design a network topology.

Design a TCP/IP networking strategy:

- Analyze IP subnet requirements.

- Design a TCP/IP addressing and implementation plan.

- Measure and optimize a TCP/IP infrastructure design.

- Integrate software routing into existing networks.

- Integrate TCP/IP with existing WAN requirements.

Design a DHCP strategy:

- Integrate DHCP into a routed environment.

- Integrate DHCP with Windows 2000.

- Design a DHCP service for remote locations.

- Measure and optimize a DHCP infrastructure design.

Design name resolution services:

- Create an integrated DNS design.

- Create a secure DNS design.

- Create a highly available DNS design.

- Measure and optimize a DNS infrastructure design.

- Design a DNS deployment strategy.

- Create a WINS design.

- Create a secure WINS design.

- Measure and optimize a WINS infrastructure design.

- Design a WINS deployment strategy.

Design a multiprotocol strategy. Protocols include IPX/SPX and SNA.

Design a Distributed file system (Dfs) strategy:

- Design the placement of a Dfs root.

- Design a Dfs root replica strategy.

Designing for Internet Connectivity

Design an Internet and extranet access solution. Components of the solution could include proxy server, firewall, routing and remote access, Network Address Translation (NAT), connection sharing, Web server, or mail server.

Design a load-balancing strategy.

Design a wide area network infrastructure.

Design an implementation strategy for dial-up remote access:

- Design a remote access solution that uses routing and remote access.

- Integrate authentication with Remote Authentication Dial-In User Service (RADIUS).

Design a virtual private network (VPN) strategy.

Design a routing and remote access routing solution to connect locations:

- Design a demand-dial routing strategy.

Designing a Management and Implementation Strategy for Windows 2000 Networking

Design a strategy for monitoring and managing Windows 2000 network services. Services include global catalog, Lightweight Directory Access Protocol (LDAP) services, certificate services, DNS, DHCP, WINS, routing and remote access, proxy server, and Dfs.

Design network services that support application architecture.

Design a plan for the interaction of Windows 2000 network services, such as WINS, DHCP, and DNS.

Design a resource strategy:

- Plan for the placement and management of resources.
- Plan for growth.
- Plan for decentralized resources or centralized resources.

HARDWARE AND SOFTWARE YOU'LL NEED

As a self-paced study guide, *MCSE Training Guide: Windows 2000 Network Infrastructure Design* will help you understand concepts that must be refined through hands-on experience. To make the most of your studying, you need to have as much background on and experience with Windows 2000 Server as possible. The best way to do this is to combine studying with work on Windows 2000 Server. The following are the minimum computer requirements you need to enjoy a solid practice environment:

- Windows 2000 Server and Professional
- A server and a workstation computer on the Microsoft Hardware Compatibility List
- Pentium 90Mhz (or better) processor
- 600MB (or larger) hard disk
- VGA (or Super VGA) video adapter and monitor
- Mouse or equivalent pointing device
- CD-ROM drive
- Network Interface Card (NIC) or modem connection to the Internet
- Presence on an existing network, or use of a 2-port (or more) miniport hub to create a test network
- Internet access with Internet Explorer 4 (Service Pack 1) or later
- 24MB of RAM (32MB recommended)
- Windows NT Option Pack recommended
- Microsoft SQL Server 6.5 (or better) optional
- Microsoft SNA Server optional

It is easier to obtain access to the necessary computer hardware and software in a corporate business environment. It can be difficult, however, to allocate enough time within the busy workday to complete a self-study program. Most of your study time will occur after normal working hours, away from the everyday interruptions and pressures of your regular job.

ADVICE ON TAKING THE EXAM

More extensive tips are found in the Final Review section titled "Study and Exam Prep Tips," but keep this advice in mind as you study:

◆ **Read all the material.** Microsoft has been known to include material not expressly specified in the objectives. This book has included additional information not reflected in the objectives in an effort to give you the best possible preparation for the examination—and for the real-world experiences to come.

◆ **Do the Step-by-Steps and complete the Exercises in each chapter.** They will help you gain experience using the specified methodology or approach. All Microsoft exams are task- and experienced-based and require you to have experience performing the tasks upon which you will be tested.

◆ **Use the questions to assess your knowledge.** Don't just read the chapter content; use the questions to find out what you know and what you don't. You also need the experience of analyzing case studies. If you are struggling at all, study some more, review, and then assess your knowledge again.

◆ **Review the exam objectives.** Develop your own questions and examples for each topic listed. If you can develop and answer several questions for each topic, you should not find it difficult to pass the exam.

Remember, the primary object is not to pass the exam—it is to understand the material. If you understand the material, passing the exam should be simple. Knowledge is a pyramid; to build upward, you need a solid foundation. This book and the Microsoft Certified Professional programs are designed to ensure that you have that solid foundation.

Good luck!

NOTE

Exam-taking Advice Although this book is designed to prepare you to take and pass the Designing a Microsoft Windows 2000 Network Infrastructure exam, there are no guarantees. Read this book, work through the questions and exercises, and when you feel confident, take the Practice Exam and additional exams using the *ExamGear, Training Guide Edition* test software. This should tell you whether you are ready for the real thing.

When taking the actual certification exam, make sure you answer all the questions before your time limit expires. Do not spend too much time on any one question. If you are unsure, answer it as best you can; then mark it for review when you have finished the rest of the questions. However, this advice will not apply if you are taking an adaptive exam. In that case, take your time on each question. There is no opportunity to go back to a question.

EXAM PREPARATION

This chapter covers the following Microsoft-specified objectives for the Analyzing Business Requirements section of the Designing a Microsoft Windows 2000 Network Infrastructure exam:

Analyze the existing and planned business models.

- **Analyze the company model and the geographical scope. Models include regional, national, international, subsidiary, and branch offices.**

- **Analyze company processes. Processes include information flow, communication flow, service and product life cycles, and decision-making.**

▶ Often network designers focus on only the technical issues that surround a design project, and they neglect the business-side issues. The first step when considering business impact and issues for a network design project is to examine the basic business model being applied. This objective teaches you how to do this.

Analyze the existing and planned organizational structures. Considerations include management model; company organization; vendor, partner, and customer relationships; and acquisitions plans.

▶ This objective helps you determine issues that will impact your design, stemming from the various business structures in place within your client's organization and from outside customers and partners.

CHAPTER 1

Analyzing Business Requirements

OBJECTIVES

Analyze factors that influence company strategies.

- **Identify company priorities.**
- **Identify the projected growth and growth strategy.**
- **Identify relevant laws and regulations.**
- **Identify the company's tolerance for risk.**
- **Identify the total cost of operations.**

▶ The purpose of this objective is to help you recognize the factors that shape your client's strategies and strategic goals, and to consider how these factors will impact your network design.

Analyze the structure of IT management. Considerations include type of administration, such as centralized or decentralized; funding model; outsourcing; decision-making process; and change-management process.

▶ This objective serves to teach you the various considerations concerning your client's Information Technology management team. Considerations made in this area help determine the success or failure of your network design project.

OUTLINE

STUDY STRATEGIES

▶ The material in this chapter is not necessarily Microsoft-specific. The approach to network design that you take in this chapter will serve you well on any network design project. Remember as you learn these techniques that many of them can be transferred to other non-Microsoft projects.

▶ Pay particular attention to the Case Study that we develop in this chapter. Case studies are an excellent way to learn and begin to understand network design concepts.

▶ As you read the material presented in this chapter, try to associate it with events in your own experience. Think about network projects that you have been involved with, and try to determine if any of the steps described in this chapter were performed for those projects. What was the outcome as a result of design-planning strategies?

INTRODUCTION

These days it is hard to imagine a business without some sort of computer network in place. Businesses of all types and sizes use computers to automate tasks and to store vital company information, such as financial data, customer data, and inventory information.

The individual computers in most companies are interconnected to form a network. Different computers on the network perform different roles. There are file servers, database servers, email servers, Internet servers, and other servers, as well as end-user workstations. These computers communicate with one another using a set of rules called a *protocol*. Depending on the type of computer systems that are in use, more than one protocol may be in use on a company network.

Each of the company's physical locations (each building or campus) will have its own Local Area Network (LAN), as shown in Figure 1.1.

Each of these sites will probably be connected to each other, or to one central site, such as the corporate headquarters, through a Wide Area Network (WAN), as shown in Figure 1.2.

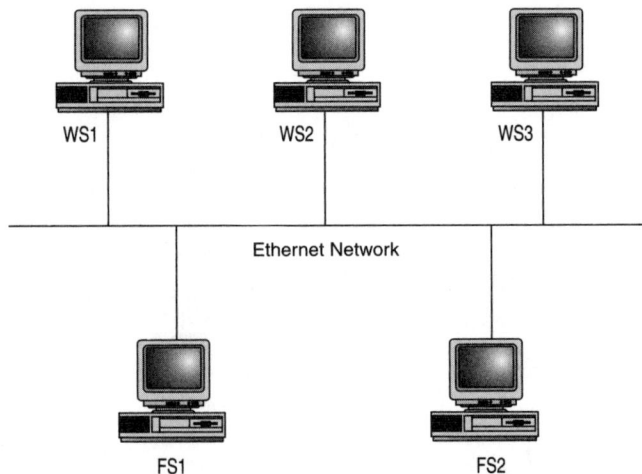

FIGURE 1.1

A Local Area Network (LAN) connects one or more computers in the same relatively small area, such as a single building, using TCP/IP in this example.

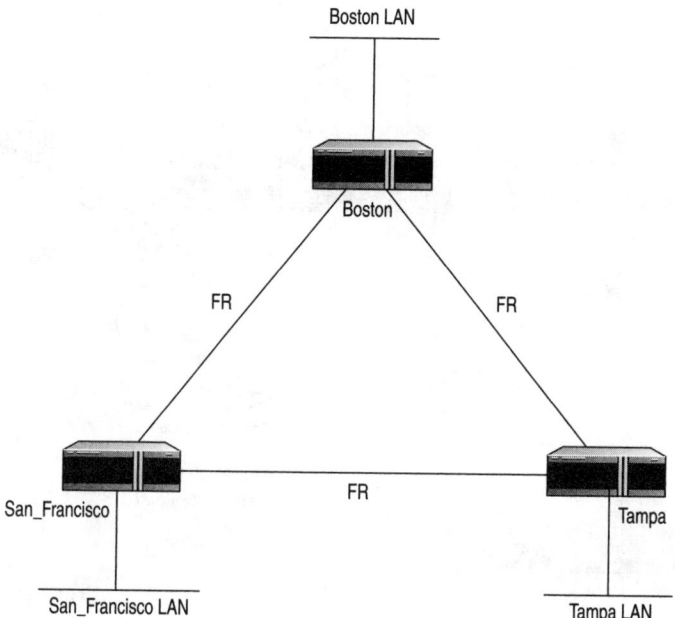

FIGURE 1.2
A Wide Area Network (WAN) connects multiple LANs over a large geographical area.

In addition, individual users might need to access the company network while working from home. These remote users may connect directly to one of the LANs by calling into a Remote Access Server via ordinary telephone lines, or they may connect over the Internet using a secure connection called a virtual private network (VPN). A VPN is shown in Figure 1.3.

The whole collection of LANs, WANs, remote users, or VPNs is referred to as the company's Enterprise network. On an Enterprise network, the protocols in use and the services offered, as well as the devices that provide the network connectivity and services, are referred to as the network infrastructure. Given the way that businesses rely on the network infrastructure, designing such an infrastructure requires considerable planning to ensure success.

FIGURE 1.3

A virtual private network (VPN) allows a remote user (or number of users) to access private corporate resources over a secure connection through the public Internet.

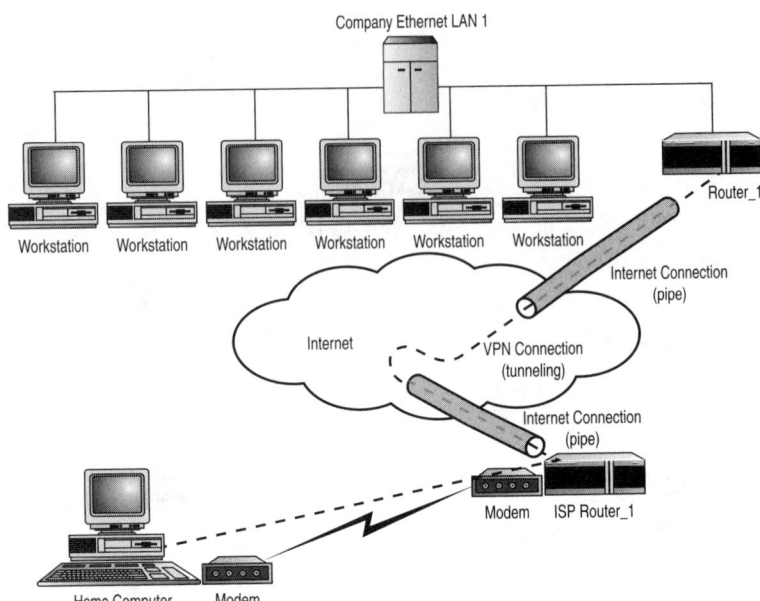

It is obvious to network professionals that the technical aspects of network infrastructure design require detailed planning, and it is easy for them to focus their efforts entirely on the technical considerations. Unfortunately, this approach is destined for failure, because it neglects to consider the crucial business elements that should be included in a network infrastructure design. If you don't thoroughly consider the business requirements for the network infrastructure, the design project is likely to result in a network that is either too simple to support the demands placed on it or too complex to deliver results efficiently and cost-effectively. Without proper consideration of business requirements, you can count on designing a network that is either too weak or too expensive.

This book will teach you the techniques you will need to know to effectively design Microsoft Windows 2000 network infrastructures that maximize performance and minimize Total Cost of Ownership (TCO). This chapter focuses on the business requirements that you will need to consider when creating your network infrastructure design.

ANALYZING BUSINESS MODELS

Analyze the existing and planned business models

One of the first elements you will examine when analyzing business requirements for a network infrastructure design project is the business model or models that the company follows. You should examine the current model as well as any model that the company plans to implement in the future.

It is rare that an engineer gets the opportunity to design a network infrastructure completely from scratch. In most cases, you must design an infrastructure that will either interoperate with or serve to upgrade an existing infrastructure. Because of this, having the documentation for previous network designs and modifications and adding your own modifications to this archive of information can be crucial. Information that you can get from examining the current business model will help you determine the services that are already in place so that you can be sure to include them in your design. Businesses will often look at a project of major impact, such as a network infrastructure design project, as an opportunity to change its strategies or business model to improve its position in the industry or change its own internal operations. In such cases, you must also examine any new business models that the company intends to employ so that your new design can incorporate them and accommodate interaction with the existing services being offered on the network.

When examining the client's business model(s), you will benefit from a very high-level understanding of the industry in which the client is doing business. Through the proper use of interviews with key personnel, research the client's business and competition. This will perhaps allow these key personnel to think of an important, but overlooked, requirement for the new network design.

Analyzing the Company Model and Geographic Scope

You will encounter different business models depending on the geographic scope of your design project. If you are designing an Enterprise network infrastructure, you will likely encounter and need to consider several different models. Microsoft emphasizes the following business models for the exam:

◆ **Branch offices.** In a branch office, you will see the smallest business model. In this model, you focus on the specific function of the branch office and what services it must offer to or receive from the company headquarters and other branch offices. In this model, typical concerns include where connections need to be made, how much they will cost, and who will have administrative control over them.

◆ **Regional.** This business model will be applied if your design includes network locations in a particular region of a single country. Regional networks often span multiple counties or states. Examples of regions in the Unites States include the Mid-Atlantic states or the states in the Pacific Northwest. This model will include considerations that are specific to the region, such as the relationship between communications providers and the environmental and landscape concerns (consider networks that must operate high in the mountains or in deeply wooded or rural areas).

◆ **National.** A national business model is applied to a business whose scope spans an entire country. This business model will involve all the types of concerns that are included in the Regional model but will also include multiple regions. This increases the importance of each region's concerns, because all regions must interoperate.

◆ **International.** Businesses that operate in multiple locations worldwide will employ the International business model. In the International model, you are likely to see all issues that could possibly be considered. This model increases the complexity of the issues in the National model by including the requirement that all National sites must interoperate. New issues that arise in this model include cultural and language barriers and international politics.

◆ **Subsidiary.** This model is somewhat different from the models discussed so far. In a Subsidiary model, concerns such as internal company politics increase in importance as you shape your design to allow the subsidiary network to interoperate with the infrastructure owned by the parent company.

Analyzing Company Processes

Once you have a thorough understanding of the business models employed, you will want to closely analyze company processes both inside and outside of the IT department. Many different processes are executed each day in the operation of any business. An example of an IT process is as follows: If a network user calls the help desk to report a computer problem, the help desk technician follows a process in which the call is logged and assigned a ticket number so that it can be tracked. Information is then gathered to aid in determining the nature of the problem. The ticket is assigned to a technician who has the appropriate skills to solve the problem, and the solution is implemented. The ticket is then closed and the resolution documented. This process is repeated for every call that is made to the help desk.

Similar processes exist for every task taking place in the day-to-day operation of the business. The execution of these processes determines who needs access to network resources, what resources they need, and when they need them. It is essential that the designer understand these processes in order to create an effective network infrastructure design. The network design must be created so that these processes can be executed most efficiently and at the least possible cost.

Microsoft refers to four major types of business process categories in its exam objectives: information flow, communication flow, service and product life cycles, and decision-making. Each of these process categories will be discussed in the following sections.

Information Flow

Information flow (or work flow) processes have to do with the way information is distributed throughout the company. They describe what information is available, who needs it, and in what order they receive it.

For example, consider a wholesale distributor who receives a phone call from a new customer, initiating the purchase of some widgets. The customer will likely call a sales representative. That representative will collect the customer's information, including name, address, phone number, credit card number, and shipping preferences. This information will be entered into a database stored on the distributor's internal network.

The salesperson will also find out what type of widgets the customer wants to purchase. In order to complete the sale, the salesperson will need to know what types of widgets are available, how many of each type are in stock, how much to charge for the widgets, and what shipping options are available. This information will also be stored in a database or, more likely, in several databases on the distributor's network. It will be made available to the salesperson when it is needed through some sort of application software interfacing with the appropriate database.

Once the order is taken, the customer's information, along with the inventory and shipping information, will be made available to an employee in the distributor's warehouse so that the widgets can be removed from inventory, packaged, and shipped to the customer. Throughout the process of accepting and fulfilling a customer order, information must flow throughout the network to various people at various locations in a specific order.

It is important to understand the information flow for all the major functions taking place within a business so that the network infrastructure can be designed to make the information available when and where it is needed. Simply delivering the information is not enough, though. The information needs to be delivered as quickly as possible and at the lowest cost possible. The network must meet these objectives and support the current demands for information flow, as well as provide for the increase in demand for information that will likely come in the future.

Communication Flow

The process of communication flow is similar to that of information flow. Communication flow tracks the path that data follows through the network infrastructure during the course of day-to-day operations of the business.

Documenting communication flow can help you describe the performance of the existing network infrastructure in specific terms. By documenting the communication flow, you have real quantified data on which to base your performance evaluation. The results of your evaluation will help you ensure that your new network infrastructure design will maintain the high performance of the existing network infrastructure or will correct the poor performance of the existing network infrastructure. You can also use this data to create a design redirecting communication flow to a more efficient pattern.

Documenting communication flow requires you to analyze the existing network infrastructure and identify data stores and destinations. Data stores include the file servers, Web servers, email/groupware servers, and database servers where information is stored for retrieval over the network infrastructure. Destinations for that data include individual hosts residing on the network infrastructure, and external hosts that access the data stores through remote network connections over the Internet.

You might want to analyze individual communication flows by dividing network traffic based on the application that generated the traffic. This can be effective, because it allows you to attribute percentages of overall network infrastructure performance to individual applications. If one application creates a disproportionate amount of the overall traffic on a network, and that network is performing poorly, you might want to develop alternative means of supporting that application, or alter your design to allow for the heavy demands that the application places on the network infrastructure.

For each individual communication flow that you trace, you will want to document several traits related to that communication flow:

◆ **Total bandwidth used.** The total bandwidth used by the communication flow, typically measured in megabytes per second (Mbps).

◆ **Percent of overall bandwidth used.** The percentage of the overall network bandwidth used by this particular communication flow. The sum of this information for all flows on the network should equal 100 percent.

◆ **Number of bytes of data.** The number of bytes of data transferred across the network for this particular communication flow.

◆ **Data source and destination.** The server or servers where the data is stored for this communication flow and the host or hosts that ultimately receive the data.

◆ **Data path and direction.** The direction and route that the data follows through the network infrastructure for this particular communication flow.

Service and Product Life Cycles

In business, any product or service that you might sell will have value for a finite period of time. At the end of that period of time, the product or service is either discontinued or has been rendered obsolete by a new product or superior service. The period of time for which a product or service has value is referred to as the "life" of the product or service.

When a company wants to offer a service or product for sale, it doesn't just pull the product or service out of thin air. Time is spent on conceptualization, research and development, design, prototyping, and production. Likewise, when a product or service is no longer of value, having reached its "end of life," it does not simply go away. The manufacturer or service provider retires the product or service gradually over a period of time (although this period is sometimes more rapid than customers would prefer).

Keep this concept in mind when thinking about networks. To have a good project, the company's network and IT systems should also have spent a significant amount of time on vision, research and development, design, and testing before being put into production.

The entire period from the initial concept of the product or service to the complete removal of the product or service from the market, and all the events that transpire in between, is called the *life cycle* of the product or service.

You should consider the life cycle of the products and/or services offered by your client when designing the network infrastructure. When evaluating life cycles, ask the following questions:

◆ Do the company's products enjoy a long life cycle, with events occurring gracefully over an extended period of time, as in the case of a car manufacturer?

◆ Do the company's products go through a very short life cycle, with events occurring in rapid succession in a matter of months or weeks, as in the case of a technical publishing company?

◆ How does each scenario affect the demands that will be placed on the network infrastructure?

You need to answer these questions before you can effectively complete your network infrastructure design.

Decision-Making

In some organizations, decisions are made quickly, and changes can occur rapidly. In others, a complicated process must be executed before the slightest thing can be done. Both extremes have their pros and cons.

Typically, there is some compromise in the approach to decision-making, allowing the company's employees to be empowered to effect change in their immediate area while still allowing the company to manage change with a reasonable degree of control. You will need to learn the company's decision-making processes and incorporate those processes into your design. As you create your design, when you present the finished design to management, and at many points in between, decisions must be made that will require you to follow some of these processes yourself. This will help you become acquainted with the way decision-making is handled within the organization.

However, you must also consider the many decisions that must be made every day, all over the company. Every business function that occurs during the day-to-day operation of the business will involve a set of decision-making processes that must be followed. Determine what role the various network resources play in those decision-making processes and at what point in the information flow decision-making processes place demands for network resources. Once you have this information, you can develop your network infrastructure design accordingly.

ANALYZING ORGANIZATIONAL STRUCTURES

Analyze the existing and planned organizational structures. Considerations include management model; company organization; vendor, partner, and customer relationships; and acquisitions plans.

These are very important considerations when designing a network infrastructure center around the organizational structures within the company. The various organizational structures already in place usually determine the distribution of network resources and the type of network management strategy that will be implemented.

Proposed changes to the company's organizational structures might have a significant impact on the network's effectiveness. You must plan for these changes and design the network with the flexibility to accommodate them. Solicit the client for input in this area. Try to get an understanding of what the current structures are and how effective they are within the organization. If there are areas that do not seem to be working from an organizational point of view, try to find out if there will be a change in that organization in the future. Always get the details of any known changes that are scheduled to occur in the future so that you can incorporate those details in your design.

In the exam objectives, Microsoft lists the following organizational structures for you to consider when creating your design:

◆ Management model

◆ Company organization

◆ Vendor, partner, and customer relationships

◆ Acquisitions plans

Each of these organization structures will be discussed in the following sections.

Management Model

First, determine if there is separation of ownership and control. Is there a board of directors, shareholders, and a chief executive officer? Alternatively, is this a family-run business? Is the CEO the founder and primary stockholder?

The former, separation of ownership and control, describes the majority of large American industries. Smaller businesses may still be owned and operated by the founders.

Even a large, publicly traded business or organization may be run as if the CEO were simply pursuing power, fame, or gratification. Many times this quest will mean success, recovery, or advancement, but it does require a charismatic individual who often maintains control by his very essence. Dissention is just not imagined.

Is the management style bureaucratic and authoritarian? Does it stress accounting and close control? Is it democratic, encouraging initiative and enterprise? Does it follow the tried and true, or is it willing to take risks?

IN THE FIELD

GETTING WORK DONE IN SPITE OF AN AUTOCRATIC MANAGEMENT STYLE

I once worked in a medium-sized company where the owners had sold the company and then agreed to stay on to run it. The former owners maintained close control while pretending to encourage initiative and discussion. Weekly management meetings were held in which each manager was required to discuss his or her progress in meeting rigid goals and to offer suggestions for improving the business.

continues

continued

Managers learned to sit to the right of the CEO, because he always started to his left. There was not usually time for everyone to speak. Any manager who had not met goals was castigated. Managers whose ideas were considered frivolous, impossible, or undesirable were belittled and mocked. Sometimes it did not seem to matter if the new idea reduced cost, increased productivity, or created new markets. Initiates soon learned to offer only ideas that reflected the CEO's thoughts (or those of his cronies). It was a contest in presenting old ideas as if they were new. Others spent time seeding the field, or somehow introducing ideas in short segments outside and prior to the meeting, and then bringing them up as something the CEO had mentioned. It was old psychology developed by the old-fashioned wife—to get what you want, make him think it was his idea.

Nevertheless, progress was made in introducing new ways of doing things. The trick was to balance something radical with something only slightly variant from the norm. This, of course, was the desired step. The radical item was ranted about; the other was ignored, but not turned down. The second part of the process was to keep introducing the desired change from other directions and to be in the right place at the right time. (Bragg, Roberta. *MCSE Training Guide (70-220): Windows 2000 Network Security Design*. New Riders Publishing, 2000)

Company Organization

The organization of the company will prove to be a major consideration for your network infrastructure design. The distribution of resources will closely follow the company organization.

Some companies are organized along the lines of business function. The various business units or departments are physically segregated. Here are some examples of ways that you might find a company segregated:

◆ Different departments in separate sections of a single floor

◆ Different departments on separate floors of a single building

◆ Different departments in separate buildings on a single campus

◆ Different departments in separate buildings in different sites

As the company organization becomes more widely segregated, you will find that you will often need to design your network infrastructure so that network resources are physically located nearest to the groups using them most. You will then build in communication paths so that other groups who need the resources less frequently will gain the access that they require.

Another typical scenario is a company that is organized along geographic lines. In this scenario, multiple business functions occupy the same space, but resources are distributed based on the location of each office that the company occupies. For example, a company might have offices in three cities: Boston, San Francisco, and Tampa. In each of these cities are representatives from the legal department, the sales department, and the accounting department.

In this scenario, you cannot simply locate accounting resources in one office, sales resources in another office, and legal resources in a third. This would result in less-than-efficient access to resources for two of the three departments in every office. In this case, you must plan your network infrastructure so that resources for each department are distributed equally to all offices or are centrally located so that each office can access them with the same efficiency.

Vendor, Partner, and Customer Relationships

The relationships that a company maintains with its vendors, partners, and customers will have an impact on the types of services the company wants to provide on its network. For instance, suppose a company maintains a call center to provide support for its customers. The company requires database servers to log the calls and provide access to customers and product information to the call center technicians. If the company sells merchandise over the Internet, it will likely want to use servers on the World Wide Web to provide an interface for its customers in business-to-consumer e-commerce (B2C). This will require that the company have a connection from its internal network to the Internet. It will also require that its internal databases provide product information to outside customers through that Internet connection.

Relationships with partners can create even more demands for network resources. In many cases, two partner companies will connect each other's networks together in some fashion for business-to-business e-commerce. The expectation of senior management (on both sides) is that the networks will interoperate. Of course, there might be significant technological, business, and political issues to overcome in order to provide that interoperability. For example, integrating a partner's network might require you to overcome interoperability issues between Windows 2000 and other operating systems, such as Novell Netware or UNIX.

Often, a company will have a relationship with one of more of the vendors supplying the materials necessary for the operation of the business. It is desirable to automate many of the repetitive tasks associated with purchasing materials and paying invoices. In order to accomplish this, special internetworking technologies might need to be applied. Knowing the relationships that exist will help you design a network infrastructure that supports the required connectivity and interoperability.

Acquisitions Plans

When designing a network infrastructure, it is always prudent to inquire about any plans that the company might have to purchase other companies. In many cases, the company might hesitate to reveal confidential business plans to an outside vendor, but these can be crucial. If a purchase is planned for the very near future, or if it is already underway, you might be able to get some details on the matter. You will greatly benefit from being aware of any acquisition plans before you create your network infrastructure design, and you should be able to communicate this in financial terms to the customer. Variations on this should always be covered in a proper project risk analysis. Furthermore, you cannot effectively deliver an internetwork design plan if you are not informed of all the requirements for that network. Company management must fill you in on all the details they can regarding any planned acquisitions.

In most cases, when one company acquires another, the network of the latter company is absorbed into that of the former. Sometimes the entire network is eliminated and replaced with an infrastructure that conforms to the standards of the purchasing company, but this is often impractical and expensive.

Usually, the company that is purchased possesses some product or information that is of extreme value to the purchasing company. The associated data and supporting network infrastructure become invaluable assets that must be preserved. Nevertheless, interoperation with the purchasing company's existing network infrastructure is crucial.

When examining a company's acquisition plans, consider the following questions after you understand the current environment:

◆ Which of the new company's systems and services will need to be retained? Why?

◆ Which of the new company's systems and services will need to be retired? Why?

◆ Which of the new company's systems and services will replace existing systems and services?

◆ Which of the existing systems and services will need to be extended into the newly acquired company?

◆ What are the support structures for the systems and services, and how will they integrate or conflict?

◆ What are the barriers to integrating the two companies' network infrastructures, and what is the magnitude of these barriers?

If you are informed of the intended purchase of another company, you can research the specific issues you will face in integrating the two networks and can design solutions to those problems from the beginning.

ANALYZING COMPANY BUSINESS STRATEGIES

Analyze factors that influence company strategies.

The purpose of any network infrastructure is to help the business perform its day-to-day activities and meet its objectives with the greatest efficiency. The day-to-day activities that must be performed will vary depending on the company's business strategies.

Consequently, the role of the network and the demands placed on the network infrastructure will vary as well.

When creating a network infrastructure design, it is important that you have an understanding of the company's business strategies and the factors that influence those strategies. Microsoft lists the following factors in its objectives for this exam:

◆ Identify company priorities

◆ Identify the projected growth and growth strategy

◆ Identify relevant laws and regulations

◆ Identify the company's tolerance for risk

◆ Identify the total cost of operations

Each of these factors will be discussed in the following sections.

Identifying Company Priorities

Designing a network infrastructure that delivers everything imaginable all the time is an impossible task. In any design project, compromises must be made. How will you determine what compromises to make in your design? You must determine which network resources align with the company's business priorities.

Meet with senior management to determine the company's priorities. Document all the business's goals, and assign a priority number to each one. You might find that several goals share the same priority. This is acceptable at this point in the design process. You need not assign a unique priority number to each of the business goals on your list. You merely need to gain some understanding of the relative priority of each goal in terms of each of the other goals.

Once you have assigned a priority level to each of the business goals, you will be able to determine if any conflicts might arise when you're trying to deliver computing services for each of the company's goals. When these conflicts occur, refer to the priority level of each of the items that are in conflict. Goals with higher priority levels get built into the design first. Goals with lower priority values are included in the design only if they can be delivered after goals at the higher priority levels have been satisfied. Always remember that the reason for an effective IT infrastructure is to help the company achieve its goals in the marketplace.

Identifying the Projected Growth and Growth Strategy

One of the most important things to do once you have identified the business requirements and priorities is to understand not only the company's projected growth, but also the company's strategy for achieving those projections. For example, let's say your company's present revenue is one million dollars a year, and you have 100 employees. The company's target for the next year is to achieve a 40 percent growth in revenue and a 20 percent growth in headcount. It is easy to do the math and figure out that you are going to have twenty additional people on the network, and so you need to include that much additional capacity in your one-year network plan. That was easy, wasn't it? Well, hang on just a minute. What the company president neglected to mention was the 40 percent growth in revenue is going to be primarily achieved through an active e-commerce site, which he expects you to maintain internally. Suddenly you need a redundant Web server design and a highly redundant, high capacity Internet connection. And firewalls, security audits, and a host of other things you never thought of.

Then there is the other side of the equation. What if the company president tells you to plan for 300 percent growth in employees and a Web site that is going to receive a million hits a day? You go and spend $500,000 building an infrastructure to support the president's vision. In three years, you have added 20 percent to your headcount, and then they decided that the e-commerce thing wasn't for them. When someone comes looking to see why you spent that money, you are going to need more justification than "Well, you told me we were going to need it." Although we certainly can't cover the detailed analysis of a business's growth in this training guide, we can discuss some of the things you will need to take into account as you start planning for company growth and its impact on the network infrastructure design.

The first thing you need to keep in mind when dealing with growth projections is the fact that it is just that—a projection. You can think of it as a "best guess" (for want of a better term). You need to ensure that your design includes enough flexibility to encompass bad projections. You may need to spend money to meet the reality, but you need to be sure that you are not locking yourself into an architecture that isn't flexible. For example, let's say you have a small office with a single file and print server. When you bought the server, there were 20 users, and you filled all three drive bays with 2GB drives and were ready to go. Then they hired 20 more people, and you were out of drive space. If you had planned appropriately, you might have selected larger drives, or you might have selected a server model that had more than three drive bays so that you could add capacity if needed. While this is a simple example, it gives you an idea of what to look for.

When you start looking at trying to project a company's growth, you need to realize that you will need input from the same business managers that identified the priorities in the last section. It is rare that a network planner or architect will be able to project the company's growth from the facts generally available to them. Make sure you involve the right people so that your projections, or your interpretations of existing projections, are as accurate as possible.

Once you have identified the correct resources, it is time to dive into the projections and then the planning. To establish accurate growth projections, you will want to look at recent trends and future planned business events as they apply to the company's growth and ask a number of questions. Here are some things you will want to determine:

◆ What growth rate has the company projected for the next year? The next three years? The next five years? The first thing you should try to discover is where the senior management of the company thinks the growth will be. Be sure to really delve into the projections. Just knowing the company is going to grow 30 percent isn't going to help your planning much if the growth is projected for a new office in Kuala Lumpur. Try to make sure that you have enough information to apply the projections to your computing architecture.

◆ How much has the company grown in the past quarter? You should be looking for information not only on revenue, but also on employees, services, locations, customers, and anything else that may be important. If they added an additional 10,000 square feet to the manufacturing plant, that is important information for you if that space requires network infrastructure. Will it be growing again in the next quarter?

◆ How much has it grown in the past year? You want to get the same information as above, but by going out to a year, you should be able to detect any trends in the company's growth patterns.

◆ Has the company been meeting its growth projections? If you work for a company that is able to predict its growth accurately (as rare as that generally is) it is important to know. If the company had been "dead on" with projection for the last 37 quarters, you can be pretty confident in your projections. If they continually miss the goal, you know to take the projections with a little common sense and plan appropriately.

◆ How does the company plan to achieve this growth? This is especially key to your planning. If the company plans to meet its goals by acquisitions, you can expect to be spending a lot of time working on integrating disparate network and systems architectures. You need to be able to ensure that your infrastructure is flexible enough to handle acquisitions. You should also make sure that a member of the IT Department is included in any acquisition or divestiture plans—to ensure you can meet the requirements. There is nothing worse than coming into the office and discovering that you have until Friday to add 1000 users to your Exchange servers because you bought a company last Friday, and the CEO wants all the employees on the same mail system ASAP.

◆ One thing that is frequently overlooked is the question, "Where will the growth be?" If you are an international company or are planning on becoming an international company, you have an entirely new set of issues to deal with, including language, available infrastructure in the country (or countries) where the growth will take place, and finding employees.

Company growth affects the demands placed on a network infrastructure in many ways. For example, the addition of new employees to the company means an increase in the number of workstations on the network and an increase in the demand for information to be carried by the network. An increase in network requests translates directly into an increased need for bandwidth. If the company expands into new markets, this might mean the addition of remote sites and campuses, placing new demands on and requiring the expansion of the Wide Area Network. If the company plans to grow by expanding its customer base through online sales, new technologies will have to be added to the network infrastructure and integrated with the existing technologies.

A company's growth plans might include extending operations into new locations. This might mean that the company will extend its geographic scope to the point that it might need to employ a different business model. For example, a U.S. company might expand its operations by building new locations overseas. This would move the company from a National to an International business model.

Following is a list of a couple of things that you should make sure you take into account as you plan for company growth:

◆ Make sure your network infrastructure is upgradeable. In a WAN environment, that means making sure you can add additional T1 lines or increase the bandwidth of existing connections as needed. This includes servers, routers, hubs, and any other computing resources in your environment. Using "maxed" equipment is seldom a good idea (unless there is a large amount of excess capacity).

◆ Make sure that management understands that you need this information for two reasons: to plan the initial design and for ongoing capacity planning. If the projections change and you are not told, you could find yourself in a tight spot when the new plans come to fruition.

◆ Make sure someone from IT is involved in any acquisitions or divestitures. It is all too frequent for senior management to acquire a company only to find out that the systems or networks are not compatible. Planning for acquisitions and divestitures is one of the most challenging facets of growth projections and capacity planning.

Keep in mind these are general guidelines that will need to be applied to your environment as necessary. But by using the methods as a guideline, you should be able to make some excellent projections of company growth and ensure that your network design can handle the load.

Identifying the Relevant Laws and Regulations

Sometimes the operation of a particular business is governed by only a few relevant laws or regulations. Other businesses, however, must adhere to a very complex and strict set of laws and regulations. Financial organizations are an example of such a business. As a business's territory expands, it finds itself governed not only by the laws and regulations local to its company headquarters, but also by laws and regulations that are local to each of its remote offices. International organizations are another good example of businesses that need to adhere to complex and strict laws and regulations.

You might not be able to (or need to) become intimately familiar with all the laws and regulations that are applicable to any given business. This is the job of an attorney, or sometimes a team of attorneys. However, you should work closely with the company's legal department to become aware of any laws and regulations that are pertinent to the network infrastructure design.

Certain areas might have regulations governing the type of wire you can use for your network and the way wiring must be installed. Certain areas have regulations regarding the frequencies and locations of any wireless communication devices you might be planning to use. In addition to the physical components of the network, you might also face regulations regarding the software you choose. For example, if you purchase high-encryption software in the United States, you most likely will not be able to export that software to international locations outside the U.S. High-encryption software is considered a form of munition by the Unites States government. Another example might be a drug company that is dealing with regulated chemical compounds. The FDA needs to know who has access to those formulas. This means that the network designer needs to ensure that the implemented infrastructure supports limiting access to certain users and auditing the nature of the access to certain resources. These features will need to be built into the network infrastructure design to ensure that the company is compliant with FDA regulations.

Partnering with the company's legal team can help make you aware of any legal issues that might apply to your project. This will allow you to take advantage of their expertise in dealing with these issues.

Identifying the Company's Tolerance for Risk

Anytime you design something as mission-critical as a network infrastructure, you must be acutely aware of the risks that are involved in implementing your design. Windows 2000 has been designed to be implemented incrementally, reducing the overall risk associated with the deployment of a Windows 2000 network infrastructure, but there are still risks involved. Knowing up front the company's position and tolerance for risk can help you avoid serious problems as the design and implementation processes unfold. A good plan for managing the risks involved, created at the design phase, can help avoid rejection of the project when it comes time to start the implementation phase.

The first step in creating a risk management plan is to conduct a risk assessment. The risk assessment will identify the risk factors that might affect the project and allow you to develop contingency plans to deal with those factors if they arise, or to prevent them from arising in the first place. The goal of an effective risk management plan is to eliminate risk factors if possible and to minimize the consequences of risk factors that cannot be eliminated.

You should consider creating a risk assessment matrix that includes the following information:

- ◆ The risk factor.
- ◆ The probability that the risk factor will actually occur.
- ◆ The impact on the project that the risk factor carries.
- ◆ Which department or group is responsible for this risk area?
- ◆ What strategy can be employed to mitigate this risk factor?

Risk management should become part of your design and should be kept up to date as your design evolves. Risk management will need to be carried out effectively by the implementation team(s) when your design is finally complete and accepted by company management.

When attempting to identify risk factors to consider in your network infrastructure design, keep in mind that soliciting input from company employees might be difficult. Most companies lack an environment that encourages employees to identify risks. Often an employee who points out risk factors is thought of as a naysayer or is not considered a team player. Other companies actually reward employees who identify risk factors and develop solutions to the problems presented by these factors. In most cases, however, this situation does not exist. Try to overcome the difficulties that identifying risk factors will present. Encourage the company's employees to share their thoughts regarding risk factors for your project, and assist in developing solutions to those problems. Your design will benefit tremendously from this input.

Identifying the Total Cost of Ownership

It is not always obvious how much a network infrastructure really costs. Beyond the purchase price of each component, many other costs are incurred over the life cycle of a network infrastructure. The aggregation of all these costs is referred to as the Total Cost of Ownership (TCO).

Consider the cost associated with putting one computer workstation on the network. Initially, there is the purchase price of the computer, the monitor, and the network cable to connect it to the LAN. There is also the cost of the electricity that powers the computer. There is also the cost of the operating system and licensing all the applications software that is installed on the computer. Of course, this leads to the labor cost that must be paid to the person who installs the operating system and applications software. Once the computer is ready for use, costs are incurred simply by using the computer.

The user might want to access resources on the Internet; this leads to the cost of an Internet connection. If the user wants to print any documents from this computer, another list of costs is incurred: purchase of a printer, printer cables, paper, and toner, and the electricity to operate the printer. There are many other costs to include, ranging from the environmental design, desk, chair, and lighting to the total training of the user population.

What if the user has a problem with the software or hardware? There are support costs for troubleshooting problems and repairing the system. At this point, you can begin to understand how a single network device can lead to a long list of costs and that the sum of these costs can be very large. Now, consider the scope of your network infrastructure design project. How many users will you need to support? 500? 1,000? 10,000? As the scope of your project expands, so do the associated costs. You can see that the Total Cost of Ownership for a large network infrastructure can be astronomical.

A major goal for a network infrastructure design project is to help reduce the Total Cost of Ownership for the company in the area of Information Technology.

ANALYZING IT MANAGEMENT

Analyze the structure of IT management. Considerations include type of administration, such as centralized or decentralized; funding model; outsourcing; decision-making process, and change-management process.

Your network infrastructure design should include an analysis of the current and proposed IT management structure within the organization. It is important to know what areas of responsibility have been established and who represents each area. You will want to solicit input from each of these representatives to ensure that each area is represented in the finished design. This input also ensures that the network infrastructure ultimately implemented delivers all that is needed to each of these groups.

Microsoft identifies the following areas for consideration in its exam objectives for this test:

- Type of administration
- Funding model
- Outsourcing
- Decision-making process
- Change-management process

Each of these considerations will be discussed in the following sections.

Centralized and Decentralized Administration

The company's approach to IT management will have a significant impact on your network infrastructure design. The company might take a centralized approach to administration in which network resources are centrally located and controlled. On the other hand, the company might take a decentralized approach in which resources are widely distributed and responsibility for administering each resource is distributed as well. In still other cases, you might find a hybrid approach in which some resources are administered centrally and the administrative responsibilities for other resources are decentralized.

Make sure that you are aware of any proposed changes to the IT administration model. Planning for these changes ahead of time will save you the effort and cost of having to make accommodating adjustments in your design.

Corporate Funding Models

Before you begin your design, you might want to consider who will pay for the network. The company's approach to funding design and implementation projects will directly impact what you can and cannot accomplish with your design.

If the company has a simple funding model in which projects are funded from a single source of money, the approval process is often simplified as well. If funding is distributed across the organization through a complicated charge-back process, responsibility for approving the project is often distributed. Under this model, each business unit is charged for a portion of the network infrastructure based on the demands that each unit places on the infrastructure. This funding model can make securing approval for your network infrastructure design a long and arduous process.

Outsourcing Network Responsibilities

In many industries, an organization's focus is not technical in nature. The employees do not have the technical expertise to design, install, administer, and maintain a network infrastructure. In the past, organizations had to hire one or more people to perform these tasks, usually at great expense.

These days, a popular alternative is to contract with another company whose focus is entirely technical. This trend is called *outsourcing*. When network responsibilities are outsourced, the contract transfers the responsibility for technical tasks that must be performed to an outsource company. The outsource company maintains the expertise to accomplish tasks with the greatest efficiency. The contract might transfer all responsibility, or only a portion of the responsibilities, for the technical work that must be performed.

In the design process, you need to ascertain whether the company for whom you are designing a network infrastructure is currently outsourcing any part of the responsibility for installing, administering, and maintaining its network. You will need to contact the company representatives who have been charged with the networking responsibilities and involve them in the design process. These people are intimately familiar with the issues currently associated with the company's network infrastructure and can be of tremendous assistance to you as you document the existing infrastructure. They can make you aware of any current issues and help you prioritize them so that you can design your new infrastructure to resolve these issues or at least accommodate them.

The Decision-Making Process

As mentioned earlier in this chapter, each organization has decision-making processes. Sometimes these processes are simple, and other times they are very complex. You will need to examine many of the company's decision-making processes while creating your network infrastructure design, but you will probably become most familiar with the decision-making process followed by the company's IT management. This is the process that your design will go through in order to gain approval and be implemented. Each proposed change to the design will be the result of this decision-making process.

In smaller organizations, the IT management's decision-making process might be as simple as discussing an issue with a single IT manager, who makes a decision on the spot. In larger organizations, you might find that the decision-making process involves many different managers or even committees with representatives from all parts of the organization. Often in large organizations that have formal and complex decision-making processes, the process that is required to be followed by IT management is very time-consuming and slow. It can often take several days or even weeks to get decisions made, even relatively insignificant ones. Being familiar with the decision-making process and planning ahead can help make the design process flow more smoothly, and bring you to the approval stage more quickly and with a great deal less stress.

The Change-Management Process

Whenever a change is made in a production network environment, however slight, there is an associated risk. The risk is that the change will result in the loss of functionality in one system or another on the network.

Loss of functionality might be due to human error of one type or another. Loss of functionality might result if the change is implemented incorrectly.

Loss of functionality might result even if the change was implemented correctly. Change might result in an incompatibility with another related system. Many times, administrators responsible for a particular system are highly knowledgeable in regard to that particular system but are not as knowledgeable when it comes to other systems. While performing configuration changes on their own systems, they might inadvertently cause a negative impact on another related system, resulting in loss of functionality. This can result in downtime and troubleshooting costs as the team responsible for the nonfunctioning system attempts to determine what happened.

In order to avoid situations like this, many companies have implemented a formal change-management process. In some organizations, the process might be a very simple one in which proposed changes submitted to a manager for approval before being implemented. In others, the process might be very involved, in which proposed changes must be thoroughly documented. Proposed changes are presented before a large group of managers from each area of the company. The proposal is discussed by these managers, allowing each department to voice its own concerns before the proposal is finally approved and scheduled for implementation. In some companies, changes that have been implemented are still reviewed by a board of managers to determine the level of success associated with the change and to evaluate whether the change was implemented with the greatest possible efficiency.

No matter what the change-management process is, its main purpose is to eliminate downtime resulting from changes made to the production network environment. You need to be aware of the change-management process that is in place when you create your network infrastructure design. It can often be beneficial to put the design through the change-management process well before you approach the implementation of your design. This offers you another opportunity to determine some of the obstacles your network infrastructure design will face as you seek approval from senior management to implement your design.

CASE STUDY: WHIRLED FOODS, INC.

ESSENCE OF THE CASE

Here are the essential elements of this case:

▶ The company has divisions in Paris, Hong Kong, and New York. They are on the verge of acquiring two large organizations and are planning for further growth.

▶ To support the merger, a new WAN must be developed.

▶ To facilitate some of this growth, the company wants to integrate its network with its suppliers and distributors via the Internet for the purposes of e-commerce.

SCENARIO

Whirled Foods, Inc. is a large parent company with five operating companies under its umbrella. Each of the five operating companies has its own network infrastructure and Information Technology standards. Each operating company is currently responsible for its own Information Technology administration. Three of the companies have hired Information Technology administration staff, and two of the companies have outsourced all of their Information Technology administration to the same Information Technology management company. The operating companies comprise a worldwide operation with multiple international sites. Whirled Foods, Inc. would like to connect each of the sites together in

CASE STUDY: WHIRLED FOODS, INC.

order to form a WAN that will facilitate more effective communication between the operating companies. The marketing department of Whirled Foods, Inc. would also like to sell its products over the Internet and allow each of the operating companies to better communicate with their suppliers and distributors. There are plans to acquire at least two more operating companies in the next year. Given its current sales projections, it is expected that Whirled Foods, Inc. will hire at least another 200 employees in the next two years.

Whirled Foods, Inc. senior management has hired you to create a new network infrastructure design to help them implement Windows 2000 throughout the entire enterprise.

ANALYSIS

Whirled Foods, Inc. and its multiple operating companies pose several challenges to a network infrastructure designer. The individual operating companies each have their own IT standards and administration. There is also the IT management company that is responsible for the outsourced IT administration from two of the operating companies. This management company should be involved in the design project in order to adequately assess the current issues that the operating companies face.

Implementing a WAN to connect the operating companies across international boundaries will necessitate the involvement of each company's legal department to determine the impact of any laws and regulations local to each company's sites. In order to allow the operating companies to interact with their suppliers and distributors, you need to address any integration issues with those network infrastructures. Internet connectivity must be included, and you must address the issues concerning the information flow from inside the corporate network to the outside through the Internet, and vice versa.

The company plans to acquire two more operating companies, so you must address all the issues surrounding the integration of those networks. Finally, you must develop a set of Enterprise-wide IT standards for implementation and administration.

CHAPTER SUMMARY

KEY TERMS

- Local Area Network (LAN)
- Wide Area Network (WAN)
- virtual private network (VPN)
- Enterprise network
- network infrastructure
- business model
- information flow
- life cycle
- Total Cost of Ownership (TCO)
- outsourcing
- change management

Although the business prospectus might seem foreign to many technical engineers, it is essential to a successful deployment of any corporate network and to Windows 2000/Active Directory in particular.

Without an in-depth analysis of the business, you cannot design a flexible, comprehensive, and scaleable network. Geographic boundaries alone do not provide adequate information for determining domain or site boundaries and domain controller placement. You must also understand the business requirements and work flow within and between geographic locations.

Understanding work flow and areas of responsibility helps you determine requirements for messaging, data replication, and storage management, as well as security and user data access. How does the company run? How are the business units divided, and how do they interact? A comprehensive study must also include entities external to the company. Vendors, partners, and customers are vital to the business and must be factored into your design. Finally, you must make special considerations beyond the usual scope of projected growth for issues, such as corporate acquisitions. Allow for flexibility in your design for integration of disparate directories, noncontiguous address space, or foreign networks into your enterprise.

The corporate network exists to facilitate the business of business. Your priorities when developing the network plan should be based on the company's priorities. Plan for the business's stated growth projections. Stay abreast of industry regulations or laws that pertain to your business, such as data archival requirements for record-keeping. Identify the company's tolerance for risk. Network redundancy is costly, but for some systems, the cost pales in comparison to extended downtime. Risk management is a common justification when calculating the Total Cost of Ownership. Plan network upgrades or implementations using a phased approach to minimize the potential risk of a new system failure.

CHAPTER SUMMARY

Finally, you need to look at how your particular IT organization functions. This information is crucial, not only for design, but also to maintain a smooth process and avoid costly delays.

In summary, you should consider the following:

◆ Know your source of funding.

◆ Understand the processes surrounding corporate decisions in your company.

◆ Allow adequate time and resources for the change-management process.

◆ Work closely with the group that will implement the changes, internal or outsourced.

APPLY YOUR KNOWLEDGE

Exercises

1.1   Documenting Information Flow

This exercise demonstrates the process of documenting information flow for a sample business process. We will use a fictitious company called Speedy Message Service, Inc. for this exercise.

Estimated Time: 15 minutes

Speedy Message Service, Inc. is a company that offers after-hours telephone answering and message delivery services to small businesses. It employs several switchboard operators who answer calls, collect messages, and deliver messages to fax machines and pagers owned by representatives of Speedy Message Service clients.

When a person calls a client of the Speedy Message Service after that client's normal business hours, the phone call is routed to the Speedy Message Service switchboard. One of the Speedy operators answers the call, collects the caller's name and phone number, and determines for which client the call was intended. The operator then reads a prewritten script describing the Speedy Message Service to the caller and asks the caller if he wants to leave a message. If the caller wants to leave a message, the operator requests and records the identity of the intended recipient of the message, as well as the message itself, from the caller. After the caller leaves his message, the call is ended. The operator then looks up the pager or fax number of the recipient of the message and either faxes a typed copy of the message to the appropriate fax number or forwards the text message to the recipient's pager. The transaction is logged in the Speedy Message Service database for billing purposes. The transaction is logged whether or not the caller chooses to leave a message.

From this scenario, document the information flows that take place during the call-answering/message-delivery process. Follow these steps:

1. Determine each individual step of the process.

2. Determine the source and destination of each piece of information that is involved in each step of the process.

3. Document the flow of information from each source to each destination. Indicate the direction of the information flow.

When you have completed step 1, you will have a list that looks like the following:

1. Answer the call and collect the caller's name and phone number.

2. Determine which client the caller wants to reach.

3. Read the script to the caller.

4. Determine if the caller wants to leave a message.

5. Request and record the recipient's name.

6. Collect the message and end the call.

7. Look up the recipient's information.

8. Forward the message to the fax or pager number.

9. Log the transaction for billing purposes.

When you have completed step 2, you will have a table that looks like this:

Step	Information Source	Information Destination
1	Caller	Operator
2	Caller	Operator
3	Operator	Caller

APPLY YOUR KNOWLEDGE

Step	Information Source	Information Destination
4	Caller	Operator
5	Caller	Operator
6	Caller	Operator
7	Client Database	Operator
8	Operator	Fax machine or pager
9	Operator	Billing database

After completing step 3, you will have an information flow for this process that looks like this:

Caller <— —> Operator

Client Database —> Operator

Operator —> Fax machine or pager

Operator —> Billing database

As you can see from this exercise, a number of information flows can be associated with a given business process. The information flow can be in one direction, or it can be two-way. Any component of the process can be an information source, an information destination, or both.

1.2 Identifying the Company Organization

In this exercise you will identify the organization of the company for the purpose of allocating network resources. In this example, we'll use a fictitious company called King Foods.

Estimated Time: 10 minutes

King Foods is a food distributorship with headquarters in Chicago. They have warehouses in Philadelphia,

Atlanta, and Portland. Their executive management resides at headquarters but occasionally travels to the other locations. Executive management, human resources, legal, and finance departments are located at headquarters. Each of the warehouses has a small human resources, shipping, receiving, and customer service department, which is responsible for handling issues with orders as well as providing order status for customers.

In addition, 20 sales offices are located throughout the United States. These offices are responsible for taking orders. One person on staff is responsible for maintenance of PCs as well as swapping backup tapes for the servers.

Each department is responsible for purchasing its own PCs and equipment, although departments with small presence are allowed to use other departments' resources.

Answer the following questions:

1. What is the organizational structure of the company (such as geographic)?

2. What network resources should be located at the following locations?

   • Corporate headquarters

   • The distribution warehouses

   • The sales offices

Answers to Exercise 1.2

1. The company is organized by business, function, or department. Headquarters, warehouses, and sales offices each perform a certain business support function.

APPLY YOUR KNOWLEDGE

2. The network resources should be located at the following locations:

- Corporate headquarters: Executive management, human resources, legal, and finance.

- The distribution warehouses: Shipping, receiving, and customer service. (Human resources will use the other departments' resources.)

- The sales offices: Sales. (Executive management will use sales resources when necessary.)

1.3   Identifying the Projected Growth and Growth Strategy

In this exercise you will identify the projected growth and growth strategy of a company. We will use a fictitious company called Healthtastic.

Estimated Time: 10 minutes

Healthtastic is a fledgling company that sells vitamins and nutritional supplements in locations in the Midwest. They have locations in Cincinnati, Cleveland, Columbus, Louisville, and Indianapolis. Sales have increased steadily by 15 to 20 percent each year for the past five years.

Because it has had success in the past, Healthtastic would like to expand into new geographic markets. Additionally, new funding has been approved to launch a radio advertising campaign. Recent market research indicates that online purchases of vitamins and nutritional supplements will increase by 300 percent in the next five years. Healthtastic currently doesn't have a Web presence but is considering starting one.

Name the factors to take into consideration when planning a network infrastructure for Healthtastic.

Answers to Exercise 1.3

▶ Sales have increased steadily by 15 to 20 percent each year. Therefore, the network infrastructure should be designed to accommodate for continued growth at this rate. This includes not only the ability to support additional bandwidth requirements, but also the potential for more offices opening in the future.

▶ Healthtastic is planning on launching a radio advertising campaign. Sales of their products should increase with this campaign. Growth may follow the increased sales. You may want to check the statistics for previous campaigns and see what impact they had on sales. You should also factor in that increased sales can frequently mean increased hours for your employees. You will need to be sensitive to planned network outages, and you may want to plan on additional support personnel for the off hours.

▶ Recent market research indicates that online purchases of vitamins and nutritional supplements will increase by 300 percent in the next five years. Healthtastic currently doesn't have a Web presence but is considering starting one. If Healthtastic decides to create a Web presence, the network infrastructure will need to be modified to accommodate this Web presence. This is always fun for a company because decisions need to be made. Do you self-host or outsource? What kind of security infrastructure will you need? How many hits will the site generate? What is the impact of system downtime? What platform will the site run on, and how fault-tolerant does it need to be? Do you have the expertise in-house to handle such an undertaking, or do you need to outsource? Do you need to start training your people and ordering equipment in order to meet the goals set?

APPLY YOUR KNOWLEDGE

▶ Healthtastic would like to expand into new geographic markets. If Healthtastic decides to build or lease new locations in the U.S., the network infrastructure will need to be modified to accommodate these locations. However, Healthtastic may create a Web presence and rely on this presence to enter new geographic markets. You need to work with senior management to determine which avenue makes sense for the company. You can expect to have to provide costs for the competing solutions, including the advantages and disadvantages, as well as a plan for supporting the new infrastructure once it is deployed.

1.4   IT Management Structure

In this exercise, you will plan the IT management structure of a company. We will use a fictitious company called Vandelay Industries.

Estimated Time: 10 minutes

Vandelay Industries is an upscale clothing manufacturer with headquarters in Paris. They also have locations in Venice, Italy; Vincenza, Italy; Bonn, Germany; and Vienna, Austria. The headquarters has 300 employees and also holds the company's main databases and Enterprise Resource Planning (ERP) system. Vincenza is a satellite office that has a staff of 20 employees. The remaining three locations have between 75 and 250 employees. All locations have PCs and PC servers. The IT department is responsible for maintaining all equipment—although department heads have requested the ability to reset their users' passwords as well as manage their own printers.

Design an IT management structure for the company.

Answers to Exercise 1.4

Suggested solution:

- Have a central IT staff located in Paris.

- Have IT staff to support the PCs in Bonn, Vienna, and Venice.

- Due to the low number of users and the close proximity to Venice, have no IT presence in Vincenza.

> **NOTE**
>
> **Regarding the Solution** There is more than one correct answer.

Review Questions

1. What is the major benefit of a formal change-management process?

2. What are some of the benefits of conducting a risk analysis?

3. What characteristics distinguish a WAN from a LAN?

4. What are some of the factors contributing to the TCO of a computer beyond the purchase price?

5. What span of time makes up a product's life cycle?

6. In what way can a company's growth plans impact a network infrastructure design project?

7. What are some of the pros and cons of a centralized approach to Information Technology administration?

APPLY YOUR KNOWLEDGE

8. What are some of the main reasons that companies outsource the Information Technology responsibilities?

9. What network design considerations must be made when a company acquisition is planned?

10. How can local laws and regulations affect a network infrastructure design project?

Exam Questions

The first five exam questions refer to the Case Study presented earlier in this chapter.

1. Which business model applies to Whirled Foods, Inc.'s corporate Enterprise network?

    A. Regional

    B. National

    C. Subsidiary

    D. International

2. When you've finished your new network infrastructure design, the Enterprise corporate network that connects each of the operating companies in the parent headquarters will be what type of network?

    A. Wide Area Network (WAN)

    B. Metropolitan Area Network (MAN)

    C. Local Area Network (LAN)

    D. Storage Area Network (SAN)

3. What is the structure of Whirled Foods, Inc.'s IT management group?

    A. Centralized

    B. Decentralized

    C. Distributed

    D. Hierarchical

4. What is Whirled Foods, Inc.'s projected growth?

    A. The company plans to reduce its size in the next two years.

    B. The company plans to increase its size in the next two years.

    C. The company plans to remain consistent over the next two years.

    D. The company has no plans or strategies with respect to growth.

5. How do Whirled Foods, Inc.'s relationships with its vendors, partners, and customers impact your considerations of network infrastructure design? (Choose two.)

    A. The company's vendor relationships have no impact on the internal network design.

    B. The company's plans to sell products over the Internet require consideration in the network design.

    C. The company's goals of better communication with its suppliers and distributors demand consideration during the network infrastructure design.

    D. The network infrastructure design will require the approval of the company's partners, vendors, and customers.

    E. The company's customer relationships have no impact on the internal network design.

6. You have been hired to create a new network infrastructure design for the Sunbeam Foods Manufacturing Company. The company has

specified a number of requirements for the network, including the following:

- The new network must help reduce the company's total cost of operations.

- The new network must help reduce the company's risk exposures.

- The new network must accommodate the company's projected growth.

You set out to create a network design that meets these corporate goals. Which of the following impact the company's TCO? (Choose all that apply.)

A. The cost of each individual network component

B. The cost of the lighting fixtures above each workstation

C. The cost of the software and operating systems on each person's computer

D. The salary cost for each help desk technician

E. The salary cost for the end user

F. The weighted salary cost for the end user

G. The research and development costs for the software manufacturer

7. You have been hired by the T.S. Allen corporation to design a new network infrastructure for its corporate headquarters. T.S. Allen management hierarchy is very structured, as is the organization's decision-making process. Each proposed change or new project must first be approved by a lower-level manager, who in turn brings it to a department head, who in turn brings it to a vice president. In what way does such a hierarchical, structured decision-making process impact your network design?

A. The decision-making process within the organization has no impact on the network design.

B. The decision-making process hinders the network design.

C. The decision-making process can slow the development of a network design.

D. The decision-making process helps speed the creation of the network design.

8. You are hired to perform a network infrastructure design for Happy Toys, Inc. While creating a network infrastructure design, you decide to perform a life-cycle analysis on the company's products and services. Your manager doesn't understand the definition of the process of a life cycle and asks you to describe the starting point and end point of a life-cycle analysis. Which of the following represent the start and end of a product's life cycle?

A. The life cycle begins on the date the product is offered for sale and hits the market and ends when the product is removed from the market.

B. The life cycle begins on the date the product is removed from store shelves and is no longer offered for sale and ends when the product is no longer supported by the manufacturer.

C. The life cycle begins on the date the product is initially conceived and ends on the date that the product is no longer sold or supported.

APPLY YOUR KNOWLEDGE

D. The life cycle begins on the date that the product enters production and ends when all supplies of the product are exhausted and support for the product no longer exists.

9. You are in the middle of creating a network design infrastructure for Sharp Pens Corporation when it acquires one of its competitors, Ball Point, Inc. Which of the following aspects of the acquisitions process will impact your design? (Choose all that apply.)

    A. The cost of acquiring the company

    B. Determining which of the company's systems or services need to be retired

    C. Determining the roles and responsibilities of IT management in the merger

    D. Determining which of the new company's systems will replace existing systems in the parent company

    E. Determining the impact of systems previously retired from Ball Point, Inc.

    F. Determining multiple iterations of past infrastructure designs for either company

10. You are in the process of creating a network infra-structure design for ABC Sewing Machine Co. During the process, you ask to meet with senior management to help develop an understanding of the company's business priorities. Management wants to know why you need to discuss this with them. What will you tell company management to help justify the meeting? (Choose two.)

    A. Understanding the company's business priori-ties will help you resolve conflicts and make compromises in your network design.

    B. Understanding the company's business priori-ties will help you create a faster network.

    C. Understanding the company's business priori-ties will help you reduce the total cost of ownership for the network.

    D. Understanding the company's business priori-ties will help you complete your design more quickly.

11. While developing a network infrastructure design for Hefty Luggage Corp., you ask to meet with their legal team to go over any legal issues that might impact your design. Members of the legal team respond that they are very busy and might not be able to meet with you. They question whether it is of the utmost importance to get together before you finish your network design. What can you tell the legal team to justify the need for meeting with them before you finish your design?

    A. The company might be breaking the law by implementing your network design.

    B. You are not an attorney, and you require their expertise in order to guarantee that the final design does not incorporate any elements that violate local laws, rules, or regulations.

    C. Senior management has mandated that you meet with the legal team, even though you really don't feel it is necessary.

    D. You require the expertise of the legal depart-ment to make sure that all the paperwork you submit for your network design conforms to the legal structure of documents of that nature.

APPLY YOUR KNOWLEDGE

12. During the design phase of the network infrastructure for New Riders, Inc., one of the company managers comes to you, expressing extreme concern that risk is being considered during the design phase. Which design component can you produce to that manager to demonstrate the incorporation of risk management in the overall network infrastructure design?

    A. Risk matrix

    B. Life cycle analysis

    C. Risk factor

    D. Legal analysis

13. You are in the process of creating a network infrastructure design for Good Foot Shoes, Inc. Currently, the company is outsourcing responsibility for IT management. What steps must you take to accommodate this outsourcing in your overall network design?

    A. You must exclude IT support from your network design.

    B. You must meet with the outsourcing company to determine its requirements and how the network design can accommodate them.

    C. You should meet with company management to try to convince them to move responsibility for IT management in-house.

    D. You should contact the outsourcing organization to have it create your network infrastructure design.

14. During the process of creating a network infrastructure design for Corporate Training, Inc., you find that you must submit your design to the change-management board for approval. Your

boss feels that this step is unnecessary because he has complete faith in your ability to create an excellent infrastructure design. However, you are glad that the change-management process exists, and you attempt to explain to your boss the benefits of an effective change-management strategy. What are some of the elements in favor of the change-management process that you can cite while explaining your position to your boss? (Choose two.)

    A. The change-management process slows down the ability to make changes in the enterprise.

    B. The change-management process ensures appropriate responsibility for changes to the production environment.

    C. The change-management process ensures adequate recovery strategy should a change implemented to the production environment create problems.

    D. The change-management processes cost more money and will therefore increase the amount you can charge for creating your network design.

    E. The change-management process is rarely implemented, so in this case, it is good practice, but nonessential.

15. You're in the process of creating a network infrastructure design for Charles Films Distribution Co. During the process, you spend considerable time documenting information flow throughout the company. Your boss considers this to be time wasted and wonders why the network infrastructure design is not completed. What will you tell him about the benefits of documenting information flow to help justify your actions?

APPLY YOUR KNOWLEDGE

A. Documenting company information flow takes considerable time, increasing the number of hours you can bill for your network infrastructure design.

B. Documenting company information flow helps you understand senior management's motivations and gain approval for your design.

C. Understanding information flow in an enterprise helps ensure that you design a network infrastructure that enables information to be delivered where it is needed, when it is needed, as quickly as possible and at as low a cost as possible.

D. Documenting the information flow within an organization helps you create charts and graphs to include in your network infrastructure design to make it seem more feasible.

Answers to Review Questions

1. A formal change-management process allows an organization to carefully analyze proposed changes and let all affected parties give input before a change is implemented in the production environment. This helps avoid implementing changes that have surprising and sometimes disastrous results. See "The Change-Management Process."

2. The major benefits of conducting a risk analysis are the ability to develop plans to prevent risk factors from happening and the ability to develop plans to help mitigate the impact of risk factors that cannot be prevented. See "Acquisitions Plans."

3. Several characteristics distinguish a WAN from a LAN. First is the geographic scope. A WAN occupies a much larger geographic region than a LAN. Another characteristic is bandwidth. WANs typically (but not always) offer much less bandwidth then LANs. Finally, LANs are usually under the complete control of the company that owns them, whereas WANs use leased lines from public carriers and are subject to control by the carrier administrators. MAN stands for Metropolitan Area Network. A MAN is a subset of a WAN, with a shorter area span, usually within the boundaries of a single city. SAN stands for Storage Area Network, which describes the newer technologies available for mass data storage where large arrays of storage are distributed across a building or campus and connected via high-speed data links. See "Introduction."

4. Many factors contribute to the TCO of a single computer beyond the purchase price. Some factors include the cost of any cables that must be purchased to connect the computer's components, the cost of the electricity to power the PC, the cost of peripherals, such as printers and scanners, the cost of the operating system and any applications software installed on the computer, the labor cost associated with assembling the computer, and installing and configuring the operating system and applications software. See "Identifying the Total Cost of Ownership."

5. A product life cycle starts when the product is initially conceived, extends through the design and production stages, and continues until the product is rendered obsolete and is finally retired or discontinued. See "Service and Product Life Cycles."

6. The company's projected growth plans are a significant factor to be considered when designing a network infrastructure. If your design assumes moderate growth for the company, and after implementation you find that the company has aggressive growth plans, your network infrastructure will be inadequate for the demands placed on it. If you plan for aggressive growth and the company plans to grow slowly or moderately, your network design will probably specify a network that is too expensive to be justified by the level of demand for network services. See "Identifying the Projected Growth and Growth Strategy."

7. Table 1.1 lists the pros and cons associated with a centralized approach to Information Technology administration.

TABLE 1.1

PROS AND CONS OF CENTRALIZED IT ADMINISTRATION

Pros	Cons
Limited risk of misconfiguration	The administration is not close to resources and the people who use them
Lower staffing costs	Lack of flexibility
Greater control over Enterprise configuration	Often unable to respond quickly to localized failures at remote sites

See "Centralized and Decentralized Administration."

8. Companies whose business focus is not a technical one tend to outsource their Information Technology responsibilities for the following reasons:

- Outsourcing is cheaper than employing and managing technical staff.

- Outsourcing eliminates the risk of losing significant administrative capabilities due to employee turnover.

See "Outsourcing Network Responsibilities."

9. Chances are that the two companies have very different and possibly incompatible network infrastructures. When designing a network infrastructure for a company that you know will be acquiring another, you will need to determine the following:

- Which of the new company's systems and services will need to be retained?

- Which of the new company's systems and services will need to be retired?

- Which of the new company's systems and services will replace existing systems and services?

- Which of the existing systems and services will need to be extended into the newly acquired company?

- What are the barriers to integrating the two companies' network infrastructures?

See "Acquisitions Plans."

10. Local laws and regulations can impact your network infrastructure design in many ways. For instance, local regulations might dictate which types of cabling you may use. Local laws might affect the placement of certain network devices, such as microwave transmission devices. See "Identifying the Relevant Laws and Regulations."

Answers to Exam Questions

1. **D.** The Whirled Foods, Inc. network is comprised of the individual networks of all the five operating companies. These operating companies are distributed worldwide, making the Enterprise network an international one. The International business model applies to Whirled Foods, Inc.'s Enterprise network. See "Analyzing the Company Model and Geographic Scope."

2. **A.** The Whirled Foods, Inc. Enterprise network would be a Wide Area Network that connects each of the operating companies' Local Area Networks. See "Introduction."

3. **B.** Each of the operating companies under the Whirled Foods, Inc. umbrella is responsible for managing its own IT resources. Some of the companies' staff manages their resources internally, and others outsource the responsibilities. This is an example of a decentralized approach to IT management. See "Centralized and Decentralized Administration."

4. **B.** Whirled Foods, Inc. plans to acquire another two operating companies within the next year and plans to hire at least 200 more employees in the next two years. Understanding ahead of time the company's growth plans and strategies allows you to incorporate and accommodate them in your network infrastructure design. See "Identifying the Projected Growth and Growth Strategy" and "Acquisitions Plans."

5. **B, C.** An understanding of the company's relationships with its partners, vendors, and customers is important prior to the design phase of a new network infrastructure. Whirled Foods, Inc.'s plans to sell products to its customers over the Internet and to communicate with its suppliers and distributors will require consideration during the design phase of its network infrastructure. You will want to make sure that the network infrastructure design accommodates these types of communication in order to ensure that the design helps the company meet its business goals. See "Vendor, Partner, and Customer Relationships."

6. **A, B, C, D.** The TCO for information technology describes not just the purchase price of each individual component, but also every other cost associated with owning and operating those components. These include lighting necessary to allow each person to use these network devices, the operating systems and software that reside on each network device, as well as the costs associated with hiring and keeping on staff appropriate support personnel. See "Identifying the Total Cost of Ownership."

7. **C.** Organizations with thorough hierarchical decision-making processes can often slow the process of creating a network infrastructure design. This is not necessarily a bad thing, because the hierarchical decision-making process helps weed out errors and potential pitfalls that might result as part of the design. Working through the decision-making process and making changes to your design as you complete each step can help ensure that the design most closely meets corporate business goals and will ultimately reach approval at the final step of the decision-making process. See "The Decision-Making Process."

APPLY YOUR KNOWLEDGE

8. **C.** The full life cycle of a product or service begins on the date that the product is conceptualized, not on the date that it is offered for sale. Much time is spent between conceptualization and the date that the final product is offered for sale. This time is spent doing research and development, design, prototyping, and, finally, manufacturing or production. The end of life for a product or service comes when all supplies of that product or service have been exhausted and the company has decided to end all support for the product or service. This usually occurs long after the date the product is no longer offered for sale. See "Service and Product Life Cycles."

9. **B, C, D.** Company acquisitions can have dramatic impact on your network infrastructure design. Here are some of the elements that you must consider regarding corporate acquisitions:

   • Which of the company's systems and services will need to be retained?

   • Which of the new company's systems and services will need to be retired?

   • Which of the new company's systems and services will replace existing systems and services?

   • Which of the existing systems and services will need to be extended into the newly acquired company?

   • What are the barriers to integrating the two companies' network infrastructures?

   See "Acquisitions Plans."

10. **A, C.** Developing an understanding of a company's business priorities will help you during the network infrastructure design phase. Creating a network infrastructure design often requires resolution of conflicting requirements on the part of each network component. Compromises must be made during the design process. Understanding a company's business priorities will help you understand where to make these compromises and resolve these conflicts. In addition, understanding a company's business priorities will help you create a design that reduces the company's total cost of ownership by maximizing their investment in the components that matter to them most and minimizing the investment in components that do not serve to meet specific business goals. See "Identifying Company Priorities."

11. **B.** Sometimes the operation of a business is governed by a very complex set of rules and regulations. Often a company requires not just a single attorney, but a team of attorneys to ensure compliance with the relevant rules and regulations. As a network designer, you can't possibly be intimately familiar with all the rules and regulations that govern the activities of all of your clients. You'll need to recruit the assistance of the company's legal team in the design process to make sure that the final design does not include components that would result in a violation of any relevant laws, rules, or regulations. See "Identifying the Relevant Laws and Regulations."

APPLY YOUR KNOWLEDGE

12. **A.** In the process of creating the network infrastructure design, you should incorporate risk management. The way to do this is to complete a risk matrix that identifies the risk factors that the company might face, the probability that the risk factor will actually occur, the impact on the project of each risk factor, which department or group is responsible for this risk area, and the strategies that can be employed to mitigate these factors should they occur. The risk matrix should be kept up to date as the network design process continues. See "Identifying the Company's Tolerance for Risk."

13. **B.** When creating a network infrastructure design for a company that outsources responsibility for IT management, you will need to meet with the company that has that responsibility to determine any issues currently associated with the company's network infrastructure. The outsourcing company that has responsibility for those issues can help you prioritize them and help you design an infrastructure that either resolves or accommodates these issues. See "Outsourcing Network Responsibilities."

14. **B, C.** An effective change-management process can help ensure that before changes are made to the corporate production environment, adequate responsibility has been assigned for those changes, and a backup recovery strategy has been developed. This helps ensure that any changes made to the production environment have been thoroughly tested and are sure to work. In the event that unforeseen problems arise and a change creates a problem, the requirement that a backup strategy exists helps to minimize the impact of these change-related problems and can eliminate or minimize downtime associated with changes made to the production environment. See "The Change-Management Process."

15. **C.** As employees in a company perform their day-to-day work, information flows to and from many different locations within the organization. Efficient and effective delivery of information to its required destinations is the job of the network infrastructure. Understanding the information flow within the organization helps you create a network infrastructure design that ensures fast delivery of information to a destination that requires it, at the time it is required, as fast as possible, and for as low a cost as possible. These are the ultimate goals of the network infrastructure design. See "Information Flow."

Suggested Readings and Resources

1. Oppenheimer, Priscilla. *Top-Down Network Design*. Indianapolis, IN: Cisco Press, 1999.

2. *Windows 2000 Deployment Guide*. Microsoft Press, 2000.

This chapter covers the following Microsoft-specified objectives for the Analyzing Technical Requirements section of the Designing a Microsoft Windows 2000 Network Infrastructure exam:

Evaluate the company's existing and planned technical environment and goals.

- **Analyze company size and user and resource distribution.**

- **Assess the available connectivity between the geographic location of work sites and remote sites.**

- **Assess net available bandwidth and latency.**

- **Analyze performance, availability, and scalability requirements of services.**

- **Analyze data and system access patterns.**

- **Analyze network roles and responsibilities.**

- **Analyze security considerations.**

▶ This objective will help you determine how to translate the goals of the business into a technical design. You will learn how to assess the existing network infrastructure from a technical point of view and compare it to the proposed goals to determine which Windows 2000 features will need to be included in your design.

CHAPTER 2

Analyzing Technical Requirements

Analyze the impact of infrastructure design on the existing and planned technical environment.

- **Assess current applications.**

- **Analyze network infrastructure, protocols, and hosts.**

- **Evaluate network services.**

- **Analyze TCP/IP infrastructure.**

- **Assess current hardware.**

- **Identify existing and planned upgrades and rollouts.**

- **Analyze technical support structure.**

- **Analyze existing and planned network and systems management.**

▶ This objective addresses the considerations that must be made to determine the impact of a new network infrastructure design on the existing network infrastructure. Windows 2000 was designed to be deployed gradually. To successfully deploy, you must fully understand the areas where changes to the existing infrastructure will be the most disruptive and plan accordingly. You must also be able to identify the areas of the existing network infrastructure requiring improvement or change.

Analyze the network requirements for client computer access.

- **Analyze end-user work needs.**

- **Analyze end-user usage patterns.**

▶ The primary function of any network infrastructure is to support the needs of the end users. This objective will help you learn to identify the needs of the end-user community and focus your network infrastructure design on meeting those needs.

Analyze the existing disaster recovery strategy for client computers, servers, and the network.

▶ This objective helps you examine the disaster recovery strategies that exist to support the current network infrastructure. You will need to consider these strategies and determine whether they are sufficient for the existing infrastructure as well as for the new network infrastructure design.

▶ The material in this chapter is not necessarily Microsoft-specific. The approach to network analysis that you take in this chapter will serve you well on any network project. Remember as you learn these techniques that many of them can be transferred to other non-Microsoft projects.

▶ Much of the material in this chapter dealing with basic networking was previously covered on the MCSE 4.0 exam Networking Essentials. Because Microsoft has eliminated this exam requirement in the MCSE 2000 track, I recommend reviewing *Network+ Certification Guide* (New Riders Publishing, ISBN 073570077X) and *Network+ Fast Track* (New Riders Publishing, ISBN 0735709041).

▶ Pay particular attention to the Case Study that we develop in this chapter. Case studies are an excellent way to learn and begin to understand network design concepts.

▶ As you read the material presented in this chapter, try to associate it with events in your own experience. Think about network projects that you have been involved with, and try to determine if any of the steps described in this chapter were performed for those projects. What was the outcome as a result of design planning strategies?

INTRODUCTION

Perhaps the most obvious planning step when creating a network infrastructure design is the analysis of technical requirements. It is not always obvious, however, how to actually perform this step.

What information should be included in a thorough technical requirements analysis? What measurements must be taken? How are these measurements made? What does the data mean? The answers to these questions will be revealed as we address the objectives that Microsoft has defined for analyzing technical requirements. Each of the objectives is covered in the following sections.

EVALUATING TECHNICAL ENVIRONMENT AND GOALS

Evaluate the company's existing and planned technical environment and goals.

Before beginning your network infrastructure design, you must be able to determine three things:

- ◆ What does the customer do with its existing network infrastructure?

- ◆ What does the customer want to do with the network infrastructure?

- ◆ What is the gap between the current infrastructure and the desired infrastructure?

Answering these questions is called performing a *gap analysis*.

A gap analysis is useful in determining what steps will need to be performed to improve the existing network infrastructure. The gap between the existing environment and the environmental goals proposed by company management will form the basis of your network infrastructure design and will help you decide which Windows 2000 features will need to be included in your design.

The first step in your gap analysis is to assess the state of the current network infrastructure. The areas to examine, and the processes for doing so, are covered in the next several sections.

Analyze Company Size and User and Resource Distribution

Examine the company size. How many users will the network infrastructure need to support? 100? 1,000? 10,000? Make sure that you consider whether the company plans to extend its infrastructure to be used by its vendors and partners. If so, determine how many users from the vendors' and partners' networks will be accessing the new network infrastructure. Make sure that you have an accurate assessment of the various user populations so that you can design for performance, reliability, and scalability, in accordance with the real demand for network services.

In addition to the user population total, you should look closely at the distribution of these users. Are they all in one building or on one campus? Are they spread out across multiple locations? Are those locations spread out across the country or around the world?

You will have different considerations depending on the distribution of the user population. If all the users are in one building, you are basically designing a LAN infrastructure. If they occupy multiple buildings within a single campus, you are working with a design known as a CAN, or campus area network. In this type of network, you must deal with the additional complexity of connecting the buildings within the campus, in addition to the individual client computers within each building.

If the population is more widely distributed, you must also include a design for WAN services in your overall infrastructure design. Each of the company sites will have its client computers connected to a LAN, and each of the LANs will be connected in some way to the WAN.

Some of the users in the total user population might be mobile users who need to access the network infrastructure from remote sites that change frequently. In this case, you will want to build in support for either the traditional RAS services or the newer VPN services in your network infrastructure design. The use of VPN services implies that some sort of Internet connectivity will be required, so you must include that connectivity in your design as well.

Once you have assessed the user population and the distribution of those users, you will need to examine the distribution of network resources on the existing infrastructure. Are the resources centrally located? Are the resources stored physically near segments of the user population that uses them most? Are all users afforded adequate access to all the network resources they require?

As you examine the existing distribution of resources and compare that to the distribution of users, you should attempt to determine if the current infrastructure is adequate. This will help you decide whether you can use the existing infrastructure as a model for the new one, or whether you must discard the layout of the existing infrastructure and design a new infrastructure from scratch.

After you've developed a clear understanding of the existing user and resource distribution, you must then work with company management to develop an understanding of their future plans. How large will the company grow? What new resources will be added? How will the distribution of users and resources change? Try to identify the differences between the existing state and the proposed future state so that you can craft your infrastructure design accordingly.

Assessing Available Connectivity

If you are working on a design for a network that is geographically distributed, you will need to become familiar with the connectivity that is available to each location. If the site is already connected to the current infrastructure, examine its current connectivity. Is it adequate? Does it meet the company's goals in terms of cost, performance, and scalability? What other options are available? You might need to check with the provider of the connectivity you are examining if it is in the form of some kind of leased line. If the connectivity is provided through Plain Old Telephone Service (POTS), you might want to inquire whether an alternative means of connecting is available. In some mountainous or rural areas, connectivity options, including POTS, might be limited.

If the location you are examining is a new one, or if it is not connected to the existing infrastructure for some other reason, you will need to investigate the connectivity options available in that area. Remember that connectivity concerns include both ends of the link. You must determine the connectivity options that are common to both the remote site and the central site that it will connect to (if, indeed, you are connecting to a central site). Different connectivity models require different approaches. Two typical connectivity models are the hub and spoke model and the mesh model.

In a hub and spoke network, one site—the hub—is selected as a central point of communication, and all other sites connect to it. The links from the remote sites to the hub sites are the spokes, resembling the spokes of a wagon wheel. Figure 2.1 depicts a hub and spoke network.

A mesh network, on the other hand, has no central point of communication. There is no hub. Instead, each location is connected to several other locations. A mesh network can be either fully meshed or partially meshed. In a fully meshed network, each site is connected to every other site. Figure 2.2 depicts a fully meshed network.

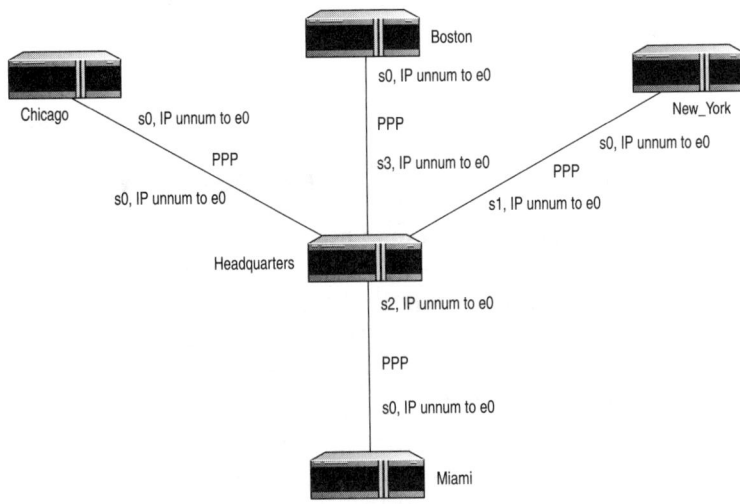

FIGURE 2.1

In a hub and spoke network topology, remote sites all connect to a central site, usually the corporate headquarters.

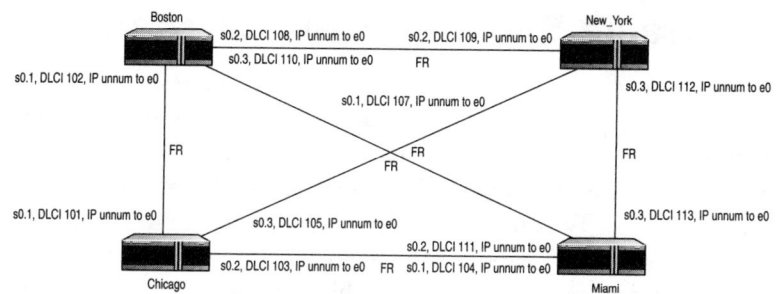

FIGURE 2.2
In a fully meshed network topology, all sites connect to all other sites.

In a partially meshed network, one or more sites are connected to every other site. However, other sites on the network are not connected to every other site; some sites might be connected to only one other site, or to several sites. Figure 2.3 shows a network that is partially meshed.

Once you have determined which model you want to use, you can investigate the connectivity that is available for each proposed link in the network design. After you determine the available options, you can decide which options provide the required level of connectivity with respect to cost, performance, scalability, and reliability.

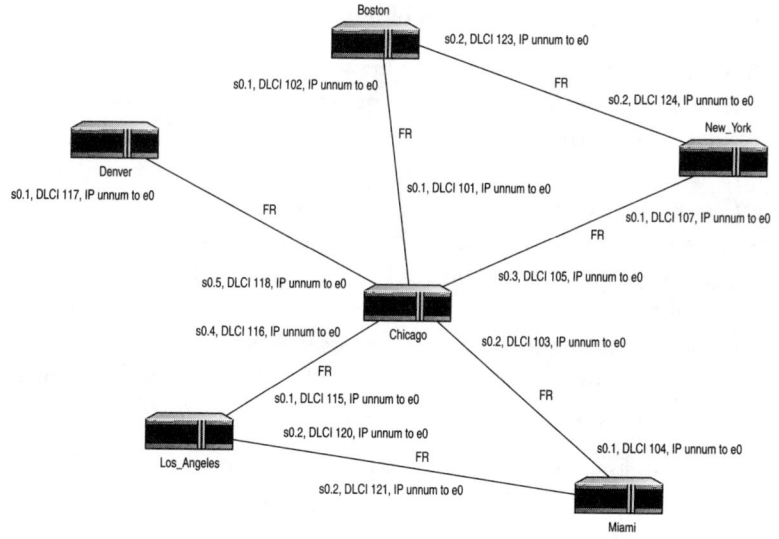

FIGURE 2.3
In a partially meshed network topology, some sites connect to every other site on the network, and other sites are not connected to every other site.

Assessing Bandwidth and Latency

A major factor in designing connectivity throughout the network infrastructure is bandwidth. Bandwidth is the measure of the amount of data that a network link can carry at any given time. Bandwidth is typically measured in bits per second (bps), or some multiple of bps. Typical multiples are kilobits per second (Kbps) and megabits per second (Mbps). A standard Ethernet network can carry 10Mbps of data, so its potential available bandwidth is also 10Mbps. Fast Ethernet offers 100Mbps of potential bandwidth. A T-1 leased line offers 1.544Mbps of bandwidth, compared to a typical modem connection across POTS lines, which can offer only a theoretical 56Kbps (in actual practice, less than 53Kbps).

These topologies offer potential bandwidth. I say potential bandwidth because, depending on the topology and the type of use to which the link is put, the actual amount of data that can cross the link will vary. The actual amount of data that crosses a link is called the *throughput* of the link. Throughput can be measured overall or on a per-user basis. When you measure throughput on a per-user basis, you are typically only concerned with user data that crosses the network link. Many other types of data will occupy the network link at any given time. This data uses up a portion of the potential bandwidth.

Other data that might occupy the network link includes control information necessary to maintain the link itself, and broadcast or multicast information put on the network by devices that offer network services. For example, file servers and print servers often broadcast across the network. Routers exchange routing protocol information with each other in order to provide network services. Bridges exchange Bridge Protocol Data Units (BPDUs) with each other. All of this data crosses the network link and uses the same bandwidth that might be available for user data. The amount of bandwidth left over for user data, after subtracting all the bandwidth used by other kinds of data, is referred to as *net available bandwidth*.

You need to assess the net available bandwidth on all network links. This will determine if the links can meet the company's performance requirements.

A related factor that affects throughput is *latency*. Latency refers to the amount of time between the moment when a network station sends the first data packet and the moment when the transmission of that packet is completed successfully. Average latency is sometimes also called *propagation delay*. Applications often have limited tolerance for latency. Increases in network latency can be the cause of application timeouts and consequently loss of functionality and increased downtime. Your network infrastructure design should be created with every effort to minimize latency.

Increases in latency often point to a network link that is overutilized and unable to meet the demands placed on it. When analyzing network links over extended periods of time, note any periods where dramatic increases in latency accompany increases in utilization. If these periods occur frequently, the link might be overutilized and will need to be improved in your new design.

How do you measure bandwidth and latency? Use a network protocol analyzer. Many protocol analyzers, such as Network Associates' Sniffer or Microsoft's Network Monitor, allow you to gather network bandwidth, utilization, and latency statistics. Some products produce charts from data collected over a long period of time. The charts are created from data that is collected by taking a "snapshot" of the traffic on the network and analyzing the traffic. Snapshots are taken at specific intervals. Most protocol analyzers allow you to specify the interval at which snapshots are taken. Depending on the interval at which the snapshots are taken, the charts can tell you different things.

For example, a network utilization chart with snapshots taken every 60 seconds will give you lists of details about those times when the network is most heavily utilized. The same chart on the same network link with snapshots taken every 60 minutes will probably not give you the same impression of the link's utilization. With longer snapshot intervals, peaks in utilization tend to get averaged out.

Performance, Scalability, and Availability

Three terms you will hear often are performance, scalability, and availability. When you design network infrastructures, these will usually be your primary concerns. Often the issues surrounding performance, scalability, and availability will be a higher priority than cost. It can also be said that keeping performance, scalability, and availability as high as possible while keeping cost as low as possible is the most difficult challenge a network designer faces. You will face this challenge on nearly every design project you undertake.

Let's define the three terms:

◆ **Performance.** The ability of the network infrastructure to effectively and efficiently meet the demands for network services.

◆ **Scalability.** The ability of the network infrastructure to expand or contract in accordance with the demand for network services.

◆ **Availability.** The percentage of time that the network infrastructure is up and running and available for use.

Performance is often a very subjective term. Appraisals of performance will vary from user to user. It is good to gather anecdotal evidence of a network infrastructure's performance to gain an understanding of the customer's position on the performance of its existing infrastructure. You will also want to collect some more concrete evidence by taking some measurements. A protocol analyzer is a good tool for this.

You will want to measure the utilization of each network link. Utilization is the measure of the amount of bandwidth actually used by all the network services traversing the link in a given period of time. In addition to utilization, you will want to examine the latency on the roundtrip time of network requests sent from client computers to servers hosting network resources and back again. You will need to collect this information over an extended period of time to make sure that you can see how the network meets its demand at various times. Demand for network services increases and decreases at various times of the day, so you will want to make sure you have collected data from all of the times when the demands on the network are high.

In addition to utilization, response time, and delay, you will want to quantify the following:

- ◆ **Capacity.** The total amount of data that the link might carry.

- ◆ **Throughput.** The actual amount of data that successfully crosses the network.

- ◆ **Accuracy.** The rate of error-free data transmissions compared to total transmissions.

- ◆ **Efficiency.** The rate of data throughput relative to the transmission overheard to achieve that throughput.

Once you have data reflecting the actual performance of the existing network infrastructure, you can assess the changes and improvements that must be made in your new network infrastructure design.

In some cases, you will have specific performance levels that must be met. Sometimes, applications developers will provide data that outlines the network performance levels that must be met in order for their applications to function properly. If you have collected accurate data on your own, it will be easy to identify areas where improvements must be made. In some cases, you might identify areas in the existing infrastructure where the available resources grossly exceed the demands placed on them. Armed with specific performance requirements, you might find that you can reduce the resources expended in these areas and save a substantial amount of money while continuing to meet the demand for network resources.

Be careful, however, that you do not sacrifice scalability. Once you have investigated the company's future growth plans and have examined the company's past growth trends, you will be able to calculate the room for expansion that you will need to design into the network infrastructure. Make sure that you design your network infrastructure with enough capacity to handle an unexpected increase in network demand, and that you give your network the ability to be adapted to support any future plans for increases in the number of users, sites, or network services.

Finally, consider the availability requirements for the network infrastructure and the services that rely on it. For example, in a medical environment, the systems that are used to monitor the patient's health must be available all the time. Loss of availability for these devices can have dire consequences. Likewise, in a financial transaction environment, network services must be readily available. Loss of functionality of a network component or service could result in transactions being lost or processed incorrectly. This could have very costly ramifications.

Availability is most often represented as a percentage with two decimal points of accuracy. For example, a typical availability goal might be 99.95 percent. If this is the goal, you are saying that in a given week the network can experience downtime only .05 percent of the time. One week has 168 hours (24 hours×7 days), or 10,080 minutes. To calculate the acceptable downtime per week, multiply the number of minutes in one week by the acceptable downtime percentage (10,080×.0005). The result is about 5 minutes. Compare this to an availability rate of 99.50 percent, which allows for nearly one hour of downtime per week. This would be totally unacceptable in most enterprises. A limit of 5 minutes of downtime per week will probably be an acceptable availability goal for company management, but it might be a lofty goal for network engineers. Nevertheless, if the company specifies an availability goal of 99.95 percent, you must create your design to provide for this availability.

When you consider the purchase of network hardware to implement your design, you might see that the manufacturer expresses the availability of its products using the following terms:

◆ **Mean Time Between Failure (MTBF).** The average amount of time that a device operates properly before a malfunction occurs.

◆ **Mean Time To Repair (MTTR).** The average time that it takes to repair a device and restore it to proper operation once a malfunction has occurred.

You will want to make sure that the devices included in your design specify a very high MTBF and a very low MTTR. Keep in mind that averages give little indication of the amount of variance in the data. Devices could frequently fail at intervals much shorter than the mean. Also, devices could take considerably more time to repair than the mean.

Data and System Access

In order to gain a complete understanding of the real demands that are placed on a network, you will need to examine how the end users use the network to access its systems and the data that is stored on them. Observing the data and system access patterns will help you determine the times and locations where the most stress is placed on the network. You will need to make sure that your network infrastructure design can support the demands that will be placed on it. You might also want to identify network access patterns that are inappropriate or inefficient and make company management aware of them before creating your design. If you can show management that money can be saved and productivity can be increased by changing an existing data or system access pattern, you might be able to simplify your network infrastructure design.

Some data and system access patterns are typical in most enterprises. For example, you might find that network traffic increases dramatically and the impact on authentication servers is most severe early in the morning. This is the time when most company employees are arriving for work and logging in to their computers.

If the company is integrating its network infrastructure with that of its partners, suppliers, or clients, you might find that you cannot accurately predict data and systems access without analyzing the behavior and interaction of the partners, suppliers, and clients, and how they make use of the company's network. If the company does business over the Internet or operates 24 hours a day, 7 days a week, you will need to examine the data and system access patterns that occur throughout the day. You will most likely need to examine these patterns over the course of a number of days to get a complete and accurate picture of the real demand for network services within the organization.

Network Roles and Responsibilities

Network roles and responsibilities are all about the systems performing server roles on the network. Each server has a role to play and a service to provide. Many of the individual services will be discussed later in this section, but this section focuses on the role of servers in the infrastructure itself. These include the following:

◆ **Global catalog servers.** This server is used to search a subset of the Active Directory in the local site and to help users locate a login server. It is a special version of a domain controller. Without this service on the network, users could have problems logging on, and remote searches of the active directory would take longer because they would need to traverse the WAN.

◆ **Name servers.** This is required to resolve computer names to IP addresses and to locate infrastructure services, such as the global catalog and Kerberos (authentication) servers on the network. These may be DNS, WINS, HOST files, LMHOST files, or the preferred method in Windows 2000, Dynamic DNS.

◆ **Domain controllers.** These are required for the purposes of logging into the domain. Domain controllers also contain a replica of the Active Directory that holds the dynamic DNS databases as well as everything else that the Active Directory stores and provides.

◆ **Security servers.** These include PK servers for Kerberos authentication and RADIUS servers for Internet standard remote access authentication.

◆ **DHCP servers.** These servers perform the functions of assigning IP addresses to clients and registering the clients' host names with the dynamic DNS service.

◆ **Remote access servers.** Whether this is traditional dial-in RAS, VPN, RRAS, or Terminal Services, this is a critical role for remote users. These servers provide connectivity over various types of third-party networks, such as the Internet, PSTN, ISDN, and other types of leased bandwidth for remote sites and users.

◆ **Operations masters.** These special domain controllers are unique to the domain in that one of each type of master must exist somewhere in the domain or forest it belongs to. There is much more information on operations masters in *Windows 2000 Directory Services Design* by Scott Archer (New Riders Publishing, ISBN 0735709831).

These operational roles include the schema master, domain naming master, relative identifier master, primary domain controller emulator, and infrastructure master.

◆ **File and print servers.** As the most common and most basic server role, these servers provide the vast majority of resources to users through shared files and network-enabled printers.

◆ **Application servers.** These servers are second only to file and print servers in terms of providing resources to end users. These can include service roles as email servers, Web servers, database servers, and a host of other third-party applications.

As you can see, there are many possible server roles, but the bottom line is that they provide the medium in which users may collaborate. Some of these provide the infrastructure across which the users can communicate securely, and others provide the group resources for the four basic categories of computing: input, processing, storage, and output.

Security Considerations

Security considerations are numerous when you're creating a new network infrastructure design. In fact, the issues surrounding network security are so numerous that, if you give them too much consideration, you might never get your design project off the ground. One way to simplify matters somewhat, and to keep security concerns in their proper perspective, is to evaluate the existing security measures against the business goals. Try to determine if the existing approach to network security has been effective, and whether it helps facilitate the company's goals or hinders them. If the security measures currently in place have not been effective, you'll need to examine the areas in which there were failures in order to develop new strategies to enhance security in those areas. Keep in mind that as tighter security procedures are put into place, the network becomes proportionally less flexible.

Some of the areas that you will want to examine when evaluating the current security measures are described in the following sections.

Physical Security

Examine the physical location of all devices that are connected to the network, as well as the locations of the wiring and other components that make up the physical network. Look at the placement of desktop computers, file servers, hubs, switches, and routers, and ask the following questions:

◆ Are the computers accessible only to those authorized to do so?

◆ Are the infrastructure components (hubs, switches, routers) kept in secure areas with access controlled in some way?

◆ Is there any way to track who has access to these devices and when they have used that access?

◆ Are there measures in place to prevent someone from removing computers or other devices from the company premises?

The answers to these questions will help you determine whether the physical security that is currently in place is effective. Desktop computers are typically an issue when it comes to physical security. Usually, there is little to stop someone from simply walking up to a desk and using the computer that is located there. For this reason, desktop computers should have access controlled by password to ensure that the person who uses a desktop computer is the person intended to do so.

File servers should be kept in a room dedicated to storing these devices. They should be kept in a climate-controlled environment where physical access is controlled. A typical datacenter where file servers are housed will have a raised floor, an industrial air conditioner, and some kind of access control method. This method might be as simple as a locking doorknob (where few people have keys), or it might be something very complicated (with keycards, fingerprint readers, or retinal scanners). The access control method used is often determined by the level of risk associated with unauthorized access to the datacenter, as well as the budget available for security. Regardless of the selected method, the main objective is to allow access to the datacenter only to those who are authorized for such access. An added benefit of some access control methods is a record of who is accessing the datacenter and when they access it.

Network infrastructure devices should also be kept behind locked doors, but they are often distributed across an enterprise due to the function they perform. These devices should be stored in wiring closets with access controlled by a method similar to that used to control access to the datacenter.

There should also be a procedure in place to prevent someone from simply carrying computer equipment off company premises. Often, sensitive data is stored on company computers. Given the trend in the technology age to provide as much information as possible to employees, the likelihood that sensitive company information could be found on a desktop or laptop computer is high. You might not be able to have much impact on company plans to take steps such as hiring security guards to inspect bags and packages as they enter and leave the building, but you can probably make a few suggestions. For example, desktop computers can be attached to the furniture in the offices by some kind of security cable. Many such cables are available for this purpose. Using such a cable, the PC is locked down to a permanent or semipermanent fixture so that it cannot be simply carried off. Laptop computers can be adapted to support these security cables as well, and rightly so. The highly portable nature of laptops makes them a prime target for theft.

Internal Access Security

Another area to examine when evaluating the existing security measures is internal network security. This defines the access to network resources that is granted to the company's own employees, as well as to contractors performing work for the company inside company facilities. In many company network environments, it is common to grant different levels of access to systems and data based on the responsibilities and job functions of the employees who are granted access. For example, senior-level executives are granted much greater access to company financial information than receptionists. The company Chief Financial Officer would be granted even greater access. Another example is the levels of access granted to the company email system. Each end user is granted complete control over his or her own mailbox but must not be granted any access to other employees' mailboxes. An exception to this might be secretaries who must access the mailboxes of their managers or email administrators who must have access to all the users' mailboxes.

When evaluating existing internal access security, ask the following questions:

◆ What are the administrative levels at which employees are granted different levels of system and data access?

◆ What are the procedures for determining and granting an appropriate access level to each employee?

◆ What procedures exist to determine if an employee has been granted greater access than is appropriate?

◆ What procedures are in place to determine successful and unsuccessful attempts to exercise inappropriate access levels?

You will need to determine the various levels of access that must be granted and ensure that your design supports these levels of access. You should also attempt to build methods for auditing access events and administrative alerts into your network infrastructure design wherever possible.

External Access Security

Perhaps the most popular perspective on network security is one that focuses on external access. Although internal security threats are more dangerous and more likely to succeed (as we have already discussed), protecting your internal systems and data from hackers on the outside is a notion that gets a lot of attention in the press these days. Remember, just because you're paranoid doesn't mean that they aren't really out to get you! The threat of system compromise from outside the organization is very real, so you should take appropriate precautions wherever your internal network borders the outside world. Areas of concern include the following:

◆ Internet connections

◆ Dial-in servers

◆ Connections to public carriers

◆ Connections to external networks owned by partners, suppliers, or clients

Anywhere that an outside user could potentially access the company's internal network is an area that must be protected. One example is a RAS server, where users connect to the company's internal network by dialing in from remote locations with modems. Care should be taken that the phone numbers associated with the modems on the RAS server do not become public knowledge. This might not be enough, however. Outsiders might use programs called war dialers that automate the task of calling hundreds of combinations of phone numbers, looking for a modem to answer. When a modem does answer, the phone number is logged for future break-in attempts.

A further step to secure dial-in servers is to configure them to automatically hang up and call the user back at a predetermined number. If an unauthorized user attempts to connect and break in using a valid user ID, the system will hang up and call the phone number that is associated with the valid user ID. In this way, an unauthorized user cannot access the network through the dial-in server unless he does so from the home of an authorized company employee.

Another example is a Web server that must be accessed by both internal employees and external customers over the Internet. In order to avoid increased costs for traffic over the company's Internet connection, it is common to connect such a server to the internal company network as well as to the Internet. In this way, internal employee traffic to the server is not first sent out over the company's connection to the Internet, only to return over that same connection to the internal network. Figure 2.4 depicts this scenario.

The danger in this situation is that any server that is connected to both the internal network and an external network could be used as a "bridge" between the two networks. An unauthorized user might use this bridge to gain access to the internal network from the outside.

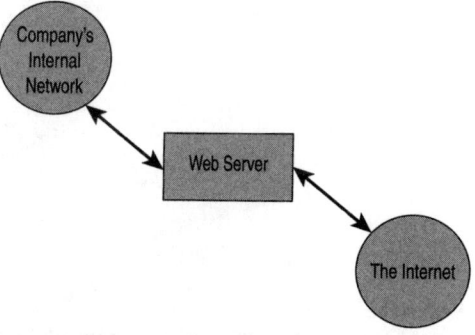

FIGURE 2.4
Company Web servers are often connected to the company's internal network as well as to the Internet.

In situations such as this, it is common to build what is known as a *demilitarized zone* (DMZ). The DMZ is an area of your network that is connected to the outside world (the Internet) as well as to your internal network. A device known as a *firewall* protects the connection to each network. The firewall is used to filter out traffic that is undesirable, preventing unauthorized access to the internal network from the Internet and preventing access from the Internet to the Web server for any service other than World Wide Web files (http access).

Web servers are not the only servers that might find themselves placed in a DMZ. Examples of other servers that are commonly placed in a DMZ are SMTP servers, which handle Internet email, and FTP servers, which allow file transfer to or from the server. Each of these servers offers its services over a particular TCP/IP channel, called a *port*.

The firewall on the Internet side of the servers is configured to allow only traffic intended for those servers and ports to access the DMZ. The firewall on the other side of the servers is configured to prevent all traffic from the Internet from entering the internal network. Figure 2.5 depicts a DMZ.

NOTE

More Information on TCP/IP   For more information on TCP/IP in general and TCP/UDP ports specifically, refer to *MCSE Training Guide: TCP/IP, Second Edition* (New Riders Publishing, ISBN 1562059203).

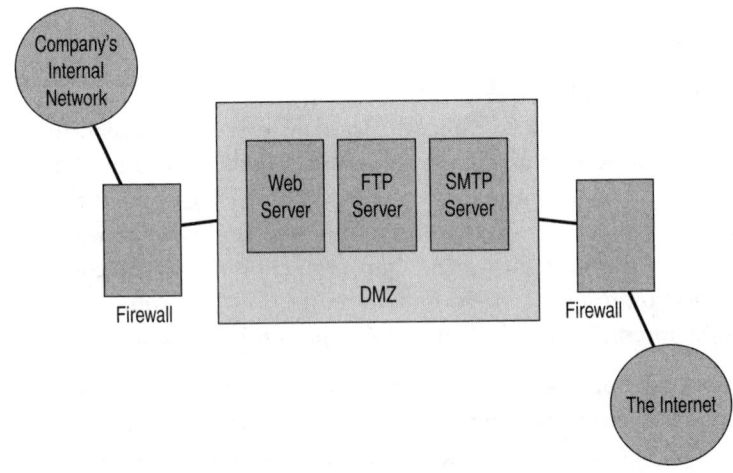

FIGURE 2.5
A DMZ is an area of the company network that is connected to the Internet as well as to the internal network. The connection to each network is protected by a firewall.

Firewalls and DMZs are also useful tactics to employ in scenarios where the company's internal network will be connected to that of its partners, suppliers, and/or clients. As you examine the existing approach to external access security, you might find these strategies already in place. If not, you will need to ask the following questions:

◆ Where is the internal network potentially vulnerable to unauthorized outside access?

◆ What methods have been employed to prevent unauthorized access in these areas?

◆ What methods are in place to identify unauthorized access attempts and to alert the appropriate people?

◆ What methods are in place to identify the source of unauthorized access attempts?

The answers to these questions will help you identify weak areas in the existing security approach and ensure that your network infrastructure design has adequate security built into it.

R E V I E W   B R E A K

This part of the chapter discussed many areas of a solid technical assessment. This is the first step in understanding the company's technical environment and providing a foundation for technical design. A technical assessment analyzes several factors in both the premigration environment and post-migration goals. These factors include company size and the geographical distribution of its users; distribution and administration (centralized versus decentralized) of network resources; and analyzing the available connectivity via LAN, WAN, and remote access. Also included are concerns about the network bandwidth of that LAN/WAN/RAS connectivity, its scalability and availability, and how data and network systems are accessed. Finally, we discussed network roles and how security affects these systems. This brings us to the next part of the chapter, where we will review the physical structure of a network in more detail and analyze the impact that various devices and services have on the network.

ANALYZING THE IMPACT OF INFRASTRUCTURE DESIGN

Analyze the impact of infrastructure design on the existing and planned technical environment.

After thoroughly examining the existing network infrastructure and matching the company's goals to the proposed network infrastructure, you can begin to determine just how drastic the changes will be when moving from the existing network infrastructure to the newly designed network infrastructure. In some cases, you might find that there is a tremendous gap between the existing network and the proposed network. In other cases, the gap will be less extensive. In either case, you will want to minimize the impact on productivity of making the change from old to new. Ultimately, the new network infrastructure design will save the company money and allow it to meet its business goals in the most effective and efficient manner. During the implementation phase, while the network is "under construction," the loss of productivity and increased costs can be significant. A great design includes an analysis of the potential impact of the implementation so that an effective implementation plan can be developed to minimize the costs associated with rolling out the new design. Some factors to consider when determining the impact of implementing your network infrastructure design are described in the following sections.

Applications

Perhaps the most important thing to keep in mind when creating a network infrastructure design is the way the customer will actually use the infrastructure once it is in place. Consider the applications that the company will be running. First, list all the applications that are currently in use by the organization. Examine each of the applications to determine its requirements in terms of the network infrastructure. Some applications will be very demanding of the network infrastructure, generating heavy traffic and requiring high throughput, and others will not.

Legacy applications, for example, might not place heavy demands on the network infrastructure with high bandwidth or quality of service requirements, but they might be challenging to support in other ways. Legacy applications might require the use of older, less-efficient protocols. You might not prefer to operate these protocols on your new network infrastructure, but you might find that you must do so in order to support legacy applications that the company refuses to replace or retire.

Once you have compiled a list of all the applications currently in use by the company, you will also want to prioritize these applications. This will help you determine which applications are critical to the company's goals and mission. Critical applications will need to be addressed first when designing the network infrastructure to support application requirements, and then you should address the needs of less-critical applications. If you find conflicts between the requirements of applications, criticality will be one criterion to help determine where to compromise.

Network Infrastructure, Protocols, and Hosts

A computer network is comprised of many parts. There are the individual computer systems that occupy the network, as well as the myriad devices used to connect those systems. This section is all about network infrastructure, which includes all workstations, servers, interconnection devices, and wiring. The most basic level of this network infrastructure consists of the wiring and connecting devices that allow data to travel from one computer to another.

Here are some examples of the types of wiring used in computer networks:

◆ **Unshielded Twisted Pair (UTP).** This type of wire is also used to connect telephones. Different categories of UTP wire exist, each with its own capacity for carrying data and resisting interference. Categories that you might see in use for computer networks include Category 3 (CAT 3) (even though it's used primarily for voice and very slow networks), Category 5 (CAT 5), and the relatively new Category 6 (CAT 6).

NOTE **Reference Material Suggestions** As you get into this material, you might want to reference the New Riders *Training Guide* and *Fast Track* on the CompTIA Network+ exam for more details. Even though Microsoft eliminated the Networking Essentials exam in the Windows 2000 MCSE Track, it still considers this prerequisite knowledge that can be tested on any exam.

◆ **Shielded Twisted Pair (STP).** This type of wire is similar to UTP, except that it includes additional protection from external interference (the "shielding"). An example of STP wire is Type 1 cable, used for Token Ring networks.

◆ **Coaxial cable.** This type of wire consists of a single conductor in the center of the cable, insulated by a protective coating and then wrapped with a stranded or meshed wire. Computer networks use different types of coaxial cable. "Thicknet" is a term that refers to the thick, heavy coaxial cable used by older Ethernet networks. "Thinnet" refers to the relatively newer, lighter, and more flexible thin coaxial cable also used in Ethernet networks.

◆ **Fiber-optic cable.** This cable type is actually a thin, hollow strand of optical fiber that is used to carry light from one end to the other. Electrical impulses, representing the 1s and 0s of binary data, are converted into pulses of light (on and off) that are carried through these optical fibers. Fiber Distributed Data Interface (FDDI) is a technology designed to use fiber-optic cable.

◆ **EIA/TIA 232.** These cables, formerly referred to as RS-232 cables, are used to connect serial devices, such as a PC to a modem. These cables might be seen connecting WAN devices.

In addition to the physical wiring, the network infrastructure also includes devices that are the connection points of the network. Such devices include the following:

◆ **Repeater.** Repeaters are devices that are placed on a computer network to extend the distance that the network may span. As data is carried across a wire, it travels in the form of an electrical signal. This electrical signal loses its intensity as it moves across the wire, so the ability to interpret the data it represents begins to degrade. This is known as *signal attenuation*. A repeater is used to receive an electrical signal before it degrades completely and repeat it to the wire at full strength. Note that a repeater simply repeats the signal it receives. If the signal is badly distorted when it is received, that distortion is simply amplified when the signal is repeated.

◆ **Hubs.** A hub is a device that interconnects multiple segments of network wiring. Usually several of those wires connect at the other end to individual PCs. An active hub is actually a kind of repeater. When an active hub receives a signal on one of the wires connected to it, it repeats that signal to every other wire that is connected to it.

◆ **Bridge.** A bridge is a device that connects multiple physical wiring segments to form a single logical segment. Unlike repeaters, which have no built-in intelligence, bridges can examine the data carried by the wire and make decisions as to where to repeat the signal. These decisions are made based on the MAC address information that the bridge receives with each data frame.

◆ **Switch.** A switch can be considered a "multiport intelligent bridge." Switches provide tremendous flexibility in deciding where and when to repeat data signals. Some of the latest switches operate at OSI layers 2 and 3 (Data Link and Network) and perform the functions of a multiport intelligent bridge as well as the functions of a multiport router, called a VLAN switch.

◆ **Router.** A router is a device that makes complex decisions regarding the optimum path that data should take from its source to its ultimate destination across the network. Routers make these decisions based on logical addressing information found at layer 3 of the OSI model. Routers can perform much more complex functions than bridges or layer 2 switches, but doing so results in more overhead and slower performance. It should be noted, however, that routers are faster at layer 3 functions than the equivalent layer 3 switches. For more information on layer 2 and layer 3 switching, refer to Cisco Systems' *Cisco IOS 12.0 Switching Services* (Cisco Press, ISBN 1578701570).

◆ **Multiplexor (MUX).** A MUX is a device that takes a broadband network segment with high bandwidth and divides it into multiple segments with less bandwidth. An inverse multiplexor (I-MUX) does the opposite: It joins multiple low-bandwidth segments to form a single high-bandwidth broadband link.

The wiring and the connecting devices form the basic network infra-structure. Connected to this basic infrastructure are the many indi-vidual computer systems that must use the network. These systems are called *hosts* because each one has the potential to host data that is of interest to the other computer systems on the network. Although it is a connecting device in applications, a router is also a host on a network. In fact, any network device with a physical or logical address on the network is considered a host. This includes all inter-networking devices above the level of an unintelligent hub at the Physical OSI layer. Hosts perform many different functions on the network:

- Server
- Client
- Router

In order for hosts to make use of the network infrastructure for communications, they must first agree to a set of rules or protocols. They might need to adopt a number of different protocols to allow multiple types of hosts to communicate with each other. Much more information on protocols can be obtained in the Network+ books referenced earlier in this chapter.

There are protocols that specify how to use the physical media to carry binary data. There are protocols that specify how to get that data from one system to another. There are also protocols that spec-ify how to present the data to the particular host that receives it.

Network Services

In the existing infrastructure, you will find that a number of net-work services are currently being offered:

- User authentication
- Directory services
- File services
- Print services
- Web services

- ◆ FTP services

- ◆ Network management services

- ◆ IP address services

- ◆ Host name resolution services

- ◆ Database services

- ◆ Gateway services

These network services make use of the network infrastructure and define the functionality of the network itself.

When designing a new network infrastructure, you need to determine the following:

- ◆ Which network services are currently in use?

- ◆ Which of the currently used network services will be retired?

- ◆ How will implementation of the new design impact the functionality of the currently used network services?

- ◆ What new network services will be added to the network in the future?

As you did with the applications currently in use, you should list all the network services that are currently in use by the organization. Include in your list the specific network requirements for each service. For example, the DNS name resolution service requires the TCP/IP protocol. After you list all the network services currently in use and the requirements for each service, consult with company management to determine how critical each service is to the business. Whenever you face conflicts with the requirements of network services, this priority level can help you resolve them or determine where to make compromises.

TCP/IP Infrastructure

The TCP/IP suite is the standard network protocol used by nearly every network in existence today. It is the default protocol used by Microsoft Windows 2000, as well as Windows NT 4.0. Many other network operating systems use TCP/IP. Myriad network devices support the TCP/IP protocol suite. A network that is based on the TCP/IP protocol has certain elements that must be considered carefully at the design stage in order for the network to operate effectively and efficiently:

◆ The IP addressing scheme

◆ The IP address assignment process

◆ The host name registration process

◆ The host name resolution process

These TCP/IP network elements must be carefully considered when creating your new network infrastructure design. We will discuss each of them in the following sections.

The IP Addressing Scheme

When you're setting up an IP network, one of the fundamental building blocks is the IP addressing scheme. Each host connected to the network must have a unique address in order for it to communicate with other hosts on the network. You have two options when creating an addressing scheme. The first is to use a public IP address assigned by a public entity. This is the option you must take if you are connecting your company to the Internet and do not have any kind of proxy server or firewall between your company's network and the Internet. The second option is to use the so-called reserved private IP addresses. The private IP addressing space is a set of IP addresses that are reserved and cannot be used in the public network. These IP addresses give you the ability to configure as many subnets and hosts as you require, regardless of the public IP assigned to your company.

The private or reserved IP addresses adhere to the following ranges. The first private network range is from 10.0.0.0 through 10.255.255.254. The second private network range is from 172.16.0.0 through 172.31.255.254. The third private network range is from 192.168.0.0 through 192.168.255.254.

Whichever addressing scheme you choose, public or private, one main concern is that your addressing strategy be a planned and organized one rather than haphazard. Standards should be developed for assigning IP addresses to devices. Set aside a range of numbers that specify certain devices. For instance, printers might fall within the host range of 25 to 46; routers might fall within the address range for hosts of 15 through 25; switches might be in the host address range 5 through 15. There are no hard and fast rules here. Just be sure that the approach you take is organized and meaningful. Always make sure that your addressing scheme is documented.

The IP Address Assignment Process

After you have arrived at an IP addressing scheme that is organized and works well throughout the enterprise, you will need to decide how to get these IP addresses assigned to each individual station on the network. This could be a manual process, which would require a lot of administration and hands-on technical work. If you take a manual approach to IP address assignment, a technician must approach each device on the network and configure its IP address. This can be very time-consuming and expensive and also introduces the possibility of human error. This will, in turn, lead to troubleshooting costs and downtime.

Another approach, which might save time and money, is to automate the assignment of IP addresses to end stations. One way of doing this is to use the Dynamic Host Configuration Protocol (DHCP). When using DHCP, you first configure a DHCP server with an address pool containing all the IP addresses that you can use to assign to hosts on your network. When DHCP clients first power up and connect to the network, they request an IP address from the server. They do this by broadcasting a DHCP request over the network. All the DHCP servers on the network seeing this request will respond with an "offer" of an IP address. The client will accept the first offer it receives, and it will lease that address for a fixed period of time.

The time frame during which a workstation may use the address it received from DHCP server is called the *lease duration*. The lease duration is a configurable parameter. Configure a long lease duration if your clients tend to stay in one place and the network topology doesn't change often. However, if your network topology changes frequently, or if you do not have an address pool with enough addresses to sufficiently meet the demand for them, configure a shorter lease duration.

N O T E

NetBIOS Computer Names Versus DNS Host Names   Although they are created for the same reason, NetBIOS computer names in downlevel clients are not the same as DNS host names. Most downlevel clients have the ability to have two different "friendly" names associated with their IP address. One is the NetBIOS or computer name, and the other is the DNS host name.

For more information on NetBIOS over TCP/IP, NetBIOS naming, and WINS name resolution, refer to New Riders' *Networking with Microsoft TCP/IP,* Third Edition, by Drew Heywood (ISBN 0735700141).

The Host Name Registration Process

TCP/IP end stations are not identified by only their IP address. For the sake of human convenience, they are also recognized by a host name.

Most people find that names are easier to remember than IP addresses. In addition, although IP addresses might be dynamically assigned and changed frequently for the same host, the host name remains consistent. So, regardless of whether the host has a new IP address or changes its IP lease frequently, you can consistently refer to the host by name, and connectivity will be ensured. It is tempting to use interesting (even wild) host names for your end stations. Individual end users might want to use a host name that reflects their personality or favorite hobbies. However, this is probably not the best approach to assigning IP host names across your enterprise, because it makes it very difficult for a user to determine what resources reside on which host. Develop a standard naming convention that is meaningful, hierarchical, and organized, and that you can apply throughout the enterprise. Once you have determined your host name scheme, you will need to deploy those names across the enterprise. This typically requires a manual visit to each end station for configuration.

The Host Name Resolution Process

Once host names have been assigned to each end station on your TCP/IP network, you will need some way to translate host names into the IP addresses associated with those end stations. The service that provides this function in a TCP/IP network is the domain name service (DNS).

Using DNS, you first configure a database on a DNS server. The database will contain all the host names for each of the end stations in your enterprise, as well as the IP addresses that are associated with each end station. When a workstation wants to establish connectivity with another, it will first request a lookup from the DNS server. It will specify the name of the host to which it is trying to connect. The DNS server will respond by providing the IP address associated with that name. Once the connecting station receives the IP address, it will begin to communicate directly with the host associated with that IP address.

In the past, the creation of the DNS database was a manual process. This required a DNS administrator to spend many laborious hours determining the IP addresses assigned to each of the hosts in the enterprise. This was further complicated by the use of DHCP protocol, because the IP addresses associated with each of the host names in the database change from time to time, perhaps frequently. Frequent changes to the IP address assignments require frequent changes to the DNS database. This can be very time-consuming and expensive, and it also introduces the opportunity for human error.

A solution to this problem has recently been developed and is being implemented in enterprises today. This solution is called dynamic DNS (DDNS). When using DDNS, clients that receive their IP address assignments through DHCP protocol communicate their host name back to the DHCP server. The DHCP server, in turn, communicates with the DNS server, indicating that an address assignment has been made as well as the host name associated with that address assignment. Through this process, the DNS database is updated dynamically each time an address assignment is made. This approach minimizes the administrative intervention required in assigning IP addresses and host names. It allows the DNS database to be kept up to date without manual intervention and minimizes the troubleshooting associated with IP address changes when the DNS database is not kept up to date.

Once you have configured your DNS servers and the database is up to date, each individual host will need to be configured to communicate with the DNS server to resolve host names. If you are using the DHCP protocol for a dynamic host IP address assignment, you can also configure an additional parameter that will specify the DNS server that the host should use for IP host name resolution.

Hardware

It is important to note that no matter what you include in your network infrastructure design, it will be completely useless if the hardware in place cannot support it. You will need to take an inventory of the hardware in the existing network infrastructure. Examine the inventory information for the hardware configuration of each of the components.

Upgrades and Rollouts

Earlier in this chapter, we discussed the need to list and prioritize the applications currently in use by the company. You should also have examined each of the applications to determine its network requirements. Where you might have found conflicting requirements between applications, the criticality of each application helped you arrive at a compromise. Two additional issues regarding applications that must be considered are application upgrades and rollouts.

If an upgrade to an existing application is available, the company might want to consider implementing the upgrade at the same time it implements the new network infrastructure. You might find that company management is inclined to combine as many changes to the environment as possible when implementing a new infrastructure. This is certainly not the wisest approach to take, because it complicates the troubleshooting process when issues arise during the implementation. Nevertheless, it is a common approach. You will need to become aware of any company plans to upgrade existing applications.

Upgrades that occur at the same time as a new network infrastructure implementation are not always bad. In fact, in the case of legacy applications or situations where there are conflicts in application requirements, an upgrade might be just the resolution you are looking for. Upgrading legacy applications might allow you to discontinue the use of older, less-efficient protocols. When two or more applications have conflicting requirements, upgrading one or more of them to a newer version might resolve the conflict. Of course, it is always possible that an upgrade to one application might introduce new conflicts in network requirements that must be resolved before your design can be implemented.

Technical Support Structure

An issue that needs to be considered when analyzing the impact of a network infrastructure design is the company's ability to support it after it is implemented. A major component of the total cost of ownership for the network infrastructure is the ongoing cost to support that infrastructure. It is important to take the time to examine the organization's technical support structure to determine if it can effectively support the new network infrastructure. Many infrastructure plans overlook support. Although support is often a post-implementation concern, preparing for it should be given a higher priority in the planning phase of the project.

Here are some questions you should ask:

◆ Do company employees perform technical support, or is it outsourced to contractors?

◆ Does the technical support structure effectively address the support needs of the existing network infrastructure?

◆ Are there new technologies in the new network infrastructure design that would pose new challenges to the existing technical support structure?

◆ How should the technical support structure be modified or enhanced in order to most effectively support the new network infrastructure?

You might find that the existing technical support structure is overworked and struggling to meet the support demands of the existing network infrastructure. This is frequently the case. Meet with company management, as well as the technical support staff, and try to determine the reason for this situation. Usually such circumstances are related to budgetary issues. Try to tactfully point out the shortcomings of the existing technical support structure to company management. While being mindful of office politics and general customer service principles, you will want to convey the shortcomings of the group without demeaning the members themselves. Point out to management how these shortcomings can be resolved by the addition of personnel or by an investment in the training of the existing staff.

Network and Systems Management

A major component in the supportability of a network infrastructure is the investment in network and systems management tools for monitoring the health of the network infrastructure components, as well as the individual systems that reside on the network. These are essential for minimizing downtime and troubleshooting costs.

Numerous tools are available for performing network and systems management. Depending on the devices and systems that comprise the company's network, you might find one or more of these tools currently in use.

When examining the company's existing network and systems management tools, you need to determine the following:

◆ Do the existing tools for network and systems management effectively provide support for the existing network infrastructure?

◆ Is the organization currently making the most effective use of the available tools for network and systems management?

◆ How will the implementation of the newly designed network infrastructure impact the effectiveness of the network and systems management tools currently in use?

◆ What changes to the systems and network management tools currently in use will need to be made in order to support the new network infrastructure?

◆ Which additional network and systems management tools will need to be implemented in order to effectively support the new network infrastructure?

REVIEW BREAK

This part of the chapter analyzed the physical makeup of a network and the impact that various systems and services have on the infrastructure design. Applications are often the most important piece of a company's infrastructure, because they are directly used by the end users for production purposes and the company's line of business. These applications can be prioritized by a number of factors, including criticality, resources required, time sensitivity, and visibility/user perception.

Network infrastructure includes all workstations, servers, interconnection devices, and even physical wiring. This book can't go into the depth that this material could cover. Instead, it gives you an overview of physical devices and cabling that can be researched further in some of the recommended texts, such as the CompTIA

Network+ books referenced earlier in this chapter. These devices include cabling, such as thinnet, thicknet, UTP, and fiber optic, as well as network devices, such as repeaters, hubs, bridges, switches, routers, gateways, and multiplexors. Another good overview reference for networking devices and protocols is Chapter 7 of *A+ Fast Track* (New Riders Publishing, ISBN 0735700281).

Network services were also touched on in this part of the chapter. These network services make use of the network infrastructure and define the functionality of the network itself. As an integral part of the network infrastructure, proposed changes to these will also need to be documented and analyzed for impact to the network infrastructure. These services include directory services, file and print services, Web services, management services, name resolution services, dynamic IP addressing, and many others.

IP addressing also was covered briefly in this section. This overview discussed IP addressing, address assignment, name registration, and name resolution. Particular attention should be paid to address assignment and name registration throughout this book. This portion of the TCP/IP infrastructure is the most affected by updates included in Windows 2000, especially DDNS. References were given for supporting books on TCP/IP due to this book's focus and space limitations. Entire libraries of books have been written on this most popular Internet protocol.

Hardware upgrades, systems support, and network systems management will all have a profound impact on the network infrastructure. After analysis, a good design for these support areas and tactics will have an extremely positive impact on the network infrastructure design.

This topic of support leads us directly into the next section on analyzing client computer access requirements.

ANALYZING CLIENT COMPUTER ACCESS REQUIREMENTS

Analyze the network requirements for client computer access.

The focus of your impact analysis should ultimately be the individual client computers that reside on the network. These computers are the workstations where end users do their work. Data flows into and out of these workstations all day long, and trends that occur here will ultimately determine the success or failure of your network infrastructure design to meet the goals set forth by the business. The work performed by end users needs to be as effective, efficient, and inexpensive as possible. Enabling this is the ultimate goal of any network infrastructure design. You should pay close attention to the activities of end users before, during, and after the creation of your network infrastructure design. Indeed, often the perceptions of the end-user community dictate the reality of your project. If the project is going well but is poorly communicated and ill-received by the user community, the project can quickly become mired in damage control and red tape. Likewise, if a project is well-received even though it is performing at a less-than-optimal level, it might still be considered a success.

End-User Work Needs

Analyzing end-user work needs involves determining who needs access to which data, when they need it, and where it should be delivered. For example, salespeople might need access to inventory information as well as customer financial information. The inventory information is likely to be stored in a database physically located in or near the company warehouse. Customer financial information, however, is likely to be stored in a different location, perhaps on a database server in the accounting department. Both of these data sets will need to be delivered to the salesperson. This salesperson might be in the headquarters office connected directly to the LAN when she needs the data, or she might be working remotely while on the road, connected to the network by modem. The salesperson might need the data while located at a customer site, connected to the network over the Internet. Regardless of the location of the data or the location of the salesperson, the data must be delivered, even when the salesperson is working from home in the middle of the night. These are the end-user work needs.

It is imperative that the network infrastructure support the work needs of the end users. If end users need to access data across an Internet connection, Internet access must be provided. If end users need to access data physically located in branch offices or other facilities, WAN connections to those locations must be provided. In order to meet end-user work needs effectively and efficiently, you must also carefully examine end-user usage patterns.

End-User Usage Patterns

Once you know what the end-user work needs are, you will want to design your network infrastructure to meet these needs. Before you can design anything specific, you need to have an understanding of end-user usage patterns.

By examining end-user work needs, you know what data is needed and by whom. You should also know where the data and its users are located. Next, you must answer questions such as these:

◆ When will end users be accessing the data?

◆ What is the duration of an average access session?

◆ How large is the data?

◆ How many end users will access the data simultaneously?

◆ How much bandwidth will need to be allocated to deliver the data to the end users?

◆ What security functions will need to be in place to protect access to the data?

Once you have answered these questions, you can begin to design the specific means of connectivity that will meet the end users' work needs.

ANALYZING DISASTER RECOVERY STRATEGIES

Analyze the existing disaster recovery strategy for client computers, servers, and the network.

As a network infrastructure designer, and particularly if you implement the designs you create, you will want to become intimately familiar with the organization's existing strategy for disaster recovery. The company's existing disaster recovery strategy will become an essential tool for protecting the company's systems and data as you implement your new design.

The company's overall disaster recovery strategy should include the following components:

- ◆ Tape backup strategies
- ◆ Hardware failure recovery strategies
- ◆ Power and other environmental failure recovery strategies
- ◆ Data line and cable failure recovery strategies
- ◆ System code failure recovery strategies
- ◆ Ultimate recovery from acts of God

Tape Backup Strategies

Tape backup strategies are strategies that allow you to recover failures that result in loss of data, such as a file deletion or a hard drive failure. These strategies include the following:

- ◆ Creating and maintaining a tape backup strategy involving full, differential, and/or incremental backups.

◆ Creating and maintaining a tape rotation strategy, such as Grandfather-Father-Son (GFS).

◆ Storing backup tapes offsite. This is to allow for recoverability in the event of an ultimate act of God, such as a tornado, earthquake, or fire. In designing an offsite storage plan, it is important to strike a balance between keeping recent backup tapes offsite for maximum recoverability in the event of a natural disaster and keeping recent tapes onsite to allow for quick restoration of data.

Hardware Failure Recovery Strategies

Hardware failure recovery strategies involve the strategies and plans that allow the company to recover from a hardware failure, such as a server system board, hard drive, or a hardware switch or router. This strategy is essential to all companies, because each piece of hardware has an estimated "life expectancy"; this is known as the Mean Time Between Failures (MTBF). With hardware components, it is not a matter of "Will you have a failure?" but rather "When will you have a failure?"

The following is a list of the most common hardware-failure recovery strategies:

◆ Negotiating Service-Level Agreements (SLAs) with hardware vendors, guaranteeing a certain response time in the event of a hardware failure.

◆ Maintaining a spare parts inventory in-house.

◆ Building fault tolerance into your hardware infrastructure, such as RAID5 drive arrays, redundant power supplies, or redundant switch configurations.

Power and Other Environmental Failure Recovery Strategies

Power and other environmental failure recovery strategies involve strategies that allow you to recover from events such as power outages or extreme climate conditions. Following is a list of the most common power and other environmental failure recovery strategies:

◆ Placing Uninterruptible Power Supplies (UPS) on mission-critical servers for short-term power outages.

◆ Maintaining power generators on mission-critical data centers for longer-term power outages.

◆ Equipping mission-critical data centers with industrial-quality climate control systems.

Data Line and Cable Failure Recovery Strategies

Data line and cable failure recovery strategies are solutions that allow you to recover from either a failure of a LAN or a WAN connection. This includes the following strategies:

◆ Building multiple links to servers.

◆ Deploying LAN devices (such as switches) that allow for multiple redundant links between devices.

◆ Purchasing multiple WAN links between different geographic sites.

◆ Purchasing backup WAN links, such as dial-on-demand links.

◆ Maintaining backup remote connectivity solutions, such as RAS servers.

System Code Failure Recovery Strategies

System code failure recovery strategies include strategies that allow you to recover from such failures as a faulty service pack or application upgrade. These strategies include the following:

◆ Backing up files prior to applying service packs or application upgrades.

◆ Keeping copies of software on hand in order to downgrade to the previous service pack level or application version if necessary.

Ultimate Recovery from Acts of God

Strategies that allow you to recover from ultimate acts of God include strategies that allow you to recover from natural disasters, such as floods, tornados, and earthquakes. These strategies fall into one of two categories:

◆ Housing systems in facilities that can withstand the rigors of a natural disaster.

◆ Maintaining a disaster recovery site that can be brought online in the event that the original site is struck by a disaster. Data is either restored to systems in the recovery site or is replicated from the original site to the recovery site in real time.

No strategy can guarantee that a company will never experience a failure. Rather, the goal should be to ensure that, if a failure occurs, the amount of downtime is kept within acceptable limits.

You should gather information about the current strategies by interviewing members of the IT staff. Document all the existing disaster recovery plans that the company has in place, or obtain its existing documents if those are sufficient. Review these plans and strategies to ensure that your proposed design won't interrupt or render useless these plans. You may need to make modifications to your design or to the disaster recovery strategies and plans in order to ensure an acceptable level of disaster recovery.

The modifications that you make may include improvement to the existing disaster recovery strategies. Windows 2000 provides a number of redesigned technologies that allow you to enhance your disaster recovery strategies, including the following:

◆ Two-way and four-way active clustering

◆ Network load balancing

◆ An enhanced backup utility

You need to know all the details regarding the processes involved in each of the company's disaster recovery strategies in order to determine the impact of your new network infrastructure design on them. You need to understand these strategies to ensure that these processes remain functional during the implementation of your network infrastructure design.

CASE STUDY: DESIGNING A NETWORK INFRASTRUCTURE FOR THE DEWEY, WINNEM, & HOWE LAW FIRM

ESSENCE OF THE CASE

Here are the essential elements of this case:

▶ The law firm has many remote sites, each with a small number of users. It will take considerable effort to determine the scope and size of the user population.

▶ The firm is concerned with the expense of connectivity between its headquarters and each remote office. An assessment will need to be made of the available methods for connectivity between all the sites.

▶ The TCP/IP infrastructure will need be examined to determine if it is optimal. If it is not, the changes that must be made to make it more efficient should be included in the design.

SCENARIO

The law firm of Dewey, Winnem, & Howe has hired you to design a network infrastructure to upgrade their existing network. The company has headquarters in Manhattan, with several satellite locations scattered across the country. Some of the locations are large offices with many employees. Others are small, partnered law firms with one or two people. The firm would like to maximize its data throughput while minimizing costs. Currently, it is running T-1 connections to every one of its remote offices and is finding that its monthly carrier bill is very expensive. The firm has no centralized network management. Each site has a representative in charge of computer problems on-site. Due to the lack of centralized administration, conflicts often arise. For instance, TCP/IP addresses are assigned statically at each location, and the company often finds that the addresses are duplicated, creating significant

CASE STUDY: DESIGNING A NETWORK INFRASTRUCTURE FOR THE DEWEY, WINNEM, & HOWE LAW FIRM

▶ The company uses a number of nonstandard proprietary applications. Each of these applications needs to be examined in order to determine its specific needs and how the network infrastructure can support them.

▶ Network services, such as DHCP and WINS, will need to be examined and a plan developed in order to extend those services throughout enterprise. The corporate headquarters is using Ethernet hubs for its fundamental network infrastructure; users are complaining of long delays to access the system. The possibility of replacing those hubs with switches should be investigated.

troubleshooting issues. The company uses standard office productivity software, such as Microsoft Office, as well as a number of proprietary database applications used to store client case information. Some of its remote offices, especially the smaller ones, have outsourced the computer support to various vendors. The company provides dial-in access to its attorneys so that they can access the client and caseload databases while in courtrooms or on the road. The company also has an Internet connection to access services such as WestLaw and Lexus/Nexus. The existing infrastructure is built on Windows NT 4.0, offering services such as DHCP and WINS through the corporate headquarters in Manhattan. In the corporate headquarters, all the servers are located on the dedicated Ethernet segment. All the workstations are connected to hubs placed on each floor of the office building. Users complain of long delays when they try to access the system during the day.

ANALYSIS

The law firm of Dewey, Winnem, & Howe is a nationwide company with many remote offices. Its user population is widely dispersed. The needs of those users, in terms of applications and connectivity, vary from site to site. When you're designing a new network infrastructure for this company, the existing infrastructure will need to be thoroughly examined. Applications will need to be listed and prioritized and their needs determined. The user population will need to be

continues

continued

counted and its needs quantified. End users' work needs and usage patterns will need to be examined in order to determine the appropriate connectivity bandwidth and functionality to be built into the network design. The existing design should be evaluated in terms of disaster recovery. Improvements or modifications to that strategy will need to support the upgrades brought upon by the implementation of the new network infrastructure you design.

CHAPTER SUMMARY

KEY TERMS

- gap analysis
- bandwidth
- latency
- throughput
- capacity
- performance
- availability
- scalability
- MTBF
- MTTR
- DMZ

As stated earlier, the focus of an analysis should ultimately be the individual end-user clients where the users do their work. You should pay close attention to the activities of end users before, during, and after the creation of your network infrastructure design.

Users' collective perceptions can have a profound impact on the reality of your project and how it is judged. Do not underestimate the power of the user community.

Analyzing end-user work needs involves determining who needs access to which data, when they need it, and where it should be delivered. It is imperative that the network infrastructure support the work needs of the end users. In order to meet end-user work needs effectively and efficiently, you must also carefully examine end-user group usage patterns. The questions to use for this phase do not consist of solid "who" and "what" questions, but rather "when," "how often," and "how much."

APPLY YOUR KNOWLEDGE

Exercises

2.1   Creating an IP Addressing Scheme

This exercise demonstrates the process of creating an IP addressing scheme that can be implemented across an enterprise. You will complete Table 2.1 to create the addressing standards for the Lighthouse, Inc. corporate network.

Estimated Time: 30 minutes

Lighthouse Inc. has corporate headquarters in Bangor, Maine and four remote sites in Nashua, N.H.; Lowell, Mass.; Providence, R.I.; and Buffalo, N.Y. Each site should adhere to the same IP addressing standards. In each location, there need to be at least eight client PCs, as well as four routers and/or switches, five servers, and five printers. You should allow for the addition of one or two of each type of device to the network to accommodate some minor anticipated growth over the next three years. There is also the possibility that one or two additional locations might be added to the network within three years. Those sites will need to adhere to the same standards within the selected IP address space.

The address space of 192.168.16.0 with a subnet mask of 255.255.255.224 has been selected for the enterprise.

TABLE 2.1

ADDRESSING STANDARDS FOR LIGHTHOUSE, INC.

Location	Subnet	Host Range for Servers	Host Range for Routers and Switches	Host Range for Printers	Host Range for Client PCs	Public or Private Address
Bangor	192.168.16.0	.6 to .12	.1 to .5	.13 to .18	.19 to .30	Private
Nashua	192.168.16.32		.33 to .37			
Lowell	192.168.16.64			.77 to .82		
Providence	192.168.16.96				.115 to .126	
Buffalo	192.168.16.128					

APPLY YOUR KNOWLEDGE

Answers to Exercise 2.1

When you have completed this exercise, you should have a completed table that looks like Table 2.2.

TABLE 2.2

ANSWERS TO ADDRESSING STANDARDS FOR LIGHTHOUSE, INC.

Location	Subnet	Host Range for Servers	Host Range for Routers and Switches	Host Range for Printers	Host Range for Client PCs	Public or Private Address
Bangor	192.168.16.0	.6 to .12	.1 to .5	.13 to .18	.19 to .30	Private
Nashua	192.168.16.32	.38 to .44	.33 to .37	.45 to .50	.51 to .62	Private
Lowell	192.168.16.64	.70 to .76	.65 to .69	.77 to .82	.83 to .94	Private
Providence	192.168.16.96	.102 to .108	.97 to .101	.109 to .114	.115 to .126	Private
Buffalo	192.168.16.128	.134 to .140	.129 to .133	.141 to .146	.147 to .158	Private

This solution meets the company's growth requirements by allowing for the following in each location (see Table 2.3).

TABLE 2.3

GROWTH REQUIREMENTS

Device Type	Number Allowed	Number Required
Servers	7	5
Routers/switches	5	4
Printers	6	5
Client PCs	12	8

The solution also allows for the addition of at least two additional sites that can follow this addressing scheme.

APPLY YOUR KNOWLEDGE

2.2   Performing a Hardware Assessment

This exercise demonstrates the process of assessing the existing hardware in a company against the goals of the new network infrastructure design. Complete Table 2.4 based on the information provided regarding the design of the Golden Gardens, Inc. network infrastructure.

Estimated Time: 15 minutes

Golden Gardens, Inc. is a small company with one location. In its offices, it has installed a network infrastructure with four file servers running Microsoft Windows NT 4.0 and 16 client workstations. Six of the workstation computers have 486 DX 100Mhz CPUs with 16MB of RAM, six have Pentium 233Mhz CPUs with 32MB of RAM, and four have Pentium II 266Mhz CPUs with 64MB of RAM.

Management at Golden Gardens, Inc. has mandated that part of the new infrastructure design include the rollout of a new application that has recently been purchased. The minimum CPU and memory requirements for this application are a 200Mhz CPU and 64MB of RAM. You want to perform an assessment of the existing hardware so that you can make recommendations to company management regarding any hardware upgrades that must be performed in order to support the new application.

Complete Table 2.4 in order to summarize your results and present your recommendations to Golden Gardens, Inc.'s management.

TABLE 2.4

RESULTS SUMMARY

Host Name	CPU Type	Amount of RAM	Upgrade CPU?	Upgrade RAM?
CompA	Pentium II 266Mhz	64MB	No	No
CompB	486 DX 100	16MB		
CompC	Pentium 233Mhz	32MB		

Answers to Exercise 2.2

When you have completed this exercise, you should have a table that looks like Table 2.5.

APPLY YOUR KNOWLEDGE

TABLE 2.5

ANSWERS TO RESULTS SUMMARY

Host Name	CPU Type	Amount of RAM	Upgrade CPU?	Upgrade RAM?
CompA	Pentium II 266Mhz	64MB	No	No
CompB	486 DX 100	16MB	Yes	Yes
CompC	Pentium 233Mhz	32MB	No	Yes

2.3 Analyzing Client Computer Access Requirements

In this exercise you will compile a list of client computer access requirements for use in your infrastructure design. We will use a fictitious company, MedEx, for this exercise.

Estimated Time: 10 minutes

MedEx sells medical equipment and supplies to various hospitals in the northeast. They are headquartered in Friendship, Maine, where they have a staff of 100 people. Approximately 30 salespeople with laptops are responsible for visiting local hospitals and taking orders.

These orders are taken using a custom-built client application. The client application collects the sales orders, and then the salesperson connects to headquarters to transmit the orders to a database located there.

Several executives located in the headquarters run large queries against the sales database in order to analyze sales information and perform growth projection. Also, purchasers run queries against the sales database in order to forecast future sales and generate orders for more products from suppliers.

List the factors in determining the requirements for the following groups:

- Sales personnel
- Executives
- Purchasers

APPLY YOUR KNOWLEDGE

Answers to Exercise 2.3

- Sales personnel: The sales staff will need dial-up connectivity from various locations in order to transmit their sales orders.

- Executives: They will need large amounts of bandwidth in order to process their queries against the sales database.

- Purchasers: They will need large amounts of bandwidth in order to process their queries against the sales database.

2.4 Analyzing the Existing Disaster Recovery Strategy for Client Computers, Servers, and the Network

In this exercise you will analyze the disaster recovery strategies and plans implemented by a company in order to ensure that your network design accommodates them. In this exercise we'll use a fictitious company called NorthWind Publishing.

Estimated Time: 10 minutes

NorthWind is a publishing company located in New York. They have their headquarters there, which holds 300 people, a mainframe, and 20 servers. Two of the servers at the headquarters hold databases that are mission-critical to the operation of the business. They have a number of other satellite offices in other cities. These offices have between 5 and 50 employees. The larger offices have a server, but the smaller offices do not. Central company functions, such as HR and finance, are done at headquarters, and the company data is stored on the servers. The satellite offices have writers, graphic artists, and administrative employees who create the books, articles, and other various documents.

Based on the preceding information, create a list of disaster recovery concerns.

Answers to Exercise 2.4

- Are the servers at headquarters and the satellite offices being backed up?

- Is there offsite storage for tape backups?

- Is there hardware fault tolerance for the servers?

- Is there failover capability for the mission-critical servers? Is the data on the server being replicated to another site?

- In the offices without servers, are client computers being backed up? If so, where are those tapes stored?

Review Questions

1. What components comprise the total user population for an organization?

2. What is the purpose of the gap analysis?

3. What are two typical network topology models?

4. What is net available bandwidth?

5. In what way does latency affect the performance of applications on a network?

APPLY YOUR KNOWLEDGE

6. What are some areas you should consider when developing a security strategy for the network infrastructure?

7. What are some of the typical wiring types used in today's network infrastructures?

8. What is the function of a repeater?

9. What is the purpose of an IP address?

10. Why is it unwise to combine the deployment of a new application or an upgrade to an existing application with the implementation of a new network infrastructure design?

Exam Questions

The first five exam questions refer to the Case Study presented earlier in this chapter.

1. Assuming that you decide to recommend a centralized approach to Dewey, Winnem, & Howe's network structure, what type of topology would you recommend?

   A. Hub and spoke

   B. Partially meshed

   C. Fully meshed

   D. Flat loop

2. What impact does the outsourcing of computer support have on the size of the end-user community within the law firm?

   A. Outsourcing has no impact on the size of the end-user community.

   B. Outsourcing reduces the size of the end-user community.

   C. Outsourcing increases the size of the end-user community.

   D. Outsourcing helps maintain consistency and the size of the end-user community.

3. What challenges are posed by Dewey, Winnem, & Howe's lack of centralized administration over TCP/IP address assignment in the remote offices?

   A. IP addresses might be duplicated.

   B. IP addresses might be assigned by a DHCP.

   C. Certain hosts won't need IP addresses.

   D. IP addresses may be assigned that are outside the scope of the company's IP addressing scheme.

4. What issues surround Dewey, Winnem, & Howe's use of proprietary database applications?

   A. High MTTR

   B. High MBTF

   C. End-user access to database resources

   D. Network latency

5. What remedies might you consider in your new infrastructure design to solve the problem of users complaining of long delays when trying to the access the system in the corporate headquarters?

   A. Decrease the end users' workload by reducing the number of applications that are run on each workstation.

   B. Purchase hardware with a lower MTTR.

   C. Consider upgrading the hubs on each floor of the headquarters building with network switches.

   D. Consider revising the company's TCP/IP addressing scheme.

APPLY YOUR KNOWLEDGE

6. You have been hired by the New Shoes, Inc. organization to create a new design for its network infrastructure. New Shoes is in the process of acquiring one of its competitors, Best Foot, Inc. Company management has stated that the new network infrastructure must be as decentralized as possible. Given this decentralized approach, how should you plan for resource distribution in the new infrastructure design?

   A. Resources should be physically located in the New Shoes corporate headquarters.

   B. Resources should be physically located in the Best Foot corporate headquarters.

   C. Resources should be distributed and physically located near the WAN links that connect the two companies.

   D. Resources should be distributed throughout the enterprise, physically located near the end users who take advantage of them.

7. You are responsible for network design and administration for your company, New Riders, Inc. The company has just informed you that it will be opening a new office in Gnome, Alaska. It wants you to establish a T1 line to connect that office as soon as possible. What issues might you face in providing this connectivity?

   A. Inclement weather might delay the installation of the T1 lines.

   B. T1 connectivity might not be available in that particular location.

   C. A T1 link might provide more bandwidth than is necessary for that particular office.

   D. A T1 line to Gnome, Alaska would be too expensive.

8. You are responsible for network design for West Coast Importers, Inc. Your manager, Pedro, comes to you trying to understand the difference between capacity and net available bandwidth. What do you tell him?

   A. Net available bandwidth is always greater than network capacity.

   B. Net available bandwidth is always less than network capacity.

   C. Net available bandwidth and network capacity are the same and therefore are always equal.

   D. Net available bandwidth equals network capacity minus protocol overhead and bandwidth used by protocols that carry nonuser data.

9. You are the network manager for a company named Saint Paul Purchasing. The management at Saint Paul Purchasing is very upset with you this week because the network had an availability rating of 99.70 percent. They are upset because 99.70 percent availability is totally unacceptable given the nature of their business and the requirements that are placed on the network infrastructure. Given that the network was available for 99.70 percent of the time over the course of one week, for how long was the network unavailable?

   A. 5 minutes

   B. 30 minutes

   C. 1 hour

   D. 3 hours

APPLY YOUR KNOWLEDGE

10. Harbor Lights, Inc. has contracted with you to design a network infrastructure. The company would like to ensure that everyone can access its data servers and email servers most efficiently. What are some typical data and system access patterns that you might expect to find while conducting your investigation of Harbor Lights?

    A. Few users actually access the servers located at corporate headquarters.

    B. Users tend to access the servers most frequently in the morning and the evening.

    C. Users access the email servers at the same frequencies all day long.

    D. The file and email servers are overworked.

11. You're designing a network infrastructure for a company named Jones Services, Inc. Management at Jones is questioning your recommendation for the use of private IP addresses. They ask you to justify your recommendation. Which of the following are benefits associated with the use of private IP addresses?

    A. Private IP addresses allow you to connect your network to the Internet.

    B. Private IP addresses give you a much broader range of subnet and host addresses.

    C. Private IP addresses are centrally managed, registered, and assigned by Internet service providers.

    D. Private IP addresses help minimize the impact on your overall internetwork should you decide to change Internet service providers.

12. The management at Good Foods, Inc. has hired you to create a new network infrastructure designed for its corporate network. They want you to focus your security efforts on protecting the internal network from external intruders. You tell company management that although this is a valid concern, there are other areas of security upon which you will need to focus your efforts. What are some of the other areas of security that will need to be addressed while you create your network infrastructure design?

    A. Physical security

    B. Telephone security

    C. Internal access security

    D. Administrative security

13. You're in the process of creating a network infrastructure design for the Sun Dial Breads Company. You develop an IP addressing scheme using private IP addresses. Sun Dial management wants you to explain the nature of an effective IP addressing scheme so that they can understand your undertaking. What are some of the elements of an effective IP addressing scheme?

    A. Hierarchical

    B. Random

    C. Private

    D. Meaningful

14. You're in the process of designing a network infrastructure for Laurel Foods, Inc. Laurel Foods is currently using Windows NT 4.0 servers to offer file and print services. It uses Internet Information Server 4.0 as its Web server platform. The client workstations in the corporate headquarters access the Windows NT file servers for data storage. Client workstations also access the NT file servers for office productivity applications, including the Microsoft Office suite and

Lotus Notes applications. The clients also use a 32/70 emulator to connect to a mainframe for corporate financial data. The company plans to open two new branches across town. It is your job to design the connectivity for the two new offices. What issues must you address in order to provide adequate connectivity for the users in the new offices?

   A. Legacy protocols must be routed to the new locations in order to give users access to the mainframe applications.

   B. You must install frame relay circuits to the remote locations in order to provide adequate bandwidth for users to run the office productivity applications.

   C. You must use private TCP/IP addresses in order to connect the remote locations to the corporate headquarters.

   D. Connectivity must be provided 24 hours a day at each location in order for users to accomplish their jobs.

15. General Services, Inc. has contracted with you to develop a new network infrastructure designed for its enterprise. General Services will be acquiring one of its competitors, T.H. Howard and Sons, and will incorporate the T.H. Howard network into its own infrastructure. T.H. Howard has several remote locations, each with many end users. Responsibility for supporting the existing General Services network, as well as the planned merged network, will fall on the General Services three-person technical support team. Consider the impact of the three-person technical support team on the design of the overall network. In what way will this affect your design?

   A. Your network design will have to incorporate a new network support team.

   B. Your network design will have to incorporate remote support tools and methods to allow this existing support team to do its job effectively.

   C. Your network design will have to include a reduction in services offered across the enterprise.

   D. Your network design will not be affected by the existing technical support structure.

Answers to Review Questions

1. When determining an organization's total user population size, consider not only its employees, but also any contractors who work on the company premises or at remote sites. In addition, you must consider any vendors, partners, or clients who will be accessing the local internal network. Any user who accesses resources of the internal corporate network must be considered in the total user population for that organization. See "Analyze Company Size and User and Resource Distribution."

2. Gap analysis allows you to determine the differences between the existing environment and the environmental goals proposed by company management. The gap analysis will form the basis of your network infrastructure design and will help you decide which features and improvements will need to be included in your design. See "Evaluating Technical Environment and Goals."

APPLY YOUR KNOWLEDGE

3. Two common topology models found in inter-network design are the hub and spoke model and the mesh model. In a hub and spoke network, one side is selected as the central point of communication, and all the other sites connect to this central point. The links from the hub to the remote sites form the "spokes," and the entire architecture looks like a wheel. In a mesh topology, there is no central hub. Each site is connected to one or more of the other sites. In a fully meshed topology, each site is connected to all the other sites on the network. In a partially meshed topology, each site is connected to one or more sites, but not necessarily to all the other sites. See "Assessing Available Connectivity."

4. Net available bandwidth is the amount of bandwidth available to end users for transmission of user data. This figure is arrived at by determining the overall available bandwidth of a network link and subtracting from it the bandwidth used by protocol overhead and other information traversing the link that does not carry user data. See "Assessing Bandwidth and Latency."

5. Latency refers to the amount of time between the moment when a network station is ready to transmit data and the moment when the transmission is completed successfully. Increases in latency can be the cause of application timeouts, which would cause the application to cease functioning. Loss of functionality, also referred to as downtime, can be very expensive. See "Assessing Bandwidth and Latency."

6. Some areas of concern while developing a security strategy for your network infrastructure design include physical security, internal access security, and external access security. See "Security Considerations."

7. Some typical wiring types in today's network infrastructures include unshielded twisted pair, shielded twisted pair, coaxial cable, and fiber-optic cable. WAN devices often use serial cables such as the EIA/TIA 232. See "Network Infrastructure, Protocols, and Hosts."

8. A repeater is a device placed on the network to extend the distance that a network may span. Data enters the repeater on one side and is amplified and sent out on the other. The use of a repeater helps restore signal strength that is diminished over long cable runs. See "Network Infrastructure, Protocols, and Hosts."

9. An IP address is a number that uniquely identifies each end station connected to the network. Each station must have an IP address, and that IP address must be unique across the network. No two stations can have the same IP address. See "The IP Addressing Scheme."

10. Should issues arise during implementation, the combination of projects such as these helps complicate the troubleshooting process. See "Upgrades and Rollouts."

Answers to Exam Questions

1. **A.** If you decide to implement a centralized approach to the network infrastructure for Dewey, Winnem, & Howe, you should recommend a hub and spoke topology. With a hub and spoke network topology, you would use the Manhattan headquarters as the hub site, and all connectivity to the remote sites would connect from the center of the hub. This provides connectivity from each site of the enterprise to the

APPLY YOUR KNOWLEDGE

others through the Manhattan headquarters, which becomes the central point of control. See "Assessing Available Connectivity."

2. **C.** Outsourcing of computer support by the various remote offices increases the overall size of the end-user community because the firms that are charged with supporting the computer systems for these remote offices will be utilizing network resources belonging to the firm. These additional users, although they aren't company employees, will place additional demands on the network infrastructure. Support employees from the outsourcing vendor may work on-site within the law firm's remote offices or may work at their own corporate headquarters with some sort of remote connectivity established from their offices to the Dewey, Winnem, & Howe internal network. If this is the case, an additional burden will be placed on the infrastructure, and you will need to investigate the type of connectivity that is established, as well as the access patterns of the support employees themselves. See "Assessing Available Connectivity."

3. **A, D.** The IP addresses are assigned by individuals in each remote location without being managed by a central authority. Therefore, there is a likelihood that duplicate IP addresses will be assigned to workstations throughout the enterprise. In addition, it is very likely that a local administrator will begin to assign IP addresses that are not within the scope of the company's selected addressing scheme. See "TCP/IP Infrastructure."

4. **C.** The company's use of proprietary database applications leads to the concern of end-user access to database resources. You'll need to ensure that database resources are accessible to all users

who need them, whether they are in corporate headquarters, in a remote location, or accessing the network via dial-up or VPN services. Answers A and B refer to hardware performance, not to software, so they are incorrect. Answer D is also incorrect because, although it's true that latency is a concern for application performance, it is a concern for all applications, not specifically for proprietary database applications. See "Analyzing Client Computer Access Requirements."

5. **C.** The company is using hubs on each floor of the corporate headquarters, so all users are sharing the total bandwidth available. Replacing the hubs with network switches will potentially allow you to provide the full Ethernet bandwidth to each end station. This will dramatically reduce the overall load on the network and will reduce the delays experienced by end users while they access the network. See "Network Infrastructure, Protocols, and Hosts."

6. **D.** Management wants the network to be decentralized. This will require you to distribute network resources throughout the enterprise physically located near the end users who take advantage of them. Each location will have an administrator who is responsible for managing each resource. The scope of that administrator's responsibilities will be limited to the single resource or few resources over which he has control. See "Security Considerations."

7. **B.** When designing connectivity between various physical work sites, you need to investigate the availability of communication between those locations. It might be easy to assume that certain types of connectivity are available in highly populated areas, such as busy city or suburban neighborhoods. However, certain types of communication facilities

APPLY YOUR KNOWLEDGE

might not be available in rural areas, mountainous areas, or other sparsely populated locations. An investigation of the types of communications available will allow you to understand the options available to you before you create your design. See "Assessing Available Connectivity."

8. **D.** Net available bandwidth refers to the total bandwidth available to end users on that particular link. You arrive at this figure by starting with the capacity of that network link and subtracting bandwidth used by protocols that do not carry end-user data. You will also want to subtract any protocol overhead associated with the protocol you've selected to carry that user data. The figure you are left with is the bandwidth that is actually available to each end user to carry data across the link. See "Assessing Bandwidth and Latency."

9. **B.** An availability rating of 99.70 percent over the course of one week results in a downtime of approximately 30 minutes. In many environments, 30 minutes downtime per week is unacceptable, especially if that downtime is experienced all at once. When measuring network availability in percentages, the 99 on the left side of the decimal point is assumed. The two digits following the decimal point represent the acceptability or unacceptability of performance and availability. Tolerances for downtime will vary from one organization to another, depending on the nature of the business organization and the requirements placed on the network infrastructure. 99.99 percent availability is always strived for but rarely achieved. See "Performance, Scalability, and Availability."

10. **B, C.** In many organizations, you might expect to find typical data and system access patterns. One such pattern is that of user access to file servers. This access tends to be most frequent first thing in morning, when users arrive for work and log into the system. Access to email servers tends to be consistent throughout the course of the day. See "End-User Usage Patterns."

11. **B, D.** Private IP addresses allow you much greater flexibility and a much wider range of subnets and host addresses compared to what is available in the remaining public address space. Private IP addresses also minimize the impact on your enterprise network should you choose to change Internet service providers. The public address assigned to you by your ISP will be configured on relatively few devices on your internetwork. Should you change ISPs and receive a new publicly assigned address, you need only change that address on those few devices. The remaining devices in your enterprise will remain the same. See "The IP Addressing Scheme."

12. **A, C.** In addition to focusing external access security to protect the internal network from external intruders, you need to focus on other areas of security while creating your network infrastructure design. These other areas include internal access security and physical security. See "Security Considerations."

13. **A, D.** An effective IP addressing scheme is one that is hierarchical in nature. An IP addressing scheme should also be meaningful, with some basis in the architecture of the company itself. Public and private addressing space can be effective in an IP addressing scheme, provided that they are applied in a hierarchical and meaningful fashion. See "The IP Addressing Scheme."

APPLY YOUR KNOWLEDGE

14. **B, C.** To provide for this scenario as stated, legacy protocols will not need to be transmitted across the network, but some form of connectivity will be required, although nothing in the scenario requires 24-hour access. In this case, answers B and C are the most likely. See "Evaluating Technical Environment and Goals."

15. **B.** Your new network infrastructure design must incorporate remote support tools and other methods to help the three-person technical support team effectively provide support across the entire organization. You can safely assume that this team will be overworked, but you might ease the support burden by building in the capability to support network services remotely and effectively. See "Technical Support Structure."

Suggested Readings and Resources

1. Adam, Kelli, and Rob Scrimger. *MCSE Training Guide: TCP/IP,* Second Edition. Indianapolis, IN: New Riders Publishing, 1998. (ISBN: 1562059203)

2. Berg, Glenn. *Network+ Exam,* Fast Track Network+ Series. Indianapolis, IN: New Riders Publishing, 1999. (ISBN: 0735709041)

3. Cisco Systems. *Cisco IOS 12.0 Switching Services.* Indianapolis, IN: Cisco Press, 1999. (ISBN: 1578701570)

4. Ratliff, Randy. *Network+ Certification Guide.* Indianapolis, IN: New Riders Publishing, 1999. (ISBN: 073570077X)

The term *network infrastructure* seems to be a rather nebulous term in the technology arena. For the purposes of the Microsoft exam, a network infrastructure is the collection of technical network components that provide the framework for data communications and other network operations. The network infrastructure includes

- Network hardware, such as cabling, routers, switches, and host computers

- Hardware and software protocols

- Network services that facilitate host communications, such as DHCP, DNS, and WINS

- Data storage and access configuration

Microsoft lists the following objectives for the network design section of the Windows 2000 Network Infrastructure exam:

Modify and design a network topology.

▶ The foundation for the design of a network is the topology. Hardware protocols are closely related to network topologies. Therefore, a portion of this objective demands understanding not only the topology, but also associated hardware protocols. This test objective requires you to understand mainstream network topologies and how each impacts the performance and scalability of a Windows 2000 network.

CHAPTER 3

Designing a Windows 2000 Network Infrastructure

Design a TCP/IP networking strategy.

- **Analyze IP subnet requirements.**

- **Design a TCP/IP addressing and implementation plan.**

- **Measure and optimize a TCP/IP infrastructure design.**

- **Integrate software routing into existing networks.**

- **Integrate TCP/IP with existing WAN requirements.**

▶ TCP/IP is the protocol of choice not only for a Windows 2000 network, but also for the vast majority of networks worldwide, including the Internet. The Microsoft exam requires a solid understanding of all aspects of TCP/IP design, configuration, and implementation, including those in the preceding list.

Design a DHCP strategy.

- **Integrate DHCP into a routed environment.**

- **Integrate DHCP with Windows 2000.**

- **Design a DHCP service for remote locations.**

- **Measure and optimize a DHCP infrastructure design.**

▶ DHCP service provides IP addresses and other configuration information to requesting hosts. The automated addressing and configuration eases the management of TCP/IP networks. This service is a necessity for all but very small networks. To meet this objective, you must be able, at a minimum, to complete the tasks in the preceding list.

Design name resolution services.

- **Create an integrated DNS design.**

- **Create a secure DNS design.**

- **Create a highly available DNS design.**

- **Measure and optimize a DNS infrastructure design.**

- **Design a DNS deployment strategy.**

- **Create a WINS design.**

- **Create a secure WINS design.**

- **Measure and optimize a WINS infrastructure design.**

- **Design a WINS deployment strategy.**

▶ Windows 2000 supports two name services, Domain Name System (DNS) and Windows Internet Name Service (WINS). DNS is the technology industry standard for TCP/IP networks. WINS, a NetBIOS-enabled name service, is a legacy product for pre–Windows 2000 networks and is supported by Windows 2000 Server for ease of integration.

Meeting this exam objective requires a thorough understanding of WINS, DNS, and Dynamic DNS (DDNS). You must know how to perform the tasks in the preceding list.

Design a multiprotocol strategy. Protocols include IPX/SPX and SNA.

▶ Networks in the real world often support hosts that have more than one protocol. Most commonly, mixed protocol networks use IPX/SPX (Novell) or SNA. Although Windows 2000 supports other protocols, the Microsoft exam concentrates on these two protocols for this objective. To meet this exam objective, you must be able to

- Choose the appropriate configuration—gateway or compatible client computer—for integrating Windows 2000 into a Novell network.

- Describe the three deployment models for Microsoft SNA Server and choose the best model for a scenario.

Design a Distributed file system (Dfs) strategy.

- **Design the placement of a Dfs root.**

- **Design a Dfs root replica strategy.**

▶ Dfs is a data access and distribution tool that enables administrators to integrate data from two or more physical locations on the network into a single hierarchical structure. This structure looks like a share point to network client computers. To meet the exam requirements for this objective, you should be able to perform the tasks listed.

Microsoft states exam objectives for several areas in the network infrastructure section of the test. Because the exam is largely scenario-based, you are expected to understand the technologies described in this chapter well enough to determine the best solution for a scenario. In addition to the aforementioned Microsoft exam objectives, you should also

▶ Understand the basics of the ATM protocol and IP over ATM (IP/ATM).

▶ Know how to subnet an IP address, how many hosts and networks a given IP address range and subnet support, and how to apply subnet masking to a network design.

▶ Be able to determine whether two IP addresses belong to the same network, given a subnet mask.

▶ Be able to determine how DHCP must be configured to provide services across a router or via a multi-homed Windows 2000 Server computer.

▶ Know how to configure DNS, including zone replication and Active Directory replication.

▶ Understand provisioning IP addresses for remote computers, including remote computer address requests.

▶ Be able to configure WINS in a routed environment. This means that you should know how WINS communicates across routers. In addition, because Windows 2000 DNS and WINS can be configured to interact, you should know the details of such a configuration.

▶ Be able to design an efficient deployment of Dfs with alternate volumes, Active Directory replication, and downlevel volumes.

INTRODUCTION

This chapter prepares you for the Network Infrastructure Design section of Microsoft's 70-221 exam. The Network Infrastructure Design section of the exam is designed to measure your "theoretical" understanding of network protocols (especially TCP/IP), naming services, distributed file services, network-level security, and network-level performance tuning. You should expect scenario questions on the exam that require you to determine the best design or configuration.

The explosion of network computing over the last decade has brought computers to many desktops in the workplace. It has also brought a great deal of complexity to network operations and configuration. Embryonic networks of the 1980s were required to share only files and print services with users. A simple protocol such as NetBIOS was sufficient to handle the relatively small number of host devices. Today, networks bring a number of services to the desktop in addition to file and print services.

To successfully design, implement, and manage today's networks, you must have technical knowledge rooted in network infrastructure. This chapter covers network infrastructure in general and TCP/IP network specifically.

NETWORK TOPOLOGIES

Modify and design a network topology.

Network topology is typically used to describe the physical configuration or structure of a network, including cabling, routers, bridges, switches, and hubs. Additionally, the data link and the physical layers of the network protocol are an integral part of the network topology. These protocol layers are closely related to the network topology because they are designed to work with specific hardware. In this section, the three most commonly used network topologies— backbone-based, ring-based, and switched networks—are described. Implementations of these types of networks are also described for hybrid networks, ATM communications, and Quality of Service (QoS) configuration.

Backbone-Based Networks

Historically, backbone-based networks were really configured with a backbone to which network hosts connected. Figure 3.1 shows an early shielded cable network. The backbone consists of *thicknet* cable that has hosts connected via *thinnet* cable.

Thinnet and thicknet networks were replaced by networks connected using unshielded twisted-pair 10BaseT networks. Figure 3.2 depicts a typical 10BaseT Ethernet network. This network consists of two segments separated by a router. In this configuration, the router serves as the network's backbone.

The most popular type of low-level (layer 2) network protocols by far, Ethernet networks offer a very good mix of flexibility, scalability, and economy. As well as being the most popular type of network, the Data Link protocol used is usually Ethernet.

Ethernet is a simple Carrier Sense Multiple Access/Collision Detection (CSMA/CD) protocol. The entire network on a segment can be viewed as a single strand of wire with all hosts attached (a shared network). All network cards connected to an Ethernet network have equal access to the network. When a client computer must send a frame across the wire, it listens for traffic from other network cards. If the wire is clear, the client computer attempts to send a frame. If two hosts attempt to access the wire simultaneously, a collision occurs. If a collision is detected, the client computer waits a while, listens for a clear wire, and tries again.

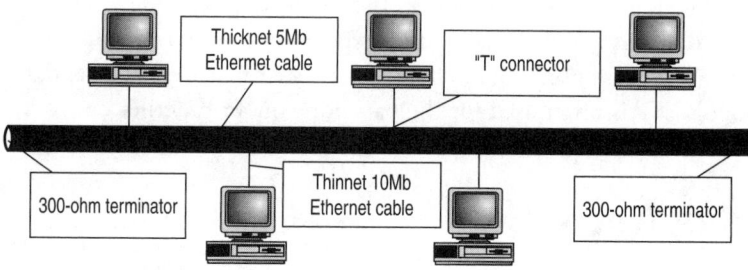

FIGURE 3.1
Early Ethernet networks were a combination of thinnet and thicknet cabling. Note that "open" ends of the thicknet backbone are terminated with resistors.

FIGURE 3.2
A typical configuration for a twisted-pair
(10BaseT) network uses one or more concen-
trators, or manageable hubs, as backbones for
a subnet.

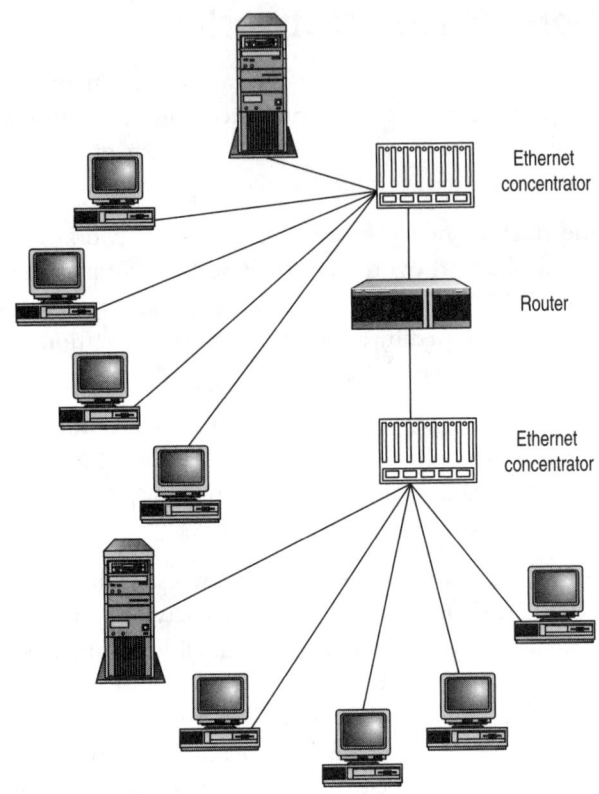

Three popular types of Ethernet are currently available: 10Mbps
Ethernet (10BaseT), 100Mbps Ethernet (100BaseT), and 1Gbps
Ethernet (1000BaseT). Cost differences between 10BaseT and
100BaseT hardware is negligible. Because it is a new technology,
1000BaseT is a substantially more expensive technology. 100BaseT
is the hardware protocol of choice for twisted-pair networks, and
1000BaseT is often used for the backbone on an Ethernet network.

Ring Networks

Two popular ring-based networks are in use today, FDDI (Fiber
Distributed Data Interface) and Token-Ring. Both of these networks
use a closed-ring topology. Both FDDI and Token-Ring networks use
token passing for traffic management. Token-passing networks tend
to perform better under heavy network traffic conditions, because
packet collisions are nonexistent on a properly working network,

whereas collisions increase exponentially with network traffic levels on a shared media access network such as Ethernet. The term *ring-based* is a logical description. Both FDDI and Token-Ring networks use Media Access Units (MAUs) that look much like an Ethernet concentrator. A MAU is, in effect, a collapsed ring.

The similarities between FDDI and Token-Ring end here. Token-Ring networks use shielded twisted-pair media. FDDI uses fiber-optic media. Additionally, FDDI rings are actually two concentric rings that ensure a level of fault tolerance. Token-Ring networks run at 4, 16, or 100Mbps. FDDI operates exclusively at 100Mbps.

Switched Networks

The most commonly used switches are Ethernet switches. Although Ethernet is described as a shared network, this paradigm is changing. The old Ethernet hub, which provides a shared conduit by which the Ethernet hosts are connected, is being replaced by switches. A switch is a "smart" hub that moves packets between hosts using virtual connections. The switch learns the hardware address of each Ethernet host and then routes data frames accordingly. These virtual connections take place on multiple-gigabit backplanes within the switches, with no potential for collisions.

The most commonly used Ethernet switches employ OSI layer 2 (Data Link) switching. The switching algorithms they used to identify Ethernet hosts are spanning-tree algorithms. Spanning-tree algorithms were originally developed for network bridging technology. Layer 2 switches can be thought of as high-speed multiport bridges. Some newer switches use OSI layer 3 (Network) switching. These switches can be though of multiport routers.

Another widely used switch uses the ATM (Asynchronous Transfer Mode) layer 2 protocol. In fact, ATM was designed as a switched protocol. Furthermore, ATM can be implemented only in a switched environment. The Windows 2000 implementation is discussed in more detail in the following section.

Windows 2000 and ATM

ATM is an emerging OSI layer 2 (Data Link) protocol that is supported by Windows 2000. ATM is designed to work optimally with switches. Although ATM can be used down to the desktop level, it is commonly used for network backbones.

ATM is ideal for use as a network backbone because it is fast, reliable, and scalable. ATM commonly operates at 155Mbps but can be implemented at up to 622Mbps. ATM packets are always the same size; therefore, ATM switches are relieved of the burden of reading packet size from the packet header and monitoring the byte count when transferring packets. A combination of the available bandwidth with ATM and the fact that this bandwidth can be partitioned into virtual LANs makes ATM an excellent protocol in terms of scalability.

The Windows 2000 implementation of ATM supports Quality of Service (QoS) for networks that handle voice, binary data, video, and audio. ATM enables each of these data types to use a single network connection. It also enables the administrator to allocate bandwidth based on several data attributes, including data type, source, and destination.

> **NOTE**
>
> **ATM LAN Emulation** Most newer routers support ATM LAN emulation.

To interoperate with conventional networks, Windows 2000 uses ATM LAN Emulation (LANE). Windows 2000 can act as a LAN Emulation Client computer (LEC) in an Emulated LAN (ELAN) environment. A LAN Emulation Client computer uses ELAN services provided by the ATM switch vendor. The ELAN emulation is associated with an ATM interface card in the Windows 2000 computer. To connect the ATM switch to an Ethernet network, for example, an Ethernet interface card is also installed in the ELAN Client computer. The Windows 2000 computer serves as a gateway to the Ethernet network.

Windows 2000 offers an alternative to ELAN: IP for ATM (IP/ATM). IP/ATM is a set of core services that communicate over an ATM network. IP/ATM enables Windows 2000 client computers to connect directly to an ATM switch with an ATM interface card using TCP/IP. Applications written for TCP/IP and QoS for Windows Sockets can be used with IP/ATM. IP/ATM offers a performance edge over LAN emulation because IP/ATM packets have smaller headers and require less evaluation by the client computer.

Windows 2000 also supports Point-to-Point Protocol for ATM (PPP/ATM). The fastest-growing communication service today is Digital Subscriber Line (xDSL), a family of high-speed residential remote access services. Most xDSL lines use PPP for the local loop that connects to an ATM switch. PPP/ATM facilitates an end-to-end ATM network over xDSL.

> **NOTE**
>
> **IP/ATM Address Resolution**
> Windows 2000 IP/ATM includes multicast and Address Resolution Protocol (ARP) services. Each segment of the network should have one—and only one—ARP/MARS server configured.
>
> Multicast Address Resolution Service (MARS) facilitates conversion of TCP/IP multicast addresses to physical addresses. MARS works in much the same manner as ARP, except that ARP is a one-for-one address resolution and MARS resolves addresses for all hosts belonging to a multicast group.

Windows 2000 Quality of Service

Network administrators can manage network resources, including bandwidth using Windows 2000 QoS. QoS is a set of tools and technologies that enables administrators to manage network communication resources:

◆ QoS Admission Control Manager is used to set network policy.

◆ Resource allocation and prioritization can be configured at the enterprise, subnet, and user level.

◆ The administrator can guarantee maximum point-to-point delivery delays.

Hybrid Networks

Most networks are not built with a single hardware protocol or topology. Certain topologies are better for particular network implementations:

◆ Token-passing protocols handle high volumes of traffic better than Ethernet; therefore, FDDI is a popular backbone topology. FDDI also offers a level of fault tolerance.

- ATM is much faster than Ethernet at high-volume levels. It supports virtual LANs, so it is often used for network backbones and is connected to Ethernet subnets.

- FDDI and ATM are expensive technologies and are not supported by a number of hardware hosts; therefore, Ethernet is the network of choice at the desktop level.

A network topology is the foundation for a network infrastructure. Many design considerations influence a network topology configuration, such as physical location, performance requirements, types of data that cross the wire, expected growth, and economics. A network topology should be designed around these and other environmental factors. To create a quality network topology design, you must understand the value of the available tools for that design. Network protocols are closely aligned with network topology. As you will see in the next section, the design of a TCP/IP network is influenced by the same factors that guide a network topology design; however, the primary influence for a TCP/IP network design is the network topology. See *MCSE Training Guide: Networking Essentials, Second Edition*, by Glenn Berg, New Riders Publishing, 1999 (ISBN: 1-56205-919-X) for more information about this topic.

PLANNING TCP/IP NETWORKING STRATEGIES

Design a TCP/IP networking strategy.

The TCP/IP protocol suite is the global standard for networking. Its robustness and scalability make it the correct choice for networks of any size, from SOHO (Small Office/Home Office) to global enterprise networks. TCP/IP has evolved as an industry standard because it supports

- Standards-based communication, facilitating connectivity among heterogenous operating systems

- A rich suite of core protocols, each optimally designed for a particular type of use, such as file transfer, reliable connections, and email communication.

◆ Flexibility and scalability

◆ Standards-based support services, such as DHCP and DNS

Windows 2000 Server supports the full implementation of the TCP/IP protocol suite, as well as connectivity and management services for TCP/IP-based networks.

Understanding the TCP/IP Architecture

Understanding the underlying architecture of TCP/IP provides a good foundation for any IT professional working with the TCP/IP protocol suite. To understand the architecture of TCP/IP, it is important to first understand the OSI (Open Systems Interconnect) Reference Model for network protocols. The OSI model is the standard for network protocol implementation and is used as a reference model to describe the architecture of network protocols.

The OSI Protocol Architecture Model and TCP/IP

The OSI model consists of seven layers. These layers work together on a host to process and transport information to and from the network and presumably other hosts. Each of the seven layers is assigned a specific function in that process. Figure 3.3 shows the OSI layers.

Table 3.1 lists and describes the core functionality of the seven OSI layers. Each layer of the OSI protocol model serves a discrete function to facilitate host-to-host communication. Layers communicate strictly with adjacent layers.

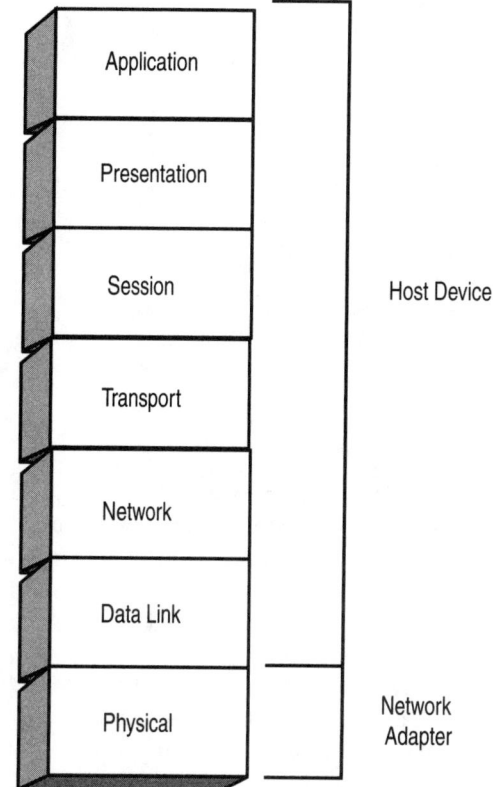

FIGURE 3.3
The OSI protocol model is often used as a comparative tool for describing network protocols.

TABLE 3.1

OSI LAYERS

OSI Layer	Description
Application	High-level data management. Any software that sends or receives "final format" data. Includes file transfer, text exchange, and virtual terminal service.
Presentation	Data conversion from network-readable to application-readable data.
Session	Manages communication between applications.
Transport	Facilitates data transfer between hosts, independent of hardware.
Network	Data packet addressing and delivery. Assembles received frames into protocol packets, and fragments outgoing protocol packets into frames.
Data Link	Sends and receives data stream from hardware.
Physical	Physical/mechanical network interface.

> **NOTE**
>
> **An OSI Model Mnemonic** It may be useful, when preparing for the exam, to memorize the OSI architecture layers in order from top to bottom. There is a mnemonic phrase for the OSI layers: "All People Seem To Need Data Processing." The first letter of each word matches the first letter of each OSI model layer in order, top to bottom.

When the layers and their respective functionality within the OSI model are understood, the OSI model can be compared to the TCP/IP architectural model. Figure 3.4 describes TCP/IP protocol suite architecture in terms of the OSI model.

The Application layer in the TCP/IP model facilitates access to the lower-level TCP/IP layers and defines the protocols that host applications use. Application layer TCP/IP protocols include HTTP, FTP, and Telnet.

The Host-to-Host Transport layer provides Application layer access to the Transport and Session layer core TCP/IP protocols—specifically, the TCP and UDP protocols.

The Internetwork layer of the TCP/IP model handles addressing, data packaging, and routing of Transport layer protocols. Internet layer protocols include IP, ARP, ICMP, and IGMP.

The Network Access layer of the TCP/IP model manages framing and read/write operations to the physical network. The Network Access layer is designed to be independent of the network media. This feature facilitates cross-platform compatibility with most network hardware.

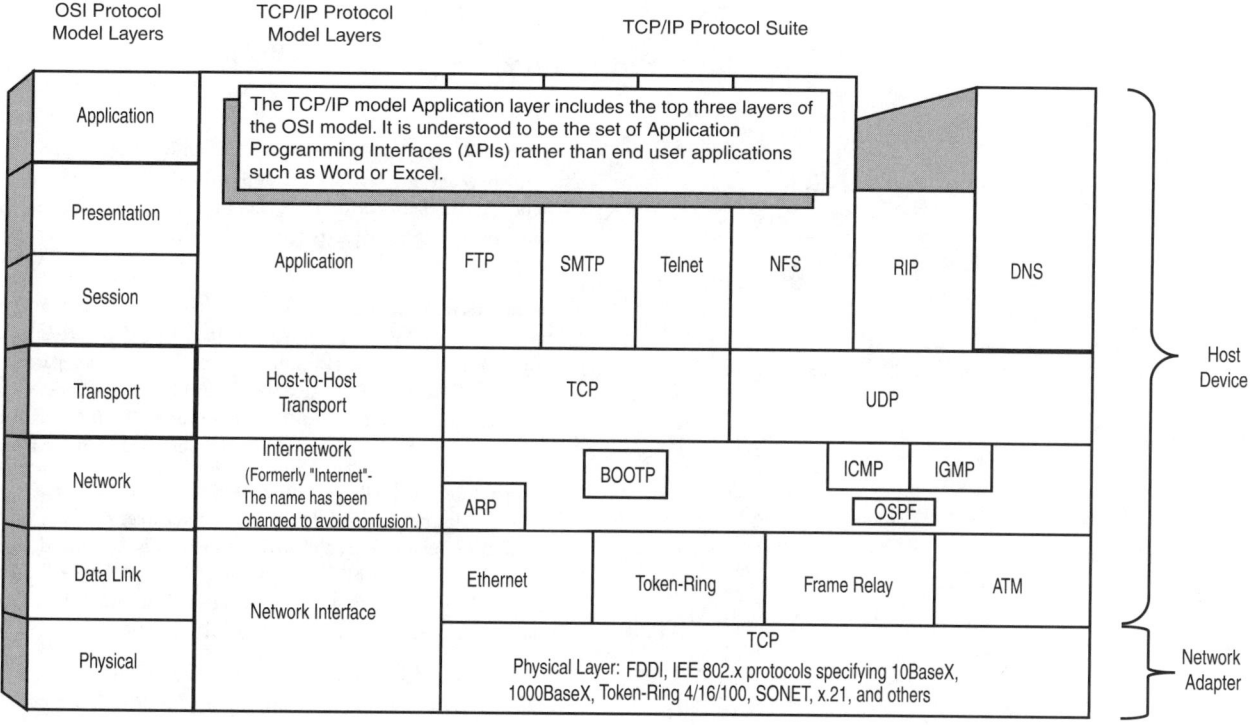

FIGURE 3.4
TCP/IP protocol compared to the OSI model shows that the TCP/IP archi-
tecture layers are integrations of more than one OSI layer for Application,
Transport, and Network Interface layers.

Understanding TCP/IP Core Protocols

All applications that use the TCP/IP protocol suite rely on a subset
of TCP/IP for basic network services. These protocols exist at the
Internetwork and Host-to-Host Transport layers and are known as
the TCP/IP core protocols. Table 3.2 describes these core protocols.

TABLE 3.2

CORE PROTOCOLS

Protocol	Description
ARP	Address Resolution Protocol: This protocol is used to resolve IP addresses to physical (MAC) addresses using MAC-level broadcasts.

continues

TABLE 3.2 | *continued*

CORE PROTOCOLS

Protocol	Description
ICMP	Internet Control Message Protocol: ICMP can be viewed as an error message and traffic control protocol. ICMP is used to report unreachable host errors, send routing redirect messages, and perform echo requests and replies. The commonly used PING tool uses ICMP.
IGMP	Internet Group Management Protocol: This protocol manages multicasts to IP groups. All hosts that belong to a particular IP host group "listen" for IP multicasts that are sent to a particular IP address. IGMP is used to join and to leave IP host groups. One of the new features of Windows 2000 DHCP is its capability of assigning multicast addresses to network hosts.
IP	Internet Protocol: IP is a connectionless, unreliable, "best effort" delivery protocol. Data delivery and receipt is not guaranteed, no session is established before data is exchanged, and packets may be lost or delivered out of order. A higher-level protocol layer is normally used in conjunction with IP to facilitate session-managed, reliable data delivery.
TCP	Transmission Control Protocol: The antithesis of IP, TCP is a reliable session- and connection-oriented protocol. Before exchange of data is initiated, TCP uses a handshake procedure to establish a session. After the session is established, all TCP packets received by a given host are checked by the receiving host for integrity and correct sequence and are then acknowledged by sending an acknowledge message (ACK) to the source host. If there is a problem with the received packet, a not acknowledged message (NACK) is sent to the source host so that the packet can be retransmitted.
UDP	User Datagram Protocol: UDP is a connectionless, unreliable protocol. Its small header size makes it useful for sending small amounts of data where acknowledgement is not required.

It is always helpful to know which core protocols, services, and Application layer protocols will be used on the network, and how they will be used in terms of broadcast traffic, retransmission, and session connections required for applications. This knowledge is useful for designing, implementing, and testing a network infrastructure.

TCP and UDP Ports

The UDP and TCP protocols communicate using ports. A port is a number between 0 and 65535 that is coded into the TCP or UDP packet. This port is an application-specific designation that is used to differentiate data streams being sent to a particular host. Typically, an application has at least one sending (source) port and at least one different receiving (destination) port.

Port numbers below 1024 are assigned by IANA (Internet Assigned Numbers Authority). Commonly known TCP ports are listed in Table 3.3; all the ports listed in this table are assigned by IANA. Commonly known UDP ports are listed in Table 3.4; UDP packets must have an IP address, a source port number, and a destination port number. Note that TCP and UDP port numbers are exclusive of each other; each protocol can use the same port number without consequences.

TABLE 3.3

COMMONLY KNOWN TCP PORTS

Port Number	Associated Application/Service
20, 21	FTP (File Transfer Protocol)
23	Telnet
25	SMTP (Simple Mail Transfer Protocol)
110	POP3 (Post Office Protocol, version 3)

TABLE 3.4

COMMONLY KNOWN UDP PORTS

Port Number	Associated Application/Service
7	Echo (used by PING)
21	FTP (File Transfer Protocol)
23	Telnet
25	SMTP (Simple Mail Transfer Protocol)
53	Domain Name System (DNS) service

continues

TABLE 3.4	*continued*

COMMONLY KNOWN UDP PORTS

Port Number	*Associated Application/Service*
69	TFTP (Trivial File Transfer Protocol)
79	Finger
80	www-http (World Wide Web HTTP)
88	Kerberos
137	NetBIOS name service
138	NetBIOS datagram service
139	NetBIOS session service
161	SNMP (Simple Network Management Protocol)
204	AppleTalk Echo

You should understand the purpose and functional description of the known TCP and UDP ports. This information is important to router configuration and is crucial to designing network security. A big part of Internet firewall security is port management.

Understanding IP Addressing and Subnetting

The Microsoft exam demands a thorough understanding of TCP/IP addressing and subnetting. Knowing how to design an IP network is crucial to the reliability and scalability of that network. After completing this section, you should be able to identify IP classes, perform binary mathematics to perform subnet calculations, and understand basic router configuration.

IP Addressing

Data networks normally require a mechanism for uniquely identifying both network segments and hosts connected to the network. At the hardware level, Ethernet uses MAC (Media Access Control) addresses and Token-Ring uses node numbers to identify hosts. At the software protocol level, Novell's IPX/SPX protocol uses MAC addresses to identify hosts and separate, administrator-assigned network numbers to identify network segments. As you will see, TCP/IP uses a single addressing scheme to identify both the network segments and hosts on a given network.

Hosts on a TCP/IP network are assigned a unique IP address that consists of four numbers, called *octets,* separated by dots. The octets are commonly represented in decimal format. A typical IP address might be

    192.168.40.7

Each octet in an IP address consists of an 8-digit binary number in the decimal range of 0 to 255 (or hexadecimal range 0x0 to 0xFF). Although each octet of an IP address obviously represents a byte, IP addresses are traditionally represented in decimal form, as shown in the previous example.

IP Subnet Masks

As stated earlier, an IP address uniquely identifies both the host and the network to which the host is connected. The leftmost portion of the IP address is the network ID, and the remaining portion is the host ID. The question that you need to ask is where to draw the line dividing left and right. The network ID is extracted from the IP address using a subnet mask. A subnet mask is a number formatted in the same way as an IP address. To extract the network ID from an IP address, a *bitwise logical AND operation* is performed using the subnet mask and the IP address. To understand how subnet masks are used to identify network and host, it is necessary to understand the bitwise logical AND operation. Bitwise logical operations compare two numbers (operands) at the binary level, yielding a result based on the value of each bit position for these numbers. When executing a bitwise logical AND, the rules are

1. If a given bit position for both operands being compared is 1, the result is 1 for that bit position.

2. All other value combinations for the operands for that bit position yield 0.

To demonstrate, perform the bitwise logical AND operation on the numbers 50 and 43. First the numbers are converted to binary format:

    50 = 110010
    43 = 101011

Then each of the bit positions are compared and the result noted below the two numbers, much in the same format as addition or subtraction:

110010
101011
_____
101010 = 34

The feature of note here is that when either of the bit positions for either operand is 0, the result is 0. The bitwise logical AND can be used to "strip away" portions of one of the operands:

10110111
11110000
_____
10110000

This is precisely how the network and host portions of an IP address are calculated. The IP address from the previous example (192.168.40.7) in binary format is

1100000.10101000.00101000.00000111

A typical subnet mask for this address is

255.255.0.0

or 11111111.11111111.11111111.00000000 in binary format. Figure 3.5 shows a bitwise logical AND performed using the address and subnet mask in the example, which is the result of the logical AND operation. When the result is converted to decimal format, it is 192.168.0.0, which is the network ID.

For more information on this topic, see *MCSE Training Guide: TCP/IP, Second Edition*, by Rob Scrimger and Kelli Adam, New Riders Publishing, 1998 (ISBN: 1-56205-920-3).

```
1100000.10101000.00101000.00000111
1111111.11111111.00000000.00000000

1100000.10101000.00000000.00000000
```

FIGURE 3.5
Determining the network ID for a given IP address is accomplished by a bitwise AND of the IP address and its associated subnet mask.

IP Classes

By current RFC standards, the universe of all possible IP addresses is divided into five classes. These five classes are listed in Table 3.5. For all practical purposes, we are concerned with only the first three classes. Classes D and E are seldom used; however, they may appear as a possible distracting answer on the Microsoft exam.

TABLE 3.5

DEFAULT IP ADDRESS CLASSES

Default IP Class	Range	Default Subnet Mask	Description
Class A	1.0.0.0 to 126.0.0.0	255.0.0.0	Supports a small number of networks and a large number of hosts.
Class B	128.0.0.0 to 191.254.0.0	255.255.0.0	Supports a large number of hosts and a large number of networks.
Class C	192.0.1.0 to 223.255.254.0	255.255.255.0	Supports a large number of networks and a small number of hosts.
Class D	224.0.0.0 to 239.255.255.255	N/A	Reserved for IP multicast addresses.
Class E	248.0.0.0 to 254.255.255.255	N/A	Reserved for future use.

Default IP classes are identified by one or more high-order bits in the binary representation of the first octet of the IP address. Table 3.6 describes the high-order bit settings for each of the classes.

TABLE 3.6

DEFAULT IP CLASSES

Default IP Class	Required High-Order Bits
Class A	0xxxxxxx
Class B	10xxxxxx
Class C	110xxxxx
Class D	1110xxxx
Class E	1111xxxx

> **NOTE**
>
> **DNS Extensions to Support IP Version 6 RFC 1886** RFC 1886 defines a new "next generation" IP addressing scheme, IP version 6 (Ipv6). This new address format is 128 bits (compared to 32 bits for the current IP version 4). An Ipv6 address is expressed as 8 sets of up to 4 hexadecimal digits:
>
> 4EF8:FFE:9888:DEBB:9:16:EAD5:708A
>
> You should be aware of this new standard; however, I would not expect to find references to Ipv6 on the exam.

The first three IP address classes are the commonly used IP addresses. Class D and E IP addresses are reserved and should not be used in network design. Table 3.7 lists the number of host IDs and network IDs available through the range of commonly used IP addresses (classes A, B, and C).

TABLE 3.7

HOST IDs AND NETWORK IDs FOR CLASSES A, B, AND C

Class	Network ID Range Subnet Mask	Number of Default Networks	Number of Default Hosts
A	1.0.0.0 to 126.0.0.0	126	16,777,214
B	128.0.0.0 to 191.254.0.0	16,384	65,534
C	192.0.1.0 to 223.255.254.0	2,097,152	254

Calculating the Number of Hosts and Networks

An important procedure when designing a TCP/IP network is choosing the appropriate IP address class. To determine the best choice (and to score points on the Microsoft exam), you must be able to enumerate a given IP address range and subnet mask combination. Enumeration is simply calculating the number of hosts and networks that a range of IP addresses and a subnet mask yield.

If you look at Table 3.7, you will notice that there is an address gap between the first two classes and that the host ID counts seem to be short by 2. This is because there are a few rules concerning assignment of IP addresses:

◆ The first octet of an IP address cannot be 127, which is reserved for local loopback procedures.

◆ Traditionally, the binary representation of the network ID cannot be all 1s, which is reserved for IP broadcasts.

◆ Traditionally, the binary representation of the network ID cannot be all 0s, which is used to represent the local network and will not be routed.

◆ The binary representation of the host ID cannot be all 1s, which is reserved for network segment broadcasts.

◆ The binary representation of the host ID cannot be all 0s, because an IP address with such a host is a representation of the network ID.

To determine the number of network IDs available for a given IP address range and subnet mask, convert the high and low network IDs to binary format. Then, count the number of bits that are used to represent the range of network IDs. Finally, calculate the difference between the value of those bits plus 1. For example, given the class C IP address range of 192.168.0.0 through 192.168.8.0 with the default subnet mask (255.255.255.0), enumeration is done as follows:

1. Convert the high and low network IDs (192.168.0.0, 192.168.8.0) to binary values. In this example, the binary conversion would look like this:

   Network ID low: 11000000.10101000.00000000.00000000

   Network ID high: 11000000.10101000.00001000.00000000

2. The highest bit used for this address range is 2^3, or the fourth bit position of the third octet. We are concerned only with the portion of the IP address that falls within the subnet mask, which in this case is the first three octets. The number of bits available for networks is four.

3. Calculate the difference between the network IDs. You need to work only with the significant bits. The difference between binary 0 (decimal 0) and binary 1000 (decimal 8) is 8. Because we are calculating the inclusive range of network IDs, increment this value by 1. Nine network IDs are available.

Finding the number of host IDs available per network is a bit (no pun intended) different. Host IDs span the available range of bits available; however, an all-1s or all-0s host ID cannot be used, so the calculation is the number of potential host IDs minus 2. Because we mathematically count all zeros (00000000) as a potential host ID and all ones as host ID 255 (11111111), there are 256 potential host IDs in this example. Removing the ID represented by 11111111 and the ID represented by 00000000 leaves you with 254 usable host IDs.

NOTE

Classless Interdomain Routing RFC 1182 There is an exception to the second and third bullet items in the list. If you are operating a CIDR-compliant routing environment, network IDs with all 0s and all 1s can be used. (CIDR is the acronym for Classless InterDomain Routing.) This exception is described in RFC 1182.

From the previous example, we know that the last octet, or 8 bits, is used for the host ID; therefore, the number of host IDs available per network is binary 256 minus minus 2. A standard class C network ID can have up to 254 hosts. IP address ranges are often assigned, either officially by InterNIC or by management in large enterprise networks. Table 3.8 shows the enumeration of hosts for this example.

TABLE 3.8

HOST BREAKDOWN FOR THIS EXAMPLE

Network ID	Host Range	Number of Hosts
192.168.0.0	192.168.0.1 to 192.168.0.254	254
192.168.1.0	192.168.1.1 to 192.168.1.254	254
192.168.2.0	192.168.2.1 to 192.168.2.254	254
192.168.3.0	192.168.3.1 to 192.168.3.254	254
192.168.4.0	192.168.4.1 to 192.168.4.254	254
192.168.5.0	192.168.5.1 to 192.168.5.254	254
192.168.6.0	192.168.6.1 to 192.168.6.254	254
192.168.7.0	192.168.7.1 to 192.168.7.254	254
192.168.8.0	192.168.8.1 to 192.168.8.254	254

You may have noticed that the preceding calculations could have been done more easily by using the decimal values. Converting the IP address to binary format is part of the process because network IDs do not always fall within octet boundaries. In the next section, nondefault subnet masks are explained.

Nonstandard Subnetting

Table 3.7 shows enumeration for all ranges of IP classes A, B, and C. With these standard subnet masks, the maximum number of hosts per network ID is limited to three values, two of which are an unnecessarily large number of hosts for most subnets. The third value (254) may be too few hosts for many subnets. Standard classes are usually not a very efficient way to allocate IP address space.

Because subnet calculation is accomplished using a bitwise logical operation, subnet masks can be defined as any number of bits. Subnet masks do not have to fall on octet boundaries. This means that you can modify a subnet mask for a standard class to change the balance of network IDs and host IDs. Subnetting allows flexible IP address allocation for network design.

For example, a class B network ID of 172.16.0.0 can be subnetted to meet the needs of a wide range of network configurations. By incrementing the number of bits of the default subnet mask of 255.255.0.0 from 16 to 31, the number of network and host IDs can be tailored to fit most network requirements. Table 3.9 shows the various subnet configurations that can be used by subnetting.

NOTE It is important to note that prior to the release of RFC 1878, "Variable Length Subnet Table For IPv4," the subnet mask, 255.255.128.0, which is referenced in Table 3.9 and the subnet mask, 255.255.255.128, which is referenced in Table 3.10 were invalid masks because of the binary makeup of the subnet mask. This fact is still referenced in many Microsoft training materials. So, be aware that although the fact is the subnet mask is valid and will work without issue in any environment, including a Windows 2000 Server with IP routing enabled, it is possible that the old information could still make its way onto a Microsoft exam.

TABLE 3.9

SUBNETTING A CLASS B NETWORK

Subnet Mask	Binary Value	Number of Network IDs	Number of Host IDs
255.255.0.0	11111111.11111111.00000000.00000000	1	65,534
255.255.128.0	11111111.11111111.10000000.00000000	2	32,766
255.255.192.0	11111111.11111111.11000000.00000000	4	16,382
255.255.224.0	11111111.11111111.11100000.00000000	8	8,190
255.255.240.0	11111111.11111111.11110000.00000000	16	4,094
255.255.248.0	11111111.11111111.11111000.00000000	32	2,046
255.255.252.0	11111111.11111111.11111100.00000000	64	1,022
255.255.254.0	11111111.11111111.11111110.00000000	128	510
255.255.255.0	11111111.11111111.11111111.00000000	256	254
255.255.255.128	11111111.11111111.11111111.10000000	512	126
255.255.255.192	11111111.11111111.11111111.11000000	1,024	62
255.255.255.224	11111111.11111111.11111111.11100000	2,048	30
255.255.255.240	11111111.11111111.11111111.11110000	4,096	14
255.255.255.248	11111111.11111111.11111111.11111000	8,192	6
255.255.255.252	11111111.11111111.11111111.11111100	16,384	2

Subnetting a class B network offers the network designer a wide range of network ID/host ID combinations to work with; however, there may be a substantial amount of wasted address space if a class B address is subnetted and applied to a small network. Subnetting a class C network is efficient for small networks, because it provides a smaller scale and more granular range of network ID and host ID combinations. Table 3.10 is an enumeration of a class C IP address.

TABLE 3.10

SUBNETTING A CLASS C ADDRESS

Subnet Mask	Binary Value	Number of Network IDs	Number of Host IDs
255.255.255.0	1111111.11111111.11111111.00000000	1	254
255.255.255.128	11111111.11111111.11111111.10000000	2	126
255.255.255.192	11111111.11111111.11111111.11000000	4	62
255.255.255.224	11111111.11111111.11111111.11100000	8	30
255.255.255.240	11111111.11111111.11111111.11110000	16	14
255.255.255.248	11111111.11111111.11111111.11111100	32	6
255.255.255.252	11111111.11111111.11111111.11111110	64	2

Planning TCP/IP Routed Networks

The Microsoft exam probably will have questions and scenarios designed to test your understanding of TCP/IP routing on Windows 2000 networks. To answer such questions correctly, and to understand routing issues on exam scenarios, you should have a good understanding of the following:

◆ Types of routed networks

◆ Routing tables

◆ Default gateways

◆ Routing protocols

◆ Windows 2000 Server routing configuration

Planning an IP Routing Infrastructure

A routed network is two or more physical network segments that are linked by one or more routers. Routers are hosts that serve as the network traffic link between these physical segments. They are intelligent store-and-forward devices that provide traffic management services for the various protocols used on the network.

To provide these traffic management services, a router must be able to forward, or retransmit, network data that it receives to the correct subnet. TCP/IP routers employ two mechanisms to determine the correct path for a TCP/IP packet: routing tables and default gateways.

Routing tables are listings of target IP addresses, subnet masks, and corresponding subnets that point to the path to the target IP address. Figure 3.6 depicts a typical network with three physical subnets that are connected by routers.

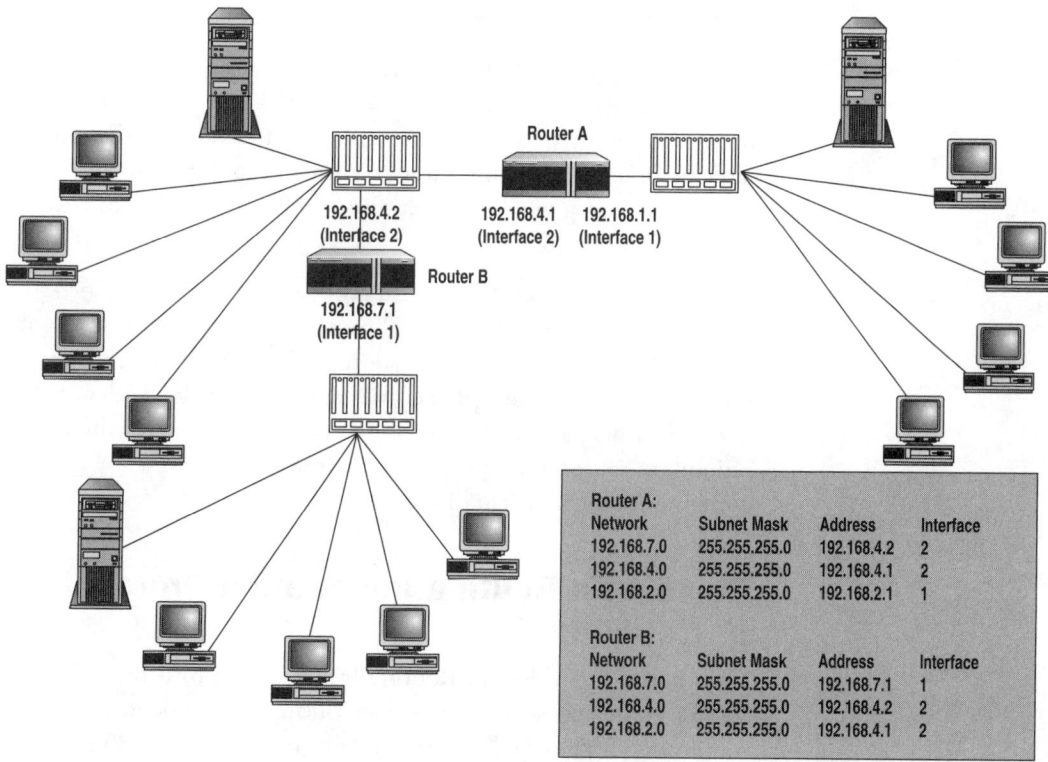

FIGURE 3.6

Routers rely on routing tables to find subnets outside of their interface connections.

The insert in Figure 3.6 shows partial routing tables for both routers. Here is what the routing table in router A says:

◆ All IP packets addressed to network ID 192.168.4.0 are sent to that network segment by way of the router interface 2, 192.168.4.1.

◆ All IP packets received that are addressed to IP network ID 192.168.7.0 are sent to router interface 1 addressed to 192.168.2.1.

◆ All IP packets addressed to network 192.168.2.0 are sent to interface 1, 192.168.2.1.

Routing table entries for IP address 0.0.0.0 represent the default gateway for that router. A default gateway is an IP address to which unknown IP addresses are sent. All types of IP hosts, workstations, routers, servers, and so forth usually have a default gateway. Default gateways tell the host to send all foreign IP addresses to that address.

There are two different types of routing table entries: static and dynamic. Static entries are permanent entries that are added by the network administrator. Dynamic addresses are added to the routing table by updates from other routers using a routing protocol. Dynamic routing table entries have a specific life span known as Time To Live (TTL).

Static routing table entries are usually used on small, stable networks. If the routing tables for all routers on the network are static entries, there is no need for the additional overhead of a routing protocol. Dynamic routing table entries are useful for large, dynamic networks where segments may not be reliably connected, there are redundant routes, traffic is redirected from time to time, or any combination of these conditions.

Planning a Routing Information Protocol for IP Network

On a network enabled for Routing Information Protocol for IP (RIP for IP), routers keep their respective routing tables updated by communicating with neighbor routers. Approximately every 30 seconds, RIP for IP routers broadcast, or announce, their list of reachable networks. Because routers do not forward broadcasts, only neighboring routers "hear" the RIP announcement. These neighboring routers update their routing tables according to the announcement information. RIP for IP is easy to implement and is adequate for small-to-medium networks. Note that RIP routes are limited to 16 hops. If a network has more than 16 hops, RIP for IP cannot be used.

The primary drawback of RIP for IP networks is bandwidth consumption due to the RIP announcements. This is especially important if RIP is being used on a network with slow WAN links or expensive bandwidth-monitored links. RIP announcements can be minimized by using autostatic RIP updates. Using autostatic updates forces the router to broadcast a RIP announcement only when its routing table changes.

RIP for IP routers use hop counts to determine the best route. If such a router has two routing table entries for a given destination and both have the same cost (hop count) associated with them, the route that is chosen is indeterminate. The router may choose the least-efficient route. The workaround for this caveat is to manually increase the hop count for the undesirable route.

Windows 2000 supports two versions of RIP for IP: version 1 and version 2. RIP for IP version 2 supports Classless InterDomain Routing (CIDR) or variable-length subnet masks. If you are using RIP for IP on a network that has one subnet mask, version 1 is adequate for the job. In other cases, unless you must use version 1 due to legacy equipment or software, version 2 is desirable.

Planning an Open Shortest Path First Network

Open Shortest Path First (OSPF) routing protocol works best with large networks. OSPF is a *link-state* routing protocol. The two main features of a link-state routing protocol are that routing table updates occur only when one or more routers on the network recognize a change, and OSPF calculates routes using a shortest-path tree. OSPF is an efficient and flexible routing protocol.

To best use the functionality of OSPF, networks should be designed hierarchically. Hierarchical network design entails defining the boundaries of the network that will be under the control of an administrative authority called an Autonomous System (AS) and then subdividing the AS into OSPF areas.

OSPF areas are contiguous groups of subnets, such as a site. OSPF areas are connected by a common backbone, forming an OSPF AS. Areas can be connected directly to the backbone via an Area Border Router (ABR), or an area can be connected to the backbone indirectly (a virtual link). Areas that are connected directly to the AS backbone that direct all foreign traffic (including other IP routing protocols) to the ABR are known as *stub areas*. There are a few guidelines for implementing OSPF that you may be asked about on the exam:

- ◆ Virtual links are not recommended for OSPF networks, because they are difficult to configure and tend to cause routing problems.

- ◆ Reduce the workload on area border routers by assigning contiguous IP network addresses within each area.

- ◆ Minimize communication between areas and domains. Avoid passing DNS, DHCP, and WINS traffic between areas, and optimize Active Directory updates.

- ◆ Use stub areas wherever possible. Stub areas are configured so that all IP traffic with targets outside the area can use a single static route.

- ◆ All inter-area traffic should cross the AS backbone.

- ◆ A high-bandwidth backbone is desirable.

If you are at all familiar with the Internet or computer networking in general, you are undoubtedly aware that the TCP/IP protocol is the de facto standard for computer networking. With the introduction of Windows 2000, Microsoft has finalized its move to TCP/IP as the native protocol for Microsoft networks. Recognizing that with Windows 2000 Microsoft has made a commitment to Internet technologies, a detailed understanding of TCP/IP is required for exam candidates. I strongly recommend that you study other sources on this subject in preparation for the exam, such as *MCSE Training Guide: Networking Essentials, Second Edition* from New Riders Publishing.

TCP/IP provides the protocol for communicating between network hosts; however, if you have ever worked with TCP/IP, you are aware that it provides basic connectivity. In order to provide reliable and manageable host communications, there are several TCP/IP-based tools that you can use. One very useful part of the TCP/IP tools is the Dynamic Host Configuration Protocol (DHCP). In the next section, you learn how DHCP is used to facilitate a manageable IP addressing strategy.

DEVELOPING DHCP STRATEGIES

Design a DHCP strategy.

DHCP was originally designed to dynamically assign IP addresses to IP network hosts. Currently, DHCP is also capable of assigning other configuration parameters to an IP host, such as default gateways, name server addresses, multicast addresses, and node type. In this section, the tools and technologies required to successfully implement DHCP are covered. The following areas are reviewed:

- ◆ IETF standard DHCP
- ◆ Windows 2000 Server implementation of DHCP
- ◆ DHCP integration into routed networks
- ◆ Integration of Windows 2000 DHCP into a legacy DHCP network
- ◆ Designing DHCP services for remote locations
- ◆ Optimizing and measuring DHCP performance

Windows 2000 Server DHCP is standards-based and is compliant with Internet Engineering Task Force (IETF) Request for Comments (RFC). Windows 2000 DHCP has several enhancements (compared to Windows NT DHCP), as defined in several IETF draft standards and RFCs. The Windows 2000 Server DHCP implementation has the following enhancements:

- ◆ DNS/DHCP integration
- ◆ Vendor-specific configuration pushdowns
- ◆ Class ID support
- ◆ Multicast address assignment
- ◆ Unauthorized DHCP server detection

Some of these enhancements are not compatible with legacy DHCP implementations, such as some UNIX versions or Windows NT 4.0. A clear understanding of IETF standards-based DHCP and Windows 2000 enhancements is required to successfully integrate Windows 2000 DHCP into a network that already uses a different flavor of DHCP. You can expect to be asked about such integration on the Microsoft exam.

The IETF DHCP Standard

DHCP for Windows 2000 supports IETF standards (RFC 2131 and RFC 2132). Under the IETF standard, DHCP supports IP address assignment and delivery of host-specific configuration information to IP hosts at boot-time. Additionally, DHCP may provide host-specific configuration information while the host is connected to the network after the host has successfully obtained an IP address from the DHCP server. The most commonly used configuration information that a DHCP server sends to a host computer includes default gateways, IP domain name, subnet mask, and name server addresses. Other important features of DHCP that are defined in RFC 2131 and RFC 2132 include the following:

- ◆ A DHCP client computer must be guaranteed a unique (to its network) IP address.

- ◆ DHCP client computers must be unaffected by a DHCP server reboot; the client computer must receive consistent configuration information regardless of DHCP server reboots.

- ◆ A DHCP client computer must be equipped to deal with multiple DHCP responses, because more than one DHCP server may be available to a given segment.

- ◆ DHCP servers must support automated assignment of configuration information to client computers and assignment of specific configuration information (including IP addresses) to specific client computers.

- ◆ Any implementation of DHCP must not require a DHCP server on each segment—that is, DHCP must work across routers or BOOTP relay hosts.

- ◆ DHCP must work in a multiprotocol environment.

NOTE

RFCs   A collection of all RFCs concerning DHCP can be found at www.dhcp.org. A library of all IETF-supported RFCs is located at www.ietf.org.

◆ DHCP must coexist on a network with statically assigned IP addresses.

◆ DHCP must interoperate with BOOTP relay agents and must support (legacy) BOOTP client computers.

You may have noticed the acronym, BOOTP, listed as part of the functionality required as part of a DHCP implementation. BOOTP (Bootstrap Protocol) was originally designed in 1985 by Bill Croft and John Gilmore to automate the configuration of network devices. In order to use BOOTP, the network administrator had to create a table with a list of clients, their IP addresses, and network configurations. When a client connected to the network, it broadcast a request to the BOOTP server for an IP address. The BOOTP server would look up the client in the table and respond with the configuration information stored in the table, allowing the client to communicate on the network. BOOTP is generally a UNIX-world protocol that was originally developed to facilitate network boots of diskless workstations. Subsequently, several extensions have been defined for BOOTP, including configuration information assignment. While this was very popular in its day, the overhead associated with administering a table of clients made this an unworkable solution in most large environments. The next generation of dynamic host addressing protocols was DHCP. There are three main differences between DHCP and BOOTP:

◆ DHCP supports IP address leasing. When a DHCP server assigns an IP address in response to a client computer request, the server may limit the length of time that the client computer may use that address (the lease time).

◆ In addition to IP address assignment, DHCP supports assignment of all IP configuration parameters required for a client computer to successfully connect to the network. These parameters include default gateways and subnet mask.

◆ DHCP does not require the configuration of client information on the server. Any client capable of issuing a DHCP request can receive an address from a DHCP server.

DHCP employs BOOTP format message packets in order to communicate between the host and the DHCP server. BOOTP packets contain a "message type" field that identifies the DHCP (or BOOTP) message as either BOOTREQUEST or BOOTREPLY. DHCP messages marked

BOOTREQUEST are messages sent from the client computer to a DHCP server. BOOTREPLY DHCP messages are messages sent from a DHCP server to a client computer. Within each BOOTREQUEST or BOOTREPLY message, there is a DHCP message type. Table 3.11 describes DHCP message types defined by RFC 2131.

TABLE 3.11

DHCP MESSAGE TYPES

DHCP Packet Type	Description
DHCPDISCOVER	Client computer broadcast message. Used to discover available DHCP servers.
DHCPOFFER	BOOTREPLY message that is a response to a DHCPDISCOVER message offering configuration information.
DHCPREQUEST	BOOTREQUEST message that requests configuration information in response to a DHCPOFFER message, confirming an IP address that was previously assigned or extending the lease on an assigned IP address.
DHCPACK	Sent to the client computer. This message contains the IP address assigned to the client computer and any other configuration parameters that the DHCP server is configured to assign to the client computer.
DHCPNAK	Server to the client computer indicating that the client computer's notion of the network address is incorrect (for example, the client computer has moved to a new subnet) or the client computer's lease has expired.
DHCPDECLINE	The DHCP standard requires that DHCP client computers "defend" their respective IP address. This message is used by the client computer to inform the server that the network address is already in use.
DHCPRELEASE	The DHCP client computer sends this message to the DHCP server to relinquish its IP address and cancel the balance of the lease on that IP address.
DHCPINFORM	Request message from the DHCP client computer that asks only for local (scope or subnet) configuration parameters because the DHCP client computer already has externally configured the network address.

When a DHCP client computer is booted, DHCP messages are exchanged between client computer and server as follows:

1. The DHCP client computer broadcasts a DHCPDISCOVER message. In a routed environment, the broadcast is limited to the physical subnet. If there is no DHCP server on the physical subnet, one or more of the routers should be configured to forward the (BOOTP) message to a known DHCP server location. The DHCPDISCOVER message can include options that request specific values for the network address and lease duration.

2. Each DHCP server that is configured to respond to the client computer's subnet should respond with a DHCPOFFER message. The DHCPOFFER message has a (presumably) available IP address as well as other configuration information. According to the IETF standard, the DHCP server should first grope the target subnet with an ICMP ECHO request to confirm that the address is available.

3. The DHCP client computer receives one or more DHCPOFFER messages from the DHCP server(s). The client computer selects one of the DHCPOFFER messages.

4. The DHCP client computer broadcasts a DHCPREQUEST message that includes a server identifier option to indicate which server it has selected. This DHCPREQEST message can include requests for specific configuration information.

5. All DHCP servers that responded to the client computer's original DHCPREQUEST broadcast should receive the second DHCPREQUEST message broadcast. The DHCP server(s) that were not selected by the client computer take no further action.

6. The selected DHCP server commits the IP address for the client computer to its list of client computers, IP addresses, and leases. It then sends a DHCPACK message that includes the (requested) configuration parameters for the DHCP client computer.

7. If the selected DHCP server cannot comply with the DHCPREQUEST message from the client computer (usually because the requested IP address is not available), the server sends a DHCPNAK message to the client computer.

8. The DHCP client computer receives the DHCPACK message from the server. The client computer normally performs a final validation of the configuration information and saves the address lease duration specified in the DHCPACK message. The client computer is configured.

9. If the DHCP client computer determines that the address is already in use, it sends a DHCPDECLINE message to the server and then begins the DHCP configuration process again with a DHCPREQUEST broadcast.

10. If the DHCP client computer does not receive a DHCPACK or a DHCPNAK message within a specified period of time, it resends the DHCPREQUEST message.

11. The client computer can relinquish its IP address lease by sending a DHCPRELEASE message to the DHCP server.

The process of obtaining network addresses and other configuration options using DHCP described previously assumes that the network is working correctly and that all equipment is configured correctly. The IETF standard includes algorithms for client computer and server timeouts and invalid messages. Windows 2000 Professional includes an automatic IP address configuration feature that sets the computer's IP address to the standard 169.254.x.x. if a DHCP server is not found on the network. This is a very useful feature for SOHO networks.

The Windows 2000 Server DHCP Implementation

Windows 2000 Server fully supports the IETF standard for DHCP, as specified in RFC 2131 and RFC 2132. This standard support includes support for the (legacy) BOOTP protocol. In addition to the IETF standards, Windows 2000 supports several enhancements, including

◆ Integration of DNS and DHCP

◆ Multicast address allocation

◆ Vendor-specific and class ID options

◆ Rogue DHCP server detection

◆ Windows Clustering

◆ Enhanced monitoring and statistical reporting

◆ Automatic client computer configuration

Each of these features is discussed in this section. To be able to cor-rectly integrate the Windows 2000 flavor of DHCP with legacy DHCP systems, such as UNIX and Windows NT, it is important to understand these features in terms of traditional DHCP. Additionally, this section presents some of the caveats of integrating Windows 2000 DHCP into an existing network.

Integrating DHCP and DNS

In order to effectively utilize the new functionality of Windows 2000 and Active Directory, it is absolutely critical that you under-stand the interaction between DHCP and DNS, and you can suc-cessfully configure the integration. Although it is true that at the time this book is being written the IETF is still working on an offi-cial RFC that defines the interaction between a DNS server(s),DHCP server(s), and hosts, the Windows 2000 implemen-tation of DNS and DHCP leverages all the new features of the draft RFC (written in large part by Microsoft) in order to successfully implement a pure Windows 2000 network.

The key feature of the new Windows 2000 DHCP server is the fact that it has the ability to register client address information in the DNS table for the Active Directory domain. This is how Microsoft has replaced WINS in a pure Windows 2000 environment. You no longer need WINS for name resolution because all Windows 2000 clients using DHCP (the Microsoft recommended architecture) are already in DNS, and their names can be resolved using that protocol instead of WINS. It is easy to say that Windows 2000 DHCP servers and client computers can register with DNS. But what exactly does that mean? A Windows 2000 DHCP server can register and update pointer (PTR) and address (A) records on behalf of its client computers. This proxy service is provided to facilitate DNS registration of legacy DHCP client computers. With a Windows 2000 Professional host, the DHCP server registers the PTR record, while the host registers its own A record with the DNS server. Windows 2000 DHCP servers can be configured to register DHCP client computers in one of three ways, or not at all:

◆ Both A and PTR records are registered with DNS.

◆ Only PTR records are registered with DNS.

◆ Both A and PTR records are registered with DNS only when requested by the workstation.

Not all DNS servers can interact with the DHCP registration feature. This means that name and address synchronization may not be reliable in a DNS environment using older DNS servers that do not support DDNS and, therefore, cannot be updated by a Windows 2000 DHCP server. To mitigate interoperability problems in such an environment, Microsoft recommends that you take the following actions:

◆ Enable WINS lookup on all DHCP client computers that use NetBIOS. WINS lookup for DHCP is covered later in this chapter.

◆ For non-NetBIOS DHCP client computers that use only DNS for name resolution, assign IP addresses with infinite lease durations.

◆ Upgrade older static DNS servers to servers that support DDNS (presumably Windows 2000 servers).

Implementing Multicast Address Allocation

As described in the section on default IP address classes, class D addresses are reserved for multicasting. Windows 2000 DHCP server includes support for multicast address allocation. This is a proposed IETF standard.

Multicast IP addresses are used to distribute data packets to a particular group of hosts. The data is broadcast on any network segments where multicast groups are connected. Hosts that are assigned a multicast address for that data pass the packets up the protocol stack to the intended recipient while "disinterested" hosts simply ignore the data. Multicasts are used primarily for streaming data distribution, such as audio broadcasts, and also for network conferencing.

The role of the DHCP server is to assign multicast IP addresses, and client computers are responsible for requesting, renewing, and releasing the addresses. Assignment of multicast addresses is configured and managed as a DHCP scope, the same way as non-multicast DHCP scopes. It is the responsibility of the client computer to request a multicast address. Note that multicast addresses are not assigned at client computer boot-time; they are assigned after the client computer is connected to the network.

Vendor-Specific and Class ID Options

The Windows 2000 DHCP server includes two features that improve the flexibility and potential for efficiency: class IDs and vendor-specific options. Class ID configuration is a proposed standard. RFC 2132 defines vendor-specific options.

Today's DHCP allows assignment of IP addresses and other configuration options based solely on scope. This means that DHCP treats all DHCP client computers on a given subnet equally. The Windows 2000 implementation of DHCP supports client computer class IDs.

Class IDs are used to differentiate types of DHCP client computers. Class ID boundaries can be based on any physical or logical client computer attribute, such as hardware, operating system, or applications installed. One way that DHCP can be used to optimize network performance is to assign different DNS servers or default gateways to two or more class IDs on a given subnet.

Conventional DHCP supports a number of configuration options that can be assigned to client computers, such as default gateway, subnet mask, and node type. At any rate, the options that may be used with DHCP are defined by the IETF. Until now, defining and implementing a new option required a change in the DHCP standard through the IETF. RFC 2132 defines a new type of configuration, the vendor-specific option.

Simply stated, DHCP can now assign vendor-specific configuration information to a client computer. For example, an option that changes the run mode of a particular application for all members of the laptop computer class can be assigned. This laptop run mode might have to do with the slower video performance typical of laptops, or limited disk space.

Rogue DHCP Servers and DHCP Server Authorization

Windows 2000 DHCP server has a "self-policing" feature that protects the network against rogue DHCP servers. When a DHCP server that is not a member of the domain is brought online, it broadcasts a DHCPINFORM message notifying the rest of the network of its existence. All other DHCP servers respond to this broadcast with a DHCPACK message that tells the new server whether one or more of the responding servers is a member of a domain. If the new server receives at least one DHCPACK from a domain server, it will not respond to any DHCP client computer requests. In other words, if a DHCP is installed on a workgroup Windows 2000 server in an Active Directory environment, it simply will not work.

In an Active Directory environment, DHCP servers must be authorized in order to operate. As with rogue server detection, Windows 2000 servers are self-policing. When a DHCP server (running on a domain member server) is brought online, it checks the Active Directory to confirm that it is a member of the directory domain. If it is, it checks the DHCP folder in Active Directory to confirm that it is authorized to operate. When the DHCP server has confirmed that it is authorized to operate in its domain, it broadcasts a DHCPINFORM message to find any other Active Directories running on the network. If any are found, the server confirms that it is authorized. If the server is not authorized in its own directory domain or at least one other Active Directory running on the network, it will not service DHCP requests.

DHCP services are managed in Active Directory using a snap-in. Because the servers are part of Active Directory, Active Directory security can be applied to them. Administrative access to DHCP servers is determined by user permissions associated with the DHCP folder. Typically, the network administrator assigns access permission to one or more users who assume the DHCP administrator role.

Designing a Highly Available, Scalable DHCP Service for the Enterprise

Microsoft provides two methods for designing a DHCP implementation in an enterprise network—a centralized implementation, where all addresses are issued from a single location, and a distributed implementation, where locations have decentralized servers that are responsible for addresses in the local network as well as any other locations or sites in the same organizational structure. Both scenarios have some things in common. In either implementation availability of DHCP services is critical. DHCP has traditionally been configured redundantly to assure a reasonable level of availability in the event a DHCP server fails. Microsoft Windows DHCP has additional tools for managing DHCP server availability: superscopes and Windows Clustering support. Before we discuss the high-availability features of the Windows 2000 DHCP server, let's take a look at the two architectures for providing DHCP services in an enterprise environment.

For the centralized approach to a DHCP service, a central site will have all the DHCP services for the enterprise. This model relies heavily on a centralized IT support infrastructure and reliable WAN connectivity between the central site and the remote locations. Some advantages to this model include the following:

◆ **Reduced support costs.** By centralizing the service, you are able to reduce the amount of administrative overhead because you will have fewer DHCP servers to support, and they will be located (generally) in a data center where support is readily available.

◆ **Reduced hardware costs.** Fewer DHCP servers generally means fewer servers, or at least less hardware intensive implementations, resulting in lower costs.

◆ **Simplified router configurations.** Because all your DHCP servers are in a central location, you can generally utilize the same BOOTP Forwarder configurations. As we will see in the decentralized model, this is not the case in other implementations.

◆ **Redundancy.** In order to make this a redundant connection (discussed in detail later in this section), you need two servers at the central location. If one server is down, the other can handle DHCP requests.

There are some disadvantages to this model as well as you can see from the following list:

◆ **Increased reliance on WAN connectivity.** If a WAN link is down, users will either need to configure static addresses, or wait for the WAN link to be re-established.

◆ **Difficult to implement in some environments.** Many companies find centralized DHCP difficult to implement because the administration of the computing environment is highly distributed and local administrators frequently prefer not to give up local control of services like DHCP.

◆ **More difficult administration.** It is generally easier for a local administrator to configure things like address reservations for printers and scopes for the local network from the local network. In many centralized implementations, the central site administrators have limited visibility into the remote networks. This requires effective communication of requirements from the remote office, which can be problematic in some environments.

The decentralized model calls for local DHCP servers in the remote sites. This can be implemented with redundant servers in a central location (a hybrid distributed environment), with multiple DHCP servers in each location, or with remote DCHP servers serving multiple locations and providing redundancy for their department, site, or region. This model also has its advantages and disadvantages. Some of the advantages to this model include the following:

◆ **Reduced reliance on WAN connectivity.** Because the DHCP servers are local, there is less of an issue in the case of WAN outages. Even in implementations where a DHCP server is serving multiple locations, the impact of an outage is not as severe as the unavailability of a central site, due to the smaller population of affected users.

◆ **Local administration.** This can ease the administrative overhead and potential delays in DHCP server configuration changes.

◆ **Fewer political issues.** If you are working in a highly distributed environment, it is often easier to provide local DHCP servers to avoid issues associated with imposing centralized control over an environment that is accustomed to distributed management.

Some of the disadvantages include the following:

◆ **Increased cost.** More DHCP servers will add cost for hardware.

◆ **Increased complexity.** Depending on the implementation, a distributed DHCP environment can be more complex than a centralized implementation.

◆ **Increased routing complexity.** Not only is there additional complexity at the DHCP level, but the BOOTP Forwarding configuration on any routers can be much more complex as well. Instead of all routers pointing to the central site, they must be configured for regional forwarding. This is not the case when every location has a DHCP server. In that model, WAN-based BOOTP forwarding is probably not needed.

Some of the factors to consider when deciding which model to implement include the following:

◆ **Network size/complexity.** The larger the network, the easier it is to justify a centralized DHCP strategy. Microsoft recommends a centralized model for any locations with three or more sites.

◆ **Existing infrastructure.** Depending on the model presently in use in the environment, you may find it is easier to continue to use whatever is in place for DHCP. In other words, if the enterprise has a DHCP server at each location, it may be easier to upgrade them to Windows 2000 instead of moving to a centralized model.

◆ **Connectivity.** If your enterprise uses low bandwidth links and has unreliable connectivity (that is, a site-to-site VPN over congested Internet connections), a distributed model may be a better idea.

The second piece of this puzzle, once you have decided on your model, is to ensure that DHCP is always available. The traditional configuration of redundant DHCP servers requires that at least two servers service each IP subnet on the network. In the event that one fails, the other server can continue to provide DHCP service to the affected subnets. The downside to this scheme is that the available

IP addresses must be split between two or more servers that service the subnet. If there are more DHCP client computers on a given subnet than one-half the available IP addresses, you risk depleting the address pool.

One workaround for this problem is to use multi-nets and super-scopes. A multi-net is a physical subnet that is actually more than one logical IP subnet. Two or more DHCP servers can be configured to service all logical IP subnets for a multi-net physical segment. The total number of available IP addresses can be increased by splitting client computers on the multi-net between two or more logical IP subnets. The address pools for these logical subnets must still be divided among the DHCP servers; however, with a multi-net, you can add enough available IP addresses so that there are less than half the client computers for each available pool.

There are two drawbacks to the multi-net solution:

◆ A DHCP server cannot determine to which of the logical sub-nets a requesting client computer belongs.

◆ A DHCPNAK response occurs when a client computer requests an address renewal from the wrong server.

The workaround is to employ class IDs and superscopes. Client computer class IDs can be used to define logical subnet assignment, and superscopes eliminate DHCPNACKS.

DHCPNAK messages are generated on a multi-net network because the DHCP servers are not aware of the scope of the other server. As a result, DHCP servers assume that requests for address updates not within their addressing scope(s) are invalid and should be rejected. Superscopes enable the administrator to define all scopes serviced by other DHCP servers. Correctly configured, superscopes ensure that all DHCP servers that service a multi-net subnet recognize all logical subnets. For example, Table 3.12 shows two DHCP servers and their respective scopes.

NOTE

Superscope Support Superscopes are supported beginning with Windows NT 4.0 Service Pack 2.

TABLE 3.12

TWO DHCP SERVERS THAT SERVICE THE SAME PHYSICAL SUBNET WITH DIFFERENT LOGICAL IP SUBNETS

Server	DHCP Scope	Subnet Mask
Server1	192.168.111.100 to 192.168.111.255	255.255.255.0
Server2	192.168.222.100 to 192.168.222.255	255.255.255.0

To create a superscope on each server, do the following:

1. On Server1, create the scope
   192.168.222.100 to 192.168.222.255.

2. On Server1, exclude the new range that you just created
   (192.168.222.100 to 192.168.222.255).

3. Start the Superscope Wizard and add the newly created scope
   and the existing scope (shown in Table 3.12).

4. On Server2, create the scope
   192.168.111.100 to 192.168.111.255.

5. On Server2, exclude the range that you just created.

6. Start the Superscope Wizard and add both ranges to the
   superscope.

Superscopes are configured so that they have *placeholder* scopes for
IP subnets they do not service; thus, the scopes not serviced by a
server have all addresses in the scope excluded. Superscoped servers
must recognize all logical IP subnets on a multi-net segment but
respond only to the IP subnets that it services.

The best way to provide high availability for DHCP (and any other
cluster-enabled services and applications) is with Microsoft clustering. A cluster is two or more servers that run cluster-enabled services
and applications as virtual services. In the case of DHCP, only one
physical server runs DHCP. All DHCP information is stored in a
remote database. If the server that is running DHCP fails, one of
the other servers in the cluster takes over almost instantly. DHCP
client computers see no change in the DHCP server, including the
IP address. Using clusters to provide DHCP services also eliminates
the need to split scopes across two or more servers.

Enhanced Monitoring and Statistical Reporting

DHCP Manager for Windows 2000 has been improved with enhanced monitoring and reporting. Features added to DHCP Manger include

◆ Address pool depletion alerts can be configured by the administrator to trigger at any threshold. Additionally, another alert that triggers when a pool is completely depleted can be enabled.

◆ SNMP-based reporting provides the administrator with detailed performance statistics, including DHCP message count, offers, acknowledgments, rejections, and releases.

◆ System statistics, such as number of addresses available, number of addresses used, total addresses, and total scopes can be viewed at the scope or server level.

One of the stated objectives for the Microsoft exam is to be able to optimize DHCP. To assess your knowledge of DHCP performance tuning, you may be given a set of statistics and asked to choose the correct actions to take to correct a problem or improve performance. Here are some of the ways that DHCP performance can be improved:

◆ Keep the number of DHCP servers on your network to a minimum. When choosing server locations on a routed network, consider using BOOTP relays to provide DHCP to segments equipped with high-speed connections. When dealing with low-speed remote connections, the number of client computers and network segments at the remote site should be factors in determining whether to deploy a DHCP server at the remote site.

◆ Configure BOOTP relays to minimize the number of DHCP messages passed to other network segments. BOOTP relays in routers are configured with a list of target networks. The relays should be configured so that a DHCP broadcast crosses each subnet only once.

◆ Manage lease durations. Longer leases reduce DHCP network traffic, and shorter leases tend to use available addresses more efficiently. Class IDs can be used to differentiate laptops from desktop computers so that shorter leases can be assigned to the laptops.

◆ Configure DHCP to update DNS.

◆ Split scopes between two or more DHCP servers.

DHCP has evolved from its modest beginnings as an IP address assignment mechanism to a robust host management tool. You can expect DHCP to continue to improve and expand to meet the needs of the ever-changing world of TCP/IP networks. Now that you know how to effectively configure and manage IP host addresses, you must be able to facilitate the communication among these hosts using name services. In the next section, you learn how to design a strategy for implementing the three name services used for Microsoft networks: Domain Name System (DNS), Dynamic Domain Name System (DDNS), and Windows Internet Name Service (WINS).

PLANNING NAME SERVICES

Design name resolution services.

Windows 2000 Server supports two name services: Domain Name System (DNS) and Windows Internet Name Service (WINS). WINS maps NetBIOS names to IP addresses. Until now, NetBIOS names have been the standard for Microsoft networks. DNS is the Internet name resolution service standard. DNS is also the name service of choice for Windows 2000.

> **NOTE**
>
> **IETF and NetBIOS Name Service** The IETF actually supports a NetBIOS name service, NetBIOS Name Server (NBNS), in RFC 1001 and RFC 1002.

WINS has been the default name service for Microsoft networks since the days of LAN Manager. Microsoft has decided to move away from WINS and embrace DNS. Therefore, you can expect that DNS questions and problems will be plentiful on the exam. You can also expect questions about WINS and DNS interoperability.

Anyone reading this book should have at least a rudimentary understanding of DNS functionality. This section describes traditional DNS basics and then builds on those basics with the introduction of Windows 2000 DNS. Windows 2000 offers some additional (standards-based) features that facilitate enhanced security, ease of integration with WINS client computers and servers, integration with older versions of DNS, and Active Directory integration.

Traditional DNS

As defined in a number of RFCs, DNS is the sole mechanism for providing hostname resolution on the Internet as well as on many private TCP/IP-based networks. This section describes the core components of DNS.

DNS Namespace

The best way to understand the hierarchical structure of DNS namespace is to describe a well-known DNS namespace, such as the Internet. Figure 3.7 depicts the structure of a small portion of the Internet DNS namespace. The entire namespace begins with an unnamed DNS node known as the *root*. All other nodes in the DNS structure are known as *labels*. The structure is called a *DNS tree*.

The physical implementation of a DNS namespace is supported by a distributed database. The namespace can be subdivided on label boundaries (subdomains) and managed by independent authorities. Such subdivisions of the DNS namespace are called *zones*.

TCP/IP hosts are identified by a Fully Qualified Domain Name (FQDN). An FQDN is comprised of DNS tree labels plus the hostname. Each label and the hostname are dot-delimited. The logical location of a host in a DNS is defined by the order of labels in the FQDM. For example, using Figure 3.7, some valid hostnames might be server1.company1.com or fileserver1.chicago.corp2.com.

DNS Zones

The smallest manageable part of the DNS namespace is known as a *zone*. A zone contains the DNS information, known as *resource records*, for a contiguous portion of the DNS namespace. They are delegations of administrative authority from their upstream DNS zone.

Keep in mind that physical configuration of the logical DNS hierarchy defines DNS zones. A zone can contain a portion of a subdomain, one subdomain, or more than one subdomain. Figure 3.8 shows how the previous DNS domain example (Figure 3.7) might be divided into zones. A single DNS server is responsible for name resolution for both the corp2.com and the chicago.corp2.com domains. corp2.com and chicago.corp2.com comprise the zone labeled Zone 2. Likewise, company1.com is the only DNS domain managed by Zone 1.

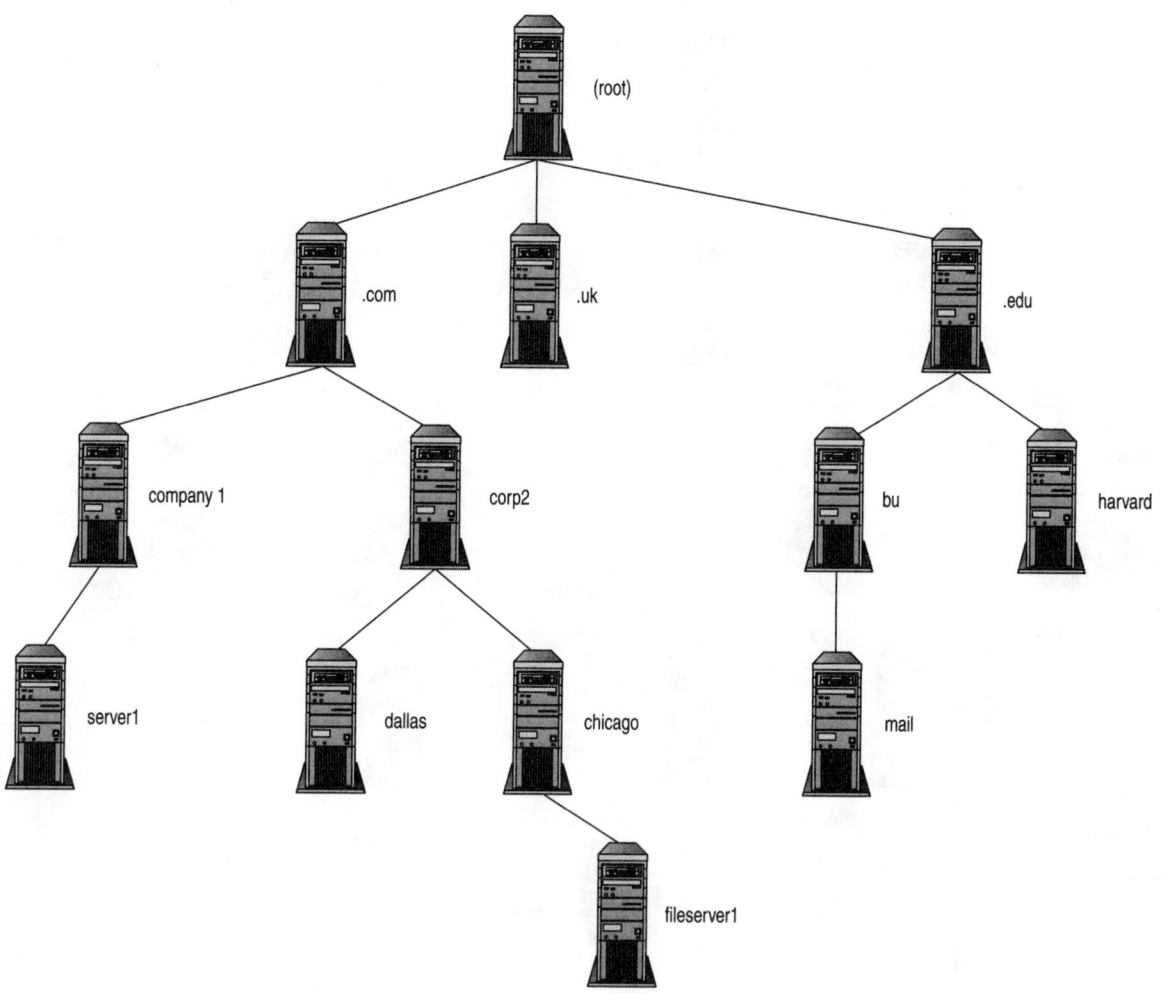

FIGURE 3.7
The location of any host in a DNS namespace can be determined by its
fully qualified DNS name.

Zone Transfer

The example of DNS zones in Figure 3.8 is a simplified depiction of
a typical DNS zone configuration. DNS zones are usually supported
by more than one DNS server. This means two or more DNS
servers must have identical databases. The mechanism for keeping
these databases synchronized—that is, database replication—is called
zone transfer. Zone transfers require two types of zones: primary and
secondary.

NOTE

Zone Databases Physical databases
for a zone are also called zones.

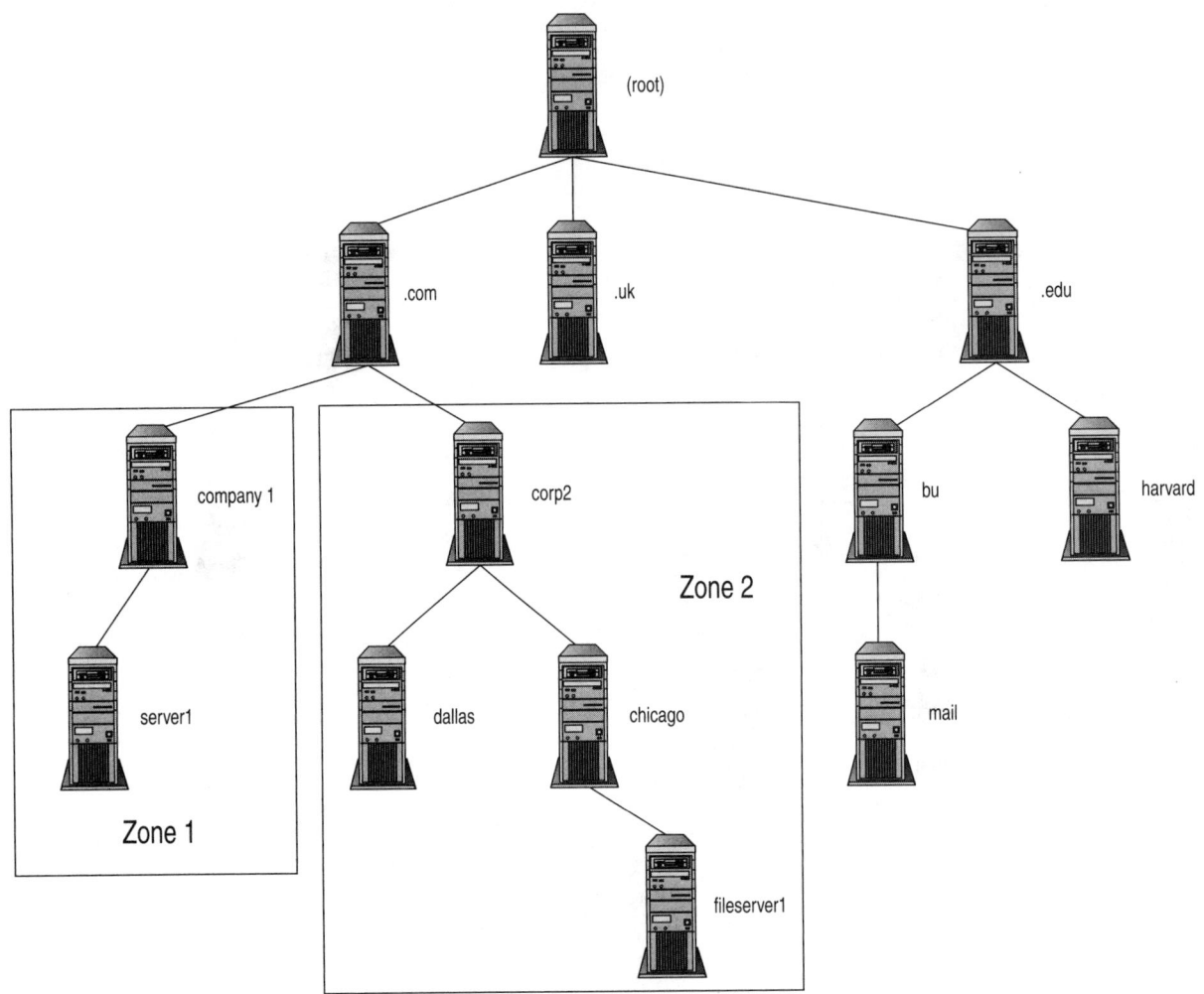

FIGURE 3.8
DNS zones are delegations of authority for a downstream namespace.

Primary zones have a read/write database. All DNS updates are registered in primary zones. There can be only one primary zone for any portion of a DNS namespace. Secondary zones are read-only databases that are updated (directly or indirectly) by the primary zone. Additionally, a single DNS server can service multiple zones. Such a server can be configured as primary for one or more zones and simultaneously configured as secondary for other zones.

DNS servers that are the source for zone transfers are known as master servers. Master servers can be either primary or secondary. A master server that contains secondary zones receives its updates from another master server. Ultimately, all update data for all secondary zones comes from a primary zone.

Not only are there two types of zones and two type of DNS servers, but there are also two types of zone transfers: full zone and incremental.

A full zone transfer, also called an AXFR, is a replication of the entire zone database. An incremental zone transfer, or IXFR, updates only information that has changed in the primary zone database. Clearly, incremental zone transfers are the best choice in most environments because less data is passed between servers.

The IXFR protocol as defined in RFC 1995 requires a specific communication process between a master (primary zone) server and a slave (secondary zone) server:

> **NOTE**
>
> **Windows 2000 Zone Transfers**
> Windows 2000 DNS server supports both AFXR and IFXR zone transfers. However, integration of Windows 2000 DNS server into an existing DNS zone may require AFXR transfers.

1. The master server sends a NOTIFY message to a slave server indicating that zone information has changed. No zone data is sent with the NOTIFY message.

2. The slave server begins the transfer process by sending an IXFR request message to the master server. The IXFR message includes the serial number of the slave server's zone file.

3. The master server checks the zone file serial number against its current version, determines which changes must be sent to the slave server, and then initiates the IXFR.

There are a few exceptions to the incremental transfer procedure. Under certain circumstances, a full zone transfer (AXFR) is executed:

◆ If the sum of the IXFR changes is larger than the entire zone file.

◆ If the master server does not recognize the IXFR request. A master server that does not recognize an IXFR message responds with the equivalent of a NAK. The slave server then requests an AFXR.

◆ If the zone file version on the slave server is too old. The master server keeps a finite number of version numbers and associated changes. If the version on the slave server is older than the oldest version on the master server, an AFXR is started.

DNS Resource Records

DNS servers store DNS data in a database comprised of resource records (RRs). There are several types of RRs in a DNS database. Table 3.13 defines the format of an RR. All DNS RRs are formatted identically except for the length of the RDATA field.

TABLE 3.13

RESOURCE RECORD FORMAT

Field Name	Purpose
NAME	Record owner: name of the associated IP host.
TYPE	2-byte field that signifies the record type.
CLASS	2-byte field containing one of the RR CLASS codes.
TTL	32-bit signed Time To Live value. Tells the host how long the RR may be cached before it is discarded. RRs that are used only for the current transaction or for highly volatile information have a **0** value.
RDLENGTH	Unsigned 16-bit value for the length of the data field (RDATA).
RDATA	Variable-length string of octets that describes the resource. The format varies, based on the TYPE and CLASS of the RR.

Table 3.14 describes DNS resource record types as defined in RFC 1035 and RFC 1183. RR types are the source information used by DNS servers to provide name services to DNS client computers. For the purposes of preparing for the Microsoft exam, most of these record types will not be discussed in any detail; however, it is a good idea to know the functions of A, PTR, SRV, and SOA records.

TABLE 3.14

DNS RESOURCE RECORD TYPES

Record Type	Description
A	The record contains a host address in the RDATA field. This is probably the most common RR, because it is used to resolve hostnames to IP addresses.
AFSDB	Special record type used only with OSF's DCE environment and AFS database environment.
CNAME	Canonical name, also known as an *alias*.
HINFO	Host information.
ISDN	Support for ISDN name routing. The RDATA field contains the ISDN telephone number. This RR enables names to be assigned to ISDN nodes that obtain their IP address via DHCP or work on an on-demand basis.
MB	Mailbox domain name (reserved, experimental).
MD	Mail destination record (obsolete, replaced by MX record type).
MF	Mail forwarder record (obsolete, replaced by MX record type).
MG	Mail group member (reserved, experimental).
MINFO	Mailbox or mail list information.
MR	Mail rename domain name (reserved, experimental).
MX	Mail exchange record.
NS	RDATA contains the address of an authoritative name server.
NULL	Null RR (reserved, experimental).
PTR	Domain name pointer. This record is the opposite of an A record. Used for reverse lookups.
RP	Responsible person for a DNS server or a zone. The RDATA field should contain email address and domain name.
RT	Route through RR. This record should point to a DNS server that keeps information about nodes with volatile names.
SOA	Start of a zone authority. This is always the first record in a zone database. It identifies the location of the primary zone.
SRV	Used to request the authoritative server for a domain name.
TXT	Text strings.
WKS	Well-known service description.
X25	Support for X.25 nodes. The RDATA field contains DNIC for the named node.

The resource record is also used by DNS to communicate with other hosts. Requests for information are called *queries*. Resolver query messages can be one of the types listed in Table 3.14, indicating to the DNS server exactly what information the resolver is requesting. Query types sent to the server from a resolver are called QTYPE codes. All RR types are also QTYPEs. In addition to the RR types listed in Table 3.14, resolvers can send several kinds of queries that are exclusive of the RR types. These additional query types are listed in Table 3.15. In other words, QTYPEs are a superset of RR types.

TABLE 3.15

QTYPE CODES

Type	Description
AXFR	Request for a full zone transfer.
IXFR	Request for an incremental zone transfer.
MAILB	Request for mailbox-related records (MB, MG, or MR records).
MAILA	Request for mail agent RRs (obsolete, replaced by MX type).
TKEY	Used to transfer security tokens (draft).
TSIG	Used to pass security signatures (draft).
*	Request for all records.

More detailed information about DNS records and resolver query format can be found in RFC 1035 and RFC 1183.

DNS Database Queries and Name Resolution

A DNS query is a request for a copy of records matching the request type and specified name. A DNS server can service two kinds of queries: recursive and iterative. The most common query issued by a resolver is a recursive query. Recursive queries force the queried DNS server to respond to the associated resolver with either a success or a failure message. Recursive queries place the responsibility for resolving the query on the DNS server.

An iterative query requires the queried name server to return any matches to the query that it has in its zone files or in cache. The returned records are known as referral records. Referral records point to name servers that hold zone files for the queried domain or subdomain. As you will see from the following example, iterative queries are typically used for name server–to–name server queries.

The following steps describe a typical name resolution process for a recursive query. Referring to Figure 3.8, follow the steps used to resolve a request for the submitted address of `mail.bu.edu`. The tasks performed by the DNS server to resolve are as follows:

1. The DNS server receives a recursive query and attempts to find the record in its zone database(s). If it's found, a copy of the requested record is returned to the resolver.

2. If the record does not exist on the server, the server issues an iterative request to the nearest parent server that may have a record for the rightmost unknown label. In this case, the requesting DNS server knows only the `.com` suffix, so it queries the DNS root server for an `edu` domain name record.

3. Because the `edu` domain is a child of the root server, the root server returns a referral record to the requesting DNS server. This referral record points to a DNS server that holds records for the edu domain.

4. The DNS server then sends an iterative query to the `edu` name server, asking for the `bu.edu` record. The `edu` server returns a referral to the `bu.edu` server.

5. Because `mail` is the last name in the FQDN for the requested record, the DNS server sends an iterative A record query to the `bu.edu` name server for `mail.bu.edu`. The `bu.edu` name server returns the A resource record to the DNS server.

6. The DNS server returns the A record for `mail.bu.edu` to the resolver.

This is a simplified example of name resolution. In the real world, the referral record returned to the `company1.com` name server is just the name of the referred server. After receiving the referral, the `company1.com` name server must send an A resource record query to the referring server to get the address of the referred server.

Because more than one DNS server often services the same zone, requesting name servers often receive referrals for more than one server and must process each referral until the first success or until all queries have failed.

There are three kinds of names that a DNS query is asked to resolve:

◆ **Fully qualified names.** A unique, dot-terminated name that specifies a certain host.

◆ **Unqualified single-label name.** An ambiguous name that has no dots.

◆ **Unqualified multilabel.** An ambiguous name that contains at least one dot.

NOTE

DNS Resolver Server Lists The DNS resolver caches DNS server lists by default. These lists are built from values provided by the TCP/IP configuration and from discovered DNS servers. A separate list is maintained for each network adapter. Servers on the list are prioritized with TCP/IP configured servers at the top of the list, followed by discovered DNS servers. If a server does not respond to a request, it is moved down the list (its priority is decreased). Server priorities can be improved if they subsequently respond to inquiries.

Resolving a fully qualified domain name is a very straightforward procedure that either succeeds or fails. To resolve a fully qualified name, the following steps are executed:

1. A query is sent to the first server on the resolver's DNS server list for the preferred network adapter.

2. The resolver waits 1 second. If no response is received, a query is sent to the first server on the DNS server list for all adapters, including the preferred adapter.

3. The resolver waits 2 seconds. If no response is received, a query is sent to all servers on all DNS server lists, including all previously queried servers.

4. The resolver waits 2 seconds. If no response is received, a query is again sent to all servers on all DNS server lists.

5. If no response is received after 4 seconds, steps 1 through 4 are repeated.

6. If there is still no response after 8 seconds, steps 1 through 4 are repeated.

When a response is received by the resolver, the procedure takes a different course:

◆ The first positive response causes the resolver to exit and return the information to the client computer.

◆ When a negative response is received, the entire list to which the responding server belongs is removed from the process. If the client computer has only one network adapter, the resolution fails. The resolver exits, returning an error code to the client computer.

◆ If a negative response is received on all adapters, the resolver exits, returning an error code to the client computer.

◆ If a server returns a failure message—that is, a message indicating that it is unable to respond to the query—the server is removed from the resolution procedure for a certain period of time.

Resolving an unqualified single label is educated guessing. The label is modified according to certain client computer configuration parameters and then processed as a fully qualified query. There are two ways that an unqualified single label name is modified to prepare it for the fully qualified name query:

◆ Using global suffix search order

◆ Using primary and per-adapter domain names

The resolver uses global suffix search order to query the name first. Upon failure, the resolver uses primary and per-adapter domain names.

Global suffix search order is configured using the TCP/IP configuration user interface. This parameter is a set of suffixes used to resolve unqualified names. These suffixes are normally the standard Internet suffixes: .com, .edu, and .org. To attempt to resolve an unqualified single label name using global suffixes, the resolver uses the following query procedure:

1. The first suffix on the search order list is appended to the name.

2. The modified name is queried using the fully qualified name procedure.

3. If a positive response is received, a positive response and the information are returned to the resolver.

4. If the query times out, an error is returned to the resolver.

5. If the query returns a negative response, the next suffix on the search order list is appended to the original unqualified name, and the query process restarts at step 2.

6. If all suffixes on the search order list have been tried, a negative response is returned to the resolver.

Windows 2000 computers have one primary domain name stored in their registry under a key named `PrimaryDnsDomainName`. Additionally, the client computer may have one or more optional domain names (`IpDomainName`), called per-adapter domain names, associated with each network adapter. Per-adapter domain names represent the binding order of TCP/IP for that adapter. The per-adapter domain name is used primarily on multi-homed computers. Upon failure of the global suffix search order query, the resolver attempts to resolve the name using the primary domain name, and if configured on the client computer, the per-adapter domain name(s):

1. The computer's primary domain name is appended to the name with a dot delimiter, if necessary.

2. The modified name is submitted as a fully qualified name query.

3. If a positive response is received, a positive response and the information are returned to the resolver.

4. If a timeout response is received, an error is returned to the resolver.

5. If a negative response is received, the next per-adapter domain name is appended to the original name, and the process continues at step 2.

6. If there are no per-adapter domain names configured, or the list of per-adapter domain names has been exhausted, and if the computer is configured for devolution, the devolution algorithm is applied to the primary domain name and the process continues at step 2. Name devolution reduces the domain name to a minimum of two labels.

7. The appropriate response is returned to the resolver.

Processing an unqualified multilabel query is a simple process because it submits the name first as only a fully qualified name query; then, if necessary, it submits it as an unqualified single-label query:

1. The name is submitted as a fully qualified name query.

2. If the name is found by DNS, a positive response is returned to the resolver.

3. If the query times out, a timeout error is returned to the resolver.

4. If DNS does not find the name, the name is submitted as an unqualified single-label query.

5. The return value of the query is returned to the resolver.

DNS Aging and Scavenging

For a number of reasons, DNS records are not always deleted correctly. The owner of a record can fail or go offline unexpectedly. A RAS client computer can be disconnected before it can delete its resource records. These records are known as *stale records*.

Stale records can present some problems for DNS. A DNS server may inadvertently respond to a query with a stale record. Stale records take up storage on the DNS server. A stale record may deny a valid client computer an update because the PTR record is owned by another object.

To help avoid stale record problems, Windows 2000 DNS supports aging and scavenging. DNS can be configured to search for and delete records in the DNS database that meet specified criteria. DNS administrators can manage aging and scavenging by managing the following parameters:

◆ **DNS servers allowed to scavenge.** DNS servers by default are configured with scavenging disabled. An administrator must enable scavenging on a per-server basis. At the risk of stating the painfully obvious, only primary servers can be enabled to scavenge.

◆ **Zones available for scavenging.** Scavenging can be enabled on a zone-by-zone basis.

◆ **Records available for scavenging.** Records are available for scavenging when they have gone a specified period without being refreshed.

To use DNS scavenging effectively, it is important to understand record aging. Record aging is based on updates and refreshes. A refresh is simply an update of the record's timestamp. Records are refreshed when

◆ The record is created.

◆ The record is updated. A record is considered updated when an update query modifies the record.

◆ An update query for a record does not change a record, such as when a DHCP client computer reregisters.

◆ The record is queried with a prerequisite-only update.

Refreshes are further restricted by no-refresh periods. No-refresh periods are part of the DNS record life cycle. During the no-refresh interval, only a record update is allowed to change the timestamp. This effectively starts the life cycle again. When the no-refresh interval expires, the record may be refreshed in any fashion for a specified period. When the refresh interval expires, the record is eligible for scavenging.

Records with a zero value timestamp are never scavenged. All records created in any manner other than dynamic update have a zero value timestamp. To make such a record available for scavenging, the administrator can change the timestamp to any non-zero value.

When a zone is scavenged, the server examines each record in the zone. If a record has a zero value, it is ignored; otherwise, if the record is stale, it is deleted. A stale record has a non-zero timestamp that is less than the current time minus the refresh interval minus the no-refresh interval.

Besides record timestamps, updates, and refreshes, there are several other parameters that the administrator can set to control scavenging. These parameters fall into two categories: server-scavenging or zone-scavenging. Server-scavenging parameters apply to primary zones enabled for scavenging on that server (see Table 3.16). Zone-scavenging parameters can be modified independent of the default values assigned to the primary server (see Table 3.17).

TABLE 3.16

SERVER-SCAVENGING PARAMETERS

Server-Scavenging Parameter	Description
Default no-refresh interval	Applies to Active Directory–integrated zones created on this server. Specifies the default no-refresh interval, which can be overridden by the zone-scavenging parameter no-refresh interval. The default value is seven days.
Default refresh interval	Applies to Active Directory–integrated zones created on this server. Specifies the default no-refresh interval, which can be overridden by the zone-scavenging parameter refresh interval. The default value is seven days.
Default enable scavenging	Applies to Active Directory–integrated zones created on this server. Specifies whether scavenging is enabled, which can be overridden by the zone-scavenging parameter refresh interval. The default value is 0 (not enabled).
Enable scavenging	Determines whether this server is allowed to scavenge primary zones on this server. The default value is 0 (not enabled).
Scavenging period	Time interval for scavenging initiation, if this server has scavenging enabled. The default value is seven days.

TABLE 3.17

ZONE-SCAVENGING PARAMETERS

Zone-Scavenging Parameter	Description
No-refresh interval	Length of time after update that a record cannot be refreshed but may be updated.
Refresh interval	Length of time after the no-refresh interval has expired when a record may be refreshed but not scavenged.
Enable scavenging	Scavenging-allowed flag for this zone.
Scavenging servers	List of servers that can scavenge this zone.
Start scavenging	Not a configurable parameter. This is a time value for when scavenging should begin for a zone, and it is set when certain events occur. The default value is 0 (never start).

The start scavenging parameter is always set by the system. It determines when scavenging begins for a zone. The start scavenging parameter is set to the current time plus the refresh interval for the zone when one of the following events occur:

◆ Dynamic Update is changed from disabled to enabled for the zone.

◆ The Enable scavenging flag is changed from false (0) to true (1).

◆ The zone is loaded and scavenging is enabled for the zone.

◆ The zone is resumed and scavenging is enabled for the zone.

Choosing effective scavenging parameters is a balancing act. You must set the refresh and no-refresh intervals long enough so that all dynamic update client computers have an opportunity to refresh their records, yet short enough so that there is never an excessive number of stale records in the zone.

The no-refresh interval protects DNS from executing unnecessary replication. When a record is refreshed, it is considered a change and is replicated to all other master servers and secondary zones. The exception to the no-refresh interval is when a record's information is really changed so that the record should be replicated. Services such as Netlogon and Windows Clustering refresh their DNS records quite often. If the no-refresh interval is set to a value to match these services, the zone would be replicating a substantial number of records several times per hour.

Selecting the best refresh interval depends a great deal upon the types of dynamic update client computers belonging to the zone. The refresh interval should be long enough to accommodate the service that has the longest time span between refreshes. For example, the default lease period for a DHCP server is three days. DHCP refreshes records at lease renewal time. Setting the default refresh interval (seven days) provides DHCP with a reasonable opportunity to refresh its records.

Understanding DDNS

In the not-so-distant past, all DNS record updates were a manual task relegated to the DNS administrator. Only statically addressed hosts had resource records in the zone. Obviously, keeping a zone updated for a host that used dynamic IP address assignments was (and still is) nearly (if not completely) impossible.

RFC 2136 defines a protocol for dynamic update of DNS records, DDNS. The core instrument of DDNS is a new record type, UPDATE, which is defined in RFC 2136. UPDATE records can add or delete DNS resource records.

Understanding the Windows 2000 Client Computer and DDNS

To develop a solid design for implementing Windows 2000 DNS, you should understand the behavior of different kinds of client computers. This section covers the DDNS update process with three types of Windows 2000 client computers: DHCP client computers, statically addressed client computers, and RAS client computers. Expect questions on this topic on the Microsoft exam.

The most commonly used Windows 2000 client computer is a DHCP client computer. The following is the default sequence of events for a new Windows 2000 DHCP client computer that boots on a Windows 2000 network:

1. The Windows 2000 client computer negotiates the update procedure with the DHCP server. By default, the DHCP client computer updates the DNS A record, and the DHCP server updates the PTR record.

2. After connecting to the network, the client computer locates the primary DNS server by issuing an SOA (Start Of Authority) query.

3. The client computer sends an assertion update to the primary server. An assertion update is a type of query that confirms whether a proposed update conflicts with any records that the server is holding.

4. If the proposed update is valid, the client computer sends an UPDATE message for the A record to the server.

In step 1, the client computer negotiates the update procedure with the DHCP server. The behavior of the DHCP server and a Windows 2000 DHCP client computer is configurable. Table 3.18 shows the possible configuration combinations and results. The DHCP server and a client computer can be configured to work together with DDNS updates.

Statically addressed Windows 2000 client computers do not interact with the DHCP server. When DDNS update is enabled, these client computers always update both the A and the PTR records on the DNS server. Windows 2000 client computers issue an update or refresh query when

◆ The client computer is rebooted.

◆ The IP address is changed.

◆ The hostname is changed.

◆ It has been 24 hours since the last refresh.

TABLE 3.18

DHCP SERVER AND CLIENT COMPUTER CONFIGURATIONS

DHCP Server Configuration	*Windows 2000 Client Computer Configuration*	*Result*
Update DNS server according to client computer request (default)	Client computer updates A record, DHCP server updates PTR record (default)	As requested by the client computer
	Client computer updates A and PTR records	As requested by the client computer
	DHCP server updates A and PTR records	As requested by the client computer
Always update forward and reverse lookups	Client computer updates A record, DHCP server updates PTR record	As DHCP server is configured
	Client computer updates A and PTR records	As DHCP server is configured
	DHCP server updates A and PTR records	As DHCP server is configured
Never update DNS server	Client computer updates A record, DHCP server updates PTR record	Client computer updates A and PTR records
	Client computer updates A and PTR records	Client computer updates A and PTR records
	DHCP server updates A and PTR records	No DNS update is attempted

When a Windows 2000 DHCP client computer is responsible for updating DNS, it will persistently attempt to update DNS on failure. If the authoritative zone is multimaster and the update attempt fails, the Windows 2000 DHCP client computer attempts to update to any and all other primary DNS servers. If all update attempts to primary servers fail, the client computer waits 5 minutes and attempts another update; then it tries again after 5 more minutes. If the client computer has not yet succeeded, the client computer attempts an update every 50 minutes.

Windows 2000 RAS client computers do not interact with the DHCP server. A RAS client computer can be either statically addressed, or its IP address is assigned by the RAS server at connection time. The Windows 2000 RAS client computer is responsible for DNS updates of its A and PTR records. The RAS client computer adds an A and PTR record to the DNS server at connect-time, and before closing a connection, the RAS client computer attempts to delete its A and PTR records. If the RAS client computer fails to delete the records, the RAS server tries to unregister the (now disconnected) client computer. If all attempts fail, the record(s) become stale and are eventually scavenged from the zone.

Another feature of DDNS updates is that both the DHCP server and Windows 2000 client computer support reregistration, or refreshes. Windows 2000 client computers reregister with the DNS server every 24 hours. Windows 2000 DHCP servers reregister client computers when their lease is renewed.

DDNS and Mixed Client Computer/Server Environments

More than likely, most implementations of Windows 2000 in the real world will be integrated into existing networks. To successfully plan for such integration, you should understand the interoperability among standard DNS, DDNS, standard DHCP, WINS, and DDNS-aware DHCP.

The one guiding tenet for integrating Windows 2000 into mixed environments is that Windows 2000 computers use DNS—and only DNS—for name resolution. Name resolution required by a Windows 2000 server or workstation must be accomplished through DNS.

This does not mean that all hosts on the network must be registered with DNS; however, all hosts and services that a given Windows 2000 client computer must access do require a DNS entry.

DDNS can integrate into a downlevel DNS environment with relative ease. DDNS is functionally identical to the downlevel product, except that it recognizes UPDATE messages. To implement DDNS into such an environment with an eye toward moving entirely to DDNS, the Windows 2000 DNS server(s) should be installed as the primary server(s). Update requests will find their way to a DDNS server, because a DDNS-aware client computer issues an SOA request that will always return the address of the primary server. In fact, even on a pure DDNS network, only primary servers perform updates.

In a mixed environment where WINS is used, Windows 2000 DNS can be configured to perform WINS lookups. When a lookup query fails, the DNS server queries WINS to resolve the name. WINS lookup provides name resolution for Windows 2000 client computers in a WINS environment where DDNS-aware DHCP is not used exclusively. WINS name resolution can be eliminated from a mixed network if the following conditions are met:

◆ All primary DNS servers are DDNS servers.

◆ All DHCP servers are DDNS-aware and are configured to perform updates on behalf of downlevel DHCP client computers.

There is one valid, but very unlikely, exception to the second condition. By default, if a Windows 2000 DHCP client computer obtains its IP address from a downlevel DHCP server, it takes responsibility for updating both its A and PTR records. A downlevel DHCP server can be used in a DDNS environment, provided that it services only Windows 2000 DHCP client computers.

Planning for Windows 2000 DNS Implementation

Windows 2000 DNS includes the following new features:

◆ Active Directory integration

◆ Incremental zone transfer (IXFR)

◆ Dynamic update and secure dynamic update

◆ Unicode character support

◆ Enhanced domain locator

◆ Enhanced caching resolver service

◆ Enhanced DNS Manager

Some of these features are not compatible with other DNS implementations, such as Windows NT 4.*x* and BIND. In addition to the description of each of these features, this section also discusses incompatibility issues and offers workarounds where applicable. You should expect questions and problems on the exam about integrating Windows 2000 DNS into a legacy DNS environment.

Windows 2000 Active Directory Integration of DNS

Windows 2000 DNS supports all IETF standards; therefore, conventional methods for replicating and managing zone files are supported. Windows 2000 DNS can optionally be integrated into Active Directory.

When integrated into Active Directory, DNS does not use conventional zone files to store records. Instead, DNS records are stored in Active Directory. Each DNS zone is represented as a container object (type DnsZone). Within the DnsZone object, a leaf object (type DnsNode) represents every unique domain name within the zone. The DnsNode object contains a DnsRecord leaf object for each record associated with the domain name. Each DnsRecord object has a multivalue attribute that contains a value for every DNS record associated with that DnsRecord object. For example, the Active Directory entry for myhost.chicago.corp1.com would include an attribute to represent the DNS A record, which contains the IP address of the host.

> **NOTE**
> **DNS Servers and Active Directory** To use Active Directory zone information directly, a DNS server must be running on a domain controller. Servers not running on DCs are configured as secondary servers and are updated using standard DNS protocols.

Understanding Zone Replication with Integrated DNS

Because the DNS records are integrated into Active Directory, any changes made to a DNS server are written to Active Directory. Active Directory in turn replicates the information to other DNS servers running on domain controllers. There are some real advantages to this replication scheme:

◆ Zone file management and replication are performed entirely by Active Directory.

◆ Replication is efficient because updates can be minimized to the per-property level for incremental zone replications.

◆ Because zone transfers are accomplished via Active Directory replication, transfers are secure.

Active Directory sees all integrated DNS servers as master servers. This means that changes can be applied to any integrated server and they are replicated to all other integrated servers. The multimaster model does present some problems:

◆ The same object can be modified on two different servers, causing an update conflict. Active Directory resolves the conflict by using the most recent update based on the timestamp.

◆ The same object name can be created on two different integrated servers. Active Directory resolves the conflict by using the most recent update.

Integrated DNS servers periodically poll Active Directory for zone updates; therefore, under either of the aforementioned circumstances, a server could return invalid information to a client computer. This is one of the reasons that the Active Directory database is "loosely consistent."

Secure Dynamic Updates

When a Windows 2000 client computer attempts to register its A record with DNS and finds that the record already exists but with a different IP address, it deletes the existing record and registers. This default behavior helps reduce stale records; however, it is a security hole. One option is to change a particular registry key so that rather than delete the existing record, the update fails and an error is written to the event log.

Another option is to use Secure Dynamic Update. Using Secure Dynamic Update, only a resource record owner or any user or group assigned write permission may update a record. Additionally, the communication between client computer and server is secure. To execute a Secure Dynamic Update, the client computer establishes a security context with the DNS server and then initiates the update process. The default process for Secure Dynamic Update is as follows:

1. The DNS client computer issues an SOA (Start Of Authority) query for the name to be updated. This is also standard for nonsecure updates.

2. The DNS server contacted in step 1 returns a reference to the authoritative DNS server.

3. The client computer contacts the authoritative server and confirms that it is authoritative for the proposed update record.

4. The client computer attempts a nonsecure update, which the server rejects.

5. The client computer and the server establish a security context. How this context is established depends on the type of security being used. Windows 2000 uses Kerberos. Establishing the security contexts involves exchanging security tokens using TKEY records to verify each other's identity, and then establishing a signature for client computer and server. For every transaction that occurs after the security context has been established, the Kerberos security context verifies message signatures.

6. Finally, the client computer sends an update request to the server.

7. If the server is able to execute the update, it does so and sends an affirmative reply to the client computer. The client computer must not only establish a security context to complete the update, but must also have write permission to the target record.

NOTE **Secure DNS Updates** This example assumes that the DNS server is configured to allow only secure updates.

To execute an update, Windows 2000 client computers can be configured to connect to a DNS server three ways:

◆ Try a nonsecure update first, and then a secure update (default configuration).

◆ Always use a secure connection.

◆ Always use a nonsecure connection.

Using the default behavior enables a client computer to connect to either a secure or a nonsecure DNS server.

Integrated DNS zones are secured by Active Directory using Access Control Lists (ACLs). The default configuration for integrated zones allows any authenticated user to create a resource record, but only the owner, other users, or groups assigned write permission can update that record. This presents a couple of problems:

◆ If a DHCP server is configured to update DNS, the server owns all the records for all client computers serviced. If the DHCP server goes offline, client computers and other DHCP servers are unable to update the resource records.

◆ If a computer is upgraded—either hardware or operating system—and the same hostname is retained, it is unable to change its own resource record(s).

The solution to this record ownership problem is a group named DNS Update Proxy. When a member of this group creates any object, that object has no security. The first user not a member of DNS Update Proxy to touch the record becomes its owner. Making DHCP servers members of the DNS Update Proxy group solves the problem for both the aforementioned scenarios.

There is a catch. Records created by the DHCP server are open to attack until they are touched by their associated client computer. If the DHCP server is installed on a domain controller, two more security holes pop up: All resource records created by Netlogon are open to attack, and DHCP has full control over all DNS records stored in Active Directory.

WARNING

DHCP Server The DHCP server should *not* be installed on domain controllers.

DNS Character Support

RFC 2044 defines DNS support for the UTF-8 character set. This extended character set includes characters for most written languages worldwide. UTF-8 is a direct translation of the Unicode character set. Windows 2000 DNS supports the UTF-8 character set.

If a Windows 2000 DNS zone is implemented with UTF-8 support enabled, the administrator must be sure that all f the protocols that interact with DNS also support UTF-8. Additionally, any DNS names that are visible to the outside world—that is, on the Internet—must use the original DNS character set as specified in RFC 1123.

Understanding the Domain Locator

The Windows 2000 Domain Locator is a service that is owned by the Netlogon service. As its name implies, it locates domain controllers for client computers attempting to log on to the network. The Domain Locator is actually two different locators wrapped into a single service. The primary locator is the IP/DNS Compatible Locator. The secondary locator is the Windows NT 4.0 Compatible Locator. The Windows NT 4.0 locator is used for downlevel compatibility in mixed environments.

The details of the Window NT 4.0 locator are not relevant to the Microsoft exam. You need to know only that it attempts to locate legacy Windows NT domain controllers when the IP/DNS Compatible Locator fails.

The core functionality of the IP/DNS Compatible Locator is DNS lookups. For IP/DNS Compatible Locator to find a domain controller and its associated Netlogon service, both the domain controller(s) and associated Netlogon service(s) must register certain records with DNS. DNS records registered by domain controllers are used by IP/DNS Domain Locator as well as other services that require access to the server. Windows 2000 domain controllers register the records shown in Table 3.19.

TABLE 3.19

DNS RECORDS REGISTERED BY DOMAIN CONTROLLERS

Record Type	NAME Field	RDATA field
A	ntdc1.company1.com	192.168.224.5
SRV	_ldap._tcp.nt.company1.com	ntdc1.company1.com
SRV	_kerberos._tcp.mycompany.com	ntdc1.company1.com
SRV	_ldap._tcp.dc._msdcs.company1.com	ntdc1.company1.com
SRV	_kerberos._tcp.dc._msdcs.company1.com	ntdc1.company1.com

The NAME field in the solitary A record in Table 3.19 is unique to the domain company1.com; however, every domain controller that registers to the company1.domain writes one of each of the SRV records. An SRV query for _ldap._tcp.dc._msdcs.company1.com returns a list of all known domain controllers.

The Netlogon service for each domain controller also registers several SRV records. These SRV records facilitate location of domain controllers using several criteria, including site name, forest name, and domain GUID. The list and description of these records is too long to cover here; however, the white paper that contains a detailed description of SVR records for Netlogon can be found at the Microsoft TechNet Web site (www.microsoft.com/technet).

In most cases, the IP/DNS Compatible Locator runs on the Windows 2000 client computer attempting to logon. The process is as follows:

1. The locator gets three parameters from the client computer configuration: the DNS name for the Active Directory name to which the client computer belongs, the Active Directory domain GUID, and the site name. Only the DNS domain name is required. The other parameters are used for alternate lookups if the domain name lookup fails.

2. If the locator fails to find a domain controller, it exits, returning an error to Netlogon. Netlogon then attempts to discover a downlevel domain controller using Windows NT 4.0 Compatible Domain Locator. If this fails, the locator exits and returns an error to Netlogon.

3. When the client computer receives the list of domain controllers, it tries to find one that belongs to the same site by querying a DNS server for a record of the found domain controllers.

4. The locator then chooses a domain controller for logon using a random ping procedure that is weighted in favor of domain controllers that belong to the same site as the client computer. Each of the domain controllers is pinged in random order and at 1/10-second intervals.

5. If no domain controllers respond affirmatively, the locator exits, returning an error code to Netlogon. Otherwise, the client computer uses the first domain controller to respond affirmatively to the ping procedure. An affirmative response to the ping is determined by the locator. When a domain controller responds, it returns parameters required to log on to the domain. If these parameters do not match the client computer's requirements, the response is thrown away.

Planning for WINS

Although Microsoft is moving to DNS as its default name service, there are still a large number of existing networks that use WINS. Most of the work that will be done in the real world will be either integration of WINS and DNS or migration of a WINS-enabled network to pure DNS. To effectively accomplish either of these tasks, you should know the functionality and the features of WINS.

How WINS Works

Like DNS, early NetBIOS networks used a text file, LMHOSTS, stored locally on each host to resolve names and to facilitate operation on routed networks. NetBIOS is broadcast-based and cannot be used on routed networks. As networks became larger and more dynamic, it was apparent that LMHOSTS files were an inadequate name resolution tool. WINS provides a solution to NetBIOS networks by offering scalability, dynamic updates, and compatibility with routed networks. WINS servers maintain a distributed database of NetBIOS mappings. Each server has a copy of the WINS database, which is synchronized using replication. WINS servers can be configured as replication partners. Replication partners can be push partners, pull partners, or both.

Push partners respond to pull partners and send updated records to the pull partners after notifying those partners that an update was available. The interval for push partner update notifications can be configured to replicate after a certain number of updates, or when an address for a name is changed. If a push partner is not configured with either of these replication triggers, it simply sends replication triggers it receives from a partner to all other partners.

A WINS pull partner requests updates from its partners by sending a request containing the highest-version ID last received during replication. The partner responds by sending all records to the pull partner with a higher-version ID. Microsoft recommends that WINS servers are both push and pull partners with all their replication partners. Furthermore, any WINS servers designated primary WINS server and secondary WINS server for any client computer must be both push and pull partners with each other.

WINS learns NetBIOS names and associated IP addresses in two ways: client computer registration and static entries. When a WINS client computer boots, it registers with its primary WINS server. At that time, WINS creates a record for the client computer that includes the NetBIOS name, IP address, a timestamp, and version ID. After a time determined by the replication configuration of the WINS server, the information is replicated to replication partners.

WINS servers communicate using the TCP protocol; therefore, they can replicate across routers on a segmented network. WINS client computers are configured with the IP address of at least one server. WINS client computers communicate with WINS servers using a TCP/IP unicast and therefore can contact servers across network segments.

When you're designing a WINS implementation, a few of the design guidelines that should be considered include

- ◆ Calculating convergence time
- ◆ Fault tolerance
- ◆ Replication traffic control
- ◆ WINS server capacity requirements

Convergence time is the longest it should take a new WINS entry to be replicated to all other WINS servers on the network. Convergence time is an important consideration because all users on a network may not have access to a particular NetBIOS-enabled host or may have wrong information for that name for a period equal to as long as the convergence time. Convergence time is effectively controlled by the frequency of WINS replication.

Convergence time is calculated by aggregating replication times between replication partners. A WINS network with a long convergence time can effectively deny access to resources for a portion of hosts, services, and applications. On the other hand, a very fast convergence time requires frequent replications, using more bandwidth and CPU cycles.

Figure 3.9 shows a typical WINS configuration. If a new client computer is added to the network and registers with WINSSvr1, only client computers that use WINSSvr1 can resolve the name of the new client computer. WINSSvr1 is configured to push to WINSSvr2 at a certain update count threshold. WINSSvr2 is configured to pull from WINSSvr1 every 20 minutes. There is no way of knowing how long it might take WINSSvr1 to reach an update count threshold; therefore, the guaranteed maximum replication time is 20 minutes. If WINSSvr1 and WINSSvr2 were the only WINS servers on the network, convergence time for the network would be 20 minutes. The administrator could guarantee users that new hosts would be available to the entire user population within 20 minutes.

WINSSvr2 is a push and a pull partner with WINSSvr3. WINSSvr3 is configured to push to WINSSvr2 at a configured update count threshold and to pull updates from WINSSvr2 every 60 minutes. WINSSvr2 is configured to push to WINSSvr3 at a specified update count and to pull from WINSSvr3 every 24 hours. The effective convergence time for WINSvr2 and WINSSvr3 is 60 minutes. Convergence time for the entire network in Figure 3.9 is 75 minutes.

FIGURE 3.9
WINS convergence times can be stated only in terms of maximums. In this configuration, convergence time for the network shown here is 75 minutes.

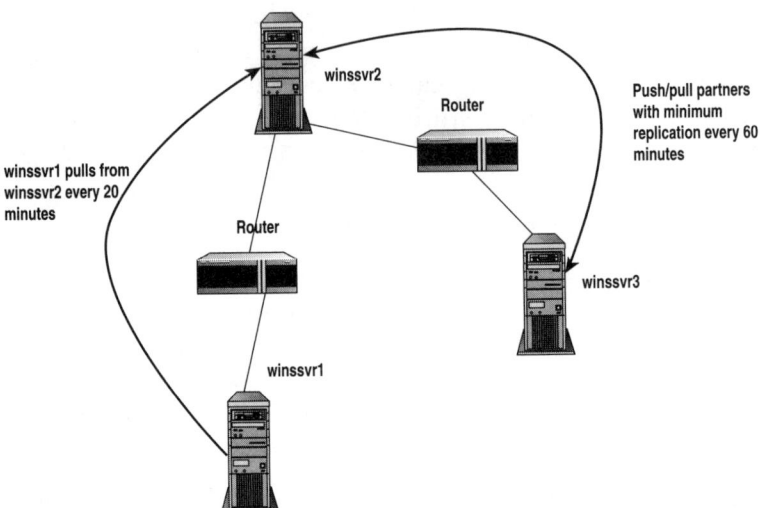

WINS server fault tolerance can be enhanced by strategic placement of WINS servers on the network and by careful planning of replication partners. The following are some WINS fault-tolerance guidelines:

◆ WINS servers should be local to remote sites. If a WAN link fails or the remote server's replication partner fails, remote users will still be able to resolve most names for local hosts. Records from other WINS servers are not deleted during scavenging because the owner of those records cannot be contacted.

◆ WINS client computers should be configured with at least a primary and a secondary WINS server. If a client computer cannot contact its primary WINS server, it will attempt to use the secondary server. Windows 2000 Professional and Windows 98 client computers can be configured with up to 12 WINS server addresses.

◆ Carefully plan and configure multiple replication paths. To compensate for potentially lost links, secondary replication partners can be created. The secondary partners should replicate at a much lower frequency than the primary partners do. Because multiple partners create more overhead and bandwidth consumption, it is better to have a fault-tolerant router/segment configuration and a simpler replication scheme.

All WINS databases on a network should be roughly the same size. Each unique entry requires 42 bytes of storage. Internet Group IDs can require more than 25 unique entries.

New WINS Features for Windows 2000

WINS features are discussed first because some of them directly impact the implementation or integration of Windows 2000 WINS.

The following are WINS features that are relevant to design and implementation:

◆ **Persistent connections.** Downlevel versions of WINS had to establish an IPC (InterProcess Communication) connection over the wire each time WINS databases were replicated. This added traffic to the network. To minimize this traffic, administrators tended to configure WINS for increased time span between replication.

Windows 2000 WINS can be configured to maintain a persistent connection with other (Windows 2000 WINS) replication partners, which eliminates CPU cycles and network traffic required to establish a connection.

◆ **Manual tombstoning.** Anyone who has attempted to delete a record from a WINS database in an environment of two or more WINS servers knows how difficult it can be. This is because a replication partner WINS server sees that record as missing, not deleted, from the database, so it replaces the removed record.

Windows 2000 WINS enables an administrator to mark records as tombstoned. The tombstoned record is replicated to WINS partners and will be removed by WINS on all servers. Only Windows 2000 WINS has manual tombstoning, but a tombstoned record is replicated to Windows NT 3.51 and Windows NT 4.0 servers.

◆ **Replication partner autodiscovery.** Windows 2000 WINS servers can be enabled to automatically detect and configure replication with other Windows 2000 WINS servers. Autodiscovery is not recommended for networks with more than three WINS servers.

◆ **Improved fault tolerance.** Both Windows 2000 Professional and Windows 98 client computers can be configured with up to 12 WINS server IP address references. If the primary or secondary servers fail to respond, the WINS client computer queries additional WINS servers. If an auxiliary WINS server provides a name resolution to the client computer, the client computer caches the response.

◆ **Dynamic reregistration.** Downlevel versions of WINS client computers can register at boot-time. Windows 2000 WINS client computers register at boot-time, but they can also reregister. When a client computer reregisters, it simply updates the version number on its WINS record, forcing replication to other WINS servers.

DNS and DDNS name services are the core name services for TCP/IP networks. WINS is supported by Windows 2000 only to provide compatibility with downlevel hosts, such as Windows NT 4 Server. Microsoft's emphasis is on TCP/IP networks; yet for purposes of interoperability, Microsoft actively supports several other protocols. In the next section, you learn about protocols supported and tools provided by Microsoft to support interoperability with non-TCP/IP networks and network devices.

DESIGNING MULTIPROTOCOL NETWORKS

Design a multiprotocol strategy. Protocols include IPX/SPX and SNA.

To meet the exam objective of designing a multiprotocol network, you should know which protocols are supported by Windows 2000. You should understand the client computer connectivity supported by these protocols. You should also know how the various client computers and gateways interoperate on a Microsoft network.

Armed with this knowledge, you should be able to develop a connectivity strategy for a multiprotocol network. Information presented in this section to help you meet this objective includes the following:

◆ **Protocols supported by Windows 2000.** The various protocols, their functionality, and their purposes are discussed.

◆ **Windows client computers, services, and gateways that use the "foreign" protocols.** These are the tools that a network designer uses to solve interoperability problems on a multiprotocol network.

The Microsoft exam will likely have at least one scenario-based problem where you will be asked to come up with the best solution for interoperability on a multiprotocol network. You will come up with the best solution if you understand the purpose of each tool and how it fits into the network design.

Network Protocols Supported by Windows 2000

Although TCP/IP is the network protocol of choice for Windows 2000, other protocols are supported. To facilitate connectivity and interoperability with other operating systems, Windows 2000 includes support for

◆ NWLink, an IPX/SPX-compatible protocol whose primary use is to provide a transport for NetWare connectivity tools and IPX/SPX client computers

◆ SNA, an IBM-specific protocol used for gateway connectivity and terminal emulator access to IBM mid- and mainframe systems

◆ AppleTalk, which is used in conjunction with File and Print Server for Macintosh

NWLink is probably the most common secondary or supplemental protocol in use today, because Microsoft networks are often integrated with Novell networks. NWLink is a routable protocol that is very easy to configure and maintain. This makes IPX/SPX a very popular protocol for small networks.

SNA is the native protocol for IBM mainframes and minicomputers. It is supported on Windows 2000 only when SNA Server is installed on a Windows NT or Windows 2000 server. SNA Server is described later in this section.

AppleTalk is the native protocol for Macintosh. As with SNA, AppleTalk is supported only when File Server for Macintosh or Print Server for Macintosh is installed on the Windows 2000 computer.

Connectivity Products for Windows 2000

Microsoft offers a variety of connectivity tools for Windows NT and Windows 2000. These tools offer network connectivity solutions for NetWare, UNIX, and Macintosh. The mainstream connectivity tools are described in this section. An implementation example is provided for each product. This example is designed to demonstrate a typical situation where the product is used effectively . As you read about these products, remember that the exam objective is to know how to use the right tool for the job.

NetWare Connectivity Products for Windows 2000

Microsoft offers several NetWare connectivity products for both Windows 2000 Professional and the Windows 2000 server family. These products offer a variety of solutions for NetWare-to-Microsoft connectivity. Because NetWare is a popular network operating system, these are the most commonly used of all Microsoft connectivity tools.

Client Computer Services for NetWare

Interoperability with Novell NetWare 3.*x* and 4.*x* on a Microsoft network can be accomplished by running an IPX/SPX-compatible protocol and a NetWare client computer on the workstation. Client computer services for NetWare should be used when only a few computers must connect to a NetWare server. Each computer that connects to one or more NetWare servers and one or more Windows servers must have both the NetWare client computer and the Microsoft client computer software installed. Additionally, if the Windows server is using TCP/IP, the client computers must also have TCP/IP installed.

Gateway Services for NetWare

Gateway Services for NetWare provides Microsoft client computers access to NetWare 3.*x* and 4.*x* servers. Gateway services for NetWare run on a Windows server. The server connects to the NetWare server(s) using NWLink and publishes NetWare resources so that these resources look like Microsoft shares to client computers. Gateway Services for NetWare should be used when a substantial number of Microsoft client computers must connect to one or more NetWare servers. Microsoft client computers need only connect to the Windows server to access the NetWare resources. Client computers need only run the Microsoft client computer software and the appropriate network protocol.

File and Print Services for NetWare v.5

File and Print Services for NetWare v.5 emulates a NetWare server so that NetWare client computers can access resources on a Windows 2000 server with no modification to the client computer configuration. This product is useful for integrating Windows 2000 into a predominantly NetWare environment.

Services for NetWare v.5

Services for NetWare v.5 is somewhat similar to File and Print Services for NetWare v.5; it includes software that emulates a NetWare server so that NetWare client computers have access to the server's resources. The real difference is that this product should be used in environments where migration to Windows 2000 is anticipated. In addition to the NetWare emulation software, Services for NetWare v.5 includes tools used for migration:

◆ Microsoft directory synchronization with NDS and NetWare 3.*x* binderies

◆ Migration from NetWare file system

◆ File and print Services for NetWare v.4

◆ Directory Service Manager for NetWare

SNA Server for Windows 2000

SNA is the standard network protocol for IBM minicomputers and mainframe computers. SNA Server provides gateway services from a Microsoft network to SNA. Here are some important features of SNA Server:

◆ The SNA side of the gateway supports X.25 and SDLC connections so that investments in legacy dedicated communications lines are not lost and other WAN links can be reserved for non-SNA traffic. Many companies have such connections in place and are not prepared to replace them with non-SNA lines.

◆ Network-side client computers need no special protocol configurations to take advantage of SNA Server. Client computers can use the same protocol used to connect to the Windows 2000 server. SNA Server supports TCP/IP, IPX/SPX, and NetBEUI connections to the SNA network.

◆ Support for three deployment models—branch-based, centralized, and distributed—is included. SNA Server can be configured to fit an existing infrastructure.

◆ Support for virtual LAN connections is included. SNA Server can connect to other SNA Server computers across an SNA network.

◆ RAS architecture integration enables the administrator to manage remote SNA connections using RAS tools. Other RAS features—such as data compression, administration, and security—are supported.

One of the real advantages of SNA Server is support for three deployment models, an important feature for network planners and designers. You should understand the relative strengths of each of the deployment models so that you can choose the appropriate model. Each of the deployment models is covered in the next three sections.

Branch-Based Deployment Model of SNA Server

The branch-based deployment model is the most commonly used model. Figure 3.10 depicts a typical branch-based model. Each branch has an SNA gateway connected to the SNA network via leased SDLC or X.25 lines. In some cases, there is also a WAN connection to the central site. If the leased lines are the only connection between branch and central office, remote SNA can be used to provide connectivity among branches and the central office.

This configuration is used where a leased SDLC or X.25 topology is already in place and the company is not prepared or has no need to move to a conventional WAN connection. Typically, the legacy architecture used a local control unit with SDLC cards installed in computers or native SDLC devices connected to the control unit.

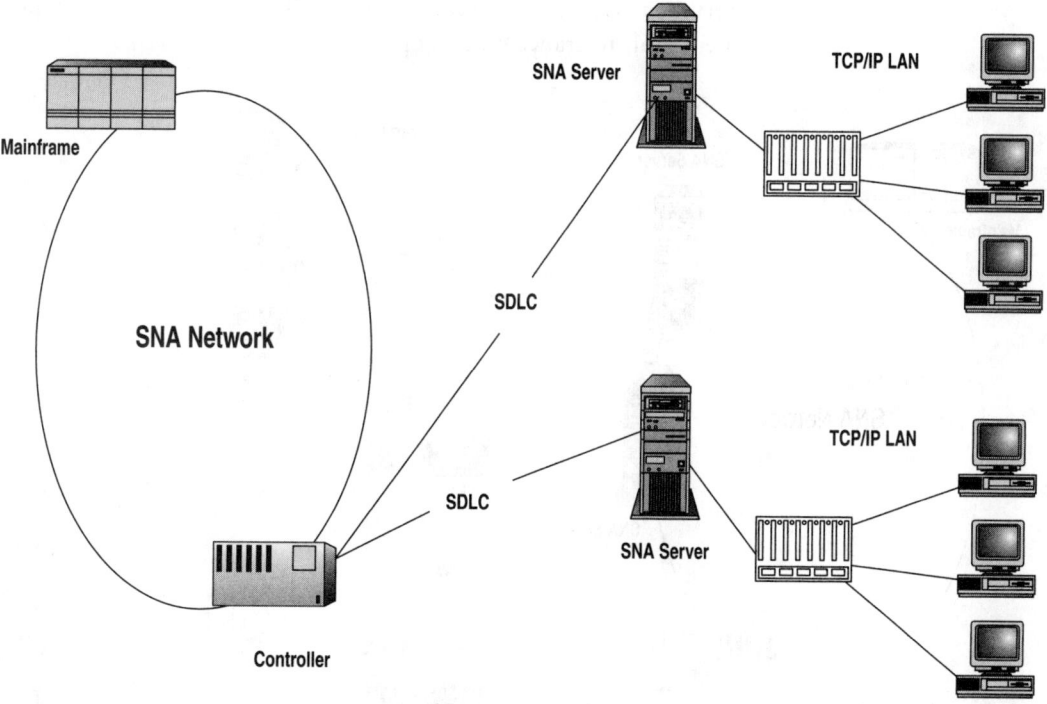

FIGURE 3.10
The distributed deployment model for SNA Server is tied to traditional remote mainframe communications configurations.

Centralized Deployment Model of SNA Server

The centralized deployment model places SNA server(s) at the central office directly connected to the SNA backbone. Branch offices communicate with the central office by way of a routed WAN connection (see Figure 3.11). This model has some advantages over a branch-based model:

◆ All SNA servers are located at one site.

◆ SNA Server expertise is not required at the remote sites.

◆ Servers on the central site can be load-balanced and configured for hot backup.

◆ Only a single protocol is required for LAN traffic.

The centralized model should be used where the goal is to eliminate leased lines, to use an existing WAN connection, to simplify SNA Server management, to service very small remote sites, or to implement fault tolerance on a budget.

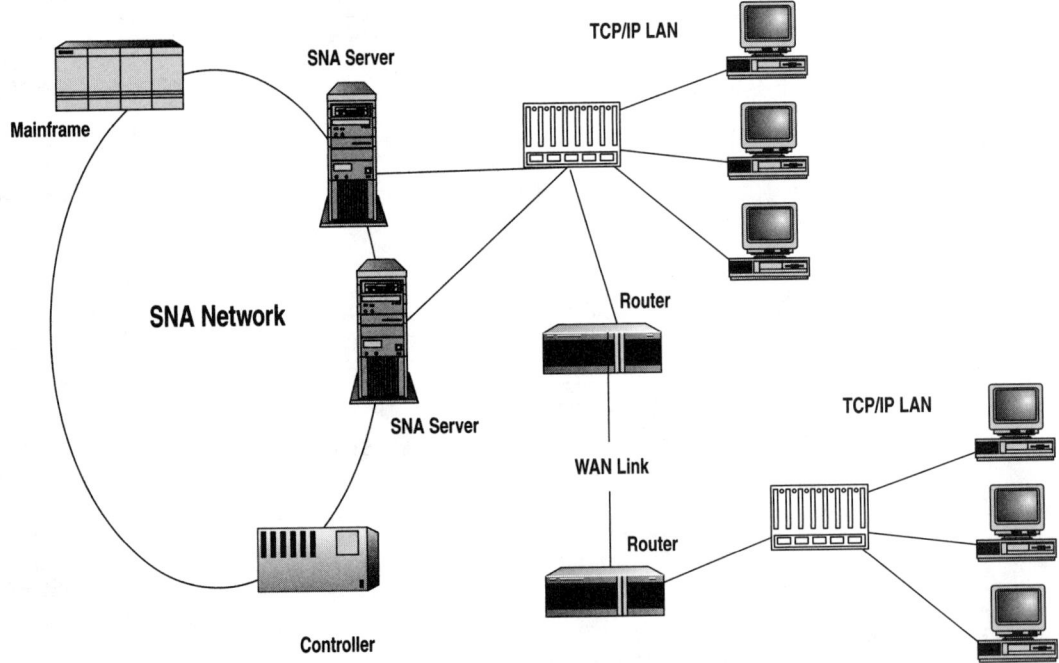

FIGURE 3.11
The centralized SNA deployment model provides on-site maintenance and administration.

Distributed Deployment Model of SNA Server

The distributed deployment model features SNA Server computers at both the central site and the branches. Figure 3.12 shows a typical distributed deployment model implementation.

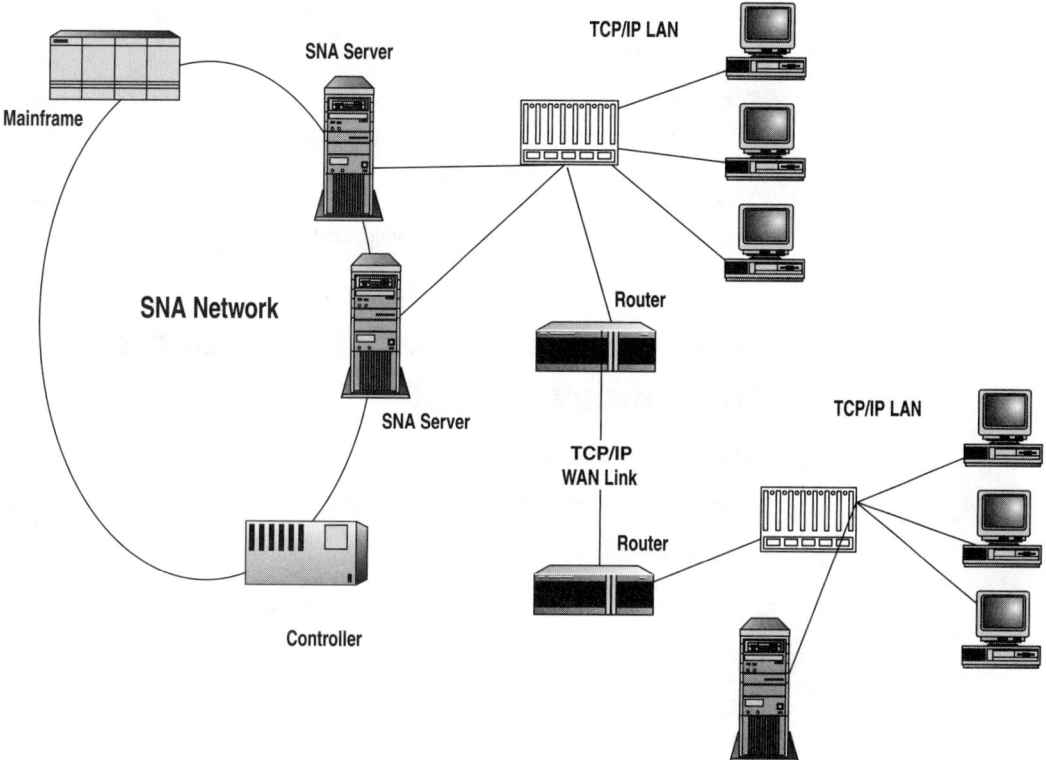

FIGURE 3.12

The distributed SNA deployment model facilitates fault tolerance using remote dialup online failure.

The addition of more SNA Server computers compared to the other deployment models offers several advantages:

◆ Because each site has a local SNA server connected to an SNA server at the central site, response time is improved and WAN bandwidth requirements are reduced.

◆ When there are multiple SNA servers at the central site, if a central site server fails, the branch SNA server automatically connects to an available server.

◆ Alternate contingency connections, such as dialup SDLC, can be configured between the branch and central SNA servers.

The distributed deployment model should be used when performance, reliability, and manageability outweigh budget considerations.

Macintosh Connectivity Products for Windows 2000

Microsoft offers three connectivity products for Macintosh:

◆ File Server for Macintosh

◆ Print Server for Macintosh

◆ Windows 2000 Server File and Print Server for Macintosh

File Server for Macintosh enables a Windows 2000 Server computer to share files with a Macintosh computer. When File Server for Macintosh is installed, a directory on an NTFS volume must be designated as a Macintosh-accessible volume. File Server for Macintosh validates NTFS-compatible filenames for files created on this volume and manages access permissions.

Print Server for Macintosh, a set of services that runs on a Windows 2000 Server computer, serves as a two-way gateway. Microsoft client computers can send print jobs to printers on an AppleTalk network, and Macintosh client computers can send print jobs to printers on a Microsoft network.

Windows 2000 Server File and Print Server for Macintosh, also a set of services that runs on Windows 2000 Server, is simply a combination of File Server for Macintosh and Print Server for Macintosh.

Windows Services for UNIX 2.0

At this time, Windows Services for UNIX 2.0 is still in beta testing. It is a rich set of tools and services designed to integrate Windows NT 4.0 and Windows 2000 servers into a UNIX environment. Integrated services to provide connectivity with UNIX hosts include the following:

◆ Gateway for NFS runs on Windows 2000 Server. It seamlessly maps exported NFS volumes to Windows shares.

◆ Server for NFS exports NTFS volumes to UNIX hosts as if they were NFS volumes.

◆ Client for NFS enables Windows client computers to map to UNIX exported NFS volumes.

◆ Server for PCNFS provides user authentication services for NFS servers. This service runs on Windows 2000 computers.

Windows Services for UNIX has more than 60 of the most widely used UNIX command-line utilities that run on Windows 2000 Server. This includes Korn Shell as well as vi, ls, grep, and awk.

Cross-platform administration is simplified. Windows Services for UNIX includes several account management services and tools:

◆ NIS to Active Directory Migration Wizard

◆ Server for NIS

◆ Two-way password synchronization

◆ Username mapping

This product should be used anywhere connectivity between UNIX and Windows is necessary. Because the tools and services included with Windows Services for UNIX are universally known to UNIX professionals, this product is also useful for moving UNIX administrators into the Windows 2000 world.

The interoperability tools for Microsoft networks described in this section are excellent tools for leveraging existing networks and devices. Without such tools, transitioning to a Microsoft network would be much more difficult both technically and economically. Another Microsoft tool not mentioned in this section that provides a degree of interoperability is Distributed file system (Dfs). In the next section, you learn how Dfs integrates network resources including foreign resources, such as NFS volumes, into manageable objects.

DISTRIBUTED FILE SYSTEM (DFS)

Design a Distributed file system (Dfs) strategy.

Distributed file system (Dfs) is a management service for file shares and directories. Dfs enables the administrator to combine network resource shares into a single namespace called a *Dfs volume*. From the users' point of view, a Dfs volume is a single Windows share that appears to be contained on a single server. From the administrator's point of view, a typical Dfs volume is a collection of directory shares distributed across two or more servers.

The immediate benefits of Dfs should be obvious. Because the distribution of directories and files is transparent to users and applications, data is accessed using a common directory structure. Users do not need to know which server or logical disk drive any data is stored on. Administrators can structure data in a logical manner regardless of physical organization. There are a number of benefits that are not so obvious:

- Shares that belong to the Dfs volume can be managed individually. They can be taken offline without impacting the rest of the volume. The share is simply unavailable to client computers until it is back online.

- Multiple shares can be created in the Dfs volume that access the same data.

- Administrators can configure Dfs volumes for load balancing and improved performance. For example, often-accessed data at a central site can have alternate copies on remote servers across slow links.

- Data can be moved from one server or disk drive to another without impacting the Dfs volume structure.

- Dfs incorporates no additional security. Windows 2000 security is used to control data access.

NOTE

Dfs Clients   Access to Dfs volumes requires Dfs client computer software. Dfs client computer software is included with Windows NT 4.0 Workstation and Windows 2000 Professional. Client computer software is available for Windows 95 and Windows 98.

◆ Dfs supports any file system that can be accessed by Windows NT 4.0 Workstation or Windows 2000 professional. For example, a NetWare volume can be shared and included in a Dfs volume by using Gateway Services for NetWare. A UNIX volume or directory can be included in a Dfs volume by using Gateway for NFS.

◆ Dfs client computer workstations can include shares in the Dfs volume so that local data is available to others on the network without using peer-to-peer sharing.

◆ Dfs can be implemented at the server level (standalone), or it can be integrated into Active Directory (Active Directory–enabled).

◆ Active Directory–enabled volumes can be configured for enhanced fault tolerance.

The benefits described here imply additional benefits. For example, because the Dfs volume appears as a single directory structure to the vast majority of applications, a Dfs volume of mission-critical data can be created for backup. In the following sections, a technical overview of Dfs is presented. Armed with knowledge of the technical underpinnings of Dfs, a network designer can develop an efficient, reliable, and user-friendly Dfs configuration.

Dfs from the User's Point of View

Dfs volumes are accessed by Dfs client computers by using standard UNC names formatted as

    \\ServerName\DfsShareName\PathName

where *ServerName* is the name of the server that is hosting the Dfs volume, *DfsShareName* is the share name assigned to the root of the Dfs volume, and *PathName* is any valid path within the Dfs volume.

When a Dfs volume is Active Directory–enabled (when it is integrated into Active Directory), Active Directory–aware client computers can access volumes using either its domain name or its fault-tolerant name:

    \\FaultTolerantName\DfsShareName\PathName

    \\DomainName\DfsShareName\PathName

> **NOTE**
>
> **Mapping Dfs Volumes** Any path within a Dfs volume can be referenced or mapped to a drive letter on a Windows NT 4.0 Dfs client computer using the NET USE command.

where *FaultTolerantName* is the Directory Service name that the administrator assigns to the Dfs share and *DomainName* is the Active Directory domain name.

Dfs Roots and Volumes

As the name implies, a Dfs root is the starting point for the hierarchical structure of one or more Dfs volumes. A Dfs root is also referred to as a Dfs volume; however, nodes referred to as volumes within a Dfs tree are not necessarily Dfs roots. Any share-point connection to the Dfs hierarchy is referred to as a volume. Figure 3.13 shows a Dfs root that contains three volumes.

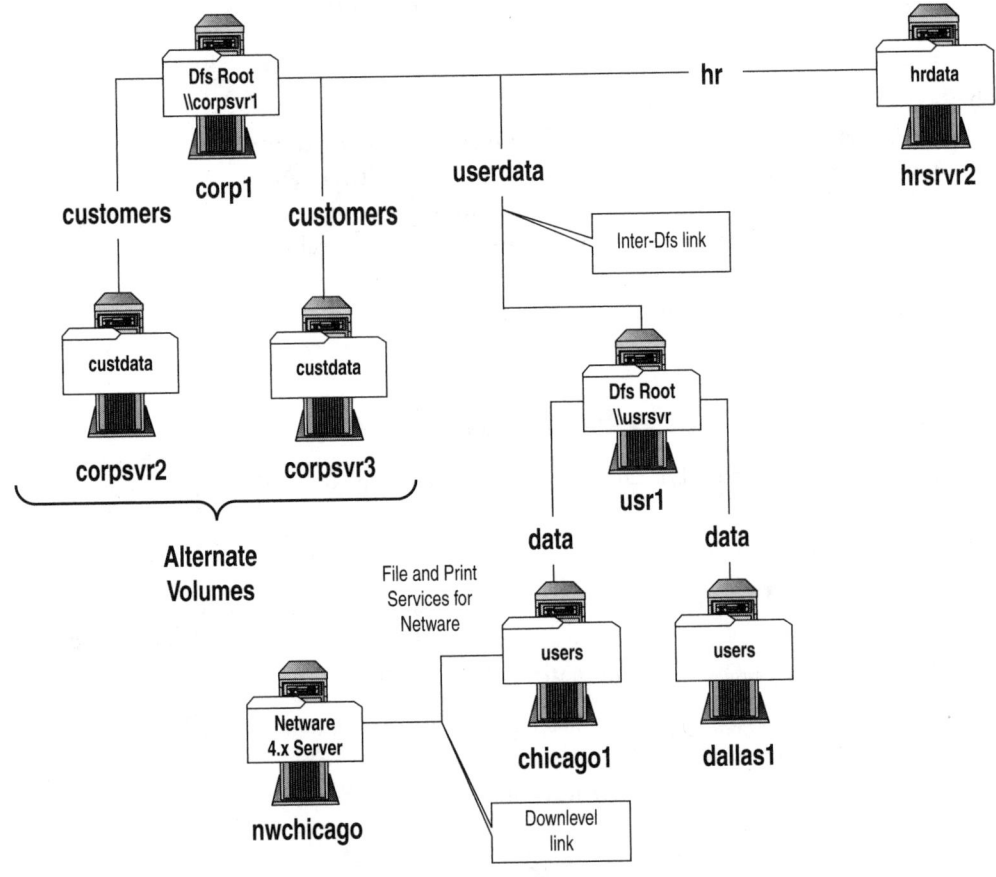

FIGURE 3.13
Dfs volumes can cross server and operating system lines using links and gateway services.

The fully qualified name for the Dfs root is \\corpsvr1\userdata.
\\corpsrv2\userdata is also a Dfs root (and volume); however, from
the point of view of \\corpsvr1, \\corpsvr2\userdata is a volume.
This is an important distinction, because there are limits on volumes
per root for Dfs. This and other resource limits are described later in
this chapter.

Dfs Junctions and Special Volume Types

Junctions are the connecting points within a Dfs volume. There are
three types of Dfs junctions (refer to Figure 3.13 for a depiction of
each junction type):

◆ A junction is a Dfs connection to an ordinary resource share.
\\corpsvr1\hr in Figure 3.13 is a Dfs junction.

◆ An inter-Dfs link junction, used with Dfs standalone roots, is
a Dfs connection to another Dfs root. \\corpsvr1\userdata is
an inter-Dfs link.

◆ A midlevel junction is a Directory Service–specific junction.
As with the inter-Dfs link, it connects a Dfs root to another
Dfs tree. The difference is in how the Dfs client computer is
referred when accessing data across such a link. Dfs referrals
are discussed later in this section.

Two special types of volumes are supported by Dfs: alternate volumes
and downlevel volumes:

◆ Alternate volumes are two or more share points that should
have the same structure and contain the same data. These
share points use the same junction in a Dfs volume. In
Figure 3.13, \\corpsvr2\custdata and \\corpsvr3\custdata
are alternate volumes that connect to the Dfs volume at
\\corpsvr1\customers.

◆ Downlevel volumes are foreign volumes that are connected to
the Dfs volume through a gateway or emulated share.
\\nwchicago\data in Figure 3.13 is a downlevel volume.

> **WARNING**
>
> **Identical Data**   It is the responsi-
> bility of the administrator to ensure
> that data is identical among alter-
> nate servers. This can be accom-
> plished with replication or if the
> data is generally static, making
> alternate directories read-only.

Walking the Dfs Tree: PKTs and Referrals

When a Dfs client computer browses or otherwise attempts to access a particular directory in a Dfs tree, the process is handled with referrals. A referral routes client computer requests for access to logical Dfs locations to a physical location.

Dfs host servers maintain a PKT (partition knowledge table), a sorted list of Dfs paths and their associated share names. Table 3.20 shows what the PKT looks like for the Dfs structure shown in Figure 3.13. When a referral is requested by a Dfs client computer, the host server looks up the requested logical location and returns a copy of the PKT entry (referral) to the client computer. The client computer chooses the best physical location to access. If the Dfs host does not find at least the first element of the logical location, an error is returned to the client computer.

TABLE 3.20

THE PKT FOR FIGURE 3.13

Dfs Path	*Physical Location*	*TTL*
\\corpsvr1	\\corp1	299
\\corpsvr1\customers	\\corpsvr2\custdata	289
	\\corpsvr3\custdata	278
\\corpsvr1\hr	\\hrsvr2\hrdata	123
\\corpsvr1\userdata	\\usrsvr1\data	277
\\usrsvr1	\\usr1	199
\\usrsvr1\data	\\chicago1\users	213
	\\dallas4\users	214

Referrals are handled differently for standalone and Active Directory–integrated Dfs volumes. When a client computer request is received by a standalone host and the host encounters an inter-Dfs link, the request is handed off to the computer hosting the associated Dfs volume. The referral is returned to the client computer indirectly by the last Dfs host in the Dfs volume that is queried. The referral information is passed in reverse order up the Dfs tree to the host for the original Dfs client computer request.

Standalone referrals are somewhat inefficient, because every time an inter-Dfs link is crossed, a new request is generated and a referral must be returned to the requester. Active Directory–enabled Dfs volumes do not use inter-Dfs links; they use midlevel junctions, which are junctions internal to Active Directory. The `DfsRoot` object in Active Directory processes the referral without handing it off.

Perhaps you noticed the TTL field for the PKT shown in Table 3.20. This is a Time To Live value. When a Dfs client computer receives a referral from a Dfs host, the client computer caches the information. The referral entry remains in client computer memory for the time specified by the referral TTL field. The default value for TTL on a referral is 5 minutes.

Alternate volumes facilitate not only load balancing, but also volume fail-over. The referral returned to a client computer by a Dfs host is actually a copy of the host's PKT record for the requested Dfs path. If one or more alternate volumes are associated with the Dfs path, the referral contains a reference to each alternate volume. This referral format provides the client computer with local fail-over information.

> **NOTE**
>
> **Referrals and Active Directory–Aware Clients**   When presented with a referral containing alternate volumes, a Directory Service–aware client computer chooses a physical volume based on site information. Selections by other client computers are purely arbitrary.

Dfs and Active Directory

Dfs takes advantage of several features of Active Directory:

- ◆ Dfs volumes can be replicated using the Active Directory replication engine. This includes Dfs roots, which cannot be replicated in a standalone configuration.

- ◆ Directory Service sites enable smart selection of alternate volumes by client computers.

- ◆ LDAP protocol is used to access Dfs objects by Directory Service–aware client computers.

Dfs Resource Limits

A Windows NT 4.0 Server computer or a Windows 2000 Server computer running the Dfs host service can host one Dfs root. Table 3.21 lists other Dfs resources and limits for Windows NT 4.0 and Windows 2000 networks. In the table, Dfs resource limits for the number of volumes per standalone root is unknown. The values listed are tested limits only.

The resource limits noted as N/A for Windows NT 4.0 Server apply only to Windows 2000 Server.

Dfs is a powerful tool for presenting data. The end user need not know anything about the location or structure of the physical data. End users access needed files by using a (preferably) well-structured directory object that makes sense to that user. On the other side of Dfs, the administrator can manage the data using technically meritorious configurations and procedures without having to worry about data presentation to the user.

> **NOTE**
>
> **Support for Multiple Dfs Roots**   The current version of Dfs for Windows NT 4.0 is version 4.1. Dfs version 4.1 limits Windows NT 4.0 Server to one root per server. Future releases are expected to allow more than one volume per server. Windows 2000 Server computers that are not domain controllers are also limited to one root. Windows 2000 Server computers that are domain controllers support multiple roots.

TABLE 3.21

OTHER DFS RESOURCES AND LIMITS FOR WINDOWS NT 4.0 AND WINDOWS 2000 NETWORKS

Resource	Windows NT 4.0	Windows 2000
Maximum fault-tolerant roots per domain	N/A	1 per computer, unlimited per domain
Maximum standalone roots per computer	1	1
Maximum Dfs volumes per domain	N/A	1,000
Maximum volumes per standalone root	6,000	10,000
Maximum root replica members	N/A	32
Maximum child replica members	255	256
Maximum characters in pathname	260	260

CASE STUDY: ROBBEM, BLINDE, AND HOWE

ESSENCE OF THE CASE

The partners recognize that to compete, they must improve their leveraging of technology in several ways:

▶ The firm would like a more consistent computing environment so that all users can be familiar with all the computers.

▶ Legal assistants often use several legal research Web sites on the Internet. They are currently using dialup Internet access, which is sometimes inadequate for document downloads. The firm requires fast, reliable, secure Internet access.

▶ The partners travel extensively and must be able to work on the office network remotely. The nature of their work requires a high level of security.

▶ All employees share files extensively. This is accomplished by sharing local drives. They would like to share information, mostly in document form, in a manner that is consistent from computer to computer.

▶ The office manager wants to reduce equipment and maintenance costs by reducing the number of printers in the office to two.

SCENARIO

Robbem, Blinde, and Howe, a law firm specializing in contract law, maintains an office in Philadelphia, PA. The office has a staff of 12, including legal assistants, secretaries, and an office manager. The firm currently uses a Lantastic peer-to-peer network with an assortment of PCs running everything from Windows for Workgroups to Windows 98. Printers are connected to computers and shared. Data files are shared between computers.

ANALYSIS

The Lantastic peer-to-peer network has to go. It was an adequate network 10 years ago, but it no longer can meet the firm's requirements. The current wire plant was recently upgraded CAT 5 twisted-pair, so a new concentrator is all that is required to move the single-segment network to 100MB Ethernet. The wire plant will then be adequate to support a Windows 2000 Server network environment.

The computing environment can be made more consistent by installing the same operating system on all computers. To do this, all the hardware must be evaluated and upgraded, as required, to support the selected client computer operating system, Windows 98.

continues

CASE STUDY: ROBBEM, BLINDE, AND HOWE

continued

DSL can provide the legal assistants with fast and reliable Internet access at a reasonable price. To meet security requirements, the Windows 2000 server can run Proxy Server. The server will have two network adapters installed. One adapter is connected to the office network concentrator, and the other is connected to the DSL router.

The DSL router has a static IP address provided by the ISP. This facilitates a VPN remote connection, which meets the partners' requirements for secure remote access to the office network. The ISP provides the VPN connection to the office network. Traveling partners can dial the ISP and establish a VPN connection that is then connected to the office network VPN.

Sharing files in an orderly fashion is accomplished with Dfs. Files located on the server and the Windows 98 client computers can be shared in a single Dfs structure. Because Windows 98 does not support directory and file-level security, permissions should be set at the share point.

A couple of laser printers with built-in network adapters round out the picture. The office manager worries only about maintaining two printers. The printers are high-speed and more than enough for this network.

It should be obvious that there is no onsite technology specialist in an office of this size, so the network is configured with TCP/IP and DHCP for address assignment. A DNS server is not required on this single-segment network. DNS for Internet browsing is provided by the ISP. Name server information is configured in the TCP/IP settings for the server adapter card attached to the DSL router.

CHAPTER SUMMARY

KEY TERMS

- Ethernet, FDDI, ATM
- IP subnetting
- IP address enumeration
- routing protocols
- route tables
- DHCP, secure DHCP
- DNS, DDNS

This chapter covered the core services and technologies that are used to plan a network infrastructure.

Knowledge of network topologies is necessary to plan an efficient and reliable network infrastructure. Topology is the driving force behind many network design decisions. Understanding the relative strengths and weaknesses of different network topologies enhances your ability to make good design decisions. The Microsoft exam will require you to make design decisions based on network topologies, or make design decisions where the network topology is an influencing factor. To meet the exam objective for planning a network topology, you must know the network topologies discussed in this chapter, their associated hardware protocols, and how they are best used.

CHAPTER SUMMARY

KEY TERMS

- WINS lookup
- zone transfer
- IPX/SPX, SNA
- gateways
- Dfs root
- inter-Dfs link

The world uses TCP/IP. IT professionals in any capacity must have working knowledge of TCP/IP, including addressing, subnetting, classes, and core protocols. The Microsoft exam will have more than a few TCP/IP problems to solve. You should be prepared to enumerate networks and hosts for a given IP address and subnet mask. You should be able to read an IP routing table and determine the destination(s) of specified IP addresses sent to that router. You should be able to choose the best subnet mask for a routed network. You should be able to choose the best routing protocol for a specified network. The IP section of the Microsoft exam is rigorous.

Name services are an indispensable component of networks today. Not only do users rely on name services to browse the networks, but applications and utilities depend on a reliable way to find network hosts. The exam objectives for planning a name service cover DNS, Dynamic DNS (DDNS), and WINS. To meet the exam objectives, you should be able to design a name service implementation for a new network, for an existing network that uses DNS, and for an existing network that uses WINS. You are expected to know how to optimize the location for the DNS server, delegation of zones, integration of DNS into Active Directory, integration of DNS with DHCP and WINS, and zone transfers. You can expect to be asked about name service security and fault tolerance.

A TCP/IP network of any substantial size must use DHCP for host address assignment.

Many networks support legacy hosts that require network protocol(s) other than TCP/IP. Windows 2000 Server supports a number of network protocols to facilitate interoperability with these legacy systems. Simply running an additional protocol does not usually provide interoperability. Microsoft supports a number of tools that work with the foreign protocols to communicate with foreign hosts. In the case of UNIX, there is no foreign protocol. TCP/IP is the native network protocol for UNIX; however, communication with Windows client computers and servers requires gateway and client computer tools. To meet the exam objectives for planning multiprotocol networks, you must know the interoperability tools available from Microsoft, what tasks they perform, and when to use them.

CHAPTER SUMMARY

Dfs is a relatively new technology, specific to newer Microsoft networks. After you have implemented Dfs on a network with more than one file server, you will wonder how you managed data access and distribution before Dfs. In this chapter, Dfs technology and terms were covered in detail. The next logical step is to use that knowledge to plan reliable, efficient, and secure Dfs volumes. The Microsoft exam will ask you to choose the best Dfs configuration for a scenario. To meet the exam objectives for planning Dfs implementations, you must know the best practices for spanning different types of volumes, implementing fault tolerance, planning Dfs security, planning for high availability, and integrating Dfs into Active Directory.

This chapter covered a lot of technical details. This information should be viewed as tools to meet the stated exam objectives. Microsoft exams emphasize scenario-based problem solving. You will probably be asked to determine the best location for a DNS server rather than asked to define the format of a DNS resource record. The following "Apply Your Knowledge" section draws on the technical knowledge presented in this chapter. To answer the questions correctly, you must use your technical knowledge to choose the best configurations and designs for a scenario.

APPLY YOUR KNOWLEDGE

Exercises

3.1 Specifying Name Search Suffixes for TCP/IP

Exercise 3.1 helps you understand the process of ambiguous name resolution discussed in the section "DNS Database Queries and Name Resolution." Name search suffixes are used when a client computer is attempting to resolve a partial IP hostname.

Estimated Time: 10 minutes

1. From Control Panel, open the Network and Dialup Connections icon. A window listing active network connection types appears.

2. Double-click the Local Area Connection icon. The Local Area Connection Status dialog box appears.

3. Click the Properties button to bring up the Local Area Connection Properties dialog box.

4. Select Internet Protocol (TCP/IP) from the components list; click the Properties button.

5. Click the Advanced button in the Internet Protocols (TCP/IP) dialog box. The Advanced TCP/IP Settings dialog box appears.

6. Choose the DNS tab from the Advanced TCP/IP Settings dialog box. You are now ready to specify suffixes for name searches.

7. Click on the Append these DNS suffixes (in order) radio button.

8. Click the Add button below the suffix list window. You are prompted to enter a suffix.

9. Enter edu and then click the Add button. The suffix edu is added to the DNS search suffix list and is displayed at the bottom of the suffix list.

10. Repeat steps 8 and 9 for the following suffixes:

    net

    org

    ca

    uk

    mil

11. Close all the dialog boxes back to the Local Area Connection Status dialog box by clicking OK. Click Close in the Local Area Connection Status dialog box.

12. Close the Network and Dialup Connections Window.

Now when the DNS server is queried for a host address and given a hostname with no suffix, the server will attempt first to append its own hostname suffix to the search name and then each of the suffixes configured in this exercise in the order listed in the Advanced TCP/IP Settings dialog box.

> **NOTE**
>
> **Rebooting Windows 2000 Server** You may have noticed that you were not required to reboot the Windows 2000 Server computer after making these changes to DNS. One of the real improvements in Windows 2000 is the reduced number of conditions under which the computer can be rebooted.

APPLY YOUR KNOWLEDGE

3.2 Creating a Dfs Root on a Windows 2000 Computer

Exercise 3.2 demonstrates creating a Dfs root in Active Directory. Active Directory Dfs volumes are preferred because of ease of replication and maintenance.

Estimated Time: 10 minutes

1. Log on to the Windows 2000 computer as Administrator.

2. Start the Distributed file system management tool by choosing Programs, Administrative Tools, Distribute File System from the Start menu.

3. From the Action menu, choose New Dfs Root. The New Dfs Root Wizard starts.

4. Click Next at the Wizard's greeting screen. You are prompted to select a Dfs root type, Domain or Standalone.

5. Click the Create a Domain Dfs Root, and then click Next. You are prompted to specify the domain name for the Dfs root with a list.

6. Select the appropriate domain name, and then click Next. You are prompted to specify the computer for the Dfs root.

7. Type in the name of the computer, or select the computer name using the Browse button, and then click Next. You are prompted for the name of the share to be assigned to the Dfs root.

8. Either specify an existing share, or create a new share by specifying a new share name, and then click Next. You are asked to specify a name for the Dfs root.

9. Enter the name for the new Dfs root or accept the default name, and then click Next.

10. Click Finish. You must restart the computer to start the new Dfs root.

After the Dfs root is created, you can use the same Dfs administration tool to add links to and remove links from the Dfs volume. Remember that other than setting an overall security policy for Dfs by selecting Administrative Tools, Domain Policies, access permissions for Dfs volumes are not managed by Dfs. Each resource share that is included in a Dfs volume must employ its own security.

3.3 Configuring DHCP for a Remote Access Computer Class

This exercise demonstrates setting up DHCP so that it will handle DHCP configuration in a special fashion for remote access (dial-in) Windows 2000 Professional computers. Because remote access is usually short-term and intermittent, it is sometimes a good idea to identify remote access connections and have DHCP assign them an IP address with a short lease duration so that DHCP scopes are not depleted by frequent dialup connections. In this exercise, you define a DHCP user class named Remote and assign that class a 10-hour lease duration for IP addresses.

Estimated Time: 15 minutes

1. Open the DHCP administrative tool by choosing Programs, Administrative Tools, DHCP from the Start menu. The administrative explorer, or MMC snap-in, appears.

2. If the listing is not expanded, expand it by selecting the DHCP icon in the left pane and then typing an asterisk (*).

3. Right-click the target server and select Define User Classes from the pop-up menu. A DHCP User Classes dialog box appears.

APPLY YOUR KNOWLEDGE

4. Click the Add button to bring up the New Class Dialog box. Enter the information into the box as follows:

    Display Name: REMOTE

    Description: Remote access computers

    ASCII ID: REMOTE

5. Click OK to return to the DHCP User Classes dialog box.

6. Click Close to return to the DHCP administrative tool.

7. Locate the scope you wish to modify, and then select the Scope Options icon.

8. From the Action menu, choose Configure Options. The Scope Options dialog box appears.

9. Choose the Advanced tab in the Scope Options dialog box, and then choose DHCP Standard Options from the Vendor Class drop-down menu and Remote from the User Class drop-down menu.

10. Locate and check the 051 Lease item in the Available Options list. A text field appears.

11. Set the lease time for the Remote class to 10 hours by entering 36000 in the Long field (10 hours = 36000 seconds).

12. Click OK to return to the DHCP administrative tools.

Another way to deal with IP address assignment for dialup computers is to configure RAS to assign the addresses. The advantage of using DHCP with Windows 2000 networks is that the dialup computer can be registered with DDNS, enabling name-level access by other IP hosts.

3.4   Creating a WINS Static Mapping

WINS static mappings are used to register IP hosts that cannot register with WINS. This enables other computers that use WINS-only name resolution to communicate at the name level with the non-WINS host. In this exercise, you add such a static mapping. If you have a computer on your network that does not register with WINS, use its IP address; if not, be sure to use an IP address that you know is not being used by any host on the network.

Estimated time: 10 minutes

1. Open the WINS administration tool by choosing Programs, Administrative Tools, WINS from the Start menu.

2. If the WINS tree in the left pane is not expanded, select the WINS icon and type an asterisk (*).

3. Locate the WINS server you want to update, and then select the Active Registration item owned by that server.

4. From the Action menu, choose New Static Mapping. The New Static Mapping dialog box appears.

5. Fill out the fields in the New Static Mapping dialog box as follows:

    Computer Name: <name of target computer>

    NetBIOS Scope: <leave blank>

    Type: Unique

    IP address: <IP address of the target computer>

6. Click OK to add the static mapping to the WINS database and to return to the WINS administrative tool.

APPLY YOUR KNOWLEDGE

The computer is registered with WINS as three types: Workstation, File server, and Messenger. This enables WINS-only computers to connect to the target computer using a name rather than an IP address. To avoid confusion, it is a good idea to use the same computer name for both WINS and DNS.

3.5   Tracing an IP Route

Frequently, an administrator must track down a routing problem. One of the tools available with Windows 2000 computers (and most other IP-based operating systems) is TRACERT (TRACE Route). In this exercise, TRACERT is used to determine the path taken by an IP packet from a subnet to a given target. The target in this example is www.yahoo.com. If you do not have an Internet connection, use a target on another subnet within your network.

Estimated Time: 5 minutes

1. Open a command prompt window by choosing Programs, Accessories, Command Prompt from the Start menu.

2. At the C:> prompt, type tracert www.yahoo.com and press Enter.

3. The output from TRACERT should look something like the following:

```
Tracing route to www.yahoo.akadns.net
[204.71.200.75]
over a maximum of 30 hops:

1    140 ms    120 ms    120 ms    206.83.96.253
2    161 ms    130 ms    110 ms    166.93.83.254
3    160 ms    120 ms    120 ms    s10-1-
➥1.ar1.DEN1.gblx.net [206.57.12.121]
4    120 ms    120 ms    120 ms    pos4-0-
➥155M.cr1.DEN1.gblx.net [206.132.117.213]
5    140 ms    140 ms    141 ms    pos3-0-
➥622M.wr2.SFO1.gblx.net [206.132.110.113]
6    160 ms    150 ms    151 ms    pos0-0-
➥2488M.wr1.SFO1.gblx.net [206.132.110.73]
```

```
7    140 ms    141 ms    150 ms    so4-0-0-
➥2488M.wr1.SNV2.gblx.net [208.48.118.118]
8    140 ms    141 ms    140 ms    pos6-0-
➥2488M.cr1.SNV.gblx.net [208.50.169.62]
9    130 ms    141 ms    150 ms    ge0-0-
➥1000M.hr8.SNV.gblx.net [206.132.254.37]
10    151 ms    150 ms    150 ms    208.178.103.62
11    160 ms    151 ms    150 ms    www10.yahoo.com
➥[204.71.200.75]
```

```
Trace complete.
```

The output from TRACERT reports each router interface that the IP packet crossed to reach the target host. Additionally, elapsed "travel times" for each segment traversed are reported. The example here works; however, most administrators use TRACERT when a target host or network cannot be reached. This utility can provide you with a point of failure in such a situation, especially if the host connection had worked in the past.

3.6   Doing Something with Network Topology

In this exercise, you design a network topology based on user requirements for bandwidth, security, and fault tolerance.

Estimated Time: 25 minutes

To create an appropriate network topology design, user requirements must be known. These requirements are as follows:

▶ **Security.** Shared processing applications running on this network require at least three Windows 2000 servers in addition to at least two domain controllers. Inter-server communications must be as secure as possible in terms of the physical network structure. Workstation connections to the network need no special security.

APPLY YOUR KNOWLEDGE

▶ **Bandwidth.** Performance of the shared processing applications is critical. Workstations will be downloading large amounts of data during off-peak hours.

▶ **Fault tolerance.** Loss of network connections by workstations are tolerable for short periods of time; however, loss of connections between servers performing shared processor tasks would require a rollback and restart of these applications of up to 15 hours.

From the stated requirements, it is clear that server fault tolerance, inter-server bandwidth, and inter-server communications security are the design priorities for the network topology. It is also clear that the level of security, fault tolerance, and bandwidth for workstations is much more relaxed and, therefore, can be treated differently in terms of topology design. This design problem should be divided into a workstation topology joined to a server topology:

1. Consider the basic topologies you might use for a server backbone: shared-wire, ring, and switched. On a piece of graph paper, draw three columns headed by each of the basic topologies.

2. Under each column, list the advantages and disadvantages of each basic topology in terms of the stated requirements.

3. List the low-level protocols that can be used with each basic topology.

4. Choose the topology and low-level protocol that best meets the stated requirements.

5. Perform steps 1 through 4 for the workstation topology.

6. Draw a simple network diagram with one server backbone and three workstation physical subnets, including any necessary routers, switches, hubs, and so forth.

There is no one correct answer for this exercise; however, the two best choices for the server backbone are a ring-based or a switched network, because token-passing or switched networks are better performers than shared-wire networks at high network traffic levels.

One of the types of ring-based physical network protocols described in this chapter is fiber-optic–based FDDI. FDDI is a good choice when a high level of security is required. It is very difficult to covertly add a connection to a fiber-optic–based network, because the network ring must be "broken" to add a network interface card. Additionally, light signals do not emit any external energy while moving through the "wire" and cannot be sniffed by proximity listening devices. FDDI has a security advantage over switched, copper-based network topologies.

Recall that FDDI uses a concentric-ring topology and is intrinsically fault-tolerant. FDDI best meets the stated requirement for fault tolerance.

Although the entire network design might be FDDI, in the real world this would be quite impractical and very expensive. Fiber-optic cable is susceptible to damage from being bent or dropped—hardly the kind of data conduit you would want to run to users' desktop computers. It would also be possible to run ATM to the desktop; however, this is also rather expensive and difficult to support. In most scenarios, the best balance of performance, economy, and ease of support is probably a copper-based switched Ethernet topology.

APPLY YOUR KNOWLEDGE

Review Questions

1. What are some advantages and disadvantages of Ethernet and 16MB Token-Ring protocols?

2. What is the best application for FDDI?

3. On a routed network of four segments, what might be the best router configuration to enable IP routing?

4. Why should a domain controller not be used as a DHCP server?

5. When are DHCP superscopes a useful tool?

6. What is the difference between a primary and secondary zone?

7. What performance trade-offs should be considered when configuring replication partners for WINS?

8. Under what circumstances might you install File and Print Services for NetWare on a Windows 2000 server?

9. What are the advantages of Active Directory–enabled Dfs over the standalone version?

10. What are the three recommended deployment models for SNA Server? When might you use each model?

Exam Questions

1. You manage the technical side of the enterprise network for your company. This enterprise network consists of two LANs connected by a T1 link. One of the LANs (LAN A) is serviced by a DHCP server cluster. The other LAN is rather small, so static IP addresses are used. Due to a recent merger, the user count on LAN B is expected to triple over the next three months. It is clear to you that static IP address administration for LAN B will soon become impractical, so you must implement DHCP on LAN B. Figure 3.14 depicts the two LANS connected using a T1 WAN connection with TCP/IP. The DHCP server cluster is connected to LAN A. What must you do to create a distributed DHCP environment?

    A. Configure one of the servers in the DHCP cluster to service client computers connected to LAN B.

    B. Disable BOOTP relay on both WAN routers.

    C. Install and configure a DHCP cluster connected to LAN B and enable BOOTP relay on both WAN routers.

    D. Install and configure a DHCP cluster connected to LAN B and disable BOOTP relay on both WAN routers.

APPLY YOUR KNOWLEDGE

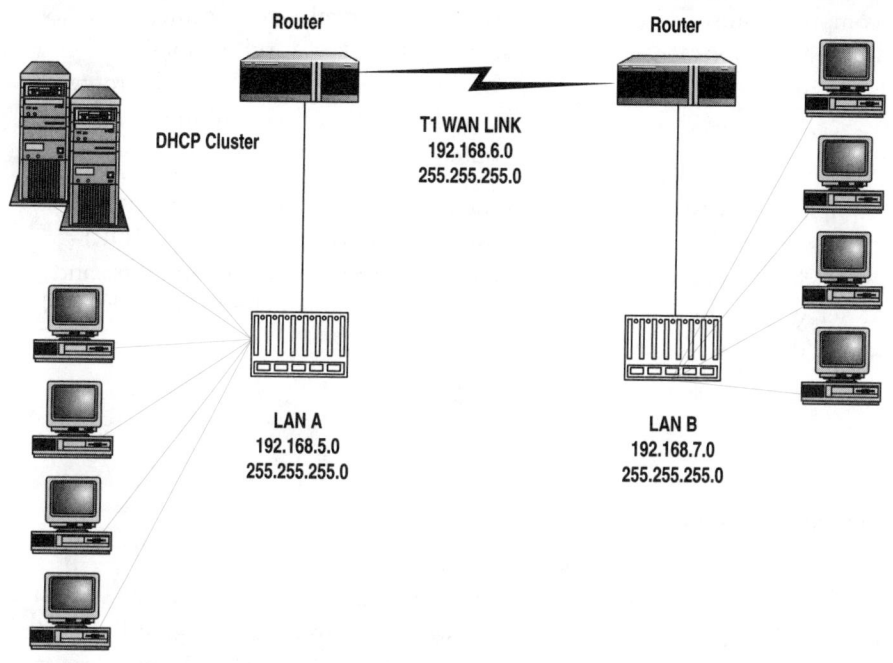

FIGURE 3.14
Although it is somewhat inefficient, DHCP servers can be configured to service remote networks.

2. Refer again to Figure 3.14. Assuming that the DHCP server cluster services both LAN A and LAN B, how can DHCP scopes be configured to avoid DHCPNAK messages for requesting client computers?

   A. Assign each logical DHCP server a unique scope for each LAN.

   B. Assign each logical DHCP server the same scopes for each LAN.

   C. Assign at least one server to service LAN A only and assign all other servers to service LAN B only.

   D. Assign at least one server to service LAN B only and assign all other servers to service LAN A.

   E. Configure both WAN routers to perform network address translation so that the DHCP server cluster recognizes the source of the request.

3. Assume that the network configuration depicted in Figure 3.14 is purely a Windows 2000 network. How must the RAS server be configured to facilitate DHCP assignment of IP addresses to dialup network client computers?

APPLY YOUR KNOWLEDGE

A. The dialup network client computers must be connected to a different subnet than LAN A. A new subnet scope must be created on at least one DHCP server on LAN A and assigned to the RAS server.

B. The dialup network client computers must get an IP address from the RAS server. A block of IP addresses must be excluded on the DHCP servers, and the RAS server must be configured to assign addresses to the client computers.

C. The RAS server must be configured as a DHCP client computer.

D. The RAS server must be configured to allow dialup network client computers to use DHCP to obtain an IP address.

E. The RAS server must be configured to use DHCP to obtain IP addresses on behalf of dialup network client computers.

4. The growth of the network described in question 1 is expected to increase the number of network hosts on LAN B to approximately 320. Given the stated IP addresses, subnet masks, and network topology described in Figure 3.14, what do you think would be the best way to increase the host capacity of LAN B?

   A. Change the subnet mask on LAN B to 255.255.128.0.

   B. Change the subnet mask on LAN B to 255.255.255.128.

   C. Add an additional logical segment to LAN B, such as 192.168.8.0, subnet mask 255.255.255.0, and configure LAN B as a multi-net LAN.

D. Add an additional logical segment to LAN B, such as 192.168.8.0, subnet mask 255.255.255.0, by adding another router or an additional interface card to the existing router.

5. Assume that the network shown in Figure 3.14 is Classless InterDomain Routing (CIDR)–compliant. Using the stated IP addresses and subnet masks, how many hosts can each LAN support?

   A. 1,024

   B. 256

   C. 254

   D. 255

6. You are planning the IP addressing scheme for a new network. The topology design calls for 30 subnets with a maximum of 125 workstations per subnet. Your company is assigned an official class B IP address block, 199.188.0.0 to 199.188.255.255. The company expects the network to grow by 30% each year over the next three years. What should you do to ensure that you do not run out of network addresses, have adequate room for hosts on each subnet, and do not waste address space?

   A. Use subnet mask 255.255.0.0.

   B. Use subnet mask 255.255.252.0.

   C. Use subnet mask 255.255.254.0.

   D. Use subnet mask 255.255.255.128.

APPLY YOUR KNOWLEDGE

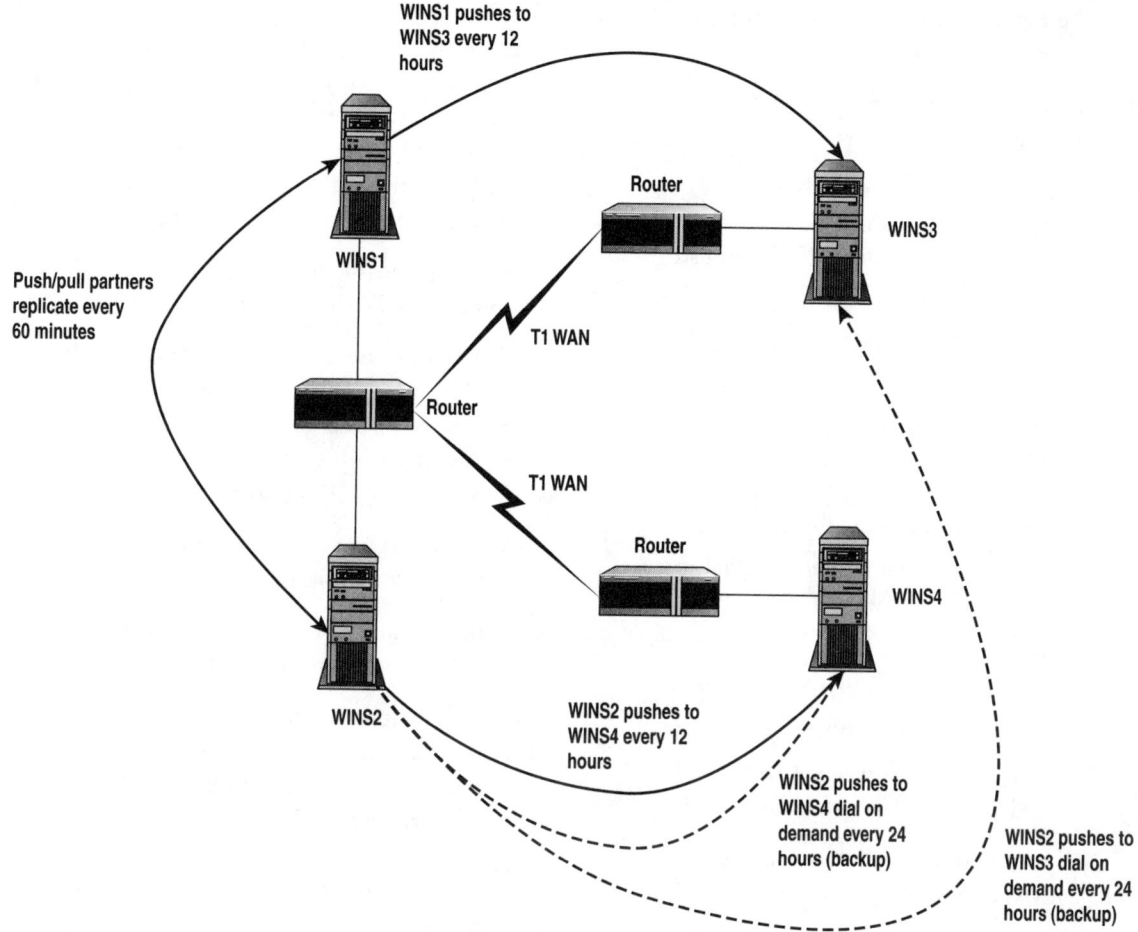

FIGURE 3.15
WINS replication partners located across a slow connection should be configured to replicate as infrequently as practical for the networking environment.

7. You administer the WINS servers for the network depicted in Figure 3.15. Several applications on the network depend on WINS to resolve dialup hostnames. Because these applications are also time-sensitive, they must be able to use WINS to contact all hosts on the network within two hours of completing their processing. How would you change the WINS configuration shown in Figure 3.15 to ensure that all WINS servers are synchronized at least every two hours?

APPLY YOUR KNOWLEDGE

A. Change the replication over T1 paths to push and pull every two hours.

B. Configure the dialup connections to update WINS3 and WINS4 two hours.

C. Configure WINS1 to push to WINS3 every 45 minutes, WINS2 to push to WINS4 every 45 minutes, and WINS1 and WINS2 to push and pull every half-hour.

D. Configure all WINS servers to push and pull every two hours.

8. Remote users in Figure 3.15 use only a primary WINS server (WINS3) in their TCP/IP configuration. What, if any, changes must be made to the network WINS configuration to allow the remote client computers to configure their dialup computers to use WINS1 as their secondary WINS server?

A. The replication interval between WINS3 and WINS1 must be reduced to one hour.

B. The replication interval between WINS4 and WINS2 must be reduced to one hour.

C. WINS4 must be configured as a replication partner with WINS 1.

D. Both WINS1 and WINS3 must be configured as both push and pull replication partners with WINS1.

E. No additional configuration is required.

9. You are the administrator for a small (200-user) Ethernet network. The network is a single-segment network with a standard IP addressing scheme. Host IP addresses are limited, so when your boss asks you to set up dialup network access for a sales crew of 10, you decide to use a different network ID for dialup client computers. You set up a domain controller Windows 2000 Server computer with a modem, and then configure RAS to assign IP addresses for dialup client computers using a different network ID. When you test the dialup procedure, you find that you can log on to the network; however, you cannot "see" the rest of the network. What did you forget to do?

A. You must enable routing in the RAS computer's TCP/IP configuration.

B. You cannot use a different network ID for RAS client computers than the network to which the RAS computer belongs. You must configure dialup client computers to use the network's DHCP services.

C. You must assign static IP addresses to the dialup client computers.

D. You must add the new network ID to the RAS computer's routing table.

10. You are the administrator for a network that uses DHCP extensively to service local clients. You also support a very busy Windows 2000 RAS computer, which uses DHCP for dialup client computers. While reviewing DHCP statistics, you notice that there are substantially more address leases taken than there are client computers on the network and that you are running dangerously short of available leases. You suspect that the excess leases were created by the RAS computer. What might you do to ensure that address leases are in adequate supply without incurring additional overhead and traffic?

A. Reconfigure the network as a multi-net IP network.

B. Reduce DHCP lease durations.

C. Increase DHCP lease durations.

D. Decrease DHCP lease durations for dialup client computers by using DHCP class IDs.

11. Your Windows 2000 network uses both DNS and WINS name services, as well as DHCP. You have noticed that the DNS servers are returning some incorrect replies to A record requests. A review of the Event Log for one of the DHCP servers indicates that Active Directory–enabled DHCP is failing to remove DNS entries for remote (dialup) client computers. Why might this be occurring, and what can be done to correct the problem?

 A. Configure the RAS computer to use DHCP to assign addresses to dialup client computers.

 B. Change the permissions on the DHCP server so that it can delete or modify DNS resource records.

 C. Change the permissions on the DNS server(s) so that the RAS computer can delete or change a DNS record.

 D. Change the permissions on the DNS server(s) so that the DHCP server(s) change(s) or delete(s) DNS resource records.

12. You are integrating the first Windows 2000 server into a TCP/IP network using six Windows NT 4.0 DNS servers in two zones. What must you do to integrate Active Directory–enabled DNS into this network?

 A. Windows 2000 DNS must be configured to emulate BSD 4.2.2 DNS until all Windows NT DNS servers are replaced.

 B. You must configure all Windows NT DNS servers as master servers, and then replace them with Windows 2000 DNS servers as master servers.

 C. You must configure the Windows 2000 DNS server as a master server for one of the zones and all Windows NT DNS servers in that zone as secondary servers. As the Windows NT DNS servers are replaced, the Windows 2000 DNS servers are added to Active Directory as secondary servers. Perform the same procedure for the other zone.

 D. You must configure the Windows 2000 DNS server as a master server for one of the zones and all Windows NT DNS servers in that zone as secondary servers. As the Windows NT DNS servers are replaced, the Windows 2000 DNS servers are added to Active Directory as master servers. Perform the same procedure for the other zone.

13. What should you do to protect a resource record from removal by DNS scavenging?

 A. Set the NOSCAVENGE field value to 1 on the resource record.

 B. Place the resource record on a secondary server that is not scavenged.

 C. Set the REFRESH field in the record to 0.

 D. Set the resource record timestamp to 0.

14. You are planning a network migration from NetWare 5.*x* to Windows 2000. You need an interim tool to service the 350 NetWare client computers while performing the (preferably) seamless migration. What should you do?

APPLY YOUR KNOWLEDGE

A. Use Services for NetWare v.5.

B. Use File and Print Services for NetWare v.5.

C. Use File and Print Services for NetWare.

D. Use NetWare Client for Windows 2000.

15. You are a consultant developing a remote access solution for a client who wants to connect to an IBM mainframe SNA network from a remote office. The remote office has a 10-user Microsoft NT 4.0 LAN running NWLink protocol. Additionally, the branch office has an IBM control unit with five IBM 5270 terminals attached. The controller is connected to the mainframe's SNA network using a leased SDLC line. The client is committed to keeping the SDLC line for at least another year; however, she wants to get rid of the IBM terminals and control unit. This is a scenario made to order for a branch-based deployment model using SNA Server. You install a Windows 2000 computer running SNA Server, connect to the SDLC line, and connect to the remote LAN. What else must you do to allow users at the branch office to log on to the IBM mainframe from their LAN workstations?

A. Change the LAN protocol to TCP/IP.

B. Configure the SDLC line for PPP tunneling for SNA.

C. Configure the mainframe SNA network for TCP/IP.

D. Configure the mainframe SNA network for TCP/IP, and then change the LAN protocol to TCP/IP.

E. Install and configure 5270 terminal emulation software on all workstations that will be used to log on to the mainframe.

16. One of the users on the network that you administer is unable to access the Engineering directory in an Active Directory–enabled Dfs volume. What must you do to provide access for this user to the Engineering directory?

A. Change the permissions for that user by changing the ACL for the Engineering directory in Active Directory.

B. Change the permissions for that user by changing the permissions at the physical server or servers where the Engineering directory is located.

C. Use Dfs manager to grant access to the Engineering directory for the user.

D. Configure the user's client computer to use an alternate volume of the Engineering directory.

Answers to Review Questions

1. Because Ethernet is by far the most popular hardware protocol in use today, it has a real economic advantage, because the cost of its hardware is typically less than comparable Token-Ring products. For the same reason, the variety of products available is greater for Ethernet-compatible hardware and software. From the standpoint of pure performance, Ethernet tends to be a better performer at normal network traffic levels, and Token-Ring works best under a heavy traffic load. See the sections "Backbone-Based Networks" and "Ring Networks."

APPLY YOUR KNOWLEDGE

2. There are several reasons why FDDI is used. Low cost is not one of them, so FDDI implementations should be carefully considered. FDDI should be used where an added measure of fault tolerance is important, because FDDI uses a redundant ring configuration. FDDI should be used where security is a priority, because fiber communications are difficult to "tap." FDDI should be used on network segments with extremely high network traffic volume, because FDDI is a token-passing protocol that performs well under heavy loads. See the section "Ring Networks."

3. If a four-segment network is very stable—that is, it is not in growth mode and servers are statically addressed—the router should be configured with a static routing table. If the network is dynamic, RIP for IP should be used. A four-segment network is much too small for link-state routing protocols, such as OSPF. See the section "Planning TCP/IP Routed Networks."

4. Domain controllers should not be DHCP servers because of access to Active Directory. Domain controllers have access to all records in Active Directory; therefore, any DNS records created by DHCP and Netlogon are open to attack if the DNS Update Proxy group is used to create these records. See the section "Developing DHCP Strategies."

5. DHCP superscopes are useful for multi-net network segments. DHCP servers handling different TCP/IP networks on the same subnet will not send NACKs to requesting client computers when the requested IP address is not recognized. See the section "Understanding Highly Available DHCP Service."

6. Secondary zones are read-only copies of a primary zone. Any update requests are written to the primary zone and then replicated to the secondary zone via zone transfer. Note that all Active Directory–enabled DNS servers are master servers (primary zone); therefore, Active Directory replication manages zone synchronization. See the section "DNS Zones."

7. Performance planning for a WINS implementation means planning replication configuration, because replication affects traffic, convergence time, and connection overhead. To plan a WINS implementation, all these factors must be balanced using the following rules:

   • The shorter the replication intervals, the higher the network traffic.

   • The more replication partners, the higher the network traffic.

   • Convergence time is dependent upon number of replication partners, network topology, and replication intervals.

   • Windows 2000 WINS servers support persistent connections, which reduces network traffic.

   • Fault tolerance requires additional replication partners or alternate routes between WINS servers. See the section "Planning for WINS."

8. File and Print Services for NetWare should be installed on a Microsoft network when access to a NetWare 3.x or 4.x server is required and it is reasonable or necessary to have only Microsoft client computers. It might make more sense, for example, to use Client Computer Services for NetWare when only a few client computers must

APPLY YOUR KNOWLEDGE

access a NetWare server. File and Print Services might make more sense when a substantial number of client computers must access the NetWare server. See the sections "Client Computer Services for NetWare" and "File and Print Services for Netware v.5."

9. The primary advantage of Active Directory–enabled Dfs is that the Active Directory replication engine can be used to provide fault tolerance. Additionally, security can be managed at the Active Directory level for Directory Service–aware client computers. See the section "Dfs and Active Directory."

10. Microsoft recommends three deployment models for SNA Server: branch-based, central, and distributed. The branch-based model should be used when SNA Server is replacing terminal controllers at remote sites and the company wishes to retain the legacy SDLC leased lines. The central deployment model might be used when there are WAN connections to the remote sites and when the company prefers to keep SNA Server security and management at the central site. The distributed deployment model is used when there are WAN connections to the remote sites and the company wants to maximize performance and fault tolerance. See the section "SNA Service for Windows 2000."

Answers to Exam Questions

1. **D.** The purpose of a distributed DHCP environment is to provide local access to a DHCP service; therefore, at least one DHCP server must be installed and configured on LAN B. When BOOTP relay is enabled on both WAN routers,

DHCP requests are passed between sites; therefore, BOOTP relay should be disabled. With answer A, servicing DHCP clients on LAN B from LAN A would certainly work; however, that would not be a distributed DHCP configuration. Answer B is only partially correct because BOOTP should be disabled between LAN A and LAN B. The key to the correct answer on this question is that you are asked to create a distributed DHCP environment, which means at least one DHCP server services each LAN in the enterprise. See the section "Developing DHCP Strategies."

2. **A.** One reason that a DHCP server would return a DHCPNAK message to a requesting client computer is that the client computer is from an IP network that does not belong to any of its scopes. To avoid this, each DHCP server reachable by a particular subnet should have a scope for that network. Duplicate scopes cannot be assigned to different DHCP servers. Servers that are dedicated to a particular subnet are the reason a client computer may receive a DHCPNAK, so answers C and D are incorrect. Even if the routers in Figure 3.14 could perform network address translation, they could only translate to an address that was foreign to the DHCP server, or the client computer would never receive a response; therefore, answer D is incorrect. See the sections "The IETF DHCP Standard" and "Understanding Highly Available DHCP Service."

3. **E.** A RAS server can be configured to obtain IP addresses from DHCP on behalf of its client computers. Answer D is almost right, but the subtle difference is that the dialup client computer does not contact DHCP directly. Answer B is close, but such a configuration does not use DHCP as the question required. Whether the

APPLY YOUR KNOWLEDGE

RAS server is a DHCP client computer has no bearing on the question. Answer A might look okay, but the dialup network client computers can use the same scope as local DHCP client computers. See the section "Understanding the Windows 2000 Client Computer and DDNS."

4. **D.** Answer A will certainly work; however, you would be using network ID bits in a default class C IP address, which is not only confusing, but could cause problems with some network hosts. Answer B would reduce the number of available hosts on LAN B. Answer C would also work; however, it is not the best answer because of the additional maintenance, administration, and confusion such a configuration would cause. Often the most obvious answer is the best answer. Answer D is the *best* answer because it is simple to implement and is the simplest to manage of all the answers offered for this question. See the sections "Understanding IP Addressing and Subnetting" and "Planning TCP/IP Routed Networks."

5. **B.** The Classless InterDomain Routing standard allows the use of all 0s and all 1s for host IDs; therefore, the entire range of 0 to 255 can be used. See the section "Calculating the Number of Hosts and Networks."

6. **C.** The first thing you must do is determine how large the network will be in three years at 30% annual growth:

Year	Subnets	Hosts per Subnet
0	30	125
1	39	125
2	51	125
3	66	125

Now that the network size in three years is known, evaluate the answers offered:

Subnet Mask	Maximum Subnets	Maximum Hosts per Subnet
255.255.255.0	1	65,534
255.255.252.0	64	1,022
255.255.254.0	128	510
255.255.255.128	512	126

Answer A, the default class B mask, is wholly inadequate in terms of subnets available. Answers B and D will work, but they leave little room for error. Answer C is the best answer. See the section "Understanding IP Addressing and Subnetting."

7. **B.** The requirement for this question is to be able to configure a two-hour convergence time. To calculate convergence time, the longest update path is identified, and update intervals are aggregated. There are two such paths in Figure 3.15: WINS3-WINS1-WINS2-WINS4 and the reverse, WINS4-WINS2-WINS1-WINS3. Either way, the aggregated times add up to 25 hours. To meet the goal of a two-hour convergence time, these update paths must total two hours. See the section "Planning for WINS."

8. **D.** Any pair of WINS servers that are designated as primary and secondary WINS servers for at least one WINS client computer must be configured as both push and pull partners. See the section "How WINS Works."

9. **A.** The modem connected to the RAS server is no different than a network interface card as far as TCP/IP is concerned. You can log on to the RAS computer because it is a domain controller;

APPLY YOUR KNOWLEDGE

however, because routing is not enabled, you are not logically connected to the rest of the network. See the section "Planning TCP/IP Routed Networks."

10. **D.** Answer A would work; however, it would certainly increase network traffic and overhead. Increasing the lease duration for all DHCP leases would exacerbate the "dead lease" problem, and shortening the lease duration would add traffic and overhead. Class IDs enable the administrator to differentiate between client computers and assign them different DHCP scopes. Different scopes can be assigned different lease durations. See the section "Vendor-Specific and Class ID Options."

11. **C.** Dialup client computers are disconnecting from the network before logging off. Dialup client computers are responsible for registering with DNS and unregistering before they disconnect. In the event of an unexpected disconnection, the RAS server attempts to unregister or reregister the records. Upon failure, an error is written to the event log. See the section "DNS Aging and Scavenging."

12. **D.** The only way that Active Directory–enabled DNS can be integrated with downlevel DNS is by configuring the Active Directory–enabled server as a master server and all downlevel servers in the zone as secondary servers. One of the advantages of Active Directory–enabled DNS is that DNS is multimaster; all DNS servers are master servers. Windows 2000 DNS cannot be configured to emulate BSD 4.2.2 (or any other) DNS. See the section "DNS Zones."

13. **D.** Statically created resource records are automatically timestamped with 0; the Active Directory DNS manager enables the administrator to change the timestamp value of any resource record. See the section "DNS Aging and Scavenging."

14. **A.** Client Computer Services for NetWare v.5 offers NetWare emulation for NetWare client computers as well as migration tools. The key to this answer is that a migration is anticipated. See the section "Client Computer Services for NetWare."

15. **E.** On the LAN side of the gateway, SNA Server supports any protocol supported by Windows 2000. SDLC is a bit stream–oriented hardware protocol that connects the remote control unit with a mainframe site control unit. The mainframe site control unit connects to the SNA network. The LAN workstations must "look" like 5270 terminals to allow user logons. See the section "Branch-Based Deployment Model of SNA Server."

16. **B.** Access to Dfs volumes is based on the permissions applied to the physical data source. This includes share permissions and NTFS file and directory permissions. See the section "Distributed File System."

APPLY YOUR KNOWLEDGE

Suggested Readings and Resources

1. Berg, Glenn. *MCSE Training Guide: Networking Essentials, Second Edition.* New Riders Publishing, 1999.

2. Cone, Boggs, Perez. *Planning for Windows 2000.* New Riders Publishing, 2000.

3. Microsoft. *Architecture and Capacity Planning, White Paper.* Microsoft, 1999.

4. Microsoft. *Distributed file system: A Logical View of Physical Storage, White Paper.* Microsoft, 1999.

5. Microsoft. *Dynamic Host Configuration Protocol for Windows 2000, White Paper.* Microsoft, 1999.

6. Microsoft. *Introduction to TCP/IP.* Microsoft Press, 1998.

7. Microsoft. *Microsoft Windows 2000 Windows Internet Name Service (WINS) Overview, White Paper.* Microsoft, 2000.

8. Microsoft. *Windows 2000 DNS, White Paper.* Microsoft, 1999.

9. Microsoft. *Windows 2000 Server Deployment Planning Guide.* Microsoft Press, 2000.

10. Miller, Mark. *Troubleshooting TCP/IP.* M&T Publishing, 1992.

    • Chapter 1: Using TCP/IP and the Internet Protocols

    • Chapter 2: Supporting TCP/IP and the Internet Protocols

11. Scrimger, Rob, and Kelli Adam. *MCSE Training Guide: TCP/IP, Second Edition.* New Riders Publishing, 1998.

This chapter covers topics associated with designing for Internet and extranet connectivity. It helps you prepare for the exam by addressing the following exam objectives:

Design an Internet and extranet access solution. Components of the solution could include Proxy Server, firewall, routing and remote access, Network Address Translation (NAT), Connection Sharing, Web server, or mail server.

▶ Microsoft offers a number of technologies that help companies connect to and benefit from the Internet. Companies require a strategy to connect their networked infrastructure to the Internet to ensure that they utilize the technology in the most efficient way possible. After they are connected to the Internet, companies must make certain that their resources are secured and managed correctly. This objective is included to ensure that you are familiar with the technologies associated with Internet connectivity.

Design a load-balancing strategy.

▶ Many technologies used on the Internet are very heavily used and must be operational 24 hours a day, 7 days a week (7×24 availability). Due to the demanding environments in which these systems operate, Microsoft provides clustering services with the Windows 2000 Advanced Server and Datacenter Server products. This objective is included to ensure that you are familiar with how these services can be used to guarantee 7×24 availability for your critical business systems.

CHAPTER 4

Designing for Internet Connectivity

STUDY STRATEGIES

▶ Remember that the focus of this chapter is designing for Internet connectivity. The key word here is "designing." You will find that there are many ways to connect to the Internet and use much of the technology covered in this chapter. You need to understand these technologies so you can evaluate different designs. I suggest that you not get too caught up in the implementation details (that is, how to actually configure different options). Understanding the capabilities and limitations of technology is essential if you are to evaluate how it can meet—or not meet—business needs.

▶ The section on firewalls is meant as a very high-level overview of the terminology. I suggest you compare the general capabilities of firewalls against the capabilities of the Microsoft Proxy Server.

INTRODUCTION

The value of the Internet is clear to many businesses. To some companies, the Internet represents a huge new market to conquer. To other companies, the Internet represents an efficient medium for the transfer of information. The Internet gives companies (both big and small) equal access to millions of potential customers 7 days a week, 24 hours a day. Whatever your motivation, connecting to the Internet is a high priority for many companies. This chapter explores the technologies associated with connecting to the Internet. Specifically, we explore how to design for Internet connectivity and for high-availability applications.

The section on Internet connectivity focuses on the use of firewalls, Proxy Servers, Connection Sharing, and Network Address Translation (NAT). Coverage of the Microsoft Clustering Service specifically looks at the Network Load Balancing capabilities of Microsoft Windows 2000.

DESIGNING FOR INTERNET CONNECTIVITY

Design for the Internet an extranet access solution. Components of the solution could include Proxy Server, firewall, routing and remote access, Network Address Translation (NAT), Connection Sharing, Web server, or mail server.

Leveraging the benefits of the Internet requires that you have a through understanding of the technologies and services commonly used on the net. Your company should have fully evaluated its business needs to determine the services that it can use and how these services can be used to assist in its operations. When implemented, these services need to be connected to the Internet in a secure manner. This section explores how to design an Internet-connecting strategy for your company. Specifically, we look at firewalls/Proxy Servers (and their importance to your environment), Connection Sharing, and NAT.

Firewalls

Security is a very real concern when a company connects to the Internet. The Internet is a large and anonymous environment that can expose your company to a number of threats. When you are connected to the Internet, you must act to ensure that your data and computer systems are not accessible by unauthorized individuals. Generally, companies draw a line between their internal (private) systems and the Internet (public resources). This line is called the firewall. Through the effective use of firewall technologies, companies can limit their exposure to the external threats found in cyberspace.

A firewall is a combination of hardware and software that can be used to reduce the risk of unauthorized access to your network. Firewalls act as a control mechanism for inbound and outbound traffic between your private and public networks. Firewalls are used to control the flow of traffic in the following situations:

◆ Between a private network (an intranet) and a public network (the Internet)

◆ An intranet linked to an external intranet (an extranet)

◆ One department accessing the intranet of another department within an organization

Inbound traffic is defined as traffic that passes from the public network to the private network. In this case, access control rules can be defined to protect your internal resources from unauthorized access from the public network.

Outbound traffic is defined as traffic that passes from the private network to the public network. In this case, access control rules can be defined to restrict internal resources from accessing resources on the public network.

It is important that companies control the flow of traffic in both directions.

Before you can implement a firewall solution for your company, you must thoroughly understand your existing environment. Your corporation will also need to clearly define the goals and objectives of the firewall solution being implemented. Firewall technologies vary in complexity and price. Your expectations must be clear about what level of protection you are planning for your environment.

EXAM TIP

Firewall Technology The following section provides a very high-level overview of firewall technology. As you study the sections on Proxy Servers, Connecting Sharing, and NAT, always remember the high-level goal of implementing a firewall. It is also useful to remember the category of firewall technology associated with each service.

NOTE

Don't Underestimate Threats to Your Organization You must understand the potential threats to your environment if you are going to protect it. Many companies underestimate the potential threats from internal staff and external sources.

Generally, the more money you spend, the more secure your environment will be. During your planning process, you need to collect the following information:

◆ The protocols being used on your network

◆ The services being used on your network

◆ Where each service is located

◆ The location of users and services they access

◆ What is considered authorized and unauthorized traffic

You need to determine all the locations on your network where you have to control the flow of traffic. Some obvious locations for firewall technologies are

◆ The connection point between your private network and the Internet

◆ The connection point between your private network and networks of your business partners (an extranet scenario)

◆ The connection points between locations connected by slow wide area links (so that the flow of traffic can be controlled to optimize bandwidth utilization)

◆ The connection between departments within your office (for example, to separate the human resources department from research and development)

Having this information enables you to determine the resources (or potential security risks) on your network. It also enables you to map the traffic patterns that can be expected on your network.

After you have clearly defined the goals and objectives for your firewall solution, you need to start shopping for it. Common firewall technologies are

◆ Packet filtering routers (level 1 firewall)

◆ Circuit-level gateways (level 2 firewall)

◆ Application-level gateways (level 3 firewall)

A firewall can be a packet filtering router, a packet filtering router combined with a circuit-level gateway, or the combination of a packet filtering router, circuit-level gateway, and application gateway. Most often, an effective firewall solution includes a combination of the three technologies.

Table 4.1 provides a summary of each type of firewall technology and how it helps secure private networks.

TABLE 4.1

FIREWALL TECHNOLOGIES

Technology	Description
Packet filtering routers	Packet filtering routers (or screening routers) can restrict incoming and outgoing traffic to the intranet by filtering unauthorized source IP addresses and port numbers.
Circuit-level gateways	Circuit-level gateways (also called circuit-level proxies) implement access control at the Session layer of the OSI model. When intranet users need access to the public network, the request is sent to a known port on a gateway server. Software at the gateway validates a TCP/UDP session before opening a connection (or circuit). The gateway services the request and substitutes its IP address to that of the requester.
Application-level gateways	Application-level gateways (also called application proxies) are generally considered the most secure type of firewall. Access control occurs at the Application layer of the OSI model. Application gateways are implemented at the Presentation and Application layers.

Another useful way to evaluate each type of firewall technology is to look at it based on the OSI model. For more information on OSI, see *MCSE Training Guide: Network Essentials, Second Edition* by Glenn Berg (New Riders Publishing, 1998). The OSI model enables you to evaluate each technology to see where it has been implemented relative to the protocols used on your network. Generally, firewall technologies implemented in the upper layers (that is,

Application, Presentation, and Session) of the OSI model offer more security and flexibility than technologies implemented in the lower levels. This comes at a price, however, because technologies implemented in the upper layers generally have higher system overhead. Table 4.2 provides a summary of how firewall technologies map to the OSI model.

TABLE 4.2

FIREWALL TECHNOLOGIES AND THE OSI MODEL

OSI Model	Description of Layer	Firewall Technology		
		Level 1	Level 2	Level 3
Application	Includes all the processes and functions specific to each network service.			X
Presentation	Transforms data into a mutually agreed-upon format understood by each application and computer involved in the transmission.			X
Session	Controls the interactions that occur between applications. This includes connection establishment, data transfer, and connection release.		X	
Transport	Responsible for the reliable delivery of transmissions information between machines.			
Network	Responsible for moving information between multiple independent networks. This function is also called routing.	X		
Data Link	Organizes the Physical layer's bits into logical groups of information called frames. This layer also detects errors, controls the flow of data, and identifies computers on the network.			
Physical	Coordinates the rules for transmitting bits. This layer defines physical network structures, mechanical and electrical specifications for the transmission medium, and bit transmission encoding and timing rules.			

Common Implementations

The following section provides details on how firewall technologies could be commonly implemented. We explore the use of packet filtering routers, circuit-level gateways, and application gateways.

Packet Filtering Routers

Most firewall implementations include some form of packet filtering router. Packet filtering routers inspect all packets and compare them to a set of incoming and outgoing rules. If the rules restrict the packet from being forwarded, the packet will be rejected. If the rules allow the traffic to pass, the packet will be forwarded. Packet filtering routers operate at the Network layer of the OSI model. Rules can be defined based on the following criteria (that is, the data typically contained in the network header of the protocol stack being filtered):

- ◆ Packet type
- ◆ Source address
- ◆ Destination address
- ◆ Source port
- ◆ Destination port
- ◆ Router interface

Suppose your company has defined a need to block users from the Internet from accessing the FTP service running on a server located on your private network. The same server, however, also runs a Web site that needs to be accessible to the public. Figure 4.1 shows how a packet filtering router could be used to address this business need.

EXAM TIP

Definition of a Proxy   You should remember the definition of a proxy. A proxy is a service that acts as an intermediary between a workstation and another machine to ensure security and administrative control.

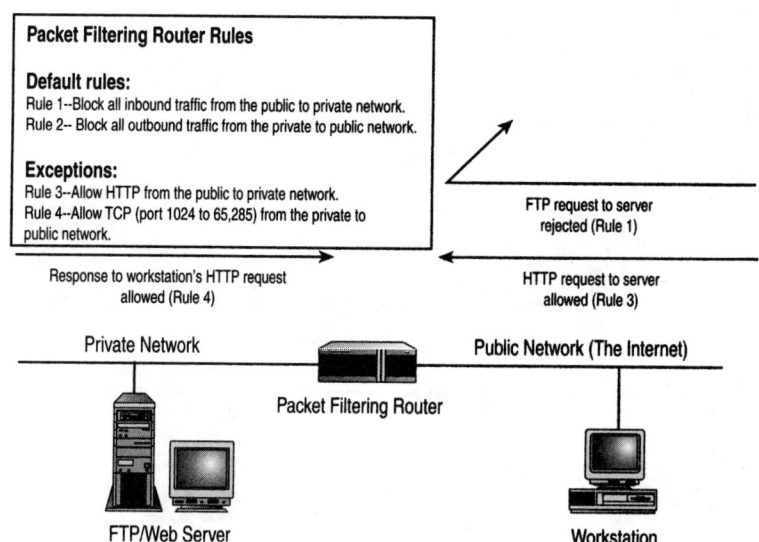

FIGURE 4.1
Common packet filtering router implementation.

Circuit-Level Gateway

Circuit-level gateways allow a user to access resources on the public network through a gateway. This allows users to access public resources without exposing their address information to the outside world. This technology also enables network administrators to apply rules about the type of request that can be passed through the gateway.

When intranet users need access to the public network, the request is sent to a known port on a gateway server. Software at the gateway validates a TCP/UDP session before opening a connection (or circuit) to the public resource being requested.

The gateway services the request and substitutes its IP address for that of the requester. Figure 4.2 shows an internal client accessing a resource on the public network through a circuit-level gateway.

FIGURE 4.2
Accessing public resources through a circuit-level gateway.

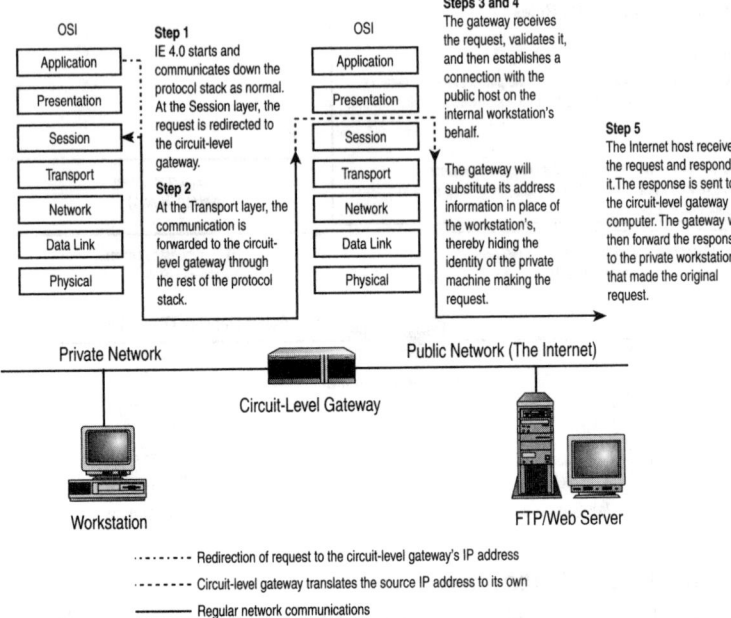

Proxy Versus Application-Level Gateway The terms *proxy server* and *application-level gateway* should be considered synonyms. Most manufacturers call their application-level gateways proxy servers. For the purposes of this text, both terms are used. Although repetitive, it helps drive home the fact that these are the same thing.

Application-Level Gateway (or Proxy)

Application-level gateways allow a user to configure applications to access public resources through a specialized gateway. This allows users to access public resources without exposing their address information to the outside world. This technology also enables network administrators to apply rules against the type of request that can be passed through the gateway. Figure 4.3 shows a user accessing a public Web server through an application-level gateway.

The Difference Between a Circuit and an Application Gateway

You should make sure you understand the difference between the circuit-level gateway and the application-level gateway. Closely examine Figures 4.2 and 4.3. On the surface, there does not appear to be much of a difference between the gateways. Technically, however, there is a great difference between the implementation of the two gateways.

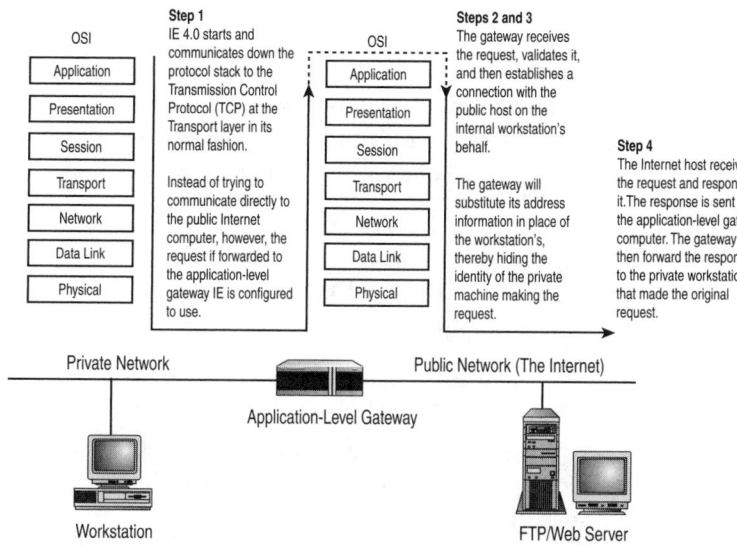

FIGURE 4.3
Accessing public resources through an
application-level gateway.

Circuit-level gateways operate at the Session layer of the OSI model. For this reason, you must configure the workstation so that its session-level protocols redirect their communications to the circuit-level gateway server for processing. With most circuit-level gateway implementations, this requires client software installed on the workstation. The software modifies the workstation's protocol stack so that it can perform this redirection.

Step by Step 4.1 demonstrates the process of installing the circuit-level gateway client for Microsoft's Proxy Server. This Step by Step assumes you have access to the Microsoft Proxy Server client software. This software is copied to your local hard drive when the Proxy Server is installed on a server.

STEP BY STEP

4.1 Installing the Microsoft Proxy Client (Circuit-Level Gateway Client)

1. Run Setup.exe from the Clients directory. You will see the MS Proxy Client installation Welcome screen (shown in Figure 4.4).

continues

> **N O T E**
>
> **Using MS Proxy Client** If you have not installed Microsoft Proxy Server on your system, you can simply copy the Clients directory from the MS Proxy installation CD to your local hard drive. You need to create an empty file called MSPLAT.TXT in the Clients directory before the installation will successfully run. This copy of MS Proxy client should be used only for the purposes of this Step by Step. The MSPLAT.TXT is usually generated during the installation of Microsoft Proxy Server.
>
> In a production environment, you will find that share is automatically created on the Proxy Server during installation (that is, \\proxyservername\mspclnt). Alternatively, you can install the proxy client using your browser by loading the following URL in your browser: http://proxyservername/msproxy.
>
> You must install the proxy client from this share, because the server keeps a series of files there for client use.

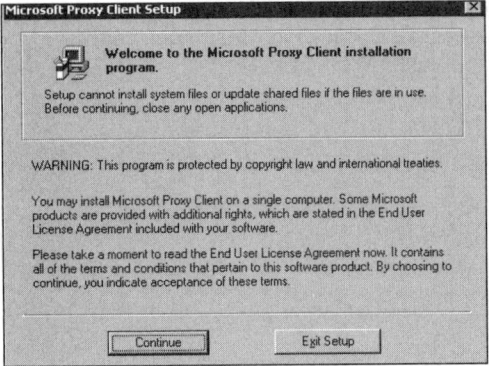

FIGURE 4.4
The Microsoft Proxy Client Setup Welcome screen.

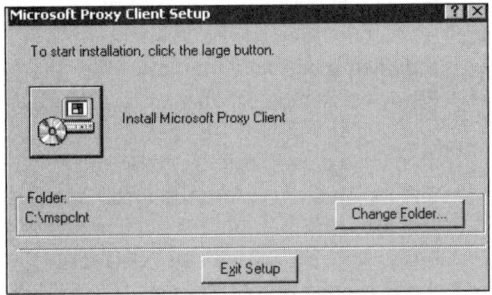

FIGURE 4.5
Microsoft Proxy Client folder configuration.

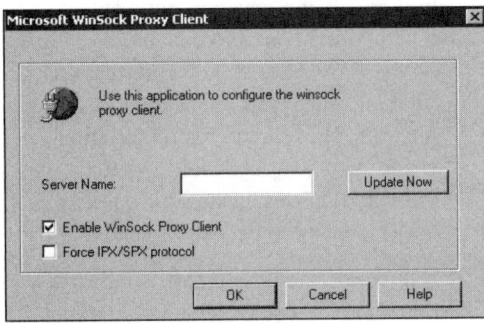

FIGURE 4.6
Winsock Proxy configuration.

continued

2. Setup searches for installed components. The installation program then prompts you for the installation folder for the client (as shown in Figure 4.5). Click the Install Microsoft Proxy Client button to start the installation.

3. A number of files are copied to your system, and you are informed that the installation is complete. At the Setup Complete dialog box, click OK. You are then prompted to reboot your computer.

4. When the computer reboots, double-click the WSP Client icon found in the Control Panel. As shown in Figure 4.6, you are prompted to configure the circuit-level gateway for this computer. (Microsoft calls its circuit-level gateway a Winsock Proxy.)

5. Uninstall the MS Proxy client from Add/Remove Programs, found in Control Panel.

Application-level gateways operate at the Application and Presentation levels of the OSI model. For this reason, you must configure specific applications to use the gateway. Generally, application-level gateways do not require the protocol stack on a workstation to be modified. The application is configured to communicate with the gateway.

Step by Step 4.2 demonstrates the process of configuring a Web browser to use an application-level proxy.

STEP BY STEP

4.2 Configuring Internet Explorer 5.0 to Use an Application Gateway

1. Start Internet Explorer. (Note: This Step by Step assumes you are running Internet Explorer 5.0.)

2. From the Tools menu, select Internet Options.

3. From the Connections Tab, choose the LAN Settings button and check the Use a Proxy Server box (as shown in Figure 4.7).

4. In the Address box, enter the address (either the IP address or DNS name) of your Proxy Server (application-level gateway). In the Port box, enter 80 (or the port where your proxy is configured to run). You have now configured your browser to use an application-level gateway (Proxy Server).

5. Uncheck the Access the Internet through a Proxy Server box, and exit Internet Explorer. This is optional depending on your environment. If you currently use a proxy in your environment, reconfigure your browser to use it. If you don't use a proxy in your environment, uncheck the box, or your browser will not function properly.

For additional information on firewall technologies, see http://www.icsa.net.

Microsoft Proxy Server

As previously discussed, connecting your network directly to the Internet is a risky business. Under Windows 2000, this risk is heightened (if the appropriate security configurations are not implemented) because Windows 2000 is specifically designed to interoperate with many different types of systems. Windows 2000 heavily uses Internet-based standard protocols, such as Domain Name System (DNS) and Lightweight Directory Access Protocol (LDAP) to accomplish this. Microsoft Proxy Server provides a number of services that can be used to assist in the management of your connection to the Internet.

The following section provides a brief overview of Microsoft Proxy Server's key features.

Isolating the Private Network from the Public Network

Microsoft Proxy Server acts as a control point between your private network and the public network. This control point enables you to isolate the private network from the public. By controlling the flow

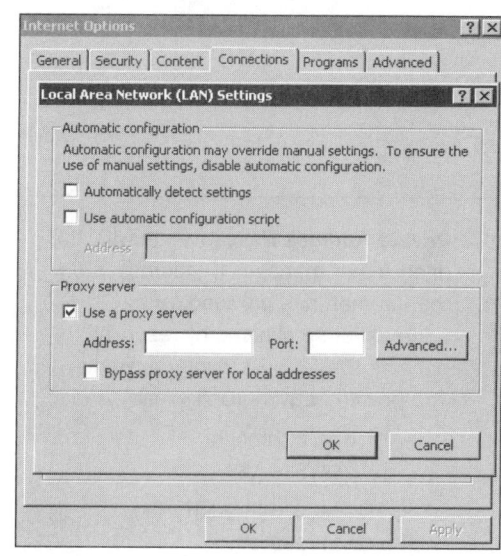

FIGURE 4.7
Internet Explorer application-level gateway configuration.

Private Address Ranges InterNIC, the agency that manages IP addresses on the Internet, has provided for an address reuse scheme by reserving network IDs for private internetworks. The private network IDs include

- 10.0.0.0 through 10.255.255.255
- 172.16.0.0 through 172.31.255.255
- 192.168.0.0 through 192.168.255.255

These address ranges can be used on your internal network and do not need to be registered (in fact, they cannot be registered). See RFC 1597, "Address Allocation for Private Internets," for details.

of traffic at this point, you can ensure your private environment is secure. The following sections provide an overview of Microsoft Proxy Server control mechanisms.

Private IP Addresses

If the IP addresses used in your private environment are never exposed to the public network, it is much more difficult to access your private systems. Any addressing information you allow to flow from your private network to the public network can be used against you. Microsoft Proxy Server enables you to use private IP addresses on your private workstations and server. Users then access public resources (on the Internet) through the Microsoft Proxy Server. Depending on the server used to access the external resource, your internal (private) IP address is never exposed to the public network. Instead, all traffic originating from the private network uses the Microsoft Proxy Server's public IP address. The Microsoft Proxy Server acts as an intermediary for internal users accessing public resources.

Access Control—Internet to Private Network Traffic

The Microsoft Proxy Server is used to block incoming traffic from accessing resources on your internal network. The Microsoft Proxy Server's public Network Interface Card (NIC) is the only public IP address that is used on the public network. For this reason, the public IP address of the Microsoft Proxy Server becomes the primary entry point (from the Internet to your private network) to your network. Because the Microsoft Proxy Server acts as the primary entry point to your network, you can configure rules that control the flow of traffic from the public to private network.

Access Control—Private Network to Internet Traffic

The Internet is a vast resource that contains many different types of information. Some of this information is considered inappropriate for corporate consumption. For this reason, many organizations are concerned about the resources their employees are accessing on the public network. The Microsoft Proxy Server allows access control rules to be defined that allow centralized administration of access to public resources. Rules can be defined that allow or deny access to specific URLs or protocols. Microsoft Proxy Server allows these rules to be applied to users and groups so that administrators can create specialized rules that apply to groups of users in their environments.

IP Packet Filtering

Microsoft Proxy Server is typically configured with two Network Interface Cards (NICs). One NIC connects to the public network, and one connects to the private network. Because no direct connection exists between the private network and the public network, the network adapters allow you to isolate traffic between the networks.

Microsoft Proxy Server examines each packet trying to pass to and from the Proxy Server. Each packet is evaluated based on packet filter criteria (also called packet filtering rules) before it is passed to the services and applications running on the Proxy Server. Based on the criteria, the request is either forwarded or dropped.

Caching Technology

Although the bandwidth available to connect businesses to the Internet is increasing at a phenomenal rate, most businesses want to ensure they get the most out of their Internet connections. To this end, Microsoft Proxy Server provides caching services. The theory behind caching is that a large portion of content on the Internet is static (that is, static text and image files). This content can be stored on local servers so that those requests are not forwarded across the Internet if content is available locally. The following lists the two primary benefits that corporations receive from caching technology:

- ◆ Bandwidth utilization to the Internet is lowered because redundant copies of information are stored locally and do not need to be downloaded.

- ◆ Copies of cached information are available to users from a source located on the Local Area Network (LAN). This can provide tremendous increases in service levels for users.

NOTE **Packet Filters and Routing** By default, when Microsoft Proxy Server is installed, IP packet forwarding is turned off. It should be noted that packet filters in the case of Microsoft Proxy Server are used to control the types of requests that can be passed to the proxy services. Although the Proxy Server looks as if it is acting as a router, it is acting as a gateway, because it will not route traffic from one network interface to the other directly. All requests must pass through one of the Proxy Services running on the server.

Microsoft Proxy Server provides caching services that support both Hypertext Transport Protocol (HTTP) and File Transfer Protocol (FTP) requests. The Proxy Server evaluates URL requests to determine whether a copy of the requested data is stored locally. The following lists the specifics of a proxy request received at the Proxy Server (Figure 4.8 displays the same process graphically):

1. The Proxy Server receives a URL request from an internal client.

2. The Proxy Server checks to see whether the requesting client is allowed to access the resource being requested. If the client is not allowed to make the request, the client receives an error message (that is, an access denied message) and ceases the process here.

   If the client is allowed, the Proxy Server checks to see whether the URL is currently in its cache.

3. If the URL is in the Proxy Server cache, the Proxy Server retrieves the information from its local cache and sends it to the client that made the request. If the URL is not in the Proxy Server cache, the Proxy Server forwards the request (on behalf of the client) to the URL on the Internet. The Internet site responds to the request and forward the requested URL to the Proxy Server. The Proxy Server places a copy of the URL in its cache and then forwards a copy to the client that made the original request.

Microsoft Proxy Server also provides a caching solution that can scale to very large environments. Microsoft Proxy Server supports proxy arrays. A proxy array is one or more proxy servers that act as a single cache source for client requests. Proxy server arrays provide fault tolerance and scalable performance benefits.

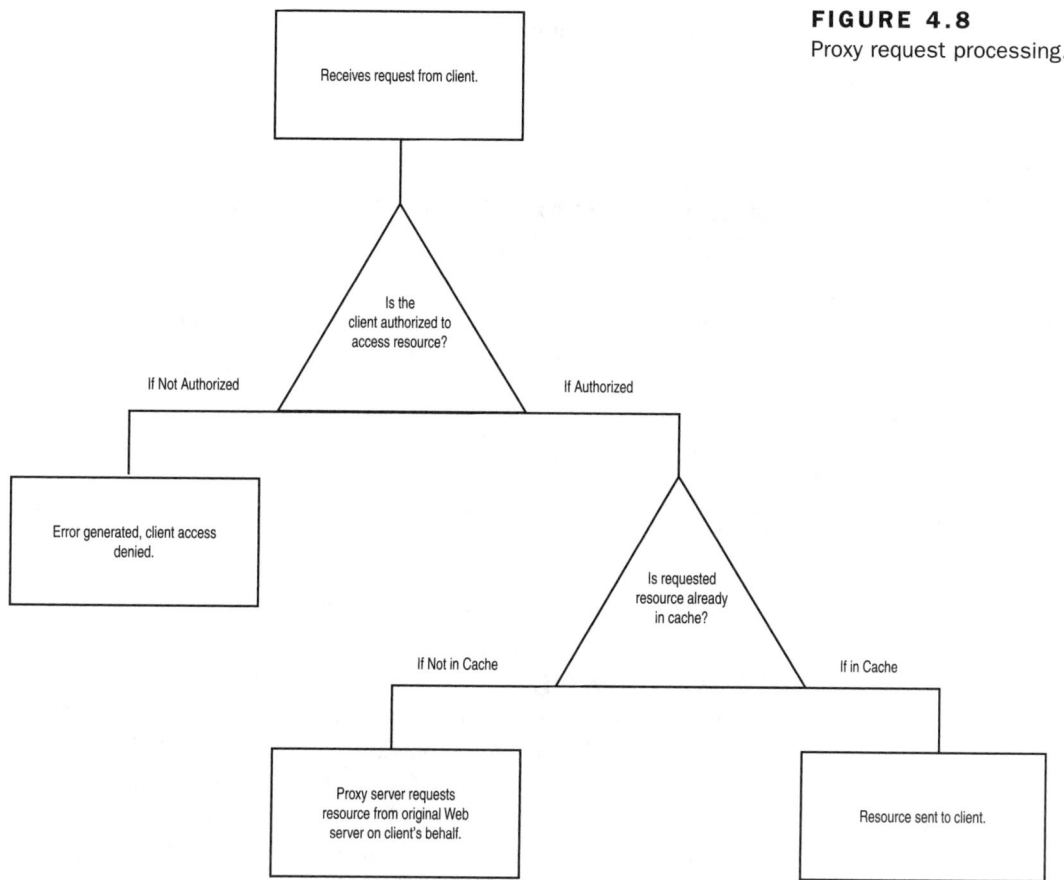

FIGURE 4.8
Proxy request processing.

Services Provided by Microsoft Proxy Server

As discussed previously, firewalls are generally made up of three primary components (packet filtering routers, circuit-level gateways, and application-level gateways). Microsoft Proxy Server is comprised of five services:

◆ Packet filtering router

◆ Web Proxy

◆ Winsock Proxy

◆ Socks Proxy

◆ Reverse Web Proxy

EXAM TIP

Remember the Role Each Service Plays in Your Firewall Solution
Each of the services Microsoft Proxy Server provides can be mapped to the generic firewall types previously discussed. Remember that each of the services provided by Microsoft Proxy Server provides one aspect of a firewall solution. You must understand the limitations of each component on its own so you can design a total solution with all the appropriate components working together.

Table 4.3 provides a listing of how these services map to the OSI model and the generic firewall components.

TABLE 4.3		
MICROSOFT PROXY SERVER PROXY SERVICES		
Service	*OSI*	*Generic Firewall Terminology*
Packet filtering router	Network	Packet filtering router
Web Proxy	Application/Presentation	Application-level gateway
Winsock Proxy	Session	Circuit-level gateway
Socks Proxy	Session	Circuit-level gateway
Reverse Web Proxy	Application/Presentation	Application-level gateway

The following sections detail each of these services.

Packet Filtering

Microsoft Proxy Server supports packet filtering. By default, packet filtering is disabled on Microsoft Proxy Server at installation. Your Proxy Server must have two NICs installed to support packet filters. When enabled, packet filters block all traffic to and from the external interface. A set of predefined filters is defined by default; these filters allow certain types of traffic to flow either to or from the Proxy Server's external interface. These exceptions are required to allow the Proxy Server services to operate.

Microsoft Proxy Server supports two packet filtering modes: dynamic and static. Under dynamic packet filtering, packets are automatically blocked from reaching services running on the Proxy Server, regardless of whether they are bound to the external interface. Ports are automatically opened and closed by the Web Proxy, Winsock Proxy, and Socks Proxy services. This minimizes the number of open ports and the length of time that a port is open.

You can also manually configure static packet filters. If you run applications that access the Internet on the same computer that is running Proxy Server, you need to configure static filters.

Web Proxy

The Web Proxy service supports Hypertext Transfer Protocol (HTTP and HTTPS), File Transfer Protocol (FTP), and Gopher communications from the private network to the public network. The Web Proxy acts as an intermediary for clients requesting resources on the public network.

The Web Proxy acts as an application-level gateway. The Web Proxy service also has the added benefit of providing caching services so that content that is accessed from the public network is stored on the Local Area Network for quick retrieval.

Winsock Proxy

The Winsock Proxy supports Windows Sockets client applications on Microsoft clients. The Winsock Proxy service is considered a circuit-level gateway.

The Winsock Proxy allows Windows-based clients running TCP/IP or IPX to access resources on the public network. As previously discussed, this is accomplished by running a Winsock Proxy Client on each computer. The Winsock Proxy client forces requests passed to the Session layer of the OSI model to be redirected to the Winsock Proxy Server. The request is then checked to ensure that the client is allowed to make it, and then the request is forwarded to the public network.

The Winsock Proxy also acts as a protocol gateway, because it supports IPX-based communications. The gateway allows clients configured with only IPX to forward their requests to the gateway using IPX. The gateway then converts the IPX request to a TCP/IP-based request and forwards it to the public network.

Socks Proxy

The Socks Proxy is a cross-platform mechanism that establishes secure communications between client and server computers. The Socks Proxy allows Windows-based and non–Windows-based clients to connect to resources on the public network.

NOTE
Reverse-Hosting   Reverse-hosting your Web site provides a limited number of benefits from a caching perspective. If your site contains a large amount of dynamic data, you may find that the performance of the site is decreased (that is, as the data is loaded into cache with each request). If your site primarily contains static information, you may find that reverse-hosting your site helps conserve bandwidth on your internal network (although this is usually not a huge concern, because the proxy and Web server typically have a 10MB or 100MB connection to one another).

Reverse Web Proxy

The Reverse Web Proxy Service allows internal Web servers to be accessed from the public network. If you have an internal Web server that needs to be accessible from the public network, you have a few options. Your first option is to move the Web server to the public side of your firewall. The problem with this is that the server is exposed to all the dangers of the Internet. The server is also difficult to update, because internal users need to pass through the firewall to get to the server. The second option is to keep the server on the private network and open a hole in the firewall to allow HTTP requests from the public network to access the Web server on the private network. The main problem with this scenario is that the Web server is still open to attack, and the holes in the firewall might be used against you by a hacker. The third option is to reverse-host your site. In this option, the Proxy Server is configured to act as an intermediary between users on the public network and the Web server on the private network. Users on the public network submit requests to the public interface of the Proxy Server, and the requests are forwarded on behalf of the user by the Proxy Server to the internal Web server. The reverse proxy process also benefits from caching technology, so content is cached at the access point to your network.

Controlling Access to Internet/Intranet Resources

One of the primary reasons to use Microsoft Proxy Server is to control network traffic between two or more networks. Microsoft Proxy Server provides a number of methods for controlling the flow of traffic between networks. The following sections define the access control methods available to each of the services provided by Microsoft Proxy Server. In general, you should be concerned with where the service should be used on your network and what level of access control it provides.

Packet Filters

The packet filtering capabilities of Microsoft Proxy Server should be used anywhere you need to control the flow of traffic between two networks. These locations include the connection points to the Internet, WAN connections, and some LAN connections.

The benefits of packet filtering at the connection point to the Internet are clear. Packet filtering enables you to block incoming traffic and control outgoing traffic. If you know what traffic needs to pass to and from the public and private networks, you can create explicit filters to allow that traffic to pass and block everything else.

Using packet filters at the connection points to your Wide Area Networks (WANs) is useful to optimize bandwidth utilization on your links. Depending on the protocols you use on your network, you may find that a large amount of WAN traffic consists of service advertisements and other background network traffic. Generally, you want to filter much of this traffic off your WAN links.

Packet filtering can also be useful within your LAN environment. If specific sections of your network must be secure (the human resources or research and development departments, for example), you can use packet filters to control the flow of traffic to those network segments.

The key to the effective use of packet filters is to fully understand the protocols and servers being used on your network. If you understand the traffic generated by these protocols and servers, you can control it. Many companies go through a process of thoroughly analyzing all network traffic. During this process, the flow of traffic is mapped for the entire network. These maps are then analyzed to determine what traffic is required and how it can be optimized. Packet filtering routers are then used to control the traffic. These routers can also be used to block traffic that does not correspond to the company's optimized network traffic design.

You also need to determine how much control you would like to exert over your environment. Packet filtering routes generally have to be configured with a default packet filtering rule. This rule states that either all traffic is blocked or all traffic is allowed. After the default is defined, exceptions are defined to allow or disallow traffic.

In high-security environments, the default rule blocks all traffic, and then "holes" are punched in the filters to allow specific types of traffic to pass. This type of configuration is critical between the connection point from your network to the Internet.

> **NOTE**
>
> **Firewalls Versus Proper Directory/Network Design** You should not use firewall technology to bypass proper directory design. It is more efficient and secure to design Windows 2000 Active Directory structures with the proper security policies than to add firewalls throughout your network.

In less-secure environments, the default rule is to allow all traffic, and then rules are defined to block specific unwanted traffic. This configuration is usually found at the connection points between LANs and WANs.

Step by Step 4.3 demonstrates how to configure a high-security configuration between a LAN and the Internet. This Step by Step assumes that you have installed Microsoft Proxy Server on a system with two network cards, as outlined in Exercise 4.1.

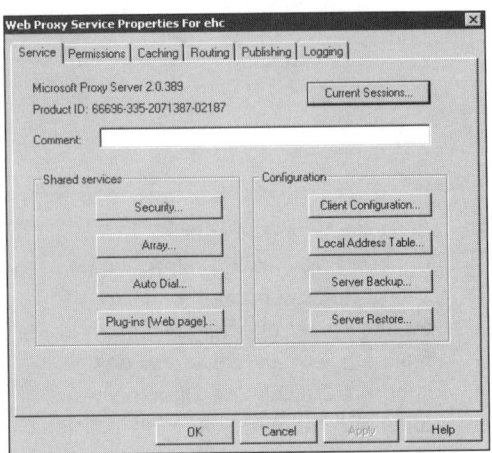

FIGURE 4.9
The Service configuration tab of a Microsoft Proxy Server service.

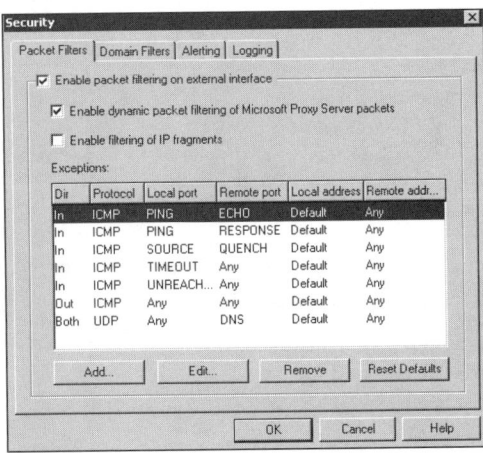

FIGURE 4.10
The Security configuration option, Packet Filters tab of Microsoft Proxy Server 2.0.

STEP BY STEP

4.3 Defining Packet Filters

1. From the Start, Programs, Microsoft Proxy Server menu, select Microsoft Management Console.

2. Packet filters are considered a shared service under Microsoft Proxy Server. You can access the packet filter configuration by right-clicking the Web Proxy, Winsock Proxy, or Socks Proxy service nodes in the MMC and selecting Properties. From the Service tab, click the Security button (as shown in Figure 4.9).

3. By clicking the Security button, you open the Security configuration page for Microsoft Proxy Server (shown in Figure 4.10). Configuration changes made on this tab affect the entire Microsoft Proxy Server.

4. To enable packet filtering, check the Enable Packet Filtering on External Interface option. This configures Microsoft Proxy Server so that no traffic will flow between the public and private interfaces on the Microsoft Proxy Server (except the packet types listed in the exceptions list).

You should note that packet filters are applied to the entire server. Filters cannot be configured so that they apply to only specific users. Packet filters have a relatively low system overhead (depending on the total number of rules being applied), but they have little flexibility when it comes to allowing or denying specific individuals from passing through the Microsoft Proxy Server.

Web Proxy

The Microsoft Proxy Server Web Proxy server is a service that can provide both security and speed. The Microsoft Proxy Server Web Proxy acts as an intermediary between clients on the private network and the public network. The Web Proxy also has the added benefit of providing caching servers. Because of the features built into the Web Proxy service, it is useful to place a Web Proxy at the connection points between networks where HTTP or FTP passes. This service is especially useful if slow links are involved.

The Web Proxy service gives network administrators the ability to restrict access to HTTP and FTP sites by name or IP address. The Web Proxy includes a permissions configuration that supports user-level access control (as shown in Figure 4.11).

Step by Step 4.4 demonstrates how to restrict a user named Mikayla from using FTP and grant access to HTTP so she can access the Web. This Step by Step assumes that you have installed Microsoft Proxy Server on a system with two network cards, as outlined in Exercise 4.1.

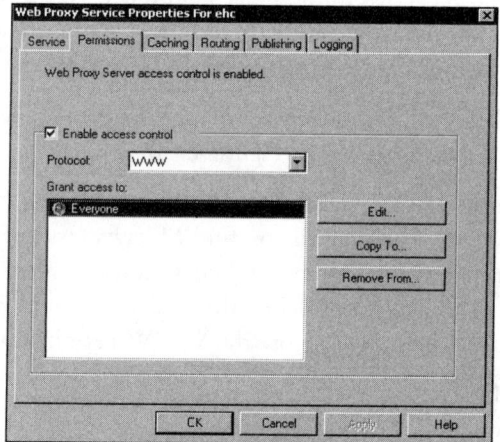

FIGURE 4.11
The Web Proxy Permissions tab.

NOTE   **Beware of Large FTP Transfers**   Be aware of large FTP transfers, because they may take up large portions of cache space. You can limit the size of cached objects. (This configuration option is found on the Advanced options button of the Cache configuration tab of the Web Proxy configuration.)

NOTE   **Time-Sensitive Date and Caching** You need to ensure that users are getting accurate information from the Web. Many Web sites contain dynamic data that changes often. If users are obtaining copies of these sites from cache, they may be getting out-of-date information. If you know users access sites that change often, you can configure Microsoft Proxy Server so it will not cache these sites. To access this configuration option, view the properties of the Web Proxy configuration, click the Advanced options button of the Cache configuration tab, and click the Cache Filters button.

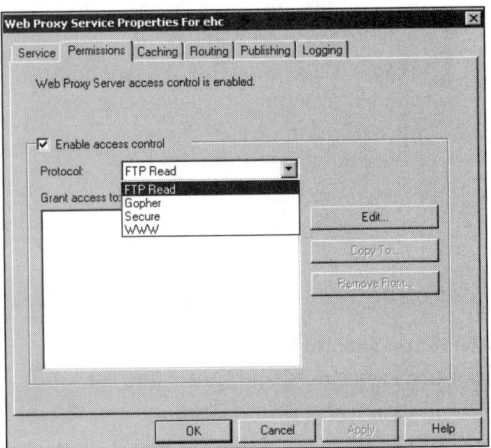

FIGURE 4.12
The Web Proxy protocol selection option.

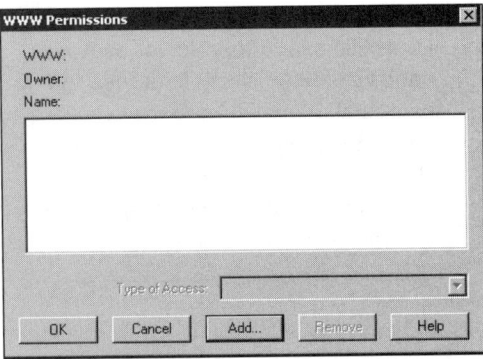

FIGURE 4.13
The WWW Permissions window.

STEP BY STEP

4.4 Restricting Access to External Web Sites

1. From the Start, Programs, Microsoft Proxy Server menu, select Microsoft Management Console.

2. Right-click the Web Proxy node and select Properties from the secondary menu.

3. Select the Permissions tab. Check the Enable Access Control box. If this box is checked, you must have access granted to your user account to use that protocol through the proxy.

4. We want to restrict Mikayla from using FTP. We can simply not grant access to the protocol through the Web Proxy (that is, do nothing).

5. We also want to give Mikayla the ability to use HTTP.

6. The first step in creating this configuration is to grant Mikayla access to the HTTP protocol. To do this, click the down arrow beside the Protocol configuration box (as shown in Figure 4.12). Select WWW from the list.

7. Click the Edit button to edit the list of users with access granted (as shown in Figure 4.13).

8. In the WWW Permissions list box, click Add. Scroll down the list of users until you find Mikayla (assuming this user exists on your system) and click Add (as shown in Figure 4.14). Click OK to close the Add Users and Groups window. Click OK to close the WWW Permissions window.

9. Mikayla is now granted access to HTTP through the Web Proxy (as shown in Figure 4.15).

For more information, see *MCSE: Implementing and Supporting Microsoft Proxy Server 2.0* by Kostya Ryvkin, David Houde, and Tim Hoffman (Prentice Hall, 1999).

Winsock Proxy

The Winsock proxy is generally placed between networks and used to help control the flow of traffic from network to network.

The Winsock Proxy server is useful in the following situations:

◆ You need to use a protocol not supported by the application proxy (that is, HTTP, HTTPS, FTP, or Gopher).

◆ Users are accessing the Internet when their workstations are not configured with TCP/IP.

◆ An administrator needs to control the protocols a user has access to.

Like the Web Proxy, the Winsock Proxy supports user-level access control. Figure 4.16 shows the Winsock Proxy Permissions tab.

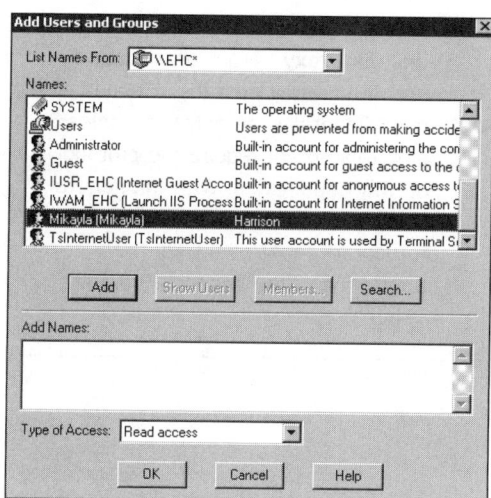

FIGURE 4.14
The Add Users and Groups window.

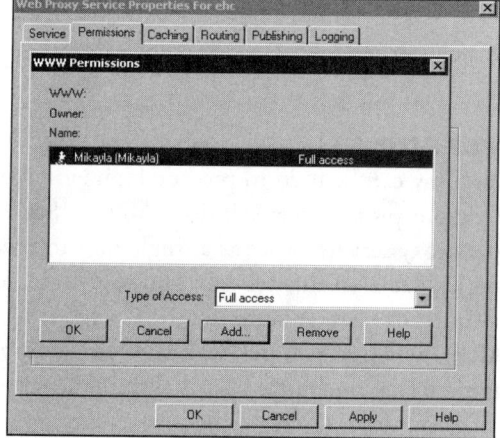

FIGURE 4.15
The final configuration.

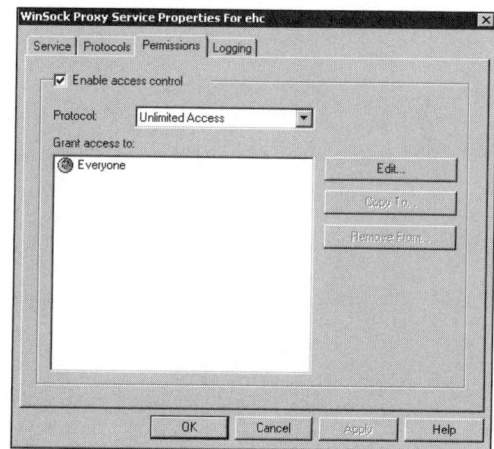

FIGURE 4.16
The Winsock Proxy Permissions tab.

NOTE

Winsock Proxy   Many organizations are moving away from the Winsock Proxy. Generally, the only companies using this server require the protocol gateway capabilities. With the general acceptance of TCP/IP as the standard protocol for most networks, the importance of the Winsock Proxy is diminishing.

Socks Proxy

The Socks Proxy server is very similar to the Winsock Proxy (that is, both services provide circuit-level gateway capabilities). The primary benefit is that the Socks Proxy does not require any additional client software to be installed on the workstations making the requests. To use the Socks Proxy, you must have Socks-compliant applications.

The Microsoft Proxy Server Socks Proxy service does not support user-level access control.

Proxy Server Availability

In the previous section, we reviewed the placement of Microsoft Proxy Servers in your environment. Microsoft Proxy Servers typically sit at critical junction points on your network. Businesses need to determine the level of "availability" they require for their Microsoft Proxy Servers. To enhance the availability of Microsoft Proxy Server, you should consider using one or more of the following technologies:

◆ Proxy Server arrays

◆ DNS round robin entries

◆ Windows clustering

Proxy Server Arrays

A Proxy Server array can be used to provide high availability and performance to your proxy server solution. A Proxy Server array allows multiple proxy servers to act as a single unit to ensure that a proxy is always available on the network and to help increase performance. Microsoft Proxy Server supports the Cache Array Routing Protocol (CARP), which distributes Web content across all proxy servers belonging to the same proxy array. Proxy client requests are sent to the array and then routed to the proxy server responsible for the requested Web content.

Proxy Server arrays provide the following benefits:

◆ Web content is cached across multiple servers so that no one server is responsible for all content.

◆ An immediate fail-over is provided if a proxy server within an array fails.

DNS Round Robin

If you have multiple Proxy Servers configured on your network and you would like to randomly assign clients to your servers, you should consider using DNS round robin. DNS allows you to create a single DNS entry in the database with multiple IP addresses. The first client to make a DNS request for your host record gets the first address in the database. The next client to request the same host gets the next IP address in the database. This process continues until the DNS reaches the last IP address in the database. At this point, the DNS server starts from the top of the list again.

The following is an example of how DNS round robin can ensure that users always have access to a proxy server. In the case of a proxy array, clients use a given member of the array to get into the array based on a DNS address. If that member of the array should fail, all clients using that member as their entry point into the array will get errors and be unable to contact the array. The DNS round robin features allow clients to connect to another member of the array. Clients using the member that failed need to close their browser and restart it. On browser restart, the client receives a new address for the proxy array (there is a chance the client will get the address of the failed server again).

Microsoft Windows Clustering

If your business goals require a proxy server design that provides the highest level of server availability, you should consider Microsoft Windows Clustering. Configuring your Proxy Servers on multiple servers belonging to the same cluster provides the following benefits:

◆ Proxy Servers share a common cache.

◆ MS Windows Clustering provides immediate fail-over if a proxy server fails.

◆ The restore process is faster because the cache does not need to be rebuilt (that is, it is not lost in case of server failure).

Proxy Server Performance

A Microsoft Proxy Server design must include an assessment of the performance issues. Microsoft Proxy Server, depending on the services used, requires specialized hardware and software configurations to perform at its best. Your design should reflect consideration of the following:

◆ Dedicated Proxy Server computers

◆ Proxy Server cache parameters

◆ Using arrays

◆ Proxy Server placement

Using Dedicated Hardware

Running Microsoft Proxy Server on a Windows 2000 server can cause performance problems. You should consider running Microsoft Proxy Server on a dedicated system to ensure that adequate resources are available to run the Microsoft Proxy Server services.

Proxy Server Cache Parameters

One of the primary benefits of using the Web Proxy service is its capability to cache Web content locally so internal users can access content without requesting it from the origin server on the public network. Depending on your environment, you may want to adjust the cache parameters for your server. As shown in Figure 4.17, Microsoft Proxy Server includes a number of settings that control how the server manages the cache.

The Web Proxy supports two methods of caching. Table 4.4 provides a summary of these methods.

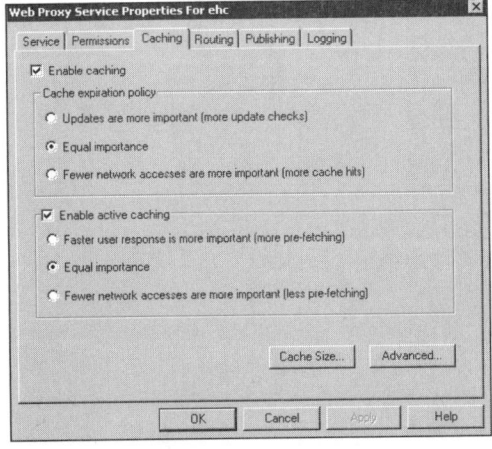

FIGURE 4.17
Microsoft Proxy Server cache configuration parameters.

TABLE 4.4

WEB PROXY CACHING METHODS

Method	Description
Passive	Uses the date and time of the most recent access to determine which content is to be overwritten first.
Active	Caches Web content based on URL and the number of requests that have been received for the content.

Passive caching requires that a user request an object to load the cache. Objects are placed in the cache, and a Time To Live (TTL) expiration value is associated with that object. During this TTL, all requests for the object are serviced from the cache without generating traffic back to the origin Web server. After the TTL has expired, client requests for the object must be forwarded to the origin Web server. The response from the Web server is stored in the cache, and a new TTL is calculated. If the Proxy Server is running low on cache space, the oldest objects in the cache are cleared out first.

Active caching is a more sophisticated method of ensuring that the cache is loaded with objects likely to be requested by clients. Active caching reduces Internet traffic by actively retrieving commonly used objects during periods of low system utilization. Active caching updates objects in the cache by having the server automatically generate requests for commonly accessed objects. Proxy Server optimizes the choice of objects for active caching based on the following:

◆ **Popularity.** Objects that are commonly accessed are likely to be re-requested during active caching. The assumption is that these commonly requested objects will continue to be requested often and therefore will be valuable objects in the cache.

◆ **TTL.** Objects with longer TTLs will be given higher priority by active caching (because objects with longer TTLs are more valuable to cache than those with shorter TTLs). The Proxy Server also checks objects that are close to expiration to see whether more current versions are available.

◆ **Server load.** During periods of low server utilization, the server will aggressively cache content.

Proxy Server Arrays

In very large environments with a large number of users accessing resources on the Web, you may want to consider a Web Proxy array. As previously discussed, a proxy array allows multiple proxy servers to act as a single unit. This allows requests to be spread across multiple servers so that no one server is overloaded with requests.

Proxy Server Placement

Proxy servers are typically placed close to a company's connection to the Internet. This helps optimize performance over the slower links to the Internet. You might also consider placing a Web Proxy in remote offices to optimize traffic over the WAN.

Proxy Server Management Strategy

After you complete your proxy server design, you need to document and implement it. You also need to include information regarding the maintenance of your Proxy Server(s). This should include event notifications and the verification of your proxy server design.

Event Notifications

One of the biggest security breaches found in many environments today is that staff members do not monitor the operations of their proxy servers. Each service provided by Microsoft Proxy Server provides a logging function that must be used to track the operation of the service. Windows 2000 also has the event logging process built into it so that operating system events are logged. You must ensure that these tools are used so that events are analyzed to determine whether potential problems exist. Table 4.5 presents some of the common events that should be included in your design.

TABLE 4.5

EVENT NOTIFICATION AREAS

Area	*Description*
High network utilization	High utilization on a public or private network link will reduce the performance of the proxy server. Network utilization can be tracked using Performance Monitor counters.
Failure of network links directly connected to Microsoft Proxy Server	If a link fails, you may need to act to fix the problem. In many situations, your staff may not be aware of any problem (if a redundant link, or back line, is available). For this reason, your design should include some form of monitoring and logging for your network links. You can use Performance Monitor, Event Viewer, or SNMP to assist with this logging.

Area	*Description*
Low cache hit ratio on for the Web Proxy Service	The cache hit ratio measures the number of client requests that were serviced from data in cache. Any request that cannot be serviced from cache requires a trip to the original server to retrieve the content. A low cache hit ratio indicates that caching is not being effective in your environment and, most likely, performance is poor. You can use Performance Monitor to track cache hits.
Saturation of a proxy server	Saturation of a proxy server occurs when it can no longer keep up the client requests. Generally, this may mean that the server does not have adequate resources to operate properly. Saturation may also occur because the number of client requests is too high. You can monitor this by using Performance Monitor to monitor the number of packets forwarded per second, or network utilization. If either value climbs significantly, you should take corrective action.
Failure of a proxy server	If a proxy server fails, you should have an automated notification process so staff can correct the problem.

Verifying Proxy Server Design

After you have implemented your proxy server design, you should test each component to ensure that it works. You should also test proxy server security to ensure that filters and other access control mechanisms are working correctly.

Routing and Remote Access

Routing and Remote Access Services provides multiprotocol routing support for Windows 2000. Through Routing and Remote Access, you can configure LAN-to-LAN, LAN-to-WAN, VPN, NAT routing services, and dialup/VPN services.

Routing and Remote Access Services are very important to companies connecting their networks to the Internet. Routing and Remote Access Services provide all the functionality required to fully support a multiprotocol environment. Many of these topics are covered in detail in the other chapters of this book. Routing and Remote Access Services also provides a Connection Sharing service. This service can be used to connect private networks to the Internet with minimal configuration. The following sections explore Connection Sharing in more detail.

Connection Sharing

Connection Sharing is the Microsoft Windows 2000 implementation of NAT (RFC 1631). The Connection Sharing service enables a company to set up a single machine to act as a shared access point to the Internet. Private clients route requests to the Connection Sharing server, and the server takes care of translating the private request into a request that can be passed onto the Internet. Connection Sharing is an excellent option for smaller organizations that need Internet connectivity. Microsoft also offers a fully configurable version of the NAT protocol for larger, more complex environments.

Connection Sharing has the following benefits for organizations:

◆ **Internet access for small networks.** You don't need to have a public IP address for every system in your office or a staff capable of managing them at each of your offices.

◆ **Conservation of a public IP address.** NAT allows multiple computers to share a single public IP address. This enables companies to conserve public IP addresses.

◆ **DHCP, DNS, and WINS services.** For smaller environments, the translation services provided by NAT include DHCP, DNS, and WINS configurations, so they do not have to be set up and configured separately.

◆ **Limited security.** NAT offers a limited form of firewall solution because it hides the internal address structure being used in your organization.

Microsoft Windows 2000 Routing and Remote Access servers support two versions of Connection Sharing: Connection Sharing and NAT. Connection Sharing and NAT are based on the same technology, but Connection Sharing is a simplified version. Connection Sharing is nearly an automatic configuration; NAT requires some configuration and planning.

Connection Sharing is made up of four primary components:

◆ **Translation component.** The Windows 2000 router on which NAT is enabled acts as a network address translator. This machine translates the IP addresses and TCP/UDP port numbers of packets that are forwarded between the private network and the Internet.

When the NAT server receives a request from the private network, it translates the private source IP address to its own public IP address. It also translates the private source TCP/UDP port number with one of its available port numbers. During this process, it builds a table of these translations so that it can reverse the process for return traffic.

◆ **Addressing component.** The NAT computer provides IP address configuration information to the other computers on the private network. The addressing component is a simplified DHCP server that allocates an IP address, a subnet mask, a default gateway, and the IP address of a DNS server. You must configure computers on the home network as DHCP clients in order to receive the IP configuration automatically.

◆ **Name-resolution component.** The NAT computer becomes the DNS server for the other computers on the private network. When name-resolution requests are received by the NAT computer, it forwards them to the Internet-based DNS server and returns responses to the private network computer.

◆ **NAT editor component.** Normal network address translation relies on the translation of the IP addresses in the IP header, the TCP port numbers in the TCP header, or the UDP port numbers in the UDP header. Translation beyond these three items requires additional processing from a component called a NAT editor. A NAT editor makes modifications to the IP packet beyond the translation of IP addresses and port numbers.

For example, File Transfer Protocol (FTP) stores the IP addresses in the FTP header for the FTP PORT command. If the NAT does not properly translate the IP address within the FTP header and adjust the data stream, connectivity problems may occur.

To develop a Connection Sharing strategy, you need to address the following issues:

◆ Installing Connection Sharing

◆ Installing NAT

◆ Configuring NAT

◆ Developing a notification and monitoring strategy

Installing Connection Sharing

Connection Sharing is a simplified version of NAT. Both Connection Sharing and NAT are based on the same technology. Connection Sharing is based on a set of simple defaults that simplify the setup and configuration process.

To install Connection Sharing, you must have a computer with two network interfaces installed in it. Typically, one interface is connected to the LAN and the other is connected to your Internet Service Provider. The LAN connection is referred to as the *private interface*. The ISP connection is referred to as the *public interface*. The public interface can be connected to a dialup networking connection to a direct connection.

Installing Connection Sharing uses the following defaults:

◆ The LAN connection used by Connection Sharing is configured to use an IP address of 169.254.0.1 and a subnet mask of 255.255.0.0.

◆ All clients on the private network will be configured to receive their IP configuration through DHCP. The range of addresses made available to them will be from 169.254.0.0 through 169.254.255.255.

◆ All clients on the private network will use the Connection Sharing computer for DNS name resolution.

Connection Sharing is enabled from the proprieties of the public interface. Step by Step 4.5 provides details about installing Connection Sharing.

NOTE

Connection Sharing Does Not Support WINS   Connection Sharing does not provide support for WINS name resolution. Clients on the private network are configured as mix-mode nodes. If you require WINS resolution, you need to manually configure it.

EXAM TIP

Remember the Shared Access Defaults   You should try to remember the default configurations for Connection Sharing implementations. This information is critical if you are presented with Connection Sharing troubleshooting questions.

STEP BY STEP

4.5 Installing Connection Sharing

  1. Right-click the My Network Places icon and select Properties from the secondary menu.

  2. Right-click the public interface of your computer and select Properties from the secondary menu.

  3. Select the Sharing tab.

  4. Check the Enable Internet Connection Sharing for this connection check box.

Installing NAT

NAT is implemented through the Routing and Remote Access Services (RRAS). Before you can enable NAT, you must install RRAS. During the Windows 2000 setup process, all the files necessary to install RRAS are copied to your hard disk. RRAS can be configured through the Installation Wizard.

Step by Step 4.6 demonstrates how to install NAT with the aid of the RRAS Installation Wizard. This Step by Step assumes you have a Windows 2000 server installed with two network interfaces.

STEP BY STEP

4.6 Installing NAT with the Assistance of the Wizard

  1. From the Start, Programs, Administrative Tools menu, select Routing and Remote Access. If this is the first time you have entered RRAS, a wizard will start. If you have already configured RRAS, jump to Step by Step 4.7, "Installing NAT Manually."

  2. From the Routing and Remote Access Server Setup Wizard, select the Internet connection server option (as shown in Figure 4.18). Click Next.

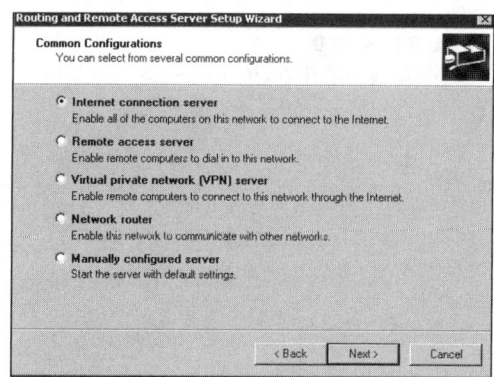

FIGURE 4.18
The Routing and Remote Access Server Setup Wizard Common Configurations window.

continues

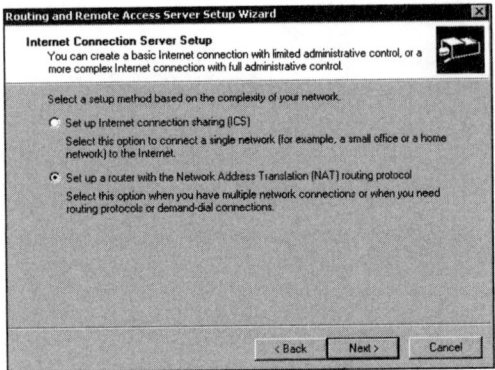

FIGURE 4.19
The Routing and Remote Access Server Setup
Wizard Internet Connection Server Setup window.

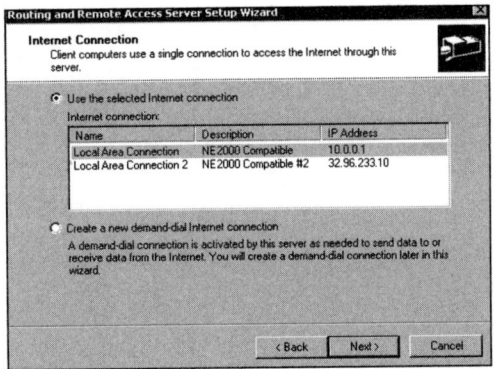

FIGURE 4.20
The Routing and Remote Access Server Setup
Wizard Internet Connection window.

continued

3. From the Internet Connection Server Setup window, select the Set up a router with Network Address Traslation (NAT) routing protocol option (as shown in Figure 4.19). If you select the Set Up Internet Connection Sharing option, you are informed you must configure that service from the properties of the public network interface. Click Next.

4. You are asked to select the public interface of your system (as shown in Figure 4.20). Select the public interface from the list and click Next.

5. The configuration of NAT is complete. Click Finish to continue.

Step by Step 4.7 demonstrates how to install NAT manually. This Step by Step assumes you have a Windows 2000 server installed with two network interfaces.

STEP BY STEP

4.7 Installing NAT Manually

1. From the Start, Programs, Administrative Tool menu, select Routing and Remote Access.

2. The RRAS MMC will launch (as shown in Figure 4.21).

3. To install NAT, click the plus sign (+) beside the IP Routing node in the scope pane (the pane on the left) of the MMC. Right-click the General node and select New Routing Protocol from the secondary menu. Select Network Address Translation (NAT) from the list of available protocols. Click OK to close the list.

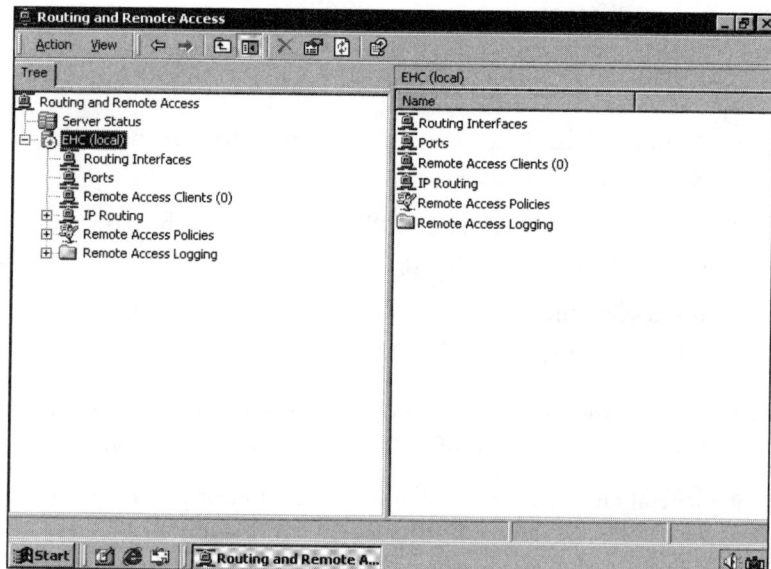

FIGURE 4.21
The RRAS MMC.

4. NAT is now installed on your system. This can be verified by looking in the list of supported routing protocols found under the IP Routing node (as shown in Figure 4.22).

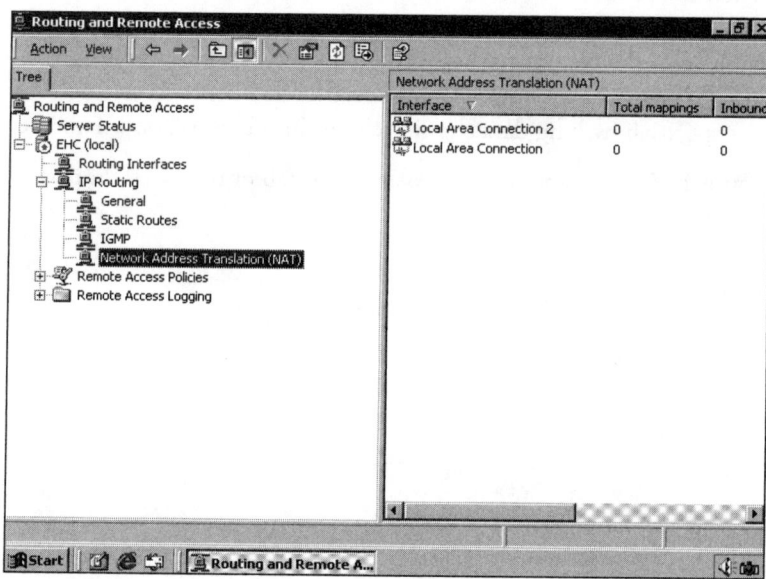

FIGURE 4.22
The RRAS MMC with NAT installed.

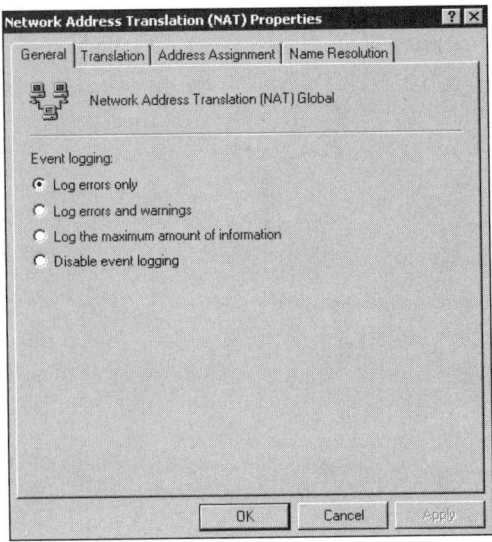

FIGURE 4.23
The NAT Properties General tab.

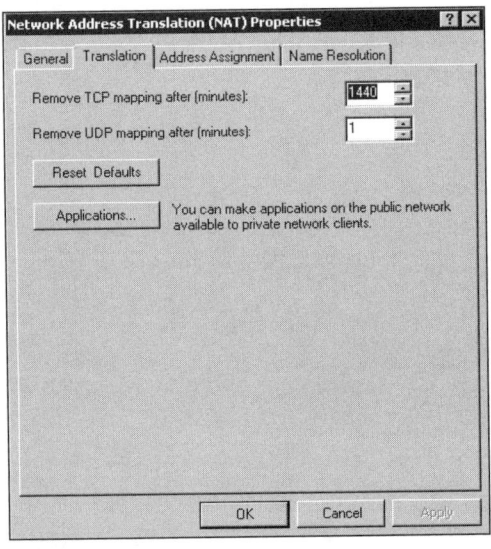

FIGURE 4.24
The NAT Properties Translation tab.

Configuring NAT

NAT can be configured from the RRAS MMC snap-in. You can view the NAT configuration options by completing the following steps:

1. From the Start, Programs, Administrative Tools menu, select Routing and Remote Access.

2. Click the + sign beside the IP Routing node in the scope pane of the MMC.

3. Right-click the Network Address Translation (NAT) node and select Properties from the secondary menu.

NAT configuration settings are broken into three categories. Figure 4.23 shows the General tab of the NAT Properties dialog box.

The General tab is used to configure the amount of detail logged to the Event Log. The default setting is Log Errors Only. This is adequate for most implementations. As the settings imply, other log settings collect more information about traffic being translated by the NAT server.

Figure 4.24 shows the Translation tab of the NAT Properties dialog box.

When the NAT server forwards packets, it translates the IP address and port values in the request. The translation data is stored in a database so that return packets can be mapped back to the original host that made the request. The Translation tab contains settings that specify how long data should remain in the translation database.

Figure 4.25 shows the Address Assignment tab of the NAT Properties dialog box.

The Address Assignment tab enables you to configure the NAT server to act as a DHCP server by setting a range of addresses.

Figure 4.26 shows the Name Resolution tab of the NAT Properties dialog box.

The Name Resolution tab enables you to choose how name resolution should be configured. Name resolution is the process of resolving a friendly (usually DNS) name into IP addresses. By enabling this option, you are telling the NAT server to forward name resolution requests to the public network. You can also check off the option to have the NAT server use a dialup interface to access the public DNS server.

After NAT is configured, you need to add the interfaces where you want NAT applied. Interfaces are added by right-clicking the Network Address Translation (NAT) node in the RRAS MMC and selecting New Interface from the secondary menu. You are presented with a list of interfaces. Select the interface you want to add and click OK.

When an interface is added, you can configure it by double-clicking it. Figure 4.27 shows the properties of a NAT interface. Table 4.6 provides details on the configuration options available on each tab.

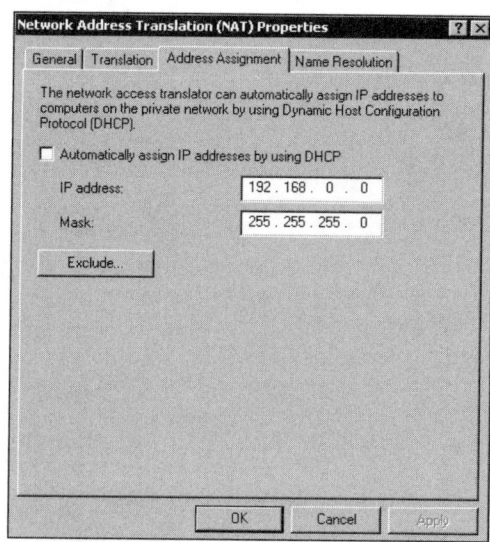

FIGURE 4.25
The NAT Properties Address Assignment tab.

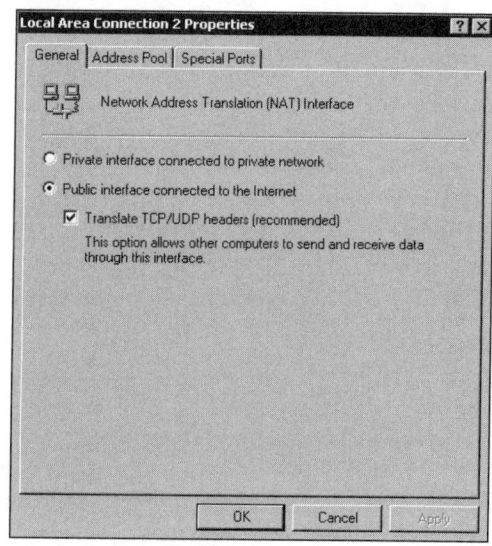

FIGURE 4.27
NAT interface properties.

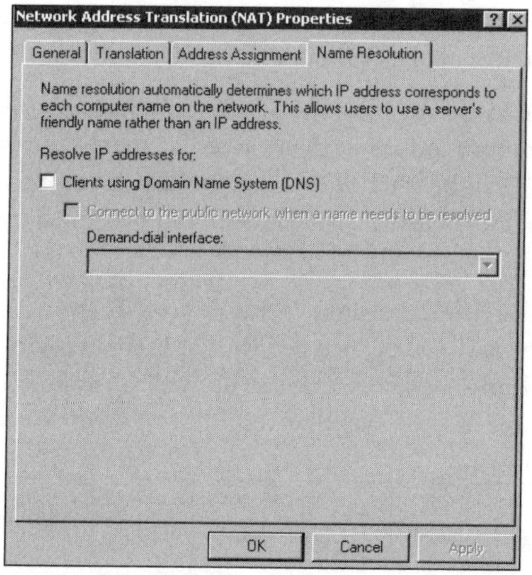

FIGURE 4.26
The NAT Properties Name Resolution tab.

TABLE 4.6	
NAT INTERFACE CONFIGURATION OPTIONS	
Configuration Tab	*Description*
General	You must specify whether an interface is public or private. Private interfaces are connected to the private network. Public interfaces are connected to your ISP. The public interface has translation enabled on it.
Address Pool	This tab enables you to specify multiple public IP addresses for use in translating private to public traffic.
Special Ports	This tab enables you to configure how you want traffic to be mapped from the public to the private network. For example, if you want to host an FTP server on your private network (accessible from the public network), you need to create a mapping from the public interface to the private address of the FTP server.

R E V I E W   B R E A K

The preceding sections presented the key technologies involved in connecting your internal network to the Internet. We defined the term *firewall* and described the role this technology plays in your connection strategy. Through the discussion on firewalls, we described the three primary types of firewall technology implemented: packet filtering routers, circuit-level gateways, and application-level gateways.

Microsoft Proxy Server is one implementation of firewall technology. In this section, we looked at the services it offers and explored how these services can be used to connect your internal network to the Internet. We also looked at the role NAT can play in your connectivity strategy.

The next section introduces the Network Load-Balancing service. Until this point, we have been concerned with only connectivity issues. Now it is time to explore a service that can be used to ensure scalability and reliability of the TCP/IP-based servers running on your network.

DESIGNING A LOAD-BALANCING STRATEGY

Design a load-balancing strategy.

Network Load Balancing is a clustering technology included with the Microsoft Windows 2000 Advanced Server and Datacenter Server products. The service enhances the scalability and availability of TCP/IP-based services. The technology allows a cluster of systems (between 2 and 32) to be created. To scale performance, Network Load Balancing distributes IP traffic across multiple cluster hosts. It also ensures high availability by detecting host failures and automatically redistributing traffic to the remaining hosts in the cluster.

Organizations that have mission-critical TCP/IP-based services—such as Web servers, terminal services, VPN, and media servers (to name a few)—will benefit from this service. The following sections provide an overview of how the Network Load Balancing server works and how to design an implementation strategy.

Overview of Network Load Balancing

Network Load Balancing (NLB) distributes IP traffic to multiple hosts configured as a cluster. Clients access the cluster through one (or more) virtual IP address. From a client's perspective, the cluster appears to be a single server that answers client requests. As the number of client requests increases, more hosts can be added to the cluster (to a maximum of 32).

NLB is superior to a load-balancing solution such as DNS round robin. DNS round robin distributes the workload among multiple servers but does not monitor server availability. This means that if a server failed under DNS round robin, the failed server's address would be provided to clients as normal. These client requests would not be serviced.

NLB also offers advantages over some other software- and hardware-based load-balancing solutions. Many load-balancing solutions use a centralized dispatcher to monitor servers and distribute client requests. This type of load balancing suffers from a single point of failure if the dispatcher system fails. This design also suffers from overhead problems. Client requests pass through a single dispatcher system and are then redirected to systems in the cluster.

Installing Network Load Balancing

NLB is automatically installed and can optionally be enabled on the Advanced Server and Datacenter Server products. NLB operates as an optional service on one network interface. When the NLB service is configured for an interface, the system becomes part of the NLB cluster.

To enable NLB on an interface, complete the following steps:

> **WARNING**
>
> **NLB Can Be on Only One Interface at a Time**   NLB can be enabled on only one network interface at a time. If an interface has NLB enabled and you enable it on another interface, NLB is automatically disabled on the original interface. No warning is provided.

STEP BY STEP

4.8 Enabling NLB on an Interface

1. Right-click the My Network Places icon and select Properties from the secondary menu. This will open the Network and Dial-up Connections window (as shown in Figure 4.28).

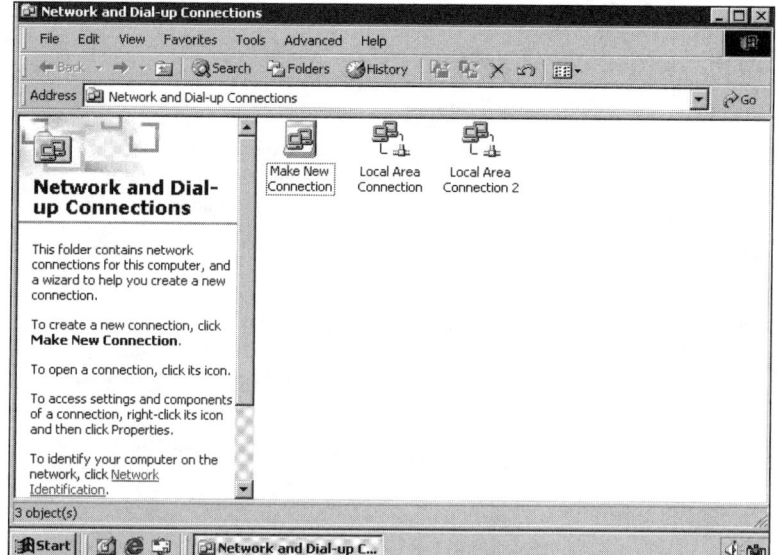

FIGURE 4.28
Network and Dial-up Connections window.

2. Right-click the interface on which you want NLB enabled, and select Properties from the secondary menu. You see the window shown in Figure 4.29. By default, NLB is disabled (unchecked). This window also shows all of the other network components for this connection.

3. Check the Network Load Balancing check box to enable NLB.

4. To see the NLB configuration properties, click the Properties button.

After NLB is enabled, you need to configure its operating parameters. Figure 4.30 shows the properties of the NLB service.

The NLB properties are divided into three categories. The first set of properties is found on the Cluster Parameters tab (shown in Figure 4.30). Table 4.7 provides details on each of the configuration options.

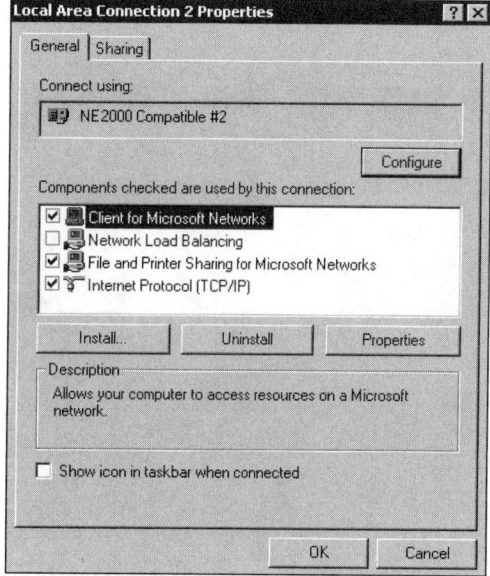

FIGURE 4.29
Network interface properties.

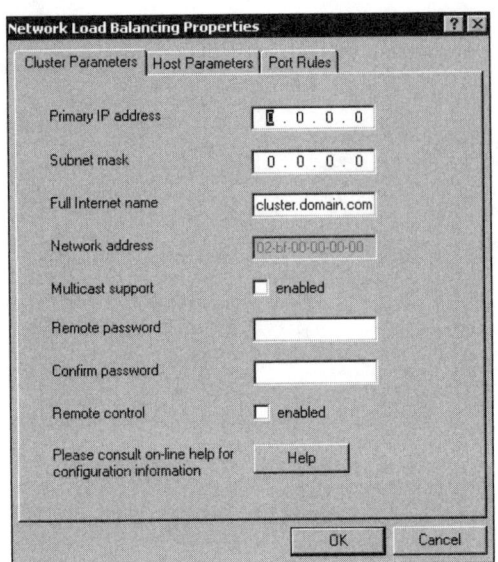

FIGURE 4.30
The NLB Properties Cluster Parameters tab.

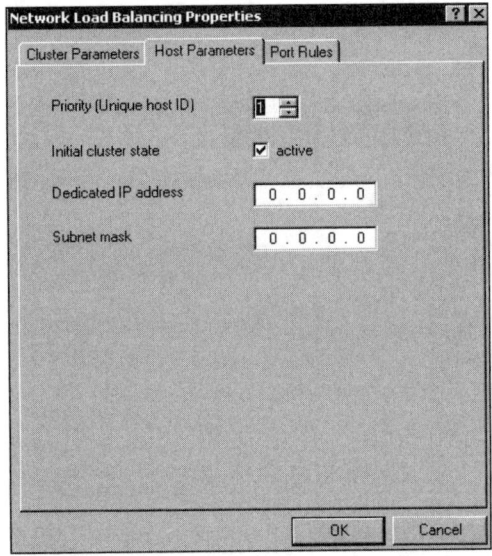

FIGURE 4.31
The NLB Properties Host Parameters tab.

TABLE 4.7

NLB CLUSTER PARAMETERS

Parameter	*Description*
Primary IP address	The primary IP address represents a virtual IP address to which all cluster hosts respond. You must ensure that all cluster hosts are configured with this address.
Subnet mask	This is the subnet mask associated with the primary IP address.
Full Internet name	This represents the Fully Qualified Domain Name for the cluster. DNS needs to contain a host record that points to the primary IP address of the cluster. All cluster hosts should be configured with the same value.
Network address	This is a noneditable option. This address represents the virtual MAC address of the cluster.
Multicast support	This parameter specifies that a multicast MAC address should be used for cluster operations. If this option is enabled, NLB converts the cluster MAC address into a multicast address. It also ensures that the Address Resolution Protocol (ARP) will resolve the multicast address. Multicasting enables the interface to which NLB is bound to retain its original MAC address.
	If multicast support is disabled, NLB converts the cluster network address to a non-multicast address. It also instructs the network adapter driver to override the adapter's built-in MAC address.
Remote password Confirm password	These parameters specify control access to the NLB cluster control program. These options do not limit the ability of a cluster host to communicate with the clusters. These parameters are used to limit access to the administrative functions of the NLB cluster. When remote control is enabled and a password is set, all management requests must include the appropriate password. See WLBS.EXE for details.
Remote control	This option enables remote control.

The second set of properties is found on the Host Parameters tab (shown in Figure 4.31). Table 4.8 provides details on each of the configuration options.

TABLE 4.8

NLB HOST PARAMETERS

Parameter	Description
Priority (Unique host ID)	This parameter specifies the host's unique priority for handling requests within the cluster. The host with the highest priority (that is, the lowest number) among the current members of the cluster handles all the cluster's default network traffic (based on the port rules discussed in the next section). If the host with the lowest-priority number fails, the next lowest value automatically takes over. If a host ever tries to join the cluster with a conflicting priority value, it will not be accepted as part of the cluster.
Initial cluster state	This option enables you to control whether the host should join the cluster when it starts up. You can use the cluster control command tool to join the cluster.
Dedicated IP address Subnet mask	These parameters specify the host's unique IP address used for traffic not associated with the cluster. Generally, this is the IP address of the computer before clustering is enabled on the computer.
	NLB references the dedicated IP address when a single NIC is used to handle both cluster network traffic and other network traffic to the dedicated IP address. In this case, both the cluster's IP address and the dedicated IP address are bound to the single NIC. NLB ensures that all traffic to the dedicated IP address is unaffected by the NLB current configuration.
	If you use separate network adapters to handle cluster traffic and network traffic to the dedicated IP address, only the cluster's Network adapter is bound to the NLB driver. Network traffic to the dedicated IP address is not associated with the NLB driver.

The last configuration option involves the configuration of port rules (as shown in Figure 4.32). NLB uses port rules to customize load balancing of consecutive port ranges. Port rules can select either multiple-host or single-host load-balancing policies.

With multiple-host load balancing, incoming client requests are distributed among all cluster hosts based on a load percentage for each host. Load percentages allow hosts with higher capacity to receive a large fraction of the total client load.

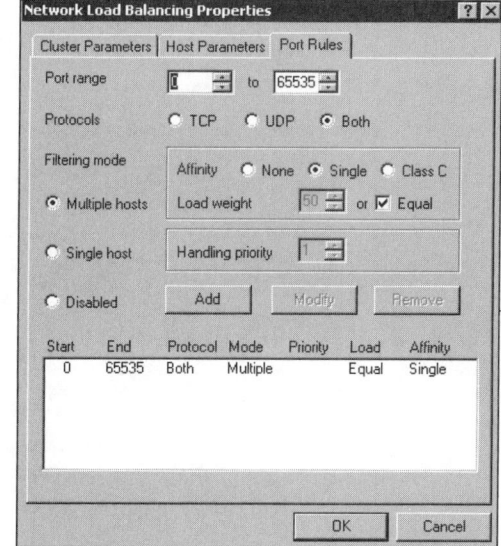

FIGURE 4.32
The NLB Properties Port Rules tab.

When a port rule uses multiple-host load balancing, one of three client affinity modes must be selected:

♦ **No affinity.** NLB balances client traffic load from one IP address and different source ports on multiple-cluster hosts.

♦ **Single-client affinity.** Client sessions from a given IP address are serviced on a single-cluster host. (This is the default configuration.)

♦ **Class C affinity.** Balances all client traffic load from a single class C address space to a single-cluster host.

Single-host load balancing directs all client requests to the host with the highest handling priority. The handling priority overrides the host priority for the port range and allows different hosts to individually handle all client traffic for specific server applications.

By default, NLB is configured with a single port rule that covers all ports (0–65,535) with multiple-host load balancing and single-client affinity.

Planning Your Network Load-Balancing Solution

Network Load Balancing is a powerful tool that can be used to ensure that your TCP/IP services are scalable and always available. You need to carefully plan your NLB implementation to ensure that it will meet your organization's needs. The next section provides an overview of planning considerations.

Identifying Your Risks

You need to take a serious look at all the services you are currently offering to your network clients to determine the ones that require NLB. The first step in this process is to inventory all the services you are running in your environment. You then need to determine which services are considered critical to the operation of your company or to service your customers. After you have identified these services, you need to determine which of the services are supported by NLB. Generally, the NLB service supports any application that is assigned to a specific port and uses TCP/IP as its network transport.

Capacity Planning

Now that you have a comprehensive list of services that you want serviced by NLB, you need to determine the number of cluster nodes required. Determining the number of NLB nodes requires that you have a thorough understanding of the services you are running and the number of clients you expect to service. This calculation also depends on the goal of your NLB implementation. Some organizations choose NLB to provide fault tolerance for the services they use. In this type of environment, you might not require a large number of nodes in your cluster (that is, two nodes will do because your only goal is to ensure availability).

The general rule is to make your best educated guess to determine an appropriate starting point for your cluster. When the cluster is running, you need to monitor the performance of each cluster node to determine how it is performing. If a specific cluster node is heavily used, you might need to adjust the NLB configuration to evenly distribute the load. If all nodes are heavily used, you might need to add more nodes to the cluster.

Optimizing Performance

Now that you have determined the services you will support through your NLB implementation, you need to optimize your hardware. Many services have specialized hardware requirements; database servers, for example, require specialized RAID controllers and disk configurations to ensure optimal performance. In general, you need to ensure that you have assessed the following to optimize service performance:

- ◆ **Hardware.** You need to optimize your hardware for the specific services you are supporting. Generally, this includes hardware RAID, server class NICs, multiple processor servers, lots of memory, and so forth.

- ◆ **Windows 2000 configurations.** You want to ensure that the configuration of your Windows 2000 server is optimized for the services you are running. This includes the placement of the page file and boot/system files. You will also find that many services can be optimized through specific registry settings.

◆ **Network performance.** The NLB services can be supported on many different types of network configurations (that is, switched networks versus nonswitched). There are a number of advantages/disadvantages of different network designs depending on the services you are supporting and how you have configured NLB (see the NLB online help for details).

CASE STUDY: MIKAYLA CONSULTING, INC.

ESSENCE OF THE CASE

Here are the essential elements in this case:

▶ 200 users to be connected to the Internet. All users require access to email and HTTP/FTP.

▶ Internal security is of primary concern.

▶ External security is of primary concern.

▶ Potential security threats come from both internal and external sources.

▶ Significant Web presence is a goal.

SCENARIO

Mikayla Consulting, Inc. (MC Inc.) develops and manufactures baby products for companies around the world. MC Inc. is in the process of connecting its offices to the Internet. The company requires a secure and manageable solution for its 200 users. All computers in the office are running Windows 2000 Professional and Internet Explorer 5.0.

The company has one office in Toronto, Ontario. The office is divided into four specific departments: Sales, R&D, Engineering, and Administration.

Security is a very real concern for MC Inc. MC Inc. is one of the largest developers of baby products and spends millions annually developing new products for the marketplace. MC Inc. also has an obligation to secure the data and designs owned by outside customers. Last year, MC Inc. had to fire a number of staff members for selling designs and data to the competition.

The company also has an extensive e-commerce Web site. Currently, the Web site is being run from an offsite location, but the IS department would like to move the site to an internal network segment. This is a critical move for MC Inc. because it will enable the Web site to be linked to the back-end billing and inventory management systems. MC Inc.'s Web presence is estimated to generate tens of millions of dollars in revenue this year as it sells its products directly to the public online.

To support the Web initiative, the company has purchased four Windows 2000 Datacenter Servers and an OC3 direct connection to the Internet. It also has a full Class C IP network address registered with InterNIC.

ANALYSIS

The key to evaluating this case is to break it down into its individual components. Each component on its own is relatively easy to assess. After you have evaluated each component and developed a reasonable design, look at the big picture and evaluate how the solutions for each component work together. It is very difficult to develop an all-encompassing solution in one step.

The first part of this case involves connecting 200 users to the Internet. Users are working on Windows 2000 Professional workstations. Options for accomplishing this objective are as follows:

- Direct connection to the Internet

- Application-level gateway (Microsoft Proxy Server Web Proxy)

- Circuit-level gateway (Microsoft Proxy Server Winsock Proxy or Socks Proxy)

For security reasons, the first option is out of the question. You need to be able to control the sites that your users are accessing. You also do not want the IP addresses of your individual workstations being used to access sites on the Internet. The second option is very easy to implement and helps control access to WWW/FTP resources. This solution also has the added benefit of caching to help speed up access to resources on the net. The last solution is also an option. All users are on Windows 2000 Professional workstations, so installing the Winsock Proxy client on each workstation can be done. The Winsock Proxy server does not have the benefit of caching associated with it.

In this case, the easiest solution for attaching the 200 users to the Internet is through the Web Proxy.

Internal and external security are the next areas to address. Internal security could be addressed by isolating the different departments within the office space and on the network. This can be accomplished by placing a packet filtering router between the network segments. External security is a bigger issue. You will look at a full firewall solution.

The next design challenge is the Web site. This is a very large and demanding Web site to host. It will require a firewall solution to control access to it from the public network. You will also need to look at Network Load Balancing (NLB) to ensure that the site is scalable and has high availability.

After you have optimal solutions for each of your design objectives, it is time to merge them to ensure that the solutions are compatible. If some of the solutions need to be revisited, you are in a position to redesign based on sound design information.

CHAPTER SUMMARY

KEY TERMS

- application-level gateways
- circuit-level gateways
- File Transfer Protocol (FTP)
- firewall
- Hypertext Transport Protocol (HTTP)
- packet filtering routers
- routing

This chapter has explored some of the technologies available to connect a network to the Internet. Specifically, this chapter looked at firewalls, Proxy Servers, Connection Sharing, and Network Load Balancing (NLB).

The section on firewalls provided a high-level overview of firewall technology and terminology. The primary goal was to provide information relating to the pros and cons of each type of firewall. The section on Microsoft Proxy Server looked at Microsoft's firewall implementation.

Connection Sharing and Network Address Translation (NAT) are very useful technologies for connecting small networks to the Internet. That section provided an overview of the technologies and the different implementations available.

The last section of this chapter looked at Network Load Balancing (NLB). NLB can be used to ensure that critical TCP/IP-based applications have high availability.

APPLY YOUR KNOWLEDGE

Exercises

4.1   Installing MS Proxy Server

The objective of this exercise is to install Microsoft Proxy Server 2 on a Windows 2000 server. Although this is not a specific objective for this exam, it is important that you understand the configuration options available to you when you design your Proxy strategy. For this reason, the installation exercise is included to assist you in getting up and running without trouble.

Estimated Time: 30 minutes

This exercise assumes you have Windows 2000 Server installed. The server can be in either a workgroup or domain. You should have two Network Interface Cards (NICs) in the computer. If you have only one NIC, you will not be able to see the packet filtering options. You also must have one partition formatted with NTFS and a minimum of 100MB of free space.

1. To install Microsoft Proxy 2 on a Windows 2000 server, you need to download the Windows 2000 Installation Wizard from Microsoft's Web site. If you try to install MS Proxy with the traditional setup.exe program that ships with Microsoft Proxy Server, you receive an error message. The Installation Wizard is available at http://www.microsoft.com/proxy.

   You also need a copy of Microsoft Proxy Server if you want to install it. An evaluation copy of the product is available at Microsoft's Web site.

2. Stop any running instances of Microsoft Management Console (MMC).

3. Run the MSP2WIZI.EXE file you downloaded in step 1.

4. Read the License Agreement. Click Yes if you agree with the agreement.

5. The Setup Wizard displays a list of tasks that are about to be completed (as shown in Figure 4.33). Click Continue.

6. Microsoft Proxy Server setup begins when the Microsoft Proxy Server Windows 2000 Setup Wizard has verified the installation of Microsoft Proxy Server on your Windows 2000 computer. Click Continue to continue the setup.

7. The Microsoft Proxy Server setup notifies you of your Product ID. Click OK to continue.

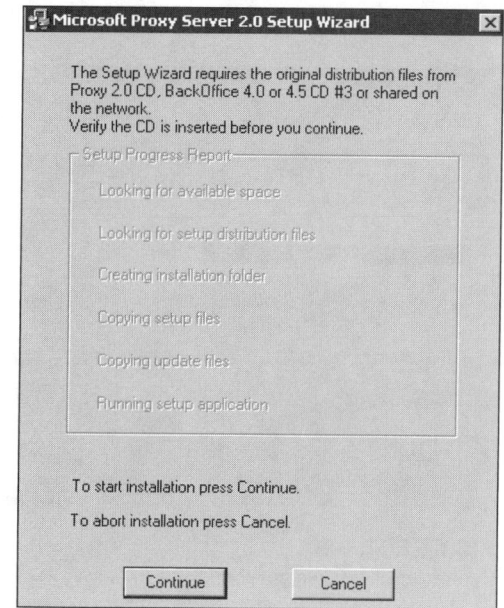

FIGURE 4.33
Microsoft Proxy Server Setup Wizard tasks.

APPLY YOUR KNOWLEDGE

8. The Microsoft Proxy Server setup verifies the installation path for the Microsoft Proxy Server files. To change the installation path, click the Change Folder button. After you have selected an appropriate folder, click the Installation button to continue.

9. You are asked which components you would like to install. Leave the defaults and click the Continue button.

10. If you would like to use the Web Proxy caching functions, you need to provide the location for the cache files. The cache must be stored on an NTFS-formatted partition (as shown in Figure 4.34). Select an NTFS-formatted partition and click OK.

11. You are prompted to list all the internal network addresses found on your network (as shown in Figure 4.35). Microsoft Proxy Server calls this information the Local Area Table (LAT). Microsoft Proxy Server uses this information to decide whether requests are destined for internal or external resources. One of the quickest ways of generating this information is to use the Construct Table button. This option enables you to select the internal NICs on your machine (as shown in Figure 4.36). Microsoft Proxy Server then automatically generates a list of internal networks based on the routing tables on your system (as shown in Figure 4.37). When you have selected your internal NIC(s), click OK.

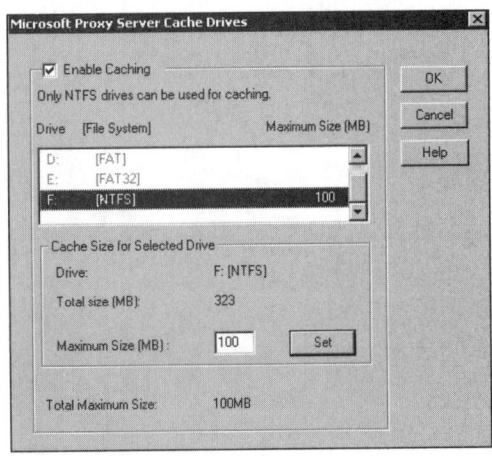

FIGURE 4.34
Cache partition configuration.

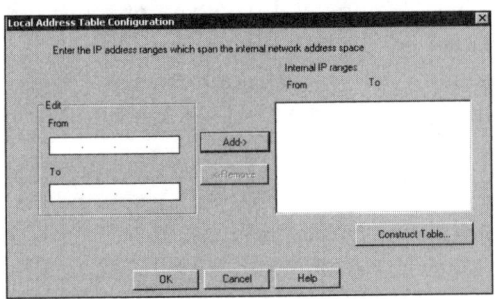

FIGURE 4.35
Initial LAT setup.

APPLY YOUR KNOWLEDGE

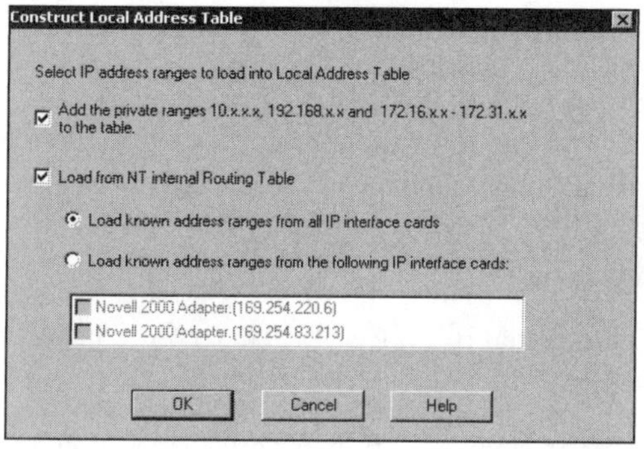

FIGURE 4.36
Automated LAT setup.

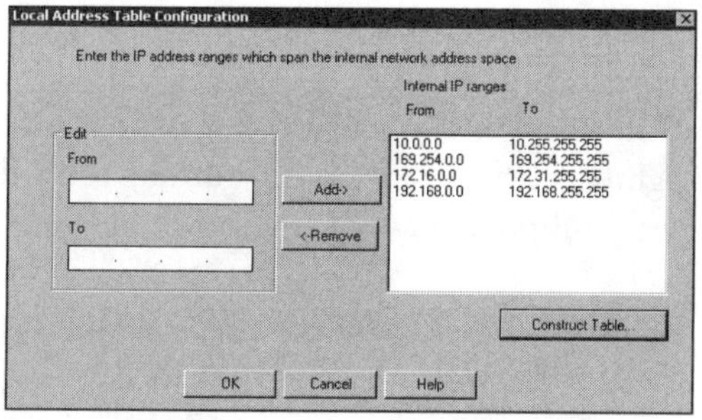

FIGURE 4.37
The completed LAT.

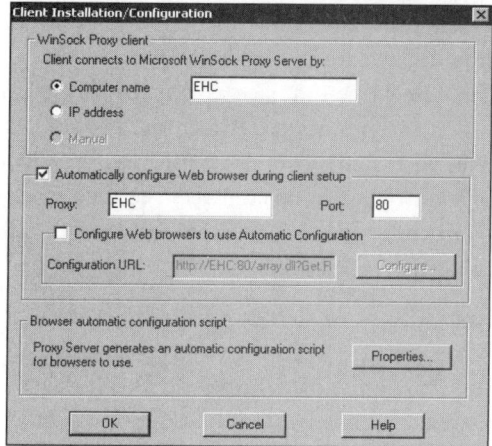

FIGURE 4.38
Microsoft Proxy Server Client configuration.

12. Setup presents a message stating the importance of the LAT. Click OK.

13. Setup confirms the LAT and allows you to add or remove networks. Click OK to continue.

14. You are asked to provide information on the default client configuration for clients that use this proxy server (as shown in Figure 4.38). Use the defaults and click OK.

15. Setup prompts you to determine whether you would like access control options to be enabled for the Web Proxy and Winsock Proxy services. Make sure both options are checked off and click OK to continue.

16. The setup manager finalizes the setup of Microsoft Proxy Server.

17. After Microsoft Proxy Server is installed, use the Internet Information Server MMC snap-in to manage the Proxy Server.

4.2   Configuring Network Load Balancing

The objective of this exercise is to configure Network Load Balancing on two Windows 2000 Advanced servers running IIS 5.0.

Estimated Time: 15 minutes

The exercise assumes you have two Windows 2000 Advanced or Datacenter servers installed. You also need a client system (Windows 95/98, Windows NT, or Windows 2000 Professional).

APPLY YOUR KNOWLEDGE

The servers can be in either a workgroup or domain. You should have two Network Interface Cards in each machine. Label one interface as internal and one as external on each computer. Attach the two internal interfaces with a crossover cable (or hub). The external interfaces also need to be connected to the same network. You connect a client to this network to test the functionality of the NLB service.

Make sure IIS is installed on each of the servers. To help distinguish between the two servers during the exercise, change the content on the Default page of each server to uniquely identify it.

We will use the IP addresses shown in Table 4.9 for the lab.

TABLE 4.9

EXERCISE 4.2 IP ADDRESS CONFIGURATION

Computer	Interface	IP Address
Computer 1	Internal	IP = 10.10.0.1 Mask = 255.255.0.0
	External	IP = 10.20.0.1 Mask = 255.255.0.0
Computer 2	Internal	IP = 10.10.0.2 Mask = 255.255.0.0
	External	IP = 10.20.0.2 Mask = 255.255.0.0
Cluster	N/A	IP = 10.10.0.3 Mask = 255.255.0.0

Testing Connectivity

1. From the workstation, start your Web browser and surf to the external interfaces of both servers. You should be able to get to each computer.

2. From each of the servers, ping the internal and external interfaces of the other system.

3. If you can get to each computer, you have verified that your systems are configured correctly.

Configuring NLB

On the external interface of each server, complete the following:

1. Right-click the My Network Places icon and select Properties for the secondary menu.

2. Right-click the external interface and select Properties from the secondary menu.

3. Check the Network Load Balancing option.

4. With the Network Load Balancing option highlighted, click the Properties button. You will see the NLB properties page (as shown in Figure 4.39).

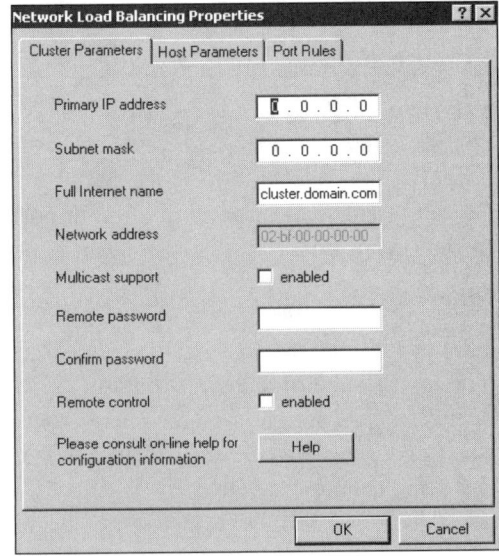

FIGURE 4.39
The NLB Properties page.

5. On the Cluster Parameters tab, enter the Cluster IP address (see Table 4.9) in the Primary IP address field. You also need to configure the mask.

6. On the Host Parameters tab, enter the External Interface IP address and mask of the computer you are working on in the Dedicated IP address field. For computer 1, set the Priority (Unique host ID) to 1. For computer 2, set the Priority to 2.

Testing NLB from the Clients

1. From the client computer, surf to the IP address of the cluster (`10.10.0.3`). You get the default IIS page from one of the servers (you should be able to tell which one based on the unique information you added to the default page previously).

2. Turn off the computer responding to your request.

3. Click the Reload button on your browser. The second system should start responding to your request.

Review Questions

1. What are the three primary firewall technologies found in most firewall solutions? What are the primary strengths and weaknesses of each?

2. On what criteria can packet filters be defined?

3. Why would you want to reverse-host a Web site?

4. Which of the Microsoft Proxy Server services cache information to better use your connection to the Internet?

5. Which of the Microsoft Proxy Server services support user-level access control?

6. What three options exist for distributing client requests across your proxy servers?

7. What services does Routing and Remote Access Services provide?

8. What is the difference between Connection Sharing and NAT?

9. Why would a company use Connection Sharing over NAT?

10. What are the primary limitations of NAT?

11. What are the suggested IP address ranges you should use on your private network?

12. What is the primary difference between installing the Network Load Balancing service on a computer with one NIC and installing it on a computer with two NICs?

13. How is Network Load Balancing different from DNS round robin?

14. What is the significance of multicasting during the configuration of the Network Load Balancing service?

15. When configuring Network Load Balancing, what is client affinity?

Exam Questions

1. You are the network administrator at a large structural design firm. You are configuring a connection to the Internet for your network, and security is of primary concern to your manager. Your environment consists of Windows 2000 Professional computers and UNIX-based systems

APPLY YOUR KNOWLEDGE

used for rendering drawings. All internal systems need access to the Internet, and you need to control which users can access Internet sites.

You purchase a dedicated 512KB connection to the Internet from a local Internet Service Provider (ISP) and install Microsoft Proxy Server between your private network and the ISP's router. You decide to install and configure only the MS Winsock Proxy service. No matter what you try, you cannot get the UNIX-based machines to connect through the Winsock Proxy. What is the cause of your problems?

A. You have not configured the browsers on the UNIX-based workstation to use the Winsock Proxy.

B. Your proxy server is not configured to let the UNIX-based systems out to the Internet.

C. There is not an MS Winsock Proxy Client for UNIX-based systems.

D. Your ISP is filtering Winsock-based traffic.

E. UNIX-based systems are not generally used to access the Internet, so this is not an issue.

2. You are the network administrator for a small insurance firm. You are directed by upper management to limit access to the Internet to authorized users (that is, the network administration group). You install MS Proxy client on all workstations and configure them to use the Winsock Proxy. You also configure all the browsers in the company to use the Web Proxy server. What can you do to limit a user's ability to surf the net (choose two)?

A. Configure a packet filter that allows only certain users to use the HTTP protocol.

B. Configure the Winsock Proxy to allow only certain users to use the HTTP protocol.

C. Configure the Web Proxy to allow only certain users to access the Web.

D. Block all users from accessing the Web and give modems to the users who need access to the Internet so that they can dial a service provider.

E. Configure a packet filter to allow the workstations of authorized users to gain access to the Web.

3. You are the security officer for a large financial institution. Your company has recently offered a number of Web-based services to your customers. Customers are allowed to access your internal system via the Web. You are very concerned about security and do not want external traffic to be able to access anything on the private network. The Web server that supports customer applications needs to access a number of your company's internal mainframes. You decide to implement Microsoft Proxy Server along with your company's Checkpoint Firewall (packet filtering and monitoring are the only components in use). Which of the following best describes how you should configure the environment?

A. You configure the Checkpoint Firewall to allow HTTP traffic to the public interface on the Microsoft Proxy Server. You then configure the Microsoft Proxy Server to reverse-host your Web site and place the Web server on the public side of the firewall.

APPLY YOUR KNOWLEDGE

B. You configure the Checkpoint Firewall to allow HTTP traffic to the public interface on the Microsoft Proxy Server. You then configure the Microsoft Proxy Server to reverse-host your Web site and place the Web server on the private side of the firewall.

C. You configure the Checkpoint Firewall to allow HTTP traffic to the private interface on the Microsoft Proxy Server. You then configure the Microsoft Proxy Server to reverse-host your Web site and place the Web server on the public side of the firewall.

D. You configure the Checkpoint Firewall to allow HTTP traffic to the private interface on the Microsoft Proxy Server. You then configure the Microsoft Proxy Server to reverse-host your Web site and place the Web server on the private side of the firewall.

4. You are the chief information officer (CIO) for your company, a large financial institution. You have just concluded a meeting with the chief financial officer (CFO) from your company. Last week your Web server was down for 30 minutes and your company lost $3,000,000 in online Internet-based trades. The CFO is less than pleased. Your systems department has indicated that the problem was with one of the Web servers (that is, it failed). You have assured the CFO that the problem will be fixed and measures will be taken to make sure this will never happen again.

The systems department has decided that adding additional Web servers is the answer to the problem. It has recommended that three additional servers be added to support the site. A redundant connection to the Internet is also proposed.

What should you do to guarantee 99% uptime?

A. Configure DNS to round-robin the IP addresses of the three Web servers to ensure that they are always available.

B. Configure the NLB service on the three Web servers to ensure that they are always available.

C. Reverse-host the Web servers to ensure that they are always available.

D. You can never make such a guarantee; it is impossible to have 99% uptime.

5. You are the head of a design team rolling out Windows 2000 to 600 offices across Canada. You are working on behalf of a company made up of franchise outlet stores. Each store needs to connect to the head office, over the Internet, to download inventory and pricing information. Each of the 600 offices has limited technical support (in most cases, none). You want to develop a standardized configuration for every store so the implementation will be easy to manage. You suggest each office use a dialup line to a local ISP. You know that Routing and Remote Access Services supports both Connection Sharing and NAT. Should you recommend Connection Sharing or NAT as part of the implementation plan?

A. NAT, because it is easier to configure and manage.

B. Connection Sharing, because it is easier to configure and manage.

C. NAT will not work in this instance, because it does not support WINS; therefore, Connection Sharing is more appropriate.

APPLY YOUR KNOWLEDGE

D. Connection Sharing will not work in this instance, because it does not support WINS; therefore, NAT is more appropriate.

E. You should go back to the drawing board, because neither technology will work.

6. Your company is designing a Web site for a financial package. The Web site will allow the application to be run online, over the Internet, for a weekly fee. The application must be available 7 days a week, 24 hours a day. There is no margin for error in the development of this site.

You want to accomplish the following goals:

- You want the site to be very fast.

- You want to ensure that the site has very high availability.

- The site must be secure, because personal customer data is stored on a database server at the site.

- No site content can be stored on the public side of the firewall.

You take the following actions:

- On a dedicated server, you reverse-host the Web site using Microsoft Proxy Server's Web Proxy capabilities.

- You house your Web site on three separate servers and configure the servers as part of a Network Load-Balanced cluster.

Which results do these actions produce (choose all that apply)?

A. The site should be very fast.

B. The site will have very high availability.

C. The site will be secure.

D. No site content will be stored on the public side of the Proxy Server.

E. None of the objectives are met.

7. Your company is designing a Web site for a financial package. The Web site will allow the application to be run online, over the Internet, for a weekly fee. The application must be available 7 days a week, 24 hours a day. There is no margin for error in the development and support of this site.

You want to accomplish the following goals:

- You want the site to be very fast.

- You want to ensure that the site has very high availability.

- The site must be secure, because personal customer data is stored on a database server at the site.

- No site content can be stored on the public side of the proxy server.

You take the following actions:

- On one server, you install a firewall solution comprised of a packet filtering router.

- You house your Web site on three separate servers and configure the servers as part of a Network Load-Balanced cluster. All equipment is placed on the private side of the firewall.

Which results do these actions produce (choose all that apply)?

A. The site should be very fast.

B. The site will have very high availability.

APPLY YOUR KNOWLEDGE

C. The site will be secure.

D. No site content will be stored on the public side of the firewall.

E. All results are produced.

8. You are the network administrator for a small manufacturing firm in Toronto. Your company has leased new office space and requires a connection to the Internet. You have been asked to design an Internet connection strategy for the company.

   Your environment contains the following equipment:

   - 200 Windows 2000 Professional workstations

   - 10 Macintosh workstations

   - 35 UNIX workstations

   - 3 Novell 4.11 servers

   - 9 Windows 2000 servers

   Your environment supports the following services:

   - Exchange 5.5 for internal and external email

   - IIS 5.0 for hosting an internal Web site and an external Web site

   - Windows file and print services for all departments except office administration

   - Novell file and print services for 20 administrative staff members

   - MS SQL 7.0

You support TCP/IP to the desktop for all workstations except the office administration department (it supports only IPX/SPX). Your organization is divided into three departments. The office administration group primarily works on Windows 2000 Professional workstations and a Novell server. The research and design group works on a combination of Windows 2000 Professional, UNIX, and Macintosh workstations. The production group works exclusively on Windows 2000 Professional workstations.

Required Result:

- All workstations require access to the Internet.

Optional Results:

- The connection to the Internet must be secure.

- Access to external Web sites must be closely monitored to ensure that users are not downloading inappropriate material.

- The total number of public IP addresses must be minimized.

- Bandwidth utilization on the connection to the Internet must be conserved.

Proposed Solution:

- You install a Microsoft Proxy Server and configure both the Web Proxy and Winsock Proxy services.

- You install the Winsock Proxy client on all computers from the administration department and enable the Winsock Proxy client.

- All browsers are configured to use the Web Proxy.

APPLY YOUR KNOWLEDGE

Which results does the proposed solution produce?

A. The proposed solution produces the required result and all the optional results.

B. The proposed solution produces the required result and produces only three of the optional desired results.

C. The proposed solution produces the required result and produces only two of the optional desired results.

D. The proposed solution produces the required result and produces only one of the optional desired results.

E. The proposed solution produces the required result but does not produce any of the optional desired results.

F. The proposed solution does not produce the required results.

9. You are the network administrator for a small manufacturing firm in Toronto. Your company has leased new office space and requires a connection to the Internet. You have been asked to design an Internet connection strategy for the company.

Your environment contains the following equipment:

- 200 Windows 2000 Professional workstations
- 10 Macintosh workstations
- 35 UNIX workstations
- 3 Novell 4.11 servers
- 9 Windows 2000 servers

Your environment supports the following services:

- Exchange 5.5 for internal and external email
- IIS 5.0 for hosting an internal Web site and an external Web site
- Windows file and print services for all departments except office administration
- Novell file and print services for 20 administrative staff
- MS SQL 7.0

You support TCP/IP to the desktop for all workstations except the office administration department (it supports only IPX/SPX). Your organization is divided into three departments. The office administration group primarily works on Windows 2000 Professional workstations and a Novell server. The research and design group works on a combination of Windows 2000 Professional, UNIX, and Macintosh workstations. The production group works exclusively on Windows 2000 Professional workstations.

Required Results:

- All workstations require access to the Internet (for HTTP and FTP).
- The connection to the Internet must be secure.

Optional Results:

- Access to external Web sites must be closely monitored to ensure that users are not downloading inappropriate material.
- The total number of public IP addresses must be minimized.
- Bandwidth utilization on the connection to the Internet must be conserved.

APPLY YOUR KNOWLEDGE

Proposed Solution:

- You install a Microsoft Proxy Server and enable packet filtering on the external interface. You also enable the Web Proxy and configure all browsers to use it.

- You add TCP/IP to all the computers in the administration department.

- You reverse-host the corporate Internet site on the Web Proxy service.

- You develop an internal IP addressing strategy using one of the public address ranges defined by InterNIC.

Which results does the proposed solution produce?

A. The proposed solution produces the required results and all the optional results.

B. The proposed solution produces the required results and produces only two of the optional desired results.

C. The proposed solution produces the required results and produces only one of the optional desired results.

D. The proposed solution produces the required results but does not produce any of the optional desired results.

E. The proposed solution does not produce the required results.

10. You are the network administrator for a small manufacturing firm in Toronto. Your company has leased new office space and requires a connection to the Internet. You have been asked to design an Internet connection strategy for the company.

Your environment contains the following equipment:

- 200 Windows 2000 Professional workstations

- 10 Macintosh workstations

- 35 UNIX workstations

- 3 Novell 4.11 servers

- 9 Windows 2000 servers

Your environment supports the following services:

- Exchange 5.5 for internal and external email

- IIS 5.0 for hosting an internal Web site and an external Web sites

- Windows file and print services for all departments except office administration

- Novell file and print services for 20 administrative staff members

- MS SQL 7.0

You support TCP/IP to the desktop for all workstations except the office administration department (it supports only IPX/SPX). Your organization is divided into three departments. The office administration group primarily works on Windows 2000 Professional workstations and a Novell server. The research and design group works on a combination of Windows 2000

APPLY YOUR KNOWLEDGE

Professional, UNIX, and Macintosh workstations. The production group works exclusively on Windows 2000 Professional workstations.

Required Results:

- All workstations require access to the Internet.

- The connection to the Internet must be secure.

Optional Results:

- Access to external Web sites must be closely monitored to ensure that users are not downloading inappropriate material.

- The total number of public IP addresses must be minimized.

- Bandwidth utilization on the connection to the Internet must be conserved.

Proposed Solution:

- You install a Microsoft Proxy Server and enable packet filtering on the external interface.

- You reverse-host the corporate Internet site on the Web Proxy service.

- You develop an internal IP addressing strategy using one of the public address ranges defined by InterNIC.

Which results does the proposed solution produce?

A. The proposed solution produces the required results and all the optional results.

B. The proposed solution produces the required results and produces only two of the optional desired results.

C. The proposed solution produces the required results and produces only one of the optional desired results.

D. The proposed solution produces the required results but does not produce any of the optional desired results.

E. The proposed solution does not produce the required results.

Answers to Review Questions

1. The three general categories of firewall technology are packet filtering routers, application-level gateways, and circuit-level gateways. Packet filtering routers enable you to create very specific rules that define what traffic can be forwarded and what traffic should be rejected. Application-level gateways act as an intermediary between an application and a host on the Internet. Application-level gateways work at the Application layer of the OSI model. Circuit-level gateways act as an intermediary between a host on the private network and a host on the Internet. Circuit-level gateways work at the Session layer of the OSI model. See the section entitled "Firewalls" for details.

2. Rules can be defined based on the following criteria (that is, the data typically contained in the network header of the protocol stack being filtered):

   - Packet type
   - Source address

- Destination address

- Source port

- Destination port

- Router interface

See the section entitled "Packet Filtering Routers" for details.

3. Reverse-hosting a Web site enables you to place the Web server on the private network. Users from the public network wanting to access the Web server can submit requests to the public interface of the Proxy Server, and it can access the Web server on the private network on behalf of the user. Reverse-hosting also benefits from the caching technology found in the Microsoft Proxy Server. See the section entitled "Reverse Web Proxy" for details.

4. The Web Proxy service is the only service supported by Microsoft Proxy Server that supports caching. See the section entitled "Services Provided by Microsoft Proxy Server" for details.

5. The Web Proxy and Winsock Proxy both support user-level access control. See the section entitled "Services Provided by Microsoft Proxy Server" for details.

6. To distribute client requests to multiple Microsoft Proxy Servers, you can use one or more of the following technologies:

  - Proxy Server arrays

  - DNS round robin entries

  - Windows clustering

See the section entitled "Proxy Server Availability" for details.

7. Routing and Remote Access Services provides multiprotocol routing support for Windows 2000. Through Routing and Remote Access you can configure LAN-to-LAN, LAN-to-WAN, Virtual Private Network (VPN), Network Address Translation (NAT) routing services, and dialup/Virtual Private Network services. See the section entitled "Routing and Remote Access" for details.

8. Connection Sharing is based on NAT technology, but it has a number of assumptions made about its installation. Connection Sharing does not have any configuration settings, whereas NAT has a number of options. Connection Sharing does not support WINS, whereas NAT does. See the section entitled "Connection Sharing" for details.

9. A company might choose to use Connection Sharing over NAT if it has a small office and does not have staff available to support a full implementation of NAT. See the section entitled "Connection Sharing" for details.

10. The primary limitation of NAT is that it has the capability to modify the source port and IP address information only when it forwards a request. Applications that embed their port and IP address information into the data area of a request do not work with NAT unless a NAT Editor exists for the protocol. See the section entitled "Connection Sharing" for details.

11. You should plan to use private network address ranges for your network. The private network IDs include

  - 10.0.0.0 through 10.255.255.255

  - 172.16.0.0 through 172.31.255.255

  - 192.168.0.0 through 192.168.255.255

APPLY YOUR KNOWLEDGE

See the Note entitled "Private Address Ranges" for details.

12. NLB references the dedicated IP address when a single NIC is used to handle both cluster network traffic and other network traffic to the dedicated IP address. In this case, both the cluster's IP address and the dedicated IP address are bound to the single NIC. NLB ensures that all traffic to the dedicated IP address is unaffected by the NLB current configuration.

    If you use separate network adapters to handle cluster traffic and network traffic to the dedicated IP address, only the cluster's network adapter is bound to the NLB driver. Network traffic to the dedicated IP address is not associated with the NLB driver. See the section entitled "Designing a Load-Balancing Strategy" for details.

13. Network Load Balancing enables a number of computers to act as clusters. If one computer fails, the cluster will adapt and client requests will still be serviced. DNS round robin is simply a listing of IP addresses for a number of computers offering services. If a computer fails, it is not reported to DNS, so the client request will still be directed to the failed machine. See the section entitled "Designing a Load-Balancing Strategy" for more details.

14. This parameter specifies that a multicast MAC address should be used for cluster operations. If this option is enabled, NLB converts the cluster MAC address into a multicast address. It also ensures that the Address Resolution Protocol (ARP) will resolve the multicast address. Multicasting allows the interface to which NLB is bound to retain its original MAC address.

If multicast support is disabled, NLB converts the cluster network address to a non-multicast address. It will also instruct the network adapter driver to override the adapter's built-in MAC address. See the section entitled "Designing a Load-Balancing Strategy" for details.

15. Client affinity determines how client requests are distributed among the nodes in the NLB cluster. See the section entitled "Designing a Load-Balancing Strategy" for details.

Answers to Exam Questions

1. **C.** You have to remember the pros and cons of each of the Microsoft Proxy Server services. The Winsock Proxy is effective only in a Microsoft-based environment, because there is a proxy client available only for Microsoft-based machines. Answer A is incorrect because the browser configuration will not impact access to the Winsock Proxy (it would impact the Web Proxy). Answer B could potentially be correct, because the UNIX-based computer cannot get to the Internet because of the Proxy. This answer, however, does not provide any specification as to why the proxy configuration is stopping the UNIX systems from accessing the net. Answer C is a better answer; it proves you know something about the Proxy product. Answer C is correct. To access the Winsock Proxy, you need an appropriate client installed on your workstation. Answer D is not possible. The only thing that an ISP could do is filter TCP or UDP traffic, but that would also stop the Microsoft-based system from

APPLY YOUR KNOWLEDGE

accessing the Internet. Answer E is incorrect. See the section entitled "The Difference Between a Circuit and an Application Gateway" for more information.

2. **B, C.** The key to this question is remembering which Microsoft Proxy Server services support user-level access control. The Web Proxy and Winsock Proxy servers support user-level access control. For this reason, answer A is incorrect, because you cannot set up packet filters based on user information. Answers D and E could technically be considered correct, but they are not preferred solutions. Answer D defeats the purpose of your connection to the Internet. Answer E is very difficult to manage and still does not verify the user-access resources on the Internet (that is, if users logged into one of the workstations included in the exceptions list, they would have access to the Internet). Answers B and C are correct because these services support user-level access control. See the section entitled "Controlling Access to Internet/Intranet Resources" for more information.

3. **B.** Trace the path! The key to this question is to understand the path HTTP traffic will take from the public to the private network. You also need to understand how reverse-hosting works. Remember that reverse-hosting is the process by which the public interface of your Proxy Server forwards requests to a Web server on behalf of users from the public network. Based on this, answers C and D are incorrect because they specify that the HTTP traffic from the public network is being allowed to pass to the private interface of the Microsoft Proxy Server. This

leaves only answers A and B. Answer A is incorrect because the Web server is being placed on the side of the Checkpoint Firewall. Placing the server in this location would not allow it to access the mainframes on the private network. This leaves only answer B. See the sections entitled "Services Provided by Microsoft Proxy Server" and "Reverse Web Proxy" for more information.

4. **B.** Answer A is incorrect because the solution does not properly distribute the load across all servers. For this reason, if one server is down, service could be impacted. Answer C is incorrect because reverse-hosting your site will not allow you to provide fault tolerance for the three servers. Pessimists would say answer D is correct. We all know, however, that Microsoft believes in its technology—if you deploy it correctly, you can get 100% uptime. Answer B is correct. Using the Network Load Balancing server, you should be able to ensure the operation of your site. See the sections entitled "Designing a Load-Balancing Strategy" and "DNS Round Robin" for details.

5. **B.** Answer A is incorrect because Connection Sharing is easier to configure than NAT. Remember that Connection Sharing is the same as NAT with a number of default assumptions made. Connection Sharing shines in environments where support is limited. Answers C and D are incorrect because WINS does not have anything to do with the problem. Answer E is incorrect because Connection Sharing and NAT were designed to support this type of environment. See the section entitled "Connection Sharing" for details.

APPLY YOUR KNOWLEDGE

6. **A, B.** Your solution includes components to speed up the site and make sure it is always available. The Network Load Balancing components satisfy the requirements of answers A and B. The solution, however, does not supply additional security. Reverse-hosting is not a substitute for a firewall; therefore, answer C is incorrect. Answer D is incorrect because site content is not being stored behind a firewall. Answer E is incorrect because answers A and B are correct. See the sections entitled "Designing a Load-Balancing Strategy" and "Firewalls" for more information.

7. **E.** You have all the bases covered with this solution. Answers A and B are correct because the site is using a Network Load Balancing solution. Answers C and D are correct because the site is behind a firewall. See "Designing for Internet Connectivity" for more information.

8. **C.** This type of question is very common on Microsoft tests. The key to answering these questions is to organize the information provided and draw a small table of the results. This will then assist you in selecting the most appropriate answer. You should also spend a couple of minutes making sure you understand the question. Often, you will find the same question repeated multiple times with a different proposed solution each time. Table 4.10 summarizes the answer to question 8.

TABLE 4.10

SUMMARY OF EXAM QUESTION 8

Result	Result Met?	Rationale
Required Result:		
All workstations require access to the Internet.	YES	The solution allows all computers to access the Internet.
		The Winsock Proxy is the key to this question. It is required to connect the administration computers to the Internet because these machines support only IPX/SPX.
Desired Optional Results:		
The connection to the Internet must be secure.	NO	The solution does not mention any technology to stop traffic from flowing from the public to the private network.
Access to external Web sites must be closely monitored to ensure that users are not downloading inappropriate material.	YES	The Web Proxy logs enable you to track where users have been visiting.
The total number of public IP addresses must be minimized.	NO	The solution does not mention the use of any public domain IP addresses.
Bandwidth utilization on the connection to the Internet must be conserved.	YES	The Web Proxy assists in the optimization of bandwidth utilization.

See the section entitled "Microsoft Proxy Server" for more information.

APPLY YOUR KNOWLEDGE

9. **A.** Table 4.11 summarizes the answer to question 9.

TABLE 4.11

SUMMARY OF EXAM QUESTION 9

Result	Result Met?	Rationale
Required Results:		
All workstations require access to the Internet.	YES	All workstations have TCP/IP installed and can therefore access the Internet through the connection.
The connection to the Internet must be secure.	YES	The solution has a packet filtering router installed that blocks traffic on the public interface.
Desired Optional Results:		
Access to external Web sites must be closely monitored to ensure that users are not downloading inappropriate material.	YES	The Web Proxy logs all sites visited on the Internet.
The total number of public IP addresses must be minimized.	YES	The solution uses an internal IP addressing strategy using public IP address ranges.
Bandwidth utilization on the connection to the Internet must be conserved.	YES	The Web Proxy caches content from the public network.

See the section entitled "Microsoft Proxy Server" for more information.

10. **E.** Table 4.12 summarizes the answer to question 10.

TABLE 4.12

SUMMARY OF EXAM QUESTION 10

Result	Result Met?	Rationale
Required Results:		
All workstations require access to the Internet.	NO	The solution proposes that public address ranges be used. These addresses are not recognized on the Internet as valid host addresses. For this reason, all internal workstations need to access the Internet through NAT or a proxy. Because they do not, no Internet access exists on the workstation.
The connection to the Internet must be secure.	YES	The solution has a packet filtering router installed that blocks traffic on the public interface.
Desired Optional Results:		
Access to external Web sites must be closely monitored to ensure that users are not downloading inappropriate material.	N/A	None of the computers can get to the Internet, so this is irrelevant.
The total number of public IP addresses must be minimized.	YES	The solution uses an internal IP addressing strategy using public IP address ranges.
Bandwidth utilization on the connection to the Internet must be conserved.	NO	No caching technology is seen in this solution.

See the section entitled "Microsoft Proxy Server" for more information.

APPLY YOUR KNOWLEDGE

Suggested Readings and Resources

1. Berg, Glenn. *MCSE Training Guide: Network Essentials, Second Edition.* Indianapolis: New Riders Publishing, 1998.

2. ICSE. *ICSA 3rd Annual Firewall Buyer's Guide,* ICSE, 1998. Available on the Web at WWW.ICSA.NET.

3. Ryvkin, Kostya, David Houde, and Tim Hoffman. *MCSE: Implementing and Supporting Microsoft Proxy Server 2.0.* Upper Saddle River, NJ: Prentice Hall, 1999.

In today's business world, one of the roles of a Microsoft professional can be ensuring that users have access to the corporate network and corporate information from anywhere in the country, or even in some cases, the world. Windows 2000 offers some unique capabilities for providing this access to users. With advanced routing capabilities, dial-in access and authentication services, and support for virtual private networks, Windows 2000 is ideally suited for supporting a Wide Area Network infrastructure.

Microsoft defines the "Designing a Wide Area Network Infrastructure" objectives as

> **Design an implementation strategy for dial-up remote access.**
>
> - **Design a remote access solution that uses Routing and Remote Access.**
>
> - **Integrate authentication with Remote Authentication Dial-In User Service (RADIUS).**

▶ One of the first widely used remote access solutions was dial-up remote access. Starting at speeds as low as 150 bits per second, dial-up access is now a ubiquitous solution for remote access. Although other technologies are becoming increasingly popular, dial-in remains one of the most reliable methods for providing remote users secure access to the corporate network. With Windows 2000, Microsoft has greatly improved the security and authentication capabilities of the Routing and Remote Access service. For this objective, Microsoft expects you to not only understand how to install and configure Routing and Remote Access service, but also how to design a reliable, secure remote access solution using the Routing and Remote Access service and RADIUS.

CHAPTER 5

Designing a Wide Area Network Infrastructure

Design a virtual private network (VPN) strategy.

▶ Although dial-in is one of the oldest and most reliable remote access solutions, virtual private networks are rapidly becoming the remote access solutions of choice in many corporations, because of the support for high-speed and wireless Internet connectivity in many employees' homes as well as in branch offices and hotels. Virtual private networks use strong encryption and authentication to ensure the security and integrity of information sent across a public network. For this objective, Microsoft expects you to understand not only the underlying technology used to create virtual private networks, but also how to design a secure, reliable VPN strategy for a corporate environment.

Design a Routing and Remote Access routing solution to connect locations.

- **Design a demand-dial routing strategy.**

▶ Another solution for providing remote connectivity is the use of a demand-dial routing strategy. This strategy is well suited for supporting small branch offices where VPN or traditional dial-up solutions are not appropriate. For this objective, Microsoft expects you to understand when this solution is applicable, how the underlying routing protocols work, and how to design and implement this solution.

▶ Be sure you have a thorough understanding of the security capabilities of all the different technologies discussed in this section. With the focus on security in the industry today, Microsoft considers security to be one of the cornerstones of Windows 2000. Because this chapter deals entirely with providing access to networks and information remotely, it is an area that demands special attention be paid to the security of each solution.

▶ Although it is important to understand how to install and configure each of these services, always keep in mind that this is a design exam. You need to be able to understand how each of these solutions could be integrated into a comprehensive network strategy. Pay close attention to the examples used in each section. These are based on real-world implementations, and will give you a good handle on when and why each of these solutions is applicable.

▶ Pay close attention to the capabilities of remote access policies. Windows 2000 includes a number of policy-based management capabilities, and understanding the policies associated with remote access will be important for this exam. You cannot design a secure dial-up or VPN solution without knowing what policies to apply, and why they are appropriate.

▶ Be sure to complete the exercises at the end of the chapter. Microsoft is striving to make certification exams more rigorous. Familiarity with not only the theory, but also the hands-on portion of the configuration and troubleshooting of remote access, will be important for this exam.

Designing an Implementation Strategy for Dial-Up Remote Access

Design an implementation strategy for dial-up remote access.

If you have ever worked in a corporate network environment, you may be asking yourself when did dial-up modems become part of a Wide Area Network (WAN)? The traditional definition of a WAN is at least two Local Area Networks (LANs) that are separated by a relatively large geographical distance. These LANs are usually connected by a point-to-point or frame relay T-1 network connection, although smaller offices sometimes take advantage of lower-speed connections such as Integrated Subscriber Digital Network (ISDN) or even constantly connected dial-up connections.

A recent innovation in WAN transport is the use of the Internet (the world's largest WAN) in conjunction with Virtual Private Networks (VPNs) and less-expensive high-speed connections such as Digital Subscriber Line (DSL) or cable modem to connect offices without the need to build a private network. We will actually discuss both of these types of WAN connections later in the chapter.

But that still doesn't explain the use of the term WAN to describe a dial-up remote access solution using Windows 2000 server. In this instance, Microsoft has recognized that the traditional definition of WAN no longer fits many computing environments. With the huge growth of the mobile worker, as a home office worker or a traveling employee, the traditional WAN has been supplanted by a new networking paradigm. Employees and businesses have conspired to redefine the term *WAN* by essentially extending the coverage of the corporate network to include anywhere an employee might be connected. So, for the purposes of this exam, (and to Microsoft's credit, for a more accurate definition of WAN) keep in mind that a WAN is more than a collection of T-1 lines.

Now that we know why we are talking about remote access dial-up as part of our corporate WAN, let's look at how we design a reliable, scalable dial-up remote access solution using Windows 2000 server.

Design a Remote Access Solution That Uses Routing and Remote Access

The basic use of the Routing and Remote Access service (RRAS) is to provide dial-up remote access to a Windows 2000 Server and the corporate network. If you have ever used a modem to connect to your ISP, you have used a form of dial-up remote access. However, instead of giving you access to www.beaniebabies.com, an RRAS server will provide you with access to your corporate resources, the corporate intranet, your mail servers, and any other networks or systems you might need to access. To set up a Windows 2000 RRAS server, all you need is at least one modem or a multiport adapter, and analog telephone lines or other WAN connections (such as ISDN). If you want the server to provide access to a network, you'll need a network adapter connected to the network you want the user to be able (see Exam Tip on this page) to which the server provides access.

The Windows 2000 RRAS provides some important new features that will make designing and supporting a remote access solution easier. These features include

♦ **Bandwidth Allocation Protocol (BAP)**. The Bandwidth Allocation Protocol (BAP) makes significant improvements to the Multilink PPP protocol supported in earlier versions of RAS. BAP can be used to dynamically add or remove aggregated dial-up connections based on the traffic flow across the connection. This is especially useful when you are paying for your connection based on bandwidth utilization or connections. (For example, if you are using ISDN as your dial-up connection, you are probably being charged for each ISDN session you initiate. If you are aggregating two 128K ISDN connections, it costs twice as much. BAP allows you to use only the second ISDN connection when it is needed, and could reduce the cost of the connection dramatically.)

EXAM TIP

Try it before you take the exam. Setting up a Windows 2000 RRAS server for dial-in is very simple and not very expensive. All you need is a PC with a modem, a phone line, network adapter, and Windows 2000 Server and you can set up and test the dial-in portion of this chapter. With Microsoft's increased focus on testing hands-on ability and experience, the more time you can spend configuring and testing RRAS, the better understanding you will have when you take the test. It will also help if you ever need to put one of these into production at your company.

◆ **RADIUS (Remote Authentication Dial-In User Service) Support**. The Windows 2000 RRAS can act as a RADIUS client to a RADIUS server. This allows you to move the authentication of remote users from the native Windows 2000 RRAS to an external RADIUS server. The benefits of this include the potential for centralized user administration using existing RADIUS servers, improved accounting and reporting information, and support for an industry-standard authentication mechanism. RADIUS is still used by virtually all Internet service providers for authenticating dial-in users. Windows 2000 also provides RADIUS server functionality with the Internet Authentication Service (IAS). An IAS server can provide centralized authentication, authorization, and accounting functions and a central location to configure remote access policies. Combine the two capabilities and you could configure a pool of standalone RRAS servers that all authenticate against a central Windows 2000 server with IAS providing RADIUS.

◆ **Active Directory Support**. The Windows 2000 RRAS provides full integration with Active Directory. User dial-in settings can be stored in Active Directory and accessed by any registered Windows 2000 RRAS servers. Active Directory–based tools such as the Routing and Remote Access console can be used to manage registered RRAS servers, reducing the administrative overhead dramatically over previous versions of RAS.

But how do you go about designing a remote access solution for your company? The first step in designing any solution is to identify the requirements. In a business environment, this usually means asking the person requesting this solution a lot of questions. In the case of a dial-up remote access solution, you should ask the following questions at a minimum:

◆ How many users will need access through the RRAS server?

◆ How many users will be accessing the RRAS server concurrently?

◆ What applications will be used through this connection?

◆ What type of security is required?

◆ What client operating systems do you need to support?

Now that you have an idea of what questions you'll need to ask, we need to think about what to do after you have answers:

◆ How many users will need access through the RRAS server? Some things you need to think about after you have a user count include

- How are you going to authenticate all these users? Will a user ID and password be adequate? If you are a bank or a nuclear power plant, you will probably need a more secure solution such as a smart card.

- Where will you authenticate the users? Should you use your Active Directory for this authentication or should you set up a dedicated domain for RRAS users? Using Active Directory is easier from an account management perspective, but using the same passwords to authenticate users for remote access and application access is not generally a good idea from a security perspective.

- Who will administer the remote access accounts? Should it be someone from the security department, someone from the Windows administration team, or someone from the network team?

- How will you keep track of who should have accounts and who shouldn't? When a new employee is hired, what will be the process to get them a new account on the remote access server? Equally important, if an employee leaves the company, how will they be removed from the remote access server? And undoubtedly the most important of all—how will you handle an employee who is being laid off or fired? Disgruntled employees are a serious security issue, especially with remote access accounts, and frequently the usual processes are not quick enough to prevent abuse. What is your process to bypass the process when needed?

◆ How many users will be accessing the RRAS server concurrently? This is an almost impossible question to answer, but without some idea you'll have a tough time determining how many lines you will need to support your users. The general rule with this question is aim high. It is better to have idle modems available for peak utilization than it is to have end users waiting for the busy signals to stop when they need to close their end of the quarter financials.

  • A good rule of thumb for an average user population is the 8:1 rule. That means for every 8 users, you will need 1 modem line. If you know your users will be very heavy users, or that they will all be connecting at the same time (to submit weekly time cards, for example), you will need to lower the ratio to something specific to these requirements.

  • After you have determined what the concurrency will be, you need to think about the hardware you will need to support these users. Can you provision enough modems in a single server for all these users or will you need to set up multiple servers to provide enough capacity? There are a number of vendors who make multiport serial adapters, which can provide up to 128 modems on a single card.

  • Do your concurrency requirements include any provisions for fault tolerance? Do you need spare parts, service contracts, additional servers, or a "hot site" remote access solution? In a company where your employees work from an office environment, and your remote access is used by a few traveling executives and some dedicated employees burning the midnight oil after they get home from work, you might not need the redundancy. If your company has a large number of traveling employees (consultants, sales people, and so on) or a large population of telecommuters, you should at least consider some sort of fault-tolerant/redundant solution.

EXAM TIP

How can you find out what modem hardware is supported by Windows 2000?   The best place to look for the correct hardware for your solution is the Hardware Compatibility List (http://www.microsoft.com/ hcl/default.asp). This will not only tell you whether the hardware you have or would like to install is certified, but it also provides an excellent resource for identifying potential vendors to meet your needs. This is a critical requirement when doing solution design.

IN THE FIELD

REDUNDANT REMOTE ACCESS SOLUTIONS

Let's talk about the real-world use of the RRAS service and redundancy for just a minute. Where will you usually find a dial-in remote access solution in today's business environment? Generally, in smaller companies or in small locations of large companies. The companies who require huge dial-in remote access solutions are becoming increasingly rare, as Internet access and VPNs become ubiquitous. So, why spend all this time on designing a solution that no one uses? Because the dial-in server has been relegated to a less prominent, but still critical position, in large networks. The dial-in server has become the preferred mechanism for providing redundancy for those ubiquitous (and sometime problematic) VPN solutions.

Here's the way one Fortune 500 company is using its RAS solution. This company has a widely distributed workforce, and access to the corporate network is critical. It has redundant Internet connections and redundant VPN servers providing remote access for about 5,000 employees. It also has a 72-line remote access server for emergencies. This is used for employees who are having VPN-client issues, employees who are traveling and aren't able to get Internet access, and for mission-critical employees in the event of a complete VPN outage. This solution is cost effective and reliable, and in the event of an outage provides a critical service for remote employees who need access to mail, sales information, documentation, and a host of other applications.

So, although you may not be designing a lot of dial-in RAS solutions for 15,000 employees, you could very easily find yourself deploying dial-in access as part of a comprehensive remote access strategy.

◆ What applications will be used through this connection? This will give you an idea not only of the type of connections to provision (although you will generally provision as high-speed a connection as possible), but also what parts of your internal network these users will need to access.

- Whenever possible, you should restrict network access for remote access users to the smallest number of systems as possible, to limit your exposure to potential attackers. You also need to take routing into account with as you design the solution. How will your remote users get from your dial-in solution to the network on which the application resides? And you need to be sure the application server is able to get back to your dial-in users. It is not unusual for dial-in solutions to use reserved or custom IP addressing, which can cause routing issues. Be sure to take this into account as you are doing your solution design.

- Applications will also tell you what protocols you need to support. Although TCP/IP is far and away the most common, you may have Macintosh users who need AppleTalk, or have a legacy application running on a NetWare server that requires IPX. You need to make sure to take these into account as part of your design.

- You should be sure to test your applications, and make sure they can be supported by the dial-up connection. Be ready to look into thin client or Web-based technologies when you encounter bandwidth-intensive applications. Running Microsoft Outlook across a slow modem connection is probably not acceptable. Using Internet Explorer to access Outlook Web Access probably is acceptable.

◆ What type of security is required? Can you just use IDs and passwords, or do you need additional security?

- Will you need to use callback? If callback is configured, the server will call your workstation modem back to complete the dial-up connection. This is useful for a couple of reasons. It allows you to log phone numbers of connecting users without relying on caller ID. This is very handy if you have a break-in. Callback can also be used to restrict what numbers people can use to connect. You can associate a specific number (or numbers) to a user. If they try to connect from outside that number or pool of numbers, they won't get a connection. Finally, callback has a non–security-related benefit. If you want to spare employees the cost of long distance connections when they are connecting via the dial-in server, you can use the callback option to shift those calls to your location. If you have better long distance rates than your employees (and you should), you can reduce costs and accounting overhead through the use of callback.

- How about encryption? You may find you need to encrypt your data to protect it from interception. Be sure to configure your security as tightly as possible. It is far better to err on the side of caution than to find out that the code for the company's new "killer app" leaked out to the world through a security flaw in your RRAS server.

◆ What client operating systems do you need to support? If you work in a very mixed environment, where users could be using a combination of Windows 98, Windows NT, Windows Me, Linux, Windows 2000, and Macintosh systems, you need to pay close attention to what protocols and authentication methods you will need to use to support them all. As with most things, the more standardized your environment, the easier it is to ensure you are able to support all your end users.

Okay, we've asked our questions and have covered what to do with the answers. Now let's discuss some of the specifics of what remote access services are supported by Windows 2000 Server that can help you in your design.

The first thing we need to look at is what exactly remote access is under Windows 2000. If you have worked with Windows NT 4, you are undoubtedly familiar with the Remote Access Service (RAS). RAS was an NT 4 add-on service, which provided the capability to receive incoming modem calls and enable the user to connect to the network. RAS was also used the other direction: You needed RAS to connect your Windows NT Server or Workstation to another host, either NT or a generic dial-in server.

This model has changed dramatically in Windows 2000. Not only is the Routing and Remote Access Service (RRAS) (the next generation of the Remote Access Service) installed automatically with the operating system, it also bundles a number of features that used to be distributed through other services under Windows NT. For example, not only are RAS services available with RRAS, but the Windows 2000 VPN service is included in RRAS as well.

To use RRAS, you will need a Windows 2000 Server with RRAS enabled and configured. This can be either a member server or a domain controller, although for security reasons it is generally a better idea to use a member server whenever possible. Providing modem-based access to your domain controller can sometimes be a security risk. Although that makes setting up an RRAS server sound easy, it is a little more complicated than that. We need to discuss a little more about the makeup of the RRAS before we jump into enabling and configuring it.

To start, you need to be familiar with the supported dial-in protocols. The Windows 2000 Server RRAS supports the Point-to-Point Protocol (PPP) for dial-in remote access. PPP provides support for several key features that you will need when you design your first remote access solution using Windows 2000 Server. These include

◆ **Dynamic Host Control Protocol (DHCP)**. DHCP is used to assign dynamic IP addresses to devices; in this case, to remote users connecting to the Windows 2000 Server through RRAS.

◆ **Compression**. Compression is used to transmit data using fewer data bits than the original data requires. This improves performance across the dial-up lines, which are relatively slow in today's networking environment.

◆ **Encryption**. Encryption is used to translate data to an unreadable format unless you have the correct key to translate the date back to a readable format. When used in conjunction with either Extensible Authentication Protocol—Transport Layer Security (EAP-TLS) or Microsoft Challenge Handshake Authentication Protocol (MS-CHAP) PPP supports the use of the Microsoft Point-to-Point Encryption (MPPE) encryption protocol. MPPE supports uses the Rivest-Shamir-Adleman (RSA) RC4 stream cipher, with 40-bit, 56-bit, or 128-bit key strengths.

We will be looking more closely at the authentication and encryption options a little later in the chapter.

Windows 2000 Server RRAS also supports other dial-up protocols, including

◆ **Serial Line Interface Protocol (SLIP)**. SLIP is an older protocol used primarily by Unix servers. Although Windows 2000 Server RRAS supports SLIP, it will act only as a SLIP client. SLIP clients cannot connect to a Windows 2000 RRAS server.

◆ **Microsoft RAS Protocol**. This Microsoft-proprietary protocol can be used only with the NetBEUI network protocol. The Microsoft RAS protocol is almost never used in production environments because of the widespread use of PPP, but it is supported.

◆ **Apple Remote Access Protocol (ARAP)**. ARAP is used to connect Apple Macintosh computers to a Windows 2000 RRAS server through dial-up.

> **EXAM TIP**
>
> **Serial Line Interface Protocol (SLIP) Support in Windows 2000**
> For the exam, be sure to remember that although Windows 2000 does support SLIP, it supports it only as a SLIP client. Windows 2000 will not act as a SLIP server. In order to connect to a Windows 2000 server with a modem, you must use the Point-to-Point Protocol (PPP).

Okay, now you know what server protocols are supported by the Windows 2000 RRAS. Let's take a second to review the network protocols that are supported through RRAS:

◆ **TCP/IP**. TCP/IP is a suite of protocols that allows hosts and network devices to communicate with each other. TCP/IP is the protocol that runs the Internet, and is rapidly becoming the de facto standard for network environments.

◆ **IPX**. IPX (Internet Packet Exchange) is the native NetWare protocol created by Novell to allow users to connect to NetWare servers. Recent releases of NetWare have fully supported TCP/IP, and the use of IPX is waning quickly. IPX is supported by Windows 2000 Server to allow access to legacy NetWare servers.

◆ **NetBEUI**. NetBEUI (NetBIOS Extended User Interface) was originally developed by IBM for use with its LAN Manager operating system. Microsoft later extended the protocol. Generally considered to be best used in small workgroups or LANs, NetBEUI is not generally used in corporate environments because of its inefficient design and lack of routability.

◆ **AppleTalk**. AppleTalk is a network architecture developed by Apple Computer. AppleTalk provided a user-friendly network protocol that allowed Apple computer users to plug in and connect to the network. This protocol has been almost entirely replaced with TCP/IP, but is still supported by Windows 2000 Server to allow Apple/Macintosh users connectivity in a Microsoft environment.

> **EXAM TIP**
>
> **What good is AppleTalk support?**
> It is important to remember that with the addition of AppleTalk support, the Windows 2000 RRAS is the first Microsoft remote access service to support Macintosh clients through dial-up PPP connections.

We know some of the features, and we have talked about the supported protocols. We need to cover the different ways of authenticating to our RRAS server before we get into some of the specifics. Windows 2000 RRAS supports the following dial-in authentication methods:

◆ **Extensible Authentication Protocol (EAP).** EAP-TLS is an extension to the Point-to-Point Protocol (PTPP). EAP provides a standard mechanism for support of additional authentication methods within PPP such as smart cards, one-time passwords, and certificates. EAP is critical for secure Windows 2000 VPNs, because it offers stronger authentication methods (such as X.509 certificates) instead of relying on the user ID and password schemes used traditionally.

◆ **Challenge Handshake Authentication Protocol (CHAP).** CHAP negotiates an encrypted authentication using MD5 (Message Digest 5), an industry-standard hashing scheme. CHAP uses challenge-response with one-way MD5 hashing on the response. This allows you to authenticate to the server without actually sending your password over the network. Because this is an industry-standard authentication method, it allows Windows 2000 to securely connect to almost all third-party PPP servers.

◆ **Microsoft Challenge Handshake Authentication Protocol (MS-CHAP).** Microsoft created MS-CHAP, an extension of CHAP, to authenticate remote Windows workstations, increasing the protocol's functionality by integrating the encryption and hashing algorithms used on Windows networks. Like CHAP, MS-CHAP uses a challenge-response mechanism with one-way encryption on the response. Although MS-CHAP is consistent with standard CHAP as much as possible, the MS-CHAP response packet is in a format specifically designed for computers running a Windows operating system. A new version of the Microsoft Challenge Handshake Authentication Protocol (MS-CHAP V2) is also available. This new protocol provides mutual authentication, stronger initial data encryption keys, and different encryption keys for sending and receiving.

◆ **Shiva Password Authentication Protocol (SPAP).** SPAP is used specifically to allow Shiva client computers to connect to a Windows 2000 Server and to allow Windows 2000 client computers to connect to Shiva servers.

◆ **Password Authentication Protocol (PAP).** PAP uses unencrypted (plain-text) passwords for authenticating users and is considered the least secure authentication protocol available. PAP is usually used as the authentication of last resort; it's used when a more secure form of authentication is not available. You might need to use this protocol when you are connecting to a non–Windows-based server.

◆ **Unauthenticated Access.** Microsoft RRAS will also support unauthenticated access, which means it can be configured to accept connections without requiring a user ID and password. This is almost always a bad idea, although Microsoft does recommend it for some very special-purpose circumstances, as when an external authentication method is being used, or when you are setting the server up for guest access to a limited number of resources.

Now let's look at what is involved in enabling and then configuring Windows 2000 RRAS.

STEP BY STEP

5.1 Enabling the Routing and Remote Access Service

1. Open the Routing and Remote Access console by going to Start, Settings, and opening the Control Panel. From within the Control Panel, open the Administrative Tools. Select Routing and Remote Access. The Routing and Remote Access console will open (see Figure 5.1).

continues

EXAM TIP

Do you need a user ID to connect to a dial-up Microsoft RRAS server? The answer for the exam is no. You can configure access without requiring any authentication. However, before you set something like that up in a production environment, make absolutely sure that you have either limited access to resources, or you are using a different authentication method before you turn on the modems.

EXAM TIP

How do you install the Routing and Remote Access Service? You don't need to install the Routing and Remote Access Service because it's installed as part of the installation of the operating system. You just need to enable it, and then configure it for the services you need.

EXAM TIP

Do you need an authentication protocol to connect to a dial-up Microsoft RRAS server? Yes. The Windows 2000 remote access client must always be configured to use at least one authentication protocol. The unauthenticated access protocol is still considered a protocol, even though you don't need a user ID or password.

continued

FIGURE 5.1
The Routing and Remote Access Service is managed using the Routing and Remote Access applet in the Administrative Tools menu. This is a Microsoft Management Console snap-in.

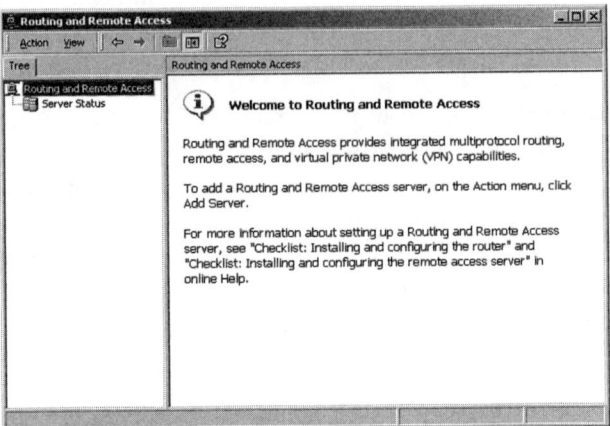

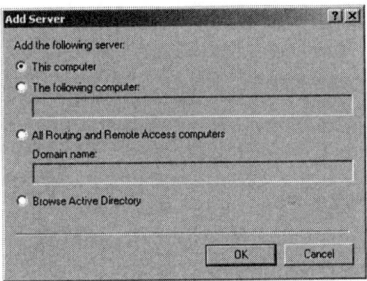

FIGURE 5.2
The Routing and Remote Access console allows you to enable the local computer, a computer by name, or all the Routing and Remote Access servers in a domain, or find the server to enable by browsing the Active Directory.

2. Click Action and select Configure and Enable Routing and Remote Access. This opens the Add Server dialog box (see Figure 5.2).

3. Select This Computer and click OK. Your computer will appear in the left pane (The Tree View) with a red arrow on the icon (see Figure 5.3). This indicates that the server has been enabled, but it is presently down. In this case, that's because we haven't configured it yet.

FIGURE 5.3
The red arrow next to the computer icon indicates that the server is running the Routing and Remote Access Service, but that it is not presently up.

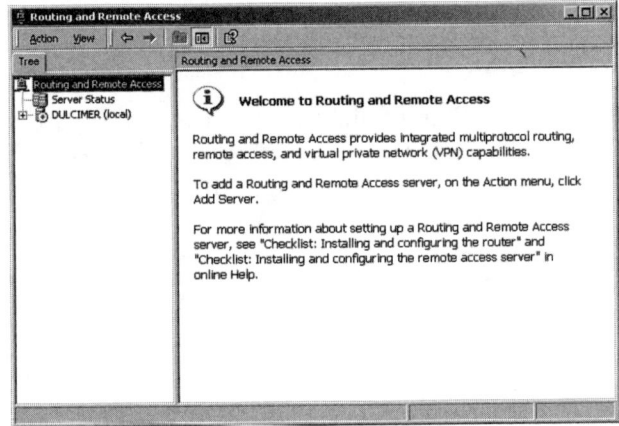

You have now successfully enabled the Routing and Remote Access Service on the local computer. Unfortunately, your server still isn't ready to start accepting dial-up connections. Now, we have to configure the Routing and Remote Access Service for dial-in.

STEP BY STEP

5.2 Configuring the Routing and Remote Access Service for Dial-In Use

1. Open the Routing and Remote Access console by going to Start, Setting, and opening the Control Panel. From within the Control Panel, open the Administrative Tools. Select Routing and Remote Access. The Routing and Remote Access console will open.

2. Right-click the server you want to configure and select Configure and Enable Routing and Remote Access (see Figure 5.4). This opens the Routing and Remote Access Server Setup Wizard (see Figure 5.5).

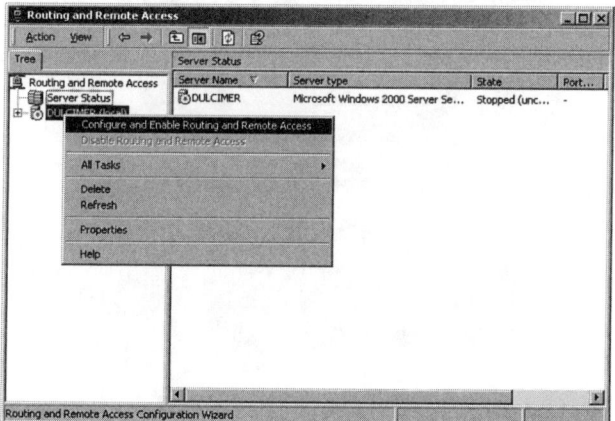

FIGURE 5.4
Configuring a Routing and Remote Access server is done with the same menu selection as adding a server to the list of Routing and Remote Access servers.

continues

continued

FIGURE 5.5
Configuring your Routing and Remote Access server is done through the familiar Windows 2000 configuration wizard interface.

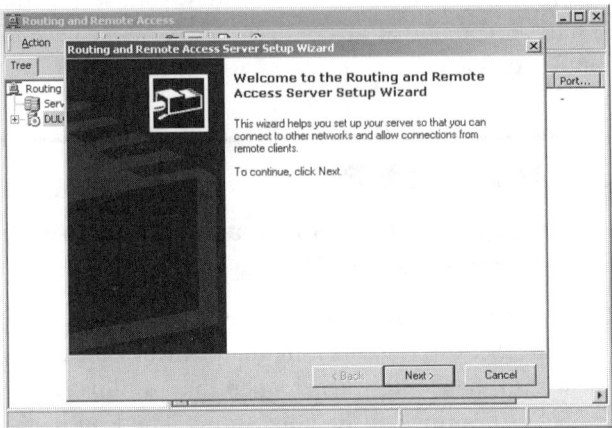

EXAM TIP

Do you need the wizard for all configurations of the Routing and Remote Access service? If you have a custom configuration for your RRAS server, or don't like the Windows 2000 configuration wizard interface, you can select Manually Configured Server. This starts the server with the default settings, and you can configure it manually to whatever configuration you need.

FIGURE 5.6
The Wizard allows you to select the most common configuration options for the Routing and Remote Access service.

3. Click Next. The list of common configurations for a Routing and Remote Access server are shown with option buttons to select which type of RRAS configuration you need (see Figure 5.6).

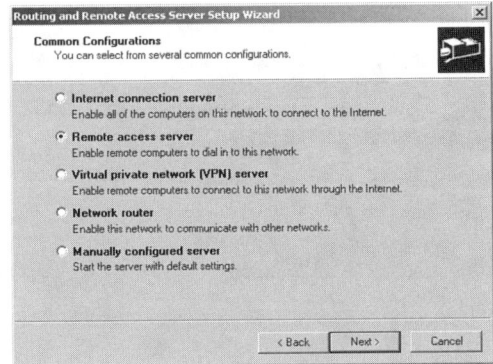

4. Select Remote Access Server and click Next. This opens the Remote Client Protocols dialog box (see Figure 5.7). The protocols shown are the supported protocols installed on the server's LAN interface. If you select the No, I Need Additional Protocols option button, you will be shown any additional installed protocols. If the protocol you need is not installed on the system, you will need to install it before it appears on this list.

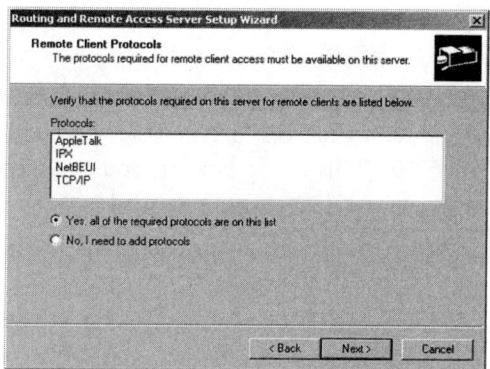

FIGURE 5.7
The Remote Client Protocols dialog box allows you to select which protocols will be supported for remote clients.

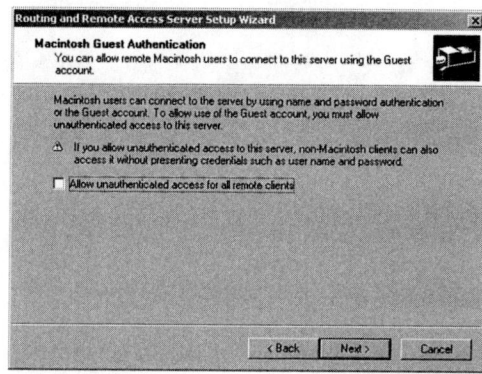

FIGURE 5.8
This dialog box allows you to determine how Macintosh authentication will be done after the server configuration is completed.

5. Click Next. If you have the AppleTalk protocol installed then the Macintosh Guest Authentication dialog box will open (see Figure 5.8). This is where you can enable unauthenticated access. Avoid this if at all possible.

6. Click Next. The IP Address Assignment dialog box opens (see Figure 5.9). If you select Automatically, the DCHP server on your network will be used to provide IP addresses to users when they connect. If you select From a Specified Range of Addresses, you will be prompted to enter a pool of addresses to be used for remote access clients when they connect.

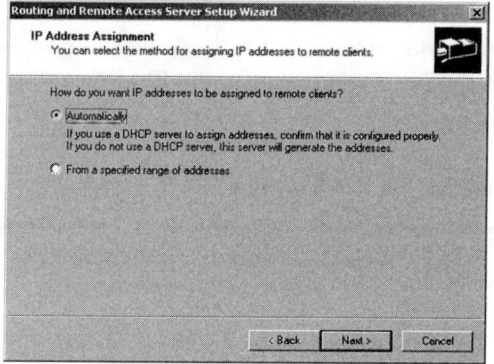

FIGURE 5.9
The IP Address Assignment dialog box allows you to decide whether to use the Dynamic Host Control Protocol (DHCP) or static IP addressing for your users when they are accessing the network via dial-up modem.

continues

continued

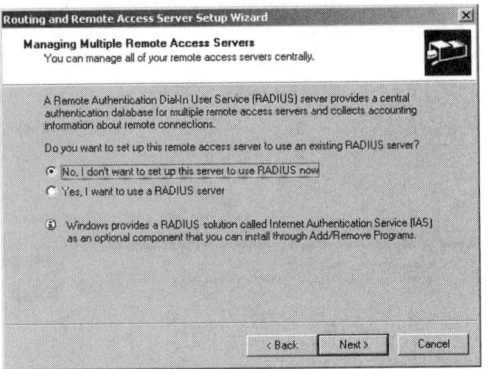

FIGURE 5.10
If you have a RADIUS server on your network for remote access authentication, you would configure it here.

FIGURE 5.11
The last dialog box of the wizard allows you to go back to correct any mistakes you might have made, or complete the configuration. You can also select to have the RRAS Help displayed when you exit the wizard.

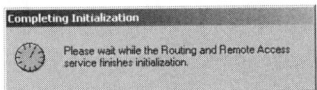

FIGURE 5.12
It can take a couple of minutes for the process to start, depending on the hardware and the configuration complexity.

7. Select Automatically and Click Next. The Managing Multiple Remote Access Servers dialog box opens (see Figure 5.10). This dialog box lets you configure authentication to a RADIUS server if needed.

8. Select No, I Don't Want to Set Up This Server to Use Radius Now and click Next. The Completing the Routing and Remote Access Server Setup dialog box opens (see Figure 5.11). You can configure a RADIUS server after this configuration is completed, if necessary.

9. Click Finish to complete your installation. You'll need to wait a couple minutes for the service to start (see Figure 5.12). When you return to the Routing and Remote Access console, you'll notice the icon now has a green arrow (see Figure 5.13). This indicates a configured and available RRAS server.

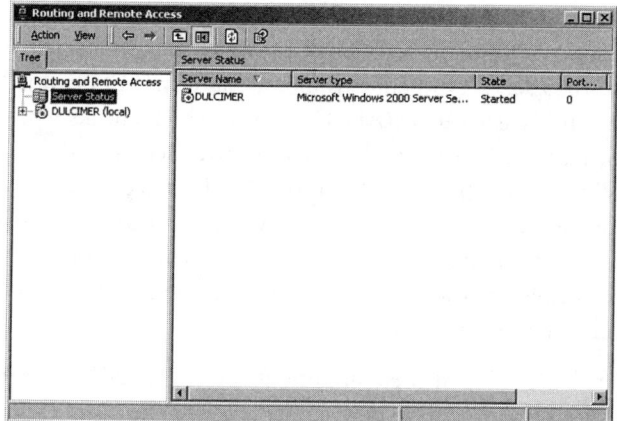

We have completed our first objective, and you should have a good idea of what goes into the planning, solution development, and eventual implementation of a Windows 2000 RRAS server for dial-in access to the network. Now we need to discuss how we could use RADIUS to centralize the management of accounts and utilization reporting for your Routing and Remote Access server(s).

Integrate Authentication with Remote Authentication Dial-In User Service (RADIUS)

Integrate authentication with Remote Authentication Dial-In User Service (RADIUS).

Now that we have talked about how to design and build a remote access dial-in solution using a Windows 2000 server and the Routing and Remote Access Service, we need to discuss one of the more popular authentication services being used in the industry today—the Remote Authentication Dial-In User Service (RADIUS). Let's start at the beginning. If you are going to use RADIUS in your solution design, you need to be sure you know what RADIUS is.

RADIUS is an industry-standard authentication and accounting system used in conjunction with Remote Access Servers. When you dial in to the RAS server, you enter your username and password. This information is passed to a RADIUS server, which checks whether the information is correct and then authorizes access to the system. With Windows 2000 Server, Microsoft has bundled RADIUS authentication as part of the Internet Authentication Service. In this chapter, we will discuss the generic makeup of RADIUS and then look specifically at how and why you would use IAS/RADIUS in your dial-in remote access designs.

Let's start by looking at the components of the RADIUS authentication architecture. RADIUS authentication is made up of three basic elements, which include

◆ **Remote Host**. This is the host (PC or other workstation) that is requesting authenticated access to the network or system resources remotely. This is typically done via a PPP dialer which is connecting to a Remote Access Server (RAS), and upon authentication will become a node on the remote network, as discussed in the "Design a Remote Access Solution That Uses Routing and Remote Access" section of this chapter. Another very popular use for RADIUS is in conjunction with some Virtual Private Network servers, which allow the user to connect to the RAS server across a public network such as the Internet. (Designing a VPN solution with Windows 2000 RRAS will be discussed at length in the "Designing a Virtual Private Network (VPN) Strategy" section of this chapter.)

◆ **The Remote Access Server (RAS)**. The Remote Access Server (or RAS) is the server that is used to provide dial-in access to network, generally through PPP dial-in calls. This server acts as the point-of-user authentication via the RADIUS Server, and after the user is authenticated, routes that user onto the network.

◆ **The RADIUS Server**. The RADIUS Server accepts authentication requests from one or more Remote Access Servers, performs the authentication, and responds with the result—either an accept or a reject. Another useful feature of most RADIUS servers is the ability to provide Accounting services. This is dependent on whether the RAS device can support RADIUS accounting.

Now that we've looked at the components of RADIUS authentication, let's look at how a typical RADIUS authentication session works:

1. A remote host dials into an RAS server and begins to negotiate a connection using PPP.

2. The RAS server passes the user ID and password (the authentication information) provided by the remote host as part of the PPP negotiation to the RADIUS server.

3. The RADIUS server checks the authentication information and if the user ID and password are good, it issues an accept response to the RAS server, along with profile information required by the RAS to set up the connection. (RADIUS profiles can be used to provide IP addressing, to restrict concurrent connections, to set idle timeouts, and a number of other connection-related information, depending on the options supported by the RAS server.) If the RADIUS server is passed bad authentication information, it issues a reject response to the RAS server, along with a text string indicating the reason. The PPP negotiation is terminated at this point. Depending on the settings and options, the reason for termination could be passed back to the remote host.

4. After the RAS server receives an accept response from the RADIUS server, it completes the PPP negotiation with the remote host. The remote host can now access the network, within the restrictions of the RAS configuration and RADIUS profile information.

USING RADIUS FOR CORPORATE ISP ACCOUNT MANAGEMENT

One thing you may be asked to do as a systems or network architect or solutions designer is to set up dial ISP accounts for the employees of your company. As we are all aware, home offices, traveling users, and wireless devices are becoming a larger part of the business-computing environment. Coupled with the rapid spread of VPNs and a large demand for access to the corporate network from all these devices, ISP accounts are moving from a benefit of working for the company to a requirement for successful employment. So, how will you manage this access?

You can always go the low-tech route, where you e-mail your ISP additions and deletions to your list of users based on new hires and terminations. This is effective if you are working for a small company, but can become very time consuming if you work for a large company where new hires and terminations can be a daily occurrence. So, what would be a better solution? Because this chapter is about RADIUS, that would be a good guess.

Most RADIUS servers will allow you to do something called *Proxy RADIUS* for authentication. What Proxy RADIUS allows you to do is manage your users on a local RADIUS server, which is then used by the ISP's RADIUS servers to authenticate users. This allows your ISP to set you up with a couple of settings on their RADIUS server, and you can then use the Windows 2000 Internet Authentication Services RADIUS to manage the authorized users for you.

This is a very common architecture, and most of the major ISPs will support it. In fact, many of them require this architecture.

One other benefit of this architecture becomes evident if you are also using the Windows 2000 RRAS as a dial-in access service for users to access your network. You can use the same RADIUS server to authenticate your dial-in users as you do your ISP users.

One other thing to be aware of is the authentication used in conjunction with RADIUS. RADIUS supports the following two forms of authentication:

◆ **PAP (Password Authentication Protocol).** PAP is a very simple authentication method. The remote host sends its password to the RADIUS server, and the RADIUS server validates it. The main drawback of this method is that the password goes from the remote host to the RADIUS server in clear text.

◆ **CHAP (Challenge Handshake Authentication Protocol).** CHAP removes the clear-text password issue found with PAP by having the RAS server generate a random number (the challenge) and send it to the user. The user's PPP client then encrypts the user's password using this challenge by creating a digest of the password concatenated with the challenge. The digest is sent to the RAS server, which forwards it to the RADIUS server. The RADIUS server cannot read the password in its encrypted digest form, so it performs the same encrypting operation using the challenge and password in its database. It then compares the result with the information it was sent by the RAS server, and if the two digests match, the user is authenticated.

Now that we have discussed how RADIUS works, let's talk about why you would want to use RADIUS in your environment. There are a number of benefits to utilizing RADIUS in conjunction with an RRAS dial-in access solution. The main benefit is that the IAS allows you to provide centralized authentication services to all your RRAS servers. This is a major boon to your traveling users, because with a single point of authentication you can dial into the New York office RRAS server on Monday, and then dial into the Los Angeles office RRAS server on Thursday. As long as you are authorized on the RADIUS server, you can connect to the server. And in addition to centralized authentication, you also get centralized accounting so that management can tell how much usage the RRAS servers are getting. This accounting information is also very useful for tracking down security violations and abuse. If the RADIUS logs show you were logged in from a number in Phoenix and a number in San Jose although you were at home in St. Paul, it's a pretty good indication that someone besides you is using your account.

Although the centralized authentication and accounting are great reasons for using RADIUS, there is a Microsoft IAS-specific benefit to using RADIUS. It is tightly integrated with the Microsoft Active Directory. This means that in order to grant a remote host appropriate access to the network, IAS authenticates against the Windows 2000 Active Directory. This means there is a single database of users, and it is the same database you are already managing for all your other access.

Now that we have covered how it works and why you would want to use it, let's look at how you would add an RRAS server to allow it to use the Internet Authentication Service for RADIUS authentication.

STEP BY STEP

5.3 Adding a Routing and Remote Access Service Server to Internet Authentication Services

1. Open the Internet Authentication Services console by going to Start, Settings, and opening the Control Panel. From within the Control Panel, open the Internet Authentication applet. The Internet Authentication Services console will open (see Figure 5.14).

FIGURE 5.14
The Internet Authentication Services console allows you to configure not only RAS authentication, but also VPN server authentication.

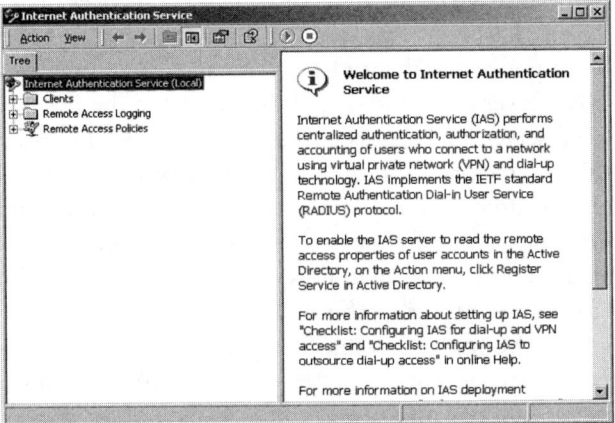

2. Right-click the Clients folder in the Tree view, and select New Client (see Figure 5.15). This opens the Add Client dialog box (see Figure 5.16).

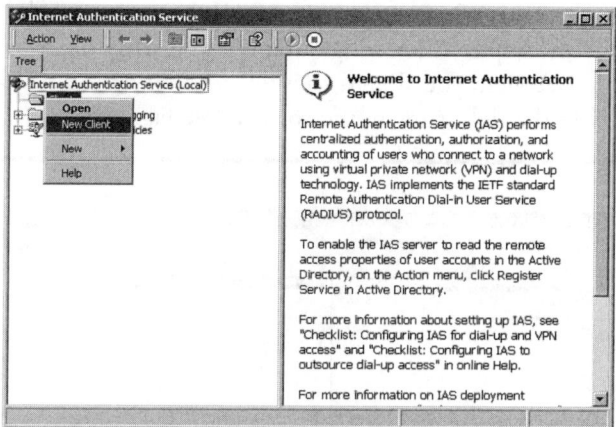

FIGURE 5.15
The context menu allows you to easily start the process of adding a new RADIUS client (RAS server) to authenticate against this server.

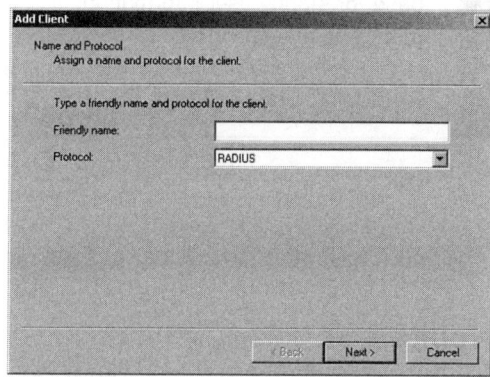

3. Enter the Friendly Name and click Next. The Client Information dialog box opens (see Figure 5.17).

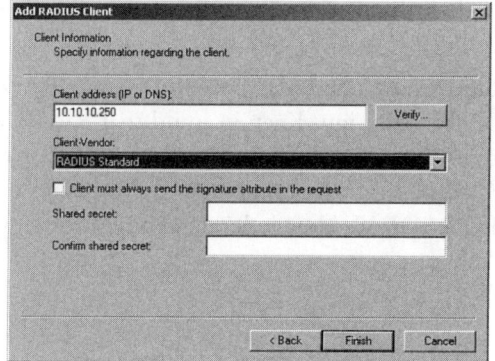

FIGURE 5.16
The Add Client dialog box prompts you for a name for your RAS server. RADIUS is the only choice available for the protocol.

FIGURE 5.17
The Windows 2000 Internet Authentication Service supports many different Client-Vendors.

continues

continued

What about fault tolerance? One other benefit of using RADIUS for authentication is that you can configure multiple RADIUS servers for authentication. So, if one server is down, the RRAS server will make its requests of the other server. Because the authentication using IAS uses the Active Directory database for storing user information, managing a second RADIUS server is very easy, and provides an excellent fault-tolerant solution.

4. Enter the IP address of your RRAS server, and select RADIUS Standard as the Client-Vendor type. Enter the Shared Secret, which is the information used to authenticate the RRAS server to the RADIUS server. Click Next to complete the configuration. If you select Clients in the Tree view, you should see the RRAS server you just added in the right pane of the console (see Figure 5.18).

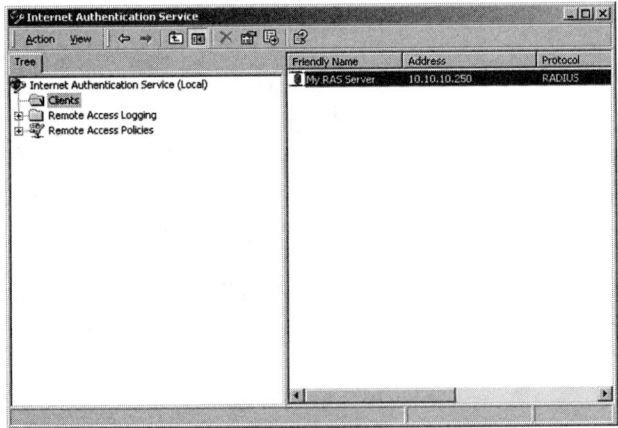

FIGURE 5.18
All your configured RRAS clients will appear in the right pane of the console.

If the question says ISP, it's probably a RADIUS question. One area in the Microsoft literature that you see RADIUS mentioned prominently is in conjunction with ISP connections. So, if you encounter a question on the exam that you have no idea about, but it references an ISP and authentication, look for an answer with RADIUS in it.

Now you should have a good idea how to integrate RADIUS into your remote dial-in solution. Keep in mind that RADIUS is an excellent solution for companies with multiple RRAS servers. If you have a single RRAS server, it is much more difficult to make a compelling case for RADIUS. Now let's talk about Virtual Private Networks.

DESIGNING A VIRTUAL PRIVATE NETWORK (VPN) STRATEGY

Design a virtual private network (VPN) strategy.

Before we dive into our set of design questions for putting together a VPN solution using the Windows 2000 Routing and Remote Access service, let's talk a little bit about VPNs in general and some of the factors that led to the creation of them.

First, let's agree on our definition of a VPN. For the sake of this discussion, a *VPN* is a private network that is constructed using encryption across a public network (such as the Internet) to connect its nodes. VPNs are used in one of two configurations. First, a user-to-network configuration, in which the remote user connects to the Internet (or to another public network) and using a VPN is able to securely become a node on the company network. This is commonly referred to as the Remote Access model for a VPN. The other configuration is when a site/office uses the VPN coupled with an Internet connection to securely connect to a network at another physical location that has an Internet connection and compatible VPN server. This is commonly referred to as a *site-to-site VPN*. The remote access VPN is used to supplant the standard remote access of dial-in or authenticated firewall access to the network. The site-to-site model is being used in places to remove the need for a Wide Area Network. Both configurations can offer significant cost savings over the more traditional access methods. VPNs come in many different types. There are hardware VPN servers, which are essentially routers with encryption cards and specialized code. Another VPN type is the firewall-based VPN, in which case a vendor has added some additional code to support the encryption and authentication needed for VPN connections. Finally, there are the solutions that run on a Network Operating System, such as the VPN bundled with Windows 2000, which is what we will discuss in this chapter.

Let's begin the discussion by covering the components and terminology Microsoft uses when discussing its VPN solutions:

◆ **VPN server**. The general definition of this is a server that accepts VPN connections from VPN clients. This server can accept host-to-network connections (remote access VPNs) or network-to-network connections (site-to-site VPN connections). Microsoft's VPN server is Windows 2000 Server with the Routing and Remote Access service configured to accept VPN connections.

◆ **VPN client**. This term actually had two meanings. The first definition is the host that initiates the VPN connection to a VPN server. Another definition of VPN client describes the software needed to initiate the VPN connection. In other words, you need to load a VPN client for your computer to become a VPN client. Windows 2000 RRAS supports Microsoft operating systems from Windows 9.x up as VPN clients. If you need to support other operating systems, you will need to look for another vendor.

◆ **Tunnel.** The term *tunnel* is used to describe the virtual connection that your data traverses. Your date is encapsulated in the encrypted data stream, to ensure it remains secure.

◆ **VPN connection**. The VPN connection is defined as the portion of the connection between the remote user and the internal network (or between the two networks in the case of a site-to-site connection) where the data is encrypted.

◆ **Tunneling protocols**. Tunneling protocols are the protocols that are used to manage the underlying data connection (the tunnel) and encapsulate private data. Windows 2000 supports the PPTP and L2TP tunneling protocols.

◆ **Encryption protocols**. Encryption protocols are the other piece of the connection. These provide the encryption of the data encapsulated by the tunneling protocols. Windows 2000 supports PPTP (this is not only a tunneling protocol, but also provides the encryption) and IPSec (Internet Protocol Security).

We have discussed how to gather the requirements needed to design a dial-in remote access solution, but what sort of questions should you ask before designing your VPN solution? In the case of a VPN solution, you should ask the following questions at a minimum (you may find these familiar):

◆ How many users will need access through the VPN server?

◆ How many users will be accessing the VPN server concurrently?

◆ Will you need a remote access VPN, site-to-site VPN, or a combination?

◆ What applications will be used through this connection?

◆ What type of security is required?

◆ What client operating systems do you need to support?

Now that we've asked our questions again, let's look at how the answers drive the creation of our VPN solution:

◆ How many users will need access through the VPN server? The challenges here are almost identical to the challenges we discussed with a dial-in solution. You need to decide how to manage the users, how you will authenticate them, and who will administer the solution after it's in place. Will you have multiple VPN servers, where using RADIUS to manage them would make sense, or should you manage your users on the VPN servers? Do the accounting capabilities of RADIUS offer any special benefits based on your requirements?

◆ How many users will be accessing the RRAS server concurrently? Unlike the dial-in server, you don't need to determine how many modems to buy. But you still need to perform some capacity planning. How much horsepower will the RRAS server need to support your users? How much bandwidth will you need to connect your remote users? If you have 200 users connected via cable modem all vying for bandwidth, the Internet access at the company could become the bottleneck. Be sure that you take into account not only your VPN users but also your users on the corporate network who might need outbound Internet access when you start provisioning your Internet connection. The good news is the cost of high-speed corporate Internet access has come down dramatically because of the amount of competition among ISPs. You can generally get a connection for around $1,200.00 per megabit of bandwidth. So, a 5Mb connection might cost you $6,000.00. This is very dependent upon region, but it is relatively cheap.

IN THE FIELD

REDUNDANT VPN SOLUTIONS

As we discuss setting up a VPN, one of the things to realize is that this is a service that will be depended on within a week of its release to your users. The question is how will you ensure that they have access? A set of redundant VPN servers is a good start, but you should also take your connectivity into account.

continues

IN THE FIELD   *continued*

Many large companies are now employing redundant Internet connections to ensure their company has access to the Internet. Although out of scope for the Microsoft exam, be ready to spend some time with the networking department when the time comes to design and implement a mission-critical VPN solution for your company.

And always keep in mind that a dial-in RRAS server makes an excellent connection of last resort as a fallback when the VPN is down. Be sure you put that on a server other than the VPN server, because you wouldn't want to have both methods of access down when the server's hard drive fails.

◆ Will you need a remote access VPN, site-to-site VPN, or a combination? A remote access VPN is an almost direct replacement for the dial-in RRAS server, whereas a site-to-site VPN can be used to replace more expensive WAN connections, either to company locations or in some cases to customers, partners, or vendors. Be sure you understand the type of VPN you need as you look at designing your solution.

◆ What applications will be used through this connection? This will give you an idea not only of the type of connections to provision (although you will generally provision as high-speed a connection as possible), but also what parts of your internal network these users will need to access. As the security surrounding access to the corporate network becomes increasingly important, it is often a good idea to restrict access to mission-critical systems to users on the corporate network. Systems such as the Research and Development or Human Resources are frequent targets for attack, and should be protected especially from potential breaches in the remote access solutions.

◆ What type of security is required? Can you just use IDs and passwords, or do you need additional security? Although more expensive than a user ID and password, certificate and smart card–based access systems are becoming more prevalent in the industry today. On the encryption front, always try to use the

EXAM TIP

Be ready for VPN questions. With the huge popularity of VPNs in the industry today, coupled with the dramatic cost savings possible, setting up VPNs is something happening at almost every company that needs remote access. Recognizing this, Microsoft considers a thorough understanding of the design considerations surrounding VPNs to be a critical component of this exam. This is a topic that would lend itself to some outside reading, if you have the time.

strongest encryption possible, unless there is absolutely no critical information traversing the VPN. With the speed of computers continuing to increase, it won't be long before some of the stronger encryption algorithms are broken by brute force. The weaker algorithms are already vulnerable to such an attack. If you want to use smart cards, you will need to enable EAP authentication, just as with the dial-in connections discussed in the last section.

Okay, we've asked our questions and covered what to do with the answers. Some of this is very similar to what we discussed with the dial-in solution, but the VPN puts a new slant on what to do with the answers you receive.

The first thing you need to be aware of when discussing the Windows 2000 VPN is the encryption protocols available. Windows 2000 has the following two main encryption protocols that are used in the VPN:

◆ **Point-to-Point Tunneling Protocol (PPTP)**. PPTP is Microsoft's legacy protocol for supporting Virtual Private Networks. Developed jointly by Microsoft Corporation, U.S. Robotics, and several remote access vendor companies, known collectively as the PPTP Forum, PPTP encountered some security issues in its original form. It has been revised by Microsoft, but has never been widely accepted by the security community. Although still supported on a variety of vendors' VPN servers, PPTP is rapidly being overtaken by the more widely adopted IPSec protocol.

◆ **Internet Protocol Security (IPSec)**. IPSec is a suite of cryptography-based protection services and security protocols that are used for the first standards-based VPN protocol. In Windows 2000, IPSec is used to provide machine-level authentication, as well as data encryption, for L2TP-based (Layer 2 Tunneling Protocol) VPN connections. Unlike some other IPSec-based VPNs, Microsoft's implementation uses the L2TP protocol for encrypting usernames, passwords, and data, although IPSec is used to negotiate the secure connection between your computer and its remote tunnel server.

NOTE

L2TP Tunneling—Part of the IPSec Standard? If you decided to read the RFP for IPSec, you may have noticed that there is no mention of L2TP anywhere in the document. L2TP is Microsoft's addition to IPSec, and actually supersedes the PPTP tunneling protocol released with Windows NT 4.0. At the writing of this book, Microsoft was petitioning the IPSec working group to include its L2TP variant in the next revision of the specification. At this time, there is no indication whether Microsoft will be successful in its efforts. However, L2TP is a joint venture between Microsoft and Cisco, and Cisco has been heavily involved in the development of the IPSec specification.

EXAM TIP

Know the differences between IPSec and PPTP. Because Microsoft uses a custom protocol configuration for its IPSec VPN implementation, you should be sure that you understand the differences between IPSec and PPTP, as well as how Microsoft implemented its version of IPSec. Table 5.1 can help you keep them straight.

TABLE 5.1

THE DIFFERENCES BETWEEN IPSEC/L2TP AND PPTP

L2TP/IPSec	PPTP
Standards based	Microsoft proprietary
Uses DES/3DES encryption	Microsoft proprietary encryption
Available on multiple platforms including Windows, Linux, Macintosh, Solaris, and others	Available for Windows OS and Linux
Requires only that the tunnel media provide packet-oriented point-to-point connectivity	Requires an IP-based transit internetwork
Supports header compression	No header compression

IN THE FIELD

I'M USING A VPN, SO I'M SECURE, RIGHT?

If only security were as easy as deploying a VPN. Although VPNs provide excellent security for the data traversing the tunnel connection, they are only part of a good security infrastructure. You need to remember that this VPN is going to be used in conjunction with a public network such as the Internet. To keep your data secure, you need a little more than just a VPN.

To create a comprehensive security environment around your VPN, be sure to investigate firewalls, virus protection, security assessment tools, intrusion detection, and, of course, make sure you have a comprehensive set of security policies for the use of the network and systems you are working to secure. If your data is important enough to encrypt using a VPN, it's important enough to keep secure after it is out of the tunnel and on a host.

Now that we know how to design our solution, let's take a look at how you can set up a VPN port using the Routing and Remote Access console.

STEP BY STEP

5.4 Adding L2TP/IPSec VPN Ports to the Routing and Remote Access Service

1. Open the Routing and Remote Access service console.

2. Double-click the server in the tree view (left pane) to expand the tree. Select the Ports icon and you should see the preconfigured VPN ports appear in the right window (see Figure 5.19).

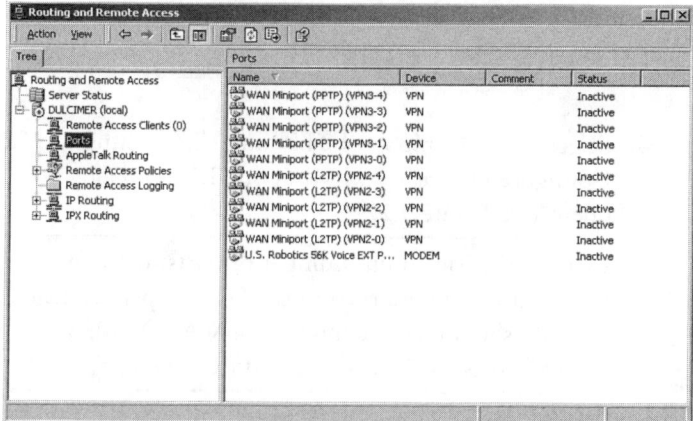

FIGURE 5.19
The Routing and Remote Access service configures five PPTP and five L2TP VPN ports by default.

3. Right-click the Ports icon and select Properties (see Figure 5.20). The Ports Properties dialog box opens (see Figure 5.21).

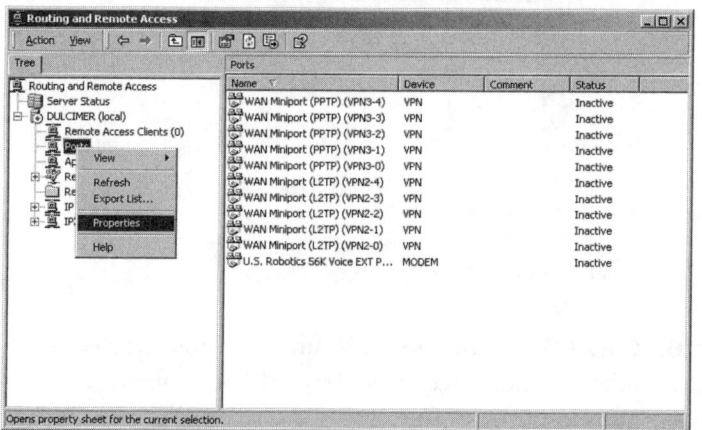

FIGURE 5.20
Selecting Properties will allow you to configure the number of ports for either PPTP or L2TP tunnels.

continues

continued

FIGURE 5.21
The Ports Properties dialog box lists all the ports enabled within the Routing and Remote Access service.

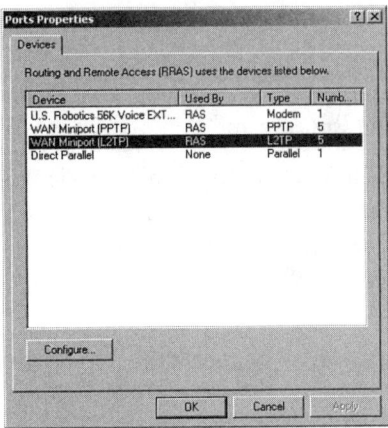

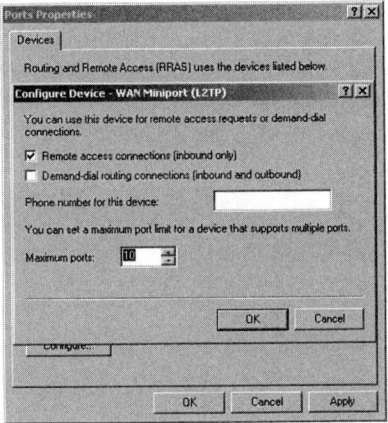

FIGURE 5.22
Not only can you change the number of ports, but you can also decide whether the ports are for remote access only or could also be used for demand-dial routing.

4. Select WAN Miniport (L2TP) and click Configure. The Configure Device WAN Miniport (L2TP) dialog box opens (see Figure 5.22).

5. Increase the Maximum number of ports to 10 and click OK. You will be returned to the Port Properties dialog box and you should see the number of WAN Miniport (L2TP) ports has increased to 10 (see Figure 5.23).

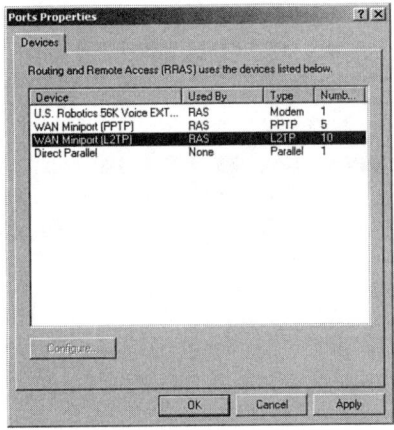

FIGURE 5.23
If you have decided to use L2TP as your protocol of choice, be sure to set the number of PPTP ports to 0.

6. Click OK to return to the Routing and Remote Access console. You should see the all 10 of WAN Miniport (L2TP) ports in the right pane of the console (see Figure 5.24).

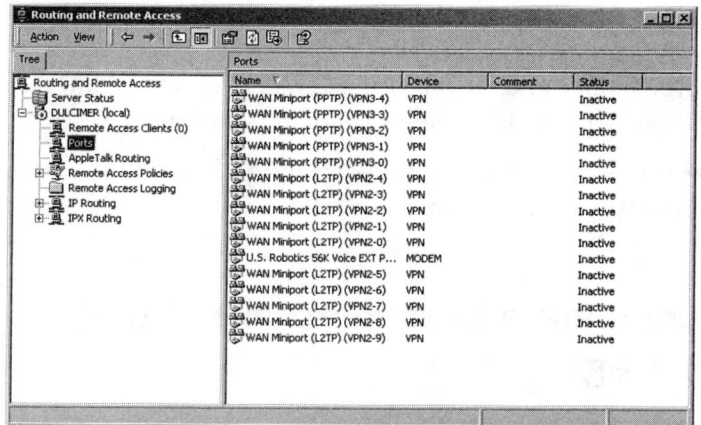

FIGURE 5.24
This view is also good for checking active VPN connections.

We have discussed how to design a VPN solution using the Routing and Remote Access service. Now let's look at the final piece of the Routing and Remote Access service WAN model, using the Routing and Remote Access service to connect locations.

DESIGNING A ROUTING AND REMOTE ACCESS ROUTING SOLUTION TO CONNECT LOCATIONS

Design a Routing and Remote Access routing solution to connect locations.

Here is the scenario. You have three office locations that occasionally need to pass data among themselves. You can either purchase some relatively expensive permanent connections with dedicated routers, or you can look into less expensive alternatives. One great alternative is to use the Windows 2000 Routing and Remote Access service to provide demand-dial connections as needed.

Demand-dial connections are opened and closed between sites on an as-needed basis. For example, when a user in Location A needs to connect to the e-mail server in Location B, a demand-dial connection is opened connecting the locations together. When the user is finished with his transaction and the connection goes idle, it is dropped.

This greatly reduces the cost of the connection, by incurring connection charges only when needed. This is usually a concern when toll charges for long distance connections or, as in the case of ISDN, bandwidth charges are a component of the solution.

Let's take a look at how you would design a demand-dial solution, and how you might implement it.

Designing a Demand-Dial Routing Strategy

Before you design a demand-dial routing strategy, you once again need to do some requirements gathering. However, because these are router-to-router connections, you don't need quite as much information as you did in the previous sections. There are no users logging in with this scenario—just two routers talking when bandwidth is needed. But you still need to gather some basic information.

◆ How many users will be using the demand-dial solution?

◆ What applications will be used through this connection?

Now for the interesting part—designing the solution. The key to designing a demand-dial routing solution is recognizing that it is useful only for low-bandwidth applications. If you have an office with 150 employees and they will all need to access your enterprise resource planning application, setting up a demand-dial connection is not a good solution.

So, when would you use demand-dial routing? There are two scenarios in which demand-dial routing is very useful. First, it makes a great solution for small office or home office connections. If you have between 1 and 10 users trying to connect, you might want to look at demand-dial. You should also take into account the applications and usage that the connection will be doing. If you have 10 users who will be connected all day long, and then starting a large file transfer at the end of the day that takes most of the night, you should look for another solution. If you have 5 users who intermittently need to check mail, a demand-dial solution is probably usable.

The second scenario in which demand-dial connections make sense is as a redundant connection for a higher-speed permanent WAN connection. In the event of an outage, even a slower demand-dial connection is better than a complete outage. This is a very cost-effective addition to your disaster-recovery design. But it brings up a good question that needs to be considered when discussing demand-dial connections. How is routing done with a connection that isn't permanent?

The Windows 2000 Routing and Remote Access service supports a number of industry-standard routing protocols, including

◆ **Routing Information Protocol (RIP).** RIP is a distance-vector protocol that uses hop count as its metric for measuring the number of routers that must be crossed to reach the desired network. Each router on the network sends a copy of the entire routing table to all the other routers on the network when it detects a change to the network. There are two versions of RIP, version 1 and version 2, and both TCP/IP and IPX use the protocol. The main weaknesses of RIP are the slow convergence times (time to find a new path in the event of an outage) and the fact that it requires that routers pass the entire routing table with each update. In a large environment, this can add substantial overhead to your network, particularly on slow connections.

◆ **Open Shortest Path First (OSPF).** OSPF is a link-state routing protocol. It functions by sending link-state advertisements (a list of its attached networks and their configured costs) to the other routers on the network. This is a much more efficient mechanism than RIP uses, and allows for much faster convergence in the event of an outage. This is accomplished at a cost of using more processing power on the router to maintain the routing information. OSPF is also more difficult to configure than RIP in most circumstances.

But how can you use dynamic routing protocols in conjunction with a demand-dial connection? Dynamic protocols need to periodically exchange information among routers to keep their routing tables up to date. If you enable dynamic routing protocols on your demand-dial server, you can cause a connection to be made each time the update process takes place or in a busy RIP environment you may inadvertently keep the connection up permanently while the router trades routing-table updates. The best place to use these dynamic protocols is when you want to use the demand-dial connection as a failover. In the event the primary connection between two sites should fail, the other routers on the network need to know that the demand-dial router is available for the connection. This works best with OSPF, which will allow you to weight the demand-dial connection to be used only in the event of a failure of the primary. But if you can't use dynamic routing, how do you get your demand-dial connection to route correctly? There are two possible solutions to this issue:

◆ **Static routes**. Static routes are a route that is entered into the routing table of the RRAS server manually using the Windows 2000 ROUTE command or through the Routing and Remote Access console. Static routes (as the name implies) are never updated dynamically, but are instead added and deleted by the server administrator. Static routes are generally useful only for very small environments, because manually maintaining a routing table can become a very tedious task.

◆ **Autostatic updates**. An autostatic update is a request from a router for all known routes or services from the router on the other side of the connection. After the request is received, the router adds the requested routes to its routing table. An autostatic update is a one-time, one-way exchange of routing information and will not occur automatically upon initiation of a demand-dial connection. Rather, the autostatic update must be manually initiated or scheduled for the routes to be updated. Autostatic updates are useful in larger environments in which there are too many routes to be maintained manually with static routes.

Now that we've discussed when and how you might use demand-dial routing in your environment, let's take a look at how you enable it.

STEP BY STEP

5.5 Enabling Demand-Dial Routing in the Routing and Remote Access Console

1. Open the Network and Dial-Up Connections by going to Start, Settings, Network and Dial-Up Connections (see Figure 5.25).

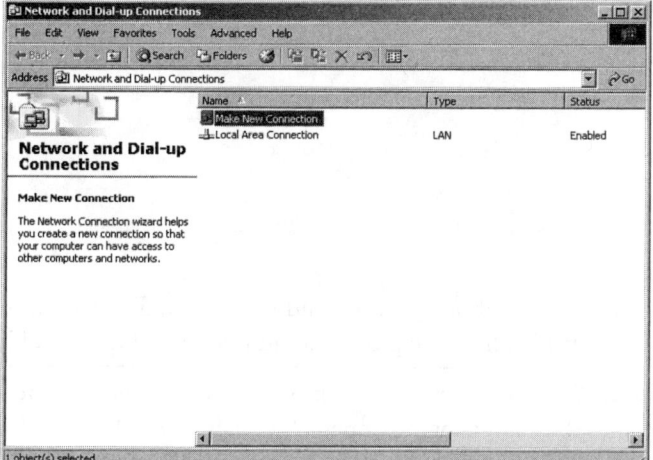

FIGURE 5.25
Before you can enable demand-dial routing, you need to create the dial-up connection.

2. Double-click the Make New Connection icon. The Network Connection Wizard will open (see Figure 5.26).

3. Click Next to continue. The Network Connection Type dialog box opens (see Figure 5.27).

FIGURE 5.26
The Network Connection Wizard will guide you through creating your connection.

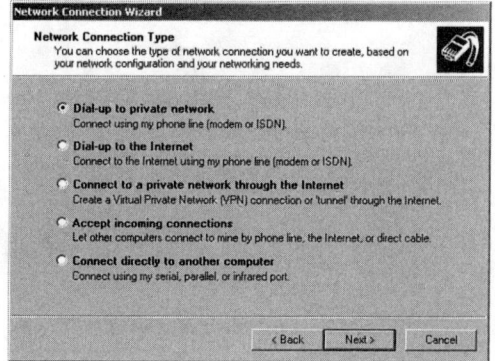

FIGURE 5.27
The Network Connection Wizard allows you to create a number of different types of connections.

continues

continued

4. Select Dial-Up to Private Network and click Next. You will be prompted to enter the phone number of the remote network (see Figure 5.28).

FIGURE 5.28
You can use the dialing rules configured with your modem or you can manually enter the area code and number of the remote RRAS server.

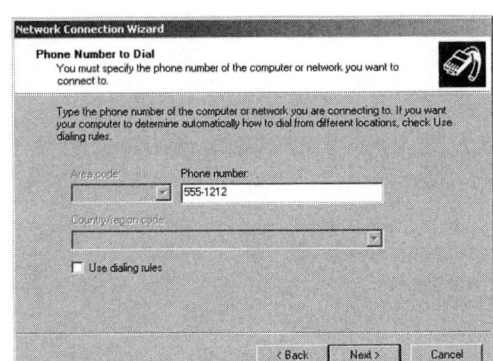

5. Enter a phone number and click Next. The Connection Availability dialog box should open (see Figure 5.29).

6. Select All users and click Next. The Internet Connection Sharing dialog box opens (see Figure 5.30). To enable on-demand connections, you must enable Internet Connection Sharing. This allows external hosts to use the RRAS server to route to the networks at the other end of the demand-dial connection.

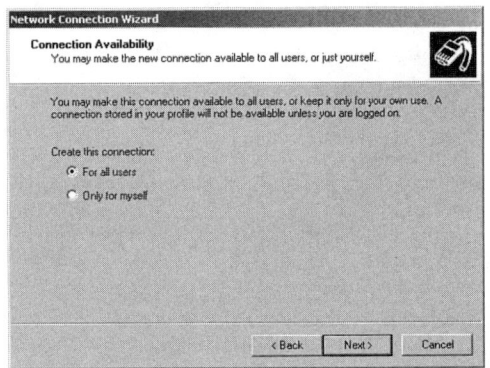

FIGURE 5.29
To successfully use this connection for demand-dial routing, you need to enable it for all users.

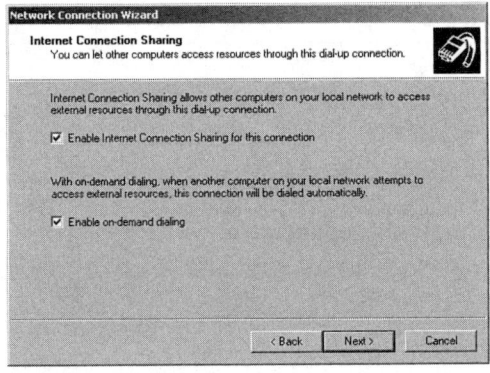

FIGURE 5.30
Internet Connection Sharing is an integral part of the on-demand connection.

7. Click Next to complete the configuration. The Network Connection Wizard will prompt you to name the connection (Figure 5.31). Click Finish to complete the configuration and activate the connection.

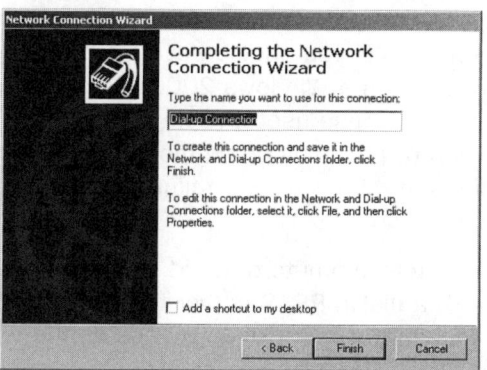

FIGURE 5.31
If you are going to have multiple demand-dial connections, be sure to select a good naming convention to ease administering them.

CASE STUDY: IMPLEMENTING ROUTING AND REMOTE ACCESS IN A COMPLEX ENVIRONMENT

ESSENCE OF THE CASE

The essence of the case is as follows:

▶ You need a cost-effective remote access solution for your new remote field office.

▶ Your newly designated telecommuters also need access.

▶ You need the access to be reliable and fault tolerant.

SCENARIO

Mount Abora Consulting is a company that manages the data cabling of home networks for new homes. The company has recently gone through a large expansion, coupled with a reduction in real estate. They closed six field offices that had fewer than five employees, and opened a new field sales office that had 20 salespeople assigned to it. Although there are rarely more than two or three of the sales staff working there at any given time, they want to use the office as an easy place to check their mail and review the new sales literature on the company intranet site. The employees who were working from the small offices have been designated telecommuters, and will need to work from home.

continues

CASE STUDY: IMPLEMENTING ROUTING AND REMOTE ACCESS IN A COMPLEX ENVIRONMENT

continued

Because Mount Abora Consulting is operating on fairly slim margins, you have been asked to cost effectively provide connectivity for the field office and the telecommuters. Naturally, the solution must be reliable and fault tolerant, and to effectively evaluate costs, management wants accounting information.

The existing Windows 2000–based network infrastructure does not have any remote access solutions at present.

All the remote users and the main corporate office have access to the Internet. The field office is not connected to the Internet, and there are not any plans to install a connection in the near future.

What solution do you propose?

ANALYSIS

Because the new field office has such intermittent usage, you should set up a demand-dial connection on a Windows 2000 RRAS server to support those users. Fault tolerance can be supplied by providing some modems and modem lines in the event of a failure of the demand-dial connection.

Your telecommuters would benefit from a VPN, with a dial-in RRAS server to provide fault tolerance in the event of an outage on the VPN.

To provide the accounting information requested by management, you should plan on leveraging RADIUS for your VPN and dial-in access. This can be either a Windows 2000 Internet Authentication Server or a legacy RADIUS server, if available.

This should be fairly straightforward after you have read the chapter. Let's take a quick chapter recap and then move on to some exercises.

CHAPTER SUMMARY

KEY TERMS

- Authentication
- Virtual Private Network
- Cryptography
- Default gateway
- Default router
- Modem

Let's review what we've discussed before we test your knowledge. In the first section, we covered designing an implementation strategy for dial-up remote access using the Routing and Remote Access service (RRAS). This solution is to allow remote users to dial into the corporate network to access resources. We started the discussion with some of the new features in the Windows 2000 RRAS that help you with this solution design and support. They included

- ◆ Bandwidth Allocation Protocol (BAP)
- ◆ RADIUS (Remote Authentication Dial-In User Service) Support
- ◆ Active Directory Support

CHAPTER SUMMARY

Next, we talked about requirements gathering before designing your solution. The main information you need to get includes

◆ How many users will need access through the RRAS server?

◆ How many users will be accessing the RRAS server concurrently?

◆ What applications will be used through this connection?

◆ What type of security is required?

◆ What client operating systems do you need to support?

After we got the information we needed for designing the solution, we discussed some of the key feature of the Point-to-Point Protocol, the most prevalent protocol used for dial-in connection. They include

◆ Dynamic Host Control Protocol (DHCP)

◆ Compression

◆ Encryption

The other supported protocols include

◆ Serial Line Interface Protocol (SLIP)

◆ Microsoft RAS Protocol

◆ Apple Remote Access Protocol (ARAP)

The Routing and Remote Access service also supports a number of network protocols, including

◆ TCP/IP (Transmission Control Protocol/Internet Protocol)

◆ IPX (Internet Packet Exchange)

◆ NetBEUI (NetBIOS Extended User Interface)

◆ AppleTalk

KEY TERMS

• Multilink Point-to-Point Protocol

• Encryption

• Dynamic Host Control Protocol (DHCP)

• Routing and Remote Access Service (RRAS)

• Callback

• Active Directory Service

• Dynamic Routing

• RIP (Routing Information Protocol)

• OSPF

• BGP

• ISP (Internet service provider)

• xDSL (Digital Subscriber Line)

• Cable Modem

CHAPTER SUMMARY

Finally, we covered the different authentication protocols support. They include

◆ Extensible Authentication Protocol (EAP)

◆ Challenge Handshake Authentication Protocol (CHAP)

◆ Microsoft Challenge Handshake Authentication Protocol (MS-CHAP)

◆ Shiva Password Authentication Protocol (SPAP)

◆ Password Authentication Protocol (PAP)

◆ Unauthenticated Access

Our next main topic of discussion was the use of RADIUS (Remote Authentication Dial-In User Service) as part of our authentication model. RADIUS is an industry-standard authentication and accounting system used in conjunction with Remote Access Servers. When you dial in to the RAS server, you enter your username and password. This information is passed to a RADIUS server, which checks that the information is correct, and then authorizes access to the system. With Windows 2000 Server, Microsoft has bundled RADIUS authentication as part of the Internet Authentication Service.

The components of a RADIUS solution include

◆ Remote Host

◆ The Remote Access Server (RAS)

◆ The RADIUS Server

The RADIUS authentication process works as follows:

1. A remote host dials into an RAS server and begins to negotiate a connection using PPP.

2. The RAS server passes the user ID and password from the remote host to the RADIUS server.

3. The RADIUS server checks the authentication information and issues either an accept or deny response.

CHAPTER SUMMARY

4. After the RAS server receives an accept response from the RADIUS server, it completes the PPP negotiation with the remote host. The remote host can now access the network.

RADIUS supports the following two forms of authentication:

◆ PAP (Password Authentication Protocol)

◆ CHAP (Challenge Handshake Authentication Protocol)

Next, we moved on to designing a VPN solution. The questions we used to gather our requirements are very similar to the remote access questions, because the solutions are so similar. Some key points to remember when designing a VPN solution are

◆ What type of VPN are you trying to create? You can create a site-to-site VPN or a remote access (user-to-site) VPN.

◆ What VPN protocol should you use? Microsoft supports the legacy PPTP protocol as well as the standards-based IPSec/L2TP protocol.

We completed the chapter with a discussion of designing a demand-dial strategy. For requirements gathering, you really need to ask only two critical questions:

◆ How many users will be using the demand-dial solution?

◆ What applications will be used through this connection?

After you know these answers, determining whether a demand-dial solution is applicable is relatively easy. This solution is well suited to small-office environments with light usage, or as a failover in the event of an outage of the primary site-to-site connection.

If you are going to use your Windows 2000 RRAS server as a router, you need to be familiar with some of the supported routing protocols, which include

◆ Routing Information Protocol (RIP)—RIP is a distance-vector routing protocol.

CHAPTER SUMMARY

◆ Open Shortest Path First (OSPF)—OSPF is a link state routing protocol.

Finally, we discussed how to support your demand-dial connections in the absence of dynamic routing protocols. The two methods are

◆ **Static routes.** Routes that are entered into the routing table manually.

◆ **Autostatic updates.** Manually or scheduled updates used when there are too many routes to be maintained manually with static routes.

And that wraps up the chapter summary. Let's take a look at some exercises and some questions.

APPLY YOUR KNOWLEDGE

Exercises

5.1   Registering IAS in the Active Directory

Exercise 5.1 is intended to let you practice registering IAS in the Active Directory.

Estimated Time: 5 minutes

1. From the Control Panel, open the Internet Authentication Service applet.

2. Click Action, Register Service in the Active Directory. This opens a dialog box warning you that IAS computers must be able to read dial-in property sheets of the users in the domain using IAS. Select OK to authorize this.

3. This presents a dialog box stating that IAS has been authorized in the Active Directory of your domain. It also notes that to authorize IAS in a different domain, you need to add this server to the RAS/IAS group in that domain.

Review Questions

1. You are the Senior Network Architect for Tony's Pizza and Hats, a small restaurant and haberdashery chain. You have been asked to design and implement a remote access service for the 75 employees in the company. What are some of the considerations you need to evaluate when trying to design a remote access solution of this type?

2. You are the Windows 2000 system administrator for Alph Electronics, a reseller of high-end audio equipment. You use Windows 2000 with the Routing and Remote Access service installed, to provide dial-in remote access for your users.

They need to access network segments other than the one the RRAS server is connected to. What is the most efficient method for your remote employees to get access to these segments through the RRAS server resides?

3. You are the Senior Windows Architect for Ye of Little Faith Airlines. You are researching different authentication methods that can be used with Windows 2000, and you have decided that the best authentication service available to you is RADIUS. What do you need to do to implement RADIUS in your Windows 2000/Active Directory environment?

4. You are a network architect working for Johnny on the Spot Delivery Services, a national chain of bicycle messengers. You have a number of remote users that want to connect to the corporate network but are located at branch locations throughout the country. You do have a local Windows 2000 server with modems and the Routing and Remote Access service loaded for dial-in access, but the long distance charges are extremely high to provide this service to all employees. However, you also provide an ISP account to all employees through a national ISP, so they can use the Internet to find directions to delivery locations. What can you do to provide access to your remote users with the RRAS server without incurring the exorbitant long distance charges?

5. You are the network administrator for Spin the Globe Travel, a small travel agency specializing in round-the-world tours. You have a Windows 2000 server with the Routing and Remote Access service installed. You have decided you want to separate your intranet servers from your file and print servers, so you have created a dedicated segment for the intranet. You are going to use your remote access server to connect the two networks.

APPLY YOUR KNOWLEDGE

To accomplish this, you add another Network Interface Card to the server. What do you need to do to get the new segment to communicate with the existing segments, as well as with the remote users?

6. You are the network administrator for Mount Abora Consulting, a financial service consulting organization. You are running a Windows 2000 infrastructure, and you are using Windows 2000 servers with the Routing and Remote Access service loaded to support your demand-dial routing strategy. Because your network was small, you manually created all the necessary routes on the servers. When you first installed the demand-dial WAN, this was a manageable architecture. Recently, the company's network has been growing rapidly. In fact, this month you had to add 12 new routes. How can this be made more manageable?

7. You are the senior security administrator for Exponent Electronics, a major manufacturer of CD and DVD trays. The Chief Information Security Officer for your company has asked you to review the authentication protocols being used by your Routing and Remote Access Server. What are the available protocols, and how do they work?

Exam Questions

1. You are the System Administrator for Phil's Phill-up Stations, a chain of gas stations. As part of the network, you maintain a Windows 2000 Routing and Remote Access server to provide remote access services to your users. You want to take full advantage of the new authentication protocols supported by Windows 2000.

Which of the following protocols would you choose?

A. EAP

B. BAP

C. RADIUS

D. MS-CHAP

2. You are the Network Administrator for Runaway Travel and you have just installed a new Windows 2000 Routing and Remote Access server to replace an old hardware RAS server. You have decided you want to use RADIUS for authentication for the new server.

When choosing to use RADIUS for RRAS authentication on your internal Windows 2000 network, which other service should you configure?

A. DHCP

B. IIS

C. IAS

D. IntelliMirror

3. You are the Network Administrator for Barry M. Deep Coffin Company and you have a requirement for a Windows 2000 Routing and Remote Access server to replace a hardware solution.

How do you install and configure the service?

A. Go to the Control panel. Open the Add/ Remove Programs icon. Select Add/Remove Windows Components. Click Add, and select the Routing and Remote Access service. Use the Wizard to complete the installation.

Chapter 5 DESIGNING A WIDE AREA NETWORK INFRASTRUCTURE   353

APPLY YOUR KNOWLEDGE

B. Open the Routing and Remote Access console. The Install Routing and Remote Access wizard will start. Use the wizard to complete the installation.

C. Install Windows 2000. Use the Routing and Remote Access console to enable the service installed with the OS.

D. Install Service Pack 2. Reboot. From the Control Panel, select the newly created Routing and Remote Access applet.

4. You are the System Administrator for Blue Cap Toothpaste Company, and you have a Windows 2000 Routing and Remote Access server providing access to your dial-in users. This server has been configured so that RAS users can access only a single network. Your network is expanding and you have added two more NIC cards to the server.

What do you need to do to get the server to now route RAS users to the new segments?

A. Open the Routing and Remote Access console. Select the server, right-click and select Configure from the context menu. Configure the additional networks.

B. Open the Routing and Remote Access console. Select the server, right-click and select Add New Static Route.

C. Nothing. Windows 2000 does this for you by default.

D. Open the Routing and Remote Access console. In the left-side tree view, expand the server options. In the same tree, expand IP routing options. Right-click static routes, and add a new static route from the context menu for each new network.

5. You are the Security Administrator for Jeff's House of Pancakes and you are responsible for providing remote access for all employees. The pancake house is a Windows 2000 shop, with two domain controllers for the Active Directory, three file and print servers, an IIS-based Intranet server, and an RRAS server for remote access. Because employee turnover is very high, you are extremely busy creating RAS accounts for new employees and removing RAS accounts for employees who have left the company.

What is the most effective way you could simplify this process?

A. Hire another administrator.

B. Integrate the RRAS server with IAS and use RADIUS and the Active Directory to authenticate users.

C. Enable account-based routing. Use the routing table to secure the network.

D. Have an external ISP manage RRAS authentication via an external RADIUS solution.

6. You are the Network Administrator for Phil 'Em Up gas stations. You have installed a Windows 2000 Routing and Remote Access server to provide access to the corporate network remotely. Your company has users scattered throughout the United States, who need access to the corporate network to access the intranet and check e-mail on the Exchange servers. Your company also provides Internet access for all employees.

What is the most secure, cost-effective way to provide these users access to the corporate network?

APPLY YOUR KNOWLEDGE

A. Make the Windows 2000 server accessible from the Internet. Configure VPN connections and user accounts. Have all your users configure VPN clients on their PCs.

B. Install a WAN and connect everyone directly to the corporate network.

C. Install a modem bank on the server, and configure RRAS to allow dial-in connections, authenticating against RADIUS and IAS.

D. Make the Windows 2000 server accessible from the Internet. Configure the server using the RRAS Wizard to allow EAP connections from remote PCs.

7. You are the security administrator for Jolly Snowmen Freezer Corporation, and your company has two locations—one in Denver, CO, and one in Indianapolis, IN. Denver and Indianapolis need to synchronize a customer-order database each night across a costly WAN link, but do not need to transfer any other data during normal business hours. The dedicated WAN Link is costly.

Which of the following would you choose to allow the sites to replicate data and still save money?

A. Install an Internet connection in each location. Put a Windows 2000 RRAS server in each location and configure a site-to-site VPN connection.

B. Install a Windows 2000 Server in the Denver office with RRAS, a RADIUS server, and a modem. Have the server in Indianapolis dial into the Denver server using an RAS account.

C. Using the Internet Authentication Service, configure a Windows 2000 server in each location to connect via a VPN connection over the WAN, and rely on the compression to drive usage of the link down.

D. Install and configure a Windows 2000 server running RRAS in each location, and use modems and dial-on-demand routing to allow the locations to connect as needed to replicate the database.

8. You are the senior network administrator for Frenetic Sound and Lights Inc., a large manufacturer of sound and light equipment for arena concerts. Your manager has been reading up on the new Windows 2000 RRAS servers you just installed for dial-on-demand routing between the warehouse and corporate headquarters. He just read a section on autostatic routing updates and he wants you to explain what protocols you can use with this feature.

Which of the following protocols would you be able to use with dial-on-demand routing, and why?

A. IP

B. IPX

C. NetBEUI

D. DLC

9. You are the security administrator for a small police force. Your network is based on Windows 2000 Server, and you are using the Routing and Remote Access service to connect two of your stations.

APPLY YOUR KNOWLEDGE

When you configured the persistent dial-on-demand interface, which routers did you need to configure?

A. Default gateway

B. PIX firewall

C. Calling router

D. Answering router

10. You are the system administrator for Run to the Hills Travel. You have a Windows 2000 Routing and Remote Access server configured for dial-in remote access. You have been asked to use encryption on your RAS connections.

Which of the following protocols can you use?

A. PPP

B. PPTP

C. L2TP

D. SPAP

E. MS-PAP

11. You have been asked to make sure that use of your demand-dial WAN link is not consumed by the company's accounting application. What protocol can you leverage to accomplish this goal?

A. BAP

B. EAP

C. IPSec

D. MSChap

12. On which router will you manage the route configuration in a one-way initiated dial-on-demand connection?

A. Default gateway

B. PIX firewall

C. Calling router

D. Answering router

13. Of the following, which would you use to monitor detailed RAS connection information?

A. Rasmon

B. RRAS plug-in

C. Performance Monitor

D. Network Monitor

14. You are the network administrator for Go to Cleveland bus company and you are using a Windows 2000 server with Routing and Remote Access Server to allow remote access to your network. This server is in the Infrastructure domain. You also have two other domains called Sales and Service, which are accessible via the remote access server. There is a two-way trust between the Sales and the Infrastructure domains, whereas the Service domain is standalone. You have created a remote access group policy in the Infrastructure domain to control access to the network.

Which servers are affected by this policy?

A. Only the RRAS servers in the Infrastructure domain.

B. The RRAS servers in the Infrastructure and Sales domains.

C. All member servers in the domains.

D. All the member servers in the Active Directory.

E. All the RRAS servers on the network.

APPLY YOUR KNOWLEDGE

15. You are the security administrator for Barb's House of Pancakes. You have been asked to implement smart cards for remote access authentication using the Windows 2000 Routing and Remote Access Service.

    What protocol do you need?

    A. EAP

    B. PPTP

    C. IPSec

    D. TCP/IP

    E. MS-CHAP v2

Answers to Review Questions

1. You need to consider a number of factors when designing any remote access solution. These include

   - Number of users—You need to know how many users will be connecting to this server. This will give you an idea of how much hardware you will need to build the server, but will also give you an idea of the administrative overhead associated with supporting this solution.

   - Number of concurrent users—This is especially critical when you are designing a dial solution, because you cannot buy a modem for each user (unless you have a very small user population). A general rule is 8:1. For every 8 users, there will be 1 connected at any given time. If your users are going to be connected for long periods of time, or if there is a time that many of them will be connecting

at the same time (end-of-the-month financial updates, and so on), you may need to reduce this ratio to avoid busy signals.

   - Where are the users located?—If all your users are local, you can set up a local phone number and you are ready. If you have users throughout the state, country, or even the world, you will need to consider a distributed RRAS solution, or maybe a toll-free access solution.

   - How they will connect?—Will they be using 56K modems, ISDN modems, or older 28.8 or 14.4K modems? This will help you determine what modems you need to purchase for these users to connect to, as well as give you an idea how much data might be transferred to the server.

   - How secure does this solution need to be?—If you are providing access to internal mail, you can probably use a user ID/password authentication method for your solution. But if you are delivering remote access to the research network of a weapons manufacturer, you will need to consider some of the more secure authentication solutions available with Windows 2000 RRAS, such as smart cards.

   - What resources need to be accessible?—Until you know to what your users will need access, you cannot design a comprehensive solution. In smaller environments, you don't need as much due diligence, because of the reduced number of resources to be accessed. A good rule is to provide access only to resources that absolutely need to be reached by remote users. Although it is easier to just provide access to the entire network, good security

APPLY YOUR KNOWLEDGE

practices dictate that you restrict this access as much as possible, to reduce the possibility of successful attacks against your network. While considered "low tech" by many, a poorly configured RRAS server is still one of the most common and serious security issues found in many networks.

- What client operating systems do you need to support?—If you work in a very mixed environment, where users could be using a combination of Windows 98, Windows NT, Windows Me, Linux, Windows 2000, and Macintosh systems, you need to pay close attention to what protocols and authentication methods you will need to use to support them all. As with most things, the more standardized your environment, the easier it is to ensure you are able to support all your end users.

Without a thorough understanding of these factors, you will not be able to design a solution that will provide optimal access. One other factor to consider is growth. Do you expect to add 100, 1,000, or 10,000 users to this solution? Be sure to design to meet not only the immediate requirements. See the section "Design an Implementation Strategy for Dial-Up Remote Access."

2. Enable the dial-in interface to use routing and remote access by establishing static routes to the other segments. This is practical only in smaller environments. In larger environments, you will need to use dynamic routing protocols to make managing the architecture easier. See the section "Design a Routing and Remote Access Routing Solution to Connect Locations."

3. To use RADIUS in your environment, you will need the Internet Authentication Service installed on one of your Windows 2000 servers. Another alternative some companies use is to outsource their RADIUS management to another source (such as an ISP). This can be done using the Windows 2000 RADIUS service or a third-party RADIUS application could also be used. See the section "Integrating Authentication with Remote Authentication Dial-In User Service (RADIUS)."

4. Because your employees have Internet access through a local ISP, you can set up and configure VPN services on your RRAS server (make sure it is accessible from the Internet) for the users. After this is set up, the user can establish a VPN connection to the corporate network by using the Windows 2000 VPN client. See the section "Design a Virtual Private Network (VPN) Strategy."

5. You need to create a static route from using the Routing and Remote Access applet in the Administrative Tools section of the Control Panel. Just right-click the server icon and select Add Static Route from the context menu. See the section "Design a Routing and Remote Access Routing Solution to Connect Locations."

6. You need to enable autostatic updates. See the section "Designing a Demand-Dial Routing Strategy."

7. The authentication protocols that can be used with the Windows 2000 Routing and Remote Access Service include

APPLY YOUR KNOWLEDGE

- **EAP-TLS**. The Extensible Authentication Protocol (EAP) is an extension to the Point-to-Point Protocol (PPP). EAP provides a standard mechanism for support of additional authentication methods within PPP, such as smart cards, one-time passwords, and certificates. EAP is critical for secure Windows 2000 VPNs because it offers stronger authentication methods (such as X.509 certificates) instead of relying on the user ID and password schemes used traditionally.

- **CHAP**. The Challenge Handshake Authentication Protocol (CHAP) negotiates an encrypted authentication using MD5 (Message Digest 5), an industry-standard hashing scheme. CHAP uses challenge-response with one-way MD5 hashing on the response. This allows you to authenticate to the server without actually sending your password over the network. Because this is an industry-standard authentication method, it allows Windows 2000 to securely connect to almost all third-party PPP servers.

- **MS-CHAP**. Microsoft created Microsoft Challenge Handshake Authentication Protocol (MS-CHAP), an extension of CHAP, to authenticate remote Windows workstations, increasing the protocol's functionality by integrating the encryption and hashing algorithms used on Windows networks. Like CHAP, MS-CHAP uses a challenge-response mechanism with one-way encryption on the response. Although MS-CHAP is consistent with standard CHAP as much as possible, the MS-CHAP response packet is in a format specifically designed for computers running a Windows operating system.

A new version of the Microsoft Challenge Handshake Authentication Protocol (MS-CHAP V2) is also available. This new protocol provides mutual authentication, stronger initial data-encryption keys, and different encryption keys for sending and receiving.

- **SPAP**. Shiva Password Authentication Protocol (SPAP) is used specifically to allow Shiva client computers to connect to a Windows 2000 Server and to allow Windows 2000 client computers to connect to Shiva servers.

- **PAP**. Password Authentication Protocol (PAP) uses unencrypted (plain-text) passwords for authenticating users and is considered the least secure authentication protocol available. PAP is usually used as the authentication of last resort—when a more secure form of authentication is not available. You might need to use this protocol when you are connecting to a non–Windows-based server.

Answers to Exam Questions

1. **D**. MS-Chap has been in use with Windows NT before Windows 2000. EAP, BAP, and RADIUS have been optimized for use with Windows 2000. See the section "Key Terms."

2. **C**. To use RADIUS internally on a Windows 2000 network, you need the Internet Authentication Service. See the section "How IAS Works."

3. **B**. RRAS is configured through the RRAS snap-in in the MMC. RRAS is installed by default in an inactive state. See the section "Design an Implementation Strategy for Dial-Up Remote Access."

APPLY YOUR KNOWLEDGE

4. **D**. Static routes are added by selecting Static Route from the context menu of the IP routing object under the RRAS server name. See the section "Design a Routing and Remote Access Routing Solution to Connect Locations."

5. **B**. By using IAS, you could allow the Active Directory administrator to manage the accounts centrally. After a user's account has been deleted from the Active Directory, they no longer have authorization to use the remote access server. New users could be enabled either by the administrators, or could still be managed by you. See the section "How IAS Works."

6. **A**. Configuring VPN is the best solution. This allows all the scattered users to have a virtual local connection to the network. See the section "Design a Virtual Private Network (VPN) Strategy."

7. **D**. A dial-on-demand routing implementation meets this need. See the section "Designing a Demand-Dial Routing Strategy."

8. **A, B**. Both A and B have autostatic updates as an option in RRAS. See the section "Autostatic Updates."

9. **C, D**. Both C and D are correct in persistent dial-on-demand connections; both the calling and answering routers need to be configured.

See the section "Components of Demand-Dial Routing."

10. **A, B, D**. L2TP does not support encryption on its own; it needs to be used in conjunction with IPSec. MS-PAP is not an actual supported protocol. PPP, PPTP, and SPAP all support encryption over a dial-in connection. See the section "Key Terms."

11. **A**. BAP is the Bandwidth Allocation Protocol. See the section "Key Terms."

12. **C**. During a one-way initiated dial-on-demand connection, the calling router contains the configuration information. See the section "Demand-Dial Routing and Routing Protocols."

13. **A**. The Rasmon utility in the Windows 2000 resource kit allows for much greater detailed monitoring. See the section "Monitoring Initiated Demand-Dial Connections with Rasmon."

14. **A**. The Remote Access Group Policy applies only to RRAS servers in the domain in which it is created. See the section "Remote Access Permission."

15. **A**. EAP is the protocol needed to support smart cards. See the section "Configure Authentication Protocols."

APPLY YOUR KNOWLEDGE

Suggested Readings and Resources

1. Tate, Steven *Windows 2000 Essential Reference.* New Riders 2000.

2. Siyan, Karanjit S. *Windows 2000 TCP/IP.* New Riders, 2000.

3. Microsoft Corporation *Microsoft Windows 2000 Server Resource Kit,* Microsoft, 2000.

4. Fortenberry, Thaddeus *Windows 2000 Virtual Private Networking* New Riders, 2001.

5. Windows 2000 Server Homepage `http://www.microsoft.com/windows2000/server/default.asp.`

6. Bixler, Dave *MCSE Training Guide (70-216): Installing and Administering Windows 2000 Network Infrastructure* New Riders, 2000.

7. Kachur, Alexander *Microsoft Windows 2000 Security Handbook* Que Publishing 2000.

OBJECTIVES

This chapter covers the Microsoft-specified objectives for the section entitled Designing a Management and Implementation Strategy included in Exam 70-221, "Designing a Microsoft Windows 2000 Network Infrastructure."

The objectives are as follows:

Design a strategy for monitoring and managing Windows 2000 network services. Services include Global Catalog, Lightweight Directory Access Protocol (LDAP) services, Certificate Services, DNS, DHCP, WINS, Routing and Remote Access, Proxy Server, and Dfs.

▶ The key to managing a network is planning. This objective is included to ensure that you are able to recognize the importance and interdependence of the various services and plan their implementation and management. This is the primary point of this chapter and the key objective in this section.

Design network services that support application architecture.

▶ This objective falls on the implementation side of the chapter and is included to ensure that you are aware of the network services that are required to support client server and where you can place them. It is also included as a general look at combining services on systems and the allocation of resources in the implementation phase.

CHAPTER 6

Designing a Management and Implementation Strategy for Windows 2000 Networking

Design a plan for the interaction of Windows 2000 network services, such as WINS, DHCP, and DNS.

▶ This objective is again focused on implementation and is included to ensure that you not only know each service individually but also how the services work together and, therefore, how they can be placed to best benefit one another. Obviously, this will cover Dynamic Host Configuration Protocol (DHCP) and Domain Name System (DNS), which now work together, as well as Windows Internet Naming Service (WINS) that played a larger role in Windows NT 4.0.

Design a resource strategy.

- **Plan for the placement and management of resources.**

- **Plan for growth.**

- **Plan for decentralized resources or centralized resources.**

▶ This objective covers the implementation, how to combine services, which services can share a computer, and so on. It also involves the management side. Here, you need to have some plan to monitor services so you know when to add resources to move resources to better service the client needs.

As suggested in the title of this chapter, there are really two parts to this objective. The first is the implementation. Implementation involves gaining a thorough understanding of the services that are available and where they can be used.

This also involves knowing how the services interact and what types of resources each will need. This information has been covered in the preceding chapters in great detail, so this chapter assumes that you already know this information. As you read this chapter, think about which services can be combined on the same physical computer, and which cannot. Think about what systems can work together and why you might need more than one method to accomplish the same objective—for example, why might you need both WINS and Dynamic DNS? Or, what circumstances might cause you to require multiple methods of dynamic name resolution and registration.

Management is actually a four-step process that you need to understand in order to be successful when tested on this material. When you understand this four-step process, you will be able to easily understand what needs to be done in your network environment. The steps are

1. Identify what you need to manage.

2. Determine how to monitor these items.

3. Determine how and when to analyze the information you gather.

4. Determine what you need to respond to and what the response should be.

INTRODUCTION

This chapter draws information from the previous chapters and adds information about how to manage the network when it is running. This chapter ties those pieces together into a total package, first presenting how to manage a network in general and then details the four-step process you should use.

You then explore designing a server rather than designing a service.

Until now, you have looked at the services and have seen a bit on how to install them and what they require—and in some cases, what other services are available. This chapter presents how to configure a computer system that will run one or more services together (and how you can decide which services should go together) and how to look at the system in the test lab and the real world to determine whether the performance is adequate.

THE MANAGEMENT PROCESS

Design a strategy for monitoring and managing Windows 2000 network services. Services include Global Catalog, Lightweight Directory Access Protocol (LDAP) services, Certificate Services, DNS, DHCP, WINS, Routing and Remote Access, Proxy Server, and Dfs.

Some might think that it is easy to manage a server or a network, but if you sit down and try to identify in detail exactly what that involves, you might be hard pressed to describe it. That is exactly what this chapter does. It describes the functions and tasks required to manage a server or a network. It is worth pointing out, however, that these are merely guidelines and not hard and fast rules. Every network is different, and you need to adjust the information to suit your working conditions. There are essentially four main steps to managing a network:

1. **Identify what to manage**. In general terms, identifying means that you must first decide what you need to manage and what you do not need to manage. For example, you might have to deal with the network infrastructure only and not have to deal with the Wide Area Network (WAN), the client systems, and the other servers on the network, such as SQL servers.

2. **Monitor the network**. Monitoring involves using the Performance Monitor and Network Monitor, among other tools, to gather information about the status of the systems that make up the network and about the physical network. You should have some idea about what aspects you need to monitor. That is, do you need to concern yourself with the CPU utilization on the DNS server, or should you be more concerned about the traffic that is hitting the server?

3. **Analyze the information**. Obviously, you will be gathering a significant amount of data as you monitor an entire network. It is important that you analyze the data in real time or close to real time; otherwise, you probably don't need to monitor. If it takes you two days to analyze a day's worth of data, the users will be the first to let you know there is a problem. Ideally, the user should never be affected by a system problem, and you should be able to recognize a problem before it becomes critical and adjust resources to compensate. This is the goal; unfortunately, very few networks get to this state.

4. **Respond to issues**. The point of monitoring and of having tools that will let you monitor a network is to detect problems and to be able to respond to them. This means you should know what you would need to do to resolve each crisis that could arise. In reality, this should be part of the disaster plan for your company, but often, this deals only with who has spending authority and where backups are kept. The time to figure out what steps are required to replace a critical network service because it crashed is before it crashes. Otherwise, you will probably have your hands full when the system does crash. Windows 2000 goes a long way toward relieving the immediacy of these crashes with many built-in redundancies. However, it can still affect users and you will still need to respond quickly. Planning the response ahead of time reduces the "chicken with its head cut off" time during an emergency.

Understanding and performing these four steps ensures that your network will run smoothly and that you will be able to take your next vacation with the peace of mind that things are running properly. The next few sections look more closely at each of these steps.

Identifying What to Manage

In a perfect world, all the servers you set up would have 32 processors and 64GB of RAM; they would have 16EB of disk that never crashed; and the entire planet would run on fiber. This is not a perfect world, however. The basic truth is that you will have servers that fail, you will have wide area links that go down, and you will have users that will accidentally delete the data on their hard disks.

The first step to making these common failures bearable is to have the policies, procedures, and processes in place to counteract the effect of a failure in the shortest possible time with little or no service interruption.

This approach is still fairly vague, however, because it does not say exactly what you will monitor. Unfortunately, it is almost never that easy. The reason is the great paradox of the computer industry: A network would run perfectly if no users were allowed on it. However, without users there would be no need for a network in the first place. The point is that you will need to work with other managers in your organization to determine what their needs are. The network is really part of the infrastructure of an organization, and as such the network services the company—not vice versa.

You need to understand what all the users of the network consider important. This should be filtered through a reality filter to come up with what is an attainable level of service. As much as people talk about 7×24 availability networking and ensuring that you can order pizza over the Internet at 3:00 a.m., the need might not justify the cost. 7×24 networking is very expensive and requires a lot of expensive equipment; 7×23 is bargain-basement.

When you have an understanding of the requirements of the users, you need to prioritize the different services based on the needs of those services. The key services are normally the ability to resolve a name and the ability to move packets from one location to another. If you can keep these basics running, most of the other problems will be manageable in proportion. The fact is very simple: If the users can communicate and perform their day-to-day activities, you will have time to verify that the servers are running up to spec or to plan network expansions. This means a problem that affects the users directly should always take priority over other activities, such as planning.

To recap, as you start to look at creating your management plans you should bear these points in mind:

◆ An important network service is one that affects users directly.

◆ Verifying that services are running exactly as they should or planning for network expansion should always take a back seat to ensuring basic functionality.

◆ This isn't a perfect world—servers will crash, links will fail. If you can detect the failure and have a plan to respond, you are well ahead of the game.

By now, you are starting to think about the services that you will need to ensure are always running—the key services that ensure your network can continue to function. Not surprisingly, there is a fairly good list of them in the main objective for this chapter. The following list is a quick recap of the material covered in previous chapters of this book:

◆ **Global Catalog service**. This server is used for searching and for locating a login server (as well as any objects outside the local domain). Without this service on the network, users could have problems logging on.

◆ **Lightweight Directory Access Protocol (LDAP)**. LDAP is the protocol used by the client to communicate with the domain controllers and the Global Catalog servers. This is required for all logons and object management.

◆ **Certificate Services**. Certificate Services provide the issuing and management of X.509 certificates. If you are using Internet Protocol Security (IPSec) on your network, you need to ensure that Certificate Services are available. These are also needed to add objects in the Active Directory.

◆ **Domain Name System (DNS) name server**. The DNS name server is required to resolve computer names and to locate the Global Catalog (gc) and Kerberos (authentication) servers, as well as any other machines, on the network.

◆ **Dynamic Host Configuration Protocol (DHCP)**. DHCP is required if you are assigning client IP addresses automatically. Because this works with the DNS server to register pointer records or possibly the host records, these servers should be able to find one another as well.

◆ **Windows Internet Name Service (WINS).** WINS is used by NetBIOS applications or down-level clients (pre–Windows 2000 clients) to register their name and IP address. This service could be configured as a name resolution source for a DNS server, and they should be able to find one another.

◆ **Routing and Remote Access Service (RRAS).** RRAS is a hot topic for the exam. RRAS notably uses IPSec, Point-to-Point Tunneling Protocol (PPTP), and Layer-Two Tunneling Protocol (L2TP), which are seen as positive ways to expand the network or provide redundancy by using demand asynchronous dialup over Public Switched Telephone Network (PSTN), Integrated Services Digital Network (ISDN), or X.25, or by using a virtual private network (VPN) over the Internet.

◆ **Proxy Server and/or Network Address Translation (NAT).** Both of these technologies allow multiple internal users to access external Internet resources. With the Microsoft philosophy of "information at your fingertips," access to the Internet is considered essential.

◆ **Distributed file system (Dfs).** Dfs is considered a good choice for storing critical files that need to be accessed by large numbers of users. Fault-tolerant Dfs, which is now known as Domain Dfs, is also a hot technology at Microsoft and will be on the exam.

As stated earlier, every network is different, and you need to look at the network presented to you during the exam and determine which of these services are in use and which are critical for the different parts of the operation. For example, if you find there is a branch office that uses an L2TP VPN to connect to the head office and the connection uses encryption, you know that in addition to basic services (LDAP, DNS, and the Global Catalog), you need Certificate Services, Routing and Remote Access Service, and possibly a routing protocol, such as RIP 2.

When you are back to the real world, you might find that you have a branch office that uses dialup; guess what—the same services are required there. So, you have identified the services that you need. Next, you should decide what information you want to monitor or test and how you plan to do it.

Monitoring the Network

To manage your network, you need to monitor various aspects of its operation. This is done for two main reasons: to find services that have failed and to ensure that the network is running at optimal efficiency. You should look not only at the overall network, but also at the individual pieces that make up the network.

One of the problems with monitoring a network is the large number of services that are required to keep a network running and the even larger amount of information that will be generated as you monitor each of these services. In cases where you attempt to log every detail about one service or another, there can be too much data to effectively manage. In some cases, you need to look at other methods that can be used to signal a service failure.

Monitoring Tools and Utilities

There are, of course, several utilities that are included with Windows 2000 that can be used to monitor the network. These tools each have a place in the overall plan, and you should become familiar with each.

How you monitor your network determines what types of responses you can have for a given situation. There are a number of tools that can be used to gather the data that will be required to ensure services are running within the proper parameters. This includes the following:

◆ Event Viewer logs

◆ Performance Logs and Alerts

◆ Network Monitor

◆ Simple Network Management Protocol (SNMP)

◆ Windows Scripting Host

◆ Command-Line Utilities

Event Viewer Logs

The Event Viewer Logs can provide you with a great deal of information for troubleshooting a problem. The logs can also be used to calculate uptime for various services and to capture problems that happened. In Windows 2000, there are six main event logs, each of which provides different information:

◆ **Applications log**. Any application that is written to Microsoft standards has the capability to record information in the Applications log. This log often tells you why the Exchange server is not working or the SQL server couldn't start.

◆ **Security log**. Events that deal with the security of the system are tracked in this log. The information that is logged depends on the settings that you select in the machine's audit Policies. (Remember that excessive auditing is likely to affect system performance.)

◆ **System log**. All the device drivers, services, and other system-related components record their errors in the system log. This is the log to look at when you get the "At least one driver or service has failed to start" message when you start Windows 2000.

◆ **Directory Service**. This log tracks events that relate to the Active Directory database and its replication.

◆ **DNS server**. This log tracks events that affect the DNS server. If you are having problems resolving network names or logging on, you should check this log.

◆ **File Replication Service**. This service manages the replication of the files in the SYSVOL. If you find that Group Policies, or other information, fails to get to all the domain controllers, you should check this log.

There are five different types of events that you might find in the event log:

◆ **Error**. This event type indicates a problem or a serious issue with some aspect of the operating system or device drivers. Usually an error event is a sign of a failed activity, a terminated service, or an inoperable device. Examples of error events include a service failing to load, not being authenticated by a domain controller, or a device driver not responding as expected.

◆ **Warning**. This event type indicates an occurrence of an incident, which may lead to a system failure or other problem. Examples of warning events include the installation of an unsigned device driver, a DHCP lease is not renewed at its 50% lifespan, or the synchronization failure of the system clock with a timeserver.

◆ **Information**. This event type indicates an occurrence of a
noncritical but informative incident. Information events are
usually confirmations of successful operations and completed
tasks. Examples of information events include when a service
enters the running state after a reboot, the joining of a
domain, or the successful installation of a new device via PnP.

◆ **Success Audit**. This audit type indicates the occurrence of a
successful completion of an audited task. Examples of a success audit include valid authentication at logon, valid access to
a restricted folder, and valid management of user accounts.

◆ **Failure Audit**. This audit type indicates the occurrence of a
failed attempt to perform an audited task. Examples of a failure audit include a user entering the wrong password at logon,
an attempt to open a file to which the user does not have
access rights, and the unauthorized alteration of group policy.

Performance Logs and Alerts Events

Using the System Monitor, you can configure alerts that can be fired
whenever a specific performance threshold is surpassed. Alerts allow
you to configure an action that should be taken, a notification to be
sent on the network, or both.

Using the System Monitor, which is found in the Performance
Console, you can view real-time data, and you can configure and
collect information in logs. The collection of data can be configured,
started, and stopped manually or can be configured and then set to
run on a schedule or in response to a performance alert.

The information that you are gathering is provided by the
Performance Objects. These are DLLs that provide measurement of
various aspects of the operating system's performance and the performance of services that are installed. Whenever a service is installed,
it should include its own Performance Monitor counters that are
then available for examples of services, such as DHCP, WINS, DNS,
and RRAS. These all provide counters when they are installed, so
they can be monitored this way.

System Monitor can be used either to gather information centrally
on one server or in a distributed fashion across many servers.

In either case, the monitoring you do will have an impact on the resources available. When reviewing the data, you should consider the impact of monitoring on the service; in the case of having a central system gather the information, you should consider the impact of monitoring on the network. The service you are monitoring needs to respond to the System Monitor at whatever frequency at which you decide to update the information. If you are looking at a large number of counters, this can seriously affect the available bandwidth on the network.

Network Monitor

The Network Monitor is used to capture the traffic that is received or sent from a single computer (the one it is running on). This allows you to actually see what packets are being generated from the services on a system and can be used to monitor or troubleshoot problems on the network.

Simple Network Management Protocol (SNMP) Events

Because you will be running TCP/IP, you can take advantage of the SNMP Agent that is built into Windows 2000. This agent can use various Management Information Bases (MIBs) to access and report the status of various parts of the operating system. The agent can then respond to a query from a third-party management station or send traps to the management station. (A trap is an occurrence of a significant event.)

Essentially, there are two main pieces to the SNMP protocol:

- ◆ **SNMP Managers**. Managers are stations that have SNMP management software installed. The management software handles querying the devices that it manages and also receives alerts from the agents.

- ◆ **SNMP Agents**. Agents are the part of the protocol that resides in Windows 2000 and responds to the requests of the management software. The agent is also responsible for sending alerts or traps to a configured manager.

SNMP is a very simple protocol. The SNMP protocol uses UDP packets on port 161 to send and receive the information. Four commands can be used in the SNMP protocol:

◆ **Get**. This command from a manager tells the agent to return the current value for a particular setting.

◆ **Get-next**. This command tells the agent to return the next value in a sequence.

◆ **Set**. This command lets a manager set a value. Because of a lack of security, very few values can be set.

◆ **Trap**. The agent sends a trap, which indicates an alert condition.

The data structure that is used by the SNMP protocol is the MIB, which defines the set of manageable objects that an agent has. It provides a common reference point that both the management station and the agent know.

There are various MIBs supported in Windows 2000, including the following:

◆ **Internet MIB II**. Used for the standard TCP/IP objects, this allows management of stations and routers through an entire intranet or on the Internet.

◆ **LAN Manager MIB II**. This MIB is a group of manageable objects that are part of Windows 2000.

◆ **Host Resources MIB**. This MIB describes the resources available on the host.

◆ **DHCP MIB**. This MIB provides management of the DHCP service.

◆ **WINS MIB**. This MIB provides management of the WINS service.

Windows 2000 comes with an SNMP Agent. However, Microsoft has not released a Management tool. It has included a Manager API, which is intended to allow others to produce management software.

There is only basic security in the SNMP protocol, and you should be aware that you could be letting information about your system be read by numerous hackers. The LAN Manager MIB, for example, can provide a list of all the users allowed on a system and the services that are running. This is very useful if a hacker is attempting to break into your computer.

An SNMP Agent will not respond to every system in the world that can run SNMP; it will respond only to other systems that have the same community name. A community name is very much like a workgroup name; it identifies a group of systems that will be managed as one unit. The management software and the agents must share the same community name before they will be able to communicate.

There are a couple of security measures that you should take. The most important measure you should take if you connect to the Internet is to filter UDP port 161 at the router. This means you cannot manage the network across the Internet. However, neither can others.

You should tell the agent to which management systems it will be allowed to respond. In this way, you can also prevent internal hackers from being able to take over workstation management. If you include SNMP solely to enable the TCP/IP performance counters, you should enter a fake IP for the nonexistent management station.

Windows Scripting Host

Windows Scripting Host (WSH) is a controller system for Windows-compliant scripting engines. WSH has low memory requirements and can be used to manage both interactive and automatic/unattended scripting operations.

WSH is a significant improvement in the scripting capabilities of the Microsoft product line. Previously, only MS-DOS batch scripting was natively supported. Now, both VBScript and JScript can be used to enhance an administrator's control over systems. WSH is not limited to just native scripting languages—any language with a Windows engine, such as Perl, can be controlled through WSH.

WSH offers two modes for its control interfaces: a GUI and a command line. The GUI mode control interface (`WSCRIPT.EXE`) allows an administrator to set script properties through standard Windows dialog boxes. The command-line mode control interface (`SCRIPT.EXE`) uses command-line switches to set script properties. Having two control interface modes makes WSH a very versatile tool.

Command-Line Utilities

Most of the graphical tools and utilities found on Windows 2000 have a command-line equivalent. The command-line tools enable a resourceful administrator to automate repetitive and tedious tasks. Simple batch files or even complicated scripting routines can take advantage of these command-line tools. The administrative overhead can be reduced even further by combining a script or batch file with the task-scheduling capabilities of Windows 2000.

The following is a list of some of the most useful Windows 2000 command-line utilities:

◆ **Ipconfig**. This tool displays IP configuration, renews or releases a DHCP lease, flushes DNS cache, and registers a system with DNS.

◆ **Nbtstat**. This tool displays which TCP/IP connections are using NetBIOS, lists the NetBIOS name cache table, purges the NetBIOS name cache table, and more.

◆ **Netdiag**. This tool is used to perform several tests of the networking infrastructure. Tests look for installed hot fixes, IP configuration, and verification of resolution services. This tool is not present on a default Windows 2000 installation; it is part of the support tools, which must be installed manually.

◆ **Netstat**. This tool displays all open connections and ports, lists Ethernet statistics, displays the service listening on each open port, and shows the routing table.

◆ **Nslookup**. This tool is used to issue interactive queries against a DNS server to test for name resolution. Nslookup can be used as a single command-line tool to obtain a single data point or result. It can also be used to enter an interactive testing session.

◆ **Pathping**. This tool combines the features of Tracert and Ping. This tool performs repeated response tests of each system or hops between the host and the destination.

◆ **Ping**. This tool is used to verify IP connectivity by testing response time between host and destination.

◆ **Tracert**. This tool displays the routers between host and destination. This tool reveals the logical path of communication between two systems.

Data Collection

When monitoring any system, you must take into consideration the effect that monitoring itself has on that system. Monitoring any object affects the performance of that object. Thus, the more objects that are monitored, the greater the overall skew of a system's performance. For a few objects, this change is negligible. However, it can quickly become significant enough to hide the true performance of a system. You must learn to balance the need to obtain the monitoring data against the amount of skew such activity causes.

When monitoring several systems on a network, you often choose to centralize the data-gathering processes on a single system. This requires that the measurement data be transported to that single system in some manner. There are two possible pathways for this transport:

◆ **In-band data collection**. The measurement data is transported across the same network on which all other normal or productive activities occur. This causes a reduction in bandwidth available for normal traffic.

◆ **Out-of-band data collection**. The measurement data is transported across a secondary or backup network or link that is specifically designated for this purpose. This does not cause a reduction in the bandwidth on the primary network.

Deploying out-of-band data collection doesn't always require a complete duplicate network. In fact, you can often get away with a few additional point-to-point connections between the central measurement system and key monitored systems.

In addition to determining whether monitoring data is gathered on a monitoring server or servers using in-band or out-of-band collection pathways, you should also consider whether to deploy a centralized or a decentralized collection scheme:

◆ **Centralized**. A single system is used to gather all measurement data. The single system also performs data storage and analysis. A single system provides a single point of failure and too much measurement data can result in missed data points or a saturated connection medium (in-band or out-of-band pathway).

◆ **Decentralized**. Multiple systems are used to gather the measurement data. Each individual gathering host can also perform initial analysis. This allows for less data transfer during possible condensing of data onto a single system for final analysis. This is the preferred methodology for distributed networks using WAN connections.

Analyzing the Information

After data has been gathered, it must be analyzed and condensed in order to provide useful perspectives on how a system is performing. The bulk of data analysis can be performed manually. However, manual data reduction is often tedious and unreliable because of the human factor. Several mechanisms for automated or scripted data reduction not only are significantly faster but are more reliable.

Manual analysis has even further drawbacks. It requires that a manual response to any problem or condition be performed by an administrator. Additionally, it does not provide a timely response to critical issues.

Automated analysis can include data-reduction tools such as spreadsheets, database systems, or programmatic solutions. The benefits of automated analysis include the possibility of automated responses to problems and the achievement of more accurate results. However, automated solutions are not without their own drawbacks. The automation process is capable of producing false-positives and false-negatives. A false-positive is the discovery of a problem when there actually is no problem. Although this is inefficient, it is typically not a significant issue. A false-negative occurs when a real problem is not discovered, and thus is not corrected. This is a significant problem and can be corrected only through periodic refining of the automated systems and manual analysis to check the automated results.

Responding to Issues

Of course, responding is the end of the cycle. You decided what you needed to monitor, gathered information about it, and analyzed the information, and now you need to respond to the situation.

This can be done manually or automatically and could be as simple as restarting a service that stopped or as complex as having to redesign your entire network.

The apparent time that it takes you to fix a network problem includes the time it takes to gather the data and then to analyze the data as far as the client is concerned. In addition, there is the time that it will take to correct the problem. In some operations, this combination of times can become unacceptably large and can have a major impact—not only in downtime but also in monetary losses and other intangible losses, such as the loss of "face" in the customer's eye.

Planning to detect and gather the correct data and analyze it in a meaningful time frame cannot ensure a smooth operation. For example, if you have programmatically configured your network to let you know within one minute if a server crashes, your users should be happy—unless the server will then be down for five hours while a replacement is purchased on the administrator's credit card at the local computer shop and then loaded from scratch because the configuration is so different.

For this reason, you should have in place the processes and policies that will prevent this scenario; spare parts alone are not an option if your company will lose $250,000 every hour the system is down. (This is quite possible if it is a SQL Server system.)

Another way to help this scenario from becoming reality is to monitor and analyze enough information so that you can proactively manage your network. In other words, if you notice that there are occasional errors on a network adapter in your Global Catalog server, replace the adapter during the next maintenance window rather than waiting for it to fail. Another option to ensure that a failure is always noncritical is to build a redundant network.

However, even in a redundant network, if a service is failed over to a second server in the cluster, you still need to notify the administrator so that the system can be repaired.

Summary of Network Management

It's important to remember that the network management plan is only one component of the overall network plan. The network plan dictates how the entire network and the applications on the network function. The network management plan includes methods for the following:

◆ Responding to network changes as they occur

◆ Verifying that current operations are within the design specifications

◆ Anticipating the need for changes to the network design

This is all accomplished through the gathering of data, its analysis, and the determination of the response it requires.

DESIGNING AND COMBINING NETWORK SERVICES

Design network services that support application architecture.

Design a plan for the interaction of Windows 2000 network services, such as WINS, DHCP, and DNS.

Many of the core networking services and BackOffice applications can be deployed onto the same server. But, even though this is possible, is it a good idea? Well, that depends on the capabilities of your hardware, the load on your network, and the applications themselves. Deploying a single server with combined network services can offer numerous benefits. However, when functionality or reliability is compromised, many of these benefits become worthless.

Therefore, determining which network services can or should be combined is an important design element. Very few organizations have the budget to deploy every network service on its own dedicated system. So, learning how to maximize the potential of combined services is usually a necessity.

There are several benefits that you can achieve by combining various network services on a single system. However, the goal is to improve performance and availability, not to overload a system and create a single point of failure. If you plan on deploying multiple network services onto a single system, consider the following items:

- Don't sacrifice security to gain ease of use.

- Don't sacrifice availability to reduce hardware costs.

- Don't sacrifice performance to improve administrative overhead.

- Ensure that the system has sufficient hardware resources, including RAM, CPU, storage, network connectivity, and so forth, to fully support the requirements of the combined services.

Service Combination Benefits

One of the primary benefits of combining multiple services onto a single system can be a reduction in the total number of physical servers required to support the network. When fewer computers are on a network, this directly reduces the amount of chatter traffic. Thus, a significant gain in usable network bandwidth is reaped.

Not all cases of combining multiple service onto a single computer result in a reduction of the number of physical servers on the network. For example, if one server is running DNS and another is running WINS, it is a better design plan to deploy both DNS and WINS on both physical servers rather than use only a single server for both. This also provides improved network fault tolerance through redundancy.

The combination of services can also offer security benefits such as deploying an authentication service and a resource distribution service on the same server. This prevents authentication information from propagating across insecure network links.

Furthermore, the combination of services can offer performance benefits such as deploying the Global Catalog and a Domain Dfs root on the same server. Combining these services onto a single system reduces the network traffic and optimizes the computer resources that are underused.

Service Combination Drawbacks

Combining multiple network services onto a single system can create a single point of failure. If your network cannot function with the combined-service system, you must consider an alternative design.

No amount of reduced hardware cost or improved administrative overhead is worth the risk of an offline network.

Not all networking services can be deployed onto the same server. For example, the global catalog server service and the infrastructure master service should be deployed on separate physical servers whenever possible. These two services do not operate efficiently when deployed on the same system.

Microsoft has even issued a specific warning against deploying any combination of SQL Server, Exchange Server, and Terminal Services onto a single system. Each of these services is so resource intensive that they will consume any and all resources present on a system and still demand more. None of these services works well on a multiservice server.

Optimizing Performance Through Combining Services

There are several different advantages that you can gain if you combine network services. You need to consider what you are trying to optimize, because often if you optimize the performance of the network, it is to the detriment of the processor or vice versa.

To gain improved performance on a combined-services system, you must ensure that each service is able to access sufficient resources in a timely manner. Without adequate resource access, performance is degraded significantly. When combining services, look for complementary opposites. For example, deploy a service that has a high-storage system usage with a service that needs significant use of system memory. When selecting services to combined, focus on preventing resource starvation and keeping network traffic to a minimum.

Service Combination Limitations

When designing a network with combined-service servers, you must take into consideration several limitations and restrictions. The physical server must be sufficiently equipped to handle the workload created by each service. This usually means adding or cumulating each service's resource requirements to build a "super-server."

Reducing a network down to too few servers can cause bottlenecking.

This is especially true if you don't deploy redundant systems.

If every member of the network must interact with a single server, the network will become saturated around that key server.

Additionally, the presence of WAN links or concentration devices, such as routers and switches, can make the placement of multiple service servers important and the need for redundant systems critical.

Service Combining on Clustered Servers

One method to ensure sufficient resources for a multiservice server is to use clustering. Clustering is often touted as an efficient solution for deploying enterprise-level SQL, Exchange, or Terminal Server. However, clustering can also be used when multiple services are deployed together. This is clearly evident in Microsoft's implementations of DHCP and DNS, which are able to directly integrate with and benefit from clustered servers.

The primary benefit of clustering is the automated failover in the event of a cluster member failure. Additionally, clustering automatically performs load balancing among all cluster members.

PLANNING RESOURCES FOR THE NETWORK

Design a resource strategy.

- ◆ Plan for the placement and management of resources.
- ◆ Plan for growth.
- ◆ Plan for decentralized resources or centralized resources.

As a last topic for this chapter and, for that matter, this text, it is worth looking at resources. These are also network services, but they are special because they interact with the clients directly, unlike services, such as DHCP, that are used by the client's system.

In general, there are two schools of thought on resources: centralized and decentralized. Which to use is the first decision to make before you can begin to plan your network. In a centralized network, there are typically fewer but larger servers, and these servers tend to be on a backbone. This makes maintaining the servers much simpler because they are physically in one location. The users will need to traverse the network more often and you will need to ensure sufficient bandwidth. On the upside, you will have good security because one of the first principles of security is physical control.

On the downside, as the number of network applications increases and as the reliance on Internet and intranet sites increases, the bandwidth that you need to accomplish centralization is harder to maintain. This might seem strange, but if you consider the cost of throwing out enough hubs, routers, switches, and other networking gear to hook up a large office—for example, 20,000 users—and replace all that gear with 100Mbps fiber, it becomes clear why this is a concern.

If you are willing to give up centralized control, you can easily accommodate your users. The simplest method is to place the resources where the users are that use them. This means that for each Active Directory site you have, you could have a file and print server, a domain controller, and any other servers that you need. This means that you still have a need for systems; however, they will be smaller. It also means that a great deal of the network traffic will stay in the same subnet or site as the user.

ESSENCE OF THE CASE

In this chapter, you looked at designing a management and implementation strategy for Windows 2000 networking. The chapter pulled together some of the information that you saw in the other chapters and gave you some insight into the questions that you might need to look at in the real world.

This case study is presented in keeping with the scenario-based nature of the exam, where you will have testlets that contain an incredible amount of information. As you read through this, think about the way that you might configure servers—centralized or decentralized. Think about the services that are required and how you will combine them, and think about the critical services and how you might deal with them.

Scenario

Sunshine Brewing is a multinational corporation with major centers in Ottawa, Sydney, Cape Town, and London. There are smaller branch offices throughout the world located in Victoria, Los Angeles, Mexico City, Houston, New York, Buenos Aires, St. John's, Paris, Moscow, Beijing, and Tokyo.

The company has decided after extensive studies that it will use Windows 2000 with Active Directory as its primary network. In addition, the company also needs to use Unix for monitoring and controlling the production facilities.

Sunshine Brewing plans on providing both Internet and intranet access to all employees. Information should flow easily from location to location because teams are often drawn up from human resources across the entire organization. Provision also has to be made for the sales and IT staffs who travel frequently but still need to access resources in their home locations.

Before you can go much further, you need to look at the physical network. You need to look at the number of users at each location and the role each plays in the organization. The physical connections between the sites should be addressed as to both speed and reliability. Table 6.2 breaks down the user community by location as a basis for the network.

TABLE 6.2

DISTRIBUTION OF USERS AT SUNSHINE BREWING

Branch	Exec.	R&D	IT	Adm.	Sales	Prod.
Ottawa	145	352	450	742	1,274	854
London	23	120	180	521	963	562
Cape Town	18	136	196	436	954	632
Sydney	32	224	251	357	965	843
Victoria	1	5	0	42	89	236
Los Angeles	2	6	0	61	109	310
Mexico City	3	12	0	72	174	400
Houston	2	15	0	66	98	350
New York	2	23	0	96	131	298

DISTRIBUTION OF USERS AT SUNSHINE BREWING

Branch	Exec.	R&D	IT	Adm.	Sales	Prod.
St. John's	1	4	0	35	64	198
Paris	1	16	0	41	134	201
Moscow	1	6	0	24	54	126
Beijing	1	2	0	88	140	320
Tokyo	2	4	0	48	98	264

As you probably guessed, the breakdown of the users into these six groups is not accidental. These represent the main roles in the company, and each of the roles has a different set of requirements from the network. The following is an overview of the different requirements for the users:

◆ **Exec. (235).** The executive users require 24-hour-a-day access from anywhere. Frequently, executives travel between the offices and to other locations. They need to be able to use email, they need an office suite, and they need to be able to connect to server-based applications internally using a Web browser.

◆ **R&D (933).** The research and development users don't travel, but they need to be able to collaborate with R&D users in other branches. In addition to email and an office suite, they need access to specialized applications. Research users also have the option of working at home or at the office, and at the office they have shared desk areas where any research user can sit down and work. They want to ensure all applications are available on each of the shared systems but would also like to have the users able to keep their own desktop settings.

◆ **IT (1,077).** The IT department in each location takes care of the local computers—both the production systems that are running Unix and the Windows-based systems that are used by the other users. The IT staff frequently travels to the branch offices to maintain and upgrade systems and will need access to email from any branch. IT users also need to be able to access troubleshooting tools that are located on various servers across the network.

◆ **Adm. (2,674).** The administration users are probably the easiest to deal with; they don't travel and need to be able to work with only email and an office suite. Each is assigned a fixed desk and computer.

◆ **Sales (5,314).** Sales users travel constantly and are rarely in the office. They use laptops exclusively to access their email, the order processing application, and an office suite. They occasionally stop by the office, and a space has been provided in each branch for about half the sales staff to be in at any time. The space provided includes only network connections and the users will work on their laptops even in the office.

◆ **Prod. (5,839).** The production users are responsible for ensuring that production and shipping are handled. They primarily use the Unix systems but also need access to email. They use Web browsers to access the production software.

As you can see, the requirement for each different type of user is varied and this should be accommodated. In addition to the local software on their systems, each type of user needs to access servers on a corporate level. This includes the Unix servers that control production and the accounting system that runs on a SQL server in the Ottawa Office. In addition, users need to access the sales tracking system that links the accounting system and the production system that has been specially built, based on the Exchange servers that are used for email. Finally, the research staff makes frequent use of Exchange public folders for collaboration.

Another consideration is the remote access for the executive and sales users. This will be handled by acquiring an account at an ISP that is local to each site (most of which will bulk discount). For some users, a global ISP will be used and this could be considered for all users depending on price. The users will then use a virtual private network to access the local office through its Internet connection.

So far, you have learned about the user community and the locations; but before you can make decisions about the domain structure, the number of subnets, the sites, or the placement of servers, you need to know about the physical network.

Sunshine Brewing has been building the network for some time and therefore doesn't have a single technology across the board. The locations vary in the type and quality of network and in the type and quality of connection to the other offices and the Internet. The following describes the technology in the different locations:

◆ **Ottawa (3,817 users).** The network in Ottawa has been upgraded a few times over the years and is now running 100Mbps Ethernet. The main protocol in use is TCP/IP, and all the desktop systems and servers are cycled out every two years. The facility is a collection of three buildings—one for production, one for warehousing, and one for offices. The three buildings are linked using a redundant-fiber backbone providing high-speed connections between them. The buildings use a combination of routing and switching so that no more than 50 desktop systems and no more than five servers are local to any segment. In cases where servers need to communicate with one another, a separate network card connects the servers; in the case of Microsoft products, this backbone runs the NetBEUI protocol.

The Ottawa location is currently connected to the Internet using a 100Mbps connection. In addition, there are T1 links between this office and London and 512Kbps Frame Relay links to Sydney and Cape Town. There is also a 512Kbps link to the St. John's office and an OC3 link to New York.

◆ **London (2,369 users).** The London office is similar to the Ottawa office but consists of two buildings—one for production and warehousing and the other for offices. The buildings are linked using a redundant-fiber backbone providing high-speed connections between them. The buildings use a combination of routing and switching so that no more than 120 desktop systems and no more than 10 servers are local to any segment. The office building uses 100Mbps Ethernet, and the production and warehousing site uses 10Mbps Ethernet.

The London office is connected to the Internet by a T1 link. A connection to Ottawa uses a T1, a connection to Paris uses a T1, and a connection to Moscow uses a 256Kbps leased line. An additional T1 connects the London office to the Tokyo office.

◆ **Cape Town (2,372 users).** The Cape Town office was acquired during a takeover of a rival brewing company. The existing Token-Ring network is still in use, although the wiring has been upgraded to allow the network to run at 16Mbps. There are two buildings, as with London, and the buildings are linked using a redundant-fiber backbone providing high-speed connections between them. The buildings use routing so that no more than 150 desktop systems and no more than 15 servers are local to any segment.

The Cape Town office is connected to the Internet using a 512Kbps leased line. In addition, it is connected to the Buenos Aires office using a 512Kbps link. The overall network diagram appears in Figure 6.1.

FIGURE 6.1

Network diagram of the Cape Town site.

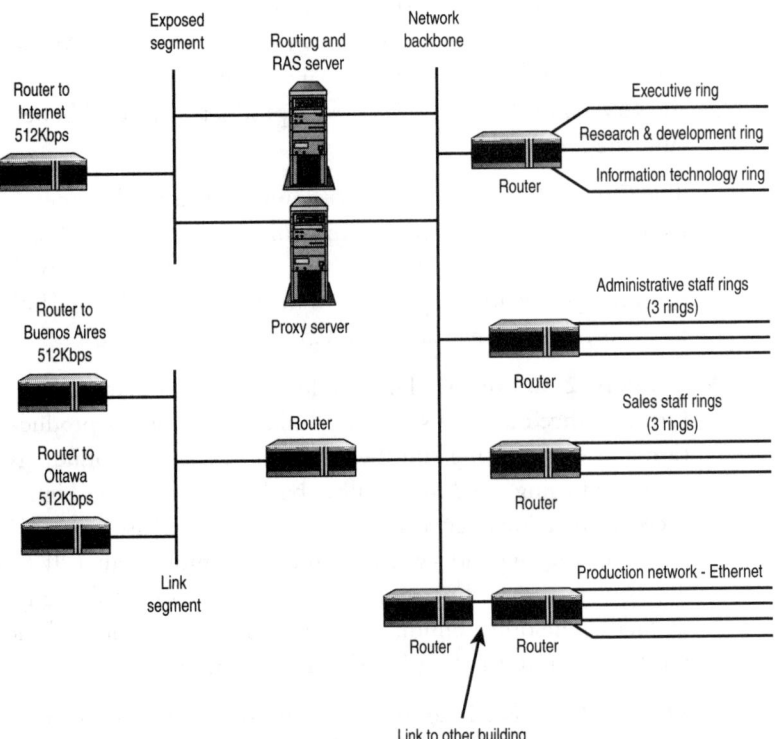

◆ **Sydney (2,672 users)**. Sydney is also broken down into two buildings; however, the buildings are connected using a leased 768Kbps line because they are not physically close enough to use fiber. This office currently uses a 10Mbps Ethernet network. The buildings uses switching so that no more than 80 desktop systems and no more than five servers are local to any segment.

The Sydney office is connected to the Internet using a T1 link. It is connected to Ottawa using a 512Kbps line and to Tokyo using a T1 line.

◆ **Victoria (373 users)**. The Victoria office, like all the branches, is a combined facility with the production, warehousing, and office space all in one location. The network is a routed 100Mbps Ethernet network with four network segments.

The Victoria office is connected to the Internet using business ADSL (768Kbps uplink speed). There is also a T1 link to the Los Angeles office.

◆ **Los Angeles (488 users)**. The Los Angeles office uses 100Mbps Ethernet. It has five segments across routers locally. There is a T1 connection to the Internet, a T1 connection to the Victoria office, a T3 connection to the New York office, and a T3 connection to Tokyo.

◆ **Mexico City (661 users)**. In Mexico City, the network is running Token Ring at 4Mbps. The network is split into 10 separate rings and routing is used between them. There is a 256Kbps link to the Internet and a 512Kbps link to the Houston office.

◆ **Houston (531 users)**. The Houston office uses 100Mbps Ethernet and uses switching between the seven network segments. There is a T1 connection to the Internet in addition to a 512Kbps link to Mexico City and a T1 connection to New York.

◆ **New York (550 users)**. This network uses a switched-fiber backbone and then uses 100Mbps to the desktop. There are six segments in the network. There is a T1 connection to the Internet in addition to the T1 connection to Houston, the T3 connection to Los Angeles, and the OC3 connection to Ottawa.

◆ **Buenos Aires (366 users).** In Buenos Aires, the network runs 10Mbps Ethernet with routers connecting the seven segments. There is a 256Kbps connection to the Internet in addition to the 512Kbps connection to Cape Town.

◆ **St. John's (302 users).** The St. John's office uses 100Mbps Ethernet with a switch between the six network segments. There is a business ADSL connection to the Internet and a 512Kbps link to the Ottawa office. Figure 6.2 shows a diagram of the network layout.

FIGURE 6.2
The St. John's office network layout.

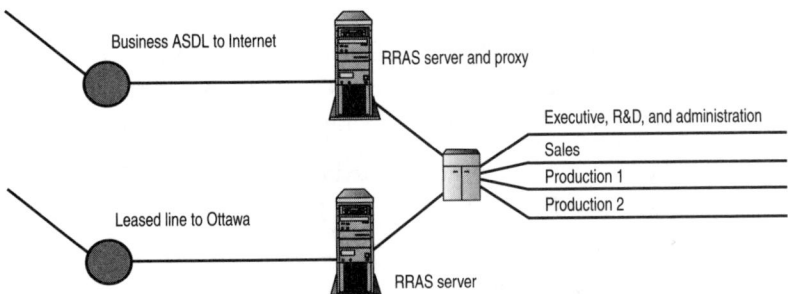

◆ **Paris (393 users).** The Paris office also uses 100Mbps Ethernet and switching technology between the eight network segments. There is a 512Kbps link to the Internet and a T1 connection to the London office.

◆ **Moscow (211 users).** The Moscow office uses ARCnet at 2Mbps and routes between the five network segments. There is a 128Kbps link to the Internet and a 256Kbps link to London.

◆ **Beijing (551 users).** The Beijing office uses 10Mbps Ethernet with bridges between the six network segments. There is a 128Kbps link to the Internet and a 256Kbps link to Tokyo.

◆ **Tokyo (416 Users).** The Tokyo office is using fiber to the desktop and connects each system directly to one of its switches. It has a T1 link to the Internet, a 256Kbps link to Beijing, a T1 link to London, a T1 link to Sydney, and a T3 link to Los Angeles.

Within North America, the WAN links tend to be 95% reliable, and elsewhere it is more like 75% reliable. Each location has demand-dial routes set up using RRAS to try to compensate for downtime, and this has brought your overall WAN link uptime to around 98%.

Corporate information is kept on each of the main sites; however, region-specific information will be kept in the appropriate branch office. This information needs to be available to all users.

Analysis

Believe it or not, there are companies with networks like this and there are some with larger networks that have even more types of users. The trick to looking at a network is really simple. Break it down. In the end, most users want to get at their files, work with an office suite, and surf the Internet.

From that standpoint, most of the information you need should be in the descriptions of what the users need. The following are key services that will make this network run:

- ◆ **Global Catalog servers**. Locate the users' home domain. You need to have one per site, which is the Microsoft recommendation. This is fine; the users should have to query it only once if they are traveling and that's it.

- ◆ **Lightweight Directory Access Protocol (LDAP)**. For those who think this list is familiar, it is. It is copied from the section on monitoring, because in most networks, regardless of size or shape, the process is essentially the same. Let's call these domain controllers and place one from each domain in each site. This will cause some replication; however, there aren't any big issues about network traffic, and the passwords aren't changed every day (in other words, there isn't much replication).

- ◆ **Certificate Services**. In this case, there is no mention of IPSec, so this wouldn't come into play. Be aware that this will come into play at least once on the exam, and make sure you understand how it works, how IPSec works, and when to use L2TP.

◆ **Domain Name System (DNS) name server**. You need the DNS name server because this will be the main name resolution method. For load balancing, you want to have multiple copies of this, and probably one per site would not be out of line—notably if the domain is Active Directory integrated.

◆ **Dynamic Host Configuration Protocol (DHCP)**. DHCP is also a requirement (even the refrigerator will need this one day). This is a small service and is locked into subnets, so it makes sense to put it at the subnet level. Then you can split the range to provide redundancy.

◆ **Windows Internet Name Service (WINS)**. You probably won't need this service. At the very least, you won't need it forever, so this is not a big issue. To make it easier to remove, you might place it centrally.

◆ **Routing and Remote Access (RRAS)**. RRAS is required and should be monitored. In offices where the Internet connection can stand it—that is, physically accept two connections—you might create a redundant server. This definitely is the case in Ottawa to allow for the dial-in VPN users.

◆ **Proxy Server and/or Network Address Translation (NAT)**. These are also requirements and services to monitor; however, because the business is not driven on these, it is probably not a big issue.

◆ **Distributed File System (Dfs)**. Dfs does not seem to be used in this design, so you can forget about it.

Now that the services are identified and you have an idea of where they are located, you could then look at the monitoring. In this case, a collection station in each physical location would make sense. You could have that collection station run Terminal Services and monitor the services in that way, or you could have the system programmatically send the data to the head office for analysis.

Obviously, this is just an overview—and it is left this way so that you might read through it again and see what else might work for this organization.

As you can see, there are no hard or fast rules for monitoring—except that it's a good thing—or for combining services—which could be a good thing or a bad thing—or for deploying resources. Successful designers tend to be flexible and to listen to their clients.

You need to decide what to monitor, how to gather the data, how to analyze it, and then just what you want to do with it.

You monitor reactively because you will have servers crash, you will get viruses, and you will have WAN links that fail; you need to react to these. When possible, you should have a system that is redundant so that the failure of a single service doesn't matter, and a system that is automatic so that even if an administrator is not around, the problem can be fixed.

APPLY YOUR KNOWLEDGE

Exercises

6.1 Planning the Network Services at the Cape Town Site

In this exercise, you decide the implementation of services within the site and then look at the management of those services that you are deploying. The goal in the design of the network is to ensure as much redundancy as possible. After you complete this exercise, consider practicing by planning the networks for the other sites.

Estimated Time: 45 minutes

1. Review the material in the case study with a particular interest in the Cape Town site.

2. Review the network diagram of the Cape Town site shown in Figure 6.1.

3. How many domain controllers should you have in this diagram? Where should they be placed?

4. Which of the domain controllers that you are locating in this site should be Global Catalog servers? Why?

5. Given that all the users will require access to file and print servers, where is the best place to locate them?

6. Where should the DHCP and DNS servers be located? How many of each should you have in this site?

7. Given that all the users need to access the Exchange servers, where should you locate them?

8. Reviewing the design choices you have made up to this point, have you provided total redundancy? Is it possible to provide total redundancy?

9. Consider and then list the systems that are critical and therefore should be monitored.

10. What other portions of the network should you be monitoring? From where should they be monitored?

Exercise 6.1 Answers

As you read through the answers that are presented here and for the following exercises, remember that they are not necessarily the only possible answers. You are given a solution that will fit with Microsoft recommendations. It is critical when you take the exam to remember that you are writing the exam—that is, you must think like Microsoft. Many very experienced people have problems with Microsoft exams because they are used to performing tasks differently or to planning networks in a different fashion.

3. As you read the case study, you should have understood that the Cape Town office is a single site in the Active Directory sense and therefore will require at least one domain controller. Wherever there is one domain controller, you should always add a second domain controller for redundancy.

   In real life, you would probably have a few extra domain controllers. Normally, Microsoft looks at a domain controller for every 2,000 users. In general, the number is somewhat closer to one domain controller for every 500 users plus 1. In this case, there are more than 2,300 users, meaning there might be closer to 5 domain controllers.

4. Because this is a site, you should have at least one Global Catalog server. This will be used for users that belong to other branches to be able to log on in this site. This will also be used to locate resources across the enterprise and if the domain is in native mode for universal groups.

APPLY YOUR KNOWLEDGE

Because of the importance of the Global Catalog server, you would probably set two in this situation. This is not yet a Microsoft recommendation; however, it probably will be the solution it comes up with in many cases. The trick here is to configure one of the servers that will be the Global Catalog server as the replication bridgehead server. This will ensure that the Global Catalog will be replicated to it over the WAN link. The chances are that the second Global Catalog server will now take its copy from the first one rather than across the WAN link.

5. In a pinch, a single server could handle file and print services for 2,372 users; however, this is not the optimal design—nor is it the Microsoft design. For years, Microsoft has been moving toward using more, cheaper boxes rather than one or two larger systems. This is how they designed Windows NT and has evolved out of the peer-to-peer networks.

   Given that Microsoft is big on Dfs, you can bet that it will probably throw these at you. If they do, go for it; it is probably the right answer. In real life, consider Dfs and compare this with just using regular file and print servers. Actually, you will still need regular print servers.

   In general, the file and print servers should be as close to the users as possible; so if you are using multiple (that is, not Dfs) file servers, the file servers should be on the same subnets as the users. This will also ensure you don't go over the 15-servers/subnet limit that is given in the case study.

6. There is one important thing to look at if the question is about these servers. Do the routers support RFC 1542, which is also known as BOOTP forwarding? If the routers do not

support this standard, you will need to either use DHCP Relay Agents or locate the DHCP servers on each of the subnets.

If it is not mentioned in the question that the routers support this standard, you should not assume the routers could forward these packets. By default, a Windows 2000 computer configured as a router does not support this standard.

If forwarding is possible or DHCP Relay Agents are available, you could get by with one DHCP server for all the systems. Microsoft always recommends two for redundancy's sake and this would be the solution. In real life, you normally have the domain controllers handle DNS and DHCP—and WINS if you use it—because this tends to balance the load well. You might notice in some of the Microsoft questions and documentation that this is probably its practice, because it seems to assume a domain controller is running these services.

If forwarding were not available, Microsoft would expect that you would have a DHCP server on each subnet and quite possibly—for the best answer—a second one for redundancy.

The DNS server is a different kettle of fish in this case. If the DNS zone is Active Directory integrated, the DNS service should be on domain controllers. This is a must for the main domain; however, the Active Directory–integrated zones do not extend to the child domains and you need to use a standard secondary DNS server in any child domains for DNS services. The system also needs to have access to a domain controller running DNS from the parent domain to be able to dynamically register. For example, if you have ScrimTech.com and this is an Active

APPLY YOUR KNOWLEDGE

Directory–integrated zone, wherever there is a child, such as `Development.ScrimTech.com`, you use standard secondary servers. When a client registers its DNS name, it reads the SOA record and finds the servers that can update the zone, which are from the `ScrimTech.com` domain. The client then registers with a domain controller from `ScrimTech.com` that is running the DNS service.

The other thing to remember about DHCP and DNS and about DNS and WINS is that they work together and can benefit from being on the same system. DHCP will, by default, update the reverse-lookup information for its clients, and DNS can be configured to query a WINS server for entries it doesn't have.

7. The simple answer is that you should put the server on the backbone. There isn't any real trick to this question except that you might not know too much about Exchange. On the exams, Microsoft generally gives you the information about any other servers that you need to consider in the questions.

   It is worth the time, however, to review the Microsoft site or to run through TechNet and get a feel for the other services. This is considered a senior exam because if you are going to be planning networks, you should understand not only the basics but also the services that you could find on the networks. In practice, the "Enterprise" exam from the Windows NT 4.0 stream was extremely easy, and Microsoft has gone out of its way to make this exam difficult.

8. The term *redundancy* has become a buzzword in the computer industry. It is not a new term, and for years certain very critical systems have been made redundant. With Microsoft looking toward the network and trying to essentially take the Sun approach of "the network is the computer," we are seeing more pressure to make everything redundant.

   This is not bad, but like the Internet and like PDAs, it is a wave that you can get caught up in. It is important in real life to sit back and decide what really needs to be redundant. Having said that, this design can be made redundant, of course. With respect to domain controllers and DNS and DHCP, you have already read about how this could be done. When it comes to the other items that you would need to add, look at where you have only one server to do it or one route to get there.

   For example, to make this scenario completely redundant, you would first need to add a second network card to every system and build a second set of identical Token Rings and backbone, including a completely separate set of routers between the rings and the backbone. Then, you would need to have a redundant RRAS server to receive and handle the VPNs coming from the field.

   There would also have to be a redundant proxy server and a redundant router to the link segment. Ideally, you'd finish all this off by adding a redundant power supply and UPS to each station. This would be stupidly expensive and points out why although redundancy is good, total redundancy is not practical.

9. There are several critical systems that make up this network and that therefore you would want to monitor:

   Domain Controllers (NetLogon service). These servers are required to validate logons. They should be monitored using the Performance Log periodically for capacity planning and to ensure the service is running, using an alert.

APPLY YOUR KNOWLEDGE

Global Catalog server. These servers are required for users from other offices to log on and to process searches. They should be monitored using the Replication Monitor to ensure they are in the right role and using the Performance Logs to ensure they have enough resources—notably, RAM and disk because of the extra information they must handle.

RRAS server. This server allows remote users to access the network using VPNs and is also used to connect over the network, using VPN, to other branches. This should be monitored using Performance Log occasionally to ensure sufficient resources and using an alert to ensure the service is available.

Proxy server. This server allows internal clients to surf the Internet. This server should occasionally be checked for sufficient resources, using the Performance Logs.

DHCP server. This provides the IP addresses for the clients. This should be checked either manually or using a script on a daily basis to ensure it is running properly. The DHCP database should be compacted monthly.

DNS server. This provides name resolution for hostnames. This service is critical in Windows 2000 and should be checked daily, and scavenging should be configured to clean up the database.

WINS server. If you are using this, you should check it daily and configure the automatic backups. The database should be compressed monthly.

Internal routers. These routers provide connectivity from the clients to central servers (on the backbone and in the Ottawa office). If they are Windows 2000 servers, they should be checked for capacity, using the Performance Logs. If your routers are not Windows 2000 systems then SNMP should be considered to ensure that they continue to be up.

File and print servers. These are Windows 2000 servers, possibly with Dfs filling these roles, which provide file and print services. These should be monitored for capacity, using the Performance Monitor, and alerts should be set for available disk space.

Plans should be made to check the event logs of all the servers on a daily basis to ensure any major problems are discovered and corrected quickly.

10. Other than the items that you are monitoring, you should keep an eye on the network use for each segment to ensure that there is enough bandwidth. In this case, there should be no problems because Token Ring can handle more hosts per segment and the overall design is based on Ethernet.

    Because there is IT staff at this location, the monitoring should be done in the branch. Probably, the stations that will perform the monitoring should be on the backbone to have easy access to all systems.

6.2 Planning a Resource Strategy for the St. John's Site

In this exercise, you make decisions about the placement of resources in one of the smaller branches. In general, this will be the same in all the branch offices.

Estimated Time: 15 minutes

1. Review the information in the case study about the St. John's branch, noting particularly the number and types of users.

APPLY YOUR KNOWLEDGE

2. Review Figure 6.2 showing the layout of the network at the St. John's office.

3. For each of the following network resources, list the users that will need access to the resource:

   - Network file storage

   - Network printers

   - Exchange server

   - Global Catalog

   - Web servers for production information

   - Exchange public folders

4. Using the information from the last question, determine the best location for each of the following (that is, which segment):

   - Exchange server

   - Domain controllers

   - File server(s)

   - Printer server(s)

   - Production Web servers

5. If the number of research and development staff members doubled, what changes might you consider in this design?

6. If the administration users find that connecting with the SQL Server in Ottawa is particularly slow, what might you consider to improve the connection speed?

Exercise 6.2   Answers

3. The following is a breakdown of users by each type of server or service:

   - Network file storage. Executive staff, research and development staff, and administrative staff.

   - Network printers. Executive staff, research and development staff, and administrative staff.

   - Exchange Server. All Staff.

   - Global Catalog. Executive staff, research and development staff, administrative staff, and sales staff.

   - Web servers for production information. Production staff.

   - Exchange public folders. Sales staff and research and development staff.

4. There are several ways that you can deal with the distribution of the servers on the network. In this case, however, the majority of active users will be on one segment; the executive, R&D, and administration segment is therefore the best place to locate your servers:

   - Exchange server. These servers should be on the executive, R&D, and administration segments.

   - Domain controllers. The domain controllers in this case should be located on the executive, R&D, administration, and sales segments. This will accommodate all but the production users. The production users, however, use only Exchange and then only as an email package. This means that they will not log on to the domain and need to be authenticated only by the Exchange server when they check their mail, which the server will do against the local domain controller.

APPLY YOUR KNOWLEDGE

- File server(s). The only users that really need to be able to connect to file services are the executive, R&D, and administrative users. The sales users keep everything local on their laptops, and the production users use only email. Therefore, the file servers are located on the executive, R&D, and administration segments.

- Printer server(s). The printer servers fall into the same category as the file servers and should be located on the same segment.

- Production Web server(s). These have to be where the production equipment is located and therefore should be on the production segments.

5. In this case, you might decide to create another segment for the R&D users to separate them from the executive and administrative users. Then, you would also consider a separate set of servers for them and possibly an Exchange server for them.

6. In this case, you could create a separate subnet for the administrative users and see whether that helps. Failing that, you would then have to put the connection to the Ottawa office on the same subnet that the administrative users are on.

6.3 Planning the Name Resolution Strategy for the Buenos Aires Office

In this exercise, you plan the name resolution strategy for the Buenos Aires office. For the purposes of this exercise, it is assumed that the organization is running as a single domain and that each branch, such as Buenos Aires, is defined as a *site*. It is also given that there is an Active Directory–integrated zone.

Further in this exercise, you need to plan to accommodate down-level systems because some of the computers are not able to load Windows 2000.

Estimated Time: 15 minutes

1. Review the material in the case study about the Buenos Aires office.

2. There are several pieces of information that affect how name resolution should be configured. Consider the following questions: How are the segments connected? Are broadcasts forwarded using this technology? Can down-level clients register with the DNS servers?

3. Because of constraints with budget and to keep the Buenos Aires office in line with the corporate standard, you intend to use two domain controllers. What does this mean with respect to supporting the clients?

4. How do you think this office should best deal with name resolution?

Exercise 6.3 Answers

2. Because the segments are connected using routers, you need to realize that broadcast traffic, such as NetBIOS name resolution and DHCP requests, will not automatically be forwarded. There are some routers that will forward, and you need to check the question to see whether you are using that type of router. You may need to use a DHCP Relay Agent, which acts as a DHCP server spokesperson on the local subnet.

The down-level clients will not be able to register with the DNS server themselves, and you need to come up with a strategy that will allow them to register or at least be available to the DNS server.

APPLY YOUR KNOWLEDGE

This can be done by configuring the DNS server to use WINS or by having the DHCP server register all the client information.

3. The down-level clients will either need a WINS server to locate the domain controllers so they can log on or they will need to each have an LMHOSTS file that is used to list the domain controllers and their addresses. This is because the down-level clients will attempt to broadcast their logon request, whereas Active Directory clients do not.

4. The best solution in this case is to use the Dynamic DNS for the Active Directory clients and to use WINS for the down-level clients. All servers have to be configured to register with the WINS servers, but the down-level clients could then find them easily. The DNS server could then be configured to look in the WINS server for the address of any down-level clients it might be trying to find.

6.4 Planning the Monitoring and Management of Services for the Ottawa Office

In this exercise, you identify the services that are used in the Ottawa branch and the appropriate type of monitoring for each service.

Estimated Time: 15 minutes

1. Review the case study, making special note of the information about the Ottawa location.

2. Make a list of all network services that are in use in the Ottawa location.

3. For each service that you have listed, decide what you need to monitor it for: security, availability, or capacity. Additionally, decide which tool you should use and what you need to look for.

Exercise 6.4   Answers

2. The following is a list of the network services that you should find in the Ottawa office:

   - File and print services
   - Exchange server
   - Proxy server
   - Routing and Remote Access server
   - SQL Server
   - Global Catalog
   - Domain controllers
   - DNS name server
   - DHCP server

3. Table 6.3 summarizes the information you should have.

APPLY YOUR KNOWLEDGE

TABLE 6.3

SERVICES IN THE OTTAWA OFFICE THAT SHOULD BE MONITORED

Service	Monitor For	Using
File and print services	Security	This could be accomplished using the auditing functionality built into the operating system and viewed in the Event Viewer.
	Availability	This should be checked on a periodic basis. It could be done using a simple alert on the Server service for the File and Print server.
	Capacity	Simply checking the free space on the drive checks this. As the drive fills, you add new space. You can also set an alert on the available disk space.
Exchange server	Availability	This can be monitored using alerts on the main Exchange services.
	Capacity	As a rough check, this should be checked in the same way as the file and print services.
Proxy server	Security	This should be checked using various tools to verify that outside users cannot break into the network. At a minimum, an attempt should be made to connect into the network using basic Microsoft networking. As with the Exchange server and the SQL server, there are other areas of security that should be checked but that are specific to those servers.
	Availability	This should be checked, and you can do so by setting an alert on the IIS Admin and Proxy services. You can also just try surfing the Net; however, if the server is caching, this might tell you.
	Capacity	Occasionally, you should monitor this server using the Performance tool to check the bandwidth utilization on both cards and to check the CPU, disk, and RAM.
Routing and Remote Access server	Security	This is obviously an important place to check the security. You should log the activity of the server and review. Notably, you should audit logon and logoff for both success and failure. These can be viewed in the Event Viewer.
	Availability	With the number of users in this company that require this service, you should ensure the availability of the service. In this case, you can set up an alert on the service so you can be notified if it fails.
	Capacity	Because of the importance of this service to your company, you want to keep a close eye on it. This is done by using the Performance tool and checking the resources available.
SQL server	Availability	This can be monitored using alerts on the SQL Server service.
	Capacity	As a rough check, this should be checked in the same way as the file and print services.
Global Catalog	Security	This shouldn't be a big concern, but you would check the Event Viewer occasionally to ensure that there are no errors caused by unknown or anonymous users.
	Availability	The availability of the Global Catalog (GC) is important for users that are searching the GC and for users that are attempting to log on in branches other than their own. However, you can check this using the Replication Monitor. Because this service is easily made redundant, you should do so.
	Capacity	The capacity can be an issue because the GC contains an entry for every object in your entire enterprise. This means checking the RAM and disk using the Performance tool.

continues

APPLY YOUR KNOWLEDGE

TABLE 6.3	*continued*

SERVICES IN THE OTTAWA OFFICE THAT SHOULD BE MONITORED

Service	*Monitor For*	*Using*
Domain controllers	Security	Auditing logon and logoffs for success or failure on the domain controller covers the domain controllers and many other servers. This should be set and viewed in the Event Viewer as a security event.
	Availability	This service can and should be redundant. You can also set an alert on the Netlogon service to verify it is running.
	Capacity	This should be checked using the Performance tool. This is often done as a result of checking another service that is also on the domain controller.
DNS name server	Security	You might monitor the server to ensure that users are not transferring your zone information through the Internet and to ensure that malicious updates to the database are not taking place. You can set up auditing of the objects in Active Directory and view the audit in the Event Viewer. You can also check the Event Viewer for zone transfers and see where they were sent.
	Availability	This is a critical service, but it is easily made redundant by adding the DNS service to more servers. The Performance tool can be used to configure an alert on the service, though, and this is a consideration for the main internal DNS server.
DHCP server	Availability	This is likely to be a problem because the lack of a DHCP server will no longer generate a user error. You should therefore set up multiple DHCP servers with the capability of backing up each other, and you should monitor the service.

As you can see, the two main tools that you will use for monitoring are the Performance tool and the Event Viewer. Make sure you have worked with both before you write the exam.

Review Questions

1. What are the four parts that make up a management plan?

2. When in-band data collection is used, what concern do you have with centralized data collection?

3. What are the two main components of an SNMP management scenario?

4. Which of the logs in the Event Viewer logs an event when a service starts up?

5. Which type of audit in the event logs are you likely to find reported about a service before it fails?

6. If you need to analyze data for trends and will be tracking the data over a period of months, what method of analysis should you use?

7. What are the main reasons you should consider combining services on a single server?

8. What are the four key resources on a server that you need to balance?

9. What are the two advantages that clustering offers?

APPLY YOUR KNOWLEDGE

Exam Questions

1. You are an administrator for the MTP network. You are responsible for the availability of servers on the network and are starting to put together a management plan for these servers. Another department will handle the Internet connections and connections to branch offices.

   Which of the following would you monitor? (Choose the best answer.)

   A. DNS servers

   B. Certificate Services

   C. RRAS servers

   D. Proxy servers

2. You want to gather specific data about a server on your network. The information that you want to gather deals with the use of the CPU overall and for a specific process. Which tool should you use?

   A. Event logs

   B. SNMP

   C. SNTP

   D. Performance Logs and Alerts

3. You are studying your network to determine whether an upgrade to Gigabit Ethernet is warranted or not. You want to be able to take a look at the traffic that is traveling on the network in various locations and then gather the information to a central location so that you can analyze the data and find what the traffic on the network is doing. Which tool will let you best perform this task?

   A. System Monitor

   B. Replication Monitor

   C. Network Monitor

   D. SNMP

4. You have loaded the MIBs that are required for Windows 2000 into your management software so that you will be able to check the status of Windows 2000 systems using it. There are seven systems that you want to manage on the network, and as you try to connect to the first few you find that you are unable to. You personally installed the SNMP Agent on the systems. What should you check?

   A. You should check the Active Directory domain name you are using.

   B. You should check the DNS name server you are using.

   C. You should check the community name you are using.

   D. You should check the WINS server you are using.

5. You are currently integrating a new application into your office network. The application is Web based and uses Microsoft Transaction Server (MTS) COM components for the business logic. Internal systems will connect to an IIS server that is running MTS with these components so internal users can use the application. The MTS COM components read and write the data for the application to the Microsoft SQL Server database.

   The network covers four locations across your state with good connectivity between the offices using VPNs over the Internet. The minimum Internet connection speed is 1.54Mbps. Which is the best way to deploy this application to the network?

APPLY YOUR KNOWLEDGE

A. Set up a central MTS server and SQL server, and then set up an IIS server in each location.

B. Set up a pool of IIS servers in the central office, each running MTS, and have them talk to a single SQL server in the head office.

C. Set up an IIS server with MTS for the application in each office. Have this system connect to a local SQL server in each office; manually synchronize the SQL servers.

D. Set up the IIS server with MTS in the central office on a subnet that is exposed to the Internet. Place the SQL server in the central office behind a firewall and configure the firewall to allow the MTS components to work the SQL server.

6. You are currently integrating a new application into your office network. The application is Web based and uses Microsoft Transaction Server (MTS) COM components for the business logic. Internal systems will connect to an IIS server that is running MTS with these components so internal users can use the application. The MTS COM components read and write the data for the application to the Microsoft SQL Server database.

The network covers four locations across your state with good connectivity between the offices, using VPNs over the Internet. The minimum Internet connection speed is 1.54Mbps. Which service will you need other than IIS, MTS, and SQL?

A. WINS

B. IPSec

C. DNS

D. DHCP

7. You have six servers that you will be installing in a new office. The office is a small branch office that will connect using dialup to the larger office that you work in. You plan on using a single subnet in the remote office, and you will create a single site for it in Active Directory.

There will be approximately 35 users in this branch office that will require network services, including file and print services, and access to email that will be provided using an Exchange server.

The servers that you are configuring are the standard type of server that you use on your network, and you know that all file and print services can be handled on a single server. You also know that one of the servers will need to be dedicated to the Exchange server.

In the configuration, you need to ensure that the following objectives are met:

- All user logons must be validated against the domain, and the user interaction with the network should be simple.

- Users in this branch must be able to connect to servers across the company.

- Users in this branch must be able to use the proxy server in your branch to connect to the Internet.

- Users that are visiting from other offices must be able to log in to this branch.

- The failure of any one server should not affect the users in this branch.

APPLY YOUR KNOWLEDGE

You decide on the following design:

- You create two domain controllers for the site and create a site link with the main site. On each of the domain controllers, you add and configure the DNS service.

- You configure two servers as file and print servers and configure the users with a mapping to each of the servers. You create a batch file that copies everything that is saved to one server to the other every night. You install DHCP on both servers and provide them with different ranges of addresses, both valid for this network.

- You configure two Exchange servers and configure them in a single site with half the users on each. You add RRAS to these servers to route between this location and the main location over a demand-dial interface.

Which of the objectives does this solution meet?

A. All user logons must be validated against the domain, and the user interaction with the network should be simple.

B. Users in this branch must be able to connect to servers across the company.

C. Users in this branch must be able to use the proxy server in your branch to connect to the Internet.

D. Users that are visiting from other offices must be able to log in to this branch.

E. The failure of any one server should not affect the users in this branch.

8. You have six servers that you will be installing in a new office. The office is a small branch office that will connect using dialup to the larger office that you work in. You plan on using a single subnet in the remote office, and you will create a single site for it in Active Directory.

There will be approximately 35 users in this branch office that will require network services, including file and print services, and access to email that will be provided using an Exchange server.

The servers that you are configuring are the standard type of server that you use on your network, and you know that all file and print services can be handled on a single server. You also know that one of the servers will need to be dedicated to the Exchange server.

In the configuration, you need to ensure that the following objectives are met:

- All user logons must be validated against the domain, and the user interaction with the network should be simple.

- Users in this branch must be able to connect to servers across the company.

- Users in this branch must be able to use the proxy server in your branch to connect to the Internet.

- Users that are visiting from other offices must be able to log in to this branch.

- The failure of any one server should not affect the users in this branch.

APPLY YOUR KNOWLEDGE

You decide on the following design:

- You create two domain controllers for the site and create a site link with the main site. You configure the two domain controllers as Global Catalog servers. On each of the domain controllers, you add and configure the DNS service. You install DHCP on both servers and provide them with different ranges of addresses, both valid for this network.

- You configure a Domain Dfs and set up two servers to act as the root for this. For every share that you create, you create a redundant copy on the other server and configure Dfs to automatically replicate the content. You then map a drive for the users to the Domain Dfs.

- You configure two Exchange servers and configure them in a single site with half the users on each. You add RRAS to these servers to route between this location and the main location over a demand-dial interface.

Which of the objectives does this solution meet?

A. All user logons must be validated against the domain, and the user interaction with the network should be simple.

B. Users in this branch must be able to connect to servers across the company.

C. Users in this branch must be able to use the proxy server in your branch to connect to the Internet.

D. Users that are visiting from other offices must be able to log in to this branch.

E. The failure of any one server should not affect the users in this branch.

9. You have six servers that you will be installing in a new office. The office is a small branch office that will connect using dialup to the larger office that you work in. You plan on using a single subnet in the remote office, and you will create a single site for it in Active Directory.

There will be approximately 35 users in this branch office that will require network services, including file and print services, and access to email that will be provided using an Exchange server.

The servers that you are configuring are the standard type of server that you use on your network, and you know that all file and print services can be handled on a single server. You also know that one of the servers will need to be dedicated to the Exchange server.

In the configuration, you need to ensure that the following objectives are met:

- All user logons must be validated against the domain, and the user interaction with the network should be simple.

- Users in this branch must be able to connect to servers across the company.

- Users in this branch must be able to use the proxy server in your branch to connect to the Internet.

- Users that are visiting from other offices must be able to log in to this branch.

- The failure of any one server should not affect the users in this branch.

APPLY YOUR KNOWLEDGE

You decide on the following design:

- You create two domain controllers for the site and create a site link with the main site. You configure the two domain controllers as Global Catalog servers. On each of the domain controllers, you add and configure the DNS service. You install DHCP on both servers and provide them with different ranges of addresses, both valid for this network.

- You configure a Domain Dfs and set up two servers to act as the root for this. For every share that you create, you create a redundant copy on the other server and configure Dfs to automatically replicate the content. You then map a drive for the users to the Domain Dfs. You install and configure RRAS on these two servers to connect automatically to the main office using a demand-dial interface located on each.

- You configure two servers with Windows 2000 Advanced Server and configure them for clustering. You install Microsoft Exchange on the cluster.

Which of the objectives does this solution meet?

A. All user logons must be validated against the domain, and the user interaction with the network should be simple.

B. Users in this branch must be able to connect to servers across the company.

C. Users in this branch must be able to use the proxy server in your branch to connect to the Internet.

D. Users that are visiting from other offices must be able to log in to this branch.

E. The failure of any one server should not affect the users in this branch.

10. You are working on a problem with communications between your branch and another branch in a different city. You are finding that at some times during the day communication is fast and that at others it is very slow. The offices are connected to each other using virtual private networks over the Internet.

    You want to gather information about the route that packets are taking at different times during the day. What utility can you use when you create a batch file to do this?

    A. Ping

    B. Tracert

    C. Netstat

    D. Nslookup

11. You have been gathering information for a period of weeks about the use of a server on your network. You now want to chart the information so that you can present it at a meeting. Which analysis method should you use?

    A. Manually analyze the data and then chart it in a presentation package such as PowerPoint.

    B. Use Excel to analyze the information and then graph it.

    C. Use Access to analyze the data and then export the results to Excel or PowerPoint to graph it.

    D. You should use a third-party program for this.

APPLY YOUR KNOWLEDGE

12. You are working on combining various services on different servers. You have decided to combine DNS and DHCP on the same server. What will this optimize?

    A. Security

    B. Server availability

    C. Server performance

    D. Network performance

13. You need to monitor the number of DNS name queries that are being handled by a server. Which of the following tools would be the best to do this?

    A. Network Monitor

    B. Performance Logs and Alerts

    C. WSH

    D. Nbtstat

14. You need to track what users are working with a server on your network. This information will be used to determine whether the server will be decommissioned or not. Which tool can you use to do this?

    A. System Monitor

    B. Windows Scripting Host

    C. Event logs

    D. Replication Monitor

Answers to Review Questions

1. A management plan addresses four key issues: assessing management needs, monitoring the components that need management, analyzing the data, and responding to the changes in the services status. See the section "The Management Process."

2. In this case, the biggest concern is that the performance data that you are collecting will use a disproportionate amount of the network bandwidth. This can cause the user data, the reason for the network, to slow down or possibly time out. See the section "Monitoring the Network."

3. The two main components are the SNMP Agent, such as the one supplied with Windows 2000, and the SNMP Manager. The management station is the manager, which can query the agent. The agent can be a Windows 2000 system or a hardware device; it responds to the manager and can send traps when serious events take place. See the section "Simple Network Management Protocol (SNMP) Events."

4. The system log is where the major system events, including device drivers or services that fail to start, are listed. See the section "Event Viewer Logs."

5. In this case, you are likely to find one or more warning message that can be used to better understand what was going wrong before the service failed. See the section "Event Viewer Logs."

6. When you will be tracking data over a long period of time looking for trends, it is best to use either a spreadsheet or a database to store the information. In the case where data will be kept over months, the database is probably the better solution. See the section "Analyzing the Information."

7. There are three key benefits that you can realize if you combine services on a server: security, availability, and performance. See the section "Service Combination Benefits."

APPLY YOUR KNOWLEDGE

8. The four key resources are disk, memory, CPU, and network speed. When you consider combining services or even when you plan the capacity of a server, you need to find a good balance among these resources. If any of the services is lacking, you will get a bottleneck. See the sections "Service Combination Drawbacks" and "Service Combination Limitations."

9. Clustering in Windows 2000 provides both the ability to perform automated failover and the ability to balance the load among servers. See the section "Service Combining on Clustered Servers."

Answers to Exam Questions

1. **A**. In this case, you are responsible only for the internal network; you are not concerned with the connections to other networks or the Internet. This means the proxy server (answer D) is definitely out. The other three could all be in use on an internal network; however, you are to choose one answer. Because this is the case and IPSec was not mentioned internally, you can rule out the Certificate Services (answer B). Because you are not told that you manage routers and routers was not mentioned in the question, you can rule out RRAS (answer C). This leaves you with the DNS server, which is required to perform name resolution internally and externally and is therefore the correct answer. See the section "The Management Process."

2. **D**. When you need detailed information about a computer, the best tool is the Performance Logs and Alerts because it lets you get down to specific information about individual processes on a system.

Event logs record information about events that have happened and not about the details of a process—although they can track the starting and stopping of a process—so answer A is incorrect. The SNMP protocol is useful to query detail settings for a service in some cases, but not specific details such as the CPU time for a process, so answer B is not right. Answer C is a distracter—a close-but-no-cigar answer; SNTP, or Simple Network Time Protocol, is used to keep the time synchronized on the network. See the section "Monitoring the Network."

3. **C**. In this case, you want to see the data that is flowing on the network; this is the job of the Network Monitor. You want to use the version that is available with SMS, not the version that comes with Windows 2000, because it can gather all the data from the network. You should also run multiple copies and then copy the network data. This way, you will not end up changing the values by monitoring. The System Monitor (answer A) could tell you the bytes in and out of a server and could even break this down as to what the bytes are for; but it could do this only for a single system, so answer A is not the best answer. The Replication Monitor is used to view Active Directory replication information and not general network traffic, so answer B is wrong. SNMP could give you some of the same information as the System Monitor, but this also looks at a system or device, not the network. See the section "Monitoring the Network."

4. **C**. The SNMP protocol is a very simple protocol, and all you should need to connect to a remote agent is the correct IP or DNS name and the correct community name. The agent should have you in its list of managers because this is the only security beyond community names that is available.

APPLY YOUR KNOWLEDGE

Answer A is irrelevant because SNMP does not use NetBIOS services. The DNS server could be a problem but the question leads you to the conclusion that other hosts are working, so B is incorrect. Answer D also might be valid if you were using NetBIOS; however, SNMP does not. See the section "Monitoring the Network."

5. **D**. Answer A is wrong because the MTS server—the business logic—should be distributed and needs to be on the IIS server. Setting up the pool of IIS servers means more data than needs to would have to cross the WAN links, and therefore B is not the best answer. Answer C involves a manual synchronization, which is never the best answer. This leaves answer D, which puts the business logic near the users and passes only finished data over the WAN links. See the section "Planning Resources for the Network."

6. **C**. The WINS server deals with NetBIOS names; Web servers use hostnames, so answer A is wrong. Using IPSec in this case might be a good idea; however, there is no mention of this in the question. Because IPSec is not required here, answer B is wrong. The ability to resolve a hostname to an IP address is always required—frankly, DNS is always required in Windows 2000; so answer C is correct. Answer D is also a possible requirement; however, it is not mentioned in the question and therefore is wrong. See the section "Designing Network Services."

7. **B, C**. All the users can be validated because there is at least one domain controller, so objective A is almost met. The file backup system is fairly automated; however, users will not get their files automatically if the main file server goes down, so this objective is not met. The inclusion of demand-dial interfaces and RRAS means that the users

will be able to connect to the main branch, so objective B is met. Because the users will be able to find (DNS) and physically get to (RRAS), the proxy server objective, C is met. For users to find their home servers when visiting, they could need a Global Catalog server and because there isn't one here, objective D is not met. Finally, a failure in an Exchange server would cause some of the users not to be able to get their mail; therefore, objective E is not met. See the section "Designing Network Services."

8. **A, B, C, D**. All the users can be validated because there is at least one domain controller, so objective A is met because the Dfs fixed the file problem. The inclusion of demand-dial interfaces and RRAS means that the users will be able to connect to the main branch, so objective B is met. Because the users will be able to find (DNS) and physically get to (RRAS), the proxy server, objective C is met. For users to find their home servers when visiting, they could need a Global Catalog server, and because there is one here, objective D is met. Finally, a failure in an Exchange server would cause some of the users not to be able to get their mail; therefore, object E is not met. See the section "Designing Network Services."

9. **A, B, C, D, E**. All the users can be validated because there is at least one domain controller, so objective A is met because the Dfs fixed the file problem. The inclusion of demand-dial interfaces and RRAS means that the users will be able to connect to the main branch, so objective B is met. Because the users will be able to find (DNS) and physically get to (RRAS), the proxy server, objective C is met. For users to find their home servers when visiting, they could need a Global Catalog server, and because there is one here,

APPLY YOUR KNOWLEDGE

objective D is met. Finally, a failure in an Exchange server would cause an automatic failover; therefore, object E is met. See the section "Designing Network Services."

10. **B**. In this case, the choice is to use Tracert, which will show the path a packet takes. Pathping might also work but is not an option. None of the other options shows the whole path. See the section "Tools and Utilities."

11. **B**. In this case, you can work directly in Excel. This will be easier than working manually, because there are weeks' worth of data. Using Access or SQL might be required for months' or years' worth of data, but it is not likely in this case. A third-party program might be nice, but Excel would do. See the section "Analyzing the Information."

12. **D**. In this case, the protocols don't really need much security unless your zone is Active Directory–integrated. In that case, it would be better to put these services on a domain controller. The server availability is not affected with these servers—only the ability to locate them. Service performance could appear better, but only because the pause for the network is gone. See the section "Designing Network Services."

13. **B**. In this case, the best bet is Performance Logs and Alerts, which has counters that will count this for the DNS server. The Network Monitor would let you see the queries on the network, but you would have to manually count them. The WMI could be used to access the performance counters, but then you would need to write a program to perform this task, which you can already do with Performance Logs. The Nbtstat command does nothing with hostnames, although it can let you see and modify the NetBIOS name cache. See the section "Monitoring the Network."

14. **C**. In this case, you want to see who was using the resource, so the System Monitor is out. The scripting host could be used, but only in conjunction with WMI to read the data. The Replication Monitor watches Active Directory replication, not server usage. This leaves the event logs, notably the security log. See the section "Monitoring the Network."

Suggested Readings and Resources

1. Bixler, Dave. MCSE Training Guide (70-216): Windows 2000 Network Infrastructure. Indianapolis, IN: New Riders Publishing. August 2000.

2. Microsoft Corporation. Microsoft Windows 2000 Server Resource Kit: Windows 2000 Deployment Planning Guide. Microsoft Press, 2000. (ISBN: 1572318058)

3. Microsoft Corporation. Microsoft Windows 2000 Server Resource Kit: Windows 2000 Internetworking Guide. Microsoft Press, 2000. (ISBN: 1572318058)

FINAL REVIEW

Fast Facts

Study and Exam Prep Tips

Practice Exam

Now that you have thoroughly read through this book, worked through the exercises, and picked up as much hands-on exposure to Windows 2000 network infrastructure design as possible, you're ready to take your exam. This chapter is designed to be a last-minute cram for you as you walk out the door on your way to the exam. You can't reread the whole book in an hour, but you will be able to read this chapter in that time. This chapter is organized by objective category and summarizes the basic facts you need to know regarding each objective. If you know what is in here, chances are the exam will be a snap.

ANALYZING BUSINESS REQUIREMENTS

It is obvious to network professionals that the technical aspects of network infrastructure design requires detailed planning, and it is easy for them to focus their efforts entirely on the technical considerations. Unfortunately, this approach is destined for failure, because it neglects to consider the crucial business elements that should be included in a network infrastructure design. Without thoroughly considering the business requirements for the network infrastructure, the design project is likely to result in a network that is too simple to support the demands placed upon it or too complex to deliver results efficiently and cost effectively. Without proper consideration of business requirements, you can count on designing a network that is either too weak or too expensive.

Fast Facts

Designing a Microsoft Windows 2000 Network Infrastructure

Analyzing Business Models

An engineer rarely gets the opportunity to design a network infrastructure completely from scratch. In most cases, you must design an infrastructure that will either interoperate with or serve to upgrade an existing infrastructure. Information that you can get from examining the current business model will help you determine the services that are already in place so that you can be sure to include them in your design. Businesses often look at a project of major impact, such as a network infrastructure design project, as an opportunity to change its strategies or business model to improve its position in the industry or change its own internal operations. In such cases, you must also examine any new business models that the company intends to employ so that your new design can incorporate them and accommodate interaction with the existing services being offered on the network. You should remember the following models for the Microsoft exam:

◆ **International.** Businesses that operate in multiple locations worldwide employ the International business model. In the International model you are likely to see all issues that could possibly be considered. This model increases the complexity of the issues in the National model by including the requirement that all national sites must interoperate. New issues that arise in this model include cultural and language barriers and international politics.

◆ **National.** A National business model is applied to a business whose scope spans an entire country. This business model involves all the types of concerns that are included in the Regional model, but includes multiple regions. This increases the importance of each region's concerns, because all regions must interoperate.

◆ **Regional.** This business model is applied if your design comprises network locations in a particular regional area of a single country. Regional networks often span multiple counties, or states. Examples of regions in the Unites States include the Middle Atlantic states or the states in the Pacific Northwest. This model includes considerations that are specific to the region, such as the relationship between communications providers, environmental concerns, and landscape concerns (consider networks that must operate high in the mountains or in deeply wooded or rural areas).

◆ **Subsidiary.** This model is a smaller scale than the models discussed so far. In a Subsidiary model, concerns such as internal company politics increase in importance as you shape your design to allow the subsidiary network to interoperate with the infrastructure owned by the parent company.

◆ **Branch Office.** In a branch office, you see the smallest business model. In this model, you focus on the specific function of the branch office and what services it must offer to or receive from the company headquarters and other branch offices. In this model, typical concerns include where connections need to be made, how much they will cost, and who will have administrative control over them.

Microsoft also lists the following company processes for you to examine and understand:

◆ **Information flow.** Information flow processes have to do with the way information is distributed throughout the company. It describes what information is available, who needs it, and in what order they receive it. Another term that describes this is "logical data flow." The way information flows logically from one part of the organization to the other happens without regard to physical structures to support it. A good example of this is a rumor. There is no particular way to predict how a rumor will go from one person to the one on the other end—it only has to get there.

◆ **Communication flow.** Communication flow tracks the path that data follows through the network infrastructure during the course of day-to-day operations of the business. This is also referred to as "physical data flow." To use the rumor example, the information has to get to the last person, but how it travels on the telephone network can be predicted based upon how the phone network is configured.

◆ **Service and product life cycles.** The entire period from the initial concept of the product or service to the complete removal of the product or service from the market, and all the events that transpire between, is called the *life cycle* of the product or service.

◆ **Decision-making.** In some organizations, decisions are made quickly and changes can occur rapidly. In others, there is a complicated process that must be executed before the slightest thing can be done. Typically, there is some compromise in the approach that allows the company employees to be empowered, but still provides management with a reasonable degree of control.

Analyzing Organizational Structures

Some very important considerations when designing a network infrastructure are the organization structures within the company. The various organizational structures in place will usually determine the distribution of network resources and the type of network management strategy that will be implemented. In the exam objectives, Microsoft lists the following organizational structures for you to consider when creating your design:

◆ **Management model.** The management philosophy prevalent in the organization has a direct impact on how the network is designed. Companies are broadly categorized as having a centralized or decentralized management structure. If management wants to centralize control, this impacts how the network is configured. If the opposite is true, this may provide for a very different network design.

◆ **Company organization.** The organization of the company will prove to be a major consideration for your network infrastructure design. The distribution of resources will follow the company organization closely.

◆ **Vendor, partner, and customer relationships.** The relationships that a company maintains with its vendors, partners, and customers has an impact on the types of services that the company wants to provide on its network.

◆ **Acquisitions plans.** Awareness of intended acquisitions or mergers enables you to research the specific issues that will be faced in integrating the networks and to design solutions to those problems from the beginning.

Analyzing Company Business Strategies

The purpose of any network infrastructure is to enable the business to perform its day-to-day activities and meet its objectives with the greatest efficiency. The day-to-day activities that must be performed will vary depending on the company's business strategies. Consequently, the role of the network and the demands placed upon the network infrastructure will vary as well. For the Microsoft exam, you should know the following factors:

◆ **Identify company priorities.** Document all the goals of the business and assign a priority number to each one. Goals with higher priority levels get built into the design first, and goals with lower priority values are included in the design only if they can be delivered after satisfying the goals at the higher priority levels.

◆ **Identify the projected growth and growth strategy.** Company growth affects the demands placed on a network infrastructure. It is crucial that you develop an understanding of the company's projected growth as well as its growth strategy to ensure that the network infrastructure design meets the demands placed upon it.

◆ **Identify relevant laws and regulations.** Sometimes the operation of a particular business is governed by only a few relevant laws or regulations. Other businesses, however, must adhere to a very complex and strict set of laws and regulations. Partnering with the company's legal team can help make you aware of any legal issues that may apply to your project, and enables you to take advantage of its expertise in dealing with these issues.

◆ **Identify the company's tolerance for risk.** Any time that you design something as mission-critical as a network infrastructure, you must be acutely aware of the risks that are involved in implementing your design. Knowing up front the company's position and tolerance for risk can help you avoid serious problems later. Companies that are very risk-averse may implement more fault-tolerant features to minimize the risk of a network failure; those less worried about network failure will not require the same level of fault tolerance.

◆ **Identify the total cost of ownership.** The aggregation of all costs associated with purchasing, implementing, supporting, and operating a network infrastructure is referred to as the *Total Cost of Ownership* (TCO) of the network infrastructure.

Analyzing IT Management

Your network infrastructure design should include an analysis of the current and proposed IT management structure within the organization. You should be aware of the following areas for consideration in Microsoft's exam:

◆ **Type of administration, such as centralized or decentralized.** Your network infrastructure design must accommodate the IT administration model, whether handled centrally in one location or distributed across the organization in a decentralized approach.

◆ **Funding model.** The company's approach to funding the design and implementation projects directly impacts what you can and cannot accomplish with your design.

◆ **Outsourcing.** If the company for which you are designing a network infrastructure is currently outsourcing any part of the responsibility for installing, administering, and maintaining its network, you need to contact the company representatives who have been charged with the responsibility. These representatives can help you prioritize any issues in the existing infrastructure so that you can design your new infrastructure to resolve these issues, or at least to accommodate them.

◆ **Decision-making process.** Being familiar with the IT decision-making process and planning ahead can help make the design process flow more smoothly and bring you to the approval stage more quickly and less stressfully.

◆ **Change-management process.** The main purpose of a change-management process is to eliminate downtime resulting from changes made to the production network environment.

ANALYZING TECHNICAL REQUIREMENTS

Perhaps the most obvious planning step when creating a network infrastructure design is the analysis of technical requirements. There are several steps to follow in order to perform a thorough and effective analysis of the technical requirements for a network infrastructure design. The sections that follow discuss each of the steps outlined by Microsoft in its objectives for exam 70-221.

Evaluating Technical Environment and Goals

Before you can begin your network infrastructure design you must be able to determine three things:

◆ What does the customer want to do with the network infrastructure?

◆ What does the customer do with its existing network infrastructure?

◆ What is the gap between the current infrastructure and the desired infrastructure?

Answering these questions is called *performing a gap analysis*. After performing a gap analysis, consider the following items:

◆ **Analyze company size and user and resource distribution.** Determine the total size of the user population and any plans for future growth. In addition to the user population total, you should look closely at the distribution of these users.

◆ **Assess the available connectivity between the geographic location of work sites and remote sites.** Examine each of the work locations in the existing and the planned network infrastructure. For each location, you need to investigate the connectivity options available in that area.

◆ **Assess net available bandwidth and latency issues.** *Bandwidth* is the measure of the amount of data that a network link may carry at any given time. *Latency* refers to the amount of time between the moment when a network station is ready to transmit data and the moment when the transmission is completed successfully. Latency is sometimes also called *delay*.

◆ **Analyze performance, availability, and scalability requirements of services.** Performance, scalability, and availability are three terms you will hear over and over again. Make sure you know the definition of these three terms for your test:

- **Performance.** The capability of the network infrastructure of meeting the demands for network services effectively and efficiently

- **Scalability.** The capability of the network infrastructure of expanding or contracting in accordance with the demand for network services

- **Availability.** The percentage of time that the network infrastructure is up and running and available for use

◆ **Analyze data and system access patterns.** Assess the peaks and valleys that exist in users connecting to different systems in the organization. For example, an intranet server might experience peak loads after new employee benefits information gets posted. Knowing when servers are going to be busy and which machines are affected has an impact on network design.

◆ **Analyze network roles and responsibilities.** Determine the types of services that parts of the network will be used for. For example, a Web server can be used for either Internet or intranet traffic, or both. The role of the server in the organization could provide a clue to its usage and can be helpful in design. If a server is used for more than one purpose, this may require more bandwidth to be allocated to it and thus impact the design.

◆ **Analyze security considerations.** Security can be physical security at the network level or logical at the file system level. In Windows 2000, secure communication can also be specified between servers or between clients and servers. The type of security requirements defined by the business practices of the organization can impact the network design.

Analyzing the Impact of Infrastructure Design

In some cases, you may find that there is a tremendous gap between the existing network and the proposed network. In other cases, the gap will be less extensive. In either case, you want to work to minimize the impact on productivity of making the change from old to new. Ultimately, the new network infrastructure design will save the company money and enable it to meet its business goals in the most effective and efficient manner; but during the implementation phase—while the network is "under construction,"—the loss of productivity and increased costs can be significant. A great design includes an analysis of the potential impact of the implementation so that an effective implementation plan can be developed to minimize the costs associated with rolling out of the new design. Consider the following factors when determining the impact of implementing your network infrastructure design:

◆ **Assess current applications.** Examine each of the applications to determine its requirements in terms of the network infrastructure. Some applications will be very demanding of the network infrastructure, generating heavy traffic and requiring high throughput, and others will not.

◆ **Analyze network infrastructure, protocols, and hosts.** A computer network is comprised of many parts: individual computer systems that occupy the network and the myriad devices used to connect those systems. The wiring and the connecting devices form the basic network infrastructure. Connected to this basic infrastructure are the many individual computer systems that must use the network. These systems are called *hosts*. For hosts to make use of the network infrastructure for communications, they must first agree to a set of rules for doing so. They may need to adopt a number of different sets of rules to enable multiple types of hosts to communicate with each other. These sets of rules are called *protocols*.

◆ **Evaluate network services.** List all the network services that are currently in use by the organization. Include in your list the specific network requirements for each service.

◆ **Analyze TCP/IP infrastructure.** A network that is based on the TCP/IP protocol has certain elements that must be considered carefully at the design stage in order for the network to operate effectively and efficiently. Some of these elements are:

  • The IP addressing scheme

  • The IP address assignment process

  • The hostname registration process

  • The hostname resolution process

◆ **Assess current hardware.** It is important to note that no matter what you include in your network infrastructure design, it is completely useless if the hardware in place cannot support it. You need to take an inventory of the hardware in the existing network infrastructure and determine which devices need to be upgraded to ensure that each device can support the demand that will be placed upon it.

◆ **Identify existing and planned upgrades and rollouts.** You need to become aware of any company plans to upgrade its existing applications. If there is an upgrade to an existing application available, the company may want to consider implementing the upgrade at the same time as it implements the new network infrastructure. Upgrading legacy applications may allow you to discontinue the use of older, less efficient protocols. When two or more applications have conflicting requirements, upgrading one or more of them to a newer version may resolve the conflict.

◆ **Analyze technical support structure.** A major component of the total cost of ownership for the network infrastructure is the ongoing cost to support that infrastructure. It is important to take the time to examine the organization's technical support structure to determine whether it can effectively support the new network infrastructure.

◆ **Analyze existing and planned network and systems management.** There are numerous tools available for performing network and systems management. Depending on the devices and systems that comprise the company's network, you may find one or more tools currently in use. Tools for monitoring the health of the network infrastructure components, as well as the individual systems that reside on the network, are essential for minimizing downtime and troubleshooting costs.

Analyzing Client Computer Access Requirements

The work performed by end users needs to be as effective, efficient, and inexpensive as possible. Enabling this is the ultimate goal of any network infrastructure design. Close attention to the activities of end users should be applied before, during, and after the creation of your network infrastructure design. Make sure you do the following:

◆ **Analyze end-user work needs.** It is imperative that the network infrastructure supports the work needs of the end users. Analyzing end-user work needs involves determining who needs access to which data, when they need it, and where it should be delivered.

◆ **Analyze end-user usage patterns.** By examining end-user work needs, you know what data is needed, and by whom. You should also know where the data and its users are located. Next, you must answer questions such as the following:

 • When will end users be accessing the data?

 • What is the duration of an average access session?

 • How large is the data?

 • How many end users will access the data simultaneously?

 • How much bandwidth needs to be allocated to deliver the data to the end users?

 • What security functions need to be in place to protect access to the data?

Knowing these elements can help you predict the load on the network (size of data and frequency of access together impact bandwidth). Knowing the load at different points on the network can help determine how the network should be segmented, thereby impacting the network design.

Analyzing Disaster Recovery Strategies

The company's existing disaster recovery strategy for client computers, servers, and the network will become an essential tool for protecting the company's systems and data as you implement your new design. You need to know all the details regarding the processes involved in each of the company's disaster recovery strategies in order to determine the impact of your new network infrastructure design on them, and to ensure that these processes remain functional during the implementation of your network infrastructure design.

Disaster recovery is often associated with performing regular backups. Although this is an important element of recovering from serious failures, other elements also need to be considered. For example, where will the backup media be stored: locally or off-site? If locally, what would happen to the network and the company's data if the building caught fire?

Disaster recovery also deals with fault tolerance of network design. Issues include the loss of a critical network component, such as a backbone switch. How can the network continue to operate without this component, or can it? Is there a way to ensure that critical systems are still available while the failed component is being replaced? What will the business impact be of network failure and how can this be minimized?

These elements and others need to be considered in designing a network structure. However, the need to provide proper recovery in the case of a disaster (that is, fault tolerance) should be balanced between the associated costs and then finally compared with the specific requirements of the organization. In other words, make sure your disaster recovery plan satisfies your business goals.

DESIGNING A WINDOWS 2000 NETWORK INFRASTRUCTURE

For the purposes of the Microsoft exam, a network infrastructure is the collection of technical network components and services that provide the framework for data communications and other network operations. The network infrastructure includes

◆ Network hardware, such as cabling, routers, switches, and host computers

◆ Hardware and software protocols

◆ Network services that facilitate host communications, such as DHCP, DNS, and WINS

◆ Data storage and access configuration

Network Topologies

There are two components to network topologies: the physical network structure and the hardware protocol. Physical structure and protocol are closely related, because hardware protocols are designed to work with specific kinds of physical networks. The three most commonly used network topologies are:

◆ **Backbone-based networks**. Backbone-based networks consist of multiple segments connected to a central segment, a backbone, through which traffic between segments flows. An example could be a thicknet (10Base5) Ethernet backbone network with multiple thinnet (10Base2) segments connected to the backbone via a router.

◆ **Ring networks.** Token-Ring and Fiber Distributed Data Interface (FDDI) are two examples of ring networks where the logical implementation of the network topology emulates a ring.

◆ **Switched networks.** Switched networks consist of a smart hub that "switches" traffic between different segments. Each port on a switch is considered a separate segment and will receive only packets destined for it. Switches can be layer 2, where the port on the switch to receive the packet is determined by the MAC—that is, hardware—address of the destination host, or layer 3, where the destination is determined by the IP address.

Planning TCP/IP Networking Strategies

The TCP/IP protocol suite is the global standard for networking. Windows 2000 Server supports the full implementation of the TCP/IP protocol suite and connectivity and management services for TCP/IP-based networks. It is important to know which core protocols, services, and application-layer protocols will be used on the network and how they will be used in terms of broadcast traffic, retransmission, and session connections required for applications.

An important procedure when designing a TCP/IP network is choosing the appropriate IP address class. To determine the best choice (and to score points on the Microsoft exam), you must be able to enumerate a given IP address range and subnet mask combination. *Enumeration* is simply calculating the number of hosts and networks a range of IP addresses and subnet mask yields.

A routed network is two or more physical network segments that are linked by one or more routers. To understand routing issues on exam scenarios, make sure you have a good understanding of the following:

◆ **Types of routed networks**. Routed networks divide a large network into two or more subnets by using a router. The router forwards packets between the two segments to ensure all traffic reaches the proper host.

◆ **Routing tables**. Entries within the router specify to which segments a particular packet is to be forwarded based upon the IP address. Routing tables can be configured manually using static routes or automatically by one of the two routing protocols: Routing Information Protocol (RIP) and Open Shortest Path First (OSPF).

◆ **Default gateways**. A default gateway is a TCP/IP configuration entry on each host specifying to which router to forward packets not destined for the local network. Hosts also have a routing table and may have multiple default gateways specified to allow for redundancy.

◆ **Routing protocols**. Routing protocols are protocols used by a router to keep its routing tables updated automatically. The two most common protocols are Routing Information Protocol (RIP) and Open Shortest Path First (OSPF).

◆ **Windows 2000 Server routing configuration**. The configuration of a Windows 2000 machine tells IP to which router to forward packets not for the local segment. This information can be retrieved by using the Ipconfig utility or the Netstat utility.

Developing DHCP Strategies

Dynamic Host Configuration Protocol (DHCP) was originally designed to dynamically assign IP addresses to IP network hosts. Currently, DHCP is also capable of assigning other configuration parameters to an IP host, such as default gateways, name server addresses, multicast addresses, and node type. A clear understanding of IETF standards–based DHCP and Windows 2000 enhancements is required to successfully integrate Windows 2000 DHCP into a network that already uses a different flavor of DHCP. The most commonly used configuration information that a DHCP server sends to a host computer is default gateways, IP domain name, subnet mask, and name server addresses. Some of the other important features of DHCP that are defined in RFC 2131 and RFC 2132 include the following:

◆ DHCP client computers must be guaranteed a unique (to its network) IP address.

◆ DHCP client computers must be unaffected by a DHCP server reboot. The client computer must receive consistent configuration information regardless of DHCP server reboots.

◆ A DHCP client computer must be equipped to deal with multiple DHCP responses, because more than one DHCP server may be available to a given segment.

◆ DHCP servers must support automated assignment of configuration information to client computers and assignment of specific configuration information (including IP addresses) to specific client computers.

- Any implementation of DCHP must not require a DHCP server on each segment—that is, DHCP must work across routers or BOOTP relay hosts.

- DHCP must work in a multiprotocol environment.

- DHCP must coexist on a network with statically assigned IP addresses.

- DHCP must interoperate with BOOTP relay agents and must support (legacy) BOOTP client computers.

Planning Name Services

Windows 2000 Server supports two name services: Domain Name System (DNS) and Windows Internet Name Service (WINS). DNS is the Internet name resolution service standard. DNS is also the name service of choice for Windows 2000. The physical implementation of a DNS namespace is supported by a distributed database. TCP/IP hosts are identified by a Fully Qualified Domain Name (FQDN). The smallest manageable part of the DNS namespace is known as a *zone*. Zones may be either primary or secondary. A zone contains the DNS information, known as resource records, for a contiguous portion of the DNS namespace. There are several types of resource records in a DNS database. The mechanism for keeping DNS server databases synchronized is called *zone transfer*. DNS servers that are the source for zone transfers are known as *master servers*.

Requests for information are called *queries*. Query types sent to the server from a resolver are called *QTYPE codes*. A DNS server can services two kinds of queries: recursive and iterative. The most common query issued by a resolver is a recursive query. *Recursive queries* place the responsibility for resolving the query on the DNS server. *Iterative queries* are typically used for name-server-to-name-server queries.

RFC 2136 defines a protocol for dynamic update of DNS records, Dynamic DNS (DDNS). The core instrument of DDNS is a new record type, UPDATE, which is defined in RFC 2136. UPDATE records can add or delete DNS resource records. A feature of dynamic DNS updates is that both the DHCP server and Windows 2000 client computer support reregistration, or refreshes. Windows 2000 client computers reregister with the DNS server every 24 hours. Windows 2000 DHCP server reregisters downlevel client computers when their lease is renewed.

Windows 2000 computers use DNS—and only DNS—for name resolution. In a mixed environment where WINS is used, Windows 2000 DNS can be configured to perform WINS lookups. When a lookup query fails, the DNS server queries WINS to resolve the name. When integrated into Active Directory, DNS does not use conventional zone files to store records. Instead, DNS records are stored in Active Directory. To use Active Directory zone information directly, a DNS server must be running on a domain controller. Servers not running on DCs are configured as secondary servers and update using standard DNS protocols. Though Microsoft is moving to DNS as its default name service, many existing networks still use WINS. Most of the work that will be done in the real world will be either integration of WINS and DNS or migration of a WINS-enabled network to pure DNS.

Designing Multiprotocol Networks

Although TCP/IP is the network protocol of choice for Windows 2000, other protocols are supported. To facilitate connectivity and interoperability with other operating systems, Windows 2000 includes support for these additional network protocols:

- ◆ NWLink is an IPX/SPX-compatible protocol used to provide a transport for NetWare connectivity tools and IPX/SPX client computers. Integration of NetWare servers in a Windows 2000 network is provided by Client and Gateway Services for NetWare on a Windows 2000 Server or Advanced Server computer. Individual Windows 2000 Professional clients can configure connectivity to a NetWare server by installing Client Services for NetWare.

- ◆ NetBEUI is a nonroutable fast and efficient protocol ideal for small networks. NetBEUI cannot be used alone if support for Windows 2000 Active Directory is required.

- ◆ DLC is an IBM-specific protocol used for gateway connectivity and terminal emulator access to IBM mid- and mainframe systems using SNA. Connectivity between SNA and Windows 2000 networks is provided in Microsoft's SNA Server, part of the BackOffice product suite. DLC can also be used to connect to network-attached printers from LexMark and other vendors.

- ◆ AppleTalk is used in conjunction with File Services for Macintosh and Print Services for Macintosh to allow Macintosh clients to use Windows 2000 Server computers for file and printer sharing.

Windows 2000 supports all NDIS-compliant protocols with drivers for the Windows 2000 operating system, including Banyan Vines IP, DECNet, and others. Not all protocols supported by Windows 2000 are shipped on the product CD, but they may be available from third parties.

Distributed File System (Dfs)

Distributed file system (Dfs) is a management service for file shares and directories. Dfs enables the administrator to combine network resource shares into a single namespace called a Dfs volume. Access to Dfs volumes requires Dfs client computer software. Dfs client computer software is included with Windows NT 4 Workstation and Windows 2000 Professional. Client computer software is available for Windows 95 and Windows 98.

A Dfs root is the starting point for the hierarchical structure of one or more Dfs volumes. When a Dfs client computer browses or otherwise attempts to access a particular directory in a Dfs tree, the process is handled with referrals. A *referral* routes client computer requests for access to logical Dfs locations to a physical location. A Windows NT Server computer or a Windows 2000 Server computer running the Dfs host service can host one Dfs root.

DESIGNING FOR INTERNET CONNECTIVITY

Leveraging the benefits of the Internet requires that you have a through understanding of the technologies and services commonly used on the 'Net. When implemented, these services need to be connected to the Internet in a secure manner.

Designing an Internet and Extranet Access Solution

Components of an Internet and extranet access solution include:

◆ **Proxy servers.** Microsoft Proxy Server provides a number of services that can be used to assist in the management of your connection to the Internet. Microsoft Proxy Server acts as a control point between your private network and the public network. This control point enables you to isolate the private network from the public. Microsoft Proxy Server is used to block incoming traffic from accessing resources on your internal network. Microsoft Proxy Server enables access control rules to be defined that allow centralized administration of access to public resources. Rules can be defined that allow or deny access to specific URLs or protocols. Microsoft Proxy Server enables these rules to be applied to users and groups so administrators can create specialized rules that apply to groups of users in their environments. Microsoft Proxy Server also enables you to optimize your connection to the Internet by caching frequently accessed pages on a local hard drive that can be accessed internally, thereby reducing the actual amount of traffic on the slower Internet connection.

◆ **Firewalls.** Security is a very real concern when a company connects to the Internet. A *firewall* is a combination of hardware and software that can be used to reduce the risk of unauthorized access to your network. A firewall can be a packet filtering router, a packet filtering router combined with a circuit-level gateway, or the combination of a packet filtering router, circuit-level gateway, and application gateway. Most often, an effective firewall solution includes a combination of the three technologies.

◆ **Routing and Remote Access Service (RRAS).** The Routing and Remote Access Service provides multiprotocol routing support for Windows 2000. Through RRAS you can configure LAN-to-LAN, LAN-to-WAN, virtual private network (VPN), Network Address Translation (NAT) routing services, and dialup/virtual private network services.

◆ **Network Address Translation (NAT).** NAT is implemented through the Routing and Remote Access Service (RRAS). Before you can enable NAT, you must install RRAS. When the NAT server forwards packets, it translates the IP address and port values in the request. The translation data is stored in a database, so return packets can be mapped back to the original host that made the request.

◆ **Connection Sharing.** The connection sharing service allows a company to set up a single machine to act as a shared access point to the Internet. Private clients route requests to the Connection Sharing server, and the server takes care of translating the private request into a request that can be passed onto the Internet. Connection Sharing is an excellent option for smaller organizations that need Internet connectivity.

◆ **Web servers and mail servers.** Web servers and mail servers offer data access services to clients that reside inside the corporate network and externally. Web servers offer data through the Hypertext Transfer Protocol (HTTP). Client software called a *browser* is used to access data on Web servers using the HTTP protocol. Web servers that offer data to internal clients form the basis of an intranet. Microsoft's Internet Information Server (IIS) included with Windows 2000 Server, Advanced Server, and Datacenter Server, includes an HTTP and SMTP server component, as well as a File Transfer Protocol (FTP) server and Network News Transfer Protocol (NNTP) server.

◆ **Mail servers.** Mail servers facilitate the transfer of electronic mail to clients internal and external to the corporate network using the Simple Mail Transport Protocol (SMTP) or the Post Office Protocol version 3 (POP3). A POP3 and SMTP server is included with Microsoft Exchange server. IIS includes an SMTP server.

Designing a Load-Balancing Strategy

Network Load Balancing (NLB) is a clustering technology included with the Microsoft Windows 2000 Advanced Server and Datacenter Server products. The service enhances the scalability and availability of TCP/IP-based services. The technology enables a cluster of systems (between 2 and 32) to be created. To scale performance, NLB distributes IP traffic across multiple cluster hosts. It also ensures high availability by detecting host failures and automatically redistributes traffic to the remaining hosts in the cluster.

NLB uses port rules to customize load balancing of consecutive numeric ranges of server ports. Port rules can select either multiple hosts or single-host load-balancing policies. With multiple-host load balancing, incoming client requests are distributed among all cluster hosts, and a load percentage can be specified for each host. Load percentages allow hosts with higher capacity to receive a large fraction of the total client load. Single-host load balancing directs all client requests to the host with the highest handling priority. When a port rule uses multiple-host load balancing, one of three client affinity modes must be selected. When no affinity mode is selected, NLB balances the client traffic load from one IP address and different source ports on multiple-cluster hosts. To assist in managing client sessions, the default single-client affinity mode balances all network traffic load from a given client's IP address and a single-cluster host. By default, NLB is configured with a single port rule that covers all ports (0–65,535) with multiple-host load balancing and single-client affinity.

DESIGNING A WIDE AREA NETWORK INFRASTRUCTURE

Beyond the considerations of the LAN network infrastructure, you must also consider connecting the individual LANs to form a WAN. WAN technologies and strategies differ from those of LANs. In configuring and designing a WAN, you need to develop a routing strategy to ensure access to all the sites that make up the WAN.

Though not directly part of designing a WAN, connections for dial-in users and virtual private networks (VPNs) also need to be designed to satisfy requirements for users who work away from the office, as well as branch office connections. The methods used to connect to the LAN and access resources are key elements of a strategy to design a network serving all types of users.

Designing an Implementation Strategy for Dialup Remote Access

In order for users to access the corporate network from remote locations, one connectivity option is a dialup connection to a Remote Access Server (RAS). This enables a remote user to connect to the network using a modem and ordinary telephone line. There are some issues that you must resolve if you incorporate this type of dialup strategy into your network infrastructure design, including the following:

- ◆ **Client IP address assignment**. Clients are assigned an IP address when they connect to the RRAS server, via DHCP or from a static pool of addresses.

- ◆ **Client name registration**. Name registration is the method used by clients to register their computer names on the network, automatically via DHCP or manually using DDNS or WINS.

- ◆ **Name resolution**. Name resolution is the method used by clients to resolve the names of hosts they want to connect to, either by DNS or WINS.

- ◆ **User authentication**. Will users be authenticated by a domain controller, the local server, or by a RADIUS (Internet Authentication Service) server?

- ◆ **Cost of long distance calls**. Do you want to configure callback to reduce the cost of long distance calls to the RRAS server, or would a VPN connection through the Internet be a better alternative?

Designing a Virtual Private Network (VPN) Strategy

Another alternative that provides remote users connectivity to the corporate network is a virtual private network (VPN) solution, which provides secure access to remote users across the Internet. Security is provided by encapsulating all transmissions across the Internet link within an encrypted data stream. Microsoft Windows 2000 VPN solutions support the Point-to-Point Tunneling Protocol (PPTP) and the Layer-2 Tunneling Protocol (L2TP). Internet Protocol Security (IPSec) can be used in conjunction with L2TP to provide an encrypted, secure tunnel across the Internet for data to travel through.

Designing a Routing and Remote Access Service (RRAS) Routing Solution to Connect Locations

The Routing and Remote Access Service (RRAS) provides multiprotocol routing support for Windows 2000. Through RRAS you can configure LAN-to-LAN, LAN-to-WAN, virtual private network (VPN), Network Address Translation (NAT) routing services, and dialup/virtual private network services.

When using RRAS to provide LAN-to-LAN or LAN-to-WAN routing services using the TCP/IP protocol, two dynamic routing protocols are supported: Routing Information Protocol (RIP) version 1 & 2 and Open Shortest Path First (OSPF). On a Routing Information Protocol for IP (RIP for IP)–enabled network, routers keep their respective routing tables updated by communicating with neighbor routers. Approximately every 30 seconds, RIP for IP routers broadcast, or announce, their list of reachable networks. The primary drawback to RIP for IP networks is bandwidth consumption due to the RIP announcements. The OSPF routing protocol works best with large networks. It is a *link-state* routing protocol. The two main features of OSPF are that routing table updates occur only when one or more routers on the network recognizes a change and that OSPF calculates routes using a shortest-path tree.

DESIGNING A MANAGEMENT AND IMPLEMENTATION STRATEGY FOR WINDOWS 2000 NETWORKING

The last step in your network infrastructure design project is to create a strategy for implementing and managing your design recommendations. A fully detailed implementation plan might be beyond the scope of your project, and is probably the responsibility of the deployment team, but a well-developed deployment strategy can give the team some direction from the start.

After the design has been implemented, it needs to be managed and supported. Because the network infrastructure is new, the team needs to become acquainted with the design before being able to do its job effectively. Including a management strategy in your design provides the team with enough information to begin its management and support tasks as soon as the implementation is complete.

There are essentially four main steps to managing a network:

- **Identify what to manage.** In general terms, this means that you must first decide what you need to manage and what you do not need to manage.

- **Monitor the network.** This involves using the Performance tool and the Network Monitor, among other tools, to gather information about the status of the systems that make up the network and about the physical network.

- **Analyze the information.** Obviously, you gather a significant amount of data as you monitor an entire network. It is important that you analyze the data in real time. Ideally, the user should never be affected by a system problem, and you should be able to recognize a problem before it becomes critical and adjust resources to compensate.

- **Respond to issues.** The point of monitoring and the point of having tools that enable you to monitor a network is to detect problems and to be able to respond to them. This means you should know what you need to do to resolve each crisis that could arise.

Being able to understand and perform these four steps ensures that your network will run smoothly and that you will be able to take your next vacation without a pager. The next few sections look more closely at each of these steps.

Designing a Strategy for Monitoring and Managing Windows 2000 Network Services

You need to devise a strategy for monitoring the key Windows 2000 services that are offered on the network infrastructure. The services need to be monitored for both availability and performance. Each service on the network needs to be managed to ensure that it is operating at peak efficiency. Some of the Windows 2000 network services that you want to monitor and manage include:

- **Global Catalog servers.** The central repository containing a subset of attributes of all objects in Active Directory, the Global Catalog is populated by Active Directory replication using Remote Procedure Calls (RPC) over either TCP/IP or SMTP.

- **Lightweight Directory Access Protocol (LDAP).** LDAP is the protocol used to search the Global Catalog and Active Directory.

- **Certificate Services.** Certificate Services is a component of Windows 2000 enabling you to issue X.509 certificates that can be used by the Encrypting File System (EFS), IIS, and other Windows 2000 services.

- **Microsoft Proxy Server.** Microsoft Proxy Server is a separate Microsoft product providing caching, filtering, and other services to optimize Internet access.

- **Domain Name System (DNS) Servers.** DNS is used by Active Directory to provide information on which services can be found on which machine—for example, which host is a domain controller and can authenticate logins. It is also used by clients to resolve hostnames to IP addresses, and is used by DHCP to update a hostname and IP address when a DHCP lease is issued or expired.

- **Dynamic Host Configuration Protocol (DHCP).** DHCP provides for the automatic assignment of IP addresses and other settings to computers on the network. It is also used by Remote Installation Services (RIS) to provide the IP address of a RIS server during client boot.

- **Routing and Remote Access Service (RRAS).** RRAS provides dialup remote access services, virtual private network (VPN) services, and Network Address Translation (NAT) services. This enables clients to access the network using the Public Switched Telephone Network (PSTN) and analog modems, ISDN, or the Internet. It also provides Internet connection sharing capabilities by masking internal IP addresses to a single external address through NAT.

- **Windows Internet Naming System (WINS).** WINS resolves NetBIOS computer names to IP addresses. This enables clients requiring NetBIOS naming to be able to connect to the right computer.

- **Distributed File System (Dfs).** Dfs enables clients to find network shares more easily by providing a central access point with information on the physical location of many shares. Clients connect to the Dfs root and then are redirected to the appropriate host instead of remembering the names of all hosts and which shares exist on them. With Windows 2000 Active Directory, Dfs can also provide for fault tolerance and replication of data in shares.

In monitoring these services, you need to collect data that enables you to determine whether the network is operating properly. You should design a data collection strategy that allows monitoring to ensure that the business requirements of the organization are satisfied.

There are many tools available for monitoring and managing network services. Many of them come in the form of a Microsoft Management Console (MMC) snap-in. The available tools include the following:

- **Performance logs and alerts.** These are a subset of the System Monitor MMC snap-in in which you can configure alerts that can be fired whenever a specific performance threshold is surpassed. Alerts enable you to configure an action that should be taken or a notification that should be sent on the network or both. You can also configure the logging of the performance of certain objects over a defined period using performance logs and then review the captured information using the System Monitor chart view.

◆ **Service Monitor events.** The Service Monitor is built into Windows 2000, and it monitors certain services that are designed to use it. It can restart a service, restart the server, or run a program to send a notification of the failure.

◆ **Simple Network Management Protocol (SNMP).** The SNMP agent service on Windows 2000 can use various Management Information Bases (MIBs) to access and report the status of various parts of the operating system. The agent can then respond to a query from a third-party management station or send traps to the management station. A *trap* is an occurrence of a significant event.

◆ **Event logs.** The Event Log Service can provide you with a great deal of information for troubleshooting a problem. The logs can also be used to calculate uptime for various services and to capture problems that happened. They report five types of events: Information, Warning, Error, Success Audit, and Failure Audit. In Windows 2000 there are six main event logs, each of which provides different information:

  • **Applications log.** Any application that is written to Microsoft standards has the capability of recording information in the Applications log.

  • **Security log.** Events that deal with the security of the system are tracked in this log.

  • **System log.** All the device drivers, services, and other system-related components record their errors in the system log.

  • **Directory service.** This log tracks events that relate to the Active Directory database and its replication.

  • **DNS server.** This log tracks events that affect the DNS server.

  • **File replication service.** This manages the replication of the files in the SYSVOL.

◆ **Network Monitor.** The Network Monitor is used to capture the traffic that is received or sent from a single computer (the one it is running on). This enables you to actually see what packets are being generated from the services on a system and to monitor or troubleshoot problems on the network.

◆ **Command-line utilities.** Windows 2000 provides a number of command-line utilities that can be integrated into a script or called using the Task Scheduler to verify network performance. Some of the most commonly used utilities are

  • **Netdiag.** This utility performs a series of tests to isolate networking and connectivity problems. It can also determine the functional state of your network client.

  • **Ping.** This utility troubleshoots IP connectivity.

  • **Tracert.** This utility displays a list of routers along the path between a source host and a destination.

  • **Pathping.** This utility is a combination of Ping and Tracert. Over a period of time, Pathping sends packets to each router on the path to a final destination, and then computes results based on the packets returned from each hop. Pathping shows the degree of packet loss at any given router or link, so you can pinpoint which routers or links might be causing network problems.

- **Nslookup.** This utility troubleshoots DNS problems.

- **Netstat.** This utility displays protocol statistics and current TCP/IP connections for each network interface in a computer.

- **Nbtstat.** This utility displays protocol statistics and current TCP/IP connections that use NetBIOS over TCP/IP (NetBT). It can also be used to verify the NetBIOS name cache.

◆ **Scripting and programming solutions.** The Windows Scripting Host is a utility available for Windows 2000 that dramatically increases the ability of an administrator to create scripts that can be used to perform monitoring or other administrative tasks. The scripting host enables you to create scripts that are written in Visual Basic Scripting edition or JScript as well as other languages, such as Perl. For more advanced and more complicated monitoring, you may want to write an application or a DLL that will monitor the specific elements you need, such as the performance of an application.

◆ **Windows Management Instrumentation (WMI).** The WMI provides a single point of integration through which you can access status information from many sources within a computer. The WMI is a service that is started by default on Windows 2000–based computers and is also available on Windows 95–and Windows 98–based computers. When developing an application with the WMI API, you can monitor many facets of the network by accessing performance logs, connecting to databases, starting and stopping services remotely, and so forth.

Analyzing the Information

In most cases, after you collect the data that you want to use to manage your network, the next item on the agenda is to analyze the data. This can be done in a number of ways depending on the type of data that you are looking at and what you are trying to find in the data. The following are some of the common methods:

◆ **Manual inspection of status.** In cases where you manually inspect data, there should be little data and the source of the data and response to conditions should be documented.

◆ **Spreadsheets, such as Microsoft Excel.** This can be used when you are looking for fluctuations or for trends. You also can automate by using the programming capabilities of Microsoft Excel.

◆ **Microsoft Access or Microsoft SQL Server.** As with using Excel, this method is useful if you are looking for trends or if you are seeking an anomaly in a large data sample.

◆ **Programmed solutions.** In cases where you are looking for a specific type of change in service or you need to ensure that there will be a response regardless of the time that the change in service took place, you can use a programmatic solution. This includes third-party software.

Responding to Issues

After you have analyzed the information, you need to establish a plan to respond to any issues that arise. You can respond in one of two ways:

◆ **Reactive response.** When responding reactively to information that you have obtained, you are essentially trying to fix a situation that has already taken place, such as a critical network component going down. You should develop a process that ensures that the reaction to a critical situation is quick and responsive.

◆ **Proactive response.** Proactive response is the correction of a potential problem before it takes place. With proper analysis of configured logs, you can track the use of network components and determine when a problem might occur, and then take action to ensure that it does not. This is preferred and will result in fewer disruptions. Design of a proper monitoring and analysis strategy is required in order for proactive response to work.

Designing Network Services That Support Application Architecture

When you deploy network services across an enterprise, you need to ensure that each service performs a function that supports the application software in use by the enterprise. The application software that an organization chooses to use serves the purpose of enabling the company employees to perform their day-to-day tasks. The network services deployed by the enterprise should serve to support the requirements of each of the applications that are used. This is the main function of the network infrastructure.

Combining Networking Services

By combining multiple networking services on a single computer you simplify the network and use hardware resources more efficiently. You can combine services onto a single system as long as you bear the following points in mind:

◆ Combining the services must meet the design criteria for security, availability, and performance on the network.

◆ The computer hardware resources—RAM, CPU, disk, and network—can support the combined services.

◆ The goal is to reduce the number of computers that must be managed.

There are times when you may combine services for other reasons, such as redundancy or perhaps security or performance. There are several cases where this could be the case, including the following:

◆ **Security.** When using remote access or a screened subnet, you can isolate the networking services that manage confidential data on a single server.

◆ **Availability.** By combining services on multiple servers, you can reduce the probability of a failure that results in the loss of the service overall.

◆ **Performance.** Where two services work closely together, such as the Global Catalog and a Domain Dfs root, you can reduce the network traffic or optimize the computer resources that are underused by combining the services on a single system.

Another method to ensure proper use of resources and fail-over support is to make use of Windows 2000 Clustering services to combine services on a cluster. When installing SQL Server or Exchange, or even for DNS and WINS, you can configure these services to run on a Windows 2000 cluster that will provide load balancing (no one server is overloaded) and automatic fail-over (if a server goes down, another assumes its role).

Designing a Plan for the Interaction of Windows 2000 Network Services such as WINS, DHCP, and DNS

Windows 2000 network services offer the essential services that provide the basic foundation of the Windows 2000 network infrastructure. Each service contributes a specific piece to the overall network infrastructure puzzle, but these services do not function completely independently. Several of the basic services found in a Windows 2000 network infrastructure rely on the presence and performance of other services. Planning the implementation of a particular service often involves planning the configuration and implementation of a number of other services. For example, in order to implement the Windows 2000 Active Directory Service, you must also implement the DNS Service. Active Directory relies on the DNS Service to perform its functions. Though DNS does not rely on Active Directory to perform its functions, considerations must be made regarding the DNS configuration if it is known that Active Directory will be deployed along with it. Some of these include support SRV or services records as well as dynamic updates in DNS. The

Windows 2000 DNS Services provides support for both, as does any BIND-compatible DNS server whose version is greater than 8.1.1.

The relationships and dependencies associated with the interaction of Windows 2000 network services need to be carefully considered when creating a network infrastructure design. You need to be aware not only of the requirements of each individual network service, but also of the requirements for proper interaction among the Windows 2000 network services that you include in your design. For example, DHCP in Windows 2000 can be used to automatically update the Windows 2000 DNS Service with the hostname and IP address of any client, including Windows 9x and Windows NT clients that have had an IP address leased to them from the Windows 2000 DHCP server. In this way, there is a strong interaction between the Windows 2000 DHCP server and the Windows 2000 DNS server.

The resource requirements of the various key Windows 2000 services are outlined in Table FF.1. You should not combine services with high-resource requirements on the same server, but many services with low-resource requirements may be combined, providing memory, processor, network, and disk resources are available. In other words, don't overload a server with many services.

TABLE FF.1
WINDOWS 2000 SERVICE RESOURCE REQUIREMENTS

Networking Service	Processor	Memory	Disk	Network
DHCP	High	Low	High	Low
DHCP Relay Agent	Medium	Low	None	Medium
DNS	Medium	Low	High	Low
WINS	Low	Low	High	Medium
WINS Proxy	Low	Low	None	Low
RRAS as a NAT server	High	High	None	High
Microsoft Proxy Server	High	High	High	High
RRAS as a router	Medium	High	None	High
IAS as a RADIUS server	Medium	High	None	Low
IPSec	High	Low	None	Low
VPN tunneling with encryption	High	Low	None	Low

Designing a Resource Strategy

When developing your implementation and management strategies, you want to examine the resources that will reside in the network infrastructure you have created. After you have enumerated them and have an understanding of the requirements for implementing and managing them, you want to do the following:

◆ **Plan for the placement and management of resources.** Care should be taken when deciding where to place each of the resources on the network. Should the resource be placed physically near the end users that will take advantage of it? The assumption is that resources physically close to the users will be able to respond more quickly to user requests because they will have more bandwidth available to them. In many cases, this may be true; however, this choice does not always meet the needs of the business or the constraints placed upon the design by company management. Network design requires that location consider the bandwidth requirements for each resource and which users will be making use of the resource in question. Then, you need to ensure that the resource is not going to use bandwidth in other parts of the network in order to satisfy user requests. Properly placing the resource in the correct physical location that allows minimal use of bandwidth is the goal. However, you need to consider all the requirements of the overall design to decide on the best physical placement of each network resource.

◆ **Plan for growth.** One of the most important aspects of an effective network design is scalability. Make sure that your plan takes into account the company's anticipated growth and growth strategy so that your design can scale accordingly.

◆ **Plan for decentralized resources or centralized resources.** When you understand the geographical and political organization of a company, you can determine whether network resources will be centralized (stored and managed in a single location or by a single administrative authority) or decentralized (physically distributed throughout the enterprise and/or managed by a number of independent administrative authorities). However, placing resources in a physically different location from the centralized management team may be the right choice to minimize network bandwidth utilization, while still allowing a centralized management model. It is not necessary to adopt a decentralized management model when resources are in many locations, nor is it necessary to have a centralized model when resources are in a single location. The physical placement of computers will not change the management style of the organization. Both have to coexist.

This element of the book provides you with some general guidelines for preparing for a certification exam. It is organized into four sections. The first section addresses your learning style and how it affects your preparation for the exam. The second section covers your exam preparation activities and general study tips. This is followed by an extended look at the Microsoft Certification exams, including a number of specific tips that apply to the various Microsoft exam formats and question types. Finally, changes in Microsoft's testing policies, and how these might affect you, are discussed.

LEARNING STYLES

To better understand the nature of preparation for the test, it is important to understand learning as a process. You probably are aware of how you best learn new material. You may find that outlining works best for you, or, as a visual learner, you may need to "see" things. Whatever your learning style, test preparation takes place over time. Obviously, you shouldn't start studying for these exams the night before you take them; it is very important to understand that learning is a developmental process. Understanding it as a process helps you focus on what you know and what you have yet to learn.

Thinking about how you learn should help you recognize that learning takes place when you are able to match new information to old. You have some previous experience with computers and networking. Now you are preparing for this certification exam. Using this book, software, and supplementary materials will not just add incrementally to what you know; when you study, the organization of your knowledge actually restructures as you integrate new information into your existing knowledge base. This will lead you to a more comprehensive understanding of the tasks and concepts

Study and Exam Prep Tips

outlined in the objectives and of computing in general. Again, this happens as a result of a repetitive process rather than a singular event. Keep this model of learning in mind as you prepare for the exam, and you will make better decisions concerning what to study and how much more studying you need to do.

STUDY TIPS

There are many ways to approach studying, just as there are many different types of material to study. However, the tips that follow should work well for the type of material covered on the certification exams.

Study Strategies

Although individuals vary in the ways they learn information, some basic principles of learning apply to everyone. You should adopt some study strategies that take advantage of these principles. One of these principles is that learning can be broken into various depths. Recognition (of terms, for example) exemplifies a more surface level of learning in which you rely on a prompt of some sort to elicit recall. Comprehension or understanding (of the concepts behind the terms, for example) represents a deeper level of learning. The ability to analyze a concept and apply your understanding of it in a new way represents a further depth of learning.

Your learning strategy should enable you to know the material at a level or two deeper than mere recognition. This will help you perform well on the exams. You will know the material so thoroughly that you can easily handle the recognition-level types of questions used in multiple-choice testing. You will also be able to apply your knowledge to solve new problems.

Macro and Micro Study Strategies

One strategy that can lead to this deeper learning includes preparing an outline that covers all the objectives and subobjectives for the particular exam you are working on. You should delve a bit further into the material and include a level or two of detail beyond the stated objectives and subobjectives for the exam. Then expand the outline by coming up with a statement of definition or a summary for each point in the outline.

An outline provides two approaches to studying. First, you can study the outline by focusing on the organization of the material. Work your way through the points and sub-points of your outline with the goal of learning how they relate to one another. For example, be sure you understand how each of the main objective areas is similar to and different from another. Then, do the same thing with the subobjectives; be sure you know which subobjectives pertain to each objective area and how they relate to one another.

Next, you can work through the outline, focusing on learning the details. Memorize and understand terms and their definitions, facts, rules and strategies, advantages and disadvantages, and so on. In this pass through the outline, attempt to learn detail rather than the big picture (the organizational information that you worked on in the first pass through the outline).

Research has shown that attempting to assimilate both types of information at the same time seems to interfere with the overall learning process. Separate your studying into these two approaches, and you will perform better on the exam.

Active Study Strategies

The process of writing down and defining objectives, subobjectives, terms, facts, and definitions promotes a more active learning strategy than merely reading the material. In human information-processing terms, writing forces you to engage in more active encoding of the information. Simply reading over it exemplifies more passive processing.

Next, determine whether you can apply the information you have learned by attempting to create examples and scenarios on your own. Think about how or where you could apply the concepts you are learning. Again, write down this information to process the facts and concepts in a more active fashion.

The hands-on nature of the step-by-step tutorials and exercises at the ends of the chapters provide further active learning opportunities that will reinforce concepts as well.

Common-Sense Strategies

Finally, you should also follow common-sense practices when studying. Study when you are alert, reduce or eliminate distractions, and take breaks when you become fatigued.

Pre-Testing Yourself

Pre-testing allows you to assess how well you are learning. One of the most important aspects of learning is what has been called "meta-learning." Meta-learning has to do with realizing when you know something well or when you need to study some more. In other words, you recognize how well or how poorly you have learned the material you are studying.

For most people, this can be difficult to assess objectively on their own. Practice tests are useful in that they reveal more objectively what you have learned and what you have not learned. You should use this information to guide review and further studying. Developmental learning takes place as you cycle through studying, assessing how well you have learned, then reviewing, and then assessing again until you feel you are ready to take the exam.

You may have noticed the practice exam included in this book. Use it as part of the learning process. The *ExamGear, Training Guide Edition* test simulation software included on the CD also provides you with an excellent opportunity to assess your knowledge.

You should set a goal for your pre-testing. A reasonable goal would be to score consistently in the 90-percent range.

See Appendix D, "Using the *ExamGear, Training Guide Edition* Software," for more explanation of the test simulation software.

EXAM PREP TIPS

Having mastered the subject matter, the final preparatory step is to understand how the exam will be presented. Make no mistake: A Microsoft Certified Professional (MCP) exam will challenge both your knowledge and your test-taking skills. This section starts with the basics of exam design, reviews a new type of exam format, and concludes with hints targeted to each of the exam formats.

The MCP Exam

Every MCP exam is released in one of three basic formats. What's being called exam format here is really little more than a combination of the overall exam structure and the presentation method for exam questions.

Understanding the exam formats is key to good preparation because the format determines the number of questions presented, the difficulty of those questions, and the amount of time allowed to complete the exam.

Each exam format uses many of the same types of questions. These types or styles of questions include several types of traditional multiple-choice questions, multiple-rating (or scenario-based) questions, and simulation-based questions. Some exams include other types of questions that ask you to drag and drop objects on the screen, reorder a list, or categorize things. Still other exams ask you to answer these types of questions in response to a case study you have read. It's important that you understand the types of questions you will be asked and the actions required to properly answer them.

The rest of this section addresses the exam formats and then tackles the question types. Understanding the formats and question types will help you feel much more comfortable when you take the exam.

Exam Format

As mentioned above, there are three basic formats for the MCP exams: the traditional fixed-form exam, the adaptive form, and the case study form. As its name implies, the fixed-form exam presents a fixed set of questions during the exam session. The adaptive form, however, uses only a subset of questions drawn from a larger pool during any given exam session. The case study form includes case studies that serve as the basis for answering the various types of questions.

Fixed-Form

A fixed-form computerized exam is based on a fixed set of exam questions. The individual questions are presented in random order during a test session. If you take the same exam more than once, you won't necessarily see the exact same questions. This is because two or three final forms are typically assembled for every fixed-form exam Microsoft releases. These are usually labeled Forms A, B, and C.

The final forms of a fixed-form exam are identical in terms of content coverage, number of questions, and allotted time, but the questions are different. You may notice, however, that some of the same questions appear on, or rather are shared among, different final forms. When questions are shared among multiple final forms of an exam, the percentage of sharing is generally small. Many final forms share no questions, but some older exams may have a 10–15 percent duplication of exam questions on the final exam forms.

Fixed-form exams also have a fixed time limit in which you must complete the exam. The *ExamGear, Training Guide Edition* software on the CD-ROM that accompanies this book provides fixed-form exams.

Finally, the score you achieve on a fixed-form exam, which is always reported for MCP exams on a scale of 0–1,000, is based on the number of questions you answer correctly. The passing score is the same for all final forms of a given fixed-form exam.

The typical format for the fixed-form exam is as follows:

◆ 50–60 questions.

◆ 75–90 minute testing time.

◆ Question review is allowed, including the opportunity to change your answers.

Adaptive Form

An adaptive-form exam has the same appearance as a fixed-form exam, but its questions differ in quantity and process of selection. Although the statistics of adaptive testing are fairly complex, the process is concerned with determining your level of skill or ability with the exam subject matter. This ability assessment begins with the presentation of questions of varying levels of difficulty and ascertaining at what difficulty level you can reliably answer them. Finally, the ability assessment determines whether that ability level is above or below the level required to pass that exam.

Examinees at different levels of ability will see quite different sets of questions. Examinees who demonstrate little expertise with the subject matter will continue to be presented with relatively easy questions. Examinees who demonstrate a high level of expertise will be presented progressively more difficult questions. Individuals of both levels of expertise may answer the same number of questions correctly, but because the higher-expertise examinee can correctly answer more difficult questions, he or she will receive a higher score and is more likely to pass the exam.

The typical design for the adaptive form exam is as follows:

- ◆ 20–25 questions.

- ◆ 90 minute testing time (although this is likely to be reduced to 45–60 minutes in the near future).

- ◆ Question review is not allowed, providing no opportunity for you to change your answers.

The Adaptive-Exam Process

Your first adaptive exam will be unlike any other testing experience you have had. In fact, many examinees have difficulty accepting the adaptive testing process because they feel that they were not provided the opportunity to adequately demonstrate their full expertise.

You can take consolation in the fact that adaptive exams are painstakingly put together after months of data gathering and analysis and that adaptive exams are just as valid as fixed-form exams. The rigor introduced through the adaptive testing methodology means that there is nothing arbitrary about the exam items you'll see. It is also a more efficient means of testing, requiring less time to conduct and complete than traditional fixed-form exams.

As you can see in Figure 1, a number of statistical measures drive the adaptive examination process. The measure most immediately relevant to you is the ability estimate. Accompanying this test statistic are the standard error of measurement, the item characteristic curve, and the test information curve.

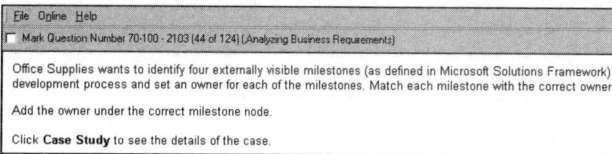

FIGURE 1
Microsoft's adaptive testing demonstration program.

The standard error, which is the key factor in determining when an adaptive exam will terminate, reflects the degree of error in the exam ability estimate. The item characteristic curve reflects the probability of a correct response relative to examinee ability. Finally, the test information statistic provides a measure of the information contained in the set of questions the examinee has answered, again relative to the ability level of the individual examinee.

When you begin an adaptive exam, the standard error has already been assigned a target value below which it must drop for the exam to conclude. This target value reflects a particular level of statistical confidence in the process. The examinee ability is initially set to the mean possible exam score (500 for MCP exams).

As the adaptive exam progresses, questions of varying difficulty are presented. Based on your pattern of responses to these questions, the ability estimate is recalculated. At the same time, the standard error estimate is refined from its first estimated value of one toward the target value. When the standard error reaches its target value, the exam is terminated. Thus, the more consistently you answer questions of the same degree of difficulty, the more quickly the standard error estimate drops, and the fewer questions you will end up seeing during the exam session. This situation is depicted in Figure 2.

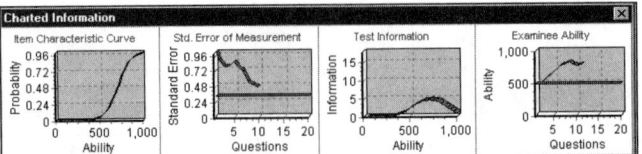

FIGURE 2
The changing statistics in an adaptive exam.

As you might suspect, one good piece of advice for taking an adaptive exam is to treat every exam question as if it were the most important. The adaptive scoring algorithm attempts to discover a pattern of responses that reflects some level of proficiency with the subject matter. Incorrect responses almost guarantee that additional questions must be answered (unless, of course, you get every question wrong). This is because the scoring algorithm must adjust to information that is not consistent with the emerging pattern.

Case Study Form

The case study-based format first appeared with the advent of the 70-100 exam (Solution Architectures). The questions in the case study format are not independent entities as they are in the fixed and adaptive formats. Instead, questions are tied to a case study, a long scenario-like description of an information technology situation. As the test taker, your job is to extract from the case study the information that needs to be integrated with your understanding of Microsoft technology. The idea is that a case study will provide you with a situation that is more like a "real life" problem situation than the other formats provide.

The case studies are presented as "testlets." These are sections within the exam in which you read the case study, then answer 10–15 questions that apply to the case study. When you finish that section, you move onto another testlet with another case study and its associated questions. There may be as many as five of these testlets that compose the overall exam. You will be given more time to complete such an exam because it takes time to read through the cases and analyze them. You may have as much as three hours to complete the exam—and you may need all of it. The case studies are always available through a linking button while you are in a testlet. However, once you leave a testlet, you cannot come back to it.

Figure 3 provides an illustration of part of a case study.

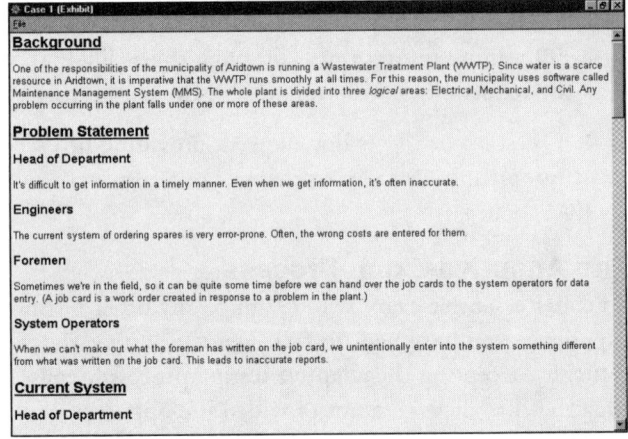

FIGURE 3
An example of a case study.

Question Types

A variety of question types can appear on MCP exams. Examples of many of the various types appear in this book and the *ExamGear, Training Guide Edition* software. We have attempted to cover all the types that were available at the time of this writing. Most of the question types discussed in the following sections can appear in each of the three exam formats.

The typical MCP exam question is based on the idea of measuring skills or the ability to complete tasks. Therefore, most of the questions are written so as to present you with a situation that includes a role (such as a system administrator or technician), a technology environment (100 computers running Windows 98 on a Windows 2000 Server network), and a problem to be solved (the user can connect to services on the LAN, but not the intranet). The answers indicate actions that you might take to solve the problem or create setups or environments that would function correctly from the start. Keep this in mind as you read the questions on the exam. You may encounter some questions that just call for you to regurgitate facts, but these will be relatively few and far between.

In the following sections we will look at the different question types.

Multiple-Choice Questions

Despite the variety of question types that now appear in various MCP exams, the multiple-choice question is still the basic building block of the exams. The multiple-choice question comes in three varieties:

- ◆ **Regular multiple-choice.** Also referred to as an alphabetic question, it asks you to choose one answer as correct.

- ◆ **Multiple-answer multiple-choice.** Also referred to as a multi-alphabetic question, this version of a multiple-choice question requires you to choose two or more answers as correct. Typically, you are told precisely the number of correct answers to choose.

- ◆ **Enhanced multiple-choice.** This is simply a regular or multiple-answer question that includes a graphic or table to which you must refer to answer the question correctly.

Examples of such questions appear at the end of each chapter.

Multiple-Rating Questions

These questions are often referred to as scenario questions. Similar to multiple-choice questions, they offer more extended descriptions of the computing environment and a problem that needs to be solved. Required and desired optional results of the problem-solving are specified, as well as a solution. You are then asked to judge whether the actions taken in the solution are likely to bring about all or part of the required and desired optional results. There is, typically, only one correct answer.

You may be asking yourself, "What is multiple about multiple-rating questions?" The answer is that rather than having multiple answers, the question itself may be repeated in the exam with only minor variations in the required results, optional results, or solution introduced to create "new" questions. Read these different versions very carefully; the differences can be subtle.

Examples of these types of questions appear at the end of the chapters.

Simulation Questions

Simulation-based questions reproduce the look and feel of key Microsoft product features for the purpose of testing. The simulation software used in MCP exams has been designed to look and act, as much as possible, just like the actual product. Consequently, answering simulation questions in an MCP exam entails completing one or more tasks just as if you were using the product itself.

The format of a typical Microsoft simulation question consists of a brief scenario or problem statement, along with one or more tasks that you must complete to solve the problem. An example of a simulation question for MCP exams is shown in the following section.

A Typical Simulation Question

It sounds obvious, but your first step when you encounter a simulation question is to carefully read the question (see Figure 4). Do not go straight to the simulation application! You must assess the problem that's presented and identify the conditions that make up the problem scenario. Note the tasks that must be performed or outcomes that must be achieved to answer the question, and then review any instructions you're given on how to proceed.

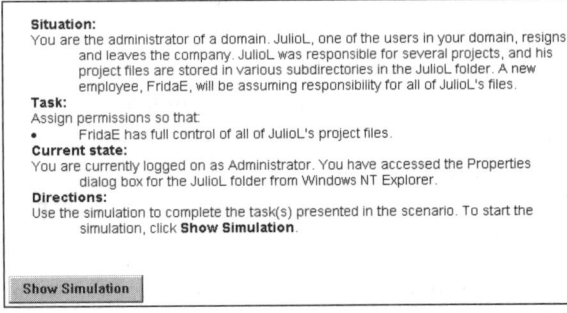

FIGURE 4
A typical MCP exam simulation question with directions.

The next step is to launch the simulator by using the button provided. After clicking the Show Simulation button, you will see a feature of the product, as shown in the dialog box in Figure 5. The simulation application will partially obscure the question text on many test center machines. Feel free to reposition the simulator and to move between the question text screen and

the simulator by using hotkeys or point-and-click navigation, or even by clicking the simulator's launch button again.

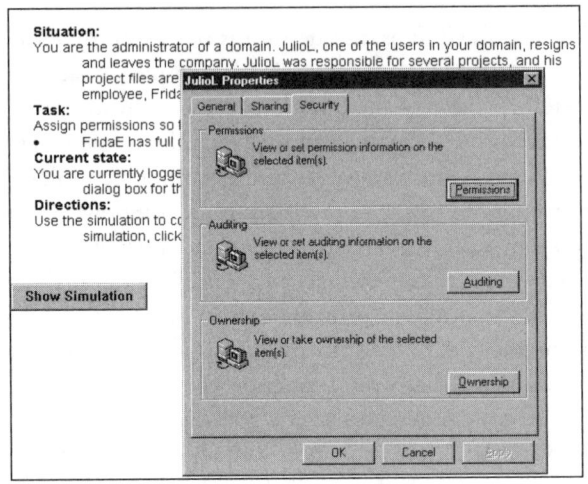

FIGURE 5
Launching the simulation application.

It is important for you to understand that your answer to the simulation question will not be recorded until you move on to the next exam question. This gives you the added capability of closing and reopening the simulation application (using the launch button) on the same question without losing any partial answer you may have made.

The third step is to use the simulator as you would the actual product to solve the problem or perform the defined tasks. Again, the simulation software is designed to function—within reason—just as the product does. But don't expect the simulator to reproduce product behavior perfectly. Most importantly, do not allow yourself to become flustered if the simulator does not look or act exactly like the product.

Figure 6 shows the solution to the example simulation problem.

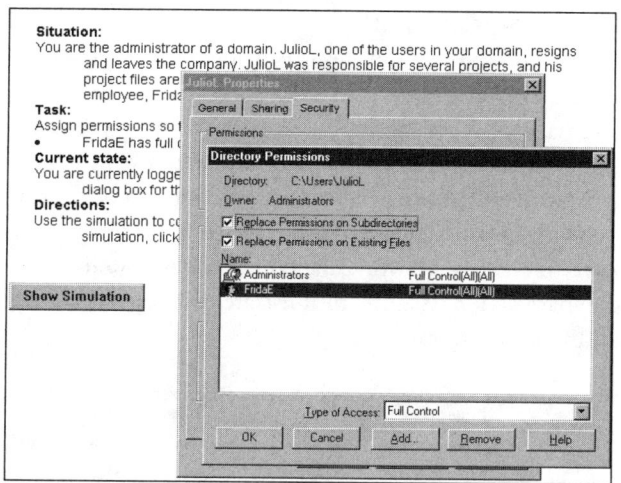

FIGURE 6
The solution to the simulation example.

Two final points will help you tackle simulation questions. First, respond only to what is being asked in the question; do not solve problems that you are not asked to solve. Second, accept what is being asked of you. You may not entirely agree with conditions in the problem statement, the quality of the desired solution, or the sufficiency of defined tasks to adequately solve the problem. Always remember that you are being tested on your ability to solve the problem as it is presented.

The solution to the simulation problem shown in Figure 6 perfectly illustrates both of those points. As you'll recall from the question scenario (refer to Figure 4), you were asked to assign appropriate permissions to a new user, Frida E. You were not instructed to make any other changes in permissions. Thus, if you were to modify or remove the administrator's permissions, this item would be scored wrong on an MCP exam.

Hot Area Question

Hot area questions call for you to click on a graphic or diagram in order to complete some task. You are asked a question that is similar to any other, but rather than clicking an option button or check box next to an answer, you click the relevant item in a screen shot or on a part of a diagram. An example of such an item is shown in Figure 7.

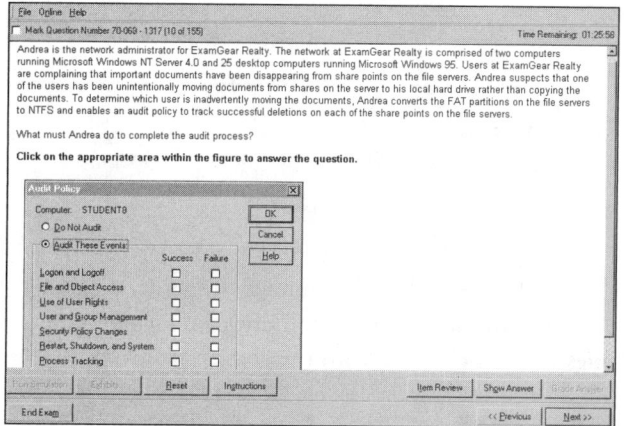

FIGURE 7
A typical hot area question.

Drag and Drop Style Questions

Microsoft has utilized two different types of drag and drop questions in exams. The first is a Select and Place question. The other is a Drop and Connect question. Both are covered in the following sections.

Select and Place

Select and Place questions typically require you to drag and drop labels on images in a diagram so as to correctly label or identify some portion of a network. Figure 8 shows you the actual question portion of a Select and Place item.

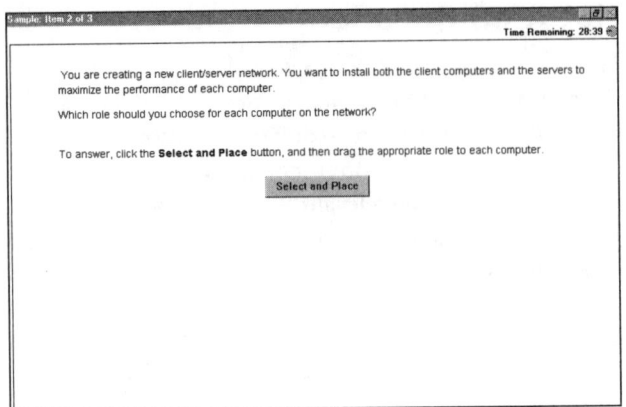

FIGURE 8
A Select and Place question.

Figure 9 shows the window you would see after you chose Select and Place. It contains the actual diagram in which you would select and drag the various server roles and match them with the appropriate computers.

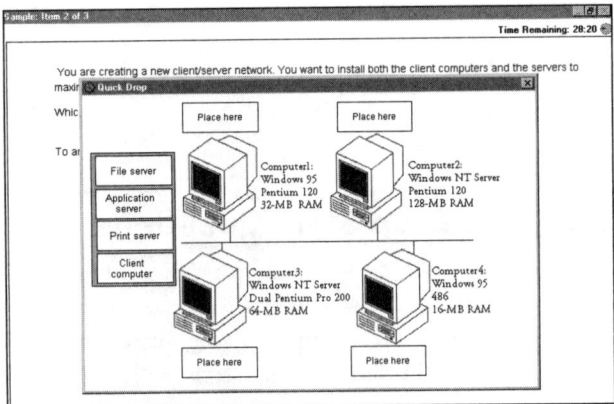

FIGURE 9
The window containing the diagram.

Drop and Connect

Drop and Connect questions provide a different spin on the drag and drop question. The question provides you with the opportunity to create boxes that you can label, as well as connectors of various types with which to link them. In essence, you are creating a model or diagram in order to answer the question. You might have to create a network diagram or a data model for a database system. Figure 10 illustrates the idea of a Drop and Connect question.

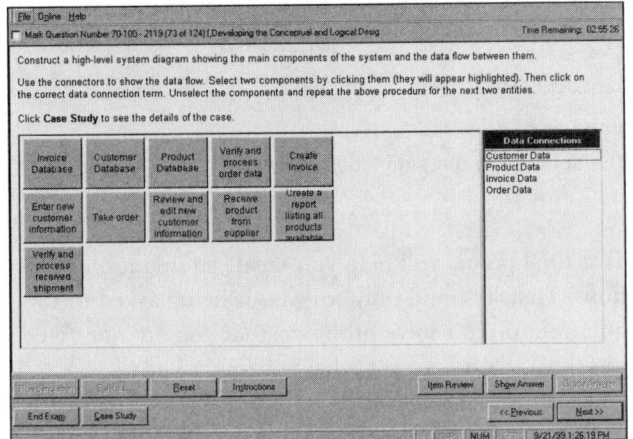

FIGURE 10
A Drop and Connect question.

Ordered List Questions

Ordered list questions simply require you to consider a list of items and place them in the proper order. You select items and then use a button to add them to a new list in the correct order. You have another button that you can use to remove the items in the new list in case you change your mind and want to reorder things. Figure 11 shows an ordered list item.

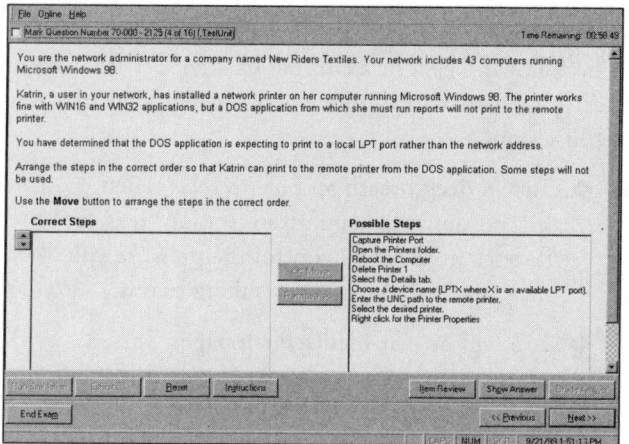

FIGURE 11
An ordered list question.

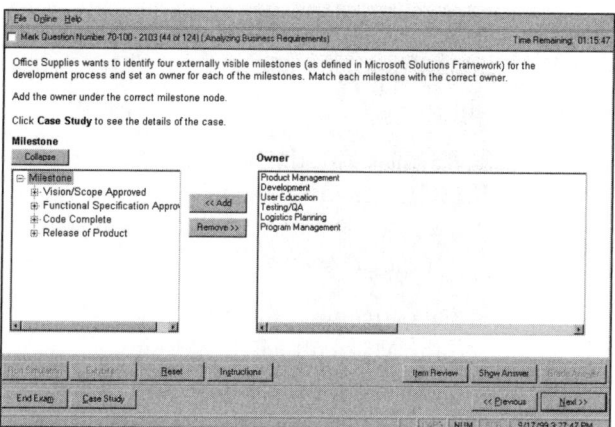

FIGURE 12
A tree question.

Tree Questions

Tree questions require you to think hierarchically and categorically. You are asked to place items from a list into categories that are displayed as nodes in a tree structure. Such questions might ask you to identify parent-child relationships in processes or the structure of keys in a database. You might also be required to show order within the categories, much as you would in an ordered list question. Figure 12 shows a typical tree question.

As you can see, Microsoft is making an effort to utilize question types that go beyond asking you to simply memorize facts. These question types force you to know how to accomplish tasks and understand concepts and relationships. Study so that you can answer these types of questions rather than those that simply ask you to recall facts.

Putting It All Together

Given all these different pieces of information, the task now is to assemble a set of tips that will help you successfully tackle the different types of MCP exams.

More Exam Preparation Tips

Generic exam-preparation advice is always useful. Tips include the following:

◆ Become familiar with the product. Hands-on experience is one of the keys to success on any MCP exam. Review the exercises and the Step by Steps in the book.

◆ Review the current exam-preparation guide on the Microsoft MCP Web site (www.microsoft.com/mcp/examinfo/exams.htm). The documentation Microsoft makes available over the Web identifies the skills every exam is intended to test.

◆ Memorize foundational technical details, but remember that MCP exams are generally heavier on problem solving and application of knowledge than on questions that require only rote memorization.

◆ Take any of the available practice tests. We recommend the one included in this book and the ones you can create using the *ExamGear* software on the CD-ROM. As a supplement to the material bound with this book, try the free practice tests available on the Microsoft MCP Web site.

◆ Look on the Microsoft MCP Web site for samples and demonstration items. These tend to be particularly valuable for one significant reason: They help you become familiar with new testing technologies before you encounter them on MCP exams.

During the Exam Session

The following generic exam-taking advice that you've heard for years also applies when you're taking an MCP exam:

◆ Take a deep breath and try to relax when you first sit down for your exam session. It is very important that you control the pressure you may (naturally) feel when taking exams.

◆ You will be provided scratch paper. Take a moment to write down any factual information and technical details that you committed to short-term memory.

◆ Carefully read all information and instruction screens. These displays have been put together to give you information relevant to the exam you are taking.

◆ Accept the non-disclosure agreement and preliminary survey as part of the examination process. Complete them accurately and quickly move on.

◆ Read the exam questions carefully. Reread each question to identify all relevant detail.

◆ Tackle the questions in the order in which they are presented. Skipping around won't build your confidence; the clock is always counting down (at least in the fixed-form exams).

◆ Don't rush, but also don't linger on difficult questions. The questions vary in degree of difficulty. Don't let yourself be flustered by a particularly difficult or wordy question.

Fixed-Form Exams

Building from this basic preparation and test-taking advice, you also need to consider the challenges presented by the different exam designs. Because a fixed-form exam is composed of a fixed, finite set of questions, add these tips to your strategy for taking a fixed-form exam:

◆ Note the time allotted and the number of questions on the exam you are taking. Make a rough calculation of how many minutes you can spend on each question, and use this figure to pace yourself through the exam.

◆ Take advantage of the fact that you can return to and review skipped or previously answered questions. Record the questions you can't answer confidently on the scratch paper provided, noting the relative difficulty of each question. When you reach the end of the exam, return to the more difficult questions.

◆ If you have session time remaining after you complete all the questions (and if you aren't too fatigued!), review your answers. Pay particular attention to questions that seem to have a lot of detail or that require graphics.

◆ As for changing your answers, the general rule of thumb here is *don't*! If you read the question carefully and completely and you felt like you knew the right answer, you probably did. Don't second-guess yourself. If, as you check your answers, one clearly stands out as incorrect, however, of course you should change it. But if you are at all unsure, go with your first impression.

Adaptive Exams

If you are planning to take an adaptive exam, keep these additional tips in mind:

◆ Read and answer every question with great care. When you're reading a question, identify every relevant detail, requirement, or task you must perform and double-check your answer to be sure you have addressed every one of them.

◆ If you cannot answer a question, use the process of elimination to reduce the set of potential answers, and then take your best guess. Stupid mistakes invariably mean that additional questions will be presented.

◆ You cannot review questions and change answers. When you leave a question, whether you've answered it or not, you cannot return to it. Do not skip any question, either; if you do, it's counted as incorrect.

Case Study Exams

This new exam format calls for unique study and exam-taking strategies. When you take this type of exam, remember that you have more time than in a typical exam. Take your time and read the case study thoroughly. Use the scrap paper or whatever medium is provided to you to take notes, diagram processes, and actively seek out the important information. Work through each testlet as if each were an independent exam. Remember, you cannot go back after you have left a testlet. Refer to the case study as often as you need to, but do not use that as a substitute for reading it carefully initially and for taking notes.

FINAL CONSIDERATIONS

Finally, a number of changes in the MCP program will impact how frequently you can repeat an exam and what you will see when you do.

◆ Microsoft has instituted a new exam retake policy. The new rule is "two and two, then one and two." That is, you can attempt any exam twice with no restrictions on the time between attempts. But after the second attempt, you must wait two weeks before you can attempt that exam again. After that, you will be required to wait two weeks between subsequent attempts. Plan to pass the exam in two attempts or plan to increase your time horizon for receiving the MCP credential.

◆ New questions are being seeded into the MCP exams. After performance data is gathered on new questions, the examiners will replace older questions on all exam forms. This means that the questions appearing on exams will regularly change.

◆ Many of the current MCP exams will be republished in adaptive form. Prepare yourself for this significant change in testing; it is entirely likely that this will become the preferred MCP exam format for most exams. The exception to this may be the case study exams because the adaptive approach may not work with that format.

These changes mean that the brute-force strategies for passing MCP exams may soon completely lose their viability. So if you don't pass an exam on the first or second attempt, it is likely that the exam's form will change significantly by the next time you take it. It could be updated from fixed-form to adaptive, or it could have a different set of questions or question types.

Microsoft's intention is not to make the exams more difficult by introducing unwanted change, but to create and maintain valid measures of the technical skills and knowledge associated with the different MCP credentials. Preparing for an MCP exam has always involved not only studying the subject matter, but also planning for the testing experience itself. With the recent changes, this is now more true than ever.

This exam consists of 65 questions reflecting the material you have covered in the chapters; the questions are representative of the types that you should expect to see on the actual exam.

The answers to all questions appear in their own section following the exam. It is strongly suggested that when you take this exam, you treat it just as you would the actual exam at the test center. Time yourself, read carefully, and answer all the questions to the best of your ability.

Most of the questions do not simply require you to recall facts but require deduction on your part to come up with the best answer. Most questions require you to identify the best course of action to take in a given situation. Many of the questions are verbose, requiring you to read them carefully and thoroughly before you attempt to answer them. Run through the exam, and for questions you miss, review any material associated with them.

Practice Exam

EXAM QUESTIONS

1. You are the newly appointed system administrator for a small law firm. The firm would like to design and implement an Internet access integration for the entire organization.

   There are 100-client workstations to configure access for the Internet. Most workstations need to securely tunnel to remote offices using VPNs.

   Required Results:

   - To make Web surfing faster, the use of some Web caching technology is required.

   - Clients will require the use of PPTP for VPN access to remote offices.

   Optional Desired Results:

   - You are required to track which clients access certain Web sites.

   - Blocking questionable Web sites would also be beneficial.

   Proposed Solution:

   - Install Microsoft Proxy Server on the server accessing the Internet and the Microsoft Proxy client on all the workstations.

   - Enable Web caching on the proxy server.

   - Enable IP filtering and add questionable Web site IPs to the filter list.

   Which results does the proposed solution produce? Choose the correct answer.

   A. The proposed solution produces the required results and produces all the optional desired results.

   B. The proposed solution produces the required results and produces only one of the optional desired results.

   C. The proposed solution produces the required results but does not produce any of the optional desired results.

   D. The proposed solution does not produce the required results.

2. As the network administrator, you want to provide the best solution for network browsing for your entire network.

   Your network is divided into two subnets. All clients in both subnets are Win 9x, Windows NT, and Windows 2000.

   Required Results:

   - Provide NetBIOS name resolution for the entire organization.

   - Provide redundancy and load balancing for name resolution.

   Optional Desired Results:

   - Assign all required client information as efficiently as possible.

   - Minimize excess network traffic from the new solution.

   Proposed Solution:

   Install a WINS server in both subnets. Configure the WINS servers as push/pull replication partners with each other. Install a DHCP server in one subnet with superscope and WINS client update information. Set all clients to use DHCP. Configure DHCP to set half of the WINS clients to use one WINS server, and to set the remainder of the WINS clients to use the other WINS server. Set the DHCP client IP lease to be short.

   Choose the correct answer.

   A. The proposed solution produces the required results and produces all the optional desired results.

B. The proposed solution produces the required results and produces only one of the optional desired results.

C. The proposed solution produces the required results but does not produce any of the optional desired results.

D. The proposed solution does not produce the required results.

3. You are a consultant working on a project at an oil company requiring high availability for a custom database application.

The oil company has provided you with three Windows 2000 servers installed fresh and with default settings. The application database currently runs from a UNIX server with no plans to move it. Clients are all remote with dialup access or ADSL connections.

Required Results:

- Allow clients to securely authenticate across the Internet to gain access to the database application.

- Create a fault-tolerant model for availability of this database application.

Optional Desired Results:

- Install a DNS server on the Windows 2000 server to provide name resolution.

- Enable dynamic disk support.

Proposed Solution:

Configure the three Windows 2000 servers with NLB and use a virtual IP to allow access to the cluster. Force the server and clients to use MS-CHAP for network access. Create a DNS round robin. Use RAID 5 for the drives in each server.

Select the correct answer.

A. The proposed solution produces the required results and produces all the optional desired results.

B. The proposed solution produces the required results and produces only one of the optional desired results.

C. The proposed solution produces the required results but does not produce any of the optional desired results.

D. The proposed solution does not produce the required results.

4. In a recent acquisition, your company merged with an industrial development company. This new company has many different sites with varying connection requirements.

Adding the industrial development company to your network introduces 150 remote Windows 2000 clients with dialup access to your existing network.

Required Results:

- Use VPN to connect all remote sites.

- Ensure all transmitted data is secure.

Optional Desired Results:

- Create seamless VPN connections that require no user intervention.

- Register all site client computers in DNS for fast name resolution.

Proposed Solution:

A VPN server running Windows 2000 at each location can establish a connection with the VPN server. The VPN servers would be configured to use the demand-dial feature of Windows 2000 to support automatic connection to your corporate network. Use IPSec in default mode to secure all data being transmitted. Use Dynamic DNS to allow changes and updates to roaming DNS clients.

Select the correct answer.

A. The proposed solution produces the required results and produces all the optional desired results.

B. The proposed solution produces the required results and produces only one of the optional desired results.

C. The proposed solution produces the required results but does not produce any of the optional desired results.

D. The proposed solution does not produce the required results.

5. You administer the network operations for a publishing company. Your company's network is about to be upgraded to Windows 2000 Server.

Upgrading the network servers to Windows 2000 is an initiative to enable e-commerce solutions and sell published books online. You've been given five servers to implement.

Required Results:

• Superior performance and reliability are required for access from the Internet.

• Active Directory integration is necessary.

Optional Desired Results:

• DHCP client updates occur automatically.

• Zone transfers must occur incrementally.

Proposed Solution:

Install a single Windows 2000 Advanced Server Domain with Active Directories, network load balancing, and clustering services and create primary Dynamic DNS servers.

Select the correct answer.

A. The proposed solution produces the required results and produces all the optional desired results.

B. The proposed solution produces the required results and produces only one of the optional desired results.

C. The proposed solution produces the required results but does not produce any of the optional desired results.

D. The proposed solution does not produce the required results.

6. You are setting up your DNS server and have created a Pointer Record for it. What types of records are found in your reverse lookup? Select the two correct answers.

A. Start of Authority

B. No such record in DNS

C. Name server

D. LDAP

7. Your company hired you to implement security on its corporate network. The company has Internet access and you decide to implement Microsoft Proxy Server. Which two proxy configurations are required to provide security on your corporate network? Choose two answers.

A. Disable IP forwarding.

B. Enable Access Control.

C. Disable packet filtering.

D. Enable RPC listening ports.

8. You've just finished installing and configuring two servers with Microsoft Windows 2000 Server Edition. These two servers are required to host a

high-availability database. What do you need to configure these servers to maintain high availability? Choose the two correct answers.

A. Install the exact Network Interface Card in both servers and connect with a crossover cable.

B. Upgrade both servers to Windows 2000 Advanced Server Edition.

C. Create a virtual IP on both servers.

D. This is not possible on Windows 2000 and requires a third-party application.

9. When establishing and deploying an Enterprise Certificate Authority, a number of components are required. Select three answers that apply.

A. Select the host server.

B. Establish private key.

C. Establish organizational naming.

D. Establish issuing policy.

E. Establish external CA trust.

10. Your company has over 10,000 users spread throughout the U.S. Hub offices are connected by high-speed links, and circuits of 56KB-or-better connect smaller satellite offices. The company wants to develop an active directory design that will allow it to manage users based on functional areas—such as marketing, sales, and HR—that spread across the various offices. Ease of manageability and replication traffic is a major concern. Which strategy meets those design goals? Choose the correct answer.

A. Use of multiple domains established by functional area (sales, marketing, HR).

B. Use of multiple domains based on geographic location to control replication patterns.

C. Single domain with users placed in OUs corresponding to their functional area. Use of sites to control replication.

D. Single domain with users divided by sites to control replication issues.

11. You have just installed Windows 2000. By default, Windows 2000 creates group and individual IPSec default policies. Select the three default policies.

A. Secure Server

B. Secure client

C. Encrypted Transport

D. Client

E. Server

12. Your ISP provides you with the IP network address of 136.124.0.0/16. You have 8 locations with 2,000, 6,000, 4,500, 7,000, 1,200, 7,200, 8,100, and 8,000 hosts, respectively. Which variable-length subnet allows you to provide all locations with enough hosts and provide for an Internet-legal scheme?

A. 22

B. 19

C. 16

D. 24

13. You have decided to implement RADIUS within your enterprise. Management wants to understand the benefit that this will bring and to know what the key features of RADIUS are that make it a more secure solution than the basic RRAS that you've been using. Pick the two features that RADIUS provides to create a secure dialup solution.

A. IPSec tunneling

B. Client authentication

C. Account logging

D. Data encryption

14. Your company wants to install DHCP, but is very frugal with expenditures for hardware. You must serve 7,000 clients, but provide redundancy in case of any DHCP server failure. What is the minimum number of DHCP servers needed in this scenario?

    A. 1

    B. 2

    C. 18

    D. 16

15. Your company has a sales force that regularly dials in to your network. Each salesperson is equipped with a laptop with Windows 2000 Professional. Regardless of where the salesperson is, he or she dials in to a predetermined ISP and then establishes a VPN to your network. You require data encryption and certified authentication. Which two technologies combined provide the most secure communication for your needs?

    A. PPTP

    B. IPSec

    C. L2TP

    D. RADIUS

16. You have implemented DHCP in your environment. Your client machines are exclusively Windows 2000 and Windows 98. Your environment is made up of five subnets with a switched VLAN. You've implemented one DHCP server and DHCP Relay Agents for communication across the virtual LAN segments.

A user sits down at one of the machines and turns it on. A relay agent has failed on this user's LAN segment. What happens with the IP stack and configuration of this machine? Choose all that apply.

    A. It supports only the local subnet.

    B. The default gateway is assigned automatically.

    C. It randomly chooses an address from the `169.254.0.0` address space using Automatic Private IP Addressing (APIPA).

    D. It does not test for IP address conflicts.

    E. It checks in the background for a DHCP offer every 5 minutes.

17. You've installed a Windows 2000 DHCP server in your Windows 2000 environment. You configure the scope and the options, and confirm that the server is communicating by pinging other hosts.

    You attempt to obtain an address from the DHCP server, but it fails and the workstation autogenerates an address.

    What is causing this issue?

    A. The DHCP scope is incorrect.

    B. The DHCP server is not authorized in Active Directory.

    C. The DNS record for the DHCP server is incorrect.

    D. The DHCP address in the client's IP Properties is incorrect.

18. Name two name resolution methods used in Windows 2000.

    A. L2TP

    B. LDAP

C. DNS

D. X.500

E. WINS

19. You have implemented DNS in Windows 2000 and intend to use Active Directory. Which record type is required for locating a specific service?

A. CNAME

B. PTR

C. SRV

D. SOA

20. You are implementing DNS within a Windows 2000 network using Active Directory. You've also implemented DHCP and WINS. You have set DHCP and DNS to do Active Directory-integrated updates. Which two main objects in the Active Directory hold the DNS information?

A. dnsObj

B. dnsZone

C. dnsNode

D. dnsPtr

E. dnsName

21. A WINS server in Los Angeles pushes a database to servers in New York, Philadelphia, and Atlanta. Which WINS replication model is implemented on this network?

A. Push replication

B. Pull replication

C. Chained replication

D. Central replication

22. Internet traffic has increased on your LAN; slow performance of your proxy server has resulted. What can be implemented on the proxy server to address the increased demand? Choose the two correct answers.

A. Add more processors to the proxy server.

B. Filter IP packets.

C. Create a proxy array.

D. Switch proxy client protocols to use IPX only.

23. IPSec in tunnel mode differs from IPSec in transport mode. Which ways are they implemented differently from one another? Choose the two correct answers.

A. Tunnel mode of IPSec requires a specific IP address or hostname for the opposite end of the tunnel.

B. Transport mode of IPSec can talk to multiple IP addresses or hostnames.

C. Tunnel mode of IPSec can talk to multiple IP addresses or hostnames.

D. Transport mode of IPSec requires a specific IP address or hostname for the opposite end of the tunnel.

24. Which authentication protocols does IPSec in Windows 2000 support? Choose the two correct answers.

A. SHA

B. 3DES

C. MKE

D. MD5

25. In what ways does IPSec enhance network security? Choose the three correct answers.

    A. Provides authentication of computers

    B. Provides Secure Socket Layer (SSL) of data

    C. Provides encryption of data

    D. Provides policy filters for individual IP address restrictions

    E. Provides management of bandwidth allocation

26. You administer a network with client computers running Windows NT 4.0 and Windows 2000 operating systems; all computers require secure access to a remote network. On your VPN server, how would you connect these operating systems? Choose the two correct answers.

    A. Use PPTP on all operating systems.

    B. Create a static route from the server to each client.

    C. Use L2TP on all operating systems.

    D. Use IKE on all operating systems.

    E. Use L2TP on Windows 2000 computers.

27. What are the primary reasons for installing RADIUS in a Windows 2000 environment? Choose three answers.

    A. Provides decentralized authentication

    B. Provides non–vendor-specific authentication

    C. Provides large-scale network deployment

    D. Provides secure access for IPSec clients

    E. Provides centralized accounting

28. To aid with name resolution, you decide to implement two WINS servers in your environment. What best practices must you set up to provide the best fault tolerance? Choose two correct answers.

    A. The two WINS servers must be configured to replicate WINS database information.

    B. The WINS clients must include the default gateway for the primary and secondary WINS server.

    C. The WINS clients must include the IP addresses for a primary and secondary WINS server.

    D. The two WINS servers must use DNS for name resolution.

29. Due to the latest threat of hackers, you require locking down your Windows 2000 server with protocol filtering. Which type of traffic can you filter out? Choose three correct answers.

    A. Internet Protocol (IP) protocol number

    B. 5056KB packets

    C. User Datagram Protocol (UDP) port number

    D. TCP port number

    E. User Datagram Protocol (UDP) protocol number

30. You need to optimize your DHCP server for performance. Which two factors must you take into consideration? Choose the two correct answers.

    A. As your DHCP server's lease length increases, network traffic increases but IP addresses on your clients release later.

    B. As your DHCP server's lease length decreases, network traffic increases but IP addresses on your clients release later.

C. As your DHCP server's lease length increases, network traffic decreases but IP addresses on your clients release later.

D. As your DHCP server's lease length decreases, network traffic increases but IP addresses on your clients release sooner.

E. As your DHCP server's lease length decreases, network traffic decreases but IP addresses on your clients release sooner.

31. Until now, you have all IPs configured through a DHCP server to be allocated to your internal corporate network. As remote access requirements have been introduced, you now must install and configure RRAS into your environment. You will initially have 15 simultaneous dialup users. How many IPs must you be prepared to allocate from your DHCP server for the RRAS clients? Choose the correct answer.

A. 15

B. 20

C. 50

D. None. RRAS won't use DHCP server for IP allocation.

32. Select which answer defines what DNS Forward Lookup does.

A. IP addresses are converted to FQDNs (Fully Qualified Domain Names).

B. It forwards DNS Queries to a DHCP server.

C. FQDNs (Fully Qualified Domain Names) are converted to IP addresses.

D. FQDNs (Fully Qualified Domain Names) are converted to the WINS database.

33. In Windows 2000, DNS can be tightly integrated with which services? Choose the three correct answers.

A. DNS database information can be replicated into the Active Directory service.

B. DHCP servers for reverse lookups can use DNS database information.

C. DNS service can forward unresolved queries to a WINS server.

D. DNS service can be automatically updated when an IP changes from DHCP services.

E. DNS services will automatically update WINS clients when IP information changes.

34. What are some of the main disadvantages of using a standard DNS infrastructure as opposed to a Windows 2000 DNS infrastructure? Choose two answers.

A. You have no ability to perform incremental zone transfers.

B. One DNS server is required at each remote location when separated by a router.

C. DNS servers involved in zone transfers may be impersonated.

D. Standard DNS infrastructures are not upward-compatible with the Windows 2000 Active Directory DNS infrastructure.

35. Under what circumstances should you consider using a DNS Caching Only server? Choose two correct answers.

A. Remote locations are on high-speed connections.

B. DNS zone information remains consistently static.

C. DNS zone replication has a low impact on network bandwidth.

D. Remote locations are on low-speed connections.

E. The primary zone is on a high-speed connection, and the secondary zones are on low-speed connections.

36. Which protocols are supported by RRAS? Choose the three correct answers.

    A. TCP/IP

    B. NetBEUI

    C. AppleTalk

    D. NWLink

    E. DLC

37. Your company requires remote access to an accounting package. Due to the sensitive nature of the data, you require implementing encryption for all remote authentication. Which of the following security protocols would you require on the server and client side? Choose the two correct answers.

    A. Unauthenticated Access

    B. EAP

    C. MS-CHAP and MS-CHAP version 2

    D. PAP

38. Which of the following is the correct implementation of a RADIUS client? Choose two correct answers.

    A. The RADIUS client allows authentication by any RADIUS server.

    B. The RADIUS client provides authentication based on the IP address database in Windows 2000.

C. The RADIUS client allows remote access information to be logged in the Event Log in Windows 2000.

D. The RADIUS client provides VPN server support for the remote clients.

39. Which services must be installed under Windows 2000 for RADIUS server services? Choose the three correct answers.

    A. TCP/IP

    B. RRAS

    C. IAS

    D. IIS

    E. RIP

40. Which services must be installed under Windows 2000 for RADIUS client services? Choose the three correct answers.

    A. IIS

    B. IAS

    C. TCP/IP

    D. RIP

    E. RRAS

41. You are installing Active Directory services in your network environment and need to use your existing DNS servers to integrate with your Active Directory service. Choose the two features that must be supported by your DNS servers?

    A. Dynamic Update Protocol for DNS

    B. PTR Update Protocol for DNS

    C. SRV (Service) Location Resource Records

    D. MPPE (Microsoft Point-to-Point Encryption)

42. What are some primary concerns when designing a network infrastructure? Choose the three correct answers.

    A. Scalability

    B. Bandwidth

    C. Performance

    D. Availability

    E. Manageability

43. DHCP services under Windows 2000 now support BOOTP protocol. What other enhanced support does Windows 2000 add to DHCP services? Choose three correct answers.

    A. Rogue DHCP server detection

    B. Windows Clustering

    C. RIP protocol integration

    D. DNS service integration

    E. OSPF (Open Shortest Path First) routing protocol integration

44. You have an existing network with Windows NT 4.0 server currently running your DNS services. Installing a new Windows 2000 server as a member server and installing DHCP server services on it may present some networking issues. What does Microsoft recommend you do for this mix of operating system services? Select the three correct answers.

    A. For non-NetBIOS DHCP clients, assign IP addresses with infinite lease durations.

    B. Enable forward lookups for DNS clients.

    C. Enable WINS lookup from DNS for all DHCP clients that use NetBIOS.

    D. Upgrade older static DNS servers to Windows 2000 servers.

    E. Disable DNS on Windows NT. Windows 2000 DHCP server can provide the required network information instead.

45. Based on a few newer remote connections that your organization requires access to, you've been given the task to create a demand-dial routing solution to help cut down the toll charges to these sites. Select three correct steps to implement this under Windows 2000.

    A. Install and configure the modem.

    B. Install and start RRAS.

    C. Create a loopback connection for routing to initialize.

    D. Configure settings by using Remote Access Policies.

    E. Set the default static route.

46. Which of the following services must be installed in Windows 2000 to use demand-dial routing? Choose the two correct answers.

    A. RRAS

    B. RIP

    C. TCP/IP

    D. OSPF

47. DNS scavenging can clean up stale records, which affects the overall data storage requirements and name resolution accuracy. What are some important factors to note about scavenging? Select two correct answers.

    A. Scavenging cannot be performed on a zone-by-zone basis.

    B. Records with a zero timestamp are never scavenged.

    C. Only primary DNS servers can be enabled to scavenge.

D. Records with a zero timestamp are always scavenged.

E. DNS servers by default are configured with scavenging enabled by default.

48. You've recently upgraded all your servers to Windows 2000 servers, and now your DHCP clients cannot receive the DDNS entries from the DHCP server. What type of areas should you look at to ensure a properly functioning service? Choose two correct answers.

A. Ensure the primary DNS server has Dynamic DNS configured correctly.

B. Ensure the primary DHCP server has Dynamic DHCP configured correctly.

C. Ensure the DHCP client is installed on Windows 2000 operating system.

D. Ensure the DHCP client is installed on at least Windows NT operating system.

E. Ensure any secondary DNS servers have Dynamic DNS configured correctly.

49. When a Windows 2000 DHCP client registers an IP, what other information can be requested or updated? Choose the two correct answers.

A. Client can update A records on DNS server.

B. DNS server updates A records on DHCP clients.

C. DHCP server updates any PTR records on the DNS server.

D. The client computer issues an SOA (Start of Authority) query and updates the DHCP server.

50. You have lost communication with your DNS servers. Your DHCP client is failing to update its DNS information to your primary servers. Initially, your DHCP client will retry to update its DNS information to the primary servers every 5 minutes for X number of tries. If it fails to update any primary DNS servers after this, how will it schedule its next update? Choose the correct answer.

A. It will try every 5 minutes until it can update the DNS servers.

B. It will try every 15 minutes until it can update the DNS servers.

C. It will try every 50 minutes until it can update the DNS servers.

D. It will try every 180 minutes until it can update the DNS servers.

51. What key characteristics does L2TP (Layer-Two Tunneling Protocol) perform for VPN connections? Choose the three correct answers.

A. L2TP provides better security than PPTP.

B. L2TP provides the highest levels of VPN security.

C. L2TP provides address assignments.

D. L2TP provides authentication.

E. L2TP requires IP connectivity between the connecting computers.

52. As the network administrator, you must plan to add WINS services to your infrastructure to aid with name resolution. What factors must you keep in mind while planning this integration? Choose two correct answers.

A. The more replication partners, the lower the network traffic.

B. The shorter the replication intervals, the lower the network traffic.

C. The more replication partners, the higher the network traffic.

D. Create persistent connections to reduce network traffic.

E. Fault tolerance requires all WINS servers to be on the same subnet.

53. You've been given the task of finding and purchasing a firewall for your network. The criterion for the firewall is that it must implement access control at the Session layer of the OSI model. What type of firewall do you require? Choose the correct answer.

A. A firewall based on packet filtering router technology

B. A firewall based on application-level gateways

C. A firewall based on circuit-level gateways

D. A firewall based on proxy services

54. To make your proxy server more efficient in distributing commonly accessed Web pages, you implement caching. Which two services support caching?

A. Web Proxy

B. Winsock Proxy

C. Socks Proxy

D. Reverse Web Proxy

E. Packet Filtering Router

55. What type of data is typically found in the network header of the protocol stack being filtered? Select the three correct answers.

A. Router interface

B. Destination port

C. Destination type

D. NLB properties

E. Source port

56. Which of the following protocols introduced with Windows 2000 are new to the Windows platform? Select the three correct answers.

A. Radius

B. BAP

C. MS-CHAP

D. PPTP

E. EAP

57. Your company has decided to use IPSec to assist in remote connectivity. You are assigned the task of evaluating how IPSec can be used in the existing network infrastructure. What types of authentication encryption can you implement with IPSec? Choose the two correct answers.

A. SHA

B. 56-bit DES

C. 3DES

D. MD5

58. After upgrading network hardware to improve reliability, you are still concerned by the availability of DHCP servers in your company's network. What DHCP solutions might you implement to ensure fault tolerance of DHCP? Choose the best answer.

A. You can create a round robin DNS configuration to do name resolution if the DHCP service fails.

B. Set the IP lease time to a shorter interval to allow faster IP allocation to DHCP clients.

C. You can split the IP addresses on two DHCP servers in case one server fails.

D. You can add a superscope to your existing DHCP server to provide redundancy.

59. Two remote sites use VPN connections across the Internet for access to your corporate intranet. Using IPSec, how could you configure Windows 2000 to provide effective security while providing access to all locations? Select the correct answer.

    A. Configure RRAS to connect all sites.

    B. Use IPSec in tunnel mode to authenticate remote computers and to encrypt data transferred.

    C. Use OSPF routing.

    D. Use IPSec in transport mode to authenticate remote computers and to encrypt data transferred.

60. You are the IS manager for your company. You've recently outsourced your network support services to a consulting firm. Your organization is configured on Active Directories and using Certificates. What types of trusted authority would you use to authenticate the consultants' access? Select the three correct answers.

    A. Private keys

    B. Certificate authorities

    C. Kerberos version 5 certificates

    D. IPSec policy

61. You are currently administering a Windows 2000 server with Active Directories installed and configured. You allow remote access by authenticating with Kerberos version 5 certificates. Due to the small size of your network, you decide to configure Internet access with Connection Sharing services. How will this new configuration effect your existing network setup? Choose the correct answer.

A. There are no issues based on this configuration.

B. The Kerberos version 5 protocol cannot be translated by Connection Sharing.

C. Connection Sharing cannot be enabled if remote users require access to internal network objects.

D. Connection Sharing will not work properly without WINS running on the server.

62. What is the maximum amount of hosts that can be configured in a cluster? Choose the correct answer.

    A. 4

    B. 16

    C. 32

    D. 128

63. To provide load balancing for network services, you implement NLB (Network Load Balancing) to distribute IP traffic to multiple hosts configured as clusters. One cluster is for DNS servers and the other for DHCP servers. One server is configured with both DNS and DHCP services, and you add an extra network interface to provide NLB to both clusters. You first enable one network interface to join the DNS cluster and then add the next network interface for the DHCP cluster. This server does not appear in the DNS cluster. Why? Choose the correct answer.

    A. To add NLB service to both network interfaces, you must install a second instance of NLB for the second interface.

    B. NLB by default allows one network interface to be configured to join a cluster; you can enable the second interface manually.

C. NLB can be enabled on only one network interface at a time.

D. When NLB is enabled on one network interface, you must add the other network interface IP address to the NLB properties found under the Cluster parameters tab.

64. Reviewing NAT as a possible solution, you discover its limitations. What are these? Select the two correct answers.

A. NAT cannot pass PPTP VPN traffic.

B. NAT cannot pass IPSec traffic.

C. NAT cannot update DHCP clients with WINS server information.

D. NAT cannot update DHCP clients with DNS server information.

E. NAT cannot modify the source port and IP address information when it forwards requests.

65. The performance of your DNS on your network is degrading. What important information plays a factor on the overall performance of DNS? Select the three correct answers.

A. Amount of DNS clients

B. Type of DNS clients

C. Network connection of DNS clients

D. Size of DNS database files

E. Location of standard primary zones

ANSWERS TO EXAM QUESTIONS

1. **D.** The requirements could not be implemented for the simple reason that most of the clients require using PPTP to provide the VPN capability to remote offices, and this protocol will not pass through the MS Proxy. NAT (Network Address Translation) would provide the VPN capability for the clients but would not provide the Web caching features that proxy would.

2. **B.** Setting the DHCP client IP addresses to expire in a short time period increases network traffic for this service.

3. **D.** To implement clustering and Network Load Balancing in Windows 2000, you must use Advanced Server Edition at the least. When Advanced Server is installed, you will be able to provide fault tolerance for the database application using NLB and clustering. NLB allows you to use a virtual IP to represent the load-balanced servers. Clustering allows the fail-over capabilities, and setting up the drives in RAID-5 enables independent server fault tolerance. MS-CHAP is a nonreversible, encrypted password authentication protocol enabling the security requirement. A DNS round robin is a valid method to provide the name resolution. Dynamic disk support is required for RAID-5.

4. **A.** Answer A is correct; the use of IPSec in a VPN connection setup to demand-dial provides the required and optional results. DDNS provides fast name resolution.

5. **A.** Answer A is correct because Windows 2000 Advanced Server provides effective Internet services and incorporates Active Directory services. Using DDNS in a NLB method provides DHCP clients with reliable, automatic updates.

6. **A, C.** A is correct because SOA is always the first record in a zone database. It identifies the location of the primary zone. See Table 3.14 in Chapter 3. C is correct because Name Server records are also found and contain the address of the authoritative name server.

7. **A, B.** A is correct because disabling IP forwarding prevents any external traffic from routing to the internal network. B is correct because enabling access control can control which internal users can access specified external addresses.

8. **B, C.** B is correct because Microsoft Windows 2000 Advanced Server and Datacenter are the only Microsoft platforms that support Network Load Balancing and clustering. Up to 32 nodes can be clustered. C is correct because when Advanced Server with Network Load Balancing is installed, you can create a virtual IP that the client will use to access the database. If one server fails, the IP will look at the other server seamlessly for the client.

9. **A, C, D.** Selection of a host server, organization naming, and external CA trusts are all components of a CA.

10. **C.** A single AD domain with users separated into designated OUs eases administration requirements and lessens overall network traffic concerns.

11. **A, D, E.** A is correct because the Secure Server requires security. D is correct because the client responds only. E is correct because the server (Request Security) is installed by default and can be modified to fit more specific requirements.

12. **B.** A variable-length subnet of /19 allows 8 networks, each with a maximum of 8,190 hosts:

    1 - 136.124.0.1–136.124.31.254
    2 - 136.124.32.1–136.124.63.254
    3 - 136.124.64.1–136.124.95.254
    4 - 136.124.96.1–136.124.127.254
    5 - 136.124.128.1–136.124.159.254
    6 - 136.124.160.1–136.124.191.254
    7 - 136.124.192.1–136.124.223.254
    8 - 136.124.224.1–136.124.255.254

13. **B, C.** B is correct because RADIUS specifically provides client authentication, which is scalable to large deployments, works with a variety of client and server platforms, and is vendor-independent. C is correct because RADIUS also is highly configurable in collecting account information on access times, who, when, and so forth.

14. **B.** Because a single DHCP server can handle up to 10,000 clients, a single server would work, but you require a backup. Cisco's "helper address" parameter acts much like the Microsoft DHCP Relay Agent and precludes the need for the additional servers per subnet.

15. **B, C.** For answer B, these two technologies combined provide a highly secure tunnel that provides data encryption from point to point and will be able to use an exchange of certificates for a high degree of authentication trust. For answer C, this scenario is currently available only for Windows 2000 server/client communication. Downlevel clients are not supported.

16. **A, C, E.** A is correct because there is no default gateway defined and a subnet mask of 255.255.0.0. C is correct because this describes the address space from the specification from Automatic Private IP Addressing (APIPA). E is correct because the client automatically checks every 5 minutes to determine whether a DHCP server has become available. If it has, it will drop the autoconfigured address and accept the DHCP offer.

    Windows 2000 uses APIPA to automate Internet Protocol (IP) configuration of network connections. By default, the computer first tries to contact a DHCP server on the network and dynamically obtain configuration for each installed network connection, as follows: If a DHCP server is reached and leased configuration is successful, TCP/IP configuration is completed.

If a DHCP server is not reached or leased config-uration fails, the computer uses APIPA to auto-matically configure TCP/IP. When APIPA is used, Windows 2000 determines an address in the Microsoft-reserved IP addressing range from `169.254.0.1` through `169.254.255.254`. This address is used until a DHCP server is located. The subnet mask is set to `255.255.0.0`.

17. **B.** To prevent rogue DHCP servers, a DHCP server must be authorized to operate. A `DHCPINFORM` is issued and must be positively acknowledged; otherwise, the DHCP service is shut down. This is known as rogue DHCP server detection.

18. **C, E.** DNS and WINS are the two correct methods for name resolution.

19. **C.** The SRV record is required in Windows 2000 Active Directory for locating servers that will pro-vide Global Catalog servers, domain controllers, and LDAP servers.

20. **B, C.** B is correct because `dnsZone` is the equiva-lent of a standard zone held as a test file. C is correct because `dnsNode` corresponds to the individual resource records. Each node contains a `dnsRecord` attribute that contains the resource record.

21. **D.** D is correct because the implementation is a single server propagating changes out to a num-ber of other servers. Push and pull replication are types of replication, not replication models.

22. **A, C.** A is correct because adding more processors increases the overall performance of the proxy server, especially if there is access control enabled and a large filter list. C is correct because the proxy array provides increased performance and availability.

23. **A, B.** A is correct because a tunnel requires a spe-cific IP or hostname to ensure a valid, secure con-nection. It can communicate only between two IP addresses or two IP subnets. B is correct because transport mode is capable of communi-cating between multiple IP addresses or hosts in order to create the IPSec tunnel.

24. **A, D.** SHA (Secure Hash Algorithm) and MD5 (Message Digest 5) are the correct answers.

> **SHA** - *n.*
> Acronym for Secure Hash Algorithm. A tech-nique that computes a 160-bit condensed rep-resentation of a message or data file, called a message digest. The SHA is used by the sender and the receiver of a message in computing and verifying a digital signature, for security purposes.

> **Message Digest Five (MD5)** –
> An industry-standard one-way, 128-bit hashing scheme, developed by RSA Data Security, Inc., and used by various Point-to-Point Protocol (PPP) vendors for encrypted authentication. A hashing scheme is a method for transforming data (for example, a pass-word) in such a way that the result is unique and cannot be changed back to its original form. The CHAP authentication protocol uses challenge-response with one-way MD5 hash-ing on the response. In this way, you can prove to the server that you know your password without actually sending the password over the network. (*Microsoft Computer Dictionary*, Fourth Edition. Microsoft Press, 1999)

25. **A, C, D.** IPSec provides machine-based authenti-cation, data encryption, and policy filters based on IP addresses.

26. **A, E.** A is correct because PPTP is supported on both Windows NT and Windows 2000. E is correct because Windows 2000 uses L2TP protocol for secure connections.

27. **B, C, E.** B, C and E are correct because Remote Authentication Dial-In User Service (RADIUS) is an industry-standard protocol based on RFCs 2138 and 2139, allowing any client platform to authenticate in a very large network environment and be centrally accounted. RADIUS is typically used by ISPs (Internet Service Providers).

28. **A, C.** A is the correct answer because the two WINS servers must replicate their database information to one another to ensure consistency and fault tolerance. C is required to ensure the clients will read the WINS database from either server in case one server goes down.

29. **A, C. D.** Three types of protocol filters you can set up on Windows 2000 to ensure secure network traffic are IP number ports, UDP ports, and TCP ports.

30. **C, D.** C is correct because shorter leases reduce network traffic and allow longer lease lengths for clients. D is correct because when you allow shorter lease lengths, your clients will renew their leases more often, therefore increasing network traffic.

31. **B.** RRAS requires blocks of 10 IPs; after 11 users are concurrently dialed in, IPs 11–20 are allocated for RRAS.

32. **C.** C is correct because the Forward Lookup uses a friendly DNS hostname to search for its IP address.

33. **A, C, D.** A is correct because Active Directory uses DNS as a locator service, resolving AD domain, site, and service names to IP Addresses. C is correct because WINS provides name resolution to DNS when it cannot resolve a name. D is correct because DHCP services can keep DNS up to date on new IP lease information, assisting with name resolution and location.

34. **A, C.** A is correct because incremental zone transfers are not supported on standard DNS implementations, making them not as flexible a solution. C is correct because Active Directory–supported DNS allows authentication between DNS zone transfers.

35. **B, D.** B and D are correct because the use of DNS Cache–only servers is recommended in environments that require static DNS records and are remote with low-speed connections.

36. **A, C, D.** TCP/IP, AppleTalk, and NWLink are all supported by RRAS.

37. **B, C.** Answers B and C are secure authentication protocols. The Extensible Authentication Protocol (EAP) is an extension to the Point-to-Point Protocol (PPP). EAP was developed in response to an increasing demand for remote access user authentication, which uses other security devices. Windows 2000 includes support for the Microsoft Challenge Handshake Authentication Protocol (MS-CHAP), also known as MS-CHAP version 1. MS-CHAP is a nonreversible, encrypted password authentication protocol.

38. **A, D.** A is correct because a RADIUS client can authenticate any RADIUS server. D is correct because you can configure any Windows 2000 router (RRAS) as a RADIUS client.

39. **A, B, C.** TCP/IP, RRAS (Routing and Remote Access Service), and IAS (Internet Authentication Service) are all requirements of a RADIUS server deployment.

40. **C, E.** TCP/IP and RRAS are the only requirements for a RADIUS client.

41. **A, C.** Any DNS service required to support Microsoft Active Directories must support Dynamic Update Protocol for DNS and SRV (Service) Locator Resource Records.

42. **A, C, D.** Scalability, performance, and availability are always the most important concerns when planning and designing any network.

43. **A, B, D.** Rogue detection is now built in, allowing automatic discovery of unauthorized DHCP servers on a network. You can implement additional DHCP server reliability by deploying a DHCP server cluster using the cluster service provided with Windows 2000 Advanced Server. For DNS integration on a Windows 2000 DHCP server, you can configure the server to perform updates on behalf of its DHCP clients to any servers that support dynamic updates.

44. **A, C, D.** A is correct because allowing non-NetBIOS clients to maintain IP address leases indefinitely enables minimal network bandwidth requirements. C is correct and enables rapid updates for name resolution, and D is correct because it enables newer DNS functionality to assist and enhance your current network environment.

45. **A, B, E.** These are the correct steps for achieving this implementation.

46. **A, C.** TCP/IP and RRAS are the minimum requirements needed to use demand-dial routing on a Windows 2000 server.

47. **B, C.** B is correct because a zero timestamp indicates that the record is not affected by the aging process and can remain without limitation until the timestamp changes or you delete them. C is

correct because only primary type zones that are loaded by DNS server services are allowed to participate in the scavenging process.

48. **A, C.** A is correct, ensuring DDNS is set up correctly. C is correct because DDNS transfers to non–Windows 2000 clients are not possible. Client computers running Windows 2000 can be configured to explicitly request that the DHCP server update only pointer (PTR) resource records used in DNS for the reverse lookup and resolution of the client's IP address to its name. These clients would then update their address (A) resource records for themselves. Clients running earlier Windows versions cannot make an explicit request for DNS dynamic update protocol preference. For these clients, the DHCP service updates both the PTR and the A resource records for the client.

49. **A, C.** The DHCP server updates both the A record and the PTR record for all Windows 2000 DHCP clients automatically.

50. **C.** After retrying to update its DNS information in 5-minute intervals twice, the client sets the update pattern to 50 minutes until it's reached the DNS server.

51. **A.** A is correct because L2TP provides better security than PPTP by providing more flexibility for secure tunneling between computers. Answer C is correct because this protocol allows address assignments, and D is correct because L2TP also provides authentication for tunneling users.

52. **C, D.** C and D are correct because the more WINS replication partners that exist, the more network traffic there will be—although if you create persistent connections, it reduces the overall traffic.

53. **C.** Circuit-level gateways provide the access control at the Session layer of the OSI model by relaying TCP connections and does no other processing or filtering of the protocol. It simply passes bytes through the firewall, providing a secure efficient environment for applications to work through.

54. **A, D.** Web and Reverse Web Proxy are the only services that support caching of commonly accessed Web sites.

55. **A, B, E.** Router interface, destination port, and source port are among the headers found on a filtered protocol stack.

56. **A, B, E.** Remote Authentication Dial-In User Service (RADIUS), Bandwidth Allocation Protocol (BAP), and Extensible Authentication Protocol (EAP) are all newly introduced protocols to the Windows platform. RADIUS is a security authentication client/server protocol widely used by Internet service providers on other remote access servers. RADIUS is the most common means of authenticating and authorizing dialup and tunneled network users. BAP is a protocol that dynamically controls the use of multilinked lines. BAP eliminates excess bandwidth by allocating lines only as they are required. The conditions under which BAP dials extra lines, when needed, and hangs up underused lines, are configured through Network and Dial-up Connections. With EAP, an arbitrary authentication mechanism validates a remote access connection (*Microsoft Computer Dictionary*, Fourth Edition. Microsoft Press, 1999).

57. **A, D.** SHA (Secure Hash Algorithm) and MD5 (Message Digest 5) are both authentication encryption methods.

58. **C.** C is correct because maintaining two DHCP servers provides the fault tolerance to produce the required results.

59. **D.** Transport mode of IPSec can talk to multiple IP addresses or hostnames.

60. **C.** C is correct because Kerberos enables secure connectivity of the consultants. Kerberos version 5 is the primary security protocol for authentication within a domain. The Kerberos version 5 protocol verifies both the identity of the user and network services (*Microsoft Computer Dictionary*. Microsoft Press, 1999).

61. **B.** Kerberos is not supported through an Internet Connection Sharing setup; you have to use Network Address Translation (NAT) instead.

62. **C.** There is a limit of 32 nodes that can be configured in a cluster.

63. **C.** The primary limitation of implementing Network Load Balancing is that you can configure only one network interface per server.

64. **C, E.** Network Address Translation (NAT) is limited by its inability to update DHCP clients with WINS server information and its inability to change source ports or IP addresses as some applications or services may require.

65. **A, D, E.** The number of DNS clients and the DNS database size and location of your primary zones greatly effect the performance of your DNS servers.

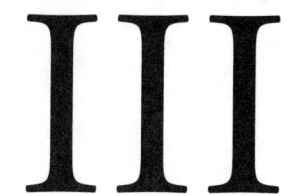

PART

III

APPENDIXES

A Glossary

B Overview of the Certification Process

C What's on the CD-ROM

D Using the *ExamGear, Training Guide Edition* Software

Glossary

10Base 10BaseT is a hardware protocol designed to operate at a maximum rate of 10Mbps.

100BaseT 100BaseT is a hardware protocol designed to operate at a maximum rate of 100Mbps.

1000BaseT 1000BaseT is a hardware protocol designed to operate at a maximum rate of 1,000Mbps (1Gbps).

A

ABR *See* Area Border Router.

Address Resolution Protocol (ARP) ARP facilitates conversion of TCP/IP network addresses to physical MAC addresses.

Application level gateway An application level gateway is a type of firewall that acts as an intermediary for clients connecting to hosts on the public network. The client and gateway servers communicate with each other at the Application layer of the International Organization for Standardization (ISO) Open Systems Interconnect (OSI) model.

Area Border Router (ABR) ABRs are OSPF-enabled routers that connect directly to the OSPF area backbone.

ARP *See* Address Resolution Protocol.

AS *See* Autonomous System.

Asynchronous Transfer Mode (ATM) ATM is a Layer 2 (Data Link) protocol that is optimized to run on switched networks. It can transmit data at up to 622Mbps.

ATM *See* Asynchronous Transfer Mode.

ATM LAN Emulation *See* LANE.

Attributes Each of the objects in the Windows 2000 Active Directory tree has a number of attributes associated with it. For example, a User account object has a name attribute, a login ID attribute, and perhaps an expiration attribute. Attributes are information that help to more completely define an Active Directory object.

Automatic Private IP Addressing (APIPA) Windows 2000 uses APIPA to automate Internet Protocol (IP) configuration of network connections. By default, the computer first tries to contact a DHCP server on the network and dynamically obtain configuration for each installed network connection, as follows: If a DHCP server is reached and leased configuration is successful, TCP/IP configuration is completed. If a DHCP server is not reached or leased configuration fails, the computer uses APIPA to automatically configure TCP/IP. When APIPA is used, Windows 2000 determines an address in the Microsoft-reserved IP addressing range from 169.254.0.1 through 169.254.255.254. This address is used until a DHCP server is located. The subnet mask is set to 255.255.0.0.

Autonomous System (AS) An AS is a logical and physical division of an OSPF-enabled network managed by a single administrative authority.

Availability Availability is the percentage of time that a network infrastructure is up and running and available for use. High availability is always a goal of effective network design. Typical availability measurements are impacted only by the values in the decimal points after 99. 99% availability is assumed; 99.99% availability is the goal.

AXFR AXFR is a mnemonic for a full DNS zone transfer.

B

Bandwidth Bandwidth refers to the data-carrying capability of the network or connection measured in bits per second.

Bandwidth Allocation Protocol (BAP) As an enhancement to multilink in Windows 2000, BAP controls the initiating or dropping of links based on demand. For example, if a dial on demand ISDN link falls below a certain threshold, BAP allows the link to be dropped. When demand increases, BAP initiates reestablishing the connection.

BAP *See* Bandwidth Allocation Protocol.

BOOTP BOOTP is a TCP/IP standard protocol for remote host booting. DHCP uses BOOTP message packets.

Business model A business model is a list of guidelines for approaching specific business goals. A business model is applied to actual business organizations to help focus the business on the most effective and efficient methods for accomplishing the goals of the organization and performing the day-to-day tasks involved in operating the business.

C

Capacity Capacity is the total amount of data that any network link may carry at a given time. This measurement is typically comparable to the bandwidth measurement, and it is often referred to in units of bits per second (bps). Capacity is typically a theoretical measurement, although it can also be reflected in real terms. You may design a network link with a theoretical capacity of 100Mbps; but given the overhead associated with some of the protocols in use on the link, the real ability to carry data across the link may be somewhat less.

Carrier Sense Multiple Access/Collision Detection (CSMA/CD) CSMA/CD is a shared access hardware protocol that relies on network hosts "listening" for data wire availability to transmit data. When host transmissions are simultaneous, a "collision" happens when two or more hosts send packets simultaneously over the same wire. This is detected by all connected hosts; hosts that have data to retransmit wait a random amount of time and attempt to send again when the wire is "clear."

Challenge-Handshake Authentication Protocol (CHAP) A classic RAS Protocol, CHAP is a way of authenticating the identity of a user on a PPP server. CHAP uses a three-way handshaking procedure and provides more security than Password Authentication Protocol (PAP). The identity of the user can be challenged at any time while a connection is open.

Change management Change management is the process of analyzing, approving, scheduling, and tracking proposed changes to a network infrastructure. Some businesses take a very formal and controlled approach to change management, and others may take a less controlled or even reckless approach to managing changes.

CHAP *See* Challenge-Handshake Authentication Protocol.

CIDR *See* Classless InterDomain Routing.

Circuit level gateway A circuit level gateway is a type of firewall that acts as an intermediary for clients connecting to hosts on the public network. The client and gateway servers communicate with each other at the Session layer of the OSI model.

Class ID In the context of Microsoft networks, a class ID is an attribute assigned to one or more IP hosts. The class ID is used to segregate DHCP clients for the purpose of custom configuration via the DHCP server.

Classless InterDomain Routing (CIDR) CIDR is a standard that defines, among other things, variable-length IP subnet masks and binary host IDs consisting of all 0s and all 1s.

Clustering Clustering is a technology in Windows 2000 that allows more than one computer to run a service. This provides fault tolerance and load balancing.

Concentrator *See* Hub.

CSMA/CD *See* Carrier Sense Multiple Access/ Collision Detection.

D

DDNS *See* Dynamic DNS.

Default gateway When an IP host is requested to send a packet that is "foreign" to its network and whose network ID is not listed in its routing table, the host sends the packet to its default gateway. If the host is not configured with a default gateway, the host reports the target address as unreachable.

Demilitarized zone (DMZ) A DMZ is an area of your network that lies between firewalls. It hosts devices that must be accessible from the outside world—for example, over the Internet—and from

inside the network. Within the demilitarized zone, there are very few protections to the servers that occupy this area.

Department of Defense (DoD) DoD is the organization responsible for the funding and initial research that resulted in many of the early network protocol standards, including the original TCP/IP specification.

Dfs junctions Junctions are the connecting points within a Dfs volume. They are the discrete file shares assigned to the Dfs volume.

DHCP *See* Dynamic Host Configuration Protocol.

DHCP lease When a DHCP server assigns an IP address to a requesting host, the time that the host may use that IP address is set to a preconfigured value, the DHCP lease duration.

DHCP scope A DHCP scope is a range of IP addresses that a DHCP server is configured to assign to requesting hosts residing on the IP subnet for that range.

DHCP superscope To facilitate a level of fault tolerance, DHCP scopes can be grouped and configured as a superscope on a DHCP server. This allows the DHCP server to respond to requests from hosts on "foreign" subnets.

Digital Subscriber Line (DSL) DSL is a digital data transmission service that is commonly implemented as a piggyback digital signal on an analog telephone line.

Directory A directory is a list of objects that comprise the network services and resources that are available on an enterprise infrastructure.

DMZ *See* Demilitarized zone.

DNS *See* Domain Name System.

DNS resolver The resolver is the portion of the IP host charged with communicating with DNS to resolve a name or address.

DNS scavenging   Scavenging is the process of cleaning stale records from a DNS zone file.

DNS zone   A DNS zone is the smallest manageable portion of a DNS name space.

DoD   *See* Department of Defense.

Domain Name System (DNS)   DNS is the TCP/IP standard for IP address/hostname resolution defined in several IETF RFCs.

DSL   *See* Digital Subscriber Line.

Dynamic DNS (DDNS)   Traditional DNS is a manual system requiring an administrator to keep the zone files up to date. Dynamic DNS enables automated update from sources such as DHCP and compliant clients and servers.

Dynamic Host Configuration Protocol (DHCP)   DHCP is the Microsoft TCP/IP standard for automated IP address and configuration information assignment to IP hosts using BOOTP.

E

EAP   *See* Extensible Authentication Protocol.

Enterprise network   The combination of all network infrastructures that comprise an entire organization is referred to as an enterprise network. Enterprise networks are made up of all LANs, WANs, and remote network connections within an organization.

Ethernet   Ethernet is the most commonly used low-level (Layer 2) protocol for LANs.

Extensible Authentication Protocol (EAP)   A Windows 2000 RAS Protocol, EAP is an extension to the Point-to-Point Protocol (PPP) that works with dial-up, PPTP, and L2TP clients. EAP allows the addition of new authentication methods known as EAP types. Both the dial-in client and the remote access server must support the same EAP type for successful authentication to occur. Windows 2000 includes an EAP infrastructure and two EAP types: EAP-MD5 CHAP and EAP-TLS. The Internet Authentication Service (IAS) implementation in Windows 2000 has the capability of passing EAP messages to a RADIUS server (EAP-RADIUS).

F

Fail-over   Fail-over is a process in which a service running on one node of a cluster automatically switches to a different node if the first node fails.

FDDI   *See* Fiber Distributed Data Interface.

Fiber Distributed Data Interface (FDDI)   FDDI protocol is a fiber-optic–based, token-passing protocol that employs a dual concentric ring topology.

File Transfer Protocol (FTP)   FTP is the protocol used to transfer files over TCP/IP-based networks.

Firewall   A firewall is a combination of hardware and software that controls the flow of traffic between network segments.

FQDN   *See* Fully Qualified Domain Name.

Fully Qualified Domain Name (FQDN)   An FQDN is the full dotted notation name for an IP host (for example, speedws.speed.com, where speedws is the IP hostname).

G

Gap analysis The gap analysis is the process of determining the differences between the existing network infrastructure and the proposed network infrastructure, based on the business and technical goals of the organization. Use the result of your gap analysis to determine which features you need to deploy, where you need to perform system and network upgrades, and where to include these changes in your design.

H

HTML *See* Hypertext Markup Language.

HTTP *See* Hypertext Transport Protocol.

Hub A hub is a device interconnecting multiple segments of network wiring. Several of those wires usually connect to individual PCs at the other end. A hub is actually a kind of repeater. When a hub receives a signal on one of the wires connected to it, it repeats that signal to every other wire that is connected to it. Sometimes a hub is referred to as a *concentrator*.

Hybrid networks Hybrid networks are networks that employ a combination of network topologies.

Hypertext Markup Language (HTML) HTML is the standard "language" used for creating documents published on the World Wide Web (WWW). HTML is not really a language, but rather a set of codes and tags used to "mark up" a document to tell a Web browser application how the document should be displayed.

Hypertext Transport Protocol (HTTP) HTTP is the protocol used to transfer hypertext and HTML information from Web servers to clients over TCP/IP-based networks.

I–K

IETF *See* Internet Engineering Task Force.

Information flow The information flow is the entire path that information follows as it moves from its source to all the points where it is needed or applied.

International Organization for Standardization (ISO) International Organization for Standardization is the governing body for international data communications standards. ISO is the creator of the OSI reference model. Although the name of the organization is the International Organization for Standardization, the acronym is ISO because standards bodies typically use two languages for their work: French and English. It has been agreed by these bodies that when referring to the organization by name, English will be used, but when using an acronym, the acronym shall represent the full name of the organization when written in French.

Internet Engineering Task Force (IETF) Internet Engineering Task Force is the standards organization for Internet-related technologies, including the TCP/IP protocol.

Internet Protocol Security (IPSec) A Windows 2000 RAS Protocol, IPSec is based on an industry standard framework that ensures secure communications over IP. IPSec uses cryptographic security services to ensure encryption of data. IPSec clients negotiate a security association that acts as a private key to encrypt data.

IP/ATM IP/ATM refers to the process of encapsulating the IP protocol inside the ATM transport.

IPSec *See* Internet Protocol Security.

ISO *See* International Organization for Standardization.

Iterative DNS query   An iterative DNS query is a DNS request that requires the DNS server to return any matches to any portion of the query name to the requester.

IXFR   IXFR is a mnemonic for an incremental DNS zone transfer.

L

L2TP   *See* Layer-Two Tunneling Protocol.

LAN   *See* Local Area Network.

LAN Emulation Client (LEC)   A LEC is a system that functions as a client on an ATM Emulated LAN. A LEC can be a workstation or server with an ATM adapter installed, or it can be a router with an ATM interface.

LANE (LAN Emulation)   ATM LAN Emulation protocol enables ATM to interoperate with conventional networks. Windows 2000 uses LANE by acting as a LAN Emulation Client (LEC). LECs use Emulated LAN (ELAN) services provided by ATM switch vendors.

Latency   Latency is a measure of the period of time between the moment when a workstation is ready to transmit data and the moment when that data transmission is completed successfully. Some applications have a very low tolerance for latency. Increases in latency often signify that a network link is overused. High latency values are recognized by end users, and they will begin to complain about delays when accessing the network.

Layer-Two Tunneling Protocol (L2TP)   A Windows 2000 RAS Protocol, L2TP is similar to Point-to-Point Tunneling Protocol (PPTP). Both create a secure tunnel through a nonsecure network—but L2TP does not provide encryption, and PPTP does. L2TP provides security by working in close association with other protocols, such as Internet Protocol Security (IPSec), to provide tunneling and encryption.

Life cycle   The life cycle is the entire life span of a project or product from the point where it was initially conceived to the point where it is rendered obsolete and retired—and all points between.

Link-state routing protocols   A link-state routing protocol is any routing protocol that initiates routing table updates only when a change in one or more network addresses is detected.

Local Area Network (LAN)   A LAN is a collection of network devices, usually under centralized administrative control, occupying a relatively small area.

M

Management   Management is the process of managing server resources and ensuring that enough resources are available for the services to run correctly.

MARS   *See* Multicast Address Resolution Service.

Mean Time Between Failure (MTBF)   MTBF is the average time that a device operates properly before a malfunction occurs. When you're investigating appropriate hardware for network infrastructure, you want high MTBF values.

Mean Time To Repair (MTTR)   MTTR is the average time it takes to repair a device and restore it to proper operation when a malfunction has occurred. When you're implementing hardware in your network infrastructure, you want to select devices with very low MTTR values.

Microsoft Challenge Handshake Authentication Protocol (MS-CHAP)   A classic RAS Protocol, MS-CHAP is the same as CHAP, but it has been modified by Microsoft for use with NT Server RAS. MS-CHAP is a variant of CHAP that does not require a plaintext version of the password on the authenticating server. In MS-CHAP, the challenge response is calculated with an MD4 hashed version of the password and the NAS challenge. This enables authentication over the Internet to a Windows 2000 domain controller (or a Windows NT 4.0 domain controller on which the update has not been installed). MS-CHAP passwords are stored more securely at the server, but they have the same vulnerabilities to dictionary and brute force attacks as CHAP.

Microsoft Management Console (MMC)   The Microsoft Management Console (MMC) is an application that provides a basic structure under which any management tool can function. The MMC provides the menuing system and object reference template for any management tool designed to work with it. The developer of the management tool provides the specific functionality that relates to the service being managed, and the MMC provides the dialog boxes, menus, and so on. This provides each management tool the capability of being modular, and of "snapping in" to the MMC. In this way, each MMC snap-in provides the user with the same look and feel, enabling the user to become productive with all MMC snap-ins more quickly.

Monitoring   The process of monitoring a service or network resource to gather data can be used to manage the service or resource.

MS-CHAP   *See* Microsoft Challenge Handshake Authentication Protocol.

MTBF   *See* Mean Time Between Failure.

MTTR   *See* Mean Time To Repair.

Multicast Address Resolution Service (MARS) MARS facilitates conversion of TCP/IP multicast addresses to physical addresses. It works much in the same manner as Address Resolution Protocol (ARP), except that ARP is a one-for-one address resolution, and MARS resolves addresses for all hosts belonging to a multicast group.

Multicast IP Addresses   Multicast IP Addresses is an addressing scheme for distributing data to IP hosts belonging to a defined IP host group.

Multi-homed   In the context of Microsoft networks, multi-homed refers to a computer that has more than one network adapter connected to one or more network segments.

Multi-net   Multi-net refers to a physical subnet that is configured as two or more IP subnets.

N

Naming service   A naming service is any service that facilitates translation from network address to hostname and/or hostname to network address. Naming services are commonly used to enable hosts to have a user-friendly name.

Network infrastructure   Network infrastructure refers to the collection of devices that house and support the provision of all network services within an organization.

Network topology   The physical topology is a picture of the physical structure of a network, including cabling, infrastructure devices, and host devices. The logical topology is a picture of the logical flow of data.

O

Objects   As they relate to Windows 2000 Active Directory, objects are any of the various network services or resources that can be represented on the Active Directory tree. Examples of Active Directory objects are Servers, Users, and Printers.

Octet   An octet is any 8-bit number. In the context of TCP/IP, an octet is a portion of an IP address bounded by the dot notation(s). TCP/IP address notation is made up of four octets.

Open Shortest Path First (OSPF)   OSPF is a hierarchical, link-state routing protocol commonly used on large, complex networks.

Open Systems Interconnect (OSI) Reference Model
The OSI reference model is a seven-layer model depicting the levels of responsibility for different layers of networking services and the interaction between them. The OSI reference model was developed initially by the International Organization for Standardization (ISO).

OSI   *See* Open Systems Interconnect Reference Model.

OSPF   *See* Open Shortest Path First.

Outsourcing   Outsourcing refers to the process of contracting with another company to transfer all or part of the responsibility for designing, installing, administering, or maintaining the corporate network infrastructure. This is becoming a popular trend in industries where the focus of a business is not of a technical nature, and the cost of employing and developing technical expertise within the company is prohibitively high.

P

Packet Filtering Router   A packet filtering router is a type of firewall that inspects packets and either forwards or drops packets based on a set of filter rules.

PAP   *See* Password Authentication Protocol.

Password Authentication Protocol (PAP)   A classic RAS Protocol, PAP is a means of authenticating passwords that uses a two-way handshaking procedure. The validity of the password is checked at login. PAP is the most flexible (and therefore least secure) authentication protocol, because passing a plaintext password to the authentication server enables that server to compare the password with nearly any storage format.

Performance   Performance is the capability of the network infrastructure to meet the demands of network services effectively and efficiently. High performance is always a goal of effective network design.

Point-to-Point Tunneling Protocol (PPTP)   A classic RAS Protocol, PPTP is a version of Point-to-Point Protocol (PPP) that has the capability of encapsulating packets of data formatted for one network protocol in packets used by another protocol.

Ports   In terms of TCP/IP, a port is an application or protocol-specific number that indicates to a host the content and application-level destination of a TCP or UDP packet.

PPTP   *See* Point-to-Point Tunneling Protocol.

Proactive   Proactive responses to service conditions provide a solution before the problem becomes critical.

Q

Quality of Service (QoS)   Commonly referred to as QoS, this is a set of tools that enables an administrator to allocate network traffic resources, which are usually based on data type, source, or destination.

R

RADIUS *See* Remote Authentication Dial-In User Service.

Reactive Reactive responses are responses to a network condition that has occurred.

Recursive DNS query The most common type of DNS query, a recursive query forces the DNS server to respond to the requester with either a success or a failure message. This forces the DNS server to perform as many queries as necessary to remote DNS servers to provide the requester an IP address for the FQDN of the requested remote host.

Remote Authentication Dial-In User Service (RADIUS) One of the many protocols used by the Windows 2000 RAS Service, RADIUS enables the integration of an external authentication service to handle authentication and authorization to a dialup server. The Microsoft Windows 2000 implementation of RADIUS uses Internet Authentication Service (IAS).

Request for Comments (RFC) Request for Comments is a standards document created by the IETF.

Resource A resource can be any device on the internetwork that provides some functionality or holds information of value. For example, a database server is a network resource because it holds data that must be made available to network users. A DHCP server is also a network resource, because it provides the functionality to dynamically assign IP addresses to end stations, allowing them to function on the network.

RFC *See* Request for Comments.

RIP *See* Routing Information Protocol.

Routing Routing on a network infrastructure refers to the process of determining the path to any device on the internetwork from any other device on that internetwork. Devices called *routers* are used to direct network traffic along its way from the source to the intended destination by forwarding packets from one network to another.

Routing Information Protocol (RIP) RIP is a simple router communication and discovery protocol that is used to dynamically update routing tables.

S

Scalability Scalability is the ability of a network infrastructure to expand or contract in accordance with the demand for network services. Although scalability includes the infrastructure's ability to contract, this is rarely tested. Most networks simply expand and never reduce in size.

Services Services are functionality that is offered over a network infrastructure. For example, the functionality that enables hostnames to be resolved to IP addresses is offered as a service, just as the functionality that enables IP addresses to be dynamically assigned to hosts is offered as a service. There are many possible services that might be offered over a network infrastructure.

Shiva Password Authentication Protocol (SPAP) A third-party protocol used in conjunction with classic RAS Protocol, SPAP is the protocol used when connecting to a Shiva proprietary RAS device like a Shiva Land Rover RAS device.

Small Office/Home Office (SOHO) SOHO refers to small networks. (You will see a lot of this acronym from Microsoft in the future.)

Snap-ins The tools that are used to administer the various network services available under Windows 2000 are made available as MMC snap-ins. Snap-ins are provided for all Microsoft Windows 2000 Network Services. Third-party vendors of Windows 2000–compatible services can provide their own snap-ins that will work under the MMC.

SOHO *See* Small Office/Home Office.

SPAP *See* Shiva Password Authentication Protocol.

Subnetting Subnetting is the process of separating the network ID from the host ID in a given IP address by using a portion of the address that has been allocated to the host ID to logically extend the network portion of the address and divide it into subnetworks (or subnets). This is accomplished by using a subnet mask to indicate which bit positions in the IP address refer to the network portion of the address. The subnet mask is "applied" to the IP address using an arithmetic operation called a *Boolean AND*.

Switches In terms of network communications, a switch is a high-speed packet routing device that uses virtual circuits to forward data at either the Data Link (layer 2) or the Network (layer 3) level.

T–U

TCO *See* Total Cost of Ownership.

Throughput Throughput refers to the amount of data that an end station can successfully transmit across a network link. One goal of efficient network design is to maximize throughput for all end stations.

Time To Live (TTL) A TTL value is assigned to many types of records, such as routing table records and IP packets. TTLs contain some value that indicates when the item should be discarded.

Token Ring Token Ring is a token-passing protocol that operates using unshielded twisted-pair (UTP) or shielded twisted-pair (STP) cabling and a logical ring configuration. Token Ring can support data transmissions of up to 100Mbps (megabits per second), but is more typically implemented at speeds of 16Mbps or 4Mbps.

Total Cost of Ownership (TCO) The TCO refers to the sum of all costs associated with the ownership and operation of a network infrastructure. These costs include both direct costs, such as purchase costs of the physical equipment, and indirect costs, such as the labor costs associated with maintaining a help desk and training users.

TTL *See* Time To Live.

V

Virtual private network (VPN) A VPN is one that links two or more private locations through links on a public network. The links between each private location are encrypted and made secure so that they appear to be on the company's own private network infrastructure. The costs associated with using a public network infrastructure are significantly lower than purchasing dedicated private links between the same remote locations.

W–Z

Wide Area Network (WAN) A WAN spans a large geographical area. WANs are typically connected through lower bandwidth links than Local Area Networks (LANs), though this is not always the case. Most often, WAN links are leased lines that cross through a carrier network, and they are subject to administrative control outside that of the company that has leased them.

Windows Internet Name Service (WINS) WINS is a NetBIOS-based name service for IP address resolution.

Zone transfer Zone transfer is the process of resource record (zone file) update between DNS zones.

Overview of the Certification Process

You must pass rigorous certification exams to become a Microsoft Certified Professional. These closed-book exams provide a valid and reliable measure of your technical proficiency and expertise. Developed in consultation with computer industry professionals who have experience with Microsoft products in the workplace, the exams are conducted by two independent organizations. Sylvan Prometric offers the exams at more than 2,000 authorized Prometric Testing Centers around the world. Virtual University Enterprises (VUE) testing centers offer exams at more than 1,400 locations as well.

To schedule an exam, call Sylvan Prometric Testing Centers at 800-755-EXAM (3926) (or register online at http://www.2test.com/register) or VUE at 888-837-8734 (or register online at http://www.vue.com/ms/msexam.html). At the time of this writing, Microsoft offered eight types of certification, each based on a specific area of expertise. Please check the Microsoft Certified Professional Web site for the most up-to-date information (www.microsoft.com/mcp/).

TYPES OF CERTIFICATION

◆ **Microsoft Certified Professional (MCP).** Persons with this credential are qualified to support at least one Microsoft product. Candidates can take elective exams to develop areas of specialization. MCP is the base level of expertise.

◆ **Microsoft Certified Professional+Internet (MCP+Internet).** Persons with this credential are qualified to plan security, install and configure server products, manage server resources, extend service to run CGI scripts or ISAPI scripts, monitor and analyze performance, and trouble-shoot problems. Expertise is similar to that of an MCP but with a focus on the Internet.

◆ **Microsoft Certified Professional+Site Building (MCP+Site Building).** Persons with this credential are qualified to plan, build, maintain, and manage Web sites using Microsoft technologies and products. The credential is appropriate for people who manage sophisticated, interactive Web sites that include database connectivity, multimedia, and searchable content.

◆ **Microsoft Certified Database Administrator (MCDBA).** Qualified individuals can derive physical database designs, develop logical data models, create physical databases, create data services by using Transact-SQL, manage and maintain databases, configure and manage security, monitor and optimize databases, and install and configure Microsoft SQL Server.

◆ **Microsoft Certified Systems Engineer (MCSE).** These individuals are qualified to analyze the business requirements for a system architecture; design solutions; deploy, install, and configure architecture components; and troubleshoot system problems.

◆ **Microsoft Certified Systems Engineer+Internet (MCSE+Internet).** Persons with this credential are qualified in the core MCSE areas and also are qualified to enhance, deploy, and manage sophisticated intranet and Internet solutions that include a browser, proxy server, host servers, database, and messaging and commerce components. An MCSE+Internet-certified professional is able to manage and analyze Web sites.

◆ **Microsoft Certified Solution Developer (MCSD).** These individuals are qualified to design and develop custom business solutions by using Microsoft development tools, technologies, and platforms. The new track includes certification exams that test the user's ability to build Web-based, distributed, and commerce applications by using Microsoft products such as Microsoft SQL Server, Microsoft Visual Studio, and Microsoft Component Services.

◆ **Microsoft Certified Trainer (MCT).** Persons with this credential are instructionally and technically qualified by Microsoft to deliver Microsoft Education Courses at Microsoft-authorized sites. An MCT must be employed by a Microsoft Solution Provider Authorized Technical Education Center or a Microsoft Authorized Academic Training site.

> **NOTE**
> For up-to-date information about each type of certification, visit the Microsoft Training and Certification Web site at http://www.microsoft.com/mcp. You can also contact Microsoft through the following sources:
>
> • Microsoft Certified Professional Program: 800-636-7544
>
> • mcp@msource.com
>
> • Microsoft Online Institute (MOLI): 800-449-9333

CERTIFICATION REQUIREMENTS

The following sections describe the requirements for the various types of Microsoft certifications.

> **NOTE**
> An asterisk following an exam in any of the following lists means that it is slated for retirement.

How to Become a Microsoft Certified Professional

To become certified as an MCP, you need only pass any Microsoft exam (with the exceptions of Networking Essentials, #70-058* and Microsoft Windows 2000 Accelerated Exam for MCPs Certified on Microsoft Windows NT 4.0, #70-240).

How to Become a Microsoft Certified Professional+Internet

To become an MCP specializing in Internet technology, you must pass the following exams:

◆ Internetworking with Microsoft TCP/IP on Microsoft Windows NT 4.0, #70-059*

◆ Implementing and Supporting Microsoft Windows NT Server 4.0, #70-067*

◆ Implementing and Supporting Microsoft Internet Information Server 3.0 and Microsoft Index Server 1.1, #70-077*

 OR Implementing and Supporting Microsoft Internet Information Server 4.0, #70-087*

How to Become a Microsoft Certified Professional+Site Building

To be certified as an MCP+Site Building, you need to pass two of the following exams:

◆ Designing and Implementing Web Sites with Microsoft FrontPage 98, #70-055

◆ Designing and Implementing Commerce Solutions with Microsoft Site Server 3.0, Commerce Edition, #70-057

◆ Designing and Implementing Web Solutions with Microsoft Visual InterDev 6.0, #70-152

How to Become a Microsoft Certified Database Administrator

There are two MCDBA tracks, one tied to Windows 2000, the other based on Windows NT 4.0.

Windows 2000 Track

To become an MCDBA in the Windows 2000 track, you must pass three core exams and one elective exam.

Core Exams

The core exams required to become an MCDBA in the Windows 2000 track are as follows:

◆ Installing, Configuring, and Administering Microsoft Windows 2000 Server, #70-215

 OR Microsoft Windows 2000 Accelerated Exam for MCPs Certified on Microsoft Windows NT 4.0, #70-240 (only for those who have passed exams #70-067*, #70-068*, and #70-073*)

◆ Administering Microsoft SQL Server 7.0, #70-028

◆ Designing and Implementing Databases with Microsoft SQL Server 7.0, #70-029

Elective Exams

You must also pass one elective exam from the following list:

◆ Implementing and Administering a Microsoft Windows 2000 Network Infrastructure, #70-216 (only for those who have *not* already passed #70-067*, #70-068*, and #70-073*)

OR Microsoft Windows 2000 Accelerated Exam for MCPs Certified on Microsoft Windows NT 4.0, #70-240 (only for those who have passed exams #70-067*, #70-068*, and #70-073*)

◆ Designing and Implementing Distributed Applications with Microsoft Visual C++ 6.0, #70-015

◆ Designing and Implementing Data Warehouses with Microsoft SQL Server 7.0 and Microsoft Decision Support Services 1.0, #70-019

◆ Implementing and Supporting Microsoft Internet Information Server 4.0, #70-087*

◆ Designing and Implementing Distributed Applications with Microsoft Visual FoxPro 6.0, #70-155

◆ Designing and Implementing Distributed Applications with Microsoft Visual Basic 6.0, #70-175

Windows NT 4.0 Track

To become an MCDBA in the Windows NT 4.0 track, you must pass four core exams and one elective exam.

Core Exams

The core exams required to become an MCDBA in the Windows NT 4.0 track are as follows:

◆ Administering Microsoft SQL Server 7.0, #70-028

◆ Designing and Implementing Databases with Microsoft SQL Server 7.0, #70-029

◆ Implementing and Supporting Microsoft Windows NT Server 4.0, #70-067*

◆ Implementing and Supporting Microsoft Windows NT Server 4.0 in the Enterprise, #70-068*

Elective Exams

You must also pass one elective exam from the following list:

◆ Designing and Implementing Distributed Applications with Microsoft Visual C++ 6.0, #70-015

◆ Designing and Implementing Data Warehouses with Microsoft SQL Server 7.0 and Microsoft Decision Support Services 1.0, #70-019

◆ Internetworking with Microsoft TCP/IP on Microsoft Windows NT 4.0, #70-059*

◆ Implementing and Supporting Microsoft Internet Information Server 4.0, #70-087*

◆ Designing and Implementing Distributed Applications with Microsoft Visual FoxPro 6.0, #70-155

◆ Designing and Implementing Distributed Applications with Microsoft Visual Basic 6.0, #70-175

How to Become a Microsoft Certified Systems Engineer

You must pass operating system exams and two elective exams to become an MCSE. The MCSE certification path is divided into two tracks: Windows 2000 and Windows NT 4.0.

The following lists show the core requirements for the Windows 2000 and Windows NT 4.0 tracks and the electives.

Windows 2000 Track

The Windows 2000 track requires you to pass five core exams (or an accelerated exam and another core exam). You must also pass two elective exams.

Core Exams

The Windows 2000 track core requirements for MCSE certification include the following for those who have *not* passed #70-067, #70-068, and #70-073:

- ◆ Installing, Configuring, and Administering Microsoft Windows 2000 Professional, #70-210

- ◆ Installing, Configuring, and Administering Microsoft Windows 2000 Server, #70-215

- ◆ Implementing and Administering a Microsoft Windows 2000 Network Infrastructure, #70-216

- ◆ Implementing and Administering a Microsoft Windows 2000 Directory Services Infrastructure, #70-217

The Windows 2000 Track core requirements for MCSE certification include the following for those who have passed #70-067*, #70-068*, and #70-073*:

- ◆ Microsoft Windows 2000 Accelerated Exam for MCPs Certified on Microsoft Windows NT 4.0, #70-240

All candidates must pass one of these three additional core exams:

- ◆ Designing a Microsoft Windows 2000 Directory Services Infrastructure, #70-219

  OR Designing Security for a Microsoft Windows 2000 Network, #70-220

  OR Designing a Microsoft Windows 2000 Infrastructure, #70-221

Elective Exams

Any MCSE elective exams that are current (not slated for retirement) when the Windows 2000 core exams are released can be used to fulfill the requirement of two elective exams. In addition, core exams #70-219,

#70-220, and #70-221 can be used as elective exams, as long as they are not already being used to fulfill the "additional core exams" requirement outlined previously. Exam #70-222 (Upgrading from Microsoft Windows NT 4.0 to Microsoft Windows 2000), can also be used to fulfill this requirement. Finally, selected third-party certifications that focus on interoperability may count for this requirement. Watch the Microsoft MCP Web site (www.microsoft.com/mcp) for more information on these third-party certifications.

Windows NT 4.0 Track

The Windows NT 4.0 track is also organized around core and elective exams.

Core Exams

The four Windows NT 4.0 track core requirements for MCSE certification are as follows:

- ◆ Implementing and Supporting Microsoft Windows NT Server 4.0, #70-067*

- ◆ Implementing and Supporting Microsoft Windows NT Server 4.0 in the Enterprise, #70-068*

- ◆ Microsoft Windows 3.1, #70-030*

  OR Microsoft Windows for Workgroups 3.11, #70-048*

  OR Implementing and Supporting Microsoft Windows 95, #70-064*

  OR Implementing and Supporting Microsoft Windows NT Workstation 4.0, #70-073*

  OR Implementing and Supporting Microsoft Windows 98, #70-098

- ◆ Networking Essentials, #70-058*

Elective Exams

For the Windows NT 4.0 track, you must pass two of the following elective exams for MCSE certification:

◆ Implementing and Supporting Microsoft SNA Server 3.0, #70-013

 OR Implementing and Supporting Microsoft SNA Server 4.0, #70-085

◆ Implementing and Supporting Microsoft Systems Management Server 1.2, #70-018

 OR Implementing and Supporting Microsoft Systems Management Server 2.0, #70-086

◆ Designing and Implementing Data Warehouse with Microsoft SQL Server 7.0, #70-019

◆ Microsoft SQL Server 4.2 Database Implementation, #70-021*

 OR Implementing a Database Design on Microsoft SQL Server 6.5, #70-027

 OR Implementing a Database Design on Microsoft SQL Server 7.0, #70-029

◆ Microsoft SQL Server 4.2 Database Administration for Microsoft Windows NT, #70-022*

 OR System Administration for Microsoft SQL Server 6.5 (or 6.0), #70-026

 OR System Administration for Microsoft SQL Server 7.0, #70-028

◆ Microsoft Mail for PC Networks 3.2-Enterprise, #70-037*

◆ Internetworking with Microsoft TCP/IP on Microsoft Windows NT (3.5–3.51), #70-053*

 OR Internetworking with Microsoft TCP/IP on Microsoft Windows NT 4.0, #70-059*

◆ Implementing and Supporting Web Sites Using Microsoft Site Server 3.0, #70-056

◆ Implementing and Supporting Microsoft Exchange Server 4.0, #70-075*

 OR Implementing and Supporting Microsoft Exchange Server 5.0, #70-076

 OR Implementing and Supporting Microsoft Exchange Server 5.5, #70-081

◆ Implementing and Supporting Microsoft Internet Information Server 3.0 and Microsoft Index Server 1.1, #70-077*

 OR Implementing and Supporting Microsoft Internet Information Server 4.0, #70-087*

◆ Implementing and Supporting Microsoft Proxy Server 1.0, #70-078

 OR Implementing and Supporting Microsoft Proxy Server 2.0, #70-088

◆ Implementing and Supporting Microsoft Internet Explorer 4.0 by Using the Internet Explorer Resource Kit, #70-079

 OR Implementing and Supporting Microsoft Internet Explorer 5.0 by Using the Internet Explorer Resource Kit, #70-080

◆ Designing a Microsoft Windows 2000 Directory Services Infrastructure, #70-219

◆ Designing Security for a Microsoft Windows 2000 Network, #70-220

◆ Designing a Microsoft Windows 2000 Infrastructure, #70-221

◆ Upgrading from Microsoft Windows NT 4.0 to Microsoft Windows 2000, #70-222

How to Become a Microsoft Certified Systems Engineer+Internet

You must pass seven operating system exams and two elective exams to become an MCSE specializing in Internet technology.

Core Exams

The following seven core exams are required for MCSE+Internet certification:

◆ Networking Essentials, #70-058*

◆ Internetworking with Microsoft TCP/IP on Microsoft Windows NT 4.0, #70-059*

◆ Implementing and Supporting Microsoft Windows 95, #70-064*

   OR Implementing and Supporting Microsoft Windows NT Workstation 4.0, #70-073*

   OR Implementing and Supporting Microsoft Windows 98, #70-098

◆ Implementing and Supporting Microsoft Windows NT Server 4.0, #70-067*

◆ Implementing and Supporting Microsoft Windows NT Server 4.0 in the Enterprise, #70-068*

◆ Implementing and Supporting Microsoft Internet Information Server 3.0 and Microsoft Index Server 1.1, #70-077*

   OR Implementing and Supporting Microsoft Internet Information Server 4.0, #70-087*

◆ Implementing and Supporting Microsoft Internet Explorer 4.0 by Using the Internet Explorer Resource Kit, #70-079

   OR Implementing and Supporting Microsoft Internet Explorer 5.0 by Using the Internet Explorer Resource Kit, #70-080

Elective Exams

You must also pass two of the following elective exams for MCSE+Internet certification:

◆ System Administration for Microsoft SQL Server 6.5, #70-026

   OR Administering Microsoft SQL Server 7.0, #70-028

◆ Implementing a Database Design on Microsoft SQL Server 6.5, #70-027

   OR Designing and Implementing Databases with Microsoft SQL Server 7.0, #70-029

◆ Implementing and Supporting Web Sites Using Microsoft Site Server 3.0, # 70-056

◆ Implementing and Supporting Microsoft Exchange Server 5.0, #70-076

   OR Implementing and Supporting Microsoft Exchange Server 5.5, #70-081

◆ Implementing and Supporting Microsoft Proxy Server 1.0, #70-078

   OR Implementing and Supporting Microsoft Proxy Server 2.0, #70-088

◆ Implementing and Supporting Microsoft SNA Server 4.0, #70-085

How to Become a Microsoft Certified Solution Developer

The MCSD certification has undergone substantial revision. Listed below are the requirements for the new track (available fourth quarter 1998) as well as the old.

New Track

For the new track, you must pass three core exams and one elective exam.

Core Exams

The core exams are as follows. You must pass one exam in each of the following groups:

Desktop Applications Development (one required)

◆ Designing and Implementing Desktop Applications with Microsoft Visual C++ 6.0, #70-016

   OR Designing and Implementing Desktop Applications with Microsoft Visual FoxPro 6.0, #70-156

   OR Designing and Implementing Desktop Applications with Microsoft Visual Basic 6.0, #70-176

Distributed Applications Development (one required)

◆ Designing and Implementing Distributed Applications with Microsoft Visual C++ 6.0, #70-015

   OR Designing and Implementing Distributed Applications with Microsoft Visual FoxPro 6.0, #70-155

   OR Designing and Implementing Distributed Applications with Microsoft Visual Basic 6.0, #70-175

Solution Architecture (required)

◆ Analyzing Requirements and Defining Solution Architectures, #70-100

Elective Exam

You must pass one of the following elective exams:

◆ Designing and Implementing Distributed Applications with Microsoft Visual C++ 6.0, #70-015

◆ Designing and Implementing Desktop Applications with Microsoft Visual C++ 6.0, #70-016

◆ Designing and Implementing Data Warehouses with Microsoft SQL Server 7.0, #70-019

◆ Developing Applications with C++ Using the Microsoft Foundation Class Library, #70-024

◆ Implementing OLE in Microsoft Foundation Class Applications, #70-025

◆ Implementing a Database Design on Microsoft SQL Server 6.5, #70-027

◆ Implementing a Database Design on Microsoft SQL Server 7.0, #70-029

◆ Designing and Implementing Web Sites with Microsoft FrontPage 98, #70-055

◆ Designing and Implementing Commerce Solutions with Microsoft Site Server 3.0, Commerce Edition, #70-057

◆ Programming with Microsoft Visual Basic 4.0, #70-065*

◆ Application Development with Microsoft Access for Windows 95 and the Microsoft Access Developer's Toolkit, #70-069

◆ Designing and Implementing Solutions with Microsoft Office 2000 and Microsoft Visual Basic for Applications, #70-091

◆ Designing and Implementing Database Applications with Microsoft Access 2000, #70-097

◆ Designing and Implementing Collaborative Solutions with Microsoft Outlook 2000 and Microsoft Exchange Server 5.5, #70-105

◆ Designing and Implementing Web Solutions with Microsoft Visual InterDev 6.0, #70-152

◆ Designing and Implementing Distributed Applications with Microsoft Visual FoxPro 6.0, #70-155

◆ Designing and Implementing Desktop Applications with Microsoft Visual FoxPro 6.0, #70-156

◆ Developing Applications with Microsoft Visual Basic 5.0, #70-165

◆ Designing and Implementing Distributed Applications with Microsoft Visual Basic 6.0, #70-175

◆ Designing and Implementing Desktop Applications with Microsoft Visual Basic 6.0, #70-176

Old Track

For the old track, you must pass two core technology exams and two elective exams for MCSD certification. The following lists show the required technology exams and elective exams needed for MCSD certification.

Core Exams

You must pass the following two core technology exams to qualify for MCSD certification:

◆ Microsoft Windows Architecture I, #70-160*

◆ Microsoft Windows Architecture II, #70-161*

Elective Exams

You must also pass two of the following elective exams to become an MSCD:

◆ Designing and Implementing Distributed Applications with Microsoft Visual C++ 6.0, #70-015

◆ Designing and Implementing Desktop Applications with Microsoft Visual C++ 6.0, #70-016

◆ Designing and Implementing Data Warehouses with Microsoft SQL Server 7.0, #70-019

◆ Microsoft SQL Server 4.2 Database Implementation, #70-021*

  OR Implementing a Database Design on Microsoft SQL Server 6.5, #70-027

  OR Implementing a Database Design on Microsoft SQL Server 7.0, #70-029

◆ Developing Applications with C++ Using the Microsoft Foundation Class Library, #70-024

◆ Implementing OLE in Microsoft Foundation Class Applications, #70-025

◆ Programming with Microsoft Visual Basic 4.0, #70-065

  OR Developing Applications with Microsoft Visual Basic 5.0, #70-165

  OR Designing and Implementing Distributed Applications with Microsoft Visual Basic 6.0, #70-175

◆ Designing and Implementing Desktop Applications with Microsoft Visual Basic 6.0, #70-176

◆ Microsoft Access 2.0 for Windows-Application Development, #70-051*

OR Microsoft Access for Windows 95 and the Microsoft Access Development Toolkit, #70-069

OR Designing and Implementing Database Applications with Microsoft Access 2000, #70-097

◆ Developing Applications with Microsoft Excel 5.0 Using Visual Basic for Applications, #70-052*

◆ Programming in Microsoft Visual FoxPro 3.0 for Windows, #70-054*

OR Designing and Implementing Distributed Applications with Microsoft Visual FoxPro 6.0, #70-155

OR Designing and Implementing Desktop Applications with Microsoft Visual FoxPro 6.0, #70-156

◆ Designing and Implementing Web Sites with Microsoft FrontPage 98, #70-055

◆ Designing and Implementing Commerce Solutions with Microsoft Site Server 3.0, Commerce Edition, #70-057

◆ Designing and Implementing Solutions with Microsoft Office (code-named Office 9) and Microsoft Visual Basic for Applications, #70-091

◆ Designing and Implementing Collaborative Solutions with Microsoft Outlook 2000 and Microsoft Exchange Server 5.5, #70-105

◆ Designing and Implementing Web Solutions with Microsoft Visual InterDev 6.0, #70-152

Becoming a Microsoft Certified Trainer

To fully understand the requirements and process for becoming an MCT, you need to obtain the Microsoft Certified Trainer Guide document from the following Web site:

http://www.microsoft.com/mcp/certstep/mct.htm

At this site, you can read the document as a Web page or display and download it as a Word file. The MCT Guide explains the process for becoming an MCT. The general steps for the MCT certification are as follows:

1. Complete and mail a Microsoft Certified Trainer application to Microsoft. You must include proof of your skills for presenting instructional material. The options for doing so are described in the MCT Guide.

2. Obtain and study the Microsoft Trainer Kit for the Microsoft Official Curricula (MOC) courses for which you want to be certified. Microsoft Trainer Kits can be ordered by calling 800-688-0496 in North America. Those of you in other regions should review the MCT Guide for information on how to order a Trainer Kit.

3. Take and pass any required prerequisite MCP exam(s) to measure your current technical knowledge.

4. Prepare to teach a MOC course. Begin by attending the MOC course for which you want to be certified. This is required so that you understand how the course is structured, how labs are completed, and how the course flows.

5. Pass any additional exam requirement(s) to measure any additional product knowledge that pertains to the course.

6. Submit your course preparation checklist to Microsoft so that your additional accreditation may be processed and reflect on your transcript.

> **WARNING**
>
> You should consider the preceding steps a general overview of the MCT certification process. The precise steps that you need to take are described in detail on the Web site mentioned earlier. Do not misinterpret the preceding steps as the exact process you must undergo.

If you are interested in becoming an MCT, you can obtain more information by visiting the Microsoft Certified Training Web site at `http://www.microsoft.com/train_cert/mct/` or by calling 800-688-0496.

What's on the CD-ROM

This appendix is a brief rundown of what you'll find on the CD-ROM that comes with this book. For a more detailed description of the newly developed *ExamGear, Training Guide Edition* exam simulation software, see Appendix D, "Using the *ExamGear, Training Guide Edition* Software." All items on the CD-ROM are easily accessible from the simple interface. In addition to *ExamGear, Training Guide Edition*, the CD-ROM includes the electronic version of the book in Portable Document Format (PDF), several utility and application programs, and a complete listing of test objectives and where they are covered in the book.

EXAMGEAR, TRAINING GUIDE EDITION

ExamGear is an exam environment developed exclusively for Que Certification. It is, we believe, the best exam software available. In addition to providing a means of evaluating your knowledge of the *Training Guide* material, *ExamGear, Training Guide Edition* features several innovations that help you to improve your mastery of the subject matter.

For example, the practice tests allow you to check your score by exam area or category to determine which topics you need to study more. In another mode, *ExamGear, Training Guide Edition* allows you to obtain immediate feedback on your responses in the form of explanations for the correct and incorrect answers.

Although *ExamGear, Training Guide Edition* exhibits most of the full functionality of the retail version of *ExamGear*, including the exam format and question types, this special version is written to the Training Guide content. It is designed to aid you in assessing how well you understand the Training Guide material and enable you to experience most of the question formats you will see on the actual exam. It is not as complete a simulation of the exam as the full *ExamGear* retail product. It also does not include some of the features of the full retail product, such as access to the mentored discussion groups. However, it serves as an excellent method for assessing your knowledge of the Training Guide content and gives you the experience of taking an electronic exam.

Again, for a more complete description of *ExamGear, Training Guide Edition* features, see Appendix D.

EXCLUSIVE ELECTRONIC VERSION OF TEXT

The CD-ROM also contains the electronic version of this book in Portable Document Format (PDF). The electronic version comes complete with all figures as they appear in the book. You will find that the search capabilities of the reader come in handy for study and review purposes.

COPYRIGHT INFORMATION AND DISCLAIMER

Que Certification's *ExamGear* test simulator:
Copyright © 2002 by Que Certification. All rights reserved. Made in U.S.A.

Using the *ExamGear, Training Guide Edition* Software

This training guide includes a special version of *ExamGear*—a revolutionary new test engine that is designed to give you the best in certification exam preparation. *ExamGear* offers sample and practice exams for many of today's most in-demand technical certifications. This special Training Guide edition is included with this book as a tool to utilize in assessing your knowledge of the Training Guide material while also providing you with the experience of taking an electronic exam.

In the rest of this appendix, we describe in detail what *ExamGear, Training Guide Edition* is, how it works, and what it can do to help you prepare for the exam. Note that although the Training Guide edition includes nearly all the test simulation functions of the complete, retail version, the questions focus on the Training Guide content rather than on simulating the actual Microsoft exam. Also, this version does not offer the same degree of online support that the full product does.

EXAM SIMULATION

One of the main functions of *ExamGear, Training Guide Edition* is exam simulation. To prepare you to take the actual vendor certification exam, the Training Guide edition of this test engine is designed to offer the most effective exam simulation available.

Question Quality

The questions provided in the *ExamGear, Training Guide Edition* simulations are written to high standards of technical accuracy. The questions tap the content of the Training Guide chapters and help you review and assess your knowledge before you take the actual exam.

Interface Design

The *ExamGear, Training Guide Edition* exam simulation interface provides you with the experience of taking an electronic exam. This enables you to effectively prepare for taking the actual exam by making the test experience a familiar one. Using this test simulation can help eliminate the sense of surprise or anxiety that you might experience in the testing center, because you will already be acquainted with computerized testing.

STUDY TOOLS

ExamGear provides you with several learning tools to help prepare you for the actual certification exam.

Effective Learning Environment

The *ExamGear, Training Guide Edition* interface provides a learning environment that not only tests you through the computer, but also teaches the material you need to know to pass the certification exam. Each question comes with a detailed explanation of the correct answer and provides reasons why the other options were incorrect. This information helps to reinforce the knowledge you have already and also provides practical information you can use on the job.

Automatic Progress Tracking

ExamGear, Training Guide Edition automatically tracks your progress as you work through the test questions. From the Item Review tab (discussed in detail later in this appendix), you can see at a glance how well you are scoring by objective, by unit, or on a question-by-question basis (see Figure D.1). You can also configure *ExamGear* to drill you on the skills you need to work on most.

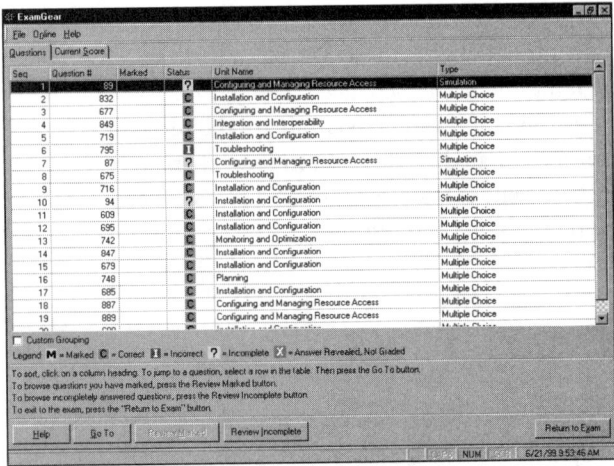

FIGURE D.1
Item review.

How *EXAMGEAR, TRAINING GUIDE EDITION* WORKS

ExamGear comprises two main elements: the interface and the database. The *interface* is the part of the program that you use to study and to run practice tests. The *database* stores all the question-and-answer data.

Interface

The *ExamGear, Training Guide Edition* interface is designed to be easy to use and provides the most effective study method available. The interface enables you to select from among the following modes:

◆ **Study Mode.** In this mode, you can select the number of questions you want to see and the time you want to allow for the test. You can select questions from all the chapters or from specific chapters. This enables you to reinforce your knowledge in a specific area or strengthen your knowledge in areas pertaining to a specific objective. During the exam, you can display the correct answer to each question along with an explanation of why it is correct.

◆ **Practice Exam.** In this mode, you take an exam that is designed to simulate the actual certification exam. Questions are selected from all test-objective groups. The number of questions selected and the time allowed are set to match those parameters of the actual certification exam.

◆ **Adaptive Exam.** In this mode, you take an exam simulation using the adaptive testing technique. Questions are taken from all test-objective groups. The questions are presented in a way that ensures your mastery of all the test objectives. After you have a passing score or if you reach a point where it is statistically impossible for you to pass, the exam is ended. This method provides a rapid assessment of your readiness for the actual exam.

Database

The *ExamGear, Training Guide Edition* database stores a group of test questions along with answers and explanations. At least three databases are included for each Training Guide edition product. One includes the questions from the ends of the chapters. Another includes the questions from the Practice Exam. The third is a database of new questions that have not appeared in the book. Additional exam databases may also be available for purchase online and are simple to download. Look ahead to the section "Obtaining Updates" in this appendix to find out how to download and activate additional databases.

INSTALLING AND REGISTERING EXAMGEAR, TRAINING GUIDE EDITION

This section provides instructions for *ExamGear, Training Guide Edition* installation and describes the process and benefits of registering your Training Guide edition product.

Requirements

ExamGear requires a computer with the following:

◆ Microsoft Windows 95, Windows 98, Windows NT 4.0, or Windows 2000.

A Pentium or later processor is recommended.

◆ Microsoft's Internet Explorer 4.01 or later version.

Internet Explorer 4.01 (or a later version) must be installed. (Even if you use a different browser, you still need to have Internet Explorer 4.01 or later installed.)

◆ A minimum of 16MB of RAM.

As with any Windows application, the more memory, the better your performance.

◆ A connection to the Internet.

An Internet connection is not required for the software to work, but it is required for online registration, product updates, downloading bonus question sets, and for unlocking other exams. These processes are described in more detail later.

Installing *ExamGear, Training Guide Edition*

Install *ExamGear, Training Guide Edition* by running the setup program that you found on the *ExamGear, Training Guide Edition* CD. Follow these instructions to install the Training Guide edition on your computer:

1. Insert the CD in your CD-ROM drive. The Autorun feature of Windows should launch the software. If you have Autorun disabled, click Start, and choose Run. Go to the root directory of the CD and choose START.EXE. Click Open and OK.

2. Click the button in the circle, and you see the welcome screen. From here you can install *ExamGear*. Click the ExamGear button to begin installation.

3. The Installation Wizard appears onscreen and prompts you with instructions to complete the installation. Select a directory on which to install *ExamGear, Training Guide Edition* (the Installation Wizard defaults to C:\Program Files\ExamGear).

4. The Installation Wizard copies the *ExamGear, Training Guide Edition* files to your hard drive, adds ExamGear, Training Guide Edition to your Program menu, adds values to your Registry, and installs test engine's DLLs to the appropriate system folders. To ensure that the process was successful, the Setup program finishes by running *ExamGear, Training Guide Edition.*

5. The Installation Wizard logs the installation process and stores this information in a file named INSTALL.LOG. This log file is used by the uninstall process in the event that you choose to remove *ExamGear, Training Guide Edition* from your computer. Because the *ExamGear* installation adds Registry keys and DLL files to your computer, it is important to uninstall the program appropriately (see the section "Removing *ExamGear, Training Guide Edition* from Your Computer").

Registering *ExamGear, Training Guide Edition*

The Product Registration Wizard appears when *ExamGear, Training Guide Edition* is started for the first time, and *ExamGear* checks at startup to see whether you are registered. If you are not registered, the main menu is hidden, and a Product Registration Wizard appears. Remember that your computer must have an Internet connection to complete the Product Registration Wizard.

The first page of the Product Registration Wizard details the benefits of registration; however, you can always elect not to register. The Show This Message at Startup Until I Register option enables you to decide whether the registration screen should appear every time *ExamGear, Training Guide Edition* is started. If you click the Cancel button, you return to the main menu. You can register at any time by selecting Online, Registration from the main menu.

The registration process is composed of a simple form for entering your personal information, including your name and address. You are asked for your level of experience with the product you are testing on and whether you purchased *ExamGear, Training Guide Edition* from a retail store or over the Internet. The information will be used by our software designers and marketing department to provide us with feedback about the usability and usefulness of this product. It takes only a few seconds to fill out and transmit the registration data. A confirmation dialog box appears when registration is complete.

After you have registered and transmitted this information to Que Certification, the registration option is removed from the pull-down menus.

Registration Benefits

Remember that registration allows you access to download updates from our FTP site using *ExamGear, Training Guide Edition* (see the later section "Obtaining Updates").

Removing *ExamGear, Training Guide Edition* from Your Computer

In the event that you elect to remove the *ExamGear, Training Guide Edition* product from your computer, an uninstall process has been included to ensure that it is removed from your system safely and completely. Follow these instructions to remove *ExamGear* from your computer:

1. Click Start, Settings, Control Panel.

2. Double-click the Add/Remove Programs icon.

3. You are presented with a list of software that is installed on your computer. Select ExamGear, Training Guide Edition from the list and click the Add/Remove button. The *ExamGear, Training Guide Edition* software is then removed from your computer.

It is important that the INSTALL.LOG file be present in the directory where you have installed *ExamGear, Training Guide Edition* should you ever choose to uninstall the product. Do not delete this file. The INSTALL.LOG file is used by the uninstall process to safely remove the files and Registry settings that were added to your computer by the installation process.

Using *ExamGear, Training Guide Edition*

ExamGear is designed to be user friendly and very intuitive, eliminating the need for you to learn some confusing piece of software just to practice answering questions. Because the software has a smooth learning curve, your time is maximized because you start practicing almost immediately.

General Description of How the Software Works

ExamGear has three modes of operation: Study Mode, Practice Exam, and Adaptive Exam (see Figure D.2).

All three sections have the same easy-to-use interface. Using Study Mode, you can hone your knowledge as well as your test-taking abilities through the use of the Show Answers option. While you are taking the test, you can expose the answers along with a brief description of why the given answers are right or wrong. This gives you the ability to better understand the material presented.

The Practice Exam section has many of the same options as Study Mode, but you cannot reveal the answers. This way, you have a more traditional testing environment with which to practice.

The Adaptive Exam questions continuously monitor your expertise in each tested topic area. If you reach a point at which you either pass or fail, the software ends the examination. As in the Practice Exam, you cannot reveal the answers.

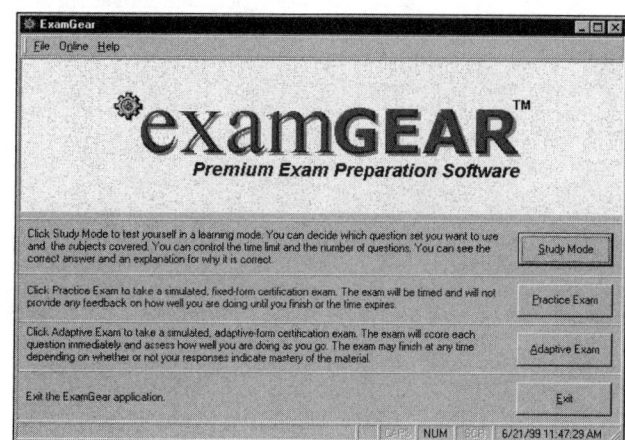

FIGURE D.2
The opening screen offers three testing modes.

Menu Options

The *ExamGear, Training Guide Edition* interface has an easy-to-use menu that provides the following options:

Menu	Command	Description
File	Print	Prints the current screen.
	Print Setup	Allows you to select the printer.
	Exit ExamGear	Exits the program.
Online	Registration	Starts the Registration Wizard and allows you to register online. This menu option is removed after you have successfully registered the product.
	Check for Product Updates	Downloads product catalog for Web-based updates.
	Web Browser	Opens the Web browser. It appears like this on the main menu, but more options appear after the browser is opened.
Help	Contents	Opens *ExamGear, Training Guide Edition's* help file.
	About	Displays information about *ExamGear, Training Guide Edition*, including serial number, registered owner, and so on.

File

The File menu allows you to exit the program and configure print options.

Online

In the Online menu, you can register *ExamGear, Training Guide Edition*, check for product updates (update the *ExamGear* executable as well as check for free, updated question sets), and surf Web pages. The Online menu is always available, except when you are taking a test.

Registration

Registration is free and allows you access to updates. Registration is the first task that *ExamGear, Training Guide Edition* asks you to perform. You will not have access to the free product updates if you do not register.

Check for Product Updates

This option takes you to *ExamGear, Training Guide Edition's* Web site, where you can update the software. Registration is required for this option to be available. You must also be connected to the Internet to use this option. The *ExamGear* Web site lists the options that have been made available since your version of *ExamGear* was installed on your computer.

Web Browser

This option provides a convenient way to start your Web browser and connect to the New Riders Web site while you are working in *ExamGear, Training Guide Edition*. Click the Exit button to leave the Web browser and return to the *ExamGear* interface.

Help

As it suggests, this menu option gives you access to *ExamGear's* help system. It also provides important information like your serial number, software version, and so on.

Starting a Study Mode Session

Study Mode enables you to control the test in ways that actual certification exams do not allow:

◆ You can set your own time limits.

◆ You can concentrate on selected skill areas (units).

◆ You can reveal answers or have each response graded immediately with feedback.

◆ You can restrict the questions you see again to those missed or those answered correctly a given number of times.

◆ You can control the order in which questions are presented (random order or in order by skill area/unit).

To begin testing in Study Mode, click the Study Mode button from the main Interface screen. You are presented with the Study Mode configuration page (see Figure D.3).

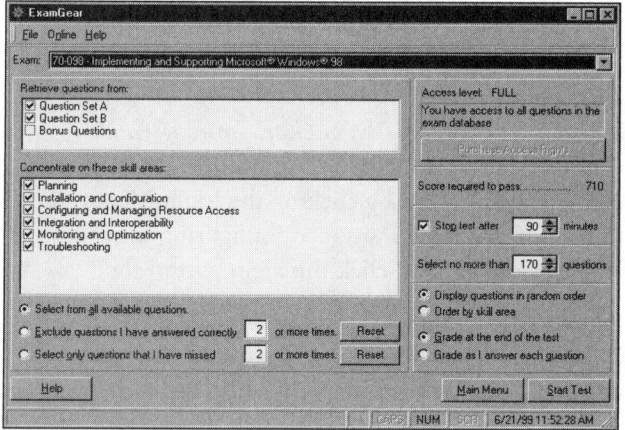

FIGURE D.3
The Study Mode configuration page.

At the top of the Study Mode configuration screen, you see the Exam drop-down list. This list shows the activated exam that you have purchased with your *ExamGear, Training Guide Edition* product, as well as any other exams you may have downloaded or any Preview exams that were shipped with your version of *ExamGear*. Select the exam with which you want to practice from the drop-down list.

Below the Exam drop-down list, you see the questions that are available for the selected exam. Each exam has at least one question set. You can select the individual

question set or any combination of the question sets if there is more than one available for the selected exam.

Below the Question Set list is a list of skill areas or chapters on which you can concentrate. These skill areas or chapters reflect the units of exam objectives defined by Microsoft for the exam. Within each skill area you will find several exam objectives. You can select a single skill area or chapter to focus on, or you can select any combination of the available skill areas/chapters to customize the exam to your individual needs.

In addition to specifying which question sets and skill areas you want to test yourself on, you can also define which questions are included in the test based on your previous progress working with the test. *ExamGear, Training Guide Edition* automatically tracks your progress with the available questions. When configuring the Study Mode options, you can opt to view all the questions available within the question sets and skill areas you have selected, or you can limit the questions presented. Choose from the following options:

◆ **Select from All Available Questions.** This option causes *ExamGear, Training Guide Edition* to present all available questions from the selected question sets and skill areas.

◆ **Exclude Questions I Have Answered Correctly *X* or More Times.** *ExamGear* offers you the option to exclude questions that you have previously answered correctly. You can specify how many times you want to answer a question correctly before *ExamGear* considers you to have mastered it (the default is two times).

◆ **Select Only Questions That I Have Missed *X* or More Times.** This option configures *ExamGear, Training Guide Edition* to drill you only on questions that you have missed repeatedly. You may specify how many times you must miss a question before *ExamGear* determines that you have not mastered it (the default is two times).

At any time, you can reset *ExamGear, Training Guide Edition*'s tracking information by clicking the Reset button for the feature you want to clear.

At the top-right side of the Study Mode configuration sheet, you can see your access level to the question sets for the selected exam. Access levels are either Full or Preview. For a detailed explanation of each of these access levels, see the section "Obtaining Updates" in this appendix.

Under your access level, you see the score required to pass the selected exam. Below the required score, you can select whether the test will be timed and how much time will be allowed to complete the exam. Select the Stop Test After 90 Minutes check box to set a time limit for the exam. Enter the number of minutes you want to allow for the test (the default is 90 minutes). Deselecting this check box allows you to take an exam with no time limit.

You can also configure the number of questions included in the exam. The default number of questions changes with the specific exam you have selected. Enter the number of questions you want to include in the exam in the Select No More than *X* Questions option.

You can configure the order in which *ExamGear, Training Guide Edition* presents the exam questions. Select from the following options:

◆ **Display Questions in Random Order.** This option is the default option. When selected, it causes *ExamGear, Training Guide Edition* to present the questions in random order throughout the exam.

◆ **Order by Skill Area.** This option causes *ExamGear* to group the questions presented in the exam by skill area. All questions for each selected skill area are presented in succession. The test progresses from one selected skill area to the next, until all the questions from each selected skill area have been presented.

ExamGear offers two options for scoring your exams. Select one of the following options:

◆ **Grade at the End of the Test.** This option configures *ExamGear, Training Guide Edition* to score your test after you have been presented with all the selected exam questions. You can reveal correct answers to a question, but if you do, that question is not scored.

◆ **Grade as I Answer Each Question.** This option configures *ExamGear* to grade each question as you answer it, providing you with instant feedback as you take the test. All questions are scored unless you click the Show Answer button before completing the question.

You can return to the *ExamGear, Training Guide Edition* main startup screen from the Study Mode configuration screen by clicking the Main Menu button. If you need assistance configuring the Study Mode exam options, click the Help button for configuration instructions.

When you have finished configuring all the exam options, click the Start Test button to begin the exam.

Starting Practice Exams and Adaptive Exams

This section describes practice exams and adaptive exams, defines the differences between these exam options and the Study Mode option, and provides instructions for starting them.

Differences Between the Practice and Adaptive Exams and Study Modes

Question screens in the practice and adaptive exams are identical to those found in Study Mode, except that the

Show Answer, Grade Answer, and Item Review buttons are not available while you are in the process of taking a practice or adaptive exam. The Practice Exam provides you with a report screen at the end of the exam. The Adaptive Exam gives you a brief message indicating whether you've passed or failed the exam.

When taking a practice exam, the Item Review screen is not available until you have answered all the questions. This is consistent with the behavior of most vendors' current certification exams. In Study Mode, Item Review is available at any time.

When the exam timer expires, or if you click the End Exam button, the Examination Score Report screen comes up.

Starting an Exam

From the *ExamGear, Training Guide Edition* main menu screen, select the type of exam you want to run. Click the Practice Exam or Adaptive Exam button to begin the corresponding exam type.

What Is an Adaptive Exam?

To make the certification testing process more efficient and valid and therefore make the certification itself more valuable, some vendors in the industry are using a testing technique called *adaptive testing*. In an adaptive exam, the exam "adapts" to your abilities by varying the difficulty level of the questions presented to you.

The first question in an adaptive exam is typically an easy one. If you answer it correctly, you are presented with a slightly more difficult question. If you answer that question correctly, the next question you see is even more difficult. If you answer the question incorrectly, however, the exam "adapts" to your skill level by presenting you with another question of equal or lesser difficulty on the same subject. If you answer that question correctly, the test begins to increase the difficulty level again. You must correctly answer several questions at a predetermined difficulty level to pass the exam. After you have done this successfully, the exam is ended and scored. If you do not reach the required level of difficulty within a predetermined time (typically 30 minutes), the exam is ended and scored.

Why Do Vendors Use Adaptive Exams?

Many vendors who offer technical certifications have adopted the adaptive testing technique. They have found that it is an effective way to measure a candidate's mastery of the test material in as little time as necessary. This reduces the scheduling demands on the test taker and allows the testing center to offer more tests per test station than they could with longer, more traditional exams. In addition, test security is greater, and this increases the validity of the exam process.

Studying for Adaptive Exams

Studying for adaptive exams is no different from studying for traditional exams. You should make sure that you have thoroughly covered all the material for each of the test objectives specified by the certification exam vendor. As with any other exam, when you take an adaptive exam, either you know the material or you don't. If you are well prepared, you will be able to pass the exam. *ExamGear, Training Guide Edition* allows you to familiarize yourself with the adaptive exam testing technique. This will help eliminate any anxiety you might experience from this testing technique and allow you to focus on learning the actual exam material.

ExamGear's Adaptive Exam

The method used to score the adaptive exam requires a large pool of questions. For this reason, you cannot use this exam in Preview mode. The adaptive exam is presented in much the same way as the practice exam. When you click the Start Test button, you begin answering questions. The adaptive exam does not allow item review, and it does not allow you to mark questions to skip and answer later. You must answer each question when it is presented.

Assumptions

This section describes the assumptions made when designing the behavior of the *ExamGear, Training Guide Edition* adaptive exam.

- ◆ You fail the test if you fail any chapter or unit, earn a failing overall score, or reach a threshold at which it is statistically impossible for you to pass the exam.

- ◆ You can fail or pass a test without cycling through all the questions.

- ◆ The overall score for the adaptive exam is Pass or Fail. However, to evaluate user responses dynamically, percentage scores are recorded for units and the overall score.

Algorithm Assumptions

This section describes the assumptions used in designing the *ExamGear, Training Guide Edition* Adaptive Exam scoring algorithm.

Unit Scores

You fail a unit (and the exam) if any unit score falls below 66%.

Overall Scores

To pass the exam, you must pass all units and achieve an overall score of 86% or higher.

You fail if the overall score percentage is less than or equal to 85% or if any unit score is less than 66%.

Inconclusive Scores

If your overall score is between 67% and 85%, it is considered to be *inconclusive*. Additional questions will be asked until you pass or fail or until it becomes statistically impossible to pass without asking more than the maximum number of questions allowed.

Question Types and How to Answer Them

Because certification exams from different vendors vary, you will face many types of questions on any given exam. *ExamGear, Training Guide Edition* presents you with different question types to allow you to become familiar with the various ways an actual exam may test your knowledge. The Solution Architectures exam, in particular, offers a unique exam format and utilizes question types other than multiple choice. This version of *ExamGear* includes cases—extensive problem descriptions running several pages in length, followed by a number of questions specific to that case. Microsoft refers to these case/question collections as *testlets*. This version of *ExamGear, Training Guide Edition* also includes regular questions that are not attached to a case study. We include these question types to make taking the actual exam easier because you will already be familiar with the steps required to answer each question type. This section describes each of the question types presented by *ExamGear* and provides instructions for answering each type.

Multiple Choice

Most of the questions you see on a certification exam are multiple choice (see Figure D.4). This question type asks you to select an answer from the list provided. Sometimes you must select only one answer, often indicated by answers preceded by option buttons (round selection buttons). At other times, multiple correct answers are possible, indicated by check boxes preceding the possible answer combinations.

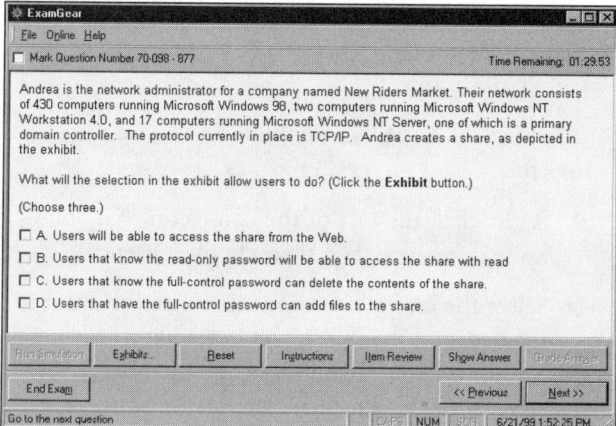

FIGURE D.4
A typical multiple-choice question.

You can use three methods to select an answer:

◆ Click the option button or check box next to the answer. If more than one correct answer to a question is possible, the answers will have check boxes next to them. If only one correct answer to a question is possible, each answer will have an option button next to it. *ExamGear, Training Guide Edition* prompts you with the number of answers you must select.

◆ Click the text of the answer.

◆ Press the alphabetic key that corresponds to the answer.

You can use any one of three methods to clear an option button:

◆ Click another option button.

◆ Click the text of another answer.

◆ Press the alphabetic key that corresponds to another answer.

You can use any one of three methods to clear a check box:

◆ Click the check box next to the selected answer.

◆ Click the text of the selected answer.

◆ Press the alphabetic key that corresponds to the selected answer.

To clear all answers, click the Reset button.

Remember that some of the questions have multiple answers that are correct. Do not let this throw you off. The *multiple correct* questions do not have one answer that is more correct than another. In the *single correct* format, only one answer is correct. *ExamGear, Training Guide Edition* prompts you with the number of answers you must select.

Drag and Drop

One form of drag and drop question is called a *drop and connect* question. These questions present you with a number of objects and connectors. The question prompts you to create relationships between the objects by using the connectors. The gray squares on the left side of the question window are the objects you can select. The connectors are listed on the right side of the question window in the Connectors box. An example is shown in Figure D.5.

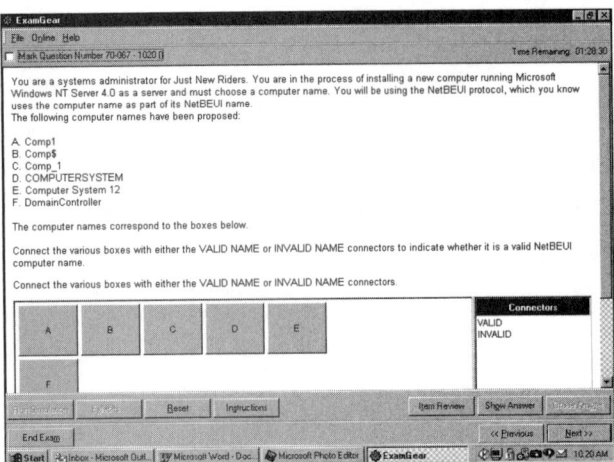

FIGURE D.5
A typical drop and connect question.

To select an object, click it with the mouse. When an object is selected, it changes color from a gray box to a white box. To drag an object, select it by clicking it with the left mouse button and holding the left mouse button down. You can move (or drag) the object to another area on the screen by moving the mouse while holding the left mouse button down.

To create a relationship between two objects, take the following actions:

1. Select an object and drag it to an available area on the screen.

2. Select another object and drag it to a location near where you dragged the first object.

3. Select the connector that you want to place between the two objects. The relationship should now appear complete. Note that to create a relationship, you must have two objects selected. If you try to select a connector without first selecting two objects, you are presented with an error message like that illustrated in Figure D.6.

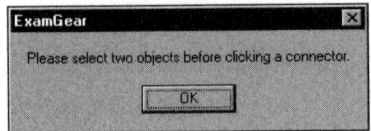

FIGURE D.6
The error message.

Initially, the direction of the relationship established by the connector is from the first object selected to the second object selected. To change the direction of the connector, right-click the connector and choose Reverse Connection.

You can use either of two methods to remove the connector:

◆ Right-click the text of the connector that you want to remove, and then choose Delete.

◆ Select the text of the connector that you want to remove, and then press the Delete key.

To remove from the screen all the relationships you have created, click the Reset button.

Keep in mind that connectors can be used multiple times. If you move connected objects, it will not change the relationship between the objects; to remove the relationship between objects, you must remove the connector that joins them. When *ExamGear, Training Guide Edition* scores a drag and drop question, only objects with connectors to other objects are scored.

Another form of drag and drop question is called the *select and place* question. Instead of creating a diagram as you do with the drop and connect question, you are asked a question about a diagram. You then drag and drop labels onto the diagram in order to correctly answer the question.

Ordered-Questions List

In the *ordered-list* question type (see Figure D.7), you are presented with a number of items and are asked to perform two tasks:

1. Build an answer list from items on the list of choices.

2. Put the items in a particular order.

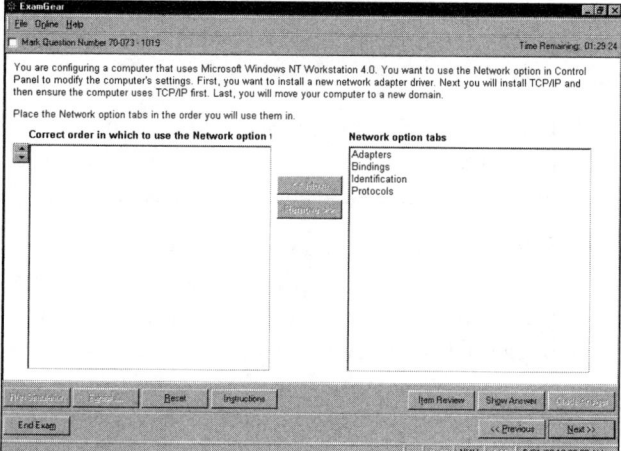

FIGURE D.7
A typical ordered-list question.

You can use any one of the following three methods to add an item to the answer list:

◆ Drag the item from the list of choices on the right side of the screen to the answer list on the left side of the screen.

◆ From the available items on the right side of the screen, double-click the item you want to add.

◆ From the available items on the right side of the screen, select the item you want to add; then click the Move button.

To remove an item from the answer list, you can use any one of the following four methods:

◆ Drag the item you want to remove from the answer list on the left side of the screen back to the list of choices on the right side of the screen.

◆ On the left side of the screen, double-click the item you want to remove from the answer list.

◆ On the left side of the screen, select the item you want to remove from the answer list, and then click the Remove button.

◆ On the left side of the screen, select the item you want to remove from the answer list, and then press the Delete key.

To remove all items from the answer list, click the Reset button.

If you need to change the order of the items in the answer list, you can do so using either of the following two methods:

◆ Drag each item to the appropriate location in the answer list.

◆ In the answer list, select the item that you want to move, and then click the up or down arrow button to move the item.

Keep in mind that items in the list can be selected twice. You may find that an ordered-list question will ask you to list in the correct order the steps required to perform a certain task. Certain steps may need to be performed more than once during the process. Don't think that after you have selected a list item, it is no longer available. If you need to select a list item more than once, you can simply select that item at each appropriate place as you construct your list.

Ordered Tree

The *ordered-tree* question type (see Figure D.8) presents you with a number of items and prompts you to create a tree structure from those items. The tree structure includes two or three levels of nodes.

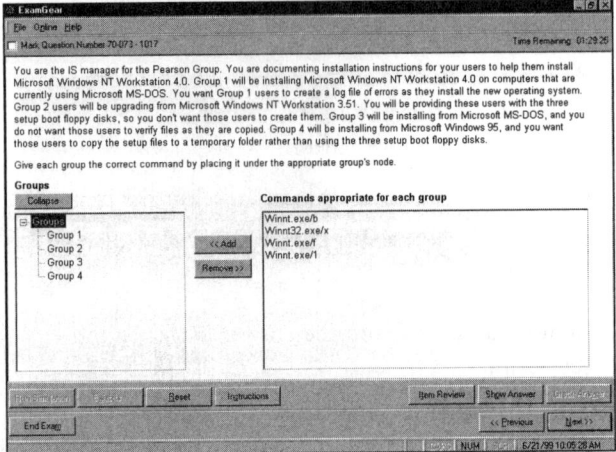

FIGURE D.8
A typical ordered-tree question.

An item in the list of choices can be added only to the appropriate node level. If you attempt to add one of the list choices to an inappropriate node level, you are presented with the error message shown in Figure D.9.

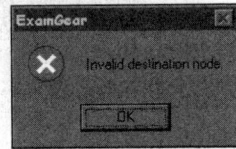

FIGURE D.9
The Invalid Destination Node error message.

Like the ordered-list question, realize that any item in the list can be selected twice. If you need to select a list item more than once, you can simply select that item for the appropriate node as you construct your tree.

Also realize that not every tree question actually requires order to the lists under each node. Think of them as simply tree questions rather than ordered-tree questions. Such questions are just asking you to categorize hierarchically. Order is not an issue.

You can use either of the following two methods to add an item to the tree:

◆ Drag the item from the list of choices on the right side of the screen to the appropriate node of the tree on the left side of the screen.

◆ Select the appropriate node of the tree on the left side of the screen. Select the appropriate item from the list of choices on the right side of the screen. Click the Add button.

You can use either of the following two methods to remove an item from the tree:

◆ Drag an item from the tree to the list of choices.

◆ Select the item and click the Remove button.

To remove from the tree structure all the items you have added, click the Reset button.

Simulations

Simulation questions (see Figure D.10) require you to actually perform a task.

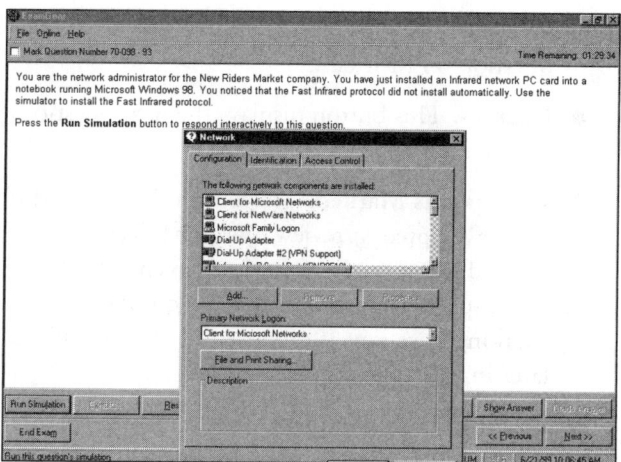

FIGURE D.10
A typical simulation question.

The main screen describes a situation and prompts you to provide a solution. When you are ready to proceed, you click the Run Simulation button in the lower-left corner. A screen or window appears on which you perform the solution. This window simulates the actual software that you would use to perform the required task in the real world. When a task requires several steps to complete, the simulator displays all the necessary screens to allow you to complete the task. When you have provided your answer by completing all the steps necessary to perform the required task, you can click the OK button to proceed to the next question.

You can return to any simulation to modify your answer. Your actions in the simulation are recorded, and the simulation appears exactly as you left it.

Simulation questions can be reset to their original state by clicking the Reset button.

Hot Spot Questions

Hot spot questions (see Figure D.11) ask you to correctly identify an item by clicking an area of the graphic or diagram displayed. To respond to the question, position the mouse cursor over a graphic. Then press the right mouse button to indicate your selection. To select another area on the graphic, you do not need to de-select the first one. Just click another region in the image.

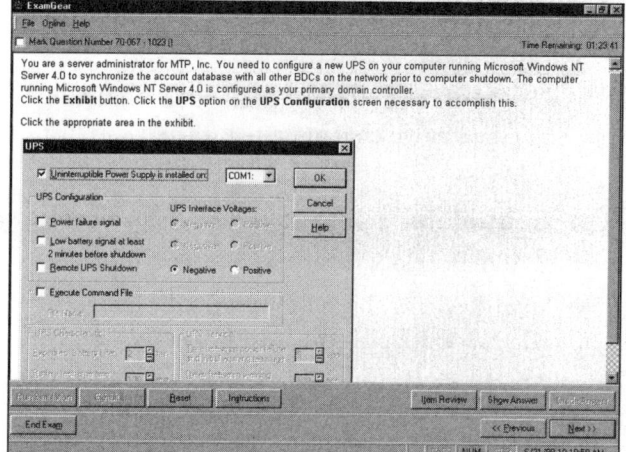

FIGURE D.11
A typical hot spot question.

Standard *ExamGear, Training Guide Edition* Options

Regardless of question type, a consistent set of clickable buttons enables you to navigate and interact with questions. The following list describes the function of each of the buttons you may see. Depending on the question type, some of the buttons will be grayed out and will be inaccessible. Buttons that are appropriate to the question type are active.

◆ **Run Simulation.** This button is enabled if the question supports a simulation. Clicking this button begins the simulation process.

◆ **Exhibits.** This button is enabled if exhibits are provided to support the question. An *exhibit* is an image, video, sound, or text file that provides supplemental information needed to answer the question. If a question has more than one exhibit, a dialog box appears, listing exhibits by name. If only one exhibit exists, the file is opened immediately when you click the Exhibits button.

◆ **Reset.** This button clears any selections you have made and returns the question window to the state in which it appeared when it was first displayed.

◆ **Instructions.** This button displays instructions for interacting with the current question type.

◆ **Item Review.** This button leaves the question window and opens the Item Review screen. For a detailed explanation of the Item Review screen, see the "Item Review" section later in this appendix.

◆ **Show Answer.** This option displays the correct answer with an explanation of why it is correct. If you choose this option, the current question will not be scored.

◆ **Grade Answer.** If Grade at the End of the Test is selected as a configuration option, this button is disabled. It is enabled when Grade as I Answer Each Question is selected as a configuration option. Clicking this button grades the current question immediately. An explanation of the correct answer is provided, just as if the Show Answer button were pressed. The question is graded, however.

◆ **End Exam.** This button ends the exam and displays the Examination Score Report screen.

◆ **<< Previous.** This button displays the previous question on the exam.

◆ **Next >>.** This button displays the next question on the exam.

◆ **<< Previous Marked.** This button is displayed if you have opted to review questions that you have marked using the Item Review screen. This button displays the previous marked question. Marking questions is discussed in more detail later in this appendix.

◆ **<< Previous Incomplete.** This button is displayed if you have opted to review questions that you have not answered using the Item Review screen. This button displays the previous unanswered question.

◆ **Next Marked >>.** This button is displayed if you have opted to review questions that you have marked using the Item Review screen. This button displays the next marked question. Marking questions is discussed in more detail later in this appendix.

◆ **Next Incomplete>>.** This button is displayed if you have opted to review questions, using the Item Review screen, that you have not answered. This button displays the next unanswered question.

Mark Question and Time Remaining

ExamGear provides you with two methods to aid in dealing with the time limit of the testing process. If you find that you need to skip a question or if you want to check the time remaining to complete the test, use one of the options discussed in the following sections.

Mark Question

Check this box to mark a question so that you can return to it later using the Item Review feature. The adaptive exam does not allow questions to be marked because it does not support item review.

Time Remaining

If the test is timed, the Time Remaining indicator is enabled. It counts down minutes remaining to complete the test. The adaptive exam does not offer this feature because it is not timed.

Item Review

The Item Review screen allows you to jump to any question. *ExamGear, Training Guide Edition* considers an *incomplete* question to be any unanswered question or any multiple-choice question for which the total number of required responses has not been selected. For example, if the question prompts for three answers and you selected only A and C, *ExamGear* considers the question to be incomplete.

The Item Review screen enables you to review the exam questions in different ways. You can enter one of two *browse sequences* (series of similar records): Browse Marked Questions or Browse Incomplete Questions. You can also create a custom grouping of the exam questions for review based on a number of criteria.

When using Item Review, if Show Answer was selected for a question while you were taking the exam, the question is grayed out in item review. The question can be answered again if you use the Reset button to reset the question status.

The Item Review screen contains two tabs. The Questions tab lists questions and question information in columns. The Current Score tab provides your exam score information, presented as a percentage for each unit and as a bar graph for your overall score.

The Item Review Questions Tab

The Questions tab on the Item Review screen (see Figure D.12) presents the exam questions and question information in a table. You can select any row you want by clicking in the grid. The Go To button is enabled whenever a row is selected. Clicking the Go To button displays the question on the selected row. You can also display a question by double-clicking that row.

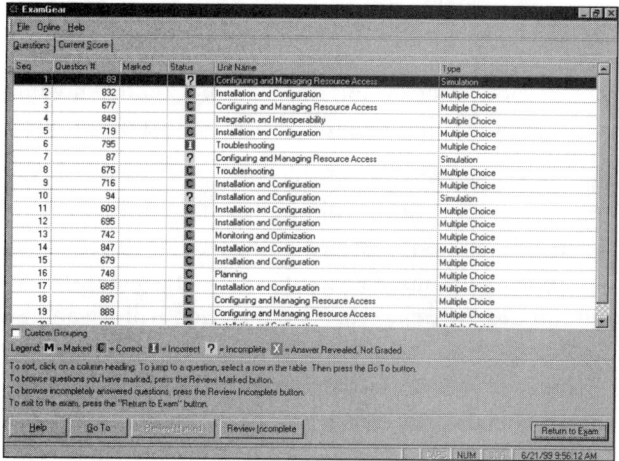

FIGURE D.12
The Questions tab on the Item Review screen.

Columns

The Questions tab contains the following six columns of information:

◆ **Seq.** Indicates the sequence number of the question as it was displayed in the exam.

◆ **Question Number.** Displays the question's identification number for easy reference.

◆ **Marked.** Indicates a question that you have marked using the Mark Question check box.

◆ **Status.** The status can be M for Marked, ? for Incomplete, C for Correct, I for Incorrect, or X for Answer Shown.

◆ **Unit Name.** The unit associated with each question.

◆ **Type.** The question type, which can be Multiple Choice, Drag and Drop, Simulation, Hot Spot, Ordered List, or Ordered Tree.

To resize a column, place the mouse pointer over the vertical line between column headings. When the mouse pointer changes to a set of right and left arrows, you can drag the column border to the left or right to make the column more or less wide. Simply click with the left mouse button and hold that button down while you move the column border in the desired direction.

The Item Review screen enables you to sort the questions on any of the column headings. Initially, the list of questions is sorted in descending order on the sequence number column. To sort on a different column heading, click that heading. You will see an arrow appear on the column heading indicating the direction of the sort (ascending or descending). To change the direction of the sort, click the column heading again.

The Item Review screen also allows you to create a *custom grouping*. This feature enables you to sort the questions based on any combination of criteria you prefer. For instance, you might want to review the question items sorted first by whether they were marked, then by the unit name, then by sequence number. The Custom Grouping feature allows you to do this. Start by checking the Custom Grouping check box (see Figure D.13). When you do so, the entire questions table shifts down a bit onscreen, and a message appears at the top of the table that reads `Drag a column header here to group by that column`.

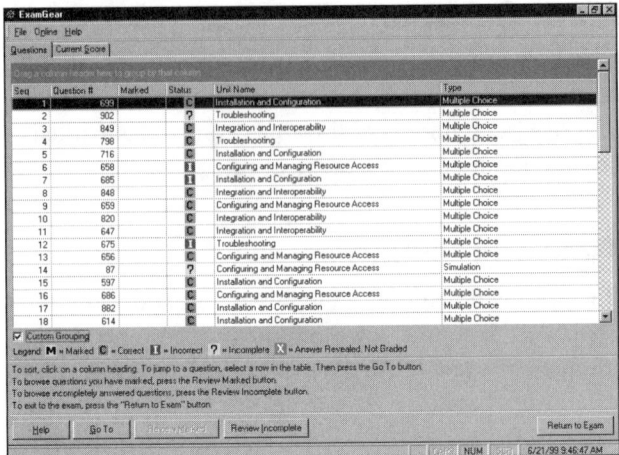

FIGURE D.13
The Custom Grouping check box allows you to create your own question sort order.

Simply click the column heading you want with the left mouse button, hold that button down, and move the mouse into the area directly above the questions table (the custom grouping area). Release the left mouse button to drop the column heading into the custom grouping area. To accomplish the custom grouping previously described, first check the Custom Grouping check box. Then, drag the Marked column heading into the custom grouping area above the question table. Next, drag the Unit Name column heading into the custom grouping area. You will see the two column headings joined together by a line that indicates the order of the custom grouping. Finally, drag the Seq column heading into the custom grouping area. This heading will be joined to the Unit Name heading by another line indicating the direction of the custom grouping.

Notice that each column heading in the custom grouping area has an arrow indicating the direction in which items are sorted under that column heading. You can reverse the direction of the sort on an individual column-heading basis using these arrows. Click the column heading in the custom grouping area to change the direction of the sort for that column heading only. For example, using the custom grouping created previously, you can display the question list sorted first in descending order by whether the question was marked, in descending order by unit name, and then in ascending order by sequence number.

The custom grouping feature of the Item Review screen gives you enormous flexibility in how you choose to review the exam questions. To remove a custom grouping and return the Item Review display to its default setting (sorted in descending order by sequence number), simply uncheck the Custom Grouping check box.

The Current Score Tab

The Current Score tab of the Item Review screen (see Figure D.14) provides a real-time snapshot of your score. The top half of the screen is an expandable grid. When the grid is collapsed, scores are displayed for each unit. Units can be expanded to show percentage scores for objectives and subobjectives. Information about your exam progress is presented in the following columns:

◆ **Unit Name.** This column shows the unit name for each objective group.

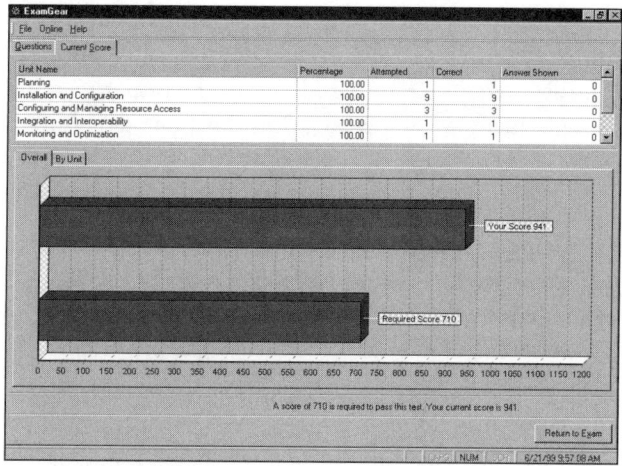

FIGURE D.14
The Current Score tab on the item review screen.

◆ **Percentage.** This column shows the percentage of questions for each objective group that you answered correctly.

◆ **Attempted.** This column lists the number of questions you answered either completely or partially for each objective group.

◆ **Correct.** This column lists the actual number of questions you answered correctly for each objective group.

◆ **Answer Shown.** This column lists the number of questions for each objective group that you chose to display the answer to using the Show Answer button.

The columns in the scoring table are resized and sorted in the same way as those in the questions table on the Item Review Questions tab. Refer to the earlier section "The Item Review Questions Tab" for more details.

A graphical overview of the score is presented below the grid. The graph depicts two red bars: The top bar represents your current exam score, and the bottom bar represents the required passing score. To the right of the bars in the graph is a legend that lists the required score and your score. Below the bar graph is a statement that describes the required passing score and your current score.

In addition, the information can be presented on an overall basis or by exam unit. The Overall tab shows the overall score. The By Unit tab shows the score by unit.

Clicking the End Exam button terminates the exam and passes control to the Examination Score Report screen.

The Return to Exam button returns to the exam at the question from which the Item Review button was clicked.

Review Marked Items

The Item Review screen allows you to enter a browse sequence for marked questions. When you click the Review Marked button, questions that you have previously marked using the Mark Question check box are presented for your review. While browsing the marked questions, you will see the following changes to the buttons available:

◆ The caption of the Next button becomes Next Marked.

◆ The caption of the Previous button becomes Previous Marked.

Review Incomplete

The Item Review screen allows you to enter a browse sequence for incomplete questions. When you click the Review Incomplete button, the questions you did not answer or did not completely answer are displayed for your review. While browsing the incomplete questions, you will see the following changes to the buttons:

◆ The caption of the Next button becomes Next Incomplete.

◆ The caption of the Previous button becomes Previous Incomplete.

Examination Score Report Screen

The Examination Score Report screen (see Figure D.15) appears when the Study Mode, Practice Exam, or Adaptive Exam ends—as the result of timer expiration, completion of all questions, or your decision to terminate early.

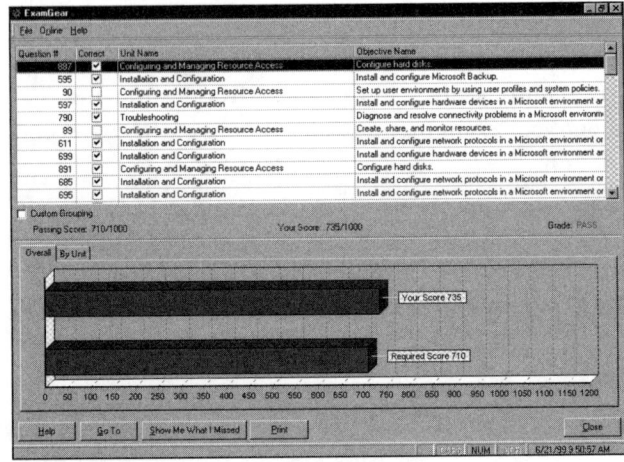

FIGURE D.15
The Examination Score Report screen.

This screen provides you with a graphical display of your test score, along with a tabular breakdown of scores by unit. The graphical display at the top of the screen compares your overall score with the score required to pass the exam. Buttons below the graphical display allow you to open the Show Me What I Missed browse sequence, print the screen, or return to the main menu.

Show Me What I Missed Browse Sequence

The Show Me What I Missed browse sequence is invoked by clicking the Show Me What I Missed button from the Examination Score Report or from the configuration screen of an adaptive exam.

Note that the window caption is modified to indicate that you are in the Show Me What I Missed browse sequence mode. Question IDs and position within the browse sequence appear at the top of the screen, in place of the Mark Question and Time Remaining indicators. Main window contents vary, depending on the question type. The following list describes the buttons available within the Show Me What I Missed browse sequence and the functions they perform:

◆ **Return to Score Report.** Returns control to the Examination Score Report screen. In the case of an adaptive exam, this button's caption is Exit, and control returns to the adaptive exam configuration screen.

◆ **Run Simulation.** Opens a simulation in Grade mode, causing the simulation to open displaying your response and the correct answer. If the current question does not offer a simulation, this button is disabled.

◆ **Exhibits.** Opens the Exhibits window. This button is enabled if one or more exhibits are available for the question.

◆ **Instructions.** Shows how to answer the current question type.

◆ **Print.** Prints the current screen.

◆ **Previous or Next.** Displays missed questions.

Checking the Web Site

To check the Que Certification Home Page or the *ExamGear, Training Guide Edition* Home Page for updates or other product information, choose the desired Web site from the Web Sites option of the Online menu. You must be connected to the Internet to reach these Web sites. When you select a Web site, the Internet Explorer browser opens inside the *ExamGear, Training Guide Edition* window and displays the Web site.

OBTAINING UPDATES

The procedures for obtaining updates are outlined in this section.

The Catalog Web Site for Updates

Selecting the Check for Product Updates option from the Online menu shows you the full range of products you can either download for free or purchase. You can download additional items only if you have registered the software.

Product Updates Dialog Box

This dialog box appears when you select Check for Product Updates from the Online menu. *ExamGear, Training Guide Edition* checks for product updates from the Que Certification Internet site and displays a list of products available for download. Some items, such as *ExamGear* program updates or bonus question sets for exam databases you have activated, are available for download free of charge.

Types of Updates

Several types of updates may be available for download, including various free updates and additional items available for purchase.

Free Program Updates

Free program updates include changes to the *ExamGear, Training Guide Edition* executables and runtime libraries (DLLs). When any of these items are downloaded, *ExamGear* automatically installs the upgrades. *ExamGear, Training Guide Edition* will be reopened after the installation is complete.

Free Database Updates

Free database updates include updates to the exam or exams that you have registered. Exam updates are contained in compressed, encrypted files and include exam databases, simulations, and exhibits. *ExamGear, Training Guide Edition* automatically decompresses these files to their proper location and updates the *ExamGear* software to record version changes and import new question sets.

CONTACTING QUE CERTIFICATION

At Que Certification, we strive to meet and exceed the needs of our customers. We have developed *ExamGear, Training Guide Edition* to surpass the demands and expectations of network professionals seeking technical certifications, and we think it shows. What do you think?

If you need to contact Que Certification regarding any aspect of the *ExamGear, Training Guide Edition* product line, feel free to do so. We look forward to hearing from you. Contact us at the following address or phone number:

Que Certification
201 West 103 Street
Indianapolis, IN 46290
800-545-5914

You can also reach us on the World Wide Web:

www.quepublishing.com

Technical Support

Technical support is available at the following phone number during the hours specified:

800-428-5331

Monday through Friday, 10:00 a.m.–3:00 p.m. Central Standard Time.

Customer Service

If you have a damaged product and need a replacement or refund, please call the following phone number:

800-858-7674

Product Updates

Product updates can be obtained by choosing *ExamGear, Training Guide Edition*'s Online pull-down menu and selecting Products Updates. You'll be taken to a private Web site with full details.

Product Suggestions and Comments

We value your input! Please email your suggestions and comments to the following address:

    certification@quepublishing.com

LICENSE AGREEMENT

YOU SHOULD CAREFULLY READ THE FOLLOWING TERMS AND CONDITIONS BEFORE BREAKING THE SEAL ON THE PACKAGE. AMONG OTHER THINGS, THIS AGREEMENT LICENSES THE ENCLOSED SOFTWARE TO YOU AND CONTAINS WARRANTY AND LIABILITY DISCLAIMERS. BY BREAKING THE SEAL ON THE PACKAGE, YOU ARE ACCEPTING AND AGREEING TO THE TERMS AND CONDITIONS OF THIS AGREEMENT. IF YOU DO NOT AGREE TO THE TERMS OF THIS AGREEMENT, DO NOT BREAK THE SEAL. YOU SHOULD PROMPTLY RETURN THE PACKAGE UNOPENED.

LICENSE

Subject to the provisions contained herein, Que Certification hereby grants to you a nonexclusive, non-transferable license to use the object-code version of the computer software product (Software) contained in the package on a single computer of the type identified on the package.

SOFTWARE AND DOCUMENTATION

Que Certification shall furnish the Software to you on media in machine-readable object-code form and may also provide the standard documentation (Documentation) containing instructions for operation and use of the Software.

LICENSE TERM AND CHARGES

The term of this license commences upon delivery of the Software to you and is perpetual unless earlier terminated upon default or as otherwise set forth herein.

TITLE

Title, ownership right, and intellectual property rights in and to the Software and Documentation shall remain in Que Certification and/or in suppliers to Que Certification of programs contained in the Software. The Software is provided for your own internal use under this license. This license does not include the right to sublicense and is personal to you and therefore may not be assigned (by operation of law or otherwise) or transferred without the prior written consent of Que Certification. You acknowledge that the Software in source code form remains a confidential trade secret of Que Certification and/or its suppliers and therefore you agree not to attempt to decipher or decompile, modify, disassemble, reverse engineer, or prepare derivative works of the Software or develop source code for the Software or knowingly allow others to do so. Further, you may not copy the Documentation or other written materials accompanying the Software.

UPDATES

This license does not grant you any right, license, or interest in and to any improvements, modifications, enhancements, or updates to the Software and Documentation. Updates, if available, may be obtained by you at Que Certification's then-current standard pricing, terms, and conditions.

LIMITED WARRANTY AND DISCLAIMER

Que Certification warrants that the media containing the Software, if provided by Que Certification, is free from defects in material and workmanship under normal use for a period of sixty (60) days from the date you purchased a license to it.

THIS IS A LIMITED WARRANTY AND IT IS THE ONLY WARRANTY MADE BY QUE CERTIFICATION. THE SOFTWARE IS PROVIDED "AS IS" AND QUE CERTIFICATION SPECIFICALLY DISCLAIMS ALL WARRANTIES OF ANY KIND, EITHER EXPRESS OR IMPLIED, INCLUDING, BUT NOT LIMITED TO, THE IMPLIED WARRANTY OF MERCHANTABILITY AND FITNESS FOR A PARTICULAR PURPOSE. FURTHER, COMPANY DOES NOT WARRANT, GUARANTEE, OR MAKE ANY REPRESENTATIONS REGARDING THE USE, OR THE RESULTS OF THE USE, OF THE SOFTWARE IN TERMS OR CORRECTNESS, ACCURACY, RELIABILITY, CURRENTNESS, OR OTHERWISE, AND DOES NOT WARRANT THAT THE OPERATION OF ANY SOFTWARE WILL BE UNINTERRUPTED OR ERROR FREE. QUE CERTIFICATION EXPRESSLY DISCLAIMS ANY WARRANTIES NOT STATED HEREIN. NO ORAL OR WRITTEN INFORMATION OR ADVICE GIVEN BY QUE CERTIFICATION, OR ANY QUE CERTIFICATION DEALER, AGENT, EMPLOYEE, OR OTHERS SHALL CREATE, MODIFY, OR EXTEND A WARRANTY OR IN ANY WAY INCREASE THE SCOPE OF THE FOREGOING WARRANTY, AND NEITHER SUBLICENSEE OR PURCHASER MAY RELY ON ANY SUCH INFORMATION OR ADVICE.

If the media is subjected to accident, abuse, or improper use, or if you violate the terms of this Agreement, then this warranty shall immediately be terminated. This warranty shall not apply if the Software is used on or in conjunction with hardware or programs other than the unmodified version of hardware and programs with which the Software was designed to be used as described in the Documentation.

LIMITATION OF LIABILITY

Your sole and exclusive remedies for any damage or loss in any way connected with the Software are set forth below.

UNDER NO CIRCUMSTANCES AND UNDER NO LEGAL THEORY, TORT, CONTRACT, OR OTHERWISE, SHALL QUE CERTIFICATION BE LIABLE TO YOU OR ANY OTHER PERSON FOR ANY INDIRECT, SPECIAL, INCIDENTAL, OR CONSEQUENTIAL DAMAGES OF ANY CHARACTER INCLUDING, WITHOUT LIMITATION, DAMAGES FOR LOSS OF GOODWILL, LOSS OF PROFIT, WORK STOPPAGE, COMPUTER FAILURE OR MALFUNCTION, OR ANY AND ALL OTHER COMMERCIAL DAMAGES OR LOSSES, OR FOR ANY OTHER DAMAGES EVEN IF QUE CERTIFICATION SHALL HAVE BEEN INFORMED OF THE POSSIBILITY OF SUCH DAMAGES, OR FOR ANY CLAIM BY ANOTHER PARTY. QUE CERTIFICATION'S THIRD-PARTY

PROGRAM SUPPLIERS MAKE NO WARRANTY, AND HAVE NO LIABILITY WHATSOEVER, TO YOU. Que Certification's sole and exclusive obligation and liability and your exclusive remedy shall be: upon Que Certification's election, (i) the replacement of our defective media; or (ii) the repair or correction of your defective media if Que Certification is able, so that it will conform to the above warranty; or (iii) if Que Certification is unable to replace or repair, you may terminate this license by returning the Software. Only if you inform Que Certification of your problem during the applicable warranty period will Que Certification be obligated to honor this warranty. SOME STATES OR JURISDICTIONS DO NOT ALLOW THE EXCLUSION OF IMPLIED WARRANTIES OR LIMITATION OR EXCLUSION OF CONSEQUENTIAL DAMAGES, SO THE ABOVE LIMITATIONS OR EXCLUSIONS MAY NOT APPLY TO YOU. THIS WARRANTY GIVES YOU SPECIFIC LEGAL RIGHTS AND YOU MAY ALSO HAVE OTHER RIGHTS WHICH VARY BY STATE OR JURISDICTION.

MISCELLANEOUS

If any provision of the Agreement is held to be ineffective, unenforceable, or illegal under certain circumstances for any reason, such decision shall not affect the validity or enforceability (i) of such provision under other circumstances or (ii) of the remaining provisions hereof under all circumstances, and such provision shall be reformed to and only to the extent necessary to make it effective, enforceable, and legal under such circumstances. All headings are solely for convenience and shall not be considered in interpreting this Agreement. This Agreement shall be governed by and construed under New York law as such law applies to agreements between New York residents entered into and to be performed entirely within New York, except as required by U.S. Government rules and regulations to be governed by Federal law.

YOU ACKNOWLEDGE THAT YOU HAVE READ THIS AGREEMENT, UNDERSTAND IT, AND AGREE TO BE BOUND BY ITS TERMS AND CONDITIONS. YOU FURTHER AGREE THAT IT IS THE COMPLETE AND EXCLUSIVE STATEMENT OF THE AGREEMENT BETWEEN US THAT SUPERSEDES ANY PROPOSAL OR PRIOR AGREEMENT, ORAL OR WRITTEN, AND ANY OTHER COMMUNICATIONS BETWEEN US RELATING TO THE SUBJECT MATTER OF THIS AGREEMENT.

U.S. GOVERNMENT RESTRICTED RIGHTS

Use, duplication, or disclosure by the Government is subject to restrictions set forth in subparagraphs (a) through (d) of the Commercial Computer-Restricted Rights clause at FAR 52.227-19 when applicable, or in subparagraph (c) (1) (ii) of the Rights in Technical Data and Computer Software clause at DFARS 252.227-7013, and in similar clauses in the NASA FAR Supplement.

Index

SYMBOLS

1Gbps Ethernet (1000BaseT), 126
10Mbps Ethernet (10BaseT), 126
100Mbps Ethernet (100BaseT), 126

A

D

F

S

U

V

Hey, you've got enough worries.

Don't let IT training be one of them.

Get on the fast track to IT training at InformIT,
your total Information Technology training network.

 | **www.informit.com** |

■ Hundreds of timely articles on dozens of topics ■ Discounts on IT books from all our publishing partners, including Que Publishing ■ Free, unabridged books from the InformIT Free Library ■ "Expert Q&A"—our live, online chat with IT experts ■ Faster, easier certification and training from our Web- or classroom-based training programs ■ Current IT news ■ Software downloads ■ Career-enhancing resources

When **IT** really matters, test with **VUE**.

You've studied the *Training Guide*. Tested your skills with *ExamGear*.™
Now what? Are you ready to sit the exam?
If the answer is yes, be sure to test with VUE.

Why VUE? Because with VUE, you get the best technology and even better service. Some of the benefits are

- **VUE allows you to register and reschedule your exam in real-time, online, by phone, or at your local testing center.**
- **Your test is on time and ready for you 99% of the time.**
- **Your results are promptly and accurately provided to the certifying agency, and then merged with your test history.**

VUE has more than 2,400 quality-focused testing centers worldwide, so no matter where you are, you're never far from a VUE testing center.

VUE is a testing vendor for all the major certification vendors, including Cisco®, Microsoft®, CompTIA®, and Novell®.

HURRY! SIGN UP FOR YOUR EXAM NOW!
TEST WITH VUE. WHEN *IT* REALLY MATTERS.

WE WANT TO KNOW WHAT YOU THINK

To better serve you, we would like your opinion on the content and quality of this book. Please complete this card and mail it to us or fax it to 317-581-4666.

Name _____

Address _____

City _____ State _____ Zip _____

Phone _____ Email Address _____

Occupation _____

Which certification exams have you already passed? _____
_____
_____
_____

Which certification exams do you plan to take? _____
_____
_____
_____

What influenced your purchase of this book?
❑ Recommendation   ❑ Cover Design
❑ Table of Contents   ❑ Index
❑ Magazine Review   ❑ Advertisement
❑ Reputation of Que   ❑ Author Name

How would you rate the contents of this book?
❑ Excellent   ❑ Very Good
❑ Good   ❑ Fair
❑ Below Average   ❑ Poor

What other types of certification products will you buy/have you bought to help you prepare for the exam?
❑ Quick reference books   ❑ Testing software
❑ Study guides   ❑ Other

What do you like most about this book? Check all that apply.
❑ Content   ❑ Writing Style
❑ Accuracy   ❑ Examples
❑ Listings   ❑ Design
❑ Index   ❑ Page Count
❑ Price   ❑ Illustrations

What do you like least about this book? Check all that apply.
❑ Content   ❑ Writing Style
❑ Accuracy   ❑ Examples
❑ Listings   ❑ Design
❑ Index   ❑ Page Count
❑ Price   ❑ Illustrations

What would be a useful follow-up book to this one for you?_____
Where did you purchase this book? _____
Can you name a similar book that you like better than this one, or one that is as good? Why?_____
_____
_____

How many Que books do you own? _____
What are your favorite certification or general computer book titles? _____
_____

What other titles would you like to see us develop?_____
_____

Any comments for us? _____
_____
_____

MCSE TRAINING GUIDE: WINDOWS 2000 NETWORK INFRASTRUCTURE DESIGN   0-7897-2794-3

Fold here and tape to mail

Que Publishing
201 W. 103rd St.
Indianapolis, IN 46290